T5-CCW-837

# READINGS
# IN
# POPULATION
# BIOLOGY

**Prentice-Hall
Biological Science Series**

William D. McElroy
and Carl P. Swanson, *editors*

PRENTICE-HALL INTERNATIONAL, INC., *London*
PRENTICE-HALL OF AUSTRALIA, PTY. LTD., *Sydney*
PRENTICE-HALL OF CANADA, LTD., *Toronto*
PRENTICE-HALL OF INDIA PRIVATE LIMITED, *New Delhi*
PRENTICE-HALL OF JAPAN, INC., *Tokyo*

# READINGS

# IN

# POPULATION

# BIOLOGY

Editors

**Peter S. Dawson**
*Oregon State University*

**Charles E. King**
*Yale University*

**Prentice-Hall, Inc., Englewood Cliffs, New Jersey**

© 1971 by Prentice-Hall, Inc.
Englewood Cliffs, New Jersey

All rights reserved. No part of this
book may be reproduced in any form
or by any means without permission
in writing from the publisher.

Current printing (last digit):

10  9  8  7  6  5  4  3  2

13–759415–1

Library of Congress Catalog Card Number 71–149171

Printed in the United States of America

# Contents

**Preface**

*I*   **Prologue**                 1

      2     Levins, R. The strategy of model building in population biology.

*II*   **Variation in Populations**           13

     18     Van Valen, L. Morphological variation and width of ecological niche.

     32     Schoener, T. W. The ecological significance of sexual dimorphism in size in the lizard *Anolis conspersus*.

     35     McNeilly, T. and A. D. Bradshaw. Evolutionary processes in populations of copper tolerant *Agrostis tenuis* Sibth.

     46     Dingle, H. and J. B. Haskell. Phase polymorphism in the grasshopper *Melanoplus differentialis*.

     48     Ashmole, N. P. Adaptive variation in the breeding regime of a tropical sea bird.

     56     Atwood, K. C., L. K. Schneider, and F. J. Ryan. Selective mechanisms in bacteria.

     66     Apirion, D. and D. Zohary. Chlorophyll lethal in natural populations of the orchard grass (*Dactylis glomerata* L.). A case of balanced polymorphism in plants.

     73     Ehrman, L. Mating success and genotype frequency in *Drosophila*.

     81     Clarke, C. A. and P. M. Sheppard. Disruptive selection and its effect on a metrical character in the butterfly *Papilio dardanus*.

     94     Milne, H. and F. W. Robertson. Polymorphisms in egg albumin protein and behaviour in the eider duck.

   100     Lewontin, R. C. and J. L. Hubby. A molecular approach to the study of genic heterozygosity in natural populations. II. Amount of variation and degree of heterozygosity in natural populations of *Drosophila pseudoobscura*.

119   Chitty, D. Population processes in the vole and their relevance to general theory.

134   Crow, J. F. and M. Kimura. Evolution in sexual and asexual populations.

146   Maynard Smith, J. Evolution in sexual and asexual populations.

151   Kettlewell, H. B. D. A résumé of investigations on the evolution of melanism in the Lepidoptera.

157   Haldane, J. B. S. The theory of selection for melanism in Lepidoptera.

159   Dobzhansky, T. and B. Spassky. Selection for geotaxis in monomorphic and polymorphic populations of *Drosophila pseudoobscura*.

168   Camin, J. H. and P. R. Ehrlich. Natural selection in water snakes (*Natrix sipedon* L.) on islands in Lake Erie.

176   Kerr, W. E. and S. Wright. Experimental studies of the distribution of gene frequencies in very small populations of *Drosophila melanogaster*: I. Forked.

182   Dobzhansky, T. and O. Pavlovsky. An experimental study of interaction between genetic drift and natural selection.

191   Ayala, F. J. Evolution of fitness in experimental populations of *Drosophila serrata*.

200   Istock, C. A. The evolution of complex life cycle phenomena: an ecological perspective.

214   Jain, S. K. and D. R. Marshall. Population studies in predominantly self-pollinating species. X. Variation in natural populations of *Avena fatua* and *A. barbata*.

229   Carrick, R. Ecological significance of territory in the Australian magpie, *Gymnorhina tibicen*.

243   Carson, H. L. The genetic characteristics of marginal populations of Drosophila.

255   Tantawy, A. O. and G. S. Mallah. Studies on natural populations of Drosophila. I. Heat resistance and geographical variation in *Drosophila melanogaster* and *D. simulans*.

269   Cody, M. L. A general theory of clutch size.

280   Johnson, M. P. and S. A. Cook. "Clutch size" in buttercups.

287   McLaren, I. A. Adaptive significance of large size and long life of the chaetognath *Sagitta elegans* in the arctic.

291   Wallace, B. and M. Vetukhiv. Adaptive organization of the gene pools of Drosophila populations.

299   Lewontin, R. C. Interdeme selection controlling a polymorphism in the house mouse.

318    MacArthur, R. and R. Levins. Competition, habitat selection, and character displacement in a patchy environment.

322    Connell, J. H. The influence of interspecific competition and other factors on the distribution of the barnacle *Chthamalus stellatus*.

336    Lerner, I. M. and E. R. Dempster. Indeterminism in interspecific competition.

342    Harper, J. L. and I. H. McNaughton. The comparative biology of closely related species living in the same area. VII. Interference between individuals in pure and mixed populations of *Papaver* species.

356    Pimentel, D., E. H. Feinberg, P. W. Wood, and J. T. Hayes. Selection, spatial distribution, and the coexistence of competing fly species.

369    Levin, D. A. and H. W. Kerster. Natural selection for reproductive isolation in *Phlox*.

378    Brooks, J. L. The effects of prey size selection by lake planktivores.

397    Breedlove, D. E. and P. R. Ehrlich. Plant-herbivore coevolution: lupines and lycaenids.

**VI    Epilogue**                                              399

400    Hutchinson, G. E. The influence of the environment.

# Preface

Historically, science has progressed through successively greater subdivision of areas of study with the result that today most scientific disciplines are highly specialized. Although this approach has had many advantages, it has frequently resulted in overspecialization and ignorance of progress in related disciplines. Fortunately, this fission process is to some extent self-limiting; it eventually becomes apparent that concepts from related areas must be integrated to fully understand common objects of study.

The latter process has led to the emergence of such fields as biochemistry, behavioral physiology, and paleoecology. It is our contention that the various population-oriented disciplines have reached a similar point and now must either merge or stagnate.

Comparable syntheses are occurring in other areas of biology and many traditional fields of specialization are being redefined. At one time, biology was subdivided in terms of the organisms being studied (e.g., botany, zoology, bacteriology, ichthyology, etc.). Later, functional divisions were incorporated (e.g., physiology, genetics, ecology, etc.) and the most recent trend is the definition of biological areas by "levels of organization" (cell, organism, and population).

The stimulus to gather these readings came from our involvement in establishing new courses in population biology. In even the most fundamental presentation of a subject, we strongly believe that the student profits by being exposed to— if not immersed in—the original literature of a field. This collection is designed to facilitate such an exposure and, in conjunction with a presentation of basic theory, to impart something of the intellectual excitement, challenge, and rigor of this nascent discipline.

Population biology encompasses all investigations above the level of the individual. We can define population biology as the study of the structure, integration, and evolution of groups of organisms belonging to one or more species. Although this definition clearly includes studies at the community and ecosystem levels of organization, we have restricted our coverage to intrapopulational phenomena and to interactions between populations. This was done partly because more than a token coverage of community and ecosystem research in a book of this size would have necessitated making the entire treatment superficial. In addition, the integration of genetic and ecological principles that forms the basis of population biology has had relatively little impact on research at these higher levels. Finally, we strongly believe that before a satisfactory understanding of ecosystem structure can be achieved, it is helpful, if not mandatory, to acquire a better knowledge of the structure of populations and their interactions with the environment.

Population biology has its deepest roots in population genetics and ecology. However, the development of a unified theory of populations must also include elements of other disciplines such as ethology, paleontology, environmental physiology, demography, and systematics. Since most research scientists now engaged in the study of populations have been trained in only one of these fields, the literature of population biology has lagged behind the realization that a synthesis of the fields is mandatory. Consequently, most of the papers in this collection do not *individually* represent the perspective of population biology. However, their relevance to the development of a unified theory of populations should become apparent when the papers in each section are viewed as an entity.

It is the nature of this type of project that no two people would independently make the same selection of papers or organize them in the same manner. This undoubtedly reflects the fact that few authors restrict their papers to a single, easily categorizable topic. Thus, many of the selected papers could justifiably be placed in other sections. However, most people in the field would probably agree that there is, or at least should be, a close interaction between the theory of population biology and evolutionary theory. Consequently, all of the selected papers bear more or less directly on problems of evolutionary significance. This is not to say that the collection can properly be considered as a "Readings in Evolution," for several important areas of evolutionary research such as paleontology and speciation theory are not represented.

The papers included in the body of this collection are organized around four types of questions:

1. How much variation is present in the population, what is its source, what is its function, and how is it maintained?
2. How does the population change through time and in response to what environmental factors does it change?
3. How is the population adapted to the prevailing environment and to withstand challenges posed by the environment?
4. How does the population interact with other populations and what are the results of these interactions?

Each of these problem areas is represented by a number of papers grouped into a section, and the sections are preceded by short introductions that identify the major contributions of each paper. The names of the authors of the included papers are capitalized in the section introductions.

All of the papers have been reprinted in their original form and their authors have been invited to add corrections or comments in footnote form. We are grateful to the authors and also to the journals in which the selected papers originally appeared for permission to reprint their articles. Since a great majority of the material in this book represents the work and writing of people other than the editors, all editors' profits resulting from the sale of this collection are being turned over to the American Society of Naturalists in recognition of its signal role in fostering the development of population biology.

In gathering these readings, we have attempted to select papers which (1) illustrate important concepts with experimental or observational results, (2) indicate some of the major approaches to research in population biology, and (3) provide a basis for class discussion. In addition we have attempted to include studies on a variety of organisms. Our emphasis has been on experimental or observational rather than theoretical papers because we feel that theory can be treated more effectively in a textbook or classroom. On the other hand, if theoretical papers had been entirely omitted, a large part of the beauty and piquancy of the field would be lost to the reader. Therefore, we have compromised by including at least one theoretical, controversial, or argumentative paper in each section with the hope that these papers will add to the value of this collection by imparting some hint of the broader flavor of population biology.

**Peter S. Dawson**
Corvallis, Oregon

**Charles E. King**
New Haven, Connecticut

# I

# Prologue

Models are among the basic working tools of population biologists. As LEVINS points out in the prologue paper, the major utility of models is to aid in reducing the vast complexity of biological systems to a manageable form. This, in turn, permits the investigator to synthesize previous knowledge and, more important, to make novel predictions that can be tested by appropriate field or laboratory experiments.

The power of the model as a tool is so great that it is not only possible but highly appropriate to trace the development of population biology by examining the history of its models. We might choose as starting points the nineteenth century models of such workers as Malthus, Verhulst, Mendel, Liebig, and Darwin, proceed through the early twentieth century models of Ross, Hardy and Weinberg, Lotka, Fisher, Wright, and Haldane, and finally approach the present with LEVINS' own model, the fitness set. The great importance of the latter model, in both forms described in the prologue paper, is that it forces an investigator to synthesize broad concepts formerly assigned to the separate disciplines of population genetics and ecology. In this sense, the fitness set constitutes one of the first general models of population biology.

# THE STRATEGY OF MODEL BUILDING IN POPULATION BIOLOGY

## By RICHARD LEVINS

ODERN population biology arises from the coming together of
what were previously independent clusters of more or less co-
herent theory. Population genetics and population ecology, the most
mathematical areas of population biology, had developed with quite
different assumptions and techniques, while mathematical biogeography
is essentially a new field.

For population genetics, a population is specified by the frequencies
of genotypes without reference to the age distribution, physiological
state as a reflection of past history, or population density. A single
population or species is treated at a time, and evolution is usually assumed to occur in a constant environment.

Population ecology, on the other hand, recognizes multispecies systems, describes populations in terms of their age distributions, physiological states, and densities. The environment is allowed to vary but
the species are treated as genetically homogeneous, so that evolution is
ignored.

But there is increasing evidence that demographic time and evolutionary time are commensurate. Thus population biology must deal
simultaneously with genetic, physiological, and age heterogeneity within
species of multispecies systems changing demographically and evolving
under the fluctuating influences of other species in a heterogeneous
environment. The problem is how to deal with such a complex system.

The naive, brute force approach would be to set up a mathematical
model which is a faithful, one-to-one reflection of this complexity. This
would require using perhaps 100 simultaneous partial differential equations with time lags; measuring hundreds of parameters, solving the
equations to get numerical predictions, and then measuring these predictions against nature. However:

(a) there are too many parameters to measure; some are still only
vaguely defined; many would require a lifetime each for their
measurement.

(b) The equations are insoluble analytically and exceed the capacity
of even good computers.

(c) Even if soluble, the result expressed in the form of quotients of
sums of products of parameters would have no meaning for us.

Clearly we have to simplify the models in a way that preserves the
essential features of the problem. The difference between legitimate and

Reprinted by permission of The Society of Sigma Xi and the author from *American Scientist*
54.421–431, 1966.

illegitimate simplifications depends not only on the reality to be described but also on the state of the science. The early pioneering work in population genetics by Haldane, Fisher, and Wright all assumed a constant environment in the models although each author was aware that environments are not constant. But the problem at hand was: Could weak natural selection account for evolutionary change? For the purposes of this problem, a selection coefficient that varies between .001 and .01 will have effects somewhere between constant selection pressures at those values, and would be an unnecessary complication.

But, for us today, environmental heterogeneity is an essential ingredient of the problems and therefore of our mathematical models.

It is of course desirable to work with manageable models which maximize generality, realism, and precision toward the overlapping but not identical goals of understanding, predicting, and modifying nature. But this cannot be done. Therefore, several alternative strategies have evolved:

1. Sacrifice generality to realism and precision. This is the approach of Holling, (e.g., 1959), of many fishery biologists, and of Watt (1956). These workers can reduce the parameters to those relevant to the short-term behavior of their organism, make fairly accurate measurements, solve numerically on the computer, and end with precise testable predictions applicable to these particular situations.

2. Sacrifice realism to generality and precision. Kerner (1957), Leigh (1965), and most physicists who enter population biology work in this tradition which involves setting up quite general equations from which precise results may be obtained. Their equations are clearly unrealistic. For instance, they use the Volterra predator-prey systems which omit time lags, physiological states, and the effect of a species' population density on its own rate of increase. But these workers hope that their model is analogous to assumptions of frictionless systems or perfect gases. They expect that many of the unrealistic assumptions will cancel each other, that small deviations from realism result in small deviations in the conclusions, and that, in any case, the way in which nature departs from theory will suggest where further complications will be useful. Starting with precision they hope to increase realism.

3. Sacrifice precision to realism and generality. This approach is favored by MacArthur (1965) and myself. Since we are really concerned in the long run with qualitative rather than quantitative results (which are only important in testing hypotheses) we can resort to very flexible models, often graphical, which generally assume that functions are increasing or decreasing, convex or concave, greater or less than some value, instead of specifying the mathematical form of an equation. This means that the predictions we can make are also expressed as inequalities

as between tropical and temperate species, insular *versus* continental faunas, patchy *versus* uniform environments, etc.

However, even the most flexible models have artificial assumptions. There is always room for doubt as to whether a result depends on the essentials of a model or on the details of the simplifying assumptions. This problem does not arise in the more familiar models, such as the geographic map, where we all know that contiguity on the map implies contiguity in reality, relative distances on the map correspond to relative distances in reality, but color is arbitrary and a microscopic view of the map would only show the fibers of the paper on which it is printed. But, in the mathematical models of population biology, it is not always obvious when we are using too high a magnification.

Therefore, we attempt to treat the same problem with several alternative models each with different simplifications but with a common biological assumption. Then, if these models, despite their different assumptions, lead to similar results we have what we can call a robust theorem which is relatively free of the details of the model. Hence our truth is the intersection of independent lies.

### Robust and Non-robust Theorems

As an example of a robust theorem consider the proposition that, in an uncertain environment, species will evolve broad niches and tend toward polymorphism. We will use three models, the fitness set of Levins (1962), a calculus of variation argument, and one which specifies the genetic system (Levins and MacArthur, 1966).

Model I assumes:

1. For each phenotype $i$ there is a best environment $s_i$, and fitness $w$ declines with the deviation of $s_i$ from the actual environment. Although the curves $W(s - s_i)$ in nature may differ in the location of the peak at $s_i$, the height of the peak, and the rate at which fitness declines with the deviation from the optimum, our model treats all the curves as identical except for the location of the peak $s_i$.

2. The environment consists of two (easily extended to $N$) alternative facies or habitats or conditions. Thus, on a graph whose axes are $W_1$ and $W_2$, the fitnesses in environments 1 and 2, each phenotype is represented by a point as in Figure 1. The set of all available phenotypes is designated the fitness set. Since a mixed population of two phenotypes would be represented by a point on the straight line joining their points, the extended fitness set of all possible populations is the smallest convex set enclosing the fitness set. In particular, if the fitness set is convex then population heterogeneity adds no new fitness points, whereas, on a concave fitness set, there are polymorphic populations represented by new points. It remains to add that, if the two environments are similar compared to the rate at which fitness declines with deviation (that is,

similar compared to the tolerance of an individual phenotype), the fitness set will be convex. But as the environments diverge the set becomes concave.

3. In an environment which is uniform in time but showing fine-grained heterogeneity in space, each individual is exposed to many units of environment of both kinds in the proportions $p$ to $1 - p$ of their oc-

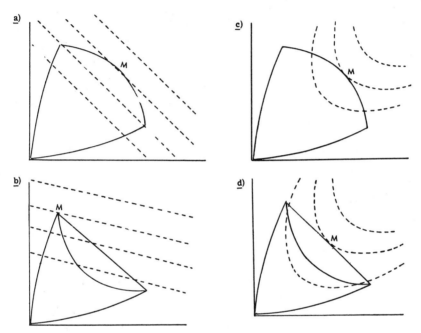

FIG. 1a. The family of straight lines $pW_1 + (1-p)W_2 = C$ are the fitness measures for a fine-grained stable environment. Optimum fitness occurs for the phenotype which is represented by the point of tangency of these lines with the fitness set.

FIG. 1b. Same for a concave fitness set.

FIG. 1c. In an uncertain environment the optimum population is the one that maximizes $p \log W_1 + (1-p) \log W_2$. On a convex fitness set this is monomorphic unspecialized.

FIG. 1d. Same for a concave fitness set. Here polymorphism creates a broad niche.

currence. Thus the rate of increase of the population is $pW_1 + (1 - p)W_2$. If the environment is uniform in space but variable in time, the rate of increase is a product of fitnesses in successive generations, $W_1^p W_2^{1-p}$. For the two situations these alternative functions would be maximized to maximize over-all fitness. The 1962 paper did not distinguish between coarse- and fine-grained environments and therefore gave the linear expression for spatial heterogeneity in general.

The rest of the argument is given in the figure. The result is that, if the environment is not very diverse (convex fitness set), the populations will all be monomorphic of type intermediately well-adapted to both environments. If the environmental diversity exceeds the tolerance of the individual (concave fitness set) then spatial diversity results in specialization to the more common habitat while temporal diversity results in polymorphism.

Model II does not fix the shape of the curve $W(s - s_i)$. Instead we fix the area under the curve so that $\int W(s)ds = C$. Subject to this restriction, we maximize the rate of increase, which is $\int W(s)P(s)ds$ for a fine-grained spatial heterogeneity and $\int \log W(s)P(s)ds$ for temporal heterogeneity. $P(S)$ is the frequency of environment $S$. In the first case, the optimum population would assign all its fitness to the most abundant environment while in the second case the optimum is $W(S) = CP(S)$. At optimum, the fitness is $\log (C) + \int \log P(s) \cdot P(S)ds$, or $\log (C)$ minus the uncertainty of the environment. Thus the more variable the environment, the flatter and more spread out the $W(S)$ curve and the broader the niche. This analysis does not mention polymorphism directly since it discusses the assignment of the fitness of the whole population. But if the $P(S)$ curve is broader than the maximum breadth attainable by individual phenotypes, polymorphism will be optimal.

These two models differ in several ways. While the first allows only discretely different environments, the second permits a continuum. While the fitness set specifies how different environments are by showing the relation between fitness in both environments for each phenotype, the second treats each environment as totally different, so that fitness assigned to one contributes nothing to survival in any other. Therefore, that they coincide in their major results adds to the robustness of the theorem. Both models are similar in that they use optimization arguments and ignore the genetic system. We did not assert that evolution will in fact establish the optimum population but only the weaker expectation that populations will differ in the direction of their optima. But even this is not obvious. Therefore, in model III, we examine a simple genetic model with one locus and two alleles. The graph in Figure 2 has, as before, two axes which represent fitnesses in environments 1 and 2. The points $A_1A_1$, $A_1A_2$, $A_2A_2$ are the fitness points of the three possible genotypes at that locus. The rules of genetic segregation restrict the possible populations to points on the curve joining the two homozygous points and bending halfway toward the heterozygote's point.

We already know from Fisher that, for rather general conditions, natural selection will move toward gene frequencies which maximize the log fitness averaged over all individuals. In a fine-grained environment, this means that selection maximizes $\log [pW_1 + (1 - p)W_2]$ which is the same as maximizing $pW_1 + (1 - p)W_2$. But as the environment

becomes more coarse-grained, each individual is exposed to fewer units
of environment until, in the limit, each one lives either in environment
1 or in environment 2 for the relevant parts of his life. Thus, in a fine-
grained environment, heterogeneity appears as an average, in a coarse-
grained environment as alternatives and hence uncertainty. Here
selection maximizes: $p \log W_1 + (1 - p) \log W_2$ or $W_1{}^p W_2{}^{1-p}$. We note
the following from the figures:

  1. In a fine-grained environment average superiority of the heterozygote is necessary for polymorphism. This has nothing to do with the
"mixed strategy" polymorphism of previous arguments.

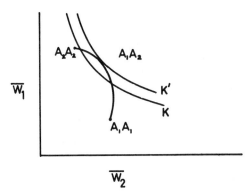

Fig. 2a. Selection in an environment with average heterosis. Possible populations are represented by points on the curve $A_1A_1$, $A_2A_2$. The curves K, K' are
samples from an infinite family of curves each connecting points with equal
fineness. In a fine-grained, stable environment, the K-curves would be *linear* and
governed by the equation $pW_1 + (1-p)W_2 = K$ for values of p between zero and
one. When these K lines are steeper (or flatter,) than the slope of the tangent
to the $A_1A_1$, $A_2A_2$ curve at the point $A_1A_1$ (or $A_2A_2$, resp.) then specialization
will replace polymorphism.

  2. If most of the environment is of type 1, there can be no polymorphism. Only when $p$ is closer to 0.5 than the slope of the curve
$A_1A_1$, $A_2A_2$ will the population become unspecialized.

  3. In a coarse-grained environment the same holds—a sufficient heterogeneity is required to broaden the niche. But now polymorphism is an
optimum strategy in the sense that a population of all heterozygotes
would not be optimal.

  4. As the two environments become more similar, $W_1$ approaches
$W_2$ for each genotype. Then the optimum is a single genotype, and
polymorphism can only come about as an imposition of the facts of
segregation when the heterozygote is superior.

  Other work on the joint evolution of habitat selection and niche
breadth, on the role of productivity of the environment, and on food-
getting procedures all converge in supporting the theorem that environ-

mental uncertainty leads to increased niche breadth while certain but diverse environments lead to specialization.

As an example of a non-robust theorem, consider the proposition that a high intrinsic rate of increase leads to a smaller average population (productivity is opposed to biomass). This result can be derived from the logistic equation for population growth

$$dx/dt = rx(K - x)/K$$

where $x$ is the population size, $r$ is the intrinsic rate of increase, and $K$, the carrying capacity or saturation level, is an environmental variable.

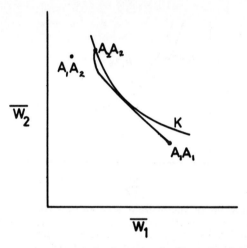

Fig. 2b. Selection in an uncertain (coarse-grained) environment without average heterosis. The points of tangency of the K curve to the curve $A_1A_1$, $A_1A_2$ are the favored gene frequencies, one specialized and one polymorphic.

Leigh (1965) showed that it also holds for a Volterra system of many prey- and predator-species without a saturation level $K$. However both results have a common explanation in the model in which high $r$ not only increases the rate of approach toward $K$ from below but also speeds the crash toward $K$ from above. This latter property was certainly not intended in the definition of $r$, and may or may not be true depending on how resources are used. Further, even in the simple logistic, the result can be reversed if we add a term $-px$ to the right hand side to indicate extraneous predation. Thus the theorem, although interesting, is fragile and cannot be asserted as a biological fact. We may be dealing here with a case of examining a map under the microscope.

## Sufficient Parameters

The thousand or so variables of our original equations can be reduced to manageable proportions by a process of abstraction whereby many terms enter into consideration only by way of a reduced number of higher-level entities. Thus, all the physiological interactions of genes in a genotype enter the models of population genetics only as part of "fitness." The great diversity in populations appears mostly as "additive genetic variance" and "total genetic variance." The multiplicity of species interactions is grouped in the vague notions of the ecological niche, niche overlap, niche breadth, and competition coefficients. It is an essential ingredient in the concept of levels of phenomena that there exists a set of what, by analogy with the sufficient statistic, we can call sufficient parameters defined on a given level (say community) which are very much fewer than the number of parameters on the lower level and which among them contain most of the important information about events on that level. This is by no means equivalent to asserting that community properties are additive or that these sufficient parameters are independent.

Sometimes, the sufficient parameters arise directly from the mathematics and may lack obvious intuitive meaning. Thus, Kerner discovered a conservation law for predator-prey systems. But what is conserved is not anything obvious like energy or momentum. It is a complicated function of the species densities which may acquire meaning for us with further study. Similarly, working with cellular metabolism and starting like Kerner with a physics background, Goodwin (1963) found an invariant which he refers to metaphorically as a biological "temperature."

In other cases, the sufficient parameters are formalizations of previously held but vague properties such as niche breadth. We would like some measure of niche breadth which reflects the spread of a species' fitness over a range of environments. Thus the measure should have the following properties: if a species utilizes $N$ resources equally, it should have a niche breadth of $N$. If it uses two resources unequally, the niche breadth measure should lie between 1 and 2. If two populations which have equal niche breadths that do not overlap are merged, their joint niche breadth should be the sum of their separate breadths. It may be less if they overlap but never more. Two measures satisfy these requirements:

$$\log B = -\Sigma\, p \log p$$

where $p$ is the measure of relative abundance of the species on a given resource or in a given habitat, and

$$1/B = \Sigma\, p^2$$

Neither one is the "true" measure in the sense that one can decide between proposed alternative structures for the hemoglobin molecule. Both are defined by us to meet heuristic criteria. The final choice of an appropriate measure of niche breadth will depend on convenience, on some new criteria which may arise, and on the extent to which the measures lead to biological predictions based on niche breadth. Meanwhile, we should use both measures in presenting ecological data so that they may be compared and studied together. In Table 1 we show some sample niche breadth measures from our study of Puerto Rican Drosophila populations.

TABLE 1

SEASONAL NICHE BREADTH OF SOME PUERTO RICAN DROSOPHILA

| species | —niche breadth during 1962— | |
|---|---|---|
| | measure I | measure II |
| D. melanogaster | 14.4 | 10.5 |
| D. latifasciaeformis | 15.5 | 15.7 |
| D. dunni | 11.0 | 7.6 |
| D. tristriata | 6.9 | 5.7 |
| D. ananassae | 11.2 | 8.6 |
| D. repleta | 5.5 | 4.2 |
| D. nebulosa | 6.5 | 6.2 |
| D. paramediostriata | 11.2 | 7.9 |
| X4 (tripunctata group) | 7.2 | 6.0 |
| X6 (tripunctata group) | 13.9 | 12.0 |

The data are based on 21 collections, so that the maximum niche breadth would be 21. Method I is $\log B = -\Sigma p \log p$ and method II is $1/B = \Sigma p^2$, where $p$ is the proportion of the given species taken in each collection.

The sufficient parameters may arise from the combination of results of more limited studies. In our robust theorem on niche breadth we found that temporal variation, patchiness of the environment, productivity of the habitat, and mode of hunting could all have similar effects and that they did this by way of their contribution to the uncertainty of the environment. Thus uncertainty emerges as a sufficient parameter.

The sufficient parameter is a many-to-one transformation of lower level phenomena. Therein lies its power and utility, but also a new source of imprecision. The many-to-one nature of "uncertainty" prevents us from going backwards. If either temporal variation or patchiness or low productivity leads to uncertainty, the consequences of uncertainty alone cannot tell us whether the environment is variable or patchy or unproductive. Therefore we have lost information. It becomes necessary to supplement our theorem with some subordinate models which explain how to go from "uncertainty" to the components of the environment and biology of the species in question. Thus general models have three kinds of imprecision:

(1) they omit factors which have small effects or which have large effects but only in rare cases;

(2) they are vague about the exact form of mathematical functions in order to stress qualitative properties;

(3) the many-to-one property of sufficient parameters destroys information about lower level events.

Hence, the general models are necessary but not sufficient for understanding nature. For understanding is not achieved by generality alone,
but by a relation between the general and the particular.

### Clusters of Models

A mathematical model is neither an hypothesis nor a theory. Unlike
the scientific hypothesis, a model is not verifiable directly by experiment.
For all models are both true and false. Almost any plausible proposed

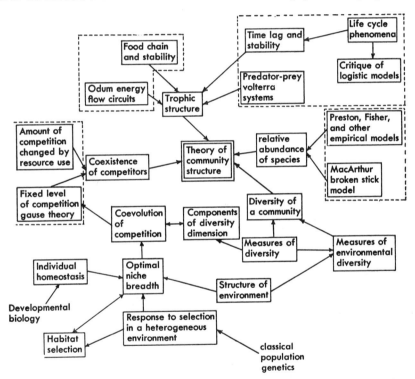

FIG. 3. Relations among some of the components in a theory of the structure of an
ecological community. Broken lines enclose alternative equivalent models.

relation among aspects of nature is likely to be true in the sense that it
occurs (although rarely and slightly). Yet all models leave out a lot
and are in that sense false, incomplete, inadequate. The validation of a
model is not that it is "true" but that it generates good testable hypotheses relevant to important problems. A model may be discarded in
favor of a more powerful one, but it usually is simply outgrown when the
live issues are not any longer those for which it was designed.

STRATEGY OF MODEL BUILDING IN POPULATION BIOLOGY    431

Unlike the theory, models are restricted by technical considerations to a few components at a time, even in systems which are complex. Thus a satisfactory theory is usually a cluster of models. These models are related to each other in several ways: as coordinate alternative models for the same set of phenomena, they jointly produce robust theorems; as complementary models they can cope with different aspects of the same problem and give complementary as well as overlapping results; as hierarchically arranged "nested" models, each provides an interpretation of the sufficient parameters of the next higher level where they are taken as given. In Figure 3 we show schematically the relations among some of the models in the theory of community structure.

The multiplicity of models is imposed by the contradictory demands of a complex, heterogeneous nature and a mind that can only cope with few variables at a time; by the contradictory desiderata of generality, realism, and precision; by the need to understand and also to control; even by the opposing esthetic standards which emphasize the stark simplicity and power of a general theorem as against the richness and the diversity of living nature. These conflicts are irreconcilable. Therefore, the alternative approaches even of contending schools are part of a larger mixed strategy. But the conflict is about method, not nature, for the individual models, while they are essential for understanding reality, should not be confused with that reality itself.

## BIBLIOGRAPHY

1. GOODWIN, B. C. Temporal Organization in Cells. Academic Press 1963.
2. HOLLING, C. S. The components of predation as revealed by a study of small-mammal predation of the European pine sawfly. *Canadian entomologist, 91* (5) 293–320, 1959.
3. KERNER, E. H. A statistical mechanics of interacting biological species. *Bull. Mat. Biophys., 19,* 121–146, 1957.
4. LEIGH, EGBERT. On the relation between productivity, biomass, diversity, and stability of a community. *PNAS, 53* (4) 777–783, 1965.
5. LEVINS, R. Theory of fitness in a heterogeneous environment, I. The fitness set and adaptive function. *Am. Nat., 96* (891), 361–373, 1962.
6. LEVINS, R. and R. H. MACARTHUR. In press.
7. MACARTHUR, R. H. and R. LEVINS. Competition, habitat selection, and character displacement in a patchy environment. *PNAS, 51* (3) 1207–1210, 1965.
8. WATT, KENNETH E. F. The choice and solution of mathematical models for predicting and maximizing the yield of a fishery. *J. Fisheries Res. Bd. of Canada, 13,* 613–645, 1956.

# II

# Variation
# in Populations

Although it has long been recognized that all biological variation is derived from either genetic or environmental sources or interactions between the two, for many years ecologists ignored genetic variation and population geneticists ignored variation derived from the environment. Quite often, ethologists have ignored both. Undoubtedly these assumptions were necessary to the development of a basic theory. However, it now seems just as clear that most of the significant theoretical advances of the future will be made by considering all sources of variation.

From a variety of research, as documented throughout these readings, we know that a considerable amount of variation exists in any population. The significance of this variation is currently a topic of great concern to many population biologists. On one hand it may be argued that there is an optimum phenotype for any environment and that deviation from this optimum reduces the overall fitness or degree of adaptation of the population. A different view, advanced by VAN VALEN in the introductory paper and by others elsewhere, is that the presence of variation may permit different individuals to exploit somewhat different microenvironments or resources with the result that population size is increased. To test this hypothesis, VAN VALEN examined morphological data from both island and mainland populations of six species of birds and found that the degree of variability in these populations was directly related to their niche breadth. This observation argues for his contention that at least part of the variation in a population is functional and is, by itself, an adaptation to the environmental mosaic.

VAN VALEN found no evidence for niche diversification based on genetic polymorphism in the populations he examined. However, many other studies have demonstrated the significance of polymorphism as a mode of adaptation. In particular, niche diversification between males and females of the same species is often observed in sexually dimorphic organisms. For instance, by discriminating between differences in size and sex of the individuals, SCHOENER was able to form four classes of the anoline lizard population living on a small island. Each class was shown to occupy a slightly different microhabitat and to feed on food items of different size. Such differences reduce the intensity of intraspecific competition by expanding the niche breadth which, in turn, can lead to an increased population size.

Each of the two preceding papers describes systems that demand the existence of an abundance of genetic variation. This variation is used by the population to diversify within a given habitat and also to adapt to a range of different habitats. We might now ask what happens to this variation. One way to answer this question is to compare the relative amounts of variation in a population before and after the action of natural selection.

It has been shown that the grass *Agrostis tenuis* is capable of adapting to the stresses imposed by high concentrations of toxic heavy metals in the soil surrounding abandoned mines. The paper by McNEILLY and BRADSHAW is a study of the effects of natural selection on genetic variation in this type of environment. Variation in such a system may be studied in a number of ways. One approach is to determine the distribution of copper tolerance in adult plants growing on soils with different quantities of copper. Seeds from these populations may then be collected and germinated under controlled conditions so that similar measures of copper tolerance are obtained for both parental and $F_1$ generations. Comparisons between these two sets of measures can be used to determine the heritability of copper tolerance and to indicate the effects of natural selection on the population structure. Other comparisons presented in the same paper are made in order to study gene flow between populations and selection against the immigrant individuals. Thus research of this type is of great value to the development of an understanding of both the genetics and ecology of variation in populations.

It is clear that all variation of evolutionary significance is a reflection of the underlying genetic variation. However, in some cases when the genotypic limits are quite broad, the phenotypic variability in a population may primarily reflect environmental variation. Ecological polymorphism, as exemplified by the grasshoppers described by DINGLE and HASKELL, demonstrates such a phenomenon. The color of many grasshoppers and locusts appears to vary with the degree of crowding of individuals during their development. Further, the color of crowded nymphs does not match the background as is normal in this grasshopper. Although no behavioral changes were noted in this study, many locusts exhibit different patterns of movement or migration along with the color phase shifts.

Another aspect of adaptive variation which is only indirectly related to the underlying genetic variation is exemplified in ASHMOLE's study of the reproductive biology of a tropical sea bird. Most birds have annual cycles of reproduction that reflect the annual cycle of environmental variation. However, while studying museum specimens of the sooty tern, ASHMOLE discovered peculiarities in the molt pattern of several birds that suggested a nonannual breeding cycle. Subsequent field experiments and observations demonstrated that the reproductive frequency of the sooty tern on Christmas Island is not an adaptation to variation in the environment but is instead related to the success of the last period of reproduction. In this case, variation in the breeding regime serves to maximize reproduction in a relatively constant environment by means of different responses to the success or failure of the previous breeding attempt.

In a closed population, all genetic variation originates through mutation. Further, it is easy to demonstrate with elementary models that if mutation is the only force acting on the gene pool of a population, equilibrium gene frequencies are attained that depend solely on the magnitude of the mutation rates. However, as ATWOOD, SCHNEIDER, and RYAN show in their study of bacterial populations, the situation is not always so simple. Under their serial transfer procedure, the population alternates between growth and stationary phases, and natural selection for adaptation to the culture medium is in continuous operation. This leads to periodic fluctuations in the composition of the gene pool as new mutant types with higher growth rates appear. Thus the genetic structure of a bacterial population under their experimental conditions is best viewed as the result of an interaction between mutation and natural selection.

If a population is not closed to migration, the genetic variation originating from mutation within the population may be augmented by gene flow from other populations. In most organisms, recombination of genes and/or chromosomes shuffles the existing variation into a tremendous array of different genotypic combinations. Counteracting the addition of variation are the forces of natural selection and random genetic drift, which usually operate to reduce variation.

The joint operation of forces acting to increase and decrease variation can result in the maintenance of genetic polymorphism within a population. However, a variety of other mechanisms can also lead to polymorphism. Perhaps the most common is environmental heterogeneity, as discussed earlier by LEVINS and VAN VALEN. Polymorphism may also result from intraspecific competition as in the case of sexual dimorphism discussed by SCHOENER. Since the existence of polymorphism has long fascinated naturalists and students of population genetics, ecology, and evolution and will undoubtedly continue to hold the attention of population biologists, we have included several papers that illustrate other aspects of the subject. Additional examples may be found throughout this collection.

One mechanism for maintaining polymorphism in populations is selection favoring heterozygotes (overdominance). For example, some natural populations of orchard grass are polymorphic for lethal genes which, when homozygous, produce chlorophyll-deficient plants. APIRION and ZOHARY concluded from a study of these populations that this polymorphism is maintained by overdominance. An important aspect of this paper is the finding that selective values of genotypes differ in populations located in different habitats. Thus the polymorphism is sensitive to the environmental conditions in which the population lives. In this case, the heterozygotes are apparently superior in both habitats; however it is not difficult to find situations in which different genotypes may be favored in different habitats. In these latter situations some populations may be monomorphic while others are polymorphic. For instance, the sickle-cell hemoglobin gene in man confers a selective advantage to heterozygotes in environments where malaria is prevalent, but is disadvantageous in nonmalarial environments. Thus populations in malarial areas tend to be polymorphic whereas populations in nonmalarial areas tend to be monomorphic for the normal allele.

One of the standard assumptions of most models in population genetics is constancy of the relative selective values associated with different genotypes. In recent years, a number of observations have called this assumption into serious question. For example, EHRMAN has shown that genotypic fitnesses may be frequency-dependent. In her study it was determined that the mating success of males possessing rare genotypes was disproportionate to their frequency in the population. Such males leave relatively more offspring than their numbers would indicate, thereby increasing the frequencies of the rare morphs. More recent evidence (Ehrman, *Evolution,* 1969) indicates that the underlying mechanism for the rare-male advantage is based on olfactory discrimination coupled with mate selection behavior by the female.

A number of other investigators have obtained results similar to those of EHRMAN. A great deal of interest in the phenomenon of frequency-dependent selection has been generated among population biologists. One reason for this interest will be pointed out after the next three papers are introduced.

Another example of polymorphism involves the phenomenon of mimicry in a natural population of swallowtail butterflies that has been intensively studied by CLARKE and SHEPPARD for many years. In the present paper they show how disruptive selection may be acting to improve the mimetic pattern. Also, their combined knowledge of both the underlying genetic system and ecological conditions has enabled them to explain the different geographic patterns of swallowtail mimicry in Africa. Like most other studies in which genetics and ecology are jointly applied, their investigation is of much greater significance than would have been possible had they chosen to look at only one aspect of this intriguing phenomenon.

One of the most significant technical advances in biology in recent years has been the development of methods that can be used to assay isoallelic variation at loci controlling the production of certain proteins. One example, taken from a rapidly increasing number of population studies that have utilized these biochemical polymorphisms, is given by MILNE and ROBERTSON. An analysis of several populations of the eider duck revealed an extensive polymorphism for egg albumen proteins, presumably involving at least two alleles at a single locus (although this was not tested by appropriate breeding experiments). The most intriguing results came from an investigation of gene frequencies in migrant and nonmigrant portions of a single population. The migratory ducks were found to have a significantly higher frequency of the rarer allele. This difference is coupled with a high degree of reproductive isolation between the two groups. Although the relationships among egg albumen protein, migratory behavior, and reproductive isolation are not known, this study shows how application of biochemical techniques can provide a means for obtaining information on problems that may otherwise be unapproachable in natural populations.

All of the mechanisms promoting polymorphism lead to the accumulation of genetic variation in populations. One of the most interesting and most important questions facing population biologists today relates to the extent of variation in natural populations. This problem has been approached in an elegant fashion by LEWONTIN and HUBBY utilizing biochemical techniques to assay for isoallelic variation at 18 loci in *Drosophila pseudoobscura.* After discussing the problems associated with previous methods of estimating the degree of polymorphism in natural populations, LEWONTIN and HUBBY present data that lead to surprisingly high estimates of the amount of variation. Although the results of their study raise more questions than they solve, the problem is clearly stated—there seems to be too much variation!

It has been argued that the proteins studied by LEWONTIN and HUBBY are not produced by loci from a representative sample of the genome. Further, errors in LEWONTIN and HUBBY's overdominance model have been pointed out by others. One possible solution to the dilemma involves the frequency-dependent selection model discussed earlier. If a substantial proportion of this isoallelic variation is maintained by frequency-dependent selection with selective neutrality at equilibrium, then the problem of intolerably high genetic loads can be circumvented, since selection occurs only when genotypes are present at nonequilibrium frequencies. Whatever explanation turns out to be the ultimate resolution of this dilemma, their insights and methods have provided a tremendous stimulus to the field of population biology.

# MORPHOLOGICAL VARIATION AND WIDTH OF ECOLOGICAL NICHE

LEIGH VAN VALEN

Department of Vertebrate Paleontology, American Museum of
Natural History, New York

How does a species maintain its genetic variability in a form suitable for adaptive evolution without an unbearable genetic load? One of the answers to this question has been that different individuals in a population may be adapted to somewhat different environments. This hypothesis normally requires the existence of all the following three conditions, where the population may be divided into sets $a$, $b$, ... $n$ and the niche inhabited by the population into more or less separable units (although complete gradation is by no means excluded for either phenotype or environment), $A$, $B$, ... $M$, at least at the time of year when population size is limited:

1) The individuals of some set $a$ survive or reproduce better than those of some set $b$ in some environment $A$, while the reverse is true in some environment $B$.

2) The above difference between $a$ and $b$ is in part genetic.

3) Some appropriate mechanism of distributional or mating preference exists. The third condition can be met by individuals of set $a$ choosing environment $A$ with a greater than random frequency, or by homogamic mating (at the limit of which $a$ and $b$ are two reproductively isolated species) if $A$ and $B$ differ spatially and there is a positive correlation between the locations of birth and mating.

It is important to note that continuous variation as well as polymorphism can be maintained by this model, the advantage of one or the other depending in part (not as an absolute condition in either direction) on the degree of regularity and continuity of the environment. Stabilizing selection is weaker with greater intra-niche diversity, and may even be absent or negative (destabilizing selection) when strong discontinuities are present within the niche.

Intrapopulation variation in niche occupied permits a greater population size than would otherwise be possible, and is advantageous even when a polymorphism is maintained by some other means. Genetic control need not be present in such cases. As an example of this advantage, if $a$ and $b$ are the sexes (however determined), equally abundant and of equal size, and eat different foods of the same abundance, and if population size is limited by the availability of food, then the population size will be twice what it would be if the sexes ate the same food.

Coexistence of morphologically or physiologically different phenotypes, as well as the behavioral or microgeographic diversity mentioned above,

Reprinted by permission of The University of Chicago Press and the author from *The American Naturalist* 99:377–390, 1965.

would be useful on both the individual and the population levels for exploitation of a diversified niche, and it is therefore probable that under the above conditions the population would be more variable than if it occupied a narrower niche.

Various aspects of the above theory have been formalized by Ludwig (1950), Levene (1953), Li (1955a, b), Lewontin (1955), Maynard Smith (1962), and Levins (1962, 1963); see also Dempster (1955). It was perhaps first explicitly proposed by Mayr (1945), although others approached it earlier. Mayr (1963) has summarized some of the evidence for the subsidiary hypotheses of the model.

The niche-variation model is compatible with a dependence of fitness on relative frequency of genotypes or phenotypes, but neither situation implies the other. For example, learning by predators can produce a frequency-dependent polymorphism in their prey, and if one part of the niche cannot be tolerated or reached by some individuals, reduction in the frequency of individuals occupying that part will not change the relative fitness of those excluded from it. Even in the more usual case, where a reduction in frequency of one form leads to an increased relative fitness in its part of the niche, this occurs only when that part of the niche remains habitable and would not apply when an environmental change reduced the frequency by reducing the parts of the niche differentially.

In the present paper I will compare the variation within populations of some birds that differ regionally as to width of niche. In one region, usually on the zoogeographic mainland, the niches of the species are relatively tightly packed together by the action of stabilizing selection imposed by ecologically adjacent species. In the other region, usually on islands, the environment available for the birds is partitioned into wider niches, which implies weaker stabilizing selection by adjacent species. The wider niches would permit greater phenotypic variation if this variation is controlled to a significant extent by the adaptive diversity of the niche. The results suggest that this is in fact the case.

By "niche width" I mean the proportion of the total multidimensional space of limiting resources used by a species or segment of a community. "Niche" is used here in an observational sense, not a theoretical one. The relative sizes of the niches in the regions compared have been studied for the species used and found to be different in the directions stated (see next section). The relative number of species in the total fauna is a related question, but one that I will not consider because it seems relevant only to the average relative width of the niches in each fauna, and the actual relative width for each species is known from direct observation.

Let us consider a segment of a community called a "trophic-A level" dependent upon some set, usually a relatively diverse set, of limiting resources. There are three extreme ways in which such a segment of a community can exploit the available supply of the limiting resources:

1) There can be relatively few species, each individual of each of which is adapted to occupy a relatively broad segment of the resource space.

Each individual may occupy this entire segment, or there may be a behavioral partitioning of the segment.

2) There can be relatively few species, but these are relatively variable and different individuals within a species are fitted to, and do in fact, occupy on the average different narrow niches (or, equivalently, different parts of a broad niche).

3) There can be a relatively large number of species, each of which is restricted to a relatively narrow segment of the resource space, more or less uniform for each individual.

These alternatives are not mutually exclusive on the community level, and most trophic-A levels of most communities probably contain more than one kind of species. Species intermediate between the extremes given are presumably common. Genetically controlled interindividual behavioral and morphological variation related to the occupation of the niche should on the average be large in the second kind of species and small in the first and third, although environmentally controlled behavioral (and in a few taxa morphological) variation may sometimes also be large in the first kind. In small and unstable communities (for example, on islets), and in stable trophic-A levels where the limiting resource changes in quality from time to time (for example, changes in composition of prey), I would expect the first kind of species to predominate. In large and exceptionally stable communities I would expect a preponderance of the third kind, which should also predominate among the rare species of most communities, excluding species maintained by immigration. The set of moderately to very stable communities should contain the greatest proportion of the second kind of species, which perhaps may never comprise a majority of the species in a community. This list is obviously suggestive rather than exhaustive, and may be compared with an analogous list, with supporting theory and involving mainly other criteria, given by Levins (1963).

I regard the fact that the present comparisons are between island and mainland populations as logically (not necessarily causally) irrelevant insofar as the relative number of species in the avifaunas is concerned. It is unknown to what extent niches are vacant or incompletely occupied on the islands, and to what extent the relative impoverishment of the island biotas is cybernetic by, in itself, restricting the number of potential niches for any trophic-A level. Because of these considerations, no *a priori* prediction of greater average niche width on the islands can be given with assurance. Island and mainland populations of most of the species on which comparisons have been made of niche width are, at the levels of resolution used, indistinguishable in niche width. I have ignored these species, although they are relevant to any consideration of relative niche width on the islands. Some species clearly have broader niches on the islands, and these species have been used here. In one case the island niche is clearly narrower than that on the mainland, and it is interesting that in this case the mainland populations, rather than the island ones, seem to be more variable.

MATERIAL

Aside from cases due to human influence or to differences in the availability of some resources (testable cases if the difference is of long standing), the only instances I know in which intraspecific differences in width of ecological niche have been demonstrated involve some of the birds inhabiting Bermuda, Curacao, the Azores, and the Canaries. Lack and Southern (1949) observed that several species on the Canaries occurred in a different (usually wider) variety of local habitats than did the same species on the mainland, and Marler and Boatman (1951) and Vaurie (1957) made similar observations for other species on the Azores. Of these species five are present in American collections in sufficient numbers for statistical tests to be made, and these five species are therefore used in the present study. They are *Phylloscopus collybita* (the chiffchaff), *Parus caeruleus* (the blue tit), and *Fringilla coelebs* (the chaffinch) from the Canaries, and *Fringilla coelebs*, *Motacilla cinerea* (the gray wagtail), and *Regulus regulus* (the goldcrest) from the Azores. C. Vaurie (verbal communication) has informed me that *F. coelebs* has a wider niche in natural habitats in the Azores than on the mainland. Marler and Boatman (1951) merely note that it has expanded its habitat into towns, a change I would otherwise ignore.

Because the above observers (except Vaurie) are British, comparison has been made with British (not Irish) specimens wherever possible. In the cases of Phylloscopus and Parus, series from Bonn, Germany, have also been included, and for Motacilla, Britain and the entire European mainland west of Russia (excluding Scandinavia and Iberia) were used. All the insular populations are placed in different subspecies from those of Europe (including Britain), and in some cases different subspecies are recognized between individual islands. Each island was treated as the locality of a single population, and on the mainland (including Britain) the maximum area used for one population was the county of Devon. The only exception was Motacilla, a very recent invader of Europe, in which all European specimens were treated as a single population because of lack of any series from a single locality. The sexes were treated separately; unsexed specimens, damaged specimens, and those with the bill clearly constricted by string were ignored.

A fortunate circumstance permits some control over factors other than width of niche. In the case of *Fringilla coelebs* of the Canaries, the niche is not wider but narrower on two islands (Gran Canaria and Teneriffe) than on the mainland. This difference is correlated with the presence on only these islands of a second species (*F. teydea*), which occupies the pineforest habitat that is part of the range of *F. coelebs* elsewhere on the Canaries and on the mainland. Therefore only specimens from Gran Canaria, Teneriffe, and the mainland were used for one comparison of *F. coelebs*. In the Azores the niche is, as with the other species used, wider than on the mainland.

The measurement used was the width of the culmen at the anterior border of the left nostril. The bill is not necessarily a constant character (no morphological character in birds has been shown to be invariant within an individual both seasonally and throughout the span of adult life), but the dates of collection were recorded for most of the specimens measured and the seasonal variation in collection time is closely comparable between island and mainland. Sample sizes and usually a scarcity of specimens collected in the middle third of the year did not permit an accurate determination of possible seasonal change within a population; any change present is not great. Davis (1954, 1961) has shown that the length of the bill of some birds varies seasonally because of differential attrition, although seasonal differences in its growth were not excluded as a contributory factor; the cycle demonstrated would presumably have less effect, if any, on bill width.

It is possible that migration may have caused some mixture of populations in mainland samples, but, as will be seen, any such effect does not eliminate the differences present.

On Curaçao and nearby islands two species have been reported by Voous (1957, p. 39) to have unusually wide niches in comparison with the rest of their range: *Mimus gilvus* (the southern mockingbird) and *Crotophaga sulcirostris* (the groove-billed ani). Voous remarked on a possible causal relation of this difference in niche in Mimus to a difference in its variation, but gave no comparative data. Crotophaga apparently reached Curaçao only in the last century, and would not necessarily be expected to have established a stable pattern of variation. Mimus is subspecifically distinct from the mainland forms. Voous (1957) gives measurements for both species from the islands, and I have made similar measurements on mainland samples of Mimus from single localities. Because there are only six degrees of freedom for each sex in Voous's data for Crotophaga (eight specimens, two localities), I did not measure mainland specimens of it. The measurement used for Mimus is length of bill. My measurement may not be exactly the same as that of Voous because of possible differences in techniques, but this should not affect the variation.

## STATISTICAL METHODS

The hypothesis to be tested is that the intrapopulation coefficient of variation is larger (except Fringilla of the Canaries) on the islands than on the mainland, including Britain. As tests are available for the variance but not for the coefficient of variation as such, the variance is used and a scaling correction made for any difference in mean.

Aside from the biological impossibility of making any other kind of correction for size in the present case, I believe that the use of coefficients of variation or their equivalent is at least as justified as assuming, with Fisher (1937) and some others, that large and small groups are biologically equally variable and then calculating an empirical relationship among the variances of groups with different means. A change of scale produces a

change in the variance and in any transformation of the variance not equivalent to the coefficient of variation; I believe that this fact is adequate
justification for use of the coefficient of variation under any circumstances
I can imagine.

Homogeneity of intrapopulation variance within a region (that is, among
the islands or mainland populations) was tested by Bartlett's test. Only
two comparisons were significant at the 5 per cent (but not at the 1 per
cent) level; such a frequency of spuriously significant results is to be expected when 26 comparisons (within region and sex) are made, and they
will be ignored. The test is probably unnecessary in any event (Box,
1953).

The intrapopulation variance for a region was obtained by the equation

$$s^2 = \frac{\displaystyle\sum_{j=1}^{m} \sum_{i=1}^{n} (x_{ij} - \overline{x}_j)^2}{\left(\displaystyle\sum n\right) - m}$$

where there are $m$ populations and $n$ individuals in one population.

Homogeneity of means within a region and species was tested approximately by a two-way hierarchical analysis of variance, with population and
sex as the variables. The probabilities for each region were then combined to give a joint probability for the region, by both Fisher's method
(1958) and Barton's modification of mine (Barton, 1964; Van Valen, 1964).
The hypothesis tested here is the presence of interpopulation variation in
one or more species on the mainland and also on the islands. The populations of Mimus from the American mainland were not used in this test; their
means are obviously heterogeneous and the distance between populations
is much greater than for the European populations.

Whether or not there was a significant difference in mean between the island and mainland populations, the mainland variance was multiplied by
the square of the ratio of the island mean to the mainland mean. This correction makes relatively little difference in the significance of the results
(it usually slightly lowers the probability of significance), and is done to
remove the usual proportionality, from scaling effects, between the mean
and standard deviation. The only other statistical effect of the correction
is a slight reduction in the power of distinguishing populations with different variation, because the means are not uniquely known. The resulting
variances were compared by the F test. Comparison of the uncorrected
variation by Levene's test (1960) gives similar results; the latter test (on
which see also Van Valen, in press) could be refined by multiplying each
mainland measurement, before testing, by the ratio of the means, but this
was not done.

Measurement error was estimated by 21 replicate measurements per species, and was assumed to be homogeneous within a species. The esti-

mated variance is the sum of the measurement variance and the true variance of the population.  Because it is the latter that is of interest, I sub-
tracted the measurement variance from each estimated variance and corrected as above for the difference in means.  A final correction on the
variance ratio, to remove a small effect of different sample size, is to divide by the appropriate F value at 50 per cent.  The resulting ratio is an
unbiased estimate of the ratio of the intrapopulation variation on the islands to that on the mainland (except Fringilla of the Canaries), although
significance tests should be performed on the ratio given in the preceding
paragraph.

### RESULTS AND DISCUSSION

From the results given in table 1 there seems to be no real room for
doubt that the species studied are on the average more variable in the region with a wider niche.  In none of the 12 independent tests are the populations with a narrower niche more variable than the others; the probability
of this happening by chance is less than 0.001.  Combining the 12 probabilities also gives a joint one-tailed probability of less than 0.001.

The unweighted mean of the 14 corrected $F$ ratios is 2.20, and the weighted
mean is 2.00.  In other words, the birds with the more variable niche are
about twice as variable in bill width or length as the others.  This suggests
that adaptation to different aspects of the environment is a major cause of
variation, at least in passerine birds.

There is significant interpopulation heterogeneity in mean bill width on
both the islands and the mainland ($P < 0.01$ in each case).  This heterogeneity did not suppress the island versus mainland difference in *Motacilla
cinerea*, if heterogeneity was present on the mainland in this species, but
may well have contributed to the failure of Crowell (1962) to find a similarly consistent difference in comparisons of three species between Bermuda
and North America.  Because of scarcity of material he was forced to use
the territory east of Indiana from Pennsylvania to Florida as a single population; any interpopulation variation within this region would increase the
mainland variance and so reduce the difference with Bermuda.  Crowell also
found little difference between island and mainland in diversity of feeding
habits in the species he studied, although the total niche was apparently
broader on Bermuda.

There is no indication of a greater difference between the sexes on the
islands than on the mainland.

The greater variation found on the islands was predicted by the hypothesis stated in the introduction, but clearly does not prove that the hypothesis is correct.  There may be correlated factors that would also lead to a
greater variation.  It is conceivable, for instance, that the food of the young
is more heterogeneous from nest to nest on the islands and that the greater
phenotypic variance found there is not related to a greater genetic variance.  The case of Fringilla of the Canaries, with a prediction and ostensi-
ble result opposite to those for the other species and the same species in

## TABLE 1

Comparative within-population statistics of bill measurements (in millimeters) for several species of birds (see text)

| | Population with wider niche | $\overline{X}$ | $s^2$ | C.V. | Corrected $F$ | $P(s_1^2 \leq s_2^2)$ | Degrees of freedom |
|---|---|---|---|---|---|---|---|
| **Phylloscopus collybita** | | | | | | | |
| males | | | | | | | |
| Canaries | x n.s | 2.28 | 0.0254 | 6.99 | | | 8 |
| mainland | | 2.14 | 0.0141 | 5.55 | 1.86 | 0.10–0.20 | 23 |
| females | | | | | | | |
| Canaries | x n.s | 2.30 | 0.0088 | 4.07 | | | 10 |
| mainland | | 2.31 | 0.0047 | 2.96 | 2.11 | 0.20–0.25 | 6 |
| **Parus caeruleus** | | | | | | | |
| males | | | | | | | |
| Canaries | x | ·3.47 | 0.0381 | 5.62 | | | 21 |
| mainland | | 3.55 | 0.0141 | 3.35 | 3.10 | 0.001–0.005 | 35 |
| females | | | | | | | |
| Canaries | x n,s | 3.37 | 0.0143 | 3.54 | | | 20 |
| mainland | | 3.46 | 0.0128 | 3.27 | 1.19 | 0.40–0.50 | 29 |
| **Fringilla coelebs** | | | | | | | |
| males | | | | | | | |
| Azores | x | 6.49 | 0.0553 | 3.62 | 1.78 | 0.01–0.025 | 87 |
| Canaries | | 6.10 | 0.0229 | 2.55 | | | 15 |
| mainland | x n.s | 5.67 | 0.0242 | 2.74 | 1.11 | 0.40–0.50 | 64 |
| females | | | | | | | |
| Azores | x | 6.05 | 0.0625 | 4.13 | 2.08 | 0.025–0.05 | 36 |
| Canaries | | 6.01 | 0.0171 | 2.28 | | | 7 |
| mainland | x n,s. | 5.37 | 0.0241 | 2.89 | 1.65 | 0.20–0.25 | 24 |
| **Motacilla cinerea** | | | | | | | |
| males | | | | | | | |
| Azores | x n.s | 3.41 | 0.0306 | 5.13 | | | 24 |
| mainland | | 3.00 | 0.0203 | 4.75 | 1.21 | 0.25–0.40 | 31 |
| females | | | | | | | |
| Azores | x | 3.33 | 0.0414 | 6.11 | | | 15 |
| mainland | | 3.06 | 0.0131 | 3.75 | 2.88 | 0.01–0.025 | 19 |
| **Regulus regulus** | | | | | | | |
| males | | | | | | | |
| Azores | x | 2.18 | 0.0417 | 9.37 | | | 32 |
| mainland | | 1.70 | 0.0123 | 6.53 | 2.33 | 0.025–0.05 | 31 |
| females | | | | | | | |
| Azores | x | 2.24 | 0.0360 | 8.47 | | | 17 |
| mainland | | 1.77 | 0.0070 | 4.73 | 4.12 | 0.025–0.05 | 10 |
| **Mimus gilvus** | | | | | | | |
| males | | | | | | | |
| Curaçao | x | 26.92 | 2.231 | 5.55 | | | 15 |
| mainland | | 21.42 | 0.362 | 2.81 | 3.94 | 0.005–0.01 | 16 |
| females | | | | | | | |
| Curaçao | x n,s, | 26.13 | 0.727 | 3.26 | | | 12 |
| mainland | | 22.10 | 0.362 | 2.72 | 1.47 | 0.20–0.25 | 17 |

the Azores, suggests that width of niche is involved in some way. Comparison with species that have similar food habits as on the mainland would be useful in testing other possibilities, but although no island-mainland differences in food or habitat are known for several species of the Canaries and the Azores, none of these species have as yet been sufficiently well studied to be sure that important differences do not exist.

It is unknown from field observations whether the greater diversity of food presumably eaten on the islands is done by largely different individuals, or whether each bird partakes of the entire array of food of its species. In the latter case no clear-cut prediction could be made. On the one hand the environmental component of the phenotypic variance is probably larger in a more diverse environment, and greater heterozygosity (related to a greater genetic variance) may be useful in coping with a more diverse environment, but on the other hand the heterozygotes themselves may be less variable. Heterozygosity may, however, be greater on the mainland because of migration.

It is possible that most of the island populations are more homozygous than those on the mainland. The effect of this possible difference on the phenotypic variance is uncertain, although it would probably not produce much increase if any. In the only direct study of this relationship Bader (1956) found almost as much phenotypic variance in laboratory-raised inbred lines of three rodents as in wild populations. The studies of the relationship between abundance and variation, cited below, show only a small average effect with large differences in abundance. *Fringilla coelebs* is a very common species in the Azores and rare in the Canaries; its pattern of variation is the reverse of that predicted by the hypothesis that canalization (insensitivity to environmental variation) is reduced in rare species.

The distributions of the measurements for the island populations give no suggestion of bimodality. The greater variation is therefore probably not maintained by any system of polymorphism but rather by the various mechanisms available for continuous variation.

In other animals there is some evidence for a relationship of variation with width of niche. In several species of Drosophila (*D. robusta, D. nebulosa, D. acutilabella, D. americana texana, D. nigromelanica, D. immigrans, D. willistoni*, parts of *D. pseudoobscura* and *D. subobscura*, and perhaps *D. euronotus*) and in *Chironomus tentans* there is a decrease of inversion polymorphism in geographically peripheral and ecologically marginal areas (da Cunha, Burla, and Dobzhansky, 1950; Townsend, 1952; da Cunha, Brncic, and Salzano, 1953; da Cunha and Dobzhansky, 1954; Brncic, 1955; Carson, 1955, 1956, 1958; da Cunha et al., 1959; Acton, 1959; Dobzhansky et al., 1963; Stalker, 1964a, b; Carson and Heed, 1964; Sperlich, 1964; Prevosti, 1964), although this is not true for all species or populations. A possibly similar situation occurs in *D. funebris* between urban and rural environments (Dubinin and Tiniakov, 1946, 1947); however, both urban and rural environments have been interpreted in the literature as more variable for Drosophila. The alternative or supplementary hypothesis of Carson (for example, 1955), involving a greater potentiality for recombination in marginal areas, does not consider the compensating increase of recombination elsewhere in the genome caused by a heterozygous inversion, and so is perhaps of less than full applicability. How to reconcile it with the apparently superior homeostasis of inversion heterozygotes and of polymorphic populations is also obscure. Genetic drift in one or more of its forms could also produce a similar pattern of distribution. In the *D. cardini* species group (Heed, 1963) there is a particularly interesting situation in that color polymorphism is less frequent in peripheral areas; the polymorphism is differently determined in different species and the two morphs even belong to different species in some areas, which strongly suggests an ecological control. Other studies are summarized by Mayr (1963); see also Sieburth (1964).

There is also some evidence (Fisher and Ford, 1928; Fisher, 1937; Dobzhansky, Burla, and da Cunha, 1950; da Cunha, Brncic, and Salzano, 1953; Salzano, 1955; data discussed but not presented by Darwin, 1859) that numerically abundant species tend to be more variable than their rarer relatives, although for the data used by Fisher (1937) and in part those used by Darwin (1859) the variation discussed is over quite wide geographic areas. This relationship is probably best explained by the variation-niche hypothesis; the evidence is not as clear-cut as for comparisons within species, and more studies are needed.

The few known examples in nature of destabilizing (centrifugal, disruptive, diversifying, fractionating) selection are presumably examples of the same phenomenon (maintenance of variation by adaptation to different parts of a niche), although destabilizing selection need not be involved in it. Different intensities of stabilizing selection could produce the same result. These cases (demonstrated or probable) of destabilizing selection are in a grasshopper (White, Lewontin, and Andrew, 1963, p. 159), butterflies (Brower, 1959; Clarke and Sheppard, 1962; Creed et al., 1959, 1962; Ford, 1964), a gull (Smith, 1964), and a mouse (Van Valen, 1963), in addition to cases such as that studied by Bradshaw (1963) and Jowett (1964) where sharp ecological boundaries cross an interbreeding population. The latter cases grade into the usual adaptive geographic ("ecotypic") variation. Variation produced by spatially varying use of pesticides and antibiotics is similar in principle. The frequently nongenetic stunted nature of plants grown on poor soil or under other adverse conditions is clearly adaptive in permitting any to survive and reproduce (see Harrison, 1959).

On the basis of the new and old evidence discussed in the present paper, it seems probable that adaptation to different aspects of the environment is a major cause of variation in at least higher animals and plants. In other words, much variation is probably adaptive in itself and is not part of the genetic or phenotypic load.

SUMMARY

In six bird species convenient for study, niches are known to be broader on some islands than on the mainland. In every case there is also greater variation in a bill measurement on the islands, except for one species in which the niche on the Canary Islands is narrower than that on the mainland. The adjusted variances average about twice as great in the broader niche. These and other results suggest that continuous variation within local populations is often adaptive in itself and is not part of the genetic or phenotypic load.

## ACKNOWLEDGMENTS

I am particularly indebted in Dr. Charles Vaurie for introducing me to birds. He and Drs. Robert H. MacArthur, George E. Watson, Richard C. Lewontin, Edward O. Wilson, and Ernst Mayr also made various useful suggestions. Dr. Vaurie, Dr. Philip S. Humphrey of the United States National Museum, and Dr. Raymond A. Paynter of the Museum of Comparative Zoology permitted measurements of specimens in their care.

## LITERATURE CITED

Acton, A. B., 1959, A study of the differences between widely separated populations of *Chironomus* (=*Tendipes*) *tentans* (Diptera). Proc. Roy. Soc. London (B) 151: 271–296.

Bader, R. S., 1956, Variability in wild and inbred mammalian populations. Quart. J. Florida Acad. Sci. 19: 14–34.

Barton, D. E., 1964, Combining the probabilities from significance tests. Nature 202: 731.

Box, G. E. P., 1953, Non-normality and tests on variances. Biometrika 40: 318–335.

Bradshaw, A. D., 1963, The analysis of evolutionary processes involved in the divergence of plant populations. Proc. XI Int. Cong. Genet. 1: 143.

Brncic, D., 1955, Chromosomal variation in Chilean populations of *Drosophila immigrans*. J. Hered. 46: 59–63.

Brower, J. vZ., 1959 (discussion after paper by Thoday). Proc. XV Cong. Zool.: 130.

Carson, H. L., 1955, The genetic characteristics of marginal populations of *Drosophila*. Cold Spring Harbor Symp. Quant. Biol. 20: 276–287.

    1956, Marginal homozygosity for gene arrangement in *Drosophila robusta*. Science 123: 630–631.

    1958, The population genetics of *Drosophila robusta*. Adv. Genet. 9: 1–40.

Carson, H. L., and W. B. Heed, 1964, Structural homozygosity in marginal populations of nearctic and neotropical species of Drosophila in Florida. Proc. Nat. Acad. Sci. 52: 427–430.

Clarke, C. A., and P. M. Sheppard, 1962, Disruptive selection and its effect on a metrical character in the butterfly *Papilio dardanus*. Evolution 16: 214–226.

Creed, E. R., W. H. Dowdeswell, E. B. Ford, and K. G. McWhirter, 1959, Evolutionary studies on *Maniola jurtina*: the English mainland, 1956–57. Heredity 13: 363–391.

    1962, Evolutionary studies on *Maniola jurtina*: the English mainland, 1958–60. Heredity 17: 237–265.

Crowell, K. L., 1962, Reduced interspecific competition among the birds of
    Bermuda.  Ecology 43: 75–88.
da Cunha, A. B., D. Brncic, and F. M. Salzano, 1953, A comparative study
    of chromosomal polymorphism in certain South American species
    of Drosophila.  Heredity 7: 193–202.
da Cunha, A. B., H. Burla, and Th. Dobzhansky, 1950, Adaptive chromo-
    somal polymorphism in *Drosophila willistoni*.  Evolution 4:
    212–235.
da Cunha, A. B., and Th. Dobzhansky, 1954, A further study of chromo-
    somal polymorphism in *Drosophila willistoni* in its relation to the
    environment.  Evolution 8: 119–134.
da Cunha, A. B., Th. Dobzhansky, O. Pavlovsky, and B. Spassky, 1959,
    Genetics of natural populations.  XXVIII. Supplementary data on
    the chromosomal polymorphism in *Drosophila willistoni* in its re-
    lation to the environment.  Evolution 13: 389–404.
Darwin, C., 1859, On the origin of species by means of natural selection.
    J. Murray, London.
Davis, J., 1954, Seasonal changes in bill length of certain passerine birds.
    Condor 56: 142–149.
    1961, Some seasonal changes in morphology of the rufous-sided towhee.
    Condor 63: 313–321.
Dempster, E. R., 1955, Maintenance of genetic heterogeneity.  Cold Spring
    Harbor Symp. Quant. Biol. 20: 25–32.
Dobzhansky, Th., H. Burla, and A. B. da Cunha, 1950, A comparative study
    of chromosomal polymorphism in sibling species of the *willistoni*
    group of *Drosophila*.  Amer. Natur. 84: 229–246.
Dobzhansky, Th., A. Hunter, O. Pavlovsky, B. Spassky, and B. Wallace,
    1963, Genetics of natural populations.  XXXI. Genetics of an
    isolated marginal population of *Drosophila pseudoobscura*.  Ge-
    netics 48: 91–103.
Dubinin, N. P., and G. G. Tiniakov, 1946, Structural chromosome varia-
    bility in urban and rural populations of *Drosophila funebris*.
    Amer. Natur. 80: 393–396.
    1947, Inversion gradients and selection in ecological races of *Droso-
    phila funebris*.  Amer. Natur. 81: 148–153.
Fisher, R. A., 1937, The relation between variability and abundance shown
    by the measurements of the eggs of British nesting birds.  Proc.
    Roy. Soc. London (B) 122: 1–26.
    1958, Statistical methods for research workers.  13th ed.  Oliver and
    Boyd, Edinburgh.
Fisher, R. A., and E. B. Ford, 1928, The variability of species in the
    Lepidoptera, with reference to abundance and sex.  Trans.
    Entomol. Soc. London 76: 367–384.
Ford, E. B., 1964, Ecological genetics.  Methuen, London.
Harrison, G. A., 1959, Environmental determination of the phenotype, p.
    81–86.  *In* A. J. Cain (ed.), Function and taxonomic importance.
    Systematics Assoc. Pub. No. 3.
Heed, W. B., 1963, Density and distribution of *Drosophila polymorpha* and
    its color alleles in South America.  Evolution 17: 502–518.

Jowett, D., 1964, Population studies on lead-tolerant *Agrostis tenuis*. Evolution 18: 70-80.

Lack, D., and H. N. Southern, 1949, Birds on Tenerife. Ibis 91: 607-626.

Levene, H., 1953, Genetic equilibrium when more than one ecological niche is available. Amer. Natur. 87: 331-333.

——— 1960, Robust tests for equality of variances, p. 278-292. *In* Olkin, Ghurye, Hoeffding, Madow, and Mann (eds.), Contributions to probability and statistics. Stanford University Press.

Levins, R., 1962, Theory of fitness in a heterogeneous environment. I. The fitness set and adaptive function. Amer. Natur. 96: 361-373.

——— 1963, Theory of fitness in a heterogeneous environment. II. Developmental flexibility and niche selection. Amer. Natur. 97: 75-90.

Lewontin, R. C., 1955, The effects of population density and competition on viability in *Drosophila melanogaster*. Evolution 9: 27-41.

Li, C. C., 1955a, The stability of an equilibrium and the average fitness of a population. Amer. Natur. 89: 281-296.

——— 1955b, Population genetics. Univ. Chicago Press, Chicago.

Ludwig, W., 1950, Zur Theorie der Konkurrenz. Neue Ergeb. Prob. Zool., Klatt-Festschrift: 516-537.

Marler, P., and D. J. Boatman, 1951, Observations on the birds of Pico, Azores. Ibis 91: 607-626.

Maynard Smith, J., 1962, Disruptive selection, polymorphism, and sympatric speciation. Nature 195: 60-62.

Mayr, E., 1945, Some evidence in favor of a recent date: symposium on the age of the distribution pattern of the gene arrangements in *Drosophila pseudoobscura*. Lloydia 8: 70-83.

——— 1963, Animal species and evolution. Harvard Univ. Press, Cambridge, Mass.

Prevosti, A., 1964, Chromosomal polymorphism in *Drosophila subobscura* populations from Barcelona (Spain). Genet. Res. 5: 27-38.

Salzano, F. M., 1955, Chromosomal polymorphism in two species of the *guarani* group of *Drosophila*. Chromosoma 7: 39-50.

Sieburth, J. M., 1964, Polymorphism of a marine bacterium (*Arthrobacter*) as a function of multiple temperature optima and nutrition. Narragansett Marine Lab., Univ. Rhode Island, Occ. Pub. 2: 11-16.

Smith, N. G., 1964, Evolution of some arctic gulls (*Larus*): a study of isolating mechanisms. Dissert. Abst. 24: 3901.

Sperlich, D., 1964, Chromosomale Strukturanalyse und Fertilitätsprüfung an einer Marginalpopulation von *Drosophila subobscura*. Z. Vererb. 95: 73-81.

Stalker, H. D., 1964a, Chromosomal polymorphism in *Drosophila euronotus*. Genetics 49: 669-687.

——— 1964b, The salivary gland chromosomes of *Drosophila nigromelanica*. Genetics 49: 883-893.

Townsend, J. I., 1952, Genetics of marginal populations of *Drosophila willistoni*. Evolution 6: 428-442.

Van Valen, L., 1963, Intensities of selection in natural populations. Proc. XI Int. Cong. Genet. 1: 153.

   1964, Combining the probabilities from significance tests. Nature 201:
        642.
   1965, Selection in natural populations.   III. Measurement and estima-
        tion.   Evolution.   (In press)
Vaurie, C., 1957, Systematic notes on Palearctic birds.   No. 25.   Motacil-
        lidae: the genus *Motacilla.*   Amer. Mus. Novitates 1832: 1–16.
Voous, K. H., 1957, The birds of Aruba, Curaçao, and Bonaire, p. 1–260.
        *In* P. H. Hummelinck (ed.), Studies on the fauna of Curaçao and
        other Caribbean islands, Vol. 7.   Martinus Nijhoff, The Hague.
White, M. J. D., R. C. Lewontin, and L. E. Andrew, 1963, Cytogenetics of
        the grasshopper *Moraba scurra.*   VII. Geographic variation of
        adaptive properties of inversions.   Evolution 17: 147–162.

## The Ecological Significance of Sexual Dimorphism in Size in the Lizard Anolis conspersus

Abstract. *Adult males of* Anolis conspersus *capture prey of significantly larger size and occupy perches of significantly greater diameter and height than do adult females; similarly, these three dimensions of the niche are significantly larger for adult females than for juveniles. Adult males on the average eat a smaller number of prey, and the range in size of prey is larger. The relationship between the average length of the prey and that of the predator is linear when the predator size is above 36 millimeters, but becomes asymptotic when it is below that value. Subadult males as long as adult females eat significantly larger food than do the latter, but only in the larger lizards is this correlated with a relatively larger head.* Anolis conspersus *selects prey from a wide range of taxa and shows no obvious intraspecific specialization not connected to differences in microhabitat and prey size. The efficiency of this system for solitary species is pointed out.*

Anoline lizards make up the most conspicuous and diversified vertebrate genus in the West Indies. There are many very small islands with at least one species, and the greatest numbers occur on the large islands of Cuba, with 22 species, and Hispaniola, with 20 species. Most species of *Anolis* which occur without congeners are about the same absolute size from island to island, the heads of adult males measuring 17 to 21 mm and the snout-vent lengths being 65 to 75 mm. Furthermore, the sexes are highly dimorphic in size, the head length of adult males averaging 1.3 to 1.5 times that of females (1). This striking convergence from at least seven different stocks (1) implies that on islands where an anoline lizard occurs without congeners, nat-

ural selection has favored an optimum size and sexual dimorphism, either because unsuitably proportioned colonists are eliminated, or because later there is an increase in size dimorphism between the sexes. Presumably this latter process, at least, is a reflection of the phenomenon of "ecological release," in which one species, in the absence of closely related species, increases the breadth of certain critical dimensions of its ecological niche.

Two nonexclusive hypotheses concerning the adaptive significance of sexual dimorphism in size were tested for one of the convergent solitary species, Anolis conspersus of Grand Cayman Island. The first, that size differences might reflect differences in structural habitat (2) such as perch size, I tested by noting the height above ground and the diameter of perches of 474 lizards in several habitats. The second, that such differences reflect a difference in the distribution of prey size, I examined by analyzing the stomachs and intestinal contents of 166 lizards collected in the same areas (3).

Differences in both prey size and microhabitat have previously been reported for age and sex classes of different sizes within other species of lizards. A greater proportion of large insects were found in larger adult males than in adult females of *Anolis lineatopus* and *Agama agama* (4, 5); similarly, juveniles take smaller food than adults (5–7). Sexual differences in the preferred microhabitat have been found in *Anolis lineatopus, A. cybotes,* and *A. sagrei* (4, 8), and juvenile-adult stratification has been observed (4, 7–9).

Grand Cayman is a flat, relatively dry island about 32 km long with a maximum width of a little over 6 km. Most of the vegetation consists of several types of mangrove associations or xeric scrub forest, some growing directly on top of bare coral rock.

*Anolis conspersus* occurs in nearly all habitats where there is shade but seems most common in moderately shaded areas with a variety of tree sizes and a relatively open forest floor. Lizards were observed and collected in areas including beach vegetation (especially *Rhizophora, Coccoloba,* and *Casuarina*), inland mangrove forests, open scrub forest vegetation (especially *Bursera,* palms, and a variety of leguminous trees and shrubs), or more closed forest vegetation (especially *Bursera, Ficus, Cassia*). Although more females than adult males were collected, the two were sampled in approximately the same proportions in all habitats.

The properties of the structural niche were determined according to the method of Rand (2), in which the diameter and height of the perch occupied by each individual is recorded. An area was covered only once, and each observation is of a different individual. To facilitate comparison, I placed the resulting data into frequency tables with intervals identical to those used by Rand (Table 1). Although there is a good deal of overlapping, adult males tended to occupy larger perches and to occur higher than did females; females, in turn, occupied larger perches and occurred at greater heights than did juveniles (lizards with snout-vent length below 33 mm). All these differences are statistically highly significant. The perches of subadult males (males the same sizes as adult females) have distributions of height and diameter intermediate between those of adult males and females (10). Therefore, the hypothesis that sexual differences in size are associated with structural differences in habitat is confirmed.

For each prey item the length and volume (length times average width times average depth) was measured or estimated. Prey from the entire length of the digestive tract were included rather than just those contained in the stomach, because the tendency for a large item to be more widely spread over the entire tract than a small one would otherwise result in a disproportionate frequency of large prey. Although both adult males and females take a much greater number of prey that are from 1 to 5 mm long than they do of larger prey, the food items of females are significantly smaller, both within the range of 1 to 5 mm ($P <.001$) and over the whole range of food size ($P <.001$). Nearly all the food items of juveniles are 1 to 5

Table 1. Frequency of perch height and perch diameter combinations for male and female adults, subadult males, and juveniles. Results are percentages observed. Five adult males, 17 adult females, 3 subadult males, and 14 juveniles were found on the ground.

| Perch height (feet) | Perch diameter in inches (1 inch = 2.54 cm) for | | | | | | | | | | | |
|---|---|---|---|---|---|---|---|---|---|---|---|---|
| | Adult males N = 133 | | | Adult females N = 222 | | | Subadult males N = 43 | | | Juveniles N = 37 | | |
| | 3 | 3–½ | ½ | 3 | 3–½ | ½ | 3 | 3–½ | ½ | 3 | 3–½ | ½ |
| >10 | 5 | 1 | 0 | 0 | 0 | 0 | 2 | 0 | 0 | 0 | 0 | 0 |
| 6–10 | 21 | 8 | 0 | 4 | 6 | 3 | 14 | 0 | 2 | 3 | 0 | 8 |
| 3–5 | 32 | 16 | 2 | 16 | 32 | 2 | 23 | 33 | 0 | 3 | 16 | 10 |
| 1–2 | 10 | 7 | 0 | 15 | 20 | 2 | 9 | 16 | 0 | 10 | 25 | 25 |

Reprinted by permission of the American Association for the Advancement of Science and the author from Science 155:474–477, 27 January 1967. Copyright 1967 by the American Association for the Advancement of Science.

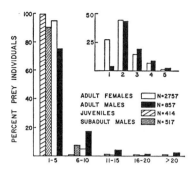 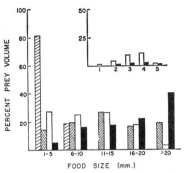

Fig. 1. Percentage of prey individuals (left) and prey volume (right) in five categories of prey size for four age and sex classes of lizards. The breakdown for the first food size category is given in the inserted graphs, which have the same axes as the main graphs.

mm long, and prey taken by subadult males are intermediate in size relative to those taken by males and females (Fig. 1, left). These compilations, in which prey items from all lizards belonging to a given size and sex class are combined, do not indicate if the distributions of prey within an individual lizard are of the same kind as the total distribution for that lizard's class, or if the total distribution is the resultant of radically different individual distributions of prey. To evaluate these alternatives, I tabulated the frequency of lizards containing large (greater than 3 mm) prey items in various percentages for each of the four classes (Fig. 2). While individual females and juveniles usually contain a large proportion of small food, in about half the

males over 50 percent of the food items were large. Thus the similarity between adult males and females with respect to frequency distribution of prey is due in part to a small proportion of males containing many small food items. On the average, the tracts of adult males contain a much smaller number of prey (18 items) than do those of females (32 items). Finally, adult males tend to take prey over somewhat greater ranges of size than do adult females, the average range in prey size of 47 males being 12.6 mm and of 84 females 8.2 mm.

A more meaningful measure of the importance of the various classes of prey size in the diets of males and females is obtained if the percentage of the total volume composed by each

of the prey classes is calculated. Relative volumes should be proportional to relative biomass, an indication of relative caloric values. This kind of tabulation results in a much neater separation by food size of the two sexes (Fig. 1, right). Adult males obtain 62 percent of their food by volume from prey over 15 mm, whereas adult females obtain only 21.1 percent from such large prey. Hence, the second hypothesis, that sexual dimorphism in size is correlated with differences in prey size, is also apparently correct.

The relationship between average prey length and predator length appears approximately linear above a certain minimum predator size, the prey length gaining about 0.5 mm for every 5-mm increase in snout-vent length (Fig. 3). Below 36 mm, there is a gradual leveling off of average prey size for females (11). This effect might be caused by a decrease in the relative abundance of extremely small prey that are acceptable to *Anolis*. For the three size classes of males whose sizes are identical to adult female classes (subadult males), distributions of prey size tend slightly but significantly toward sizes larger than those of prey taken by females in all cases (Fig. 3; $P < .05$; $P < .005$; $P < .05$). In the larger two classes, heads of males are significantly longer than those of females of the same snout-vent length ($P < .001$ by the $t$ test), thus being a better indicator of food size than snout-vent length. But in the smallest size class (36 to 41 mm), head lengths of males and females are almost exactly the same, yet the males' prey distribution was significantly larger (12). The most likely hypothesis explaining this finding is that males are genetically predisposed to take relatively larger food

Table 2. Percentage of total individuals (I) and total volume (V) of various prey taxa.

| | Adult males (N = 857) | | Adult females (N = 2757) | | Subadult males (N = 517) | | Juveniles (N = 414) | |
|---|---|---|---|---|---|---|---|---|
| | I | V | I | V | I | V | I | V |
| Hymenoptera: Formicidae | 64.4 | 7.1 | 40.8 | 10.2 | 67.1 | 12.9 | 63.7 | 27.9 |
| Other Hymenoptera (winged adults) | 1.3 | 2.8 | 1.9 | 0.7 | 3.0 | 5.2 | 2.8 | 1.1 |
| Diptera | 2.5 | 1.0 | 10.5 | 2.8 | 5.1 | 0.3 | 12.3 | 9.9 |
| Coleoptera (adults) | 8.6 | 4.6 | 9.0 | 5.3 | 5.5 | 3.8 | 2.4 | 6.0 |
| Coleoptera (larvae) | 0.1 | 0.0 | 0.0 | 0.0 | 0.4 | 0.2 | | |
| Psocoptera | 1.8 | .0 | 11.0 | 1.2 | 2.8 | .2 | 3.5 | 1.1 |
| Isoptera | 4.3 | 1.3 | 9.1 | 12.8 | 3.0 | 2.5 | 1.7 | 12.8 |
| Homoptera | 1.1 | 0.6 | 2.5 | 2.1 | 1.3 | 1.7 | 5.7 | 3.2 |
| Hemiptera | 0.3 | .3 | 0.3 | 0.4 | 0.2 | 0.0 | 0.2 | 3.0 |
| Lepidoptera (adults) | .3 | .0 | .6 | 1.6 | .4 | 1.8 | .5 | 1.3 |
| Lepidoptera (larvae) | .6 | 1.4 | 1.7 | 0.6 | .2 | 0.3 | .5 | 0.3 |
| Neuroptera (adults) | | | 0.3 | .2 | | | | |
| Neuroptera (larvae) | .1 | 0.0 | 0.1 | .0 | 0.2 | .0 | | |
| Thysanoptera | .2 | .0 | .2 | .0 | .2 | .0 | 0.9 | .1 |
| Orthoptera-Blattaria | 4.8 | 73.6 | 1.7 | 52.5 | 2.3 | 55.6 | .2 | 7.8 |
| Araneida | 1.6 | 1.7 | 2.5 | 4.1 | 2.4 | 6.7 | 2.1 | 18.5 |
| Pseudoscorpionida | 0.1 | 0.0 | 0.3 | 0.3 | 0.9 | 0.5 | 0.9 | 4.8 |
| Chilopoda | .3 | .8 | .0 | .0 | | | | |
| Acarina | .2 | .0 | 1.2 | .0 | | | .5 | 0.1 |
| Isopoda | | | | | .4 | .0 | | |
| Mollusca | | | 0.0 | .0 | | | | |
| *Anolis* | | | | | .2 | 6.6 | | |
| Plant matter | 1.6 | 2.1 | .7 | .3 | .9 | 0.3 | 0.2 | 1.1 |
| Unidentified material | 5.4 | 2.7 | 5.8 | 4.7 | 3.6 | 1.1 | 1.9 | 1.0 |

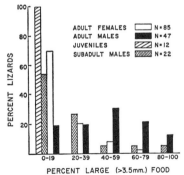

Fig. 2. Percentages of lizards containing various percentages of large food.

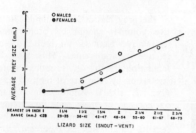

Fig. 3. Relationship of predator size to prey size for male and female lizards.

sizes, although there could also be differences arising from a mere trial and error mechanism connected with ease of manipulation.

Almost the entire diet of *Anolis conspersus* consists of animal food (Table 2). The small percentage of plant matter may be partially ingested by accident, but in the case of large berries and certain other plant items intentional consumption seems likely. All four classes of anoles eat more ants than members of any other taxon listed in Table 2. Adult females eat considerably fewer ants than do juveniles or either class of males and have their prey items more evenly distributed over the categories of available prey. Some of the major differences in the kinds of food ingested are explainable on the basis of microhabitat and size differences. Males are more likely to encounter ants on the trunks of large trees than are females, which frequent much smaller trees and shrubs and are more likely to encounter insects inhabiting foliage. Juveniles, which spend a large part of their time on the ground, are also relatively likely to encounter ants. The Orthopterans, which are more numerous in the diet of adult males, tend to be larger than other insects. Psocopterans and flies, nearly all minute, are taken much more frequently by females.

In adult females and both classes of males, the Orthoptera form over half the diet by volume. These probably belong to only three or four species, but females tend to eat the smaller nymphs much more often. In addition, other groups such as termites and ants compose a greater proportion of the volume of the food of females than of the food of adult males. Juveniles depend largely on ants, spiders, and termites (*13*).

A. S. Rand (*4, 14*) first pointed out differences in prey size between the sexes of a dimorphic species of lizard (*Anolis lineatopus* of Jamaica) and stressed the importance of such a system in increasing the efficiency of the total exploitation of its habitat. In *Anolis conspersus*, differences between the sexes with respect to microhabitat combined with differences with respect to prey size are probably largely instrumental in allowing the species to build up the extremely dense populations in which it is sometimes found, especially in areas with varied perch sizes. Such an ability is of particular value to colonizing species and those in other ecologically marginal situations. As has been shown, sexual differences in size are correlated with differences with respect to both microhabitat and prey size. Although perhaps not the only selective pressures operating, the advantage of a more thorough utilization of environmental resources combined with a lack of closely related species is probably the cause of the similar size and dimorphism of the anoles which occur alone on islands.

THOMAS W. SCHOENER

*Biological Laboratories,*
*Harvard University,*
*Cambridge, Massachusetts 02138*

**References and Notes**

1. An article including a detailed description of this pattern is in preparation.
2. A. S. Rand, *Ecology* **45**, 745 (1964).
3. This study was carried out during the period 1 to 8 April 1966.
4. A. S. Rand, *Smithsonian Inst. Misc. Collections,* in preparation.
5. V. A. Harris, *The Life of the Rainbow Lizard* (Hutchinson, London, 1964).
6. *Eumeces fasciatus,* see H. S. Fitch, *Univ. Kansas Publ. Museum Nat. Hist.* **8**, 1 (1954); *Sceloporus olivaceus,* see J. P. Kennedy, *Texas J. Sci.* **8**, 328 (1956).
7. *Basiliscus vittatus,* see H. F. Hirth, *Ecol. Mono.* **33**, 83 (1963).
8. A. S. Rand, *Breviora Museum Comp. Zool.* **154**, 1 (1962); *Anolis porcatus* and *A. sagrei,* see B. B. Collette, *Bull. Museum Comp. Zool.* **125**, 137 (1961).
9. *Tropidurus torquatus,* see A. S. Rand, *Smithsonian Inst. Misc. Collections* **151**, 2 (1966); *Sceloporus olivaceus,* see W. F. Blair, *The Rusty Lizard, A Population Study* (Univ. of Texas Press, Austin, 1960); *Uta stansburiana,* see D. W. Tinkle, D. McGregor, S. Dana, *Ecology* **43**, 223 (1962); *Iguana iguana* and *Basiliscus plumifrons,* see H. F. Hirth, *Ecology* **44**, 613 (1963).
10. Chi-square tests were performed for perch height and diameter separately. Using the intervals 1 to 2 feet, 3 to 5 feet, and > 6 feet, I found significantly different height distributions for adult males compared with adult females and adult females compared with juveniles ($P < .001$) but not for subadult males compared with adult females or subadult males compared with adult males ($P < .25$; $P < .10$). Using the intervals > 3 inches, 3 to ½ inches, and < ½ inches, I found significantly different perch diameter distributions for the first two categories ($P < .001$) and also for subadult males compared with adult males ($P < .025$) but not for subadult males compared with females ($P < .10$).
11. I did not have enough material available for males of this size to see if a similar asymptote occurs, because five of every six juveniles collected were females.
12. Chi-square values were computed for the intervals 1, 2, and > 2 mm, which is the largest combination of intervals in which at least ten prey items occur in each category for all comparisons.
13. The method of analyzing both stomach and intestinal contents probably resulted in fewer of certain soft-bodied insects, such as some Homopterans, larvae, and spiders, being recognized than actually occurred, but the effect on the total distributions would be slight.
14. A. S. Rand, unpublished.
15. I thank E. E. Williams and E. O. Wilson for their assistance in a variety of ways, including a critical reading of the manuscript, A. S. Rand for allowing me to see unpublished manuscripts, and J. A. Peters for bibliographical information. Supported by NSF grant GB-2444 to E. E. Williams.

31 October 1966

34

# EVOLUTIONARY PROCESSES IN POPULATIONS OF COPPER TOLERANT *AGROSTIS TENUIS* Sibth.

T. McNeilly[1] and A. D. Bradshaw

*Department of Agricultural Botany, University College of North Wales, Bangor*

Received February 5, 1967

A considerable number of genecological studies on many plant species have described differentiation into local populations, amongst which those of Turesson, Gregor, and Clausen Keck and Hiesey are of note. These, and the majority of subsequent works on this subject assumed the paramount importance of natural selection in the evolutionary process. Because differences in morphology, physiology, etc., could be found between populations, natural selection was assumed to have brought about such differences; evidence for the occurrence of natural selection was indirect. In the plant kingdom direct evidence in the form of data showing changes in gene frequencies between generations is scant. The studies of Kemp (1937), Sylvén (1937), Charles (1964), Barber (1966), and Aston and Bradshaw (1966), are exceptions. In the animal kingdom by contrast, the early work of Bumpus (1898), and di Cesnola (1907) on the snail *Helix abustorum* showed the occurrence of such changes. In more recent years, the role of natural selection in animal populations has received considerable attention, of which the works of Kettlewell (1961) on Lepidoptera, Sheppard (1958) on *Cepea nemoralis*, and Kurtén (1964) on *Ursus spelaeus* are notable examples.

The adult plants found in any natural population represent the resultant of the interaction of natural variation, gene flow, and natural selection, in other words, the *status quo*. Plants raised from seed produced by such populations, by contrast, show the potential variability of the population before the operation of selection. A comparison of adults and seed will therefore show the possible ways in which any such existing situation might change. But since it can be presumed that the situations examined have been in existence for a long time without change, such comparisons must indicate the magnitude of the selection maintaining the *status quo*. This technique was used by Aston and Bradshaw (1966).

Populations of *Agrostis tenuis* Sibth., tolerant of lead, or zinc, or nickel, or copper, occurring on abandoned heavy metal mine workings, have been described by Bradshaw (1952), Wilkins (1957), Jowett (1958), and the subject of heavy metal tolerance has been reviewed more recently by Gregory and Bradshaw (1965). Such populations provide a readily available opportunity of studying population variability and natural selection in relation to a specific and well defined environmental factor, the ability to withstand toxic levels of a particular heavy metal.

The present work describes the general variation in copper tolerance found within and between populations of *Agrostis tenuis*, and compares the pattern of variation of copper tolerance of seedlings and adults for several of these populations, thereby revealing the power of natural selection in such situations.

## THE MEASUREMENT OF TOLERANCE

*Adults.*—The measurement of copper tolerance of an adult plant is based on the method described by Jowett (1964) for the measurement of lead tolerance. It depends upon the fact that heavy metals suppress root growth at moderately low concentrations and totally inhibit it at slightly higher

---

[1] Present Address: The Hartley Botanical Laboratories, The University, Liverpool 3.

Reprinted by permission of The Society for the Study of Evolution and the authors from *Evolution* 22:108–118, 1968.

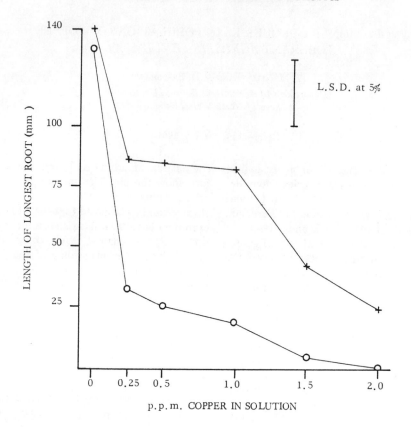

○    Normal non copper tolerant clone

+    Copper tolerant clone

FIG. 1. The effect of copper concentration on length of longest root of two clones of *Agrostis tenuis*.

concentrations. An appropriate level of copper can distinguish tolerant and non-tolerant materials very easily (Fig. 1).

For any particular plant, twenty tillers of comparable size and age were selected. These were rooted in 6 mm glass tubing suspended in 300 ml plastic beakers, 10 in a solution containing calcium nitrate solution at 0.5 g.p.l., and 10 in a solution containing calcium nitrate (0.5 g.p.l.) and also copper as copper sulphate equivalent to 0.5 p.p.m. copper. The index of copper tolerance of the plant was then calculated as follows:

$$\text{Index} = \frac{\text{Mean length of longest root in solution with copper}}{\text{Mean length of longest root in solution without copper}}$$

Using this method indices of tolerance range from 5–30% for non-tolerant populations, to 40–80% for tolerant populations. *Seedlings.*—The method used for the testing of tolerance of seed material has been adapted from the previous method, and from the method of Wilkins (1957) for measuring the lead tolerance of *Festuca ovina* seedlings.

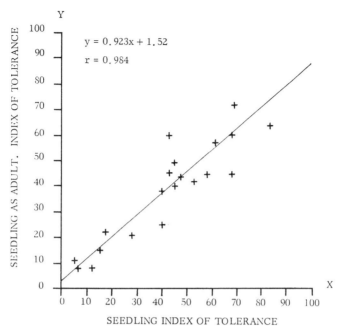

Fig. 2. Correlation: Seedling/Seedling as adult index of copper tolerance.

Ten pregerminated seedlings were sown on fine nylon mesh suspended in a beaker at the surface of 300 ml of calcium nitrate solution (0.5 g.p.l. as in the method for adults), and allowed to grow for 10 days. At the end of this period the length of the longest root was measured, and growth was allowed to continue for a further 5 days, when the length of the longest root was again measured. The calcium nitrate solution was then changed, and to the new calcium nitrate solution copper was added as copper sulphate solution equivalent to 0.5 p.p.m. as in the method for adults. After a further 2 days, root growth made was again measured. Values for daily increase in length of the longest root had thus been obtained after 17 days for seedlings grown in calcium nitrate alone, and with copper. The index of tolerance was then calculated by expressing the growth rate in calcium nitrate with copper, as a percentage of the growth rate in calcium nitrate alone.

The legitimacy of using two treatments on the same root consecutively is demonstrated by a successive series of measurements which have shown that the change produced by copper is of immediate and lasting effect (McNeilly, 1966; Barker, pers. comm.). Further justification comes from a comparison of the tolerance of individual plants determined as seedlings, then allowed to grow in ordinary soil and tested as adults (Fig. 2).

### MATERIAL

Adult populations of *A. tenuis* from three sites having toxic levels of copper in the soil, and six populations from uncontaminated soils were collected in North Wales in Autumn 1961. One further adult population from a toxic site in Ireland was included, collected in Summer 1962 (Table 1).

Thirty tiller plants were taken from each site, collections being made over an area of approximately 30 yards diameter. A single tiller of each plant was selected and grown for at least 12 weeks in an experimental garden prior to testing for copper tolerance.

TABLE 1.—*Populations Collected.*

| Population | Population number | Vegetation cover | pH | Total Soil Copper p.p.m. | Generation Collected |
|---|---|---|---|---|---|
| Parys Mountain Anglesey | 1[+] | Extremely Isolated plants, frequent bare patches | 3.5 | 1800 | Adults & Seed |
| | 2[+] | Somewhat isolated plants bare patches | 3.6 | 2300 | Adults & Seed |
| | 3 | Adjacent pasture | 6.0 | 150 | Adults |
| | 4 | Adjacent pasture | 5.8 | 129 | Adults |
| Drws y Coed, Caernarvonshire | 5[+] | Fairly continuous turf | 4.2 | 2600 | Adults & Seed |
| | 6 | Adjacent pasture | 4.7 | 156 | Adults & Seed |
| St. Patrick's, Wicklow | 7[+] | Isolated plants, bare patches | 4.6 | 960 | Adults |
| Mynydd Llandegai, Caernarvonshire | 8 | Rough upland grazing on peat | 4.4 | 50 | Adults & Seed |
| Llandegfan Common, Anglesey | 9 | Very poor acid lowland heath | 4.1 | 45 | Adults & Seed |
| Llandegfan Pasture, Anglesey | 10 | Fertile pasture | 6.1 | 47 | Adults & Seed |

[+] Denotes tolerant population

## RESULTS AND DISCUSSION

*Adults.*—The results for adults (Fig. 3) show that the populations from contaminated soil show a high level of copper tolerance while those from uncontaminated areas do not, e.g. between populations 5 and 6 from Drws y Coed. A great deal of similarity is found between all contaminated sites and particularly between the two Parys Mountain populations 1 and 2. Population 1 from Parys Mountain is near the middle of the mine and population 2 is from the edge of the mine. There thus seems to be no fall off of copper tolerance at the edge of mine areas adjoining normal uncontaminated soils. At the same time population 5 from the much smaller mine at Drws y Coed, is very similar to these two populations, and provides a remarkable example of a small yet distinct population. Jowett (1964) found distinct populations of *Agrostis tenuis* which were lead tolerant growing on areas of contamination which were no more than 45 meters in diameter. More recently Clarke and Gaunt (pers. comm.) have described a copper tolerant population only 15 meters across. This would seem to indicate the operation of very high levels of selection to maintain such populations against the smothering effects of gene flow from surrounding normal populations (Jain and Bradshaw, 1966).

The mines at Parys Mountain and Drws y Coed are of sufficient age (over 600 years) for copper tolerance genes to have spread into adjacent and possibly more distant uncontaminated areas. Yet the spatial pattern of distribution of copper tolerance appears to be very precise. Thus populations 3 and 4 from uncontaminated sites near Parys Mountain are both less than 730 meters from the contaminated area, and are not separated from it by physical boundaries and Population 6 from Drws y Coed is only 15½ meters away from the mine. In none of these is there any trace of copper tolerance such as might be

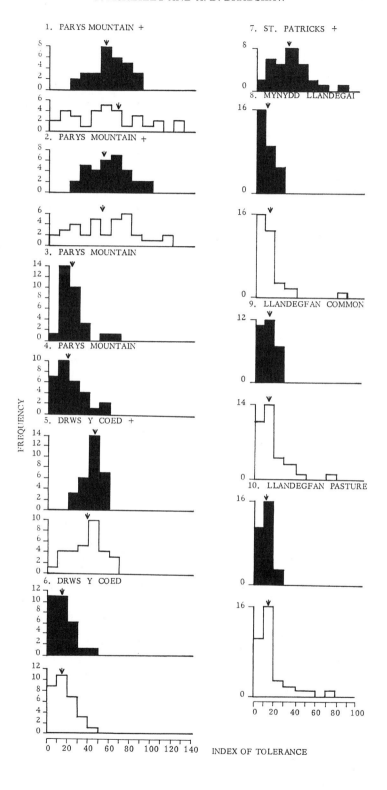

expected because of gene flow out of the tolerant mine populations. This suggests that selection must be operating against copper tolerant individuals on normal soils.

The variance in copper tolerance of the normal non-tolerant populations is very small and constant (Table 2). This is, no doubt, mainly due to the lack of tolerant individuals in such populations. However it is possible that variation does exist within non-tolerant populations, but the method of testing for tolerance does not permit its detection since only one level of copper was used in testing for tolerance. Lower levels of copper in the solution used for measuring tolerance might reveal greater variability in normal populations.

By contrast there is a considerable variance within copper tolerant populations. Surprisingly there even exist plants which show no tolerance to copper *in vitro*, but which nevertheless are found growing happily on apparently contaminated soils. This is particularly true in St. Patrick's Mine, population 7. There also occur fairly extensive bare patches on contaminated soils. Absence of colonization may be explained on the basis of low availability of seed in the more isolated sites. However this cannot hold for all sites. Such patches devoid of vegetation often occur in close proximity to fairly dense stands of copper tolerant *A. tenuis*, and the supply of seed should be adequate to promote the colonization of such adjacent areas. It would appear from this that such sites are too toxic for colonization, or that some factor or combination of factors in addition to copper tolerance, such as extreme dryness of the habitat, presence of other toxic metals, precludes colonization. All this suggests that there is considerable variability in the mine habitats to which variability of the mine populations may be ascribed.

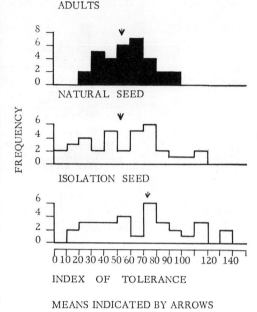

MEANS INDICATED BY ARROWS

FIG. 4. The distribution of copper tolerance in adults, a natural seed sample population, and isolation seed sample of Parys Mountain population 2.

Jowett (1958) and McNeilly (1966) have shown respectively, that lead tolerant and copper tolerant *A. tenuis* populations are better adapted to growth at lower levels of certain essential soil nutrients than non-tolerant populations. Mine soils are low in essential nutrients. It might therefore be argued that poor uncontaminated soils would permit the occurrence of tolerant plants. However populations 8 from Mynydd Llandegai, and 9 from Llandegfan Common, are both from low nutrient soils, yet show no apparent difference in copper tolerance from population 10 from Llandegfan Pasture, a fairly rich soil. This suggests that poor soil conditions do not in any way select for copper tolerance.

*Seedlings.*—Samples of seed produced under natural conditions in the field, and of

←

FIG. 3. The distribution of copper tolerance in adult and seed sample populations of *A. tenuis*. Means indicated by arrows; + signifies population from contaminated soil; adults—black histograms; seed samples—open histograms.

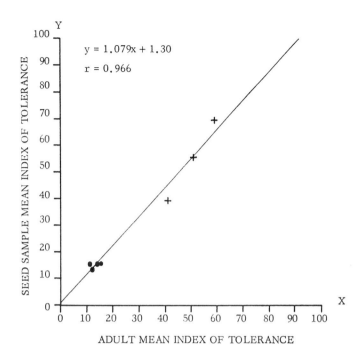

$$y = 1.079x + 1.30$$
$$r = 0.966$$

●    Normal non copper tolerant populations

+    Copper tolerant populations

FIG. 5. Correlation: Mean adult/mean seed sample index of copper tolerance.

seed produced by six adult individuals allowed to flower in isolation (i.e. with no gene flow), were tested for index of tolerance (Fig. 4). Such data, together with those for adult material, provide three types of comparison and information.

| Comparison | Information about |
|---|---|
| a) Adults and natural seed | Gene flow; segregation, selection.[1] |
| b) Natural seed and isolation seed | Gene flow and genetics of tolerance; selection. |
| c) Adults and isolation seed | Heritability; segregation; selection. |

[1] Used by Aston and Bradshaw (1966)

a) *Adults and natural seed.*—A highly significant correlation, ($r = 0.966$, Fig. 5), is found between mean index of copper tolerance of adult populations and their corresponding seed samples taken from the field.

The sample regression indicates that the seedling sample mean indices of copper tolerance are generally higher than those of the corresponding adult populations. Population 5 from Drws y Coed is an exception however, adults having a higher mean index of tolerance than the seed sample population. This suggests the occurrence of gene flow from normal into the copper tolerant population at Drws y Coed. Non-tolerant plants do occur in seed sample populations 1 and 2 from Parys Mountain. These may be the product of segregation or gene flow or a combination of both. Gene flow cannot account for the presence of copper tolerant individuals in normal seed sample populations, since distances between them are large. Such individuals are probably the products of segregation.

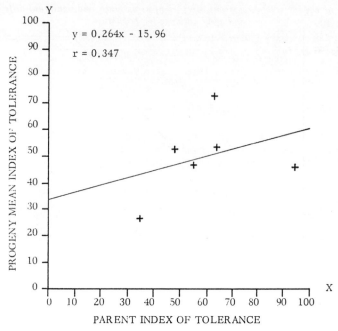

F ig. 6. Regression: Parent/mean isolation progeny sample index of copper tolerance for Parys Mountain population 2.

When the data are examined in detail, the two sites at Parys Mountain appear somewhat anomalous. Population 1 is near the center of the mine, whereas population 2 is at the extreme edge of the mine. It might reasonably be expected from such a difference in situation that there would be a greater degree of contamination from adjacent non-tolerant populations of the plants comprising population 2 than those in population 1, which is more isolated. Evidence that contamination is normally greater at mine boundaries is presented elsewhere (McNeilly, 1966). However, at Parys Mountain 2 the plant cover is relatively continuous, whereas at Parys Mountain 1 the plants are small and extremely sparsely distributed. It is reasonable to suppose that the sparsely distributed plants are more likely to be pollinated by the background rain of pollen carried from several miles away than the more densely spaced plants. This would follow from the leptokurtic distribution of pollen shown by Bateman (1947) giving high values for

pollen frequency at long distances, and the effects of density on contamination of *Lolium perenne* shown by Griffiths (1952). In plants placed in small groups, contamination (= gene flow) at 90 m was of the order of 5% whereas in a continuous broad arm of plants, reduction of contamination to 5% might occur within 18 to 30 m. The mid-mine data parallel the findings of Jensen and Bøgh (1941) who found that contamination was fairly constant at 5% at distances from 600 to 1200 m from the contaminant source.

b) *Natural and isolation seed.*—Figure 4 compares the tolerance of a seed sample produced when six individuals from Parys Mountains 2 were allowed to flower in isolation, with that of natural seed also from Parys Mountain 2.

The mean index of tolerance of the isolation seed is significantly greater ($p < 0.05$), than that of the seed collected in the field. This confirms the suggestion made earlier that gene flow does occur into this population. The natural population is the

116                    T. McNEILLY AND A. D. BRADSHAW

TABLE 2. *Index of copper tolerance means, coefficient of variance, and significant differences between seed and adult variance for populations.*

| Population Name | Population Number[1] | Mean | Coefficient of Variance | Variance ratio[2] $\frac{\text{seed variance of log}}{\text{adult variance of log}}$ | p[3] |
|---|---|---|---|---|---|
| Parys Mountain | 1 A[+] | 56.8 | 33 | | |
| | 1 S[+] | 68.3 | 50 | 2.13 | * |
| | 2 A[+] | 53.8 | 31 | | |
| | 2 S[+] | 55.1 | 53 | 2.70 | ** |
| | 2 IS[+] | 72.9 | 198 | 17.04 | *** |
| | 3 A | 23.0 | 85 | – | |
| | 4 A | 20.3 | 67 | – | |
| Drws y Coed | 5 A[+] | 45.0 | 24 | | |
| | 5 S[+] | 39.0 | 48 | 2.66 | ** |
| | 6 A | 15.3 | 67 | | |
| | 6 S | 15.0 | 75 | 1.21 | N.S.D. |
| St. Patrick's | 7 A[+] | 32.9 | 61 | – | |
| Mynydd Llandegai | 8 A | 10.6 | 66 | | |
| | 8 S | 14.5 | 103 | 1.99 | * |
| Llandegfan Common | 9 A | 14.2 | 53 | | |
| | 9 S | 14.6 | 79 | 2.02 | * |
| Llandegfan Pasture | 10 A | 12.4 | 58 | | |
| | 10 S | 12.9 | 74 | 1.51 | N.S.D. |

S.E. differences between means = 9.25

[+] Denotes tolerant population.
[1] A–adults; S–seed; IS–isolation seed.
[2] After Lewontin (1966).
[3] *–significant difference at $p = 0.05$; **–significant difference at $p = 0.01$; ***–significant difference at $p = 0.001$; N.S.D.–no significant difference.

product of intrapopulation crossing and gene flow from non-tolerant adults in adjacent populations. A similar situation has been described at Drws y Coed for natural and isolation seed (McNeilly, 1966). The intensity of gene flow from adjacent non-tolerant populations tending to dilute the character of copper tolerance is apparently considerable.

c) *Adults and isolation seed.*—Figure 6 shows the regression of the six parents against their mean progeny produced in isolation. The data are only for a group of tolerant plants, but nonetheless give an estimate of half the heritability of 0.35. Copper tolerance is clearly inherited and has a high heritability. Data comparing adults and natural seed (Fig. 4) also point to a high heritability of copper tolerance, as does the rapid response to selection in normal populations of *A. tenuis*, for copper tolerant

plants. (Data from J. Antonovics, pers. comm.).

The pattern of distribution of copper tolerance in this isolation seedling sample also provides evidence of:

1) Continuous variation—the number of genes involved may be few however, since there is some degree of error in the measurement of tolerance which may mask the different classes of phenotype;

2) heterozygosity of parents—since there is a considerable amount of variation in the offspring;

3) no obvious dominance—since variation is in both directions.

SELECTION

Adult populations from copper contaminated soils show the character of copper tolerance, whereas populations from normal soils do not. This is true even for populations separated by distances of up to 30 miles. This is strong circumstantial evidence for the operation of natural selection in the evolution of these populations.

In addition to sampling adult populations, seed samples have been tested for tolerance. The difference in mean index of copper tolerance between seed and adult samples of mine populations towards greater tolerance can only be maintained by different survival rates of tolerant and non-tolerant seed which comprise the seed populations. Thus, in spite of the probable occurrence of considerable gene flow into tolerant populations, selection is able to maintain the *status quo*. To do this selection pressures must be high.

In non-tolerant populations the agreement between mean index of tolerance of adults and seed is closer, suggesting that selection is not operating. However, there is perhaps some evidence for selection against individuals which are copper tolerant, since from Figure 2, in normal seed samples some 3% of the individuals are copper tolerant, whereas in corresponding adult populations less than 1% of the individuals were copper tolerant.

The results further show that a greater variance in copper tolerance is found within all seed samples than is found within the corresponding adult populations. Copper tolerant seedling populations contain individuals showing both smaller and larger indices of copper tolerance than the corresponding adult populations. The former represent those individuals which natural selection eliminates because of lack of copper tolerance. For the latter, it can only be concluded that the genotype which confers copper tolerance on an individual, confers also some deleterious effect, and that there is some threshold beyond which copper tolerance proceeds at the expense of some essential function or functions. This may reduce the ability of the individual so endowed to survive in the field. Selection in copper tolerant populations thus appears to be stabilizing (Schmalhausen, 1949;

Mather, 1953). This is similar to the findings of Bumpus (1899) with the introduced sparrow in New York; di Cesnola (1907) on the snail *Helix arbustorum*; and Aston and Bradshaw (1966) on local populations of *Agrostis stolonifera*.

The non-tolerant populations are all rather uniform, but there are a few individuals showing copper tolerance. A similar situation has been reported for lead tolerance by Bradshaw (1960). That such tolerant individuals do occur in normal seedling populations is interesting. In a small experiment, one hundred seeds from population 10 from Llandegfan Pasture were sown on toxic Drws y Coed soil, from which population 5 was sampled. Three individuals survived to mature plants. Their indices of tolerance were 63, 58, and 62. These fall within the range covered by the tolerant individuals examined. It would thus appear that in areas well away from any known contaminated sites, individuals may occur from which, with levels of heritability pointed to earlier, complete tolerance might arise in a very few generations should the environment demand such a population. Selection in non-tolerant populations appears to be directional (Mather, 1953).

While it is true that the adult plants tested were not produced from the same generation of seed as was tested, seedlings can readily be found on the mine sites in late summer, yet the number of individuals in any population has remained constant over a period of several years. *A. tenuis* is of perennial habit, and there is evidence that grass species may persist for many years in upland habitats (Harberd, 1962). Nonetheless a certain amount of turnover in individuals must have taken place in the long history (more than 600 years) of these mine sites. Natural selection is the only process which can have maintained distinct populations in such situations.

## SUMMARY

Populations of *Agrostis tenuis* Sibth. were collected from disused copper mines and nearby ordinary pasture in North Wales and Ireland. These populations were sampled as tillers and as seed.

Tests for copper tolerance on these populations showed that:

a) All populations growing on copper mines have copper tolerance.

b) Populations taken from uncontaminated sites removed by as little as 15½ meters from contaminated sites with tolerant populations show absence of copper tolerance. The reverse situation is equally true.

c) The character of copper tolerance has high heritability.

d) There is evidence of gene flow into mine populations, and also for genetic segregation within such populations. By contrast there is very little evidence of gene flow into non-tolerant populations. This can be explained in terms of the spatial relationships of the populations concerned.

e) There is strong evidence for the operation of natural selection in favor of copper tolerance on copper contaminated soils, and against it on uncontaminated soils, maintaining the *status quo*.

f) The differences found between seedling and adult data for the same population, point to the dangers and values of using plants grown from collections of spontaneous seed material in population studies.

## Acknowledgments

This work was financed by a grant from the Sir William Roberts Fund, which is gratefully acknowledged. Thanks are also due to Professor John L. Harper for facilities in his Department.

## Literature Cited

ASTON, J. L., AND A. D. BRADSHAW. 1966. Evolution in closely adjacent plant populations II. *Agrostis stolonifera* in maritime habitats. Heredity 21:649–664.

BARBER, H. N. 1965. Selection in natural populations. Heredity 20:557–572.

BATEMAN, A. J. 1947. Contamination in seed crops. II. Wind pollination. Heredity 1:235–246.

BRADSHAW, A. D. 1952. Populations of *Agrostis tenuis* resistant to lead and zinc poisoning. Nature 169:1089.

BUMPUS, H. C. 1899. The elimination of the unfit as illustrated by the introduced sparrow. Bird. Lect. Woods Hole 1898:209.

CESNOLA, A. P. DI. 1907. A first study of natural selection of *Helix arbustorum*. Biometrika 5:387–399.

CHARLES, A. J. 1964. Differential survival of plant types in swards. J. Brit. Grassl. Soc. 19:198–204.

GREGORY, R. P. G., AND A. D. BRADSHAW. 1965. Heavy metal tolerance in populations of *Agrostis tenuis* Sibth. and other grasses. New Phytol. 64:131–143.

GRIFFITHS, D. J. 1952. The liability of crops of perennial rye grass (*Lolium perenne*) to contamination by wind borne pollen. J. Agric. Soc. 40:19–37.

HARBERD, D. J. 1962. Some observations on natural clones in *Fustuca ovina*. New Phytol. 61:85–100.

JAIN, S. K., AND A. D. BRADSHAW. 1966. Evolutionary divergence among adjacent plant populations. Heredity 21:407–441.

JENSEN, I., AND H. BØGH. 1941. On conditions influencing the danger of crossing in the case of wind pollinating cultivated plants. Tidsskr. Planteavl. 46:238–266.

JOWETT, D. 1958. Populations of *Agrostis* spp. tolerant of heavy metals. Nature 182:816–817.

——. 1964. Population studies on lead tolerant *Agrostis tenuis*. Evolution 18:70–80.

KEMP, W. B. 1937. Natural selection within plant species as exemplified in a permanent pasture. J. Hered. 28:329–333.

KETTLEWELL, H. B. D. 1961. The phenomenon of industrial melanism in the Lepidoptera. Ann. Rev. Ent. 6:245–262.

KURTÉN, B. 1964. Population structure in Paleoecology. *In* J. Imbrie and N. Newell, [eds.] *Approaches to Palaeoecology*. John Wiley & Sons, New York.

LEWONTIN, R. C. 1966. On the measurement of relative variability. Syst. Zool. 15:141–142.

MATHER, K. 1953. The genetical structure of populations. Symp. Soc. Exp. Biol. 7:66–95.

McNEILLY, T. 1966. The evolution of copper tolerance in *Agrostis tenuis* Sibth. Ph.D. Thesis, University of Wales.

SHEPPARD, P. M. 1958. Natural selection and heredity. Hutchinson, London.

SYLVÉN, N. 1937. The influence of climatic conditions on type composition. Imp. Bureau Plant Genetics, Herbage Bull. 21.

WILKINS, D. A. 1957. A technique for the measurement of lead tolerance in plants. Nature 180:37.

# Phase Polymorphism in the Grasshopper Melanoplus differentialis

Abstract. *Individuals of* Melanoplus differentialis *raised in isolation or in a crowded environment show conspicuous morphological differences indicating phase polymorphism. Isolated nymphs are pale brown at low humidities and green at high; crowded ones show extensive black pigmentation. Isolated adults are larger than crowded, while crowded adults show maturational color changes that are not present in the isolated. No behavioral differences have been noted in the one generation.*

Since phase polymorphism, resulting from population density, was first described over 40 years ago, it has been extensively studied in Old World locusts, especially of the genera *Locusta*, *Normadacris*, and *Schistocerca* (Orthorptera, Acrididae) (*1*). Yet the general subject of phases in grasshoppers and locusts has received comparatively little attention in North America: the only study conclusively demonstrating distinct phases resulting from isolation or crowding of individuals seems to be that by Faure (*2*) of the lesser migratory grasshopper *Melanoplus sanguinipes*, although there is evidence that such phases may occur in other forms as well (*3*). Faure predicted that phases would be found in other North American grasshoppers also. We have now substantiated that prediction by producing morphological phases in *M. differentialis* (Orthoptera, Acrididae, Catantopinae) raised under controlled conditions of isolation or crowding. The occurrence of distinct forms in *M. differentialis* is interesting because, although when in large numbers it has been recorded as a crop pest (*4*), we find no records of its migrating with or without swarming. Most other polymorphic species undertake migratory flights, especially as swarms of the gregarious phase.

The grasshoppers used by us were the offspring of field-caught females that had deposited egg pods in the laboratory. Diapause was broken by immersion of the eggs in mineral oil (*5*), and the resulting hatchlings were reared in one of three ways: For crowded conditions, approximately 50 hoppers were placed in a 14 by 14 by 14 cm wooden cage having a wire-screen back and top and a removable glass front. For isolated rearing, a single hopper was placed in a cage of this type, while some isolates were reared in jars approximately 8 cm in diameter and 15 cm high. With damp cotton continually present, the relative humidity was 70 to 90 percent as opposed to 10 to 20 percent in the cages. The photoperiod was 16 hours of light and 8 hours of darkness;

temperature 23°C. Cages or jars were arranged around a 60-watt light bulb that provided radiant heat for 8 hours daily. Cracked corn was constantly available and fresh oat seedlings were provided daily; food was always abundant. Animals in jars were not supplied with corn, which became moldy at high humidities; this factor had no obvious effect on the results.

First-instar hoppers are uniformly colored, with a small amount of black pigment scattered through the integument, giving them a gray appearance. Coloration of the second to sixth instars depends on rearing conditions, although in a few instances the effects of rearing did not appear before the third instar. Hoppers reared isolated in a brown box were a uniform pale brown, with a slight black chevron pattern on the hind femur and a faint black horizontal stripe on the pronotum; some abdomens were speckled with black. Crowded hoppers,

on the other hand, showed the same brown background color, but with a much greater amounts of dispersed black pigment; the pronotum had a conspicuous black horizontal stripe, the wing buds were dark, and the abdomen was mottled with black; thus the crowded hopper was conspicuously the darker (Fig. 1). Occurrence of a melanic pattern in artificially crowded hoppers seems to be fairly common (*1*), even in species that show no other apparent effects of density (*6*).

Of the 15 nymphs raised isolated but at high humidities, eight (53.3 percent) became green in the fourth or fifth instar, with a small amount of black pigment similar in distribution to that of low-humidity isolates raised in boxes. The remaining 46.7 percent also had very little black pigment and were pale-fawn or creamy-white in color—not brown. A control group, reared in similar jars on an identical diet but at low relative humidity (30 to 40 percent), all became creamy white.

An essential feature of phase polymorphism is that isolated nymphs adjust their color to the surroundings

Table 1. Means of four measurements (mm) taken from isolated and crowded adult *M. differentialis*. All differences between phases are statistically significant at $p < .001$ or better.

| Sex | Head width (C) | Length | | |
|---|---|---|---|---|
| | | Wing (E) | Femur (F) | Prono-tum (P) |
| | | *Crowded* | | |
| Male | 5.00 | 25.03 | 16.09 | 6.69 |
| Female | 5.83 | 28.47 | 19.29 | 7.86 |
| | | *Isolated* | | |
| Male | 5.41 | 28 07 | 18.01 | 7.54 |
| Female | 6.78 | 32.78 | 22.88 | 9.69 |

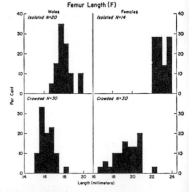

Fig. 2. Distribution of measurements of femur length (*F*) in isolated and crowded adult *M. differentialis*.

Fig. 1. Crowded (left) and isolated sixth-instar female nymphs of *M. differentialis*. Note that the crowded individual is smaller and darker. Scale, 1 cm.

Reprinted by permission of the American Association for the Advancement of Science and the authors from *Science* 155:590–592, 3 February 1967. Copyright 1967 by the American Association for the Advancement of Science.

whereas crowded nymphs do not (*1*). The isolated nymphs reared at low humidity in our experiments did tend to match the background (brown in a brown box and creamy-white or pale-fawn in a glass jar), while crowded ones were much darker. Our results also show that green coloration is produced at high relative humidities—above about 70 percent. Similarly, in two of the best-known polymorphic genera, *Locusta* and *Schistocerca*, high humidity makes hoppers become green (*7*). Faure (*2*) reported that 9 percent of isolated hoppers of *M. sanguinipes* given succulent food became green; he reared no controls.

Both green and fawn hoppers of *M. differentialis* collected in the field are in appearance typical of those raised isolated in the laboratory. Along a damp, marshy, river bank more than 95 percent of nymphs were green, whereas along a roadside bordering a small upland meadow the population was approximately 70 percent green and 30 percent fawn. Both green and fawn forms were brought into the laboratory and raised crowded in jars; after two molts, all developed the black pigment and brown background of typical crowded hoppers.

A further characteristic of isolated locusts is an extra nymphal instar. In the present instance, of a total of 43 nymphs raised in isolation at either low or high humidity, 15 had an extra stage between the fourth and fifth instars (wing-bud eversion first occurs in the fifth instar). The fact that 12 of the 15 were females could partly account for the particularly large size of isolated adult females. Extra instars have been reported in other species of *Melanoplus* (*8*), but in *M. differentialis* the phenomenon appears to be correlated with phase since crowded hoppers showed no extra stages.

Adult isolates are conspicuously larger than crowded specimens in all respects. For direct morphological comparisons, head width (*C*), pronotum length (*P*), elytron length (*E*), and hind-femur length (*F*) were measured by Dirsh's (*9*) standard procedures (Table 1). The distribution of *F* is shown in Fig. 2. Because all parameters varied in the same direction, ratios such as $E{:}F$, often used to distinguish locust phases, were not useful to us. Only isolated adults reared at low humidity were used for these measurements because the smaller jars used for high humidity may have affected size. The strong sexual dimorphism associated with phase change in *Locusta* and *Schistocerca* was not present, but the phase effect is somewhat more pronounced in females of *M. differentialis* than in males. There seem to be no previous records of isolated individuals of both sexes showing an increase in size over crowded individuals. In *Dociostaurus* and *Locustana,* for example, the converse is true; gregarious adults are larger than isolated ones (*1*).

Crowded adults of *M. differentialis* show color changes associated with sexual maturation that do not occur in isolated adults; Uvarov (*1*) considers these changes also to be a characteristic of phase polymorphism. Newly molted crowded adults are bright yellow, with a black chevron pattern on the hind femur and scattered spots of black pigment on the pronotum and dorsal surface of the abdomen. After approximately 2 weeks, under our conditions, copulation occurs and the cuticle darkens to olive green. The ventral surface of the abdomen, however, may remain yellow for several weeks longer. Adults live approximately 4 months; the integument darkens throughout adult life, passing from olive green, through brown, to a dark brown that is almost black in some individuals. Isolated adults are more variable in color and do not show the sequence of color changes mentioned. Newly molted adults may be bright yellow, dark green, or brown, and most individuals darken somewhat during adult life. Some females develop a pink tinge to the hind femurs when they become older.

At least so far we have failed to produce crowded adults with relatively longer wings; nor have we observed typically gregarious behavior in either nymphs or adults. Temperature may be a factor in wing length since *M. sanguinipes* does develop relatively longer wings when raised at high temperatures (*10*). Regarding behavior, although we have seen no differences between isolated and crowded animals, one should note that, in locusts, phase differences often appear only after several generations. Since we have raised *M. differentialis* through only one generation, final assessment of possible phase-specific behavior is still premature.

HUGH DINGLE
JEAN B. HASKELL
*Department of Zoology, University of Iowa, Iowa City*

**References and Notes**

1. B. Uvarov, *Grasshoppers and Locusts* (Cambridge Univ. Press, London, 1966), vol. 1.
2. J. C. Faure, *J. Econ. Entomol.* **26**, 706 (1933).
3. N. C. Criddle, *Can. Entomol.* **65**, 97 (1933); J. M. Grayson, "Studies of some factors influencing coloration of the grasshopper, *Melanoplus bivittatus* Say," thesis, Iowa State College, Ames, 1941); A. B. Gurney, *Proc. Entomol. Soc. Wash.* **51**, 267 (1949); C. Wakeland, *Tech. Bull. U.S. Dept. Agr.* **1167** (1958); O. L. Barnes, *J. Econ. Entomol.* **53**, 721 (1960).
4. J. R. Parker, *J. Econ. Entomol.* **26**, 102 (1933); R. C. Froeschner, *Iowa State Coll. J. Sci.* **29**, 163 (1954).
5. E. H. Slifer, *J. Exp. Zool.* **138**, 259 (1958); *Nature* **184**, 1424 (1959).
6. H. B. Johnston, *Bull. Entomol. Res.* **23**, 49 (1932); L. G. Duck, *J. Kansas Entomol. Soc.* **17**, 105 (1944).
7. D. L. Gunn and P. Hunter-Jones, *Anti-Locust Bull.* **12** (1952); P. Hunter-Jones, *Entomol. Monogr. Mag.* **98**, 89 (1962).
8. R. L. Shotwell, *Tech. Bull. U.S. Dept. Agr.* **774** (1941).
9. V. M. Dirsh, *Anti-Locust Bull.* **16** (1953).
10. C. H. Brett, *Tech. Bull. Oklahoma Agr. Exp. Sta. T-26* (1947).
11. Supported by NSF grant GB-2949 to H.D.

28 September 1966 ∎

# ADAPTIVE VARIATION IN THE BREEDING REGIME
## OF A TROPICAL SEA BIRD*

BY N. PHILIP ASHMOLE

PEABODY MUSEUM OF NATURAL HISTORY, YALE UNIVERSITY

*Communicated by G. E. Hutchinson, December 7, 1964*

The sooty tern (*Sterna fuscata*) is one of the most widely distributed of tropical sea birds, breeding on islands round the world between about 28°N and 31°S.[1] Within this range, different populations of the species show remarkable differences in breeding periodicity, demonstrating unusually clearly the potential evolutionary flexibility of this character, in spite of the apparent adherence by the vast majority of birds to annual regimes under rigid proximate[2] control.

Most populations of sooty terns breed at annual intervals, and in areas where sea-surface temperatures are above 23°C for only part of the year, breeding occurs during this period.[1] However, on Ascension Island in the equatorial Atlantic a population of sooty terns returns to breed at intervals of 9–10 months.[3-5] This was for a time the only proved example of a population of birds which had sexual cycles (defined here as the whole series of events occurring between the production of a fertile egg in two successive breeding periods) with a periodicity independent of any annual variation in the environment: recently it has become clear that in several other tropical sea birds members of certain populations breed at intervals of less than a year, and in different seasons in successive years.[6-8]

It has long been known, however, that on certain islands in the Pacific sooty terns have yet another breeding regime, the colonies being active at two distinct seasons in each year, roughly six months apart. It was at first suggested, by Hutchinson[9] and Chapin,[4] that on such islands there might be two separate populations of sooty terns, each breeding at annual intervals, but at opposite seasons—a situation which has since been found to occur in two forms of the petrel *Pterodroma*

Reprinted by permission of the National Academy of Sciences and the author from *Proceedings of the National Academy of Sciences* 53:311–318, 1965.

49

312                    *ZOÖLOGY: N. P. ASHMOLE*                    Proc. N. A. S.

*mollis* on Madeira.[10]   However, in the sooty tern a study of museum specimens showed that the populations from islands where breeding occurred at 6-month intervals had peculiarities in the molt which suggested that some individuals were involved in successive breeding periods only 6 months apart.[11]

Recent work which I undertook on Christmas Island (in the Pacific at about 2°N, 157°W) has confirmed this hypothesis, and has shown that some or all of the individuals which are unsuccessful in raising a chick in one breeding period lay again in the next, only six months later.   In contrast, individuals which are successful in raising a chick in one breeding period are absent in the next, but return to breed again 12 months later.   The data supporting this conclusion are given in this paper, together with a description of the molt adaptation which is involved and a discussion of the significance of the three different regimes of breeding and molt found in different populations of this single species, all in tropical seas.

*Results from Christmas Island.*—Between March 1963 and June 1964 eight visits of about three weeks each were made to Christmas Island.   The work was done mainly on Cook Island, in the entrance to the lagoon of Christmas Island, where there is a colony of sooty terns probably numbering between 25,000 and 50,000 birds.   Laying on Cook Island starts about June and December of each year;[1] sooty terns in the other colonies on Christmas Island breed in approximate synchrony with those on Cook Island, but were not studied in detail.   During the breeding period lasting from June through September 1963, individuals were caught at known stages in their breeding cycle and marked with numbered aluminum and red plastic bands (the latter to increase conspicuousness); details were recorded of any molt which was in progress, and of the condition of the wing and tail feathers. In the following two breeding periods, 6 and 12 months later, the colony was searched intensively for banded individuals, which were caught and examined after it had been ascertained that they were again breeding.   The results are summarized in Table 1.[12]

The first group is of 210 birds banded when incubating their single eggs during the second half of June and early July of 1963.   Some of these birds hatched chicks, and some are known to have reared young successfully.   However, since it was not practicable to follow the history of all the nests, these birds are considered as comprising a more or less random sample of the incubating population.   The 32 of these birds which were found breeding again six months later did not include any of the few known to have succeeded in rearing chicks in the previous breeding period.   A second group is of 100 incubating birds banded in early July 1963, whose

TABLE 1

Sooty Terns Banded on Christmas Island: Returns in Subsequent Breeding Periods

|  | No. of birds banded June–Sept. 1963 | No. (and %) Found Breeding in the Two Subsequent Breeding Periods | |
|---|---|---|---|
|  |  | Dec. 1963– Jan. 1964 | June 1964 |
| Birds banded when incubating; subsequent history variable | 210 | 32 (15.2%) | 18 (8.6%) |
| Birds banded when incubating; eggs then destroyed | 100 | 11 (11.0%) | 5 (5.0%) |
| Birds banded when brooding newly hatched chicks; subsequent history variable | 61 | 9 (14.8%) | 10 (16.4%) |
| Birds banded when feeding well-grown chicks | 170 | 0 | 20 (11.8%) |

eggs were then destroyed: it is unlikely that a significant proportion laid replacement eggs in the same breeding period, and it may be assumed that they did not rear chicks.   In the following breeding period, six months later, 11 of these birds were found breeding again, a proportion not significantly different from that in the first group.   A third group, of 61 birds, were banded when brooding newly hatched chicks (including a few up to four or five days old, and two eggs on the point of hatching); it is not known how many of the chicks were reared.   Nine of these birds were found breeding again six months later; this proportion is not significantly different from those in the first two groups.   It is thus clear that a bird which completes incubation and hatches a chick may yet breed again six months later.

The final group comprised 170 birds banded in August and September 1963 while they were feeding (or were apparently on the point of feeding) large young, which were probably all at least a month old, and most were considerably older. To catch adults while feeding well-grown young was the best available way to obtain a sample of adults, nearly all of which could be assumed to have been successful in their breeding.   Of these "successful" birds, none were found in the colony during the next breeding period, despite careful search.   This result is significantly different ($P < 0.001$) from the results in the other three groups, indicating that birds which are successful in rearing a chick in one breeding period do not breed again in the next, six months later.   A three-week visit to Christmas Island in June 1964, at the start of the laying period 12 months after that in which the banding was done, led to the capture of a number of banded birds which were breeding again (Table 1, right-hand column).   These included 20 of the 170 birds that had bred successfully 12 months before, and had been unrepresented in the intervening breeding period.

Since only a minority of both successful and unsuccessful banded individuals were found breeding again either 6 or 12 months later (probably because the colonies on the main island were not searched), it cannot be shown whether all birds which are unsuccessful in one breeding period breed again six months later, or whether all birds which are successful in one breeding period return a year later.   In both cases, however, it is clear that a substantial proportion do so.

It is thus established that the length of the sexual cycle in a member of the Christmas Island population can be sometimes 6 and sometimes 12 months, depending on the success or failure of the bird in the breeding period which is included. This means that the nonbreeding period lasts about four or five months in unsuccessful birds, but about eight months in successful ones.   Unfortunately there is little chance of determining the details of the gonad cycles in successful and unsuccessful birds, because both groups leave the island soon after breeding is completed.   However, it is probably safe to assume that the recrudescence of the gonads before fertilization and the regression afterwards are both rapid processes, as in the Ascension Island population,[1] and that it is the intervening quiescent period which varies drastically in length.

Although the ability of individual sooty terns to complete a sexual cycle in either 6 or 12 months, according to their breeding success, may be unique among birds, sexual cycles lasting either 12 or 24 months, again according to breeding success are found in at least two species of sea birds, the royal albatross (*Diomedea epomophora*)[13] and the king penguin (*Aptenodytes patagonica*).[14]   In these species successful birds take so long to rear their chick that they cannot breed in the next season,

51

twelve months later, while unsuccessful birds can do so. Other species which probably have a similar breeding regime are the wandering albatross (*Diomedea exulans*), the Andean and California condors (*Vultur gryphus* and *Gymnogyps californianus*), and certain species of large eagles.[15]

Since it was the curious distribution of old and new wing feathers in sooty tern skins from islands where breeding occurs at 6-month intervals which first suggested that some of the same birds were involved in successive breeding periods,[11] a special effort was made to elucidate the program of molt in the Christmas Island population. The results, which will be presented in detail elsewhere, show that birds in this population have evolved unusual flexibility in their molt as a part of the adaptation enabling them to maintain their specialized breeding regime.

Sooty terns from areas where breeding is annual, and from Ascension Island, apparently undergo a single replacement of their main wing feathers, the primaries and secondaries, between successive breeding periods; the tail feathers may be replaced twice. Replacement of the primaries occurs in a steady sequence from the innermost feather outward, while in the secondaries molt starts with the innermost and outermost feathers, the middle ones being the last to be replaced. On the other hand, birds from populations where breeding occurs every six months commonly show breaks or "discontinuities" in the normal age-sequence of the primaries and secondaries, such that outer feathers are strikingly older (or newer) than inner ones, instead of forming a smooth graded series.[11]

Of 52 birds banded while breeding in June and July 1963 which were breeding again six months later, 43 (83%) replaced all their primaries in the interval, while the remainder retained a few old ones; 18 out of 50 replaced all their secondaries in the interval. In contrast, of six birds which made breeding attempts in December–January 1963–1964 and which were breeding again in June 1964, only one replaced all its primaries in the interval and not one replaced all its secondaries: the difference is significant for the primaries ($P < 0.01$). This suggests that there may be considerable variation in the proportion of birds which are able to replace all their wing feathers in the short intervals between breeding attempts. Such variation might be correlated with availability of food, or might result from differences in the average period the birds spent in their unsuccessful attempts to breed.

Of 24 birds which bred successfully in June–September 1963 and returned 12 months later, none retained any of the old primaries. However, 18 of them had discontinuities among the primaries as a result of having replaced some feathers a second time. As one might expect, nearly all these birds (20 out of 24) had replaced all their secondaries in the 12-month interval between banding and return; three had apparently replaced a few secondaries twice. The fact that in these successful birds, whose sexual cycle on this occasion had a period of 12 months, molt of the flight feathers did not stop at the time when all the feathers had been replaced once, as it does in the annual-breeding populations, provides a clue to the nature of the molt adaptation which has been evolved in the Christmas Island population. Since molt ceases when breeding starts, and the time available for molt between successive breeding periods of an individual is sometimes four or five months and sometimes about eight months, it is clearly impracticable for the members of the population to follow any rigid molt program. Instead, they molt the flight feathers continuously, in the normal regular sequence, throughout any period when they are not breeding. Thus molt starts as soon as breeding is finished (in the case of successful birds it is initiated shortly before the chick is fledged) and continues until shortly before the start of the next breeding period in which the bird will participate; it then stops at whatever stage it has reached. After breeding, molt starts again, usually at the beginning of the sequence rather than at the point where it stopped; this results in the inner primaries being replaced, on the average, more often than the outer ones, although the latter deteriorate more quickly.

*Discussion.*—Most birds live in environments which show pronounced seasonal changes and in which food is much more abundant in one season than in others. In such environments birds have sexual cycles with annual periodicity; breeding generally occurs in the early part of the season when food is abundant and is followed by a major molt of adults and young. Such a regime allows the birds to devote all their energy to maintenance during the less favorable part of the year. On the other hand, one would expect that in an environment in which seasonal changes were negligible, selection would have led to the evolution of the shortest interval between the successive breeding periods of each individual which was consistent with continuing reproductive success. In fact, however, in the few populations of birds in which breeding is independent of season, and which have been studied in detail, the breeding periods of individuals are separated by considerable periods when the gonads are inactive, and when molt is generally in progress.[1, 6, 8] Thus it appears that continuous breeding is prevented either by the need for a quiescent period in the pituitary-gonad cycle, or by the need for periodic feather replacement.

Recently it has become clear, especially through Miller's work on *Zonotrichia capensis*,[16] that the length of the inactive period of the gonads can be greatly modified by the selective forces acting on particular populations. Miller[17, 18] has suggested that in seasonal environments the length of the refractory period in the pituitary-gonad cycle is adapted to prevent wasteful sexual activity throughout that part of the year in which breeding attempts would not lead to the successful raising of young. Extension of this reasoning leads to the hypothesis that the very existence of a quiescent period in the pituitary-gonad cycle may depend on selection favoring the avoidance of sexual activity (including maintenance of the gonads) at times when it would not be profitable. In seasonal environments the quiescent period prevents sexual activities at inappropriate seasons, but in environments in which breeding is possible at any season the quiescent period could still be of value in preventing wasteful sexual activity during the molt.

It has only recently been realized, mainly through the work of Pitelka,[19, 20] that the need for periodic feather replacement (molt) is a factor having an important influence on the evolution of the particular breeding regime of a bird population. Feathers deteriorate with use, so that the efficiency of the wing and tail feathers for flight, and of the body feathers as an insulating layer and as a basis for signal patterns, decreases with time. Thus regular molt is vital for all birds, and in practice feathers are generally replaced once or twice each year. Apart from normal maintenance, breeding activities and molt provide two of the major demands on the nutritional (and especially protein) resources of birds, so it is not surprising to find that they are nearly always mutually exclusive. The implication is that it is generally uneconomic to molt while breeding, even though the separation

53

316                    *ZOÖLOGY: N. P. ASHMOLE*                    Proc. N. A. S.

of the two activities may limit the time available for breeding. The demonstration[21, 1, 6, 8] that even in populations of several tropical birds which have sexual cycles lasting less than 12 months, breeding and molt tend not to occur together, is in full accord with the hypothesis[22] that in most tropical sea birds the mechanism by which population size is regulated ensures that there is competition for food in the breeding season, so that it is difficult for adults to raise even one slow-growing chick. Clearly under these circumstances parents which molted while breeding would be less likely to rear their chick.

Thus it seems likely that continuous breeding among sea birds in seasonless environments is prevented by selection favoring a regime in which breeding activities alternate continuously with minimal feather replacement, rather than by any fundamental physiological need for a quiescent period in the pituitary-gonad cycle.

In populations of birds in which the periodicity of breeding is not determined by seasonal changes in the environment, and in which breeding and molt alternate continuously, one would expect that individuals could be found breeding at any time of year; that is to say, one would expect there to be no synchrony in the sexual cycles of the members of the population. Such a situation was first described by Stonehouse[6] among the tropic birds (*Phaethon* spp.) on Ascension Island, where the length of the sexual cycle of each individual was determined by the length of time for which it was involved in breeding activities (varying according to whether or not it bred successfully) plus a roughly constant period spent at sea, which was apparently fully occupied by molt. A similar situation has now been found among the fairy terns (*Gygis alba*) on Christmas Island, in which molt certainly occupies all the time between the end of one breeding period and the start of the next.[8] The fact that sooty terns on Ascension breed at intervals of 9–10 months implies that they also are independent of seasonal changes in the environment, but they breed in rough synchrony with each other. The reasons for the synchrony are not fully understood,[1] but it is known that this breeding regime allows birds to breed in successive breeding periods; it is thus clearly more efficient than annual breeding in an environment in which there are no important (and consistent) seasonal changes.

On the other hand, the breeding and molt regime found in the sooty terns on Christmas Island allows individuals to breed more frequently than once a year and yet to remain in phase with seasonal changes in the environment, thus taking advantage of any tendency for certain seasons to be more (or less) favorable than others. Unfortunately, seasonal changes in the marine environment of Christmas Island are not sufficiently well marked or well known[23] to enable one to make a realistic assessment of the extent of changes in the availability of food for the birds.[24] Furthermore, since sooty terns are involved in breeding on Christmas Island for nearly eight months in each year and since it is not yet known what part of the breeding cycle requires the greatest food-collecting effort by the birds, it is not possible to say which are likely to be the critical months.

It may thus be seen that although we now have factual knowledge of some of the special breeding regimes which enable sooty terns to breed more frequently than once a year in equatorial environments, we have no precise information on the ultimate[2] control of breeding times in different populations. It should also be remembered that no start has yet been made in the investigation of the proximate mechanisms used by sooty terns in timing their breeding: changes in day-length may well be important in annual-breeding populations distant from the equator, but it is not easy to see what external factors could be used as timing mechanisms for two separate breeding periods, June and December of each year, on Christmas Island at 2°N.

*Summary.*—On Christmas Island, near the equator in the Pacific, sooty terns (*Sterna fuscata*) sometimes breed at six-month intervals: individuals which fail to raise a chick in one breeding period try again six months later, while successful breeders miss the next breeding period and return after 12 months. Molt is continuous during the nonbreeding period, but stops when breeding starts. Unsuccessful birds often do not complete replacement of their wing feathers before they start to breed again, but successful birds have generally completed one molt, and started a second, by the time they return to breed. This regime is contrasted with that found on Ascension Island, where breeding starts every 9–10 months and all birds complete a molt in the interval, and with the annual cycle found in most other populations of the species, which again involves a complete molt after breeding.

It is concluded that the differing regimes of breeding and molt which occur in different populations of this widespread species are adaptations leading in each case to the greatest frequency of breeding which is practicable in that environment. This species thus demonstrates the extreme evolutionary flexibility of sexual cycles, although environments where this can be exploited are relatively rare.

* This study was undertaken while the author was the holder of a fellowship from Yale University to the Bishop Museum, Hawaii: grateful acknowledgment is made to these institutions and to Dr. S. Dillon Ripley, Dr. Roland Force, and others who helped to make the work possible. Thanks are also due to the members of the R.A.F. Officers' Mess, Christmas Island, for assistance and warm hospitality.

[1] Ashmole, N. P., *Ibis*, **103b**, 297 (1963).

[2] The "proximate" causes of breeding seasons are the factors which act as timing mechanisms enabling birds to breed each year close to the optimum time; the "ultimate" causes provide the selective pressures favoring breeding at that time; see Baker, J. R., in *Evolution: Essays on Aspects of Evolutionary Biology Presented to Professor E. S. Goodrich*, ed. G. R. de Beer (Oxford: Clarendon Press, 1938), p. 161.

[3] Chapin, J. P., *Natural History*, **55**, 313 (1946).

[4] Chapin, J. P., *Auk*, **71**, 1 (1954).

[5] Chapin, J. P., and L. W. Wing, *Auk*, **76**, 153 (1959).

[6] Stonehouse, B., *Ibis*, **103b**, 124 (1962).

[7] Dorward, D. F., *Ibis*, **103b**, 174 (1962).

[8] Ashmole, N. P., unpublished information on *Gygis alba* on Christmas Island.

[9] Hutchinson, G. E., *Am. Scientist*, **38**, 613 (1950).

[10] Bourne, W. R. P., *Ibis*, **99**, 182 (1957).

[11] Ashmole, N. P., *Postilla*, No. 76 (1963).

[12] In the sooty tern the male and female are alike and both participate in incubation and care of the young; they are therefore not distinguished in the results.

[13] Richdale, L. E., *Biological Monographs* (Dunedin, N.Z.), No. 4 (1952).

[14] Stonehouse, B., *F.I.D.S. Sci. Reports*, No. 23 (1960).

[15] Amadon, D., *Evolution*, **18**, 105 (1964).

[16] Miller, A. H., these PROCEEDINGS, **45**, 1095 (1959).

[17] Miller, A. H., *XIIth International Ornithological Congress, Helsinki, 1958*, p. 513 (1960).

[18] Miller, A. H., *Condor*, **61**, 344 (1959).

[19] Pitelka, F. A., *Ecology*, **38**, 176 (1957).

55

318                    *ZOÖLOGY: N. P. ASHMOLE*                    Proc. N. A. S.

[20] Pitelka, F. A., *Condor*, **60,** 38 (1958).

[21] Miller, A. H., *Condor*, **63,** 143 (1961).

[22] Ashmole, N. P., *Ibis*, **103b,** 458 (1963).

[23] King, J. E., and T. S. Hida, *U.S. Fish Wildlife Serv., Fishery Bull.*, **57** (118), 365 (1957).

[24] Some information on seasonal changes in food supplies will be provided by a current study of the food items taken at different seasons during 1963–1964 by various species of sea birds on Christmas Island.

# SELECTIVE MECHANISMS IN BACTERIA[1]

## K. C. ATWOOD, LILLIAN K. SCHNEIDER AND FRANCIS J. RYAN

### Department of Zoology, Columbia University, New York

The objective in population genetics is to reconstruct the possible, or more rarely the actual, sequence of events in the evolution of organisms in terms of changes resulting from the interplay of mutation and selection. The possibility of entirely succeeding in this is of course dependent on a valid and complete assessment of the attributes of the genetic systems involved. Failing in this, we may empirically examine the genetic constitution of populations before specifying any precise basis for the variability observed. The non-sexual bacteria offer good opportunities along these lines, because the immediate source of genetic variability resides in the capacity of the existing genotype to mutate, and not in the emergence of recombinant types. In other words, the reservoir of variability is not concealed, but is directly represented by the components of heterogeneous populations.

By selection we shall understand those factors other than mutation which influence the frequencies of mutants in populations. Many forms of selection can be imagined which would tend to alter the proportions of mutants. These, for convenience, can be divided into two categories which we can call specific and non-specific. In the case of specific selection, the selective differential between mutant and parental type is a direct consequence of the mutation itself, whether primarily or as part of some pleiotropic complex. The mechanisms involved in imposed or specific selection must be separately considered for individual cases and some explanations, mostly on a biochemical level, have been offered by Braun (1947), Braun, Goodlow and Kraft (1950) and Guthrie (1949). Non-specific selection, on the other hand, consists of those factors which operate to alter the frequencies of a variety of unrelated mutants simultaneously.

In considering the role of selection as a factor determining the constitution of bacterial popula-

tions, it is instructive to imagine a hypothetical situation in which no selection operates and the population is giving rise to a number of mutants. These would, in the course of time, accumulate until an equilibrium ratio of the alternative types would be reached, where the ratio for each mutant is determined by its forward and reverse mutation rates. To assume that these forward and reverse mutation rates would be equal would provide a rather unrealistic model, so let us assume, for example, that there is a tenfold difference between the forward and reverse rates on the average for each mutant. If we consider only twenty such mutants simultaneously at equilibrium the most frequent genotype in the population would have a frequency of $(0.9)^{20}$. In other words, the population would be so heterogeneous that even the most frequent type present would be relatively infrequent.

Now let us introduce specific selection which would, in sufficient time, alter the equilibrium value for each pair of alternatives in some unspecified direction. If the equilibrium ratios were generally brought closer to unity, the population would become even more heterogeneous. On the other hand, if they were, on the average, brought closer to zero, a particular genotype would become predominant at the expense of the other possibilities, and cultures initiated from bacteria of other genotypes would be unstable, the populations becoming predominantly the selected genotype.

All of these situations would be regarded as exceptional if encountered in the handling of the various auxotrophs, phage pattern, fermentation, drug resistance, and other mutants used by the bacterial geneticist, despite the fact that stocks of widely divergent genotype are commonly maintained on the same nutrient media (Ryan, 1948).

While we cannot uphold specific selection as the cause of the apparent stability of divers bacterial stocks, it can be effectively argued that the observed values for mutation rates, combined with weak selection pressures, would lead to low rates of change in the genetic constitution of populations. Under these conditions, a high degree of stability would result from the action of a potent non-specific selective procedure; namely,

[1] This work was supported in part by an American Cancer Society grant recommended by the Committee on Growth of the National Research Council and by a research grant from the Division of Research Grants and Fellowships of the National Institutes of Health, U. S. Public Health Service.

The authors are grateful to Dr. Amos Norman for his help in formulating the equations.

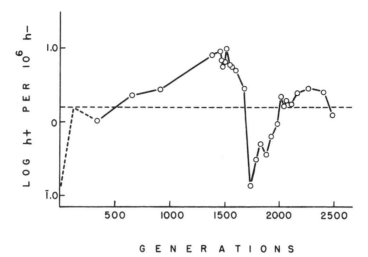

FIG. 1. h⁺ / h⁻ ratio during serial transfer for 2760 generations. The horizontal broken line indicates the equilibrium ratio based on this and other experiments.

the isolation at intervals of one or few cells from a population in order to start a new population. One might not suppose offhand that this would be an important factor in bacterial evolution except under laboratory conditions, but we are now acquainted with the fact that even if such isolations are not externally imposed, they occur as a result of the inherent dynamics of the evolving system. This process, known as periodic selection, has been encountered with respect to antigenic variants in Salmonella, (Stocker, 1949), bacteriophage resistant mutants in *E. coli*, (Novick and Szilard, 1950) and reversions of an auxotrophic mutant in *E. coli* (Schneider, 1950; Atwood et al., 1951). The purpose of the present paper is to attempt a further clarification of the mechanism of periodic selection and its consequences for bacterial evolution.

### PERIODIC SELECTION IN THE h⁻ ⇌ h⁺ SYSTEM

Our conclusions are based largely on the results of serial transfer experiments (STs) in which cultures of *E. coli* have been maintained over times ranging from a few weeks to more than six months. Transfers of 0.5 cc of undiluted cultures were made at twelve-hour intervals into 50 cc of fresh medium contained in 125 cc Erlenmeyer flasks. These were incubated at 37°C. Under these conditions the one hundred fold increase (6.64 generations) of bacteria permitted by the medium is completed within six to seven hours and the cultures are in stationary phase for the remaining time until the next transfer. The viable

count remains constant during this stationary phase. The fully grown cultures contain about $2.5 \times 10^{10}$ bacteria, and about $2.5 \times 10^{8}$ of these are transferred.

This procedure was followed using a histidineless (h⁻) mutant of strain 15 of *E. coli* transferred through G and T synthetic medium supplemented with 25 micrograms L-histidine monohydrochloride per cc. The inoculum into the first flask was small ($5 \times 10^{3}$) so that no histidine independent (h⁺) bacteria were initially introduced. Thereafter the regular inoculum of $2.5 \times 10^{8}$ bacteria was used. The h⁺ bacteria which accumulated due to mutation and growth were counted at various times by plating washed aliquots in agar without histidine (H⁻ agar). Platings were done immediately before transfer. The h⁻ bacteria in the same aliquots were counted by plating in H⁺ agar after appropriate dilution. The proportion of h⁺ bacteria was found to increase for fifteen to twenty transfers (100 to 130 generations) and then reach a rough equilibrium at about 1.3 h⁺/10⁶ h⁻. This ratio often has large temporary fluctuations, but has shown no consistent trend in our longest experiment, 2760 generations (Fig. 1).

Mutation rate determinations for h⁻ → h⁺ by the $P_0$ method of Luria and Delbrück (1943) and the median method of Lea and Coulson (1949) have averaged $2.86 \times 10^{-8}$ and $2.70 \times 10^{-8}$ respectively, where these rates are uncorrected for both phenotypic lag and segregation lag, or specific selection. Lieb (1951) has measured the rate for h⁺ → h⁻ by applying the median method to estimates of the numbers of mutants made by a quantitative modification of the penicillin screening technique (Davis, 1948; Lederberg and Zinder, 1948), and found an average of $1.17 \times 10^{-6}$. Thus, in the absence of selection we would expect to approach an $h^+/h^-$ equilibrium ratio of the order of $10^{-2}$ rather than the observed $10^{-6}$. The effect of selection in producing this large discrepancy was explored by two methods: first, by observing the return to equilibrium of STs started with an inoculum containing $h^+/h^-$ ratios from ten to one hundred fold higher than the equilibrium ratio; and second, by introducing $h^+$ bacteria bearing an additional genetic marker to distinguish them from those arising by mutation of $h^-$ to $h^+$. When both of these conditions were produced in the same ST the marked and unmarked $h^+$ remain at approximately the initial level for 150 to 250 generations, then the unmarked $h^+$ quite suddenly drop

to equilibrium and the marked $h^+$ bacteria disappear from the culture (Fig. 2). Apparently selection pressure against $h^+$ is absent or negligible for a time, then suddenly becomes very strong.

Accordingly, $h^+$ and $h^-$ bacteria were isolated during and after the period of strong selection and tested in various combinations to see whether the behavior of the population could be attributed to any new stable properties of its components. The results of many experiments with isolates taken at various times are summarized in Figure 3. In Diagram A the original stocks, designated $h_0^+$ and $h_0^-$ are placed in competition at a ratio above equilibrium. At the time Y, $h_Y^+$ and $h_Y^-$ are taken from the population and placed in competition with each other and with $h_0^+$ and $h_0^-$.

The results are shown in diagram B where $h_Y^+$ is immediately selected against in the presence

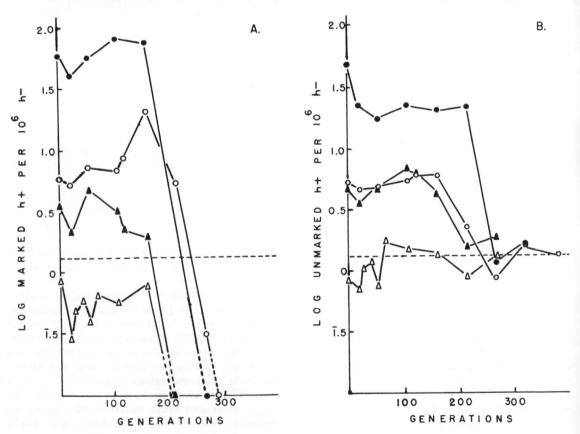

FIG. 2. Simultaneous behavior of marked and unmarked $h^+$ bacteria in serial transfers started at $h^+ / h^-$ ratios above equilibrium.

A. Various starting ratios of $h^+$ which differ in lactose fermentation character from the $h^-$.

B. Various starting ratios of $h^+$ having the same lactose fermentation character as the $h^-$. Solid circles in A are samples from the *same* cultures as solid circles in B. Likewise for open circles, triangles. Broken line indicates equilibrium.

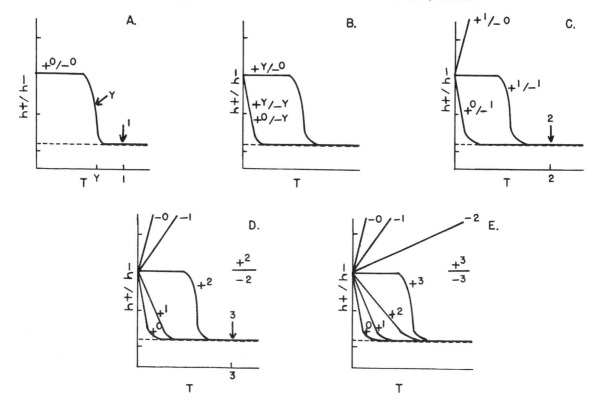

FIG. 3. Diagrammatic representation of tests of successive isolates from STs started at high initial $h^+$ / $h^-$ ratios. The curves in A, B and C are labelled with the strains tested. One of the components tested in D and E is labelled in the right margin, the opposite is marked on each curve.

of $h_Y^-$. Thus, it appears that the $h^-$ possesses a selective advantage at time Y, which it did not possess at time O, but the $h^+$ has remained unchanged. Diagram C summarizes the results of similar experiments using components isolated at time 1. We see that $h_1^+$ is no longer the equivalent of $h_0^-$, but is now selectively equal to $h_1^-$ and superior to $h_0^-$. Diagram D shows the same experiments done using components isolated at time 2, and diagram E components from time 3. It appears that the population is being replaced periodically by new types which can be distinguished by their ability to select against the pre-

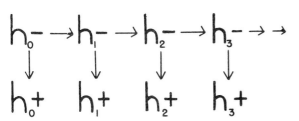

FIG. 4. The mutation pattern involved in periodic selection in the $h^- \rightleftharpoons h^+$ system.

vious types, and that the sudden fall of the $h^+/h^-$ ratio to equilibrium is an indication that replacement has occurred. The selective character of the new types, 1, 2 and 3, is stable, and the results of placing various types in competition are reproducible after the strains have been kept in stock for many months. We have concluded from these experiments that we are dealing with the mutation pattern shown in Figure 4, where mutants O, 1, 2, etc., always arise in $h^-$ because the latter are $10^6$ times more numerous than $h^+$. If an initial population is completely eliminated some time after a new type appears, the accumulation of $h^+$ in the culture has in effect taken its departure from a new starting point, a time somewhat in advance of the initial starting point. Obviously, a mutational equilibrium will not be reached while the culture continues to undergo this process at sufficiently frequent intervals.

The non-specific character of periodic selection is shown in Figure 5. Here a population of histidineless-methionineless ($h^- m^-$) serially transferred in $H^+ M^+$ medium (25 micrograms L-histidine monohydrochloride and 50 micrograms

DL-methionine per cc.) gives rise by spontaneous mutation to $h^+m^-$ and to $h^-m^+$. The $h^+/h^-$ ratio and the $m+/m-$ ratio show parallel behavior. This parallel behavior is not due to fluctuations in the total number which is the denominator for both ratios, since the reciprocal of the total shows less fluctuation than either ratio. The relatively higher number of $m^+$ at each point indicates that the rate of increase of $m^+$ is greater than that of $h^+$. It is interesting that the uncorrected median method determinations of $h^-m^- \rightarrow h^+m^-$ and $h^-m^- \rightarrow h^-m^+$ mutation rates were $1.4 \times 10^{-8}$ and $6 \times 10^{-9}$ respectively, yet we have not been able to demonstrate specific selection by independent methods. While non-specific selection is clearly demonstrated, specific selection must also be postulated here to reconcile the difference in the equilibrium values with the data on short-term increase rates obtained with the median method determinations.

## THEORY OF PERIODIC SELECTION

Regardless of the underlying causes, selection can be expressed in terms of a difference in relative growth rates of the components under examination. This applies even to selection in a stationary phase where one or both growth rates have a negative sign. Thus in the mutation pattern shown in Figure 4, the types 1, 2, 3, etc., may be regarded as growing at successively higher rates $K_1$, $K_2$, $K_3$, etc. In a population of unlimited size these types would coexist indefinitely, although their ratios would always be changing in favor of the more recent types. In a population of

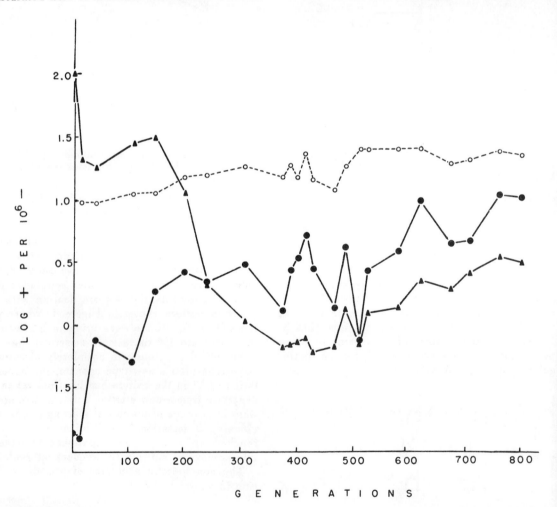

FIG. 5. Simultaneous equilibria for $h^-m^+/h^-m^-$ (solid circles) and $h^+m^-/h^-m^-$ (solid triangles). Parallel behavior begins after both equilibria have been reached. The dotted line is the reciprocal of the number of $h^-m^-$.

350       K. C. ATWOOD, LILLIAN K. SCHNEIDER AND FRANCIS J. RYAN

fixed size the older types would be eliminated by sampling. Consider the following segment of a more general mutation pattern:

(I)
$$
\begin{array}{ccc}
N_1 & \to & N_2 \\
\downarrow & & \downarrow \\
X_1 & & X_2
\end{array}
$$

where $N_1$ and $X_1$ grow at a rate $K_1$, and $N_2$ and $X_2$ at a rate $K_2$; and the mutation $1 \to 2$ occurs at a rate a, and the mutation $N \to X$ at a rate b. Evidently the pattern (I) depends upon the initial condition that X be present in sufficiently small number so that the mutation $1 \to 2$ does not occur in X, but only in N. We may now inquire whether there is selection against X if $K_2 > K_1$, or in other words whether the growth rate of N is greater than that of X.

We choose for convenience a discontinuous model for the appearance of $N_2$, thus $N_2$ will appear when $N_1 \approx 1/a$. Where $\delta$ is the time interval before the appearance of $N_2$,

(II)             $N_2 = e^{K_2(t - \delta)}$

and at times greater than $\delta$, i.e., where $N_1$ and $N_2$ coexist, the growth rate of N is

(III)   $\bar{K}_N = \dfrac{K_1 e^{K_1 t} + K_2 e^{K_2(t - \delta)}}{e^{K_1 t} + e^{K_2(t - \delta)}} = \dfrac{K_1 + K_2 g}{1 + g}$

where         $g = e^{-K_2 \delta} \cdot e^{(K_2 - K_1)t}.$

The mutation $N \to X$ is handled by the usual continuous model, thus the growth rate of X (for $t > \delta$) is

(IV)   $\bar{K}_X = \dfrac{K_1 t b e^{K_1 t} + K_2 (t - \delta) b e^{K_2(t - \delta)}}{t b e^{K_1 t} + (t - \delta) b e^{K_2(t - \delta)}} = \dfrac{K_1 + K_2 g l}{1 + g l}$

where $l = \dfrac{1 - \delta/t}$. Evidently where $t > \delta$, $0 < l < 1$ and $\bar{K}_N > \bar{K}_X$, consequently the mutation pattern (I) leads to selection against X.

The extension to include mutations $2 \to 3$, $3 \to 4$, etc., is obvious. It is important to note that the specific character of the mutant, X, is irrelevant so long as it does not lead to specific selection of the order of magnitude of $K_2 - K_1$. In other words, all mutants are selected against except the current type responsible for the selection.

NATURE OF THE ADAPTIVE LEAPS

The occurrence of a succession of types each of which selects against the previous types raises

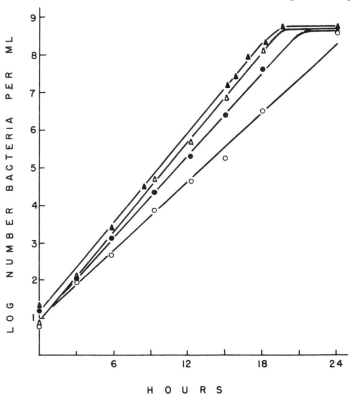

FIG. 6. Growth of stocks 0 (open circles), 1 (closed circles), 2 (open triangles), and 3 (closed triangles) on H$^+$ medium, measured by plating.

TABLE 1. PERCENT INCREASE IN RATIO OF $h_o-$ TO VARIOUS DERIVED TYPES ON DIFFERENT MEDIA

| Strain | H+ | Casamino Acids | Yeast Extract | Casamino Acids Yeast Ext. | Nutrient Broth |
|---|---|---|---|---|---|
| 1A– | –88.4 | –12.2 | +52.2 | +44.4 | +49.4 |
| 1B– | –83.3 | – 3.6 | –18.0 | –19.5 | –37.6 |
| 1C– | –66.0 | –76.5 | –93.8 | –100.0 | –100.0 |
| 1D– | –89.8 | +56.9 | –31.3 | + 7.1 | –39.5 |
| 2E+ | –73.8 | –17.2 | –11.3 | + 7.0 | +65.4 |
| 2F+ | –90.6 | –40.6 | – 7.7 | +35.7 | +100.0 |
| 2G– | –91.8 | –15.8 | –20.9 | +51.9 | +100.0 |
| 3J+ | –81.7 | –60.9 | – 0.4 | +78.3 | +100.0 |
| 3K+ | –66.4 | –24.5 | –20.5 | +34.3 | +100.0 |
| 3L+ | –74.2 | –50.0 | –31.4 | +71.9 | +51.1 |
| 3M+ | –86.4 | –53.8 | –100.0 | –91.1 | +100.0 |

several questions. First, we must account for the selective status of the initial type 0. If the observed sequence 1, 2, 3, etc., is simply a stepwise increase in intrinsic growth rate, one would suppose that this process should have evolved to completion during the course of evolution prior to our experiments. Two possible explanations can be offered for the continued potentiality for the production of new types possessing selection advantage. One is that the selection can be due to some interaction between the components of the population. This would make possible a circular mutation pattern such as previously suggested by the present authors. Alternately, the selection may be due to a successively better adaptation to the conditions of the medium. If the latter hypothesis is correct, the time over which periodic selection could operate in a constant medium would be finite, but occasional changes in the character of the environment could perpetuate the process. These two notions are not mutually exclusive, and it is conceivable that the mode of action of different mutational steps may be quite dissimilar.

In attempting to clarify the immediate basis for periodic selection, we have used stocks obtained from the first three mutational steps of a serial transfer experiment. Experiments were done with these stocks to decide whether selection operates through higher growth rate on H⁺ medium, differential viability in stationary phase, or production of substances by some stocks which influence the growth rate of others. No evidence for selection in stationary phase and no evidence of activity of culture filtrates has been found. However, in the case of steps 0, 1, and 2 there was a demonstrable increase in growth rate as shown

in Figure 6. We were unable to demonstrate a growth rate difference between 2 and 3.

The fact that at least some of the steps are due to intrinsic growth rate differences in the medium in which selection occurs suggests that the growth rate difference is medium dependent, for otherwise these steps would likely have occurred in the previous history of the strain. To demonstrate medium dependence, pairs of stocks were placed in competition at ratios above equilibrium and allowed to pass through 21 generations. At the end of this time the ratio of the stocks was determined. Lactose fermentation markers were used to identify the stocks, and the ratios were obtained by plating on Endo agar. When grown in H⁺ medium, all such mixtures showed the expected shift in ratio in favor of the more advanced com-

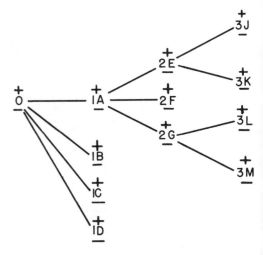

FIG. 7. Chart showing origin of stocks used in Tables I and II.

ponent. However, on complex media this shift was not merely offset, but often completely reversed.

The per cent change in ratio of mixtures of various stocks on different media is shown in Table 1. The stock numbers indicate as usual the number of mutational steps by which the stock differs from the original (o) strain, and the letters are used to distinguish stocks taken from different serial transfer experiments running in parallel. These results suggest that the mutations involved in increasing the growth rate in

$H^+$ medium have altered the genotype in such a way as to decrease the growth rate in nutrient broth.

They also suggest that the mutation involved in a given step is not always the same in different series, but on this point we cannot be certain because the quantitative pattern of response to various media is not reproducible in some stocks. It is to be hoped that a knowledge of the medium constituents involved in the reversal of selection may help clarify the nature of the reactions which are rate-limiting for bacterial growth. Thus far,

### TABLE 2. RESULTS OF DIFFERENT COMBINATIONS OF ISOLATES RECONSTRUCTED AT HIGH h+/h– RATIO

The (x) indicates the component with the advantage.

| Combination | h+ | Intermediate + | Equal | Intermediate – | h– | Combination | h+ | Intermediate + | Equal | Intermediate – | h– |
|---|---|---|---|---|---|---|---|---|---|---|---|
| 1A–/0+ | | | | | x | 2G–/2E+ | | | | | x |
| 1A+ | | | x | | | 2F+ | | | x | | |
| 1B+ | | | x | | | 3J+ | | x | | | |
| 1D+ | | | x | | | 3K+ | | | x | | |
| 2E+ | x | | | | | 3L+ | x | | | | |
| 3J+ | x | | | | | 3M+ | | | | | x |
| 1A+/0– | x | | | | | 3J–/0+ | | | | | x |
| 1B– | | | x | | | 1A+ | | | | | x |
| 1C– | | | | | x | 2E+ | | | x | | |
| 1D– | | | x | | | 2F+ | | | x | | |
| 2E– | | | | | x | 3J+ | | | x | | |
| 3J– | | | | | x | 3K+ | | | | | x |
| 1B–/2E+ | x | | | | | 3L+ | | | x | | |
| 1C–/1C+ | x | | | | | 3M+ | | x | | | |
| 2E+ | x | | | | | 3J+/0– | x | | | | |
| 1D–/2E+ | x | | | | | 1A– | x | | | | |
| 2E–/0+ | | | | | x | 2E– | x | | | | |
| 1A+ | | | | | x | 2G– | | x | | | |
| 2E+ | | | x | | | 3K– | | x | | | |
| 2F+ | | x | | | | 3K–/2E+ | | | | | x |
| 3J+ | | x | | | | 2F+ | | | | | x |
| 2E+/0– | x | | | | | 3J+ | | | x | | |
| 1A– | x | | | | | 3K+ | | | | | x |
| 1B– | x | | | | | 3L+ | | x | | | |
| 1C– | x | | | | | 3M+ | | | x | | |
| 1D– | x | | | | | 3K+/2G– | | | x | | |
| 2E– | | | x | | | 3L–/2E+ | | | | | x |
| 2G– | | | | | x | 2F+ | | | x | | |
| 3J– | | | | x | | 3L+ | x | | | | |
| 3K– | | | | | x | 3M+ | | | x | | |
| 3L– | | | | | x | 3L+/2G– | x | | | | |
| 3M– | | | | | x | 3J– | | | x | | |
| 2F+/2E– | | x | | | | 3K– | | x | | | |
| 2F– | x | | | | | 3M–/2E+ | | | | | x |
| 2G– | | | x | | | 2F+ | | | x | | |
| 3J– | | | | x | | 3M+/2G– | | | | | x |
| 3K– | | | | | x | 3J– | | | x | | |
| 3L– | | | x | | | 3K– | | | x | | |
| 3M– | | | | x | | 3L– | | | x | | |
| | | | | | | 3M– | | | x | | |

it appears that no amino acid, vitamin, purine, or pyrimidine can, by itself, duplicate the effect of a complex medium.

Direct tests have been made of whether stocks obtained from the same stage of different parallel serial transfer experiments are selectively equivalent to one another. The stocks were obtained by using the $h^- \rightarrow h^+$ system described above, where the criterion for an adaptive step is the fall to equilibrium of an artificially constructed high $h^+/h^-$ ratio. Each time this occurred, ten different strains of $h^-$ and $h^+$ bacteria were isolated from the equilibrium mixture and the high $h^+/h^-$ ratio reconstructed and used to start two or more parallel STs. Figure 7 shows the lineage of stocks obtained in this way. Appropriate pairs of $h^+$ and $h^-$ from this lineage were then placed in competition with each other at $h^+/h^-$ ratios above equilibrium. Immediate shifts in ratio indicate selective difference while a plateau followed by a fall indicates equivalence. From the results shown in Table 2 it is clear that parallel stocks are not necessarily equivalent. Moreover, selective differences are found between parallel stocks which are much weaker than those between single steps in a series. Such cases are designated in the table as "intermediate."

It is possible that these results have been influenced by inhomogeneity of some of the stocks with respect to adaptive value. The finding of selective differences between $h^+$ and $h^-$ taken simultaneously from equilibrium populations is suggestive of this complication, as is the fact that in many experiments where a high $h^+/h^-$ ratio is initiated a small and variable fraction of the $h^+$ population is eliminated in the first few transfers after which the usual plateau is established. However, if these data are taken at face value, they show that there is no predetermined sequence of mutational steps, but rather that the selective

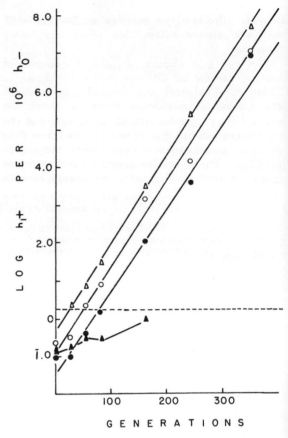

FIG. 8. Increase in $h_1^+$ on $H^+$ medium following the addition of one or few $h_1^+$ cells to a population predominantly $h_0^-$. The solid triangles are $h_0^+/h_0^-$ as determined in the same experiment as the $h_1^+/h_0^-$ (closed circles). Open circles and open triangles are repetitions of the rate of increase of $h_1^+$.

status of a stock isolated after a long period of growth is caused by the summation of a number of mutations which may occur in any temporal order, implying that at a given time there are several

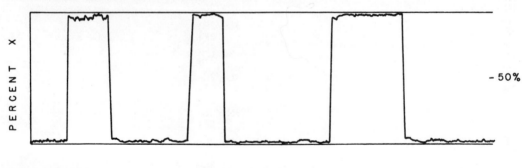

FIG. 9. Evolutionary history of a (selectively unimportant) marker as a result of periodic selection.

different ways in which a selective advantage may be conferred by mutation.

## EVOLUTIONARY CONSEQUENCES OF PERIODIC SELECTION

The principal difference between periodic selection and externally imposed periodic isolations lies in the progressive remodeling of the genotype which necessarily occurs in the former in contrast to the static condition possible in the latter case. This environmentally determined progression suppresses, but does not of course completely eliminate mutants which are not directly concerned with increase in adaptive value. Since the accumulation of mutations leading to superior performance in one environment occurs at the cost of inefficiency in others, strains invading new environments would rapidly diverge and soon reach a point where they could no longer coexist if returned to a common ecological situation. This would lead to profound strain differences which could not necessarily be detected by the usual criteria of bacterial taxonomy.

The establishment during periodic selection of a mutant which is selectively weak or neutral is an improbable event which might happen if a mutation conferring selective advantage occurred in a bacterium of rare genotype. In the case of $h^+$ the probability of this is about $10^{-6}$ per mutation. To decide whether this event would actually result in the replacement of the entire population by $h^+$, experiments were performed in which one or few $h_1{}^+$ (obtained by dilution) were added to $2.5 \times 10^8$ $h_o{}^-$, then serially transferred. The proportion of $h_1{}^+$ increased immediately as shown in Figure 8, and continued to increase until the entire population was essentially $h_1{}^+$. It is interesting that the time required for replacement in these experiments is about the same as the time between replacements (including plateau region) in normal STs. Figure 9 shows the hypothetical evolutionary history with respect to an unselected mutant, X, of a culture undergoing sustained periodic selection. The composition of the population shifts from nearly no X to nearly all X and back again very infrequently, the average length of the intervals depending on the two equilibrium ratios.

## SUMMARY

Long term population studies in *Escherichia coli* have revealed a class of mutations controlling small differences in adaptive value. The occurrence of these causes the existing population to be replaced by a new population comprised of the mutant organisms. This event, when repeated at intervals, has the effect of non-specific selection against all mutants which are eliminated during the population turnover. The selective differentials involved can be reversed by altering the environment.

## REFERENCES

ATWOOD, K. C., SCHNEIDER, L. K., and RYAN, F. J., 1951, Periodic selection in *Escherichia coli*. Proc. Nat. Acad. Sci. Wash. *37*: 146—155

BRAUN, W., 1947, Bacterial dissociation. Bact. Rev. *11*: 75—114

BRAUN, W., GOODLOW, R., and KRAFT, M., 1950, The role of metabolites in bacterial variation. Genetics *35*: 656

DAVIS, B. D., 1948, Isolation of biochemically deficient mutants of bacteria by penicillin. J. Amer. Chem. Soc. *70*: 4267

GUTHRIE, R., 1949, Studies of a purine-requiring mutant strain of *Escherichia coli*. J. Bact. *57*: 39—46

LEA, D. E. and COULSON, C. A., 1949, The distribution of the numbers of mutants in bacterial populations. J. Genet. *49*: 264—285

LEDERBERG, J., and ZINDER, M., 1948, Concentration of biochemical mutants of bacteria with penicillin. J. Amer. Chem. Soc. *70*: 4267—4268

LIEB, M., 1951, Forward and reverse mutation in a histidine-requiring strain of *Escherichia coli*. Genetics *36*: 460—477.

LURIA, S. E., and DELBRUCK, M., 1943, Mutations of bacteria from virus sensitivity to virus resistance. Genetics *28*: 491—511

NOVICK, A., and SZILARD, L., 1950, Experiments with the chemostat on spontaneous mutations of bacteria. Proc. Nat. Acad. Sci. Wash. *36*: 708—719

RYAN, F. J., 1948, On the stability of nutritional mutants of bacteria. Proc. Nat. Acad. Sci. Wash. *34*: 425—435

SCHNEIDER, L. K., 1950, Population dynamics in *Escherichia coli*. Biol. Bull. *99*: 331

STOCKER, B. A. D., 1949, Measurements of rate of mutation of flagellar antigenic phase in *Salmonella typhi-murium*. J. Hyg., Camb. *47*: 398—413.

# CHLOROPHYLL LETHAL IN NATURAL POPULATIONS OF THE ORCHARD GRASS (DACTYLIS GLOMERATA L.). A CASE OF BALANCED POLYMORPHISM IN PLANTS[1,2]

DAVID APIRION AND DANIEL ZOHARY

*Department of Botany, The Hebrew University, Jerusalem, Israel*

Received September 30, 1960

IN recent years extensive information has been gathered as to the occurrence and evolutionary significance of recessive lethal genes in natural panmictic populations (for details see reviews by DOBZHANSKY 1951, 1955, 1959). Work has concentrated almost exclusively on several Drosophila species, undoubtedly due to the fact that extraction techniques in this genetically well-studied genus are highly developed. Strikingly high frequencies of recessive lethals have been found to be a common feature in natural populations of various Drosophila species, and a model of balanced polymorphism has been suggested to account for these facts.

Compared to the genus Drosophila, information concerning the occurrence and distribution of recessive lethals in other organisms is rather meagre. An exception is the case of man; here high frequencies of the sickle cell factor in some human populations (ALLISON 1954, 1956) as well as those of several other deleterious recessive genes (NEEL 1956), have been explained on the basis of a model of balanced polymorphism.

In the present paper data are brought forward which indicate a case of balanced polymorphism, involving a recessive lethal in plants. It deals with the occurrence and distribution of a chlorophyll-deficiency factor in natural populations of diploid ($2n = 14$) orchard grass (*Dactylis glomerata*) in Israel. The study was initiated after it had been noted that certain seed samples collected for breeding purposes from individual wild Dactylis plants in the vicinity of Jerusalem, yielded a high proportion of white, chlorophyll-deficient seedlings (up to 12–15 percent). Since Dactylis is self-incompatible, such progeny should have originated from cross-pollination of a heterozygous parent by pollen carrying the mutant gene. On the assumption that an albino seedling is homozygous for a single recessive lethal locus, the appearance of up to 12–15 percent of albino seedlings among progeny of a given plant seemed to indicate that chlorophyll-deficiency genes were widely distributed in the local Dactylis populations.

[1] The authors are indebted to the Ford Foundation for a research grant which supported this study.

[2] The data presented are taken from the M.S. thesis submitted by the first author to the Dept. of Botany, The Hebrew University, Jerusalem.

Genetics 46: 393–399 April 1961.

Reprinted by permission of the Genetics Society of America, Inc. from *Genetics* 46:393–399, 1961.

## MATERIAL

Both diploid (2n = 14) and tetraploid (2n = 28) forms of *Dactylis glomerata*
L. occur in Israel (for details on their geographical distribution see Nur and
Zohary 1959). The present work deals only with natural populations of the local
diploid form: *D. glomerata* ssp. *judaica*. Tetraploids have not been investigated.

*D. glomerata* ssp. *judaica* occurs in Israel mainly in three areas: (a) the
Judaean Hills around Jerusalem, (b) Nazareth Hills, (c) the area of Safad,
Upper Galilee. Here, occurring on several different soil types, this perennial
grass constitutes a common component of the dwarf shrub and herbaceous plant
communities (Mediterranean "batha" formations) which are a characteristic
vegetational feature of these areas.

As to its breeding system, *Dactylis glomerata* ssp. *judaica* is a truly panmictic
or cross-pollinated plant. Seed is produced sexually, and the plants are entirely
self-incompatible. The latter fact has been verified by the present authors in
numerous breeding experiments. No seed has ever been obtained upon the selfing
of local Dactylis plants.

## EXPERIMENTAL PROCEDURE AND RESULTS

The frequencies of chlorophyll-deficiency genes have been investigated in 14
samples taken from 13 chosen localities occupied by natural populations of
*Dactylis glomerata* ssp. *judaica*. They are representatives of the main areas in
which diploid orchard grass is known to occur in Israel and constitute a cross
section of the various Israeli habitats occupied by this grass.

Sampling and seed harvesting were carried out at the end of the growing
season, in July 1958 (8100-series) and in June 1959 (9100-series). Sampling
procedures were as follows: At each station 100 plants were chosen for examination of their progeny, and seed from each plant was harvested separately in
the field. Plants were sampled at each station along three or four transects which
were 15–20 meters apart. Plants were sampled in pairs. The distance between
pairs was 5–10 meters, within pairs 1–2 meters. The sampling of pairs of adjacent
plants was employed to check on homogeneity of spread of heterozygotes in the
examined areas. This was checked by means of a binomial test, the two events
being identical pairs (i.e. both partners homozygous normal or both heterozygous) *versus* heterogeneous pairs (i.e. one partner homozygous normal, the
second heterozygous). These tests indicated that the homozygous and heterozygous plants were distributed at random, with no local concentrations of one or
the other genotype. There was no indication of uneven spread in the populations
sampled.

Estimates of the frequencies of chlorophyll-deficiency genes in the various
populations were obtained in two ways: (a) heterozygous plants were detected
by means of progeny tests; (b) plants whose heterozygosity had been established
were used as natural testers.

*Detection of heterozygous plants by means of progeny tests:* The seed sample
collected from each respective plant was sown in the winter following harvesting

BALANCED POLYMORPHISM

under greenhouse conditions in Jerusalem. The germinating seedlings were examined 3–4 weeks after sowing. The number of green (or normal) and albino (or chlorophyll-deficient) progeny obtained from each plant was recorded. A plant was assumed to be heterozygous for a chlorophyll-deficiency factor, when there was at least one albino seedling among its progeny.

The number of plants, in each locality, heterozygous for a chlorophyll-deficiency recessive, as detected by means of progeny tests is given in Table 1.

Naturally, the numbers of seeds that could be harvested from the individual parents varied greatly from plant to plant and from locality to locality. An effort was made to secure at least 50 seeds from each plant, but this was not possible in every case. Individuals which yielded less than ten seedlings were discarded from

TABLE 1

*Detection of heterozygous plants: Results of progeny tests*

| Sample number | Locality and soil type | Total number of plants tested | Number of normal homozygous plants | Number of heterozygous plants | Percent of heterozygotes in sample | Estimated gametic frequency of albino gene (percent) |
|---|---|---|---|---|---|---|
| Jerusalem Hills: | | | | | | |
| DC 8101: Matzleva Valley | terra-rossa | 47 | 35 | 12 | 26 | 13 |
| DC 8102: Ora | rendzina | 79 | 65 | 14 | 18 | 9 |
| DC 8103: Aminadav | rendzina | 94 | 81 | 13 | 14 | 7 |
| DC 8104: Schneller Camp | terra-rossa | 78 | 55 | 23 | 29 | 14.5 |
| DC 8105: University campus | terra-rossa | 64 | 58 | 6 | 9 | 4.5 |
| DC 8106: Qiryat Anavim | terra-rossa | 80 | 66 | 24 | 30 | 15 |
| DC 9101: Qiryat Anavim | terra-rossa | 94 | 66 | 28 | 30 | 15 |
| DC 9102: Kastel | terra-rossa | 100 | 72 | 28 | 28 | 14 |
| Nazareth Hills: | | | | | | |
| DC 8110: Kefar Hahoresh | rendzina | 82 | 79 | 3 | 4 | 2 |
| DC 8111: Nazareth | rendzina | 95 | 90 | 5 | 5 | 2.5 |
| Upper Galilee: | | | | | | |
| DC 8107: Ein Zeitim | rendzina | 79 | 76 | 3 | 4 | 2 |
| DC 8108: Safad | rendzina | 88 | 77 | 11 | 13 | 6.5 |
| DC 8109: Biriya | mixed soil | 86 | 76 | 10 | 12 | 6 |
| DC 8112: Miar | rendzina | 97 | 82 | 15 | 15 | 7.5 |

further considerations, whether they produced only green—or both normal and albino seedlings. This is the cause for the discrepancy between the 100 plants originally sampled at each locality and the results of the progeny tests presented in Table 1.

In some stations and particularly in the Jerusalem area, strikingly high percentages (26–30 percent) of plants yielded albino seedlings, thus indicating a large proportion of heterozygotes. It is probably safe to regard the plants which yielded albino progeny as heterozygous for a recessive chlorophyll-determining factor. But it is obviously impossible, solely by means of that method, to decide whether these plants are heterozygous for the same deficiency gene, or whether they represent several chlorophyll-determining factors at different loci. Yet the values obtained from utilization of heterozygotes as natural testers (see next section) strongly indicate that, at least within a respective locality, most of the plants which had yielded albino seedlings were actually heterozygous for the same recessive gene. The estimates of the gametic frequencies given in Table 1 were therefore calculated on the basis of such an assumption.

*Heterozygotes as natural testers:* Since plants of this taxon are self-incompatible and necessarily cross-pollinated, any individual whose heterozygosity had been established could be used as a natural tester for estimating the proportion of pollen, carrying the albino gene, produced in its vicinity. Any such pollen grain germinating on the stigma of a heterozygous plant has a 50 percent chance to produce a homozygous albino progeny. Assuming that there is no selective elimination (either in gametes or in zygotes), the percentage of albino seedlings in the progeny of a given heterozygote thus represents one half of the gametic frequency of the chlorophyll-deficient lethal and one fourth of the percentage of heterozygous plants within the sampled area.

In each locality, the data on progeny of plants which yielded albino seedlings (and were therefore assumed to be heterozygous) were also utilized for such an estimate of the gametic frequency of the chlorophyll-deficiency gene. To avoid complications, only heterozygotes which yielded 30 seedlings or more were included in these estimates. Table 2 summarizes the estimates of the gametic frequencies of the chlorophyll-lethal obtained upon utilization of the heterozygotes in each locality as natural testers.

In the majority of stations these estimates agree quite closely with the percentages of heterozygous plants as detected by means of the first method (compare Tables 1 and 2). The only major exception is sample DC 8105, where the values based on natural testers are exceptionally high and disagree entirely with the low number of detected heterozygotes. This general agreement between the two sets of data strongly suggests that at least within a given locality one is dealing mainly with a single lethal gene. Obviously, if several different factors for chlorophyll-deficiency had been present in a respective population, the frequency values as calculated from the testers (Table 2) would have been considerably lower than those based on detected heterozygotes (Table 1).

*Ecological differences:* The Dactylis populations examined were growing on two main types of soils. Some localities were characterized by typical mediterranean red-soil or "terra rossa". This soil type develops on a hard limestone and dolomite bed-rock. In other localities the soil was a light colored rendzina. This is a highly calcareous soil which is formed, in the mediterranean areas of Israel, on soft marls and chalks. Only in one case (DC 8109) the sample was collected in a place where the two soil types formed a mosaic. The soil type of each locality is noted in Table 1 and 2. Further ecological details on each sample may be obtained by any interested reader, by writing to the junior author.

As can be seen from the data set out in Tables 1 and 2, the frequency of the chlorophyll-blocking gene is much higher in Dactylis populations occupying terra rossa than in those occupying rendzina soil. In the Jerusalem area these

TABLE 2

*Frequencies of the chlorophyll-deficiency gene as estimated by use of heterozygotes as natural testers*

| Sample number | Locality and soil type | Number of testers employed | Total number of green progeny | Total no. of chlorophyll deficient progeny | Total number of progeny | Estimated gametic frequency (percent) | Estimated frequency of heterozygotes (percent) |
|---|---|---|---|---|---|---|---|
| Judaean Hills: | | | | | | | |
| DC 8101: | Matzleva Valley terra-rossa | 7 | 375 | 25 | 400 | 12.5 | 25 |
| DC 8102: | Ora rendzina | 12 | 868 | 22 | 890 | 5 | 10 |
| DC 8103: | Aminadav rendzina | 13 | 1511 | 32 | 1543 | 4 | 8 |
| DC 8104: | Schneller Camp terra-rossa | 21 | 2069 | 145 | 2214 | 13 | 26 |
| DC 8105: | University campus terra-rossa | 5 | 318 | 43 | 361 | 24 | 48 |
| DC 8106: | Qiryat Anavim terra-rossa | 21 | 1448 | 95 | 1543 | 13 | 26 |
| DC 9101: | Qiryat Anavim terra-rossa | 20 | 2290 | 111 | 2401 | 9.5 | 19 |
| DC 9102: | Kastel terra-rossa | 18 | 3795 | 167 | 3962 | 8.5 | 17 |
| Nazareth Hills: | | | | | | | |
| DC 8110: | Kefar Hahoresh rendzina | 3 | 160 | 3 | 163 | 3.5 | 7 |
| DC 8111: | Nazareth rendzina | 5 | 432 | 5 | 437 | 2.5 | 5 |
| Upper Galilee: | | | | | | | |
| DC 8107: | Ein Zeitim rendzina | 3 | 420 | 7 | 427 | 3.5 | 7 |
| DC 8108: | Safad rendzina | 11 | 733 | 28 | 761 | 7.5 | 15 |
| DC 8109: | Biriya mixed soil | 10 | 718 | 16 | 734 | 4.5 | 9 |
| DC 8112: | Miar rendzina | 15 | 2995 | 70 | 3065 | 4.5 | 9 |

398               D. APIRION AND D. ZOHARY

differences are highly indicative, since stations on different soil types are geographically in close proximity (distances of 3–4 km), and the Dactylis cover of this area is more or less continuous.


DISCUSSION

The most plausible explanation of the results obtained in the progeny tests is the occurrence of a recessive, chlorophyll-blocking allele in relatively high proportions in some natural populations of the diploid orchard grass in Israel. That one is dealing mainly with a single locus in each respective population is indicated by the agreement between the number of detected heterozygotes (Table 1) and the estimates based on natural testers (Table 2). Although the most likely situation is that of a simple Mendelian trait, this has yet to be verified. The final evaluation of the results obtained can be made only after genetic analysis has been carried out in at least some of the albino-producing plants, and after it has been confirmed that they are actually simple heterozygotes, and that one is dealing with the same locus in the various samples.

As to the detection technique employed, it is realized that some heterozygotes could have been missed, and erroneously considered as normal homozygotes, because a limited and variable number of progeny (ten to several hundreds) were raised from each tested plant. This is particularly true in populations where the frequency of the albino allele was found to be low. However, such errors would not change the general picture obtained.

The high proportions of the recessive lethal gene are best explained on the assumption of a higher selective value of heterozygous plants as compared to that of homozygous normal individuals. An equilibrium of adaptive polymorphism for a recessive lethal is proposed to account for the results obtained. This assumption of higher selective values of heterozygotes is further supported by the differences noted between populations occupying terra rossa and these growing on light colored rendzina soil, which indicate different selective values in different ecological niches.

Finally, attention should be drawn to the possibility that a chlorophyll-blocking class of mutations might be of general evolutionary significance in plants. The studies of WILLIAMS and BROWN (1956) on the cherry demonstrate that selection for quantitative economic traits has favored heterozygosity for chlorophyll-blocking recessives. Apparent vegetative vigor was found by GUSTAFSSON (1946) and GUSTAFSSON, NYBOM and VON WETTSTEIN (1950) in barley heterozygotes for induced, recessive chlorophyll mutations. The diploidization of the Ws locus in Nicotiana tabacum reported by CLAUSEN and CAMERON (1950) might be regarded as being of similar significance. The data presented in this paper indicate that such lethals can maintain themselves in a panmictic population. Adaptive polymorphism involving chlorophyll-deficiency factors is probably not restricted to the orchard grass alone. It may be of a more general occurrence in cross-pollinated plant species.

## SUMMARY

Natural populations of diploid ($2n = 14$) orchard grass (*Dactylis glomerata*) native in Israel were examined as to the frequency of recessive chlorophyll-deficiency lethal in them. Frequencies up to 30 percent of heterozygous plants (yielding albino progeny) were found in some localities. It was also noted that populations growing on terra-rossa soils show higher proportions of the lethal gene than populations occupying rendzina soils.

The most likely explanations for the results obtained is that in certain habitats, heterozygotes for a chlorophyll-blocking lethal have a higher selective value than normal homozygotes. Apparently a condition of balanced polymorphism with regard to this locus is present in the populations of the orchard grass tested.

## ACKNOWLEDGMENT

We are indebted to DR. R. MOAV for valuable comments and for statistical advice.

## LITERATURE CITED

ALLISON, A. B., 1954   Notes on sickle cell polymorphism. Ann. Human Genet. **19**: 39–49.
  1956   The sickle cell and haemoglobin C genes in some African populations. Ann. Human Genet. **21**: 67–89.

CLAUSEN, R. E., and D. R. CAMERON, 1950   Inheritance in *Nicotiana tabacum*. XXIII. Duplicate factors for chlorophyll production. Genetics **35**: 4–10.

DOBZHANSKY, TH., 1951   *Genetics and the Origin of Species*. 3rd Ed. Columbia Univ. Press. New York.
  1955   A review of some fundamental concepts and problems of population genetics. Cold Spring Harbor Symposia Quant. Biol. **22**: 385–393.
  1959   Variation and evolution. Proc. Am. Phil. Soc. **103**: 252–263.

GUSTAFSSON, A., 1946   The effect of heterozygosity on viability and vigour. Hereditas **32**: 263–286.

GUSTAFSSON, A., N. NYBOM, and U. WETTSTEIN, 1950   Chlorophyll factors and heterosis in barley. Hereditas **36**: 383–392.

NEEL, J. V., 1956   The genetics of human haemoglobin differences: problems and perspectives. Ann. Human Genet. **21**: 1–30.

NUR, U., and D. ZOHARY, 1959   Distribution patterns of diploid and tetraploid forms of *Dactylis glomerata* L. in Israel. Bull. Research Council Israel **7D**: 13–22.

WILLIAMS, W., and A. G. BROWN, 1956   Genetic response to selection in cultivated plants: Gene frequencies in *Prunus avium*. Heredity **10**: 237–245.

# MATING SUCCESS AND GENOTYPE FREQUENCY IN *DROSOPHILA*

## By LEE EHRMAN

### *The Rockefeller University, New York City*

Petit (1958) found that the mating success of two classical mutants of *Drosophila melanogaster*, *Bar* and *white*, depends on their frequencies in relation to the wild-type. In a mixture of *Bar* and wild-type flies, *Bar* males are less successful in mating; their disadvantage is, however, reduced when only few of them are present, and increases as their frequency in relation to wild-type males becomes greater. With *white*, the mating success is greater when *white* males are rare or are predominant, and least when this proportion in the population is between 40 and 80 per cent. Ehrman, Spassky, Pavlovsky & Dobzhansky (1965) found a similar situation in experiments with *Drosophila pseudoobscura*. Experimental populations, kept in population cages, were started in each generation with twenty pairs of flies from one cage, to which were added five pairs of 'migrants' from another cage. The flies were selected for positive or for negative geotaxis in a specially constructed maze (Hirsch, 1961). Some cage populations originally contained flies monomorphic for the AR gene arrangement in their third chromosomes, and other populations were monomorphic for CH chromosomes. When the donor population was CH and the recipient AR, the frequency of CH chromosomes increased far more rapidly than expected on the basis of other experiments started with equal numbers of AR and CH. The mating success of the carriers of CH and AR chromosomes was then studied by observing them in special chambers, constructed according to Elens & Wattiaux (1964) and discussed and photographed by Ehrman (1965). With equal numbers of females and males of both karyotypes random mating was observed. With twenty pairs of one and five pairs of the other karyotype, the rarer one had a distinct advantage. The advantages and disadvantages were reversed when the frequencies were reversed.

The above findings were entirely unexpected to us. Preferential mating correlated with frequency may evidently be of considerable importance in evolutionary processes. The present communication describes experiments designed to obtain further evidence that might throw light on this phenomenon. It should be treated as a progress report, since it is realized that much more work will be needed to understand the ethological basis as well as the genetic and evolutionary consequences of preferential mating. Sexual discrimination is a trial-and-error affair among the drosophilids observed here. Males will court females (sometimes, even other males) of any species and will try to repeat courting and mating. The acceptance is controlled mainly by the female, and so are other 'turning points' in the courtship–mating–insemination sequence, such as termination of the mount. The females have three sperm-storing organs and will only mate a second time if their supply of stored sperm is diminished (Manning, 1962). For a description of the courtship and mating behaviour in *Drosophila pseudoobscura*, see Spieth (1952); (for a pictorial description, Ehrman & Strickberger, 1960; Ehrman, 1964).

## Materials and Methods

The ARrowhead and CHiricahua populations utilized here have been described in detail by Ehrman *et al.* (1965); the section of Table I in the present article, labelled 'AR Mather, 16° *v.* 25°C' refers to this one particular population grown at either of these two temperatures to test for possible mating advantages induced by raising flies in different environments.

The Tree Line stock was a composite one made up from five strains homozygous for this gene arrangement collected at Mather, California. TL was selected because it is rare, occurring at a frequency of about 10 per cent in the population of the Mather locality. Similarly, the STandard stock is also a composite of five strains collected at Mather. Standard, however, is not rare in nature. The mutant Delta ($\triangle$) is an autosomal dominant affecting wing venation, lethal when homozygous; orange (or.) is an autosomal recessive affecting eye colour. Both mutants have good viability and are easy to classify.

All of the above are *Drosophila pseudoobscura*. Two strains of *Drosophila paulistorum* were tested; one from Cantareira São Paulo, Brazil, belonging to the Andean-South Brazilian race of the species (item 24, Dobzhansky & Spassky, 1959), and the other from Simla, Trinidad, a

Reprinted by permission of Baillère, Tindall and Cassell, Ltd. and the author from *Animal Behaviour* 14:332–339, 1966.

member of the same race (item 17, Dobzhansky, Ehrman, Pavlovsky & Spassky, 1964b).

The technique of direct observation of mating used here has been devised by Elens & Wattiaux (1964), and employed by Ehrman (1965) and Ehrman *et al.* (1965). This method is superior to the old 'male-choice' technique for several reasons, the most important of which is that it permits the observation of four types of mating, i.e. A♀ × A♂, A♀ × B♂, B♀ × A♂, B♀ × B♂. It is also possible to record the time when each mating occurs, and its sequence among the other matings.

Females and males, aged separately for at least 3 days, are introduced into a chamber, and are observed at 6 min intervals for approximately 6 hr. Most of the matings take place within the first hour, when the observations are spaced at 4 min intervals or less. To make the flies from different strains distinguishable through the glass of the observation chamber (with the aid of a 4× hand lens), the margin of one wing is clipped in one of the strains; the strains marked and unmarked are alternated in successive runs. The wing clipping is done in lightly etherized flies, which are then left to recover for at least 24 hr before being placed in the observation chamber, the transfer being made without etherization.

### Results

Table I summarizes the results of the experiments in which a total of twenty-four or twenty-five pairs (twenty-five females and twenty-five males) of *Drosophila pseudoobscura* were introduced into each observation chamber. They belonged to two different strains, or to the same strain raised under two different conditions, denoted as A and B. The columns in the table headed 'A' and 'B' give the numbers and the nature of the strains used. Several runs were made for each experiment. The four columns headed 'Matings' report the numbers of each of the four possible kinds of mating observed in a given experiment. The columns 'Have Mated' show the numbers of the females and the males of each kind which were observed to mate; a female can mate only once during the period of observation, while a male can mate several times. The columns 'Chi-squares' test the significance of the observed deviations in the numbers of the matings from what would be expected on the assumption of randomness, i.e. on the assumption that the probability of a fly mating is independent of what other flies of the same sex and

species are present in the observation chambers. These Chi-squares have one degree of freedom, making the deviation from randomness of 3·841 significant at the 5 per cent level, and 6·635 at the 1 per cent level. Calculations based on the performance of the females have been omitted where almost 100 per cent of them have mated once during the course of the observations. The rare type mating advantage, if it exists in the females tested here, is much smaller than that recorded in males (see Ehrman *et al.*, 1965); even if only the first half of the matings are considered, few significant Chi-squares for the rare type females are obtained.

The lines Nos. 1–6 in Table I report the experiments in which some of the flies observed came from strains derived from ancestors collected originally at Mather, California ('Cal.'), and others at Austin, Texas. All flies were homozygous for the AR gene arrangement in their third chromosomes. With twelve pairs of California and twelve pairs of Texas flies per chamber, no significant deviation from randomness of mating is observed. With twenty California and five Texas pairs, the Texas males are significantly more successful in mating than are California males, and this is even more striking when the ratio is twenty-three California : two Texas. With twenty Texas : five California, not only the California males but also California females mate more often than do the Texas flies. The ratio ten California : fifteen Texas confers a small, but still significant, advantage on California males, despite their somewhat lower frequency. With the exception of this last observation, then, results confirm and extend the findings of Ehrman *et al.* (1965) on the mating advantages of the genotypes which are less frequent than other genotypes in the observation chambers.

The mating advantage appears to be a property of minority males, and only rarely and to a lesser extent of minority females. Experiments were accordingly arranged in which the observation chambers contained twenty-five California females, twenty-three California males and two Texas males. The matings observed (in six runs) were: Cal. ♀ × Cal. ♂ = 102; Cal. ♀ × Texas ♂ = 18.

In other eight runs, the chambers contained twenty-five Texas females; twenty-three Texas and two California males, and the matings observed were: Texas ♀ × Texas ♂ = 86; Texas ♀ × Cal. ♂ = 19.

Table I. Numbers of Matings Recorded in Observation Chambers Containing Two Kinds of *D. pseudoobscura*

| Pair per chamber | | | | Matings | | | | Have mated | | | | $\chi^2$ |
|---|---|---|---|---|---|---|---|---|---|---|---|---|
| No. | A | B | Runs | A♀×A♂ | A♀×B♂ | B♀×A♂ | B♀×B♂ | A♀ | B♀ | A♂ | B♂ | ♂ |
| 1 | 12 Cal. | 12 Texas | 7 | 29 | 21 | 26 | 28 | 50 | 54 | 55 | 49 | 0·35 |
| 2 | 20 Cal. | 5 Texas | 6 | 57 | 27 | 13 | 12 | 84 | 25 | 70 | 39 | 16·96 |
| 3 | 5 Cal. | 20 Texas | 7 | 13 | 17 | 26 | 48 | 30 | 74 | 39 | 65 | 19·91 |
| 4 | 23 Cal. | 2 Texas | 5 | 73 | 20 | 4 | 4 | 93 | 8 | 77 | 24 | 34·75 |
| 5 | 2 Cal. | 23 Texas | 10 | 4 | 8 | 26 | 62 | 12 | 88 | 30 | 70 | 65·76 |
| 6 | 10 Cal. | 15 Texas | 11 | 16 | 44 | 23 | 46 | 60 | 69 | 39 | 90 | 5·13 |
| AR Mather, 16° *v.* 25° | | | | | | | | | | | | |
| 7 | 12–16° | 12–25° | 8 | 44 | 18 | 28 | 28 | 62 | 56 | 72 | 46 | 5·72 |
| 8 | 20–16° | 5–25° | 6 | 67 | 18 | 15 | 1 | 85 | 16 | 82 | 19 | 0·09 |
| 9 | 5–16° | 20–25° | 6 | 11 | 12 | 21 | 57 | 23 | 78 | 32 | 69 | 8·61 |
| 10 | 23–16° | 2–25° | 10 | 67 | 29 | 13 | 3 | 96 | 16 | 80 | 32 | 64·26 |
| 11 | 2–16° | 23–25° | 9 | 3 | 11 | 20 | 72 | 14 | 92 | 23 | 83 | 27·02 |
| Raised separately | | | | | | | | | | | | |
| 12 | 12 + | 12 or. | 7 | 40 | 5 | 30 | 27 | 45 | 57 | 70 | 32 | 14·16 |
| 13 | 20 + | 5 or. | 6 | 64 | 10 | 14 | 12 | 74 | 26 | 78 | 22 | 0·25 |
| 14 | 5 + | 20 or. | 8 | 7 | 8 | 38 | 47 | 15 | 85 | 45 | 55 | 39·06 |
| 15 | 23 + | 2 or. | 7 | 85 | 11 | 6 | 1 | 96 | 7 | 91 | 12 | 1·87 |
| 16 | 2 + | 23 or. | 8 | 6 | 5 | 31 | 71 | 11 | 102 | 37 | 76 | 94·27 |
| Raised together | | | | | | | | | | | | |
| 17 | 12 + | 12 or. | 8 | 43 | 2 | 43 | 12 | 45 | 55 | 86 | 14 | 51·84 |
| 18 | 20 + | 5 or. | 8 | 78 | 11 | 14 | 5 | 89 | 19 | 92 | 16 | 1·82 |
| 19 | 5 + | 20 or. | 9 | 16 | 4 | 39 | 42 | 20 | 81 | 55 | 46 | 74·94 |
| 20 | 23 + | 2 or. | 8 | 104 | 2 | 9 | 7 | 106 | 11 | 113 | 4 | 3·34 |
| 21 | 2 + | 23 or. | 7 | 7 | 7 | 37 | 50 | 14 | 87 | 44 | 57 | 173·38 |
| Raised separately | | | | | | | | | | | | |
| 22 | 12 + | 12△ | 5 | 32 | 23 | 29 | 24 | 55 | 53 | 61 | 47 | 1·81 |
| 23 | 20 + | 5△ | 4 | 64 | 16 | 14 | 6 | 80 | 20 | 78 | 22 | 0·25 |
| 24 | 5 + | 20△ | 5 | 12 | 12 | 40 | 45 | 24 | 85 | 52 | 57 | 52·30 |
| 25 | 23 + | 2△ | 5 | 80 | 21 | 7 | 3 | 101 | 10 | 87 | 24 | 27·98 |
| 26 | 2 + | 23△ | 5 | 3 | 7 | 27 | 72 | 10 | 99 | 30 | 79 | 56·55 |

**Table I** *continued*

| Pair per chamber | | | | Matings | | | | Have mated | | | | $\chi^2$ |
|---|---|---|---|---|---|---|---|---|---|---|---|---|
| No. | A | B | Runs | A♀×A♂ | A♀×B♂ | B♀×A♂ | B♀×B♂ | A♀ | B♀ | A♂ | B♂ | ♂ |
| Raised together | | | | | | | | | | | | |
| 27 | 12 + | 12△ | 5 | 26 | 28 | 33 | 19 | 54 | 52 | 59 | 47 | 1·36 |
| 28 | 20 + | 5△ | 4 | 63 | 17 | 14 | 6 | 80 | 20 | 77 | 23 | 0·56 |
| 29 | 5 + | 20△ | 4 | 10 | 10 | 45 | 35 | 20 | 80 | 55 | 45 | 76·56 |
| 30 | 23 + | 2△ | 6 | 76 | 17 | 7 | 5 | 93 | 12 | 83 | 22 | 23·93 |
| 31 | 2 + | 23△ | 5 | 6 | 6 | 28 | 80 | 12 | 108 | 34 | 86 | 67·41 |
| 32 | 12 ST | 12 TL | 6 | 48 | 16 | 21 | 30 | 64 | 51 | 69 | 46 | 4·60 |
| 33 | 20 ST | 5 TL | 7 | 63 | 26 | 16 | 13 | 89 | 29 | 79 | 39 | 12·56 |
| 34 | 5 ST | 20 TL | 5 | 9 | 10 | 24 | 57 | 19 | 81 | 33 | 67 | 10·56 |
| 35 | 23 ST | 2 TL | 6 | 74 | 26 | 5 | 4 | 100 | 9 | 79 | 30 | 56·55 |
| 36 | 2 ST | 23 TL | 6 | 2 | 8 | 19 | 81 | 10 | 100 | 21 | 89 | 18·38 |

In both cases the rare males are involved in more matings than expected by chance (Chi-squares 7·99 and 14·39 respectively for the two experiments).

The question that now logically presents itself is whether the mating advantage of a rare form requires that the rare and the common types be genetically different. Flies of Texas origin (AR gene arrangement in the third chromosomes) were made to oviposit at room temperature, and then some cultures were allowed to develop at 16°C and others at 25°C. When equal numbers (twelve pairs) of the flies developed at both temperatures were placed in observation chambers (line 7, Table I), the males brought up at the lower temperature were significantly more successful in mating. This advantage was erased when the males developed at the higher temperature were a minority of 5 : 20 (line 8), and became a pronounced disadvantage with a ratio of 2 : 23 (line 10). On the contrary, the flies developed at the lower temperature increased their mating advantage when they became a minority (lines 9 and 11). The flies brought up at the lower temperature are on the average larger in size and more vigorous than those developed at the higher temperature. This makes the greater mating success of the former when the two are equal in frequencies not unexpected (Ewing, 1961). The dependence of the mating success on frequency is, however, an unexpected and interesting finding.

Experiments were made comparing the mating success of the flies raised together from egg to adult in the same culture bottle on the same culture medium, and of flies raised in different cultures. For this purpose, inseminated females of the mutant orange (bright-red eyes, a third chromosome recessive), and of the wild-type (several strains, all with the ST gene arrangement, from Mather, California, intercrossed) were allowed to oviposit, of course without males, together in the same cultures, or separately in different cultures. When the flies hatched, they were selected and aged as usual, and their behaviour was studied in the observation chambers. When orange and wild-type are equally numerous the orange males are much inferior in mating success to the wild-type males (lines 12 and 17, Table I). This is analogous to the lowered mating success of the males raised at the high temperature (line 7). And again, just as with the males raised at the high temperature, the mating disadvantage of the orange males is removed when they become a minority 5 : 20 (lines 13 and 18) or 2 : 23 (lines 15 and 20). The advantage of the wild-type males is, on the contrary, accentuated when they are a minority (lines 14, 16, 19 and 21). There is, however, no appreciable difference between the flies developed together (lines 17–21) and those raised in separate cultures (lines 12–16).

It seems desirable to test the independence of the mating success from the medium in which flies develop from egg to the adult stage by using a mutant which does not adversely affect the mating propensity when present in equal numbers with the wild-type. The mutant orange does, as we have seen, produce such an effect. The third-chromosome dominant mutant Delta ($\triangle$), is more suitable; its use was suggested by Professor R. C. Lewontin, University of Chicago. Being lethal when homozygous, Delta cultures produce mutant as well as wild-type individuals as sibs. On the other hand, the wild-type segregants can be bred by themselves in separate cultures, yielding only wild-type progeny. Observation chambers with twelve pairs of Delta and an equal number of wild-type flies show uniform mating success in both sexes. This is independent of whether the two kinds of flies were raised together or separately (lines 22 and 27, Table I). When Delta : wild-type ratio is 1 : 4, the mating is still uniform (lines 23 and 28), but with a ratio of 2 : 23 Delta males have a very significant advantage (lines 25 and 30). When wild-type is a minority, the males are strikingly successful in mating (lines 24, 29, 26, 31). No difference is observed between mating success of flies developed in the same or in different cultures (compare lines 22–26 with the corresponding combinations in the lines 27–31).

The remainder of Table I (lines 32–36) reports the results of testing flies with standard (ST) and with Tree Line (TL) give arrangements in the third chromosomes of the Mather, California population. The rationale of this experiment is as follows. In nature the ST chromosomes have much higher frequencies than TL (Dobzhansky et al., 1964a). It is then possible that TL flies may be at a disadvantage in mating compared to ST flies. Such differences between *Drosophila pseudoobscura* karyotypes have been demonstrated in certain other strains by Spiess

& Langer (1964). Indeed, in chambers with equal numbers of ST and TL flies significantly more of the former than of the latter have mated (line 32). Yet, both ST males (lines 34 and 36) and TL males (lines 33 and 35) are preferred as mates when they are a minority.

In an attempt to find out how widespread mating advantages of minority males may be, experiments have been made with two strains of the Andean–South Brazilian race of *Drosophila paulistorum* coming respectively from Sâo Paulo, Brazil, and from Simla, Trinidad. These are nearly the geographic extremes of the distribution region of this race. With twelve pairs of each strain in the observation chamber (Table II, line 1), the intra-strain matings (A × A and B × B) greatly outnumber the inter-strain ones (A × B and B × A). The joint isolation index, computed according to the method of Malogolowkin, Simmons & Levene (1965) is $0.69 \pm 0.07$, a very pronounced ethological isolation. The question at issue is now this: Does the rarity of the males of a given strain help to overcome the ethological isolation between the strains? The data in Table II suggest a negative answer; the only significant Chi-square in Table II is in line 4, where the males of the Trinidad strain seem to have been more successful than expected for their numbers.

Two more experiments can be reported in the present communication, designed to explore the possible causes of the mating advantages of the minority class males. As shown above, the mating success of a class of males does not depend on whether these males were raised in the same cultures with their potential mates or in different cultures. This makes it improbable that the sensory cue involved may be acquired from the environment in which the individuals develop between the egg and the adult stages.

**Table II. Numbers of Matings Recorded in Observation Chambers Containing *D. paulistorum* from Sâo Paulo, Brazil (A), and from Simla, Trinidad (B)**

| No. | Pairs per chamber A | B | Runs | A♀×A♂ | A♀×B♂ | B♀×A♂ | B♀×B♂ | A♀ | B♀ | A♂ | B♂ | ♀ | ♂ |
|-----|-----|-----|------|-------|-------|-------|-------|----|----|----|----|------|------|
| | | | | Matings | | | | Have mated | | | | Chi-squares | |
| 1 | 12 | 12 | 6 | 40 | 4 | 12 | 45 | 44 | 57 | 52 | 49 | 1·68 | 0·90 |
| 2 | 20 | 5 | 7 | 68 | 12 | 12 | 10 | 80 | 22 | 80 | 22 | 0·16 | 0·16 |
| 3 | 5 | 20 | 7 | 17 | 10 | 9 | 68 | 27 | 77 | 26 | 78 | 2·31 | 1·63 |
| 4 | 23 | 2 | 7 | 85 | 7 | 2 | 8 | 92 | 10 | 87 | 15 | 0·45 | 6·23 |
| 5 | 2 | 23 | 6 | 4 | 6 | 4 | 108 | 10 | 112 | 8 | 114 | 0·00 | 0·34 |

The possibility that this cue may come from the adult flies themselves must be considered. One experiment used a 'double chamber' technique. Two regular observation chambers are used, separated only by a cheesecloth partition, which forms the ceiling of the lower and the floor of the upper chamber. The two chambers are taped and tied securely together. In the upper chamber five pairs of some 'rare' type, A, and twenty pairs of a 'common' type, B, are introduced. In the lower chamber about fifteen pairs of the 'rare' type are introduced, as nearly as possible simultaneously. Matings occur in both the lower and the upper chambers, but only the matings in the latter are recorded in the usual manner. Observations of the behaviour of the flies in single chambers are used as controls. The double chambers and the control chambers are run, of course, simultaneously or nearly so. *Drosophila pseudoobscura* strains with AR and with CH third chromosomes, selected for positive or for negative geotaxis, were used as experimental animals. The mating success of the males of these strains has been shown by Ehrman *et al.* (1965) to be frequency dependent, the rare type enjoying an advantage.

The results are reported in Table III. Lines 2 and 4 show the outcomes of the control experiments, in single chambers. As before, the minority type males are involved in very significantly more matings than would be expected from their frequencies. The Chi-squares are large enough to have negligible probabilities of being due to chance. The mating advantage of the 'rare' males disappears in double chambers (lines 1 and 3); here these males are no longer a real minority, because many males of the same kind are present under the cheesecloth partition in the lower chamber.

Another experimental technique is to use a single observation chamber twice in succession, with as little time as possible between the two runs. For the first run, the chamber contained about fifteen pairs of AR flies selected for the positive, or for the negative geotaxis (lines 5 and 6 in Table III). After about 1 hr, these flies were discarded, five pairs of AR and twenty pairs of CH flies introduced into the chamber, and observed as usual. Comparison of the control and experimental runs (lines 2 and 5, and 4 and 6 respectively) shows that the mating advantages of the rare type males persist, although perhaps weakened in comparison with the controls.

Finally, the possibility, however remote, had to be ruled out that the mating success of the flies is somehow influenced by marking them. In many experiments one of the types was marked by notching one of its wings, to make it recognizable. In successive runs the kind of flies so marked was alternated. Wild-type flies (segregants from the cultures of the mutant Delta) were taken, some of them had one of their wings notched and the other entire. Then observation chambers received groups of twenty-three pairs which were designated as 'common' and two pairs which were designated as 'rare'. Either the 'common' (C), or the 'rare' (R) flies had wings notched. In five runs the results obtained were as follows: C ♀ × C ♂ = 87; C ♀ × R ♂ = 5; R ♀ × C ♂ = 7; R ♀ × R ♂ = 2.

The Chi-squares for the deviations from the uniform mating success are 0·109 for the females and 0·163 for the males. Neither comes close to being significant. Notching of a wing does not make any difference in mating success.

**Table III. Numbers of Matings Recorded in 'Double Chambers' (items 1 and 3), in Single Control Chambers (items 2 and 4), and in Chambers Previously Occupied (items 5 and 6)**

| No. | Pairs per chamber | | Runs | Matings | | | | Have mated | | | | Chi-square ♂ |
|---|---|---|---|---|---|---|---|---|---|---|---|---|
| | A | B | | A♀×A♂ | A♀×B♂ | B♀×A♂ | B♀×B♂ | A♀ | B♀ | A♂ | B♂ | |
| 1 | 5 AR+ | 20 CH+ | 5 | 9 | 15 | 12 | 84 | 24 | 96 | 21 | 99 | 0·47 |
| 2 | 5 AR+ | 20 CH+ | 5 | 18 | 7 | 34 | 63 | 25 | 97 | 52 | 70 | 39·02 |
| 3 | 5 AR− | 20 CH− | 5 | 4 | 15 | 14 | 79 | 19 | 93 | 18 | 94 | 1·08 |
| 5 | 5 AR− | 20 CH− | 5 | 14 | 11 | 34 | 55 | 25 | 89 | 48 | 66 | 34·81 |
| 5 | 5 AR+ | 20 CH+ | 5 | 10 | 15 | 35 | 63 | 25 | 98 | 45 | 78 | 21·15 |
| 6 | 5 AR− | 20 CH− | 5 | 10 | 15 | 26 | 74 | 25 | 100 | 36 | 89 | 6·05 |

## Discussion

The experiments of Petit (1958) on *Drosophila melanogaster*, of Ehrman *et al.* (1965), and those described in the present communication on *D. pseudoobscura*, have brought to light a most interesting phenomenon. When two kinds of males are present in an environment, the mating success of each kind depends upon its frequency in relation to the other kind. Within the range of frequencies investigated, the rare male mates relatively more frequently than the common males.

This is true with strains with different chromosomes, strains of different geographic origins, mutant versus wild-type flies, and flies of the same strain raised in different environments (different temperatures). This is, however, not true of the strains of *D. paulistorum* of different geographic origin which show an incipient ethological isolation.

If the mating success of the representatives of a given genotype is greater when it is rare than when it becomes common, important genetic and evolutionary consequences might follow. A greater mating success confers upon the genotype a higher Darwinian fitness. This fitness will, however, decrease as the frequency increases, until an equilibrium is established. This mechanism, if at all frequent in a species, will cause the population of that species to be highly polymorphic. The polymorphism will be balanced even if the heterozygous genotypes do not possess an advantage compared to the homozygotes.

The physiological basis of the mating advantage of rare forms is quite obscure. In *Drosophila*, the females are believed to be responsible for 'choosing' their mating partners, while the males are more nearly promiscuous and attempt to court, or at least to investigate, individuals of about their size irrespective of strain, species, and even sex. The numbers of courtships observed in the mating chambers are considerably greater than the numbers of copulations. Although a few females copulate with the first male that approaches them, others are courted several times. It is therefore possible that the females acquire some information concerning the relative frequencies of the different kinds of available males before they finally accept one. The cues involved are, however, unclear. The experiment with the 'double chamber', described above, suggests that either auditory, or olfactory, or a combination of both kinds of stimuli may be involved. More conclusive evidence can, however, be obtained only by further experiments, which are being planned. It is evidently also important to know whether the dependence of the mating success on the frequency is widespread or we just happened to choose materials in which it is observed. If it is widespread, the phenomenon will have to be given a serious consideration as an evolutionary agent.

An indication that this type of mating preference does indeed exist in higher animals has been provided by Professor Konrad Lorenz, who kindly permits me to quote from his letter: 'We have repeatedly seen in our greylag goose colony that males start to court with explosive suddenness a female that has been absent from the colony for a few months or who is a perfect stranger. We have had a dramatic example of this happening a few weeks ago when fifteen greylags coming from another colony arrived in Seewiesen. Four of our ganders started to court three of the strange females with the explosive suddenness of 'falling in love'. One of them even deserted his former mate to do so, a thing extremely rare in greylag geese . . . where . . . the choice of mate lies with the male rather than with the female.' Professor Lorenz also states, 'Of course I believe that this phenomenon is quite widespread among higher animals. I suspect that the extremely variable song of some songbirds is selected for by the female's tendency of being more strongly attracted by a song which is "somehow different".'

## Summary

The mating success of different strains of *Drosophila pseudoobscura* and *D. paulistorum* has been studied in Elens–Wattiaux observation chambers. When two kinds of females and of males are present, the mating success depends upon their relative frequencies. The less frequent kind, especially of males, is more successful in mating. In *D. pseudoobscura* this is so when strains with different chromosomes, of different geographic origins, mutant *v.* wild-type flies, and flies raised at different temperatures are tested. The frequency effect is not observed with two sexually isolated strains of *D. paulistorum*. The mating advantage fostered by rarity may increase the genetic diversity on the population concerned.

## Acknowledgments

This work was supported in part by Contract No. AT-(30-1)-3096, U.S. Atomic Energy Commission.

The author was in receipt of U.S. Public Health Service Research Career Development Award 1K3 HD-9033-01.

## REFERENCES

Dobzhansky, Th., Anderson, W. W., Pavlovsky, O., Spassky, B. & Wills C. J. (1964a). Genetics of natural populations. XXXV. A progress report on genetic changes in populations of *Drosophila pseudoobscura* in the American southwest. *Evolution*, **18**, 164–176.

Dobzhansky, Th., Ehrman, L., Pavlovsky, O. & Spassky, B. (1964b). The superspecies *Drosophila paulistorum*. *Proc. natn. Acad. Sci. U.S.A.*, **51**, 3–9.

Dobzhansky, Th. & Spassky, B. (1959). *Drosophila paulistorum*, a cluster of species in *statu nascendi*. *Proc. natn. Acad. Sci. U.S.A.*, **45**, 419–428.

Ehrman, L. (1964). Courtship and mating behavior as a reproductive isolating mechanism in Drosophila. *Am. Zool.*, 4, 147–153.

Ehrman, L. (1965). Direct observation of sexual isolation between allopatric and between sympatric strains of the different *Drosophila paulistorum* races. *Evolution*, **19**, 459–464.

Ehrman, L., Spassky, B., Pavlovsky, O. & Dobzhansky, Th. (1965). Sexual selection, geotaxis, and chromosomal polymorphism in experimental populations of *Drosophila pseudoobscura*. *Evolution*, **19**, 337–346.

Ehrman, L. & Strickberger, W. (1960). Flies mating: a pictorial record. *Nat. Hist.*, **69**, 28–33.

Elens, A. A. & Wattiaux, J. M. (1964). Direct observation of sexual isolation. *Drosoph. Inf. Serv.*, **39**, 118–119.

Ewing, A. W. (1961). Body size and courtship behavior in *Drosophila melanogaster*. *Anim. Behav.*, **9**, 93–99.

*Hirsch, J. (1961). Sign of taxis as a property of the genotype. *Science, N.Y.*, **22**, 835–836.

Malogolowkin-Cohen, Ch., Solima-Simmons, A. & Levene, H. (1965). A study of sexual isolation between certain strains of *Drosophila paulistorum*. *Evolution*, **19**, 95–103.

Manning, A. (1962). A sperm factor affecting the receptivity of *Drosophila melanogaster* females. *Nature, Lond.*, **194**, 252–253.

Petit, C. (1958). Le déterminisme génétique et psycho-physiologique de la compétition sexuelle chez *Drosophila melanogaster*. *Bull. biol. Fr. Belg.*, **92**, 1–329.

Spiess, E. B. & Langer, B. (1964). Mating speed control by gene arrangements in *Drosophila pseudoobscura* homokaryotypes. *Proc. natn. Acad. Sci. U.S.A.*, **51**, 1015–1019.

Spieth, H. T. (1952). Mating behavior within the genus *Drosophila* (Diptera). *Bull. Am. Mus. nat. Hist.*, **99**, 395–474.

(*Received* 22 *November* 1965; *Ms. number*: ᴀ388)

* Hirsch, J. & Erlenmeyer-Kimling, L. (1961).

## APPENDIX

Professor E. B. Spiess, University of Pittsburgh, has permitted me to include the following data, collected in February 1964. The data are relevant here because the species tested, *Drosophila persimilis*, is a very close relative—a sibling species, of *D. pseudoobscura*. Also, the technique was similar to the one employed above: twenty males and twenty females were observed mating in a chamber. Here, however, only the ratio of the two types of male was altered, the females were always ten Klamath and ten Whitney (KL and WT are two autosomal inversions in *D. persimilis* which are always present in the homozygous condition in these experiments). Professor Spiess observed each chamber for 1 hr and ran six chambers for each ratio tested. The inversions were distinguished by the appropriately marked wings of their carriers. He presents his data as the number of males that have mated out of the number of males of that karyotype available.

| WT/KL ♂ Ratio | ♂♂ mated | |
|---|---|---|
| | KL | WT |
| 9/1 | 0·50 | 0·51 |
| 8/2 | 0·54 | 0·48 |
| 7/3 | 0·42 | 0·63 |
| 6/4 | 0·15 | 0·67 |
| 5/5 | 0·15 | 0·67 |
| 4/6 | 0·15 | 0·54 |
| 3/7 | 0·33 | 0·72 |
| 2/8 | 0·20 | 0·88 |
| 1/9 | 0·34 | 0·83 |

Clearly, KL males are doing proportionately better when they are rare; reciprocally, WT has a greater success in mating when it is rare.

# DISRUPTIVE SELECTION AND ITS EFFECT ON A METRICAL CHARACTER IN THE BUTTERFLY *PAPILIO DARDANUS*

C. A. Clarke and P. M. Sheppard

*Department of Medicine and Sub-Department of Genetics, University of Liverpool, England*

Received August 23, 1961

The swallowtail butterfly *Papilio dardanus* Brown is highly polymorphic in the female, but monomorphic in the male. Over most of Africa the females are unlike the males in wing pattern and many of the forms are mimetic. These females also lack on the hind wings the characteristic *Papilio* tails which are found in the males. In Madagascar the females are monomorphic, have a black and yellow pattern similar to that of the males, and like the males have tails. In Abyssinia most of the females are non-mimetic, tailed, and like the males in pattern. A minority have mimetic patterns similar to those found in the rest of Africa, but differing from them in having tails like the non-mimetic forms. Thus, the Abyssinian mimetic females appear to be less satisfactory mimics of their models than are females in the rest of Africa, since the models are everywhere tailless.

It has been argued by Clarke and Sheppard (1960a) and Sheppard (1959) that there must be selection against the tailed condition in the mimics, but in favor of it in the non-mimetic male-like females as well as in the males. If this hypothesis be true, then in Abyssinia there is disruptive selection acting on the females and favoring the reduction in tail length in the mimetic forms, but discouraging it in the male-like females.

We have shown (Clarke and Sheppard, 1959a, 1960b, 1960c, and unpublished) that the various wing patterns are controlled by at least twelve allelomorphs at a single autosomal locus, and the presence or absence of tails is controlled by another autosomal locus unlinked with the first. We have also presented evidence that the disruptive selection postulated above is in fact acting and has resulted in a difference in the mean tail length of the Abyssinian

mimetic and non-mimetic females. The work has been continued, and the present paper summarizes the evidence for such selection and for the nature of the genetic control of the difference in tail length between the female forms.

## MATERIALS AND METHODS

The butterflies used in this investigation consisted both of dead specimens in museums and private collections, and of living butterflies collected in Madagascar, Abyssinia, and South Africa, and sent to us by airmail. The living material was used to obtain breeding stocks which were maintained for a number of generations by the methods described by Clarke and Sheppard (1959b). The race crosses produced from these stocks included (1) the $F_1$, $F_2$, $F_3$, and $F_4$ between the South African and Abyssinian races; (2) the backcross of the South African-Abyssinian $F_1$ to both the South African and the Abyssinian races; (3) the $F_1$ and $F_2$ between the South African and Madagascan races; (4) the cross between the Madagascan-South African $F_1$ and the Abyssinian-South African $F_2$.

Each female was scored for its phenotype and for the length of its tail. The latter character was measured to the nearest 0.25 mm by the method described by Clarke and Sheppard (1960a). The left hind wing was always measured if it was undamaged, but if it was not complete the right wing was used. It was not possible to measure both wings and take the mean, since in a number of specimens, particularly the rarer forms from collections, one or other wing was nearly always damaged. Where both wings could be measured it was found that there was a very high degree of symmetry. The tail length was taken to extend from the

Reprinted by permission of The Society for the Study of Evolution and the authors from *Evolution* 16:214–226, 1962.

TABLE 1. *Variance in tail length*

| Origin | Sex | Phenotype | No. | Mean adjusted tail length in mm[1] | Variance |
|---|---|---|---|---|---|
| S. Africa | ♂ | - | 22 | 14.46 | 0.92 |
| Abyssinia | ♂ | - | 62 | 13.48 | 1.12 |
| Madagascar | ♂ | - | 75 | 13.87 | 0.78 |
| Madagascar | ♀ | Male-like | 50 | 14.38 | 1.05 |

[1] Tail length adjusted for wing size by taking the ratio of the tail to hind-wing length and multiplying by 34 mm.

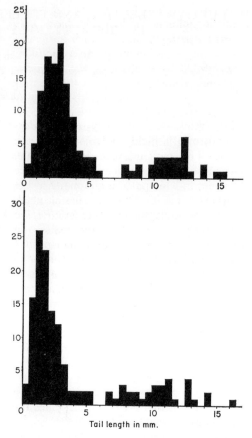

FIG. 1. The frequency histograms of tail length in mm have been plotted for the $F_1$, $F_2$, $F_3$, and $F_4$ combined of the South African-Abyssinian hybrids. The results from the mimetic females (below) and the male-like females (above) are given separately. Note the antimode in the region of 6.5 mm which allows a distinction to be made between the tailed and the "tailless" individuals.

tip of vein four to a part of the vein which is intersected by a straight line from the tip of vein three to that of vein five. The length of the wing was taken from this spot to the base of the wing.

The length of the tail is correlated with the size of the wing, and the different races and hybrids have different mean wing sizes. Consequently it seemed necessary to adjust tail length in order to be able to compare this character in different families. In the first analysis (tables 1 and 3) the ratio of tail length to wing length was calculated and multiplied by 34. This constant was selected because it is close to the average wing length of all the stocks examined. Thus, in the initial analysis the relative length of tail to wing size was investigated. This seemed an appropriate adjustment because the conspicuousness of the tails depends on the size of the hind wings.

After the results from the adjusted tail length had been analyzed in the various races and hybrids a second analysis was undertaken. In this the tail length was adjusted for wing length by calculating the regression of tail length on wing length within each race and hybrid group, and using this regression to adjust the tail length to a wing size of 34 mm. The unadjusted tail lengths were also examined to see if conclusions from them differed from those of the two sets of adjusted tail lengths.

## RESULTS

The ratio adjusted mean tail lengths of the South African males, the Abyssinian males, the Madagascan males, and the Madagascan females together with the variances of the populations are given in table 1.

The presence of tails is a semi-recessive, and the variance of tail length in hybrids is sometimes large. Consequently there could be some misclassification of heterozygotes and homozygous tailed individuals in hybrids. The length of the tails of females of the combined $F_1$, $F_2$, $F_3$, and $F_4$ families of the Abyssinian-South African hybrids are plotted in fig. 1. The mimetic and non-mimetic individuals have been plotted separately, since, if their antimodes had come at different points, combining them would have obscured the reality of the bimodal distributions. In the diagram there is a clear antimode at 6 to 6.5 mm indicating the division between heterozygotes and homozygous tailed butterflies. An examination within the families showed that an even clearer antimode existed in this region. The division between the tailed homozygotes and the rest was therefore taken at 6 mm, and an examination of the $F_2$ hybrids between the South African and Abyssinian races showed a very good agreement with the expected mendelian ratio of three "tailless" to one tailed individual on the basis of this division (62 tailless to 19 tailed male-like females; 65 tailless to 21 tailed mimics). The demarcation line is also consistent with the Abyssinian × South African $F_1$ data, since no heterozygote of this type has a tail length greater than 5.5 mm, and none of the Abyssinian tailed females that we have examined has had a tail length less than 6 mm.

The adjusted tail length of the male-like and mimetic females together with the population variances of the Abyssinian race and the various hybrids are given in table 3. The results of the Abyssinian-South African $F_2$, $F_3$, and $F_4$ have been combined since they are homogeneous, both with respect to mean tail length and variance.

## Analysis of Results

In *P. dardanus* the males of all races have long tails, as do the non-mimetic male-like females from Madagascar (table 1). However, on the African continent south of Abyssinia the vast majority of females are mimetic and all are tailless as are the distasteful models. These facts strongly indicate that the absence of tails is advantageous in the mimics since it increases the resemblance to the models, but is disadvantageous in butterflies with the black and yellow male-like pattern. This hypothesis is further strengthened by the situation found in Abyssinia. Here both the

mimetic and non-mimetic females are tailed and the mimics comprise only about 20% of the female population (table 6). Now if the absence of tails is advantageous in the mimics and not disadvantageous in the male-like forms one would expect all the females in Abyssinia to be tailless. If the presence of tails is advantageous in the male-like forms one would expect all the Abyssinian females to be tailed, as in fact they are, since the gene for the absence of tails is unlinked with the locus controlling color pattern, and therefore would be at a disadvantage in about 80% of the females and at an advantage in only about 20% of them.

An examination of the variance of tail length in the males and Madagascan females (table 1) also indicates that stabilizing selection is acting on tail length. If there were no selection acting one might expect greater variances than the rather small ones observed.

This view can be investigated more easily by examining coefficients of variation rather than variances. It can hardly be disputed that some degree of stabilizing selection is acting on wing length. A comparison of the coefficients of variation of wing length and unadjusted tail length should indicate whether the variation in the latter is consistent with an equal degree of stabilizing selection on both wing and tail dimensions. These estimates are given in table 2. The values are extremely similar to one another for tail length, but less so for wing length. Moreover, they are slightly smaller for tail length than for wing length in the Madagascan males and females, but larger in the Abyssinian and South African males. In general therefore, the data are at least in agreement with the view that stabilizing selection is acting on tail length in the Madagascan females and the Madagascan, Abyssinian, and South African males.

It therefore appears valid to assume not only that the absence of tails is advantageous in the mimetic forms, but also that their presence is advantageous in those but-

TABLE. 2. *Coefficients of variation of wing and of unadjusted tail length*

|  | Wing | Tail |
|---|---|---|
| Madagascan ♂ | 10.3 | 9.2 |
| Madagascan ♀ | 10.2 | 10.0 |
| Abyssinian ♂ | 6.8 | 9.5 |
| S. African ♂ | 8.7 | 9.4 |

terflies which have the male pattern. If this assumption be true, then there is disruptive selection tending to select for long tails in the Abyssinian non-mimetic females, but against them in the mimics.

Thoday (1959a, 1960) and Thoday and Boam (1959) have shown that under various mating systems in *Drosophila melanogaster*, strong disruptive selection for bristle number leads to an increased variance and can result in a bimodal distribution of bristle number. Consequently, if such selection were acting on *P. dardanus* in Abyssinia one might expect the variance of tail length in both the mimetic and non-mimetic females to be greater than in the males of all races and in the Madagascan females. Moreover, one might also expect a difference in the mean tail length of the male-like and the mimetic females, the latter having the shorter tails. From table 3 it will be seen that both these predictions are fulfilled, the variance being significantly higher than in the males or Madagascan females (table 1), and the difference in tail length between the mimetic and non-mimetic forms also being highly significant ($P < 0.001$). Even the non-

mimetic females have a mean tail length shorter than that of the males, a feature not true of the Madagascan race. This suggests that selection on tail length in the mimics has not only resulted in an increased variance and a difference in mean tail length between the two forms, but even in some reduction in the length of the tails of the non-mimetic females themselves.

It might be argued that the difference in mean tail length between the forms, but not of course the increased variance, is not due to the evolution of a co-adapted gene-complex as a result of disruptive selection, but is due to a pleiotropic effect of the allelomorphs controlling color pattern, in all gene-complexes. Now the South African females are all tailless, therefore there can be no disruptive selection for the accumulation of modifiers reducing tail length in the mimetic but not in the male-like females, although such selection may have acted in the distant past. Consequently if our hypothesis of disruptive selection be true we can assume that the South African race will not have a co-adapted gene-complex giving a difference in mean tail length between mimetic and non-mimetic forms. It follows therefore that in the $F_2$, $F_3$, and $F_4$ generations of an Abyssinian-South African cross, there should be a reduction in this difference in mean tail length as a result of the segregation of modifiers if our hypothesis be true. In the results (table 3) such a reduction is apparent. Since the variances of the four sub-classes concerned

TABLE 3. *Variance in tail length in crosses*[1]

| Origin | Sex | Phenotype | No. | Mean adjusted tail length | Variance | Difference between means |
|---|---|---|---|---|---|---|
| Abyssinian race | ♀ | Male-like | 46 | 12.24 | 3.019 | 3.10 |
|  |  | Mimetic | 13 | 9.14 | 5.857 |  |
| Abyssinian–S. African $F_1$ | ♀ | Male-like | 13 | 10.00 | 1.719 | 1.44 |
| × Abyssinian race |  | Mimetic | 7 | 8.56 | 4.451 |  |
| Abyssinian–S. African $F_2$, | ♀ | Male-like | 30 | 11.20 | 3.722 | 0.69 |
| $F_3$, and $F_4$ |  | Mimetic | 32 | 10.51 | 5.647 |  |
| Madagascan–S. African $F_1$ | ♀ | Male-like | 6 | 11.92 | 15.434 | 0.01 |
| × Abyssinian–S. African $F_2$ |  | Mimetic | 5 | 11.91 | 8.798 |  |
| Madagascan–S. African $F_2$ | ♀ | Male-like | 4 | 13.64 | 4.546 |  |

[1] Only homozygous tailed individuals as judged by the fact that their adjusted tail length is greater than 6.0 mm are included.

TABLE 4. *Analysis of variance*

| Source of variance | Degrees of freedom | Sum of squares | Mean square |
|---|---|---|---|
| Sub-classes | 3 | 119.78 | |
| Individuals | 117 | 489.11 | 4.18 |

Interaction mean square   35.31   $F = 8.45$,
  D.F.   1 and 117   $P < 0.01$

are homogeneous ($\chi^2_3 = 4.56$; $P > 0.2$), an analysis of variance can be used to investigate the reality of this apparent decrease in the difference in mean tail length in the combined $F_2$, $F_3$, and $F_4$ hybrids compared with pure Abyssinian stock (table 4). The interaction between stocks and patterned phenotype is highly significant ($P < 0.01$) using the method for $2 \times 2$ tables with disproportionate sub-classes (Snedecor, 1959, p. 379). This shows that there is a significant reduction in the difference in tail length in the hybrids, and suggests that the Abyssinian stocks in fact possess modifiers, absent in the South African race, which enhance the difference in mean tail length between mimics and non-mimetic females.

Besides the hybrids already discussed there are a number of others which give information on the presence of modifiers in the Abyssinian race of *P. dardanus*. These modifiers will ensure that the $F_1$ Abyssinian-South African hybrid backcrossed to the Abyssinian race will have a larger difference in mean tail length between the forms than does the $F_2$. Furthermore, a backcross to the South African race would show an even smaller difference than is found in the $F_2$. However, such a hybrid will be tailless and therefore the character cannot be measured. Nevertheless, we have produced a hybrid which is almost equivalent and does produce some tailed individuals. The tailed Madagascan race is monomorphic, and therefore on our hypothesis possess none of the special modifiers found in the Abyssinian race. The Madagascan-South African $F_1$ was crossed to a South African-Abyssinian $F_2$ individual, and the brood produced some mimetic and some non-mimetic tailed individuals. Since only one of the four grandparents was

of the Abyssinian race, the difference in mean tail length between the two forms should be less than in the $F_2$ Abyssinian-South African cross. Table 3 shows that the difference in tail length of the two forms is in fact greater in the backcross to the Abyssinian race than in the $F_2$. Moreover, the hybrid equivalent to a backcross to the South African race has an even smaller difference than that found in the $F_2$.

The data therefore seem to confirm the hypothesis that the Abyssinian race but not the Madagascan or South African race possesses special modifiers that reduce tail length in the mimetic forms but less or not at all in the non-mimetic females. There are two difficulties in the estimation of the significance of this apparent regression of tail length difference on the proportion of the Abyssinian genotype in the stock. (1) The effect exerted by an Abyssinian genecomplex in each hybrid will depend on the dominance relationships of the modifiers. (2) If all the variances of tail length in the eight sub-classes are compared, there is a significant heterogeneity ($\chi^2_7 = 15.58$; $P < 0.05$). In view of these two difficulties the most reasonable approach to the problem of the estimation of the significance of this regression seems to be to calculate an unweighted regression on the assumption that the modifiers show no dominance (fig. 2). If this is done the regression coefficient $b$ is 4.0 with $P < 0.03$. This result again indicates that the Abyssinian race possesses modifiers not found in the Madagascan and South African races. The $F_2$ between the Madagascan and South African races should be particularly informative in this investigation. Unfortunately the cross between the $F_1$ individuals is very infertile and none of the tailed $F_2$ butterflies produced was of the mimetic form (table 3). However, the significant difference between the mean tail length of the individuals in this cross and of the male-like forms of the Abyssinian $F_2$ ($P < 0.05$) does indicate that the Abyssinian race possesses modifiers which re-

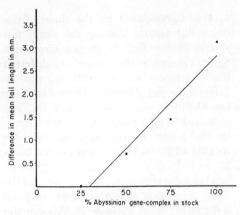

FIG. 2. The regression is of the difference in mean tail length in mm between the mimetic and male-like females on the per cent of the Abyssinian gene-complex in the stock.

duce tail length even in the male-like forms; a conclusion which was also reached from a comparison of the length of the tails of the Abyssinian males and the male-like females.

In a previous paper (Clarke and Sheppard, 1960a) we included among the Abyssinian-South African $F_1$ backcross to the Abyssinian race three insects which had tail lengths shorter than 6 mm. These three insects are the only ones of all the females examined whose status is doubtful, since the difference between their tail length and those of the undoubtedly tailed individuals of the brood is less than the difference between them and the tailless butterflies. Their inclusion in the tailed group increases the difference between the mean tail length of the mimetic and non-mimetic forms to 2.02 mm. The increase in this value fits the regression of the difference in tail length on the proportion of Abyssinian gene-complex in the stock, even better than the previous value of 1.44 mm. Consequently the doubtful status of these three insects does not alter the conclusions in any way.

Before the modifier hypothesis can be accepted unconditionally there is one other possibility that must be excluded. It is possible that the difference in the tail length situation between the pure Abys-

sinian stock and the various hybrids is due to additively acting effects on tail length of the pattern-controlling genes. The differences between the various stocks could result from differences in the proportions of homozygotes and heterozygotes among the non-mimetic individual and not to differences in the rest of the gene-complex. This seems to be an unlikely possibility because the backcross to the Abyssinian race shows a larger difference in mean tail length between the two phenotypes than the $F_2$ and fits the regression remarkably well, despite the fact that all the male-like forms in this family are heterozygous for an allelomorph controlling a mimetic pattern. Moreover, the Madagascan-Abyssinian hybrid also fits the regression, and it also has male-like forms all of which are heterozygotes.

To investigate the matter further we raised a special family. A mimetic female, the product of crosses between several races other than the Abyssinian race, was mated with a pure Abyssinian male. The female was heterozygous for the gene producing the tailed condition, this allelomorph having been derived from the Madagascan race. The mating produced both tailed and tailless offspring, and from this family the backcross was obtained to an Abyssinian male homozygous for the gene producing the mimetic pattern. The mean tail length and the variance of the tailed individuals in this backcross are given in table 5. It will be seen that the apparent difference in tail length between the mimics and non-mimetic females is greater than in the Abyssinian-South African $F_2$ as was that of the other similar backcross. The variances of the four sub-classes in the backcross and $F_2$ are homogeneous ($\chi_3^2 = 5.48$), and there is a non-significant interaction in the analysis of variance ($P > 0.05$). Since all the male-like females in the backcross are heterozygotes for one of the mimetic pattern producing genes, a significant interaction would have shown conclusively that the difference between the $F_2$ and backcross families is not only the

220                    C. A. CLARKE AND P. M. SHEPPARD

TABLE 5. *Results from the tailed female offspring of a hybrid of mixed origin backcrossed to a pure Abyssinian male homozygous for the allelomorph producing a mimetic pattern*

| Phenotype | No. | Mean ratio adjusted tail length | Variance | Difference in means |
|---|---|---|---|---|
| Male-like | 4 | 13.53 | 0.774 | |
| | | | | 3.08 |
| Mimetic | 8 | 10.45 | 8.782 | |

result of a pleiotropic effect of the allelomorphs controlling pattern, but must also depend on the rest of the gene-complex. However, despite the non-significant interaction the brood helps to support the hypothesis that modifiers are present, since the interaction is in the correct direction and the difference in mean tail length between the two phenotypes agrees with the other backcross and fits the regression of difference of mean tail length on the proportion of Abyssinian gene-complex in the stock.

The possibility that the differences shown between the Abyssinian race and the several hybrids results from the various mimetic genes themselves having different modifying effects on tail length is not sustained by the data. Only allelomorphs which are known to produce mimetic patterns in Abyssinia as well as South Africa have been used in the hybrids reported. Moreover, the tail length of the three mimetic forms concerned are all consistent with one another, both within each hybrid type in which they have occurred and within the Abyssinian race itself. Furthermore, nearly all the mimics were of one form *hippocoonides*. This is the only common mimic in Abyssinia, where it is called *niavioides*. Although the form is given different names in different races, it

is in fact controlled by the same allelomorph throughout Africa; the slight differences in the effect of the gene on pattern in them is due to the presence of different modifiers in the various races.

There are yet other reasons for accepting the modifier hypothesis. From the frequency of the recessive mimetic forms (table 6) one can calculate the gene frequency, and therefore the expected number of homozygotes among the Abyssinian male-like females. A second estimate of the number of homozygotes can be obtained from the genetic analysis of living males sent from Abyssinia (table 6). This is in good agreement with the previous independent estimate of gene frequency, and the combined estimate suggests that there are about 17 homozygotes in the 46 measured male-like females from Abyssinia. By ignoring the 17 insects with the longest tails one can again get an estimate of the mean difference in tail length between male-like heterozygotes and the mimetic homozygotes in the Abyssinian race. This will be a gross underestimate, since, of the 17 insects excluded, a large number will be heterozygotes because of the large variance in this population. The mean tail length of the male-like heterozygous females so calculated is 11.37 mm. An analysis of variance shows that even with the 17 insects excluded there is still a significant interaction between genotype and stock $P = 0.05$. Thus, once again the data do not support the conclusion that the significant interaction in the full data is due to the fact that there are more homozygotes in the Abyssinian sample than in the $F_2$. This is particularly apparent when it is remembered that the $F_2$ contains at least some homozygotes. We must conclude

TABLE 6. *Gene frequency in Abyssinian specimens*

| Abyssinian females | Male-like form 67 | | Mimics 17 | Gene-frequency of dominant 0.550 ± 0.049 |
|---|---|---|---|---|
| Males | Homozygotes 3 | Heterozygotes 10 | Homozygotes 3 | 0.500 ± 0.088 |
| Combined data | 80 | | 20 | 0.538 ± 0.042 |

TABLE 7. *Variance of tail length in crosses*

| Origin | Sex | Phenotype | No. | Mean unadjusted tail length in mm | Variance | Difference between means |
|---|---|---|---|---|---|---|
| Abyssinian race | ♀ | Male-like | 46 | 13.21 | 3.704 | 3.50 |
|  |  | Mimetic | 13 | 9.71 | 7.561 |  |
| Abyssinian–S. African F₁ ✕ Abyssinian race | ♀ | Male-like | 13 | 10.56 | 2.793 | 1.27 |
|  |  | Mimetic | 7 | 9.29 | 6.738 |  |
| Abyssinian–S. African F₂, F₃, and F₄ | ♀ | Male-like | 30 | 10.56 | 5.331 | 0.40 |
|  |  | Mimetic | 32 | 10.16 | 5.224 |  |
| Madagascan–S. African F₁ ✕ Abyssinian–S. African F₂ | ♀ | Male-like | 6 | 12.50 | 19.250 | 1.00 |
|  |  | Mimetic | 5 | 11.50 | 14.438 |  |

therefore that the difference in mean tail length between mimetic and non-mimetic types in the various stocks is due to an interaction between the main genes controlling pattern and the gene-complex. There are special modifiers in Abyssinia which increase the difference in mean tail length between the mimetic and the non-mimetic forms.

It might be argued that the results do not reflect the presence of modifiers of tail length, but of differences in insect size between mimetic and non-mimetic Abyssinian forms, since a correction of tail length dependent on wing size was applied. However, the unadjusted tail length shows the same trend (table 7). The increased difference in the mean tail length of the two phenotypes in the Madagascan F₁ ✕ Abyssinian F₂ brood is due entirely to the inclusion of one very small insect with wing size of only 23 mm.

It might also be argued that the adjustment of tail length for wing size should be based on the estimated regression of the two measurements within each race or type of hybrid. However, such estimations will be very unsatisfactory except for the Abyssinian F₂ and the Abyssinian male-like females because of the small amount of data available. If such adjustments are made (table 8) it is seen that the same regression of mean tail length difference between the pattern types on the amount of Abyssinian gene-complex is still apparent.

DISCUSSION

The genetic results, however analyzed, give clear evidence that the shorter mean tail length of the mimetic compared with the non-mimetic females in Abyssinia is due to the presence of specific sex-controlled modifiers not present, or not present at high frequency, in the Madagascan and South African races. It cannot be proved that the presence of these modifiers in the Abyssinian race is the result of disruptive selection without information on selection

TABLE 8. *Variance in adjusted tail length in crosses*[1]

| Origin | Sex | Phenotype | No. | Regression coefficient b | Adjusted mean in mm | Variance along regression line | Difference between means |
|---|---|---|---|---|---|---|---|
| Abyssinian race | ♀ | Male-like | 46 | +0.208 | 12.64 | 3.612 | 3.65 |
|  |  | Mimetic | 13 | +0.349 | 8.99 | 7.418 |  |
| Abyssinian–S. African F₁ ✕ Abyssinian race | ♀ | Male-like | 13 | +0.518 | 9.61 | 1.868 | 2.98 |
|  |  | Mimetic | 7 | +0.978 | 6.63 | 4.941 |  |
| Abyssinian–S. African F₂, F₃, and F₄ | ♀ | Male-like | 30 | +0.627 | 11.90 | 2.801 | 1.57 |
|  |  | Mimetic | 32 | +0.175 | 10.33 | 5.091 |  |
| Madagascan–S. African F₁ ✕ Abyssinian–S. African F₂ | ♀ | Male-like | 6 | +0.770 | 11.31 | 20.335 | −1.03 |
|  |  | Mimetic | 5 | +0.522 | 12.34 | 9.200 |  |

[1] The mean tail length in each sub-class has been adjusted using the regression of tail length on wing length.

222 C. A. CLARKE AND P. M. SHEPPARD

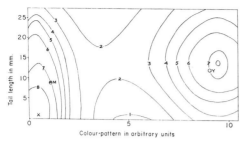

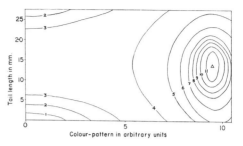

FIG. 3. The contours give the selective values of the various phenotypes in arbitrary units. Color pattern is also in arbitrary units with the mean of the model's pattern at 0.5, that of the Abyssinian mimics at 1.1, the Abyssinian male-like females at 9.0, and the Madagascan females at 9.5. Tail length is in mm with the mean of that of the model at 0.5, of the Abyssinian mimics at 9.14, of the Abyssinian male-like females at 12.24, and of the Madagascan females at 14.38.

FIG. 4. The figure is similar to fig. 3 except that no model with a pattern between 0 and 10 units exists in this area. This is the situation found in Madagascar.

in the field, which is not at the moment available. However, the inference that the disruptive selection has resulted in the presence of these modifiers seems valid for at least three reasons: (1) The predicted difference in the mean tail lengths of the mimics and non-mimetic forms is in fact found. (2) The variance of tail length in the Abyssinian females but not in the males is far higher than in Madagascan females. (3) The difference in tail length is controlled by modifiers not found in the non-mimetic Madagascan race or the tailless South African race, in both of which the disruptive selection cannot be acting.

It has already been pointed out by Clarke and Sheppard (1960a) that there is also disruptive selection acting on color pattern. Intermediates between mimetic patterns or between mimics and non-mimetic male-like forms are at a disadvantage, hence the presence of dominance between most sympatric but not between most allopatric forms. Thus, the male-like pattern is dominant to the mimetic form in Abyssinia, but the dominance tends to break down in hybrids with the South African race. In contrast, dominance is almost completely absent in the $F_2$ between the Madagascan and South African races as would be expected, since in the Madagascan race there would have been no op-

portunity for the evolution of dominance, there being no mimics to provide heterozygotes.

These considerations make it likely that there are two types of disruptive selection acting in Abyssinia, one tending to keep the non-mimetic pattern distinct from the mimetic ones, and the second tending to cause divergent tail lengths in insects of the two phenotypes. The system of relative selective values in Abyssinia can be illustrated diagrammatically using contour maps, somewhat analogous to those of Wright (1932) but differing in a number of important respects (see below). Such maps have been constructed by recording adjusted tail length along the Y axis and color pattern in arbitrary units along the X axis (figs. 3, 4, and 5). It will be realized that in practice color pattern cannot be measured on a scale in one dimension, and that the situation can be further compli-

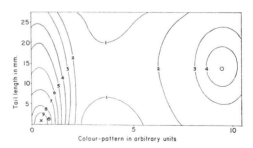

FIG. 5. Diagram is similar to figs. 3 and 4, except that the model is very abundant. This is the situation in South Africa. In the diagram the mimic has a mean color pattern of 0.75 and a tail length of 1.0 mm.

cated by the presence of more than one mimic, which would require yet more dimensions. However, for the purposes of illustration it is necessary to use only one dimension for color pattern and one mimic. The selective value of each phenotype (including both pattern and tail length) can be indicated by contour lines of selective value in the diagram. In his contour maps Wright used gene-frequencies and the average selective value of the population, so that at any one time the population is represented by a single point on the adaptive surface. We have used individual phenotypes and their particular selective value. Consequently in our maps a polymorphic population covers more than one discrete area on the diagram with different densities of individuals at various positions within these areas. Our diagrams can be made more comparable with those of Wright if the average phenotype of each form is plotted, but a polymorphic population will still be represented by more than one spot on the adaptive surface.

The diagram (fig. 3) represents the situation in Abyssinia, and on it the mean phenotypes of the model, the mimic, and the male-like form of *P. dardanus* have been plotted. For the purpose of illustration we have assumed that there is only one mimetic form in Abyssinia, the other forms being ignored, and that the frequencies of the forms are stable. The mean phenotype of the model is marked by a cross, and that of the most advantageous male-like pattern as judged by the length of the tail of the males and the pattern-phenotype of the Madagascan females is marked by a O. The mimetic form is by no means an exact copy of the model, and has features which show a strong tendency towards the non-mimetic pattern, whereas the non-mimetic male-like pattern shows some tendencies towards the mimetic one, as judged from the phenotype of the Madagascan females. Thus, it seems likely that the mean phenotypes (M indicates the mimetic form, Y indicates the male-like form in the diagram) do not correspond exactly

with the most advantageous phenotypes. Since we have no data on the intensity of selection in the wild and since pattern but not tail length is in arbitrary units, the contours of selective value are also arbitrary but the deep valley of poorly adapted phenotypes between the mimetic and non-mimetic types is real if our interpretation is correct.

The selective values indicated by the contours of the map are of course dependent on the ecological conditions prevailing at any one time. If the model were to disappear gradually from Abyssinia the adaptive peak for the mimic would tend to disappear but would be restored, probably with slightly different contours, as the mimic became correspondingly rarer and restored the stable equilibrium. However, when the model finally disappeared the adaptive peak would vanish giving a situation illustrated in fig. 4. This is the situation in Madagascar as far as the model *Amauris niavius* is concerned. Of all the models utilized in Africa only one, *Danaus chrysippus*, is present in Madagascar, and there is reason to believe that in *P. dardanus* a convincing approach to its mimicry, subsequently to be improved by selection, cannot easily be derived at one step by mutation, but requires first the evolution of the mimic of *Amauris niavius* (Sheppard, 1959).

The next circumstance to consider is one in which the model becomes exceedingly abundant. The mimic might then gain an overall advantage over the male-like form as in South Africa, and would replace it. This situation is illustrated in fig. 5. It seems probable that a slight adaptive peak would remain in the region of the non-mimetic pattern, but since it would be lower than that of the mimetic form the gene controlling the male-like pattern would be lost from the population.

These illustrations show that a non-mimetic population living in an area where there is a model present will not be able to move the higher adaptive peak of the mimetic pattern unless a mutant occurs which produces a phenotype on the slope of the mimetic adaptive peak at a point higher than the non-mimetic peak. Any small change away from the male-like pattern towards the mimetic pattern would be at a lower point on the non-mimetic peak and therefore disadvantageous. The large change which is necessary to cross the valley accounts for the frequent control of mimetic patterns in both monomorphic and polymorphic butterflies by single major genes. It would also account for the absence in *P. dardanus* of a mimic of the model *D. chrysippus* in Madagascar (see above). Once a major gene has occurred by mutation which gives such a resemblance to a model, the resemblance can be improved by the selection of modifiers or of other major genes.

Mimicry illustrates how effective stabilizing, directional and disruptive selection can be in bringing about micro-evolutionary changes. It also shows how adaptive peaks can and do appear and disappear as a result of ecological changes, thus allowing continuous evolutionary change to occur. Moreover, it illustrates how a population can move from one adaptive peak to a higher one by utilizing a new mutant having a large effect.

Changes in the adaptive surface may be very rapid. A new adaptive peak (whether defined by phenotype or by gene-frequencies and average selective values) can appear in what was previously a valley by the spread of a distasteful model into a new locality where the potentially mimetic species is already present. Any evolutionary changes in the phenotype of the model will cause gradual changes in the contours of the particular adaptive peak concerned. But alterations in the abundance of the mimetic species, the model, or the number of predators will produce violent and rapid changes in the adaptive surface. What constituted a peak in one generation may even be a deep valley in the next.

Now although it is relatively easy to show how ecological changes can rapidly alter the adaptive surface in the case of mimicry, it is much less easy with respect to most aspects of an organism's ecology. Nevertheless, it can hardly be doubted that many such aspects are causing much more profound changes in the adaptive surface than those suggested with respect to mimicry. We have some grounds for asserting therefore that a large population will not be "trapped" and confined to a single adaptive peak as was at one time suggested, but can evolve rapidly and continuously. The contour maps of Wright (1932) must not be considered merely as static or slowly changing as is the topography of land masses, but large sections must be considered as more like the topography of a rough sea or perhaps the unstable sand dunes on the sea coast, where peaks will be converted into troughs, and troughs will develop peaks. Although genetic drift must undoubtedly produce evolutionary changes, it is not imperative that it is acting for continuous evolution. Any adaptive trough sufficiently shallow for a population to pass across it as a result of genetic drift is likely to be shallow enough to be obliterated or converted into an adaptive peak by changes in the environment.

Finally, Thoday (1959b) pointed out that disruptive selection could lead to sympatric speciation. Now that there is evidence that disruptive selection can cause divergences between phenotypes in what was originally a character under multifactoral control, the occurrence of sympatric speciation seems even more likely. Any inherited factors tending to produce assortative mating would be at a slight advantage, since they would allow a greater divergence between forms, and therefore a closer approach to the optimum phenotypes than can be realized in the presence of random mating.

SUMMARY

(1) The males of *Papilio dardanus* are monomorphic, tailed, and non-mimetic. In most of Africa the females are polymorphic, tailless, and unlike the males in appearance. Moreover, most of the female forms are mimetic. In Madagascar all the females

are tailed, non-mimetic, and like the males in appearance. In Abyssinia they are all tailed, but only about 80% are male-like, the rest being mimetic.

(2) Because the models are tailless it is argued that in Abyssinia but not elsewhere there will be disruptive selection acting on tail length to reduce it in the mimics but not in the male-like females. This selection, if acting, should increase the variance of tail length in the Abyssinian females compared with the females in Madagascar and the males. It might also result in a difference in mean tail length between the mimetic and non-mimetic females, as a consequence of the readjustment of the gene-complex in Abyssinia.

(3) There is a greater variance of tail length in the Abyssinian females as predicted, and the mean tail length of the mimetic forms is less than that of the male-like females.

(4) Genetic analysis reveals that this pleiotropic effect of the allelomorphs controlling pattern results from the presence of specific sex-controlled modifiers at high frequency in Abyssinia. This result suggests that the postulated disruptive selection is in fact acting, and has resulted in a readjustment of the gene-complex in this area. In the polymorphic races of *P. dardanus* there is a second form of disruptive selection which helps to maintain the distinct color patterns of the morphs. Consequently in Abyssinia there are two types of disruptive selection acting, one on tail length, the other on color pattern.

(6) Because of the disadvantageous nature of intermediate phenotypes, the evolution of a new mimetic form usually requires the appearance of a new major mutant, since any small change in pattern is likely to be disadvantageous compared with the ancestral pattern. After the mutant has appeared the phenotype can be improved subsequently by the selection of modifiers.

(7) Contour maps were constructed in which tail length was measured in mm and pattern phenotype and selective value in arbitrary units. It appears that a polymorphic population will occupy two (or more) discrete areas on the adaptive surface of such a map. Changes in the ecological conditions, such as the prevalence of models or of predators, will result in alterations in the contours and therefore in the gene pool of the population and allow the population to evolve rapidly without the necessity of the intervention of genetic drift.

(8) The apparent effectiveness of disruptive selection in the wild suggests that on rare occasions partial or complete reproductive isolation between forms within a population may be evolved, as pointed out by Thoday.

## ACKNOWLEDGMENTS

We are very grateful to Dr. W. F. Bodmer, Dr. E. B. Ford, F.R.S., Dr. P. A. Parsons, Professor J. M. Thoday, and Dr. D. West, for reading the manuscript in detail, and for their helpful comments. We should also like to thank the many collectors who sent us living material from Africa, particularly Mr. C. G. C. Dikson, Mr. P. R. A. Mansfield, Dr. V. G. L. van Someren, Mr. J. W. Tiffin, Mr. R. W. Wells, and Mr. M. Wells, without whose material this investigation would have been impossible. We should also like to express our thanks to the Nuffield Foundation, whose continued support has been essential to this work.

### LITERATURE CITED

CLARKE, C. A., AND P. M. SHEPPARD. 1959a. The genetics of *Papilio dardanus* Brown. I. Race *cenea* from South Africa. Genetics, **44**: 1347–1358.

———. 1959b. The breeding of *Papilio dardanus* Brown in England. Technique and some results. Entomologist, **92**: 89–95.

———. 1960a. The evolution of dominance under disruptive selection. Heredity, **14**: 73–87.

———. 1960b. The genetics of *Papilio dardanus* Brown. II. Races *dardanus, polytrophus, meseres,* and *tibullus*. Genetics, **45**: 439–457.

———. 1960c. The genetics of *Papilio dardanus* Brown. III. Race *antinorii* from Abyssinia and race *meriones* from Madagascar. Genetics, **45**: 683–698.

226                    C. A. CLARKE AND P. M. SHEPPARD

SHEPPARD, P. M. 1959. The evolution of mimicry: a problem in ecology and genetics. Cold Spring Harbor Symp. Quant. Biol., **24**: 131–140.

SNEDECOR, G. W. 1959. Statistical methods. 5th ed. Iowa State College Press, Ames, Iowa.

THODAY, J. M. 1959a. Effects of disruptive selection. Heredity, **13**: 187–218.

——. 1959b. Effects of disruptive selection. Proc. 15th Int. Cong. Zool. 127–130.

——. 1960. Effects of disruptive selection. III. Coupling and repulsion. Heredity, **14**: 35–49.

—— AND T. B. BOAM. 1959. Effects of disruptive selection. II. Polymorphism and divergence without isolation. Heredity, **13**: 205–218.

WRIGHT, S. 1932. The roles of mutation, inbreeding, crossbreeding and selection in evolution. Proc. 6th Int. Cong. Genet., **1**: 356–366.

# POLYMORPHISMS IN EGG ALBUMEN PROTEIN AND BEHAVIOUR IN THE EIDER DUCK

By Dr. HENRY MILNE

Department of Natural History, University of Aberdeen

AND

Dr. FORBES W. ROBERTSON

Institute of Animal Genetics, Edinburgh

BIOCHEMICAL polymorphism in animal populations presents several aspects. When the polymorphism is balanced we have the well-recognized problem of the role of natural selection, and this requires a search for correlations between gene frequency and differences in habitat, behaviour, susceptibility to disease and exposure, etc. On the other hand, heterogeneity in gene frequency between populations may often afford a useful indication of reproductive isolation, and the greater the number of loci at which such variation occurs the more precise are the tests for restriction of gene flow. This communication deals with a particularly well-marked example of the latter aspect; it is chiefly concerned with genetic polymorphism in egg-white proteins in the eider duck (*Somateria mollissima mollissima* L.).

Using starch-gel electrophoresis[1] and a two-phase buffer system[2], and staining with amido-black, Robertson (unpublished) has examined several species of birds to see whether the kind of egg-white differences, reported by Lush[3] for the domestic fowl, commonly occur in wild species and, if so, whether this can be turned to advantage to shed light on the population structure of the species concerned. To ensure freshness, eggs were collected early in the laying season or before incubation had started. Generally one egg per clutch was examined after earlier work had shown that intra-clutch variation was unimportant; the phenotype of the albumen is determined by the genotype of the female parent. The species and the number of females scored in this way were as follows: herring gull (*Larus argentatus argentatus*), 196; lesser black-backed gull (*Larus fuscus graellsii*), 100; gannet (*Sula bassana*), 52; starling (*Sturnus vulgaris*), 30; great tit (*Parus major*), 19; and eider duck, 258. For the two gulls and the eider duck the eggs were collected from several widely separated localities. Only the eider showed evidence of egg-white variation. It is, of course, possible that minor differences were overlooked in the other species, since only one system of electrophoresis

Reprinted by permission of Macmillan (Journals) Limited and the authors from *Nature* 205:367–369, 1965.

was used, but the heterogeneity in the eider duck was so well defined that it was the obvious candidate for further study.

This polymorphism presents an apparently simple Mendelian situation of one locus with two common alleles which control differences in mobility of two protein types, as shown in Fig. 1. The alleles are referred to as $a$ and $b$ according to whether the protein they determine moves faster or slower. Equal mixture of albumen from the two alternative single-banded, presumably homozygous, types produces two less intensely stained bands which are indistinguishable from the naturally occurring double-banded, presumably heterozygous, types. In all but one of the samples from different localities, the frequencies of the alternative phenotypes conform to the Hardy–Weinberg distribution and this apparent exception is based on only a small sample (11 individuals). In addition to the three types just described, a fourth phenotype occurs very rarely (3 out of a total of 258 clutches scored) with two bands, one in the anterior position corresponding to the $a$ band and the other behind the $b$ position, as shown in Fig. 1. This slowest-moving band probably represents the effect of a third allele, $c$. So far no individuals have been found which would be identified as $cc$ or $bc$.

Gene frequency has been estimated for five different breeding areas, namely Forvie (Aberdeenshire), Tentsmuir (Fife), and sites in Orkney, Iceland and Holland; the distribution of sites is shown in Fig. 2. The number of females scored and gene frequencies are set out in Table 1, which shows considerable variation between European populations. Excluding the Forvie samples, for the reasons described below, $\chi^2$ for the differences between the other four localities is 20·9 for 3 degrees of freedom, $P < 0·01$. Types $ab$ and $bb$ were grouped in the analysis since the frequency of the $bb$ type is very low. From these data, there is no evidence of a latitudinal cline since the gene frequency at the most southerly site in Fife ($b = 0·09$) is very similar to that in the Iceland sample ($b = 0·10$) and both populations conform to the Hardy–Weinberg distribution. We must now consider the situation in the Forvie colony, for which we have more detailed information.

The breeding population of eiders on the Sands of Forvie is one of the largest, if not the largest, mainland colony in Britain. During summer the present population totals more than 3,000 birds, of which an estimated 1,000

Table 1. Gene Frequency in Eider Populations

| Site | $N$ | Frequency of $b$ |
|---|---|---|
| Tentsmuir | 24 | 0·10 |
| Orkney | 36 | 0·35 |
| Iceland | 50 | 0·09 |
| Holland | 11 | 0·09* |

* Significant departure from Hardy–Weinberg distribution.

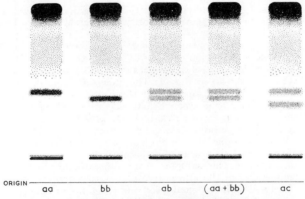

ORIGIN

aa   bb   ab   (aa + bb)   ac

Fig. 1. The appearance presented by the different genotypes in starch-gel section, stained with amido-black. Equal mixture of albumen from the homozygotes is labelled as (aa + bb)

pairs breed. About two-thirds of the population is migratory. The migrant birds leave the breeding grounds in July and August to overwinter apparently in the Firth of Tay. By marking individual birds, Milne (unpublished) has shown that the same individuals migrate south each autumn and return to breed the following spring, while the non-migrant birds remain at Forvie throughout the year. These two groups are referred to as 'migrant' and 'sedentary'. Field study of the sedentary flocks in the estuary of the River Ythan during winter showed that pair formation takes place during the period October–March inclusive, and that by April, when the migrants return, most of the sedentary group are already paired. The migrants pair during the period they are away from the breeding grounds. In three successive years they have been recorded arriving back at Forvie within a period of 2–3 days and 95 per cent were already paired. In view of this field evidence of reproductive isolation we decided to estimate the gene frequency in the two groups, and this posed the problem of distinguishing the nests of sedentary and migrant birds.

The Sands of Forvie National Nature Reserve, in which the eiders breed, is a wedge-shaped area of some 1,700 acres, bounded to the south and west by the estuary of the River Ythan and to the east by the North Sea. In winter most of the sedentary birds are to be found in the estuary with a few along the adjacent coast. Field observations suggested a strong tendency for the sedentary birds to nest on the west side of the moor near the estuary, while the migrants nest on the east side, nearer the sea; they overlap in the middle of the moor and records of marked individuals illustrate this difference (Table 2). In the seasons 1962 and 1963 eggs were collected

3

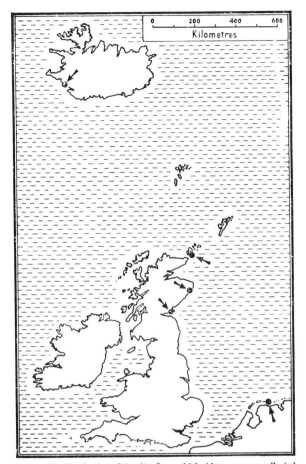

Fig. 2. The distribution of the sites from which eider eggs were collected. The Forvie colony is the more northerly of the two mainland Scottish sites

separately from the estuary and the seaward area and the gene frequencies were compared. In 1962 an additional sample was taken from the middle region where over-lapping was expected. Dealing first with the gene frequencies in the successive seasons on the west and east sides of the breeding area, we find no statistically significant difference in gene frequency between seasons within breeding areas (Table 3). The values of $\chi^2$, with $ab$ and $bb$ grouped, are 0·9 and 2·0 for a single degree of freedom in the estuary and seaward areas, respectively, and so the samples have been combined for the seasons to give a total of 51 and 67 clutches for the alternative groups

4

Table 2. Nest Sites of Sedentary and Migrant Eider Duck at Forvie

|  | Nesting near estuary | Nesting near sea |
|---|---|---|
| Resident on estuary in winter | 15 | 2 |
| Not resident on estuary in winter * | 1 | 14 |

\* This group refers to marked birds which were never recorded in the estuary during the period November to March inclusive.

which are believed to comprise almost entirely sedentary and migrant individuals. The gene frequencies are significantly different in the two groups, being respectively 0·14 and 0·27 for the less frequent $b$ allele. Combining the $ab$ and $bb$ types as before, $\chi^2$ for 1 degree of freedom $= 5·7$ ($P < 0·5 > 0·02$). In addition, for season 1962, we have a sample of 19 from the middle region where overlap occurs, and for this the frequency of $b$ was estimated as 0·21, an intermediate value which is consistent with the general interpretation. Thus there is excellent evidence of effective reproductive isolation between the two groups of eiders which occupy the Forvie breeding area.

The nature and adaptive significance of this widespread protein polymorphism in the eider are at present unknown, but to clarify the situation the survey is being extended to other populations and geographical races. It would be particularly interesting to know whether there are other races with a high incidence of the $c$ allele which is so rare in the European populations already sampled. In addition to the protein polymorphism we have also the behavioural polymorphism in the Forvie colony, and it remains to be seen whether this phenomenon also occurs in other colonies. The origin of this behavioural difference, and whether or not it has a genetic basis, is a matter for speculation. Lack[4] has directed attention to the common occurrence of partial migration in various passerine and limicoline species. In the cases considered by Lack, the migrants travel much farther than the migrant eiders, generally to France, Spain and Portugal, while in some species there is a further group which migrates westward to Ireland, that is, the population may be di- or tri-morphic with respect to where the winter is spent. It is not yet known whether heterogeneity in behaviour is a regular feature of eider populations or peculiar to this local population due to particular historical or ecological factors. Con-

Table 3. Gene Frequency in Sedentary and Migrant Eiders in the Forvie Colony

| Year | aa | ab | bb | N | Frequency of b |
|---|---|---|---|---|---|
| Sedentary | | | | | |
| 1962 | 18 | 3 | 1 | 22 | 0·11 |
| 1963 | 21 | 7 | 1 | 29 | 0·16 |
| Migrant | | | | | |
| 1962 | 16 | 12 | 1 | 29 | 0·24 |
| 1963 | 21 | 12 | 5 | 38 | 0·29 |
| Seasons combined | | | | | |
| Sedentary | 39 | 10 | 2 | 51 | 0·14 |
| Migrant | 37 | 24 | 6 | 67 | 0·27 |

ceivably migration might reduce food competition in the more sheltered estuary during winter, so that there could be some advantage to the population as a whole in limiting such (admittedly quite hypothetical) inter-individual competition. In view of their relevance to the stability of population size and density-determining factors, it would be valuable to check the proportions of sedentary and migrant birds in future seasons and record, at the same time, the frequency of the egg-white alleles in the two groups.

These observations illustrate the advantages of combining ecological and genetic data in the study of animal populations. There is little doubt that the detection of biochemical variation of various kinds will be of great help in the analysis of population structure, not least by providing critical evidence for reproductive isolation in situations where this may be unsuspected or difficult to assess by more usual ecological methods.

We thank the various people who assisted in the collection of eider material or in other ways, especially Drs. H. N. Kluyver and J. Westhoff (Holland), Dr. F. Gudmundsson (Iceland), Mr. E. Balfour (Orkney) and members of the Scottish division of the Nature Conservancy.

[1] Smithies, O., *Biochem. J.*, **61**, 629 (1955).
[2] Poulik, M. D., *Nature*, **180**, 1477 (1947).
[3] Lush, I. E., *Nature*, **189**, 981 (1961).
[4] Lack, D., *British Birds*, **37**, Part 1: 122 (1943); Part 2: 143 (1943).

# A MOLECULAR APPROACH TO THE STUDY OF GENIC HETERO-
## ZYGOSITY IN NATURAL POPULATIONS. II. AMOUNT OF
## VARIATION AND DEGREE OF HETEROZYGOSITY IN
## NATURAL POPULATIONS OF *DROSOPHILA PSEUDOOBSCURA*[1]

R. C. LEWONTIN AND J. L. HUBBY

*Department of Zoology, University of Chicago, Chicago, Illinois*

Received March 30, 1966

A S pointed out in the first paper of this series (HUBBY and LEWONTIN 1966), no one knows at the present time the kinds and frequencies of variant alleles present in natural populations of any organism, with the exception of certain special classes of genes. For human populations we know a good deal about certain polymorphisms for blood cell antigens, serum proteins, and metabolic disorders of various kinds but we can hardly regard these, *a priori*, as typical of the genome as a whole. Clearly we need a method that will randomly sample the genome and detect a major proportion of the individual allelic substitutions that are segregating in a population. In our previous paper, we discussed a method for accomplishing this end by means of a study of electrophoretic variants at a large number of loci and we showed that the variation picked up by this method behaves in a simple Mendelian fashion so that phenotypes can be equated to homozygous and heterozygous genotypes at single loci.

It is the purpose of this second paper to show the results of an application of the method to a series of samples chosen from natural populations of *Drosophila pseudoobscura*. In particular, we will show that there is a considerable amount of genic variation segregating in all of the populations studied and that the real variation in these populations must be greater than we are able to demonstrate. This study does not make clear what balance of forces is responsible for the genetic variation observed, but it does make clear the kind and amount of variation at the genic level that we need to explain.

An exactly similar method has recently been applied by HARRIS (1966) for the enzymes of human blood. In a preliminary report on ten randomly chosen enzymes, HARRIS describes two as definitely polymorphic genetically and a third as phenotypically polymorphic but with insufficient genetic data so far. Clearly these methods are applicable to any organism of macroscopic dimensions.

## The Populations Studied

We have chosen populations of *D. pseudoobscura* for a number of reasons. This species is not commensal with man, as is *D. melanogaster*, and so can be

---

[1] The work reported here was supported in part by grants from the National Science Foundation (GB 3112 and GB 3213) and the Public Health Service (GM 11216).

Genetics **54**: 595–609 August 1966.

Reprinted by permission of the Genetics Society of America, Inc. and the authors from *Genetics* 54:595–609, 1966.

said to be truly "wild." It has a wide distribution in Western North and Central America from British Columbia to Guatemala with a recently discovered outlier as far south as Bogotá, Colombia. *D. pseudoobscura* is genetically well known, at least to the extent of having marker genes and inversions on all of its four major chromosomes, and there exists a vast literature on the population genetics of the inversion systems on chromosome 3 of this species by DOBZHANSKY and his school. No species of Drosophila is really well understood in its ecological aspects, but for *D. pseudoobscura* 30 years of study of natural populations has led to a fair knowledge of population size fluctuation, kind of vegetation with which the species is associated, diurnal activity and temperature tolerance. Numerous samples from wild populations exist in the laboratory, and new samples are constantly becoming available. All of these reasons suggested to us that *D. pseudoobscura* would be a good species for our first survey of natural genic variation. It seemed to us that the variation found within and between populations of this species ought to be typical of a common, relatively widespread, sexually reproducing organism.

The populations in this study are represented by a number of separate lines each stemming from a single fertilized female caught in nature. For example, nine separate single-female lines maintained separately in the laboratory since 1957 represent the population from Flagstaff, Arizona. Because we were unable to get fresh samples (except for one case) we preferred these separate lines to any mixed population. Such separate lines may each suffer homozygosis because of inbreeding, but the differences *between* lines will preserve some portion of the original population variance. If the lines had been pooled and kept since 1957 as a mixture, more of the variability originally introduced would have been lost. As our results will show, most, but not all, lines are in fact homozygous but differences between lines have been preserved. Nevertheless, the loss of variation because of inbreeding needs to be kept in mind when we analyze the results.

The population samples in the study were as follows: (1) Flagstaff, Arizona. Nine lines collected in a ponderosa pine forest above 5,000 feet elevation in 1957. The natural population is virtually pure for the Arrowhead gene arrangement on the third chromosome and all lines are Arrowhead homozygotes (see DOBZHANSKY and EPLING 1944). (2) Mather, California. Seven lines collected between 1957 and 1960 in a Transition Zone forest at 4,600 feet elevation. This population is highly polymorphic for third chromosome inversions in nature. All strains used were homozygous Arrowhead (see DOBZHANSKY, 1948). (3) Wildrose, California. Ten strains collected in 1957 in the Panamint Range at 8,000 feet elevation in a piñon Juniper forest. The population is highly polymorphic for inversions, but the strains tested were all homozygous Arrowhead (see DOBZHANSKY and EPLING 1944). (4) Cimarron, Colorado. Six lines collected in a *Quercus gambelii* grove at about 7,000 feet elevation in 1960. All lines are homozygous Arrowhead. (5) Strawberry Canyon (Berkeley), California. Ten strains from a much larger collection made in 1965 at an elevation of 800 feet. This population is highly polymorphic for third chromosome inversions, and the strains used were also polymorphic, being the $F_2$ and $F_3$ from the wild females. (6) A single strain from Bogotá, Colombia. A much larger sample is planned for this extreme outlier of the species range, but the single strain collected in 1960 was included since it was available. The population occurs between 8,000 and 10,000 feet elevation and has two inversions, Santa Cruz and Treeline in proportions 65:35 (see DOBZHANSKY *et al.* 1963).

The natural and laboratory history of these various strains is thus rather different. Two, Cimarron and Flagstaff, are from the eastern part of the species distribution where chromosomal (inversion) variability is low. All but Strawberry Canyon have been in the laboratory for 5 to 8 years as separate strains, while Strawberry Canyon is a fresh sample from nature, and is polymorphic for inversions. One strain, Bogotá, represents a geographically remote population that surely represents the extreme southern part of the species distribution. All in all, the sample was chosen to give a diversity of histories so that the results could be given some generality.

The laboratory maintenance of all strains was the same. They were kept at 18°C in half-pint culture bottles with an average of about 50 parents each generation, but with considerable variation in size. At times in their culture, most, if not all, suffered one or more extreme breeding size bottlenecks. Thus, there has been inbreeding to an unknown extent. At the culture temperature of 18°C, there is little or no difference in selective values among third chromosome inversion types, although nothing can be said in this respect about other segregating gene systems.

## RESULTS

The methods of electrophoretic separation and detection of enzyme systems are fully explained by HUBBY and LEWONTIN (1966) and we will take it as demonstrated in that paper that the phenotypes we see are reflective of simple allelic substitutions at single genetic loci. Therefore, in what follows in this paper, we will refer to "alleles" and "loci" without again referring to the phenotypic appearance of the electrophoretic gels.

In every case, five or more individuals were tested from each strain. A strain is classified as homozygous for an allele if all individuals tested were homozygous, while the strain is classified as segregating for two alleles if any of the individuals was heterozygous or if homozygotes of two different kinds were found. The notation .95/1.07, for example, means that the allele .95 and the allele 1.07 for a gene were found segregating among the tested individuals of the strain. Throughout we use the relative electrophoretic mobilities as names of alternate alleles (see HUBBY and LEWONTIN 1966).

The observations are summarized in Table 1. The body of the table shows the number of strains (not individuals) either homozygous or segregating for various alleles at various loci. Of the ten enzyme systems discussed in HUBBY and LEWONTIN (1966), two (ap-1 and ap-2) are not included here because they appeared on the gels infrequently and are not sufficiently reliable to be used in a population study. For the same reason, only ten of the 13 larval proteins are included in the present study. The decision whether to include a band in the study was made solely on the basis of reliability, and independently of whether it showed electrophoretic variants.

The entry in Table 1 for Leucine aminopeptidase (lap) is different in meaning from the others. The relative mobilities of the variant forms are so close for this locus that it is not possible to make the proper cross assignments between populations. There are at least four alleles at the locus, but we do not at present know unambiguously which are present in which populations. Therefore, in Table 1 we have simply indicated how many alleles are present among the strains of that population.

Table 1 shows some remarkable results. First, of the 18 loci represented, there is some genetic variation in some population for nine of them. Second, genetic variation is found in more than one population for seven of the loci: malic dehydrogenase (mdh), esterase-5 (e-5), leucine aminopeptidase (lap), alkaline phosphatase-7 (ap-7), pt-7, pt-8 and pt-10. This variation in more than one popu-

## TABLE 1

*Number of strains from each population either homozygous or segregating for various alleles at different loci*

| Locus | Allele | Strawberry Canyon | Wildrose | Cimarron | Mather | Flagstaff | Bogotá |
|---|---|---|---|---|---|---|---|
| esterase-5 | .85 | 0 | 0 | 0 | 1 | 0 | 0 |
| | .95 | 0 | 1 | 0 | 1 | 1 | 0 |
| | 1.00 | 0 | 3 | 3 | 0 | 4 | 1 |
| | 1.03 | 0 | 1 | 0 | 2 | 0 | 0 |
| | 1.07 | 0 | 0 | 2 | 1 | 4 | 0 |
| | 1.12 | 0 | 1 | 0 | 2 | 0 | 0 |
| | .95/1.00 | 1 | 0 | 0 | 0 | 0 | 0 |
| | .95/1.07 | 1 | 0 | 0 | 0 | 0 | 0 |
| | .95/1.12 | 0 | 0 | 1 | 0 | 0 | 0 |
| | 1.00/1.07 | 4 | 1 | 0 | 0 | 0 | 0 |
| | 1.00/1.12 | 3 | 1 | 0 | 0 | 0 | 0 |
| | 1.03/1.07 | 1 | 1 | 0 | 0 | 0 | 0 |
| | 1.03/1.12 | 0 | 1 | 0 | 0 | 0 | 0 |
| | 1.07/1.12 | 1 | 0 | 0 | 0 | 0 | 0 |
| malic dehydrogenase | .90 | 0 | 0 | 0 | 1 | 0 | 0 |
| | 1.00 | 6 | 10 | 6 | 4 | 8 | 1 |
| | 1.11 | 2 | 0 | 0 | 0 | 0 | 0 |
| | 1.22 | 0 | 0 | 0 | 0 | 1 | 0 |
| | .90/1.00 | 0 | 0 | 0 | 2 | 0 | 0 |
| | 1.00/1.11 | 2 | 0 | 0 | 0 | 0 | 0 |
| glucose-6-phospate dehydrogenase | 1.00 | 9 | 10 | 4 | 6 | 9 | 1 |
| alkaline phosphatase-4 | .93 | 0 | 0 | 0 | 0 | 1 | . |
| | 1.00 | 9 | 11 | 6 | 7 | 8 | . |
| alkaline phosphatase-6 | + | 9 | 10 | 5 | 7 | 9 | . |
| | —/+ | 0 | 0 | 1* | 0 | 0 | . |
| alkaline phosphatase-7 | + | 9 | 9 | 5 | 7 | 9 | . |
| | —/+ | 0 | 1 | 1* | 0 | 0 | . |
| α-glycerophosphate dehydrogenase | 1.00 | 10 | 10 | 6 | 6 | 8 | 1 |
| leucine aminopepidase | .95<br>.97<br>1.00<br>1.02 | 2† alleles | 3‡ alleles | 2 alleles | 2§ alleles | 3 alleles | 1 allele |
| pt-4 | .45 | 10 | 10 | 6 | 6 | 8 | 1 |
| pt-5 | .55 | 1 | 4 | 4 | 6 | 2 | 1 |
| pt-6 | .62 | 10 | 10 | 6 | 6 | 8 | 1 |
| pt-7 | .73 | 0 | 0 | 0 | 0 | 1 | 0 |
| | .75 | 9 | 10 | 5 | 5 | 6 | 1 |
| | .77 | 0 | 0 | 0 | 0 | 0 | 0 |
| | .73/.75 | 0 | 0 | 0 | 0 | 1 | 0 |
| | .75/.77 | 1 | 0 | 1 | 1 | 0 | 0 |
| pt-8 | .80 | 0 | 0 | 0 | 0 | 0 | 1 |
| | .81 | 2 | 2 | 3 | 2 | 1 | 0 |
| | .83 | 1 | 4 | 1 | 1 | 5 | 0 |
| | .81/83 | 7 | 4 | 2 | 3 | 2 | 0 |
| pt-9 | .90 | 3 | 8 | 4 | 1 | 0 | 0 |

HETEROZYGOSITY IN NATURE

TABLE 1—Continued

*Number of strains from each population either homozygous or segregating*
*for various alleles at different loci*

| Locus | Allele | Strawberry Canyon | Wildrose | Cimarron | Mather | Flagstaff | Bogotá |
|-------|--------|-------------------|----------|----------|--------|-----------|--------|
| *pt-10* | *1.02* | 0 | 0 | 0 | 0 | 0 | 0 |
| | *1.04* | 4 | 9 | 6 | 4 | 8 | 0 |
| | *1.06* | 0 | 0 | 0 | 0 | 0 | 1 |
| | *1.02/1.04* | 0 | 1 | 0 | 0 | 0 | 0 |
| | *1.04/1.06* | 6 | 0 | 0 | 2 | 0 | 0 |
| *pt-11* | *1.12* | 4 | 10 | 6 | 6 | 8 | |
| *pt-12* | *1.18* | 5 | 10 | 6 | 6 | 8 | 1 |
| *pt-13* | *1.30* | 7 | 10 | 6 | 6 | 8 | 1 |

\* Both loci segregating in the same strain.
† Three strains segregating.
‡ One strain segregating.
§ Two strains segregating.

lation must be characterized as polymorphism in the usual sense because variant alleles occur with some appreciable frequency in more than an isolated case.

Third, and most remarkable of all, is the widespread occurrence of segregation in strains that have been in the laboratory for as many as seven years. As might be expected, the Strawberry Canyon strains are segregating at those loci that are polymorphic. In fact, not a single strain of Strawberry Canyon is homozygous for an allele of *e-5*. But four strains of Wildrose are also segregating for alleles at this locus, as is one strain of Cimarron. Most striking of all is the case of the *.81/.83* polymorphism at the *pt-8* locus where there are segregating strains in every population (not including the single strain from Bogotá). Despite the segregation at many of these loci, Table 1 definitely gives the impression of an effect of inbreeding over the many generations during which the strains have been maintained in the laboratory. The Strawberry Canyon strains segregate far more frequently than any of the others, and, in general, more of the genetic variation in the other populations is between homozygous strains.

Fourth, the genotype of the single strain from Bogotá is sometimes unusual. In most cases, the Bogotá strain is homozygous for the allele most commonly found in other localities. This is not the case for *pt-8*, however, where Bogotá is homozygous for an allele not found elsewhere, and *pt-10* where Bogotá is homozygous for one of the less common alleles.

In order to make the pattern of genic variation simpler to perceive, Table 2 has been constructed from the data in Table 1. In Table 2 *very approximate* gene frequencies are calculated for the alleles shown in Table 1 by using the following convention. Each of the original strains carried four independent doses of each gene when it was brought into culture. A large proportion of the strains still have more than one of these original doses since so many strains are still polymorphic and therefore carry at least two of the original four alleles. How many of the original alleles are still represented in any strain can only be guessed at, however. We make an arbitrary convention that each line shall be counted

600                           R. C. LEWONTIN AND J. L. HUBBY

TABLE 2

*Approximate gene frequencies calculated from the data of Table 1*

| Locus | Allele | Strawberry Canyon | Wildrose | Cimarron | Mather | Flagstaff | Bogotá |
|---|---|---|---|---|---|---|---|
| esterase-5 | .85 | 0 | 0 | 0 | .14 | 0 | 0 |
| | .95 | .09 | .10 | .08 | .14 | .11 | 0 |
| | 1.00 | .36 | .40 | .50 | 0 | .44 | x |
| | 1.03 | .05 | .20 | 0 | .29 | 0 | 0 |
| | 1.07 | .32 | .10 | .33 | .14 | .44 | 0 |
| | 1.12 | .18 | .20 | .08 | .29 | 0 | 0 |
| malic dehydrogenase | .90 | 0 | 0 | 0 | .29 | 0 | 0 |
| | 1.00 | .70 | 1.00 | 1.00 | .71 | .89 | x |
| | 1.11 | .30 | 0 | 0 | 0 | 0 | 0 |
| | 1.22 | 0 | 0 | 0 | 0 | .11 | 0 |
| glucose-6-phosphate dehydrogenase | 1.00 | 1.00 | 1.00 | 1.00 | 1.00 | 1.00 | x |
| alkaline phosphatase-4 | .93 | 0 | 0 | 0 | 0 | .11 | . |
| | 1.00 | 1.00 | 1.00 | 1.00 | 1.00 | .88 | . |
| alkaline phosphatase-6 | + | 1.00 | 1.00 | .92 | 1.00 | 1.00 | . |
| | − | 0 | 0 | .08 | 0 | 0 | . |
| alkaline phosphatase-7 | + | 1.00 | .95 | .92 | 1.00 | 1.00 | . |
| | − | 0 | .05 | .08 | 0 | 0 | . |
| α-glycerophosphate dehydrogenase | 1.00 | 1.00 | 1.00 | 1.00 | 1.00 | 1.00 | x |
| leucine aminopeptidase | .95 .97 1.00 1.02 | 2 alleles | 3 alleles | 2 alleles | 2 alleles | 3 alleles | 1 allele |
| pt-4 | .45 | 1.00 | 1.00 | 1.00 | 1.00 | 1.00 | x |
| pt-5 | .55 | 1.00 | 1.00 | 1.00 | 1.00 | 1.00 | x |
| pt-6 | .62 | 1.00 | 1.00 | 1.00 | 1.00 | 1.00 | x |
| pt-7 | .73 | 0 | 0 | 0 | 0 | .19 | 0 |
| | .75 | .95 | 1.00 | .92 | .92 | .81 | x |
| | .77 | .05 | 0 | .08 | .08 | 0 | 0 |
| pt-8 | .80 | 0 | 0 | 0 | 0 | 0 | x |
| | .81 | .55 | .40 | .67 | .58 | .25 | 0 |
| | .83 | .45 | .60 | .33 | .42 | .75 | 0 |
| pt-9 | .90 | 1.00 | 1.00 | 1.00 | 1.00 | 1.00 | x |
| | 1.02 | 0 | .05 | 0 | 0 | 0 | 0 |
| pt-10 | 1.04 | .70 | .95 | 1.00 | .83 | 1.00 | 0 |
| | 1.06 | .30 | 0 | 0 | .17 | 0 | x |
| pt-11 | 1.12 | 1.00 | 1.00 | 1.00 | 1.00 | 1.00 | x |
| pt-12 | 1.18 | 1.00 | 1.00 | 1.00 | 1.00 | 1.00 | x |
| pt-13 | 1.30 | 1.00 | 1.00 | 1.00 | 1.00 | 1.00 | x |

One strain = 2 alleles. No gene frequency estimate can be made for Bogotá, so the allele present is marked with an x.

equally and, since many of the strains are segregating, each allele in such lines is given a weight of one half. So, for example, in Strawberry Canyon, for locus *pt-8*, there are two strains homozygous for allele *.81*, seven strains segregating *.81/.83*, and one strain homozygous *.83*. Then the gene frequency of allele *.81* is $q_{.81} = (2 + 7/2)/(2 + 7 + 1) = .55$. Such a method can give only a very crude estimate of the frequency of alleles in the original sample brought into the laboratory, except for Strawberry Canyon where the sample was examined in the $F_2$ and $F_3$ generations from the wild. Since these original samples were themselves small, we cannot take our gene frequency estimation in Table 2 too seriously. They are meant only to give a qualitative picture of the variation, yet they show certain patterns and on the basis of these crude estimates we can characterize the variation at each locus as falling into certain broad categories.

1. *Monomorphism.* In a sufficiently large population, no locus can be completely without variant alleles. However, we class as monomorphic those loci that are without variation in our sample and those with only a single variant allele in a single strain. It might be argued that the presence of even a single variant allele in such a small sample as ours is evidence that in the population this variant is at reasonably high frequency. Nevertheless, we prefer to err on the side of conservatism and class such isolated variants as newly arisen mutations that have not yet been eliminated from the population by natural selection or genetic drift. Using the criterion that a variant must be present in more than one strain in more than one population in order for a population to be considered polymorphic, we find 11 out of 18 loci monomorphic. Of these, nine are completely without variation in our sample: glucose-6-phosphate dehydrogenase, α-glycerol phosphate dehydrogenase, *pt-4*, *pt-5*, *pt-6*, *pt-9*, *pt-11*, *pt-12*, and *pt-13*. The other two, alkaline phosphatase-4 and alkaline phosphatase-6 each have a single variant allele in a single strain. In the case of alkaline phosphatase-4, the strain is homozygous for the variant allele so it is likely that it has been in the strain for some time, probably from the original sample from the wild. Nevertheless, we do not count this locus as polymorphic.

2. *Widespread polymorphism with one allele in high frequency.* In this class there are three loci in our sample: *ap-7* which has the same variant allele in two different geographical regions but in low frequency, *pt-7* which is similar, but has the polymorphism more widespread and which also has a second variant allele restricted to one population, and *pt-10* which is like *pt-7* except that the rarer allele is found fixed in the Bogotá strain. These three loci are clearly polymorphic, but one allele in each case is found in high frequency in every population and so may be considered the "typical" allele. For *pt-10* the "type" concept is shaky since in Strawberry Canyon the atypical allele is in a frequency of 30% and the allele is fixed in the single Bogotá strain.

3. *Ubiquitous polymorphism with no wild type.* This class includes three loci. The most extreme case is the esterase-5 gene which has six alleles so far recovered. Populations are segregating for between three and five of these and no one allele is most common. Allele *1.00* comes close to being most common, but it is completely lacking in the Mather sample. Only one allele, *.85*, is restricted to a single population, all others being found in a minimum of three populations. *pt-8* has about a 50:50 polymorphism of alleles *.81* and *.83* in all the populations and this is related to the fact that all populations had some strains still segregating for these two alleles. In addition, *pt-8* has a unique allele in Bogotá. *Leucine amino-*

602                    R. C. LEWONTIN AND J. L. HUBBY

*peptidase* appears to fall in this group, although there is some suspicion, not yet confirmed, that allele *1.00* is most common in all populations.

4. *Local indigenous polymorphism.* Only one locus is completely of this sort, malic dehydrogenase. Three of the five populations have a local variant in high frequency, but it is a different variant in each case. Allele *1.00* would appear to be a "type" allele or at least a most common form. In addition to *mdh*, we have already noted an occasional local variant, such as the allele *.80* of *pt-8* in the Bogotá strain, the allele *.73* of *pt-7* found only in Flakstaff, and the allele *.85* of esterase-5 known only from Mather. In these last two cases, it is impossible to distinguish them from the single homozygous variant of alkaline phosphatase-4 which we have classed as nonpolymorphic.

5. *Local pure races.* A class of variation that is completely lacking in our sample of loci is the local pure race. In no case do we find some populations homozygous for one allele and other populations homozygous for a different one. We expect such a pattern if the alleles were functionally equivalent isoalleles not under any natural selection pressure. The failure to find such cases is important to our hypotheses about the forces responsible for the observed variation.

To sum up these classes, out of 18 loci included in the population study, seven are clearly polymorphic in more than one population and two are represented by rare local variants in a single population which, to be conservative, are not considered polymorphic. Thus, conservatively 39% of loci are polymorphic. This takes account of all populations and does not give an estimate of the polymorphism in any given population, which will be less. Table 3 is a summary of the information for each population separately. The populations are very similar to each other in their degree of polymorphism with an average of 30% of the loci varying in each. It is interesting that Strawberry Canyon, a fresh sample from the wild, is not different from the others. We can assume that most of the variation from nature has been preserved in the laboratory stocks but has been converted to variation between strains by the inbreeding attendant on laboratory culture. Another point of interest is that the great similarity in *proportion* of loci polymorphic in each population is not entirely a result of identity of poly-

TABLE 3

*Proportion of loci, out of 18, polymorphic and proportion of the genome estimated to be heterozygous in an average individual for each population studied*

| Population | No. of loci polymorphic | Proportion of loci polymorphic | Proportion of genome heterozygous per individual | Maximum proportion of genome heterozygous |
|---|---|---|---|---|
| Strawberry Canyon | 6 | .33 | .148 | .173 |
| Wildrose | 5 | .28 | .106 | .156 |
| Cimarron | 5 | .28 | .099 | .153 |
| Mather | 6 | .33 | .143 | .173 |
| Flagstaff | 5 | .28 | .081 | .120 |
| Average |  | .30 | .115 | .155 |

morphisms. Thus, although Wildrose and Flagstaff are both polymorphic at five out of 18 loci, only three of these are common to both populations. Flagstaff is polymorphic at two loci, *mdh* and *pt-7*, for which Wildrose is monomorphic, but Wildrose is polymorphic for *ap-7* and *pt-10*, while Cimarron is monomorphic at these loci.

Yet another question that can be asked from the data is, "At what proportion of his loci will the average individual in a population be heterozygous?" In fact, this can be described without exaggeration as the central problem of experimental population genetics at the present time. A complete discussion of the conflicting results on this question is not possible here, but the issue is very clearly drawn by WALLACE (1958). The results reported by WALLACE in that paper, in previous papers (WALLACE 1956) and in subsequent works by WALLACE (1963), WALLACE and DOBZHANSKY (1962), DOBZHANSKY, KRIMBAS and KRIMBAS (1960), and many others, all point, although indirectly, toward a high level of heterozygosity in natural populations. On the other hand, theoretical considerations by KIMURA and CROW (1964) and experiments of HIRAIZUMI and CROW (1960), GREEN-BERG and CROW (1960), MULLER and FALK (1961) and FALK (1961) among others, point in the opposite direction. These latter authors interpret their results as showing that the proportion of loci heterozygous in a typical individual from a population will be quite small and that polymorphic loci will represent a small minority of all genes.

Our data enable us to estimate the proportion of heterozygosity per individual directly. This is estimated in the next to the last column of Table 3 for each population separately. This estimate is made by taking the gene frequencies of all the alleles at a locus in a population, calculating the expected frequencies of heterozygotes from the Hardy-Weinberg proportions, and then averaging over all loci for each population separately. For example, at the *e-5* locus in Flagstaff there are three alleles at frequency .44, .44, and .11, respectively. The expected frequency of heterozygotes at this locus in Flagstaff is then given by:

$$\textit{Proportion heterozygotes} = 2(.11)(.44) + 2(.11)(.44) + 2(.44)(.44) = .581.$$

This value is then averaged with similarly derived values from each of the other loci for Flagstaff, including the monomorphic ones which contribute no heterozygosity. Obviously, for a given number of alleles the proportion of heterozygosity is maximized when all are in equal frequency. In such a case

$$\textit{maximum proportion heterozygosity} = (n-1)/n$$

where $n$ is the number of alleles present. This value is given for comparison in the last column of Table 3.

As Table 3 shows, between 8% and 15% of the loci in an average individual from one of these populations will be in a heterozygous state and this is not very different from the maximum heterozygosity expected from the number of alleles actually segregating in the population. It is interesting that the two populations with the lowest amount of chromosomal polymorphism, Flagstaff and Cimarron (DOBZHANSKY and EPLING 1944) also have a slightly lower genic heterozygosity than the chromosomally highly polymorphic populations of Mather, Strawberry Canyon, and Wildrose. More extensive data on chromosomally polymorphic and monomorphic populations are being taken now.

DISCUSSION

*Biases:* Before we attempt to explain the amount of polymorphism shown in Table 3, we need to ask what the biases in our experiment are. There are four sources of bias in our estimates and they are all in the same direction.

1. The method of electrophoretic separation detects only some of the differences between proteins. Many amino acid substitutions may occur in a protein without making a detectable difference in the net charge. We do not know what proportion of substitutions we are detecting but it is probably on the order of one half. Depending upon the protein, different results have been observed. For tryptophan synthetase about 7/9 of all mutations tested are electrophoretically detectable (HENNING and YANOFSKY 1963), but none of the forms of cytochrome-c are electrophoretically separable despite extensive amino-acid substitution over the plant and animal kingdoms (MARGOLIASH, personal communication). Presumably in the latter case, net charge is critical to proper function. At any rate, our estimate of the number of variant alleles is clearly on the low side.

2. Our lines have preserved only a portion of the variation originally present in them when they were taken from nature. Because of the inbreeding effect of maintaining small populations with occasional bottle necks in breeding size, some of the alleles originally present must have been lost. This causes our estimate of variation to be on the low side.

3. The original lines were only a small sample of the natural populations. We have tested very few lines, as few as six in the case of Cimarron, so that we are only sampling a portion of the natural variation. Alleles at frequencies of say 5% or 10% may easily be lacking in such samples. Again our experiment underestimates the variation within each population.

4. We have deliberately excluded as polymorphic two loci in which only a single variant allele was found. This coupled with the fact that only five individuals were surveyed in each strain will leave out of account real polymorphisms at low frequencies. Had we included the two rare variants in Table 3, both Cimarron and Flagstaff would have had 33% of loci polymorphic which would change the overall average to 32%. The proportion of loci heterozygous per individual in these populations would be increased from .09 and .081 to .107 and .092, respectively, bringing the average over all populations to 12%, a very small change.

All these sources of bias cause us to underestimate the proportion of loci polymorphic and the proportion of heterozygous loci per individual, but by how much we cannot say. At present we are studying a large sample of over 100 $F_1$ lines from females caught in Strawberry Canyon over the course of a year. This study will eliminate biases 2 and 3 above and give us an appropriate correction for our present estimates.

One other possible source of bias is in the choice of enzyme assays. If there were some subtle reason that the enzymes we have chosen to use tended to be more or less genetically variable than loci in general, our results would not be referable to the genome as a whole. Our chief protection against this sort of bias is in the use of the larval proteins in addition to the specific enzyme assays. Both of these classes of genes give about the same degree of polymorphism: three out of ten polymorphic loci for larval proteins and four out of eight for the enzymes. While it might be argued that the very existence of a published method for the detection of an enzyme on a gel is a bias in favor of variable enzymes, no such argument can be made for the larval proteins, all of which are developed on the same gel by a general protein stain. Moreover, two of the enzymes, malic dehydrogenase and $\alpha$-glycerophosphate dehydrogenase, were developed in this laboratory simply because suitable coupling methods are known for dehydrogenases.

In order to avoid the bias that might arise from considering only a particular enzyme function, we have deliberately not assayed a large number of proteins associated with similar functions. For example, there are ten different sites of esterase activity, presumably representing ten different genes, but we have only assayed the one with the greatest activity. To load our sample with more esterases might introduce a bias if there were some reason why esterase loci were more or less polymorphic than other genes.

*The source of the variation:* It is not possible in this paper to examine in detail all of the alternative explanations possible for the large amount of genic variation we have observed in natural populations. Our observations do require explanation and we already have some evidence from the observations themselves.

Genetic variation is destroyed by two forces: genetic drift in populations under going periodic size reductions and selection against recessive or partly dominant deleterious genes. Genetic variation is increased or maintained by three factors: mutation, migration between populations with different gene frequencies, and balancing selection usually of the form of selection in favor of heterozygotes. On the basis of combination of these factors, we can distinguish three main possibilities to explain the variation we have seen.

(1) The alleles we have detected have no relevance to natural selection but are adaptively equivalent isoalleles. In such a case, genetic drift will drive populations to homozygosity, but will be resisted by recurrent mutation and migration. We have some idea of the effective breeding size, $N$, in populations of *D. pseudoobscura* from the experiments of DOBZHANSKY and WRIGHT (1941, 1943) and WRIGHT, DOBZHANSKY, and HOVANITZ (1942). Various estimates agree that "panmictic unit" has an effective size, $N$, of between 500 and 1,000 in the Mount San Jacinto populations where the species is most dense and successful. At Wildrose the population size is between one-fifth and one-tenth of that at Mount San Jacinto and, although there is no published evidence, the same is true at Cimarron where flies are rare even in summer. For the dense populations the conclusion of DOBZHANSKY and WRIGHT (1943) is that "the effective size of the panmictic unit in *D. pseudoobscura* turns out to be so large that but little permanent differentiation can be expected in a continuous population of this species owing to

genetic drift alone." For Cimarron and Wildrose, however, this is not true, yet we find these populations with the same average heterozygosity as other populations. The lack of any loci showing pure local races in nature is against the selective equivalence of isoalleles. It can be argued, however, that genetic drift in the marginal populations is producing local pure races but that migration from the other populations and mutation (of unknown magnitude for these alleles) is preventing differentiation. As a matter of fact, very little migration, of the order of one individual per generation, will effectively prevent homozygosis by drift. We must also take account of the observation that many lines in the laboratory are still segregating for several loci and that effective population size of these lines has been very small and migration (contamination) close to nil. The continued segregation of alleles in the laboratory might be caused by mutation rates much higher for isoalleles than for dysgenic alleles, and we are checking the mutation rate for a few alleles. All in all, however, complete selective neutrality is not a satisfactory explanation of all the observations.

(2) Selection tends to eliminate alternative alleles but mutation restores them. This hypothesis comes close to the neutral isoallele theory because our observed gene frequencies of alternate alleles would require that mutation rates and selection coefficients be of the same order of magnitude. That is, the equilibrium gene frequency for an allele selected against with intensity $t$ in heterozygotes (we can ignore the rarer homozygotes) is approximately equal to $u/t$, where $u$ is the mutation rate. Since our rarer alleles at each locus vary in frequency from 5% to 45%, $u$ and $t$ must be of about the same order of magnitude. This in turn suggests extraordinarily high mutation rates or very, very weak selection *on the average*. But an average selection coefficient of .001 implies that in some populations at some times the gene in question is selected for rather than against so that local pure race formation should be promoted. Again we must check to see that mutation rates are not higher than $10^{-3}$.

(3) Selection is in favor of heterozygotes. This hypothesis satisfies all the objections to (1) and (2) above, since heterosis, if strong enough, can maintain genic variation in any size population, irrespective of mutation and migration. However, two different problems are raised by the assumption of nearly universal heterosis. First, unless we assume that the two homozygotes are very weakly selected against, in which case we are back effectively to alternatives (1) and (2), the total amount of differential selection in a population with many heterotic loci is tremendous. For example, suppose two alleles are maintained by selecting against both homozygotes to the extent of 10% each. Since half of all individuals are homozygotes at such a locus, there is a loss of 5% of the population's reproductive potential because of the locus alone. If our estimate is correct that one third of all loci are polymorphic, then something like 2,000 loci are being maintained polymorphic by heterosis. If the selection at each locus were reducing population fitness to 95% of maximum, the population's reproductive potential would be only $(.95)^{2000}$ of its maximum or about $10^{-46}$. If each homozygote were 98% as fit as the heterozygote, the population's reproductive potential would be cut to $10^{-9}$. In either case, the value is unbelievably low. While we cannot assign

an exact maximum reproductive value to the most fit multiple heterozygous genotype, it seems quite impossible that only one billionth of the reproductive capacity of a Drosophila population is being realized. No Drosophila female could conceivably lay two billion eggs in her lifetime.

There is a strong possibility that the intensity of heterosis decreases as the number of loci heterozygous increases (VANN 1966). This does not really solve the problem, however, since drift will fix loci until the heterosis per locus still segregating is high enough to resist random fixation.

We then have a dilemma. If we postulate weak selective forces, we cannot explain the observed variation in natural populations unless we invoke much larger mutation and migration rates than are now considered reasonable. If we postulate strong selection, we must assume an intolerable load of differential selection in the population.

Some most interesting numerical calculations have been made by KIMURA and CROW (1964) relating the mutation rate, population size, heterozygosity, and genetic load of isoallelic systems. Their conclusions on the theoretical implications of widespread heterosis are similar to ours. One possible resolution of this dilemma is to suppose that in any given environment, only a portion, say 10% or less, of the polymorphisms are actually under selection so that most polymorphisms are relics of previous selection. If this is coupled with a small amount of migration between populations sufficient to retard genetic drift between periods of selection, we might explain very large amounts of variation without intolerable genetic loads. Such a process needs to be explored theoretically, while tests for heterosis need to be made under controlled conditions in the laboratory for a variety of loci and environments. Such tests are now under way. One such test by MacINTYRE and WRIGHT (1966) on esterase alleles in *D. melanogaster* was ambiguous in its result, but pointed in the direction of selective neutrality for the alleles tested.

Second, if we are to postulate heterosis on such a wide scale, we must be able to explain the adaptive superiority of heterozygotes for so many different functions. Heterozygotes differ from homozygotes in an important respect: they have present in the same organism both forms of the protein, and, in some cases they also have a third form, the hybrid protein. Only some of our enzyme proteins and none of our larval proteins show hybrid enzyme formation, so that hybrid enzyme *per se* cannot lie at the basis of general heterosis. But variation in physico-chemical characteristics of the same functional protein might very well enhance the flexibility of an organism living in a variable environment. One of the best evidences that such heteromorphy of protein structure is adaptive in evolution is the occurrence of polymeric proteins made up of very similar but not identical subunits. Obviously the genes responsible for the $\alpha$ and $\beta$ subunits of hemoglobin or the subunits of lactic dehydrogenase tetramers must have arisen by a process of gene duplication since the polypeptides they produce are so similar in amino acid sequence. The advantage of duplicate genes with slight differentiation over a single gene with different alleles is that in the former case every individual in the population can have the advantage of polymorphism. Gene duplication pro-

608              R. C. LEWONTIN AND J. L. HUBBY

vides the opportunity for fixed "heterozygosity" at the functional level while allelic variation always suffers from segregation of less fit homozygotes. Heterozygosis, then, is a suboptimal solution to the problem that duplicate genes solve optimally. An excellent presentation of this argument may be found in the last chapter of FINCHAM (1966).

We are greatly indebted to Dr. SUMIKO NARISE and Mr. ALAN NOVETSKY for their contribution to the survey of the strains. Dr. CHRISTOPHER WILLS and Mr. ALAN WICK have provided us most generously with flies from Strawberry Canyon. A number of illuminating comments and criticisms of the ideas were provided by BRUCE WALLACE, ROSS MacINTYRE, JAMES CROW, and HERMAN LEWIS, to all of whom we are most grateful.

## SUMMARY

Using genetic differences in electrophoretic mobility, demonstrated by HUBBY and LEWONTIN (1966) to be single Mendelian alternatives, we have surveyed the allelic variation in samples from five natural populations of D. pseudoobscura. Out of 18 loci randomly chosen, seven are shown to be clearly polymorphic in more than one population and two loci were found to have a rare local variant segregating. Thus, 39% of loci in the genome are polymorphic over the whole species. The average population is polymorphic for 30% of all loci. The estimates of gene frequency at these loci enable us to estimate the proportion of all loci in an individual's genome that will be in heterozygous state. This value is between 8% and 15% for different populations, with an average of 12%. A suggestion of a relationship has been observed between the extent of this heterogeneity and the amount of inversion polymorphism in a population.—An examination of the various biases in the experiment shows that they all conspire to make our estimate of polymorphism and heterozygosity lower than the true value. There is no simple explanation for the maintenance of such large amounts of genic heterozygosity.

### LITERATURE CITED

DOBZHANSKY, TH., 1948 Genetics of natural populations. XVI. Altitudinal and seasonal changes produced by natural selection in certain populations of D. pseudoobscura and D. persimilis. Genetics **33**: 158–176.

DOBZHANSKY, TH., and C. EPLING, 1944 Contributions to the genetics, taxonomy and ecology of Drosophila pseudoobscura and its relatives. Carnegie Inst. Wash. Publ. **554**:

DOBZHANSKY, TH., A. S. HUNTER, O. PAVLOSKY,, B. SPASSKY, and BRUCE WALLACE, 1963 Genetics of natural populations. XXXI. Genetics of an isolated marginal population of Drosophila pseudoobscura. Genetics **48**: 91–103.

DOBZHANSKY, TH., C. KRIMBAS, and M. G. KRIMBAS, 1960 Genetics of natural populations. XXX. Is the genetic load in Drosophila pseudoobscura a mutational or balanced load? Genetics **45**: 741–753.

DOBZHANSKY, TH., and S. WRIGHT, 1941 Genetics of natural populations. V. Relations between mutation rate and accumulation of lethals in populations of Drosophila pseudoobscura. Genetics **26**: 23–51. —— 1943 Genetics of natural populations. X. Dispersion rates in Drosophila pseudoobscura. Genetics **28**: 304–340.

FALK, R., 1961 Are induced mutations in Drosophila overdominant? II. Experimental results. Genetics **46**: 737–757.

FINCHAM, J. R. S., 1966   *Genetic Complementation*. Benjamin, New York.

GREENBERG, R., and J. F. CROW, 1960   A comparison of the effect of lethal and detrimental chromosomes from Drosophila populations. Genetics **45**: 1153–1168.

HARRIS, H., 1966   Enzyme polymorphisms in man. Proc. Roy. Soc. Lond. B **164**: 298–310.

HENNING, V., and C. YANOFSKY, 1963   An electrophoretic study of mutationally altered A proteins of the tryptophan synthetase of *Escherichia coli*. J. Mol. Biol. **6**: 16–21.

HIRAIZUMI, Y., and J. F. CROW, 1960   Heterozygous effects on viability, fertility, rate of development, and longevity of Drosophila chromosomes that are lethal when homozygous. Genetics **45**: 1071–1083.

HUBBY, J. L., and R. C. LEWONTIN, 1966   A molecular approach to the study of genic heterozygosity in natural populations. I. The number of alleles at different loci in *Drosophila pseudoobscura*. Genetics **54**: 577–594.

KIMURA, M., and J. F. CROW, 1964   The number of alleles that can be maintained in a finite population. Genetics **49**: 725–738.

MacINTYRE, Ross, and T. R. F. WRIGHT, 1966   Responses of esterase 6 alleles of *Drosophila melanogaster* and *D. simulans* to selection in experimental populations. Genetics **53**: 371–387.

MULLER, H. J., and R. FALK, 1961   Are induced mutations in Drosophila overdominant? I. Experimental design. Genetics **46**: 727–735.

VANN, E., 1966   The fate of X-ray induced chromosomal rearrangements introduced into laboratory populations of *D. melanogaster*. Am. Naturalist (in press)

WALLACE, B., 1956   Studies on irradiated populations of *D. melanogaster*. J. Genet. **54**: 280–293. —— 1958 The average effect of radiation induced mutations on viability in *D. melanogaster*. Evolution **12**: 532–552. —— 1963 Further data on the overdominance of induced mutations. Genetics **48**: 633–651.

WALLACE, B., and TH. DOBZHANSKY, 1962   Experimental proof of balanced genetic loads in Drosophila. Genetics **47**: 1027–1042.

WRIGHT, S., TH. DOBZHANSKY, and W. HOVANITZ, 1942   Genetics of natural populations. VII. The allelism of lethals in the third chromosome of *Drosophila pseudoobscura*. Genetics **27**: 363–394.

# III

# Changes
# in Populations

A basic premise of both population genetics and ecology is that populations change in response to changes in their environment. Yet in spite of the common agreement on this point, probably no other major area of research has been subject to quite so much parochial myopia. On one hand, ecologists have in general concentrated on changes derived from the biotic environment and most of the theory of this area is based on interactions within and between species (see Section V). On the other hand, geneticists have concentrated on responses to changes in the physical environment. Another distinction between the two approaches is that the ecologist has been primarily concerned with short-term changes in populations, whereas the geneticist has focused his attention on long-term responses. Fortunately, this pattern is changing. Consider for instance the regulation of population size.

It is generally agreed that populations of infinite size do not exist, primarily because any environment is finite. It is also generally agreed that population size is regulated at or below some level which is termed the carrying capacity of the environment. Here the agreement ends. Not only do investigators working on different groups of organisms disagree on the relative significance of the various mechanisms which may act to regulate population size, but there can even be hearty discourse concerning the mechanisms operating in particular taxonomic groups. Nowhere is this better illustrated than in the longstanding debate on the causes of periodic fluctuations in population size of microtine rodents. In the opening paper of this section, CHITTY presents his outlook on several of the proposed hypotheses for regulation of vole populations. He then advances another hypothesis which, unlike earlier mechanisms, demands that population size regulation be obtained through the active operation of both genetic and ecological factors.

It should perhaps be noted that this paper is argumentative and that at least some of CHITTY's points can be countered. Moreover, his proposed mechanism has received no general test. It has, however, added two new elements to the debate—genetic variation and recurrent selection for different optima. Whether or not his proposal is correct, CHITTY has led the research in this area across the ecological ramparts into the realm of population biology.

The rate at which a population can change is important in determining its ability to adapt to environmental challenges. Two theoretical papers included in this section are directed at the question of the rate at which evolution can occur in asexual versus sexual populations.

CROW and KIMURA argue that the rate of gene frequency change for two or more favorable mutants is greater in sexual populations because they can be brought together from separate individuals by recombination. MAYNARD SMITH takes exception to their results and presents a different model which he uses to show that the rate of evolution is identical in asexual and sexual populations. MAYNARD SMITH contends that the CROW and KIMURA model is misleading because it does not take recurrent mutation into account. However, the crux of the disagreement (as pointed out by Crow and Kimura, *American Naturalist*, 1969, in a reply to MAYNARD SMITH's critique) lies in the frequency of beneficial mutants. If they are frequent enough in the population so that individuals with all of the favorable mutants already exist, then MAYNARD SMITH's argument is correct. Recombination is of value when the mutations occur or exist singly in different individuals, and this value increases as the number of mutations being simultaneously selected increases.

MAYNARD SMITH argues that the advantage of sexual reproduction lies in the increased rate of change of gene frequency possible when two mutants, each favored in one of two environments, are brought together in a third environment where the double mutant type is superior. In this case, recombination would be more efficient than mutation in producing the double mutant.

These two papers forcefully demonstrate the divergent results that can be obtained for the same general problem with models that employ different assumptions.

The fact that the gene pool of a population changes in response to environmental change severely restricts the direct observation of selection in nature because of the time dimension required to obtain changes of any magnitude. This is particularly true for quantitative traits. Most recorded examples of directional changes in natural populations are related to alteration of the environment by man.

One of the best documented instances of selection in natural populations comes from studies of the phenomenon of industrial melanism, which has been observed in many of the Lepidoptera in both England and North America. For example, alteration of the environment by industrial pollution has been accompanied by a very rapid and almost complete replacement of the light-colored morph of the peppered moth, *Biston betularia*, by a dark morph. Since this moth is nocturnal and rests on tree trunks during the day, and since the darkening of tree trunks by smoke and soot presumably makes the light morph more conspicuous to predators that hunt by sight, it is easy to postulate a selective advantage to the dark form in polluted areas. Although many biologists would be content with such an explanation, the proof (or disproof) of an hypothesis like this one comes only from properly conducted laboratory or field experiments. In this paper KETTLEWELL summarizes his field experiments on the peppered moth in England which conclusively demonstrate differential survival of light and dark morphs in polluted and nonpolluted habitats.

In the companion paper, HALDANE shows how a relatively simple selection model can account quite well for the observed changes in gene frequency through time. In spite of HALDANE's pessimism, his estimate of 37 years is not far from the known length of time involved in the change (about 50 years). By modifying his assumptions to allow for gradual darkening of the environment and changes in dominance relationships, it is possible to come even closer to the actual figure.

One way to escape the problems inherent in trying to observe selection in natural populations, particularly for quantitative traits, is to carry out artificial selection experiments. Most of our knowledge of directional selection has come either from studies of artificial selection in domestic plants and animals or from studies in the laboratory with such organisms as *Drosophila*. As a model for the operation of natural selection on a quantitative trait, we have chosen a paper by DOBZHANSKY and SPASSKY based on selection for geotactic behavior in *D. pseudoobscura*.

As has been the case with most quantitative traits studied, selection for both positive and negative geotaxis in a maze was successful. Thus the behavioral preference of a fly for upward or downward movement clearly has a genetic component, and further, there was genetic variability for this trait in the populations studied. One interesting response occurred in the geotactic behavior of the selected populations when artificial selection was suspended or reversed in direction. The observed return towards the original state indicates that natural selection favors an intermediate geotactic behavior. However, in an environment where either positive or negative geotaxis was advantageous, it is clear that these populations would be able to adapt through directional selection.

In addition to directional selection for adaptation to a new or changing environment, two other forms of natural selection are recognized. Stabilizing selection involves elimination of deviants from the mean of the population in both directions, and therefore does not lead to change. It would be the predominant mode of selection in a relatively constant environment to which a population has previously become adapted. An example is given in the paper by BROOKS in Section V with respect to body size in planktonic crustaceans.

The third major mode of selection is disruptive (or diversifying) selection, which occurs when there are two or more optima toward which selection is directed. This is illustrated in the paper by CLARKE and SHEPPARD in Section II.

Natural selection does not, of course, operate in the absence of other forces such as gene flow, mutation, and random genetic drift. One of the major concerns of population biologists is to investigate, quantify, and model the interactions among the various evolutionary forces and their effects on the gene pools of populations. In general, however, we lack the techniques to investigate these interactions in nature so most of our data have of necessity come from laboratory experiments. One exception to this generality is presented in the paper by CAMIN and EHRLICH which illustrates the interaction between gene flow and selection in island populations of water snakes. In this study, a selective elimination of banded snakes on the islands is counterbalanced by continual immigration of banded individuals from the mainland populations.

Although selection is the major force that reduces genetic variation in populations, random genetic drift may also be important under some circumstances. This results from sampling errors in the processes of gamete and zygote formation in populations of finite size and leads to random fluctuations in gene frequencies. The paper by KERR and WRIGHT provides a demonstration of random genetic drift resulting from inbreeding in an experimental system where selection is, for all practical purposes, unimportant. In this experiment, 120 *Drosophila* populations were established in which the frequencies of forked, a sex-linked recessive gene, and its wild-type allele were 0.5. By artificially reducing population size to 8 randomly selected flies in each generation, gene frequencies in the replicate populations fiuctuated greatly from one generation to the next. At the end of the experiment (16 generations), over 70 percent of the populations had been fixed, and less than 30 percent were still segregating for the two alleles. Thus, in extremely small populations, random genetic drift alone may be a potent force in changing gene frequencies.

Random genetic drift may occur in nature whenever a population undergoes a severe reduction in size. Examples of such "bottlenecks" may be found in insect populations that overwinter in small numbers, or when a new habitat is colonized by a small propagule from the parental population. As the size of a propagule decreases (in the extreme case to a single fertilized female), the probability that it will carry a representative sample of the gene pool of the original population also decreases. Because of this, a new population will probably have a different initial gene pool and, in most cases, it will also be subjected to different selective pressures. Thus a founding population, if it survives, is expected to diverge from the original population. This phenomenon, known as the founder effect, has been used to help explain some peculiar features of the evolution of island floras and faunas.

The paper by DOBZHANSKY and PAVLOVSKY, one of the most elegant (and most quoted) papers published in experimental population biology, provides a beautiful demonstration of the interaction between selection and random genetic drift. Although strong selection was operating in their *Drosophila* populations, the outcome of selection in replicate populations was significantly more variable in populations initiated with small numbers than with large numbers of founders. These results may be taken to indicate that the major importance of random genetic drift is probably to be found in its interaction with other evolutionary forces.

In the final paper of this section, AYALA shows that populations of *Drosophila serrata* subjected to intense crowding, and therefore to strong selective pressures, gradually increase in size by evolving a greater ability to survive the crowded conditions. This adaptation occurs at a higher rate in populations formed by crossing two different strains, presumably because a greater amount of genetic variation is available to natural selection.

# POPULATION PROCESSES IN THE VOLE AND THEIR RELEVANCE TO GENERAL THEORY[1]

## Dennis Chitty

## Abstract

No animal population continues to increase indefinitely, and the problem is to find out what prevents this. Increase among voles is halted by declines that recur fairly regularly, and can be identified by certain associated characteristics as belonging to a single class of events. By examining enough of these instances, and contrasting them with control populations that are expanding, conventional types of answer to the problem can be eliminated. According to field evidence the individuals in a declining vole population are intrinsically less viable than their predecessors, and changes in the severity of their external mortality factors are insufficient to account for the increased probability of death. On the assumption that vole populations are a special instance of a general law, the hypothesis is set up that all species are capable of regulating their own population densities without destroying the renewable resources of their environment, or requiring enemies or bad weather to keep them from doing so. The existence of such a mechanism would not imply that it is always efficient, especially in situations to which a species is not adapted, or that species do not also occur in environments where the mechanism seldom, if ever, comes into effect. The hypothesis states that, under appropriate circumstances, indefinite increase in population density is prevented through a deterioration in the quality of the population. The hypothesis can be falsified, or shown to be irrelevant to a particular situation, by proving that there are no significant differences between expanding, stationary, and declining populations in the distribution of the properties of the individuals. Tests of this hypothesis are relevant to all theories about the factors limiting animal numbers, since the effects of most mortality factors depend upon properties of the organisms, and it cannot safely be assumed that so important an environmental variable as population density has no effect on the physiology of the individual or the genetics of the population. Contrary to the assumption often made, it is therefore a priori improbable that the action of the physical factors is independent of population density. It is therefore postulated that the *effects* of independent events, such as weather, become more severe as numbers rise and quality falls. This hypothesis, if true, overcomes two of the difficulties often met with in population studies: that there is no consistent evidence of (*a*) the mortality factors that are themselves influenced by population density in the manner required by one system of thought, or (*b*) the climatic catastrophes required by other systems.

## Introduction

Populations of animals such as the vole (*Microtus agrestis*), which fluctuate more or less regularly in numbers, are not easy to fit into general theories about the natural regulation of animal numbers. This must mean either that these species are exceptional, and facts about them can safely be ignored, or else that the theories need to be modified, which is the alternative discussed in the present paper.

## Defining the Problem

The object of many field studies is to find out (1) why population density does not go on rising indefinitely, and (2) why it varies from one type of environment to another. The first enquiry concerns a common property of all populations, the second concerns differences between them. To illustrate these definitions we may imagine two different types of environment, each

[1]Manuscript received October 5, 1959.
Contribution from Bureau of Animal Population, Department of Zoological Field Studies, Oxford University, Oxford, England.

Can. J. Zool. Vol. 38 (1960)

Reprinted by permission of the National Research Council of Canada and the author from the *Canadian Journal of Zoology* 38:99–113, 1960.

starting off with the same low numbers of a certain species of animal (Fig. 1, A and B). We may also suppose that both populations expand at different rates and eventually maintain different levels of abundance. We need to explain why the populations are alike in failing to keep up their initial rates of increase, and why they differ in the levels attained.

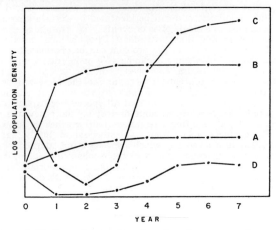

FIG. 1. Curves A–D show the results of an imaginary annual census of four populations occupying different types of habitat. The problem is to find out if there is a common explanation for failure of the populations to go on increasing indefinitely. Comparisons may be made within areas at different times (B in year 0–1 compared with year 4–5, for example) and between areas at the same time (A and B compared with C and D in years 0–1 or 4–5, for example). The present paper is not concerned with methods of enquiry into the differences between good and bad habitats (B and C compared with A and D).

The reason for recognizing two distinct problems is that it is not necessarily true, as is sometimes assumed, that factors associated with a difference in abundance between populations also prevent unlimited increase within them. Differences in food supply, weather, parasitism, etc. are often associated with differences in abundance, but we cannot infer that these are the factors preventing unlimited increase. Or to reverse the argument, although epidemics, or frosts, may not normally prevent unlimited increase, we cannot infer that such factors do not affect abundance. These matters must be decided empirically.

In the present paper I shall discuss only the first of the two problems mentioned above, which is seen as an attempt to discover the factors associated with failure to go on expanding at the higher rates observed within habitats, these rates being regarded as a control for all other rates of change. For proper controls, however, observations must also be made on a random selection of populations that are expanding at the same time as those that are not (Fig. 1).

Few populations are likely to conform to the simplified pattern so far imagined; indeed the majority will have more or less severe or prolonged declines, which may or may not have to be taken into account when searching for the factors that prevent unlimited increase. Population density may be

expected to fall if the resources of the environment are reduced or the climate
deteriorates, and an instance of this sort would be a special case of the second
of the two problems; but other declines, whether they occur at regular or
irregular intervals, must be considered as possible instances, in more obvious
form, of the general phenomenon of failure to maintain a high rate of increase.
Thus the problem is here assumed to be the same whether an initial rise in
numbers is followed by a systematically recurring decline, irregular fluctuations, or a more stationary state, and the sharp distinctions drawn by some
authors are not accepted.

Just as no single factor is associated with all differences in average abundance, no single factor is likely to be common to all departures from the maximum observed rates of increase. We must nevertheless avoid giving different
explanations for effects that merely differ superficially, but are in fact the
same. It is fortunate that in voles a specific kind of decline can be recognized,
not merely by its typical periodicity, but by various other criteria, especially
those based on the distribution of body weight (4, 31). Given enough instances of a recognizable class of events it is then possible to replace unfalsi-
fiable propositions about *some* declines by hypotheses about *all declines of a
certain kind*, and hence to eliminate explanations that do not fit the facts in
every case.

Throughout this paper it will be assumed that we are dealing with closed
systems. As will become clear, the conclusions arrived at would not apply
to populations recruited from areas in which there were fundamental differences in the conditions determining population density.

## Evidence Against Proposed Hypotheses

The present section gives reasons for rejecting some of the explanations
that have been advanced to explain recurrent declines in numbers in voles.
The observations were made at Lake Vyrnwy in Wales, in 1936–9 (4, 5), and
1945–59 (largely unpublished).

### (a) Infectious Disease

The most reasonable hypothesis consistent with the facts available before
1938 was that overcrowded vole populations were regularly decimated by
epidemics. However, the lack of any consistent association between infectious disease and population changes (14), and the discovery of vole
tuberculosis (30), helped to destroy the basis for the belief that the populations were controlled by epidemic diseases. In one part of Lake Vyrnwy
two-thirds of the animals were tuberculous at a time of severe mortality
This association of circumstances was similar to others described in the litera*
ture; but since several independent populations were being studied at Lak**
Vyrnwy it could be shown that the association was not invariant (5). The
disease was not a necessary condition for the decline of the populations, as it
was almost entirely absent from other areas from which they disappeared;
nor was it a sufficient condition, as some populations remained abundant in
spite of being heavily infected.

* litera-
** Lake

Field work on tuberculosis was terminated in 1939 and no further attempt was made to study other infectious diseases, since it was realized that the original belief about the role of epidemics in the decline of animal numbers was based only on the fact that the two were sometimes associated.   Although it is to be expected that diseases of various sorts are involved in most declines in numbers, there is no evidence that they are a sufficient condition for the type with which we are concerned.

*(b) Predation*

If certain properties are assigned to an imaginary predator and prey, the numbers of predators and prey can be made to fluctuate in a manner superficially similar to fluctuations in nature.   This superficial resemblance, however, is the same whether the predator destroys its own food supply, as in the model, or whether the prey disappears first for other reasons.   In any study of predator–prey relations it is therefore essential to distinguish between these alternatives.   In the case of the vole there is no reason to suppose that predation is sufficient to account for recurrent declines in numbers, since these take place whether predation is light or heavy; nor can predators be responsible for the failure of the animals to grow and sometimes to reproduce, nor for the differential survival of the sexes (6).   Similar conclusions were reached by Godfrey (17) and Lockie (23).

When predators are suddenly deprived of their normal food they may perhaps deplete some alternative.   In testing this possibility care must be taken to see that any association of events is not fortuitous, especially as short-term fluctuations in the numbers of small rodents are bound to coincide with all sorts of unrelated events.   An example of this occurred at Lake Vyrnwy, where foxes have always been plentiful.   In 1955 large numbers of rabbits died with myxomatosis.   Voles also became scarce; but this had been predicted from a knowledge of their populations in 1954. Furthermore there were other parts of Lake Vyrnwy where populations continued to build up their numbers in spite of any additional attention from the foxes.   The disappearance of the rabbits thus had no detectable influence on the population trends of the voles.

*(c) Food Supply*

When voles are exceptionally abundant they destroy a great deal of their food and cover; but nobody knows the proportion of occasions on which this happens, as only the abnormal instances receive attention out of several thousands of vole populations that presumably reach temporary abundance every 4 years or so.   Outbreaks attended by destruction of the vegetation have thus attracted a disproportionate amount of attention, and writers who base most of their conclusions on such instances run the risks usually associated with biased sampling.

At Lake Vyrnwy it is usual to find local patches of damage to vegetation at times of maximum abundance, but the subsequent scarcity of voles seems to be independent of the state of the vegetation.   Thus although serious damage is sometimes associated with high numbers there are so many instances when it is not that there is no reason to suspect that malnutrition or starvation play any necessary part in the recurrent mortality. Nor are there any signs of emaciation in the animals, whose numbers may decline throughout the growing season of the vegetation, in all types of plant community, in wet and dry areas, and regardless of how few voles may be left to compete for food.

At the time of the marking-recapture study described by Leslie et al. (21) a botanic survey was undertaken by Mr. W. E. J. Milton of the Welsh Plant Breeding Station, and Mr. J. Lewis of the Department of Animal Health, Aberystwyth. The data from this survey have not been published but were kindly made available for use at Oxford. Damage to the vegetation was too slight to have caused any general food shortage during 1948–50, a period covering a change from great abundance to great scarcity, but the survey showed that there was an annual shortage of green material. Some areas, for example, provided only 3% green material in March 1949. It is easy to imagine that there might be competition for this seasonally reduced food supply, and that the higher the numbers of the overwintered population the higher their mortality rate from starvation; but no supporting evidence could be found. On the special study area, for example (21, Fig. 1), the verges of the road running through it provided 35–85% green material even at this time of year, and total tillers of 300 per 36 sq. in. Yet the voles living along the road did not grow or survive any better than they did anywhere else at Lake Vyrnwy.

The results of this survey thus confirmed the common-sense impression from other occasions that a general shortage of food is neither a necessary nor a sufficient condition for the recurrent type of mortality, and the findings of Summerhayes (27) that voles did not seriously reduce the total amount of vegetation, in spite of having a pronounced effect on its composition.

### (d) Weather

In order to get some idea of the influence of weather it is helpful to study populations that are fluctuating in opposite directions in neighboring habitats. Let us suppose that some populations decline in a given year, while others nearby do not (Fig. 1, year 0–1). Then, if all were similarly exposed to bad weather, we may conclude that it was not a sufficient mortality factor. This type of evidence was provided at Lake Vyrnwy, where one group of populations declined in 1938 while another group remained abundant until the following year (4), and similar evidence has been obtained since. However, although bad weather alone may not be a sufficient condition for a decline in numbers it may be sufficient in conjunction with some other condition. Random variations in weather may indeed be one of the principal factors affecting populations, and are probably a necessary part of the mechanism that tends to make them fluctuate in phase (4, 6). Leslie (20) has constructed a numerical example to show how this effect may be produced.

(e) *Shock Disease*

Determinations were made of the liver glycogen content of wild voles taken simultaneously from declining and expanding populations. The animals were killed in the field, often within an hour of capture, and their livers were put immediately into a hot solution of potassium hydroxide; other voles were kept for a few weeks in isolation before being killed. No evidence was discovered to suggest that any of them had a pathological condition that impaired their ability to store glycogen. Elsewhere (8) I have discussed the claim that a condition of this sort (shock disease) occurs among natural populations of snowshoe hares (*Lepus americanus*) and tried to show that inferences from the laboratory data are not only unjustified, but are actually contradicted by the field evidence. The conclusion of Frank (15, 16) that shock disease occurs in *Microtus arvalis* applies only to animals that had been ill-treated in captivity; the condition has not been shown to explain the natural death rate.

(f) *Adrenopituitary Exhaustion*

Christian (9) wrote as follows: "Exhaustion of the adreno-pituitary system resulting from increased stresses inherent in a high population, especially in winter, plus the late winter demands of the reproductive system, due to increased light or other factors, precipitates population-wide death with the symptoms of adrenal insufficiency and hypoglycemic convulsions."

This generalization is partly based on the belief, which I believe to be false (8), that shock disease occurs among snowshoe hares in nature; but the picture of adult mortality given above is not that described by Green and Evans (18), who believed that the decline in numbers could be attributed to a high juvenile death rate, probably during the summer, and continuing even at low population densities. There are no data to suggest that Christian's explanation applies to wild vole populations; nor did Clarke (12) succeed in producing a decline in numbers in his outdoor enclosures, in spite of the fact that his animals were overcrowded, and that intraspecific strife was almost certainly limiting their increase.

More recently Christian (10) has expanded his original suggestions about stress to include an effect on later generations. This he believes to come about through the impaired lactation of stressed females, which occurs fairly readily in the laboratory (6, 11). Indeed there is no difficulty at all in interfering experimentally with reproductive processes; the difficulty comes in producing an effect which corresponds to anything going on in nature. Although Godfrey (17) found some young that were underweight at weaning during a decline, the principal problem is still to account for the disappearance of animals that seem to be perfectly normal when they first enter the active population. Their body weights do not support the idea that they are undernourished, and although there are other ways in which faulty lactation might affect them there is no evidence that it does so in nature.

Nevertheless, while I question the validity of Christian's conclusions about the mechanisms involved, his general point of view (10) has much in common with that discussed in the next section.

## An Alternative Hypothesis

The present section restates an hypothesis which, though still not established, has not yet been falsified, and describes the difficulties of getting the evidence that would do so. Some of the facts that have to be taken into account (4–7, 14, 17, 21, 23, 27) are that declines in the numbers of voles can take place even though the environment seems to be favorable; that high population density is not sufficient to start an immediate decline, nor low population density to halt it; that the vast majority of animals die from unknown causes, males more rapidly than females; that the death rate can be greatly reduced by isolating the animals in captivity, and that the adult death rate, as in the snowshoe hare (8, 18), is not abnormally high during the years of maximum abundance. These facts are consistent with the proposition that susceptibility to natural hazards increases among generations descended from animals affected by adverse environmental conditions. In one form or another this idea has been put forward by writers from 1868 onwards (6), and although it cannot be accepted until a mechanism has been discovered, it fits the facts and cannot be refuted at the present time. Three components need to be considered: the original adverse changes in the environment, the resultant physiological changes, and the external factors that affect the subsequent probability of dying, or actually kill the animals.

*1. Environmental Changes*

As shown above no success was met with in the search for relevant changes in any environmental factors that included food, cover, weather, enemies, disease, etc., but excluded other animals of the same sort. For some purposes it is probably convenient to think of the environment of the population in this limited sense, but it neglects the fact that each individual is surrounded by others that differ from it, and towards which it may react differently from the way they react towards it. "Every individual in a population of animals is part of the environment of other individuals. . . . The population is then understood as a group of individuals each having an environment which resembles those of its neighbors but differs from theirs if only because the environment of an individual includes its neighbors but not itself" (Andrewartha and Birch (2, pp. 13–14)). According to this definition, even a complete knowledge of total numbers and of all factors in the "environment of the population" would give inadequate grounds for prediction, unless it could also be assumed that every individual was identical with every other alive then and at any other time. In many mathematical models this is assumed to be the case, and as a first approximation it is sometimes convenient to think of real populations in terms of total numbers or degree of crowding. The approximation, however, may be no more informative than counting a number of coins without observing their denominations or realizing that currencies may depreciate.

The inadequacy of the idea that population processes can always be related to numbers is clearly shown in experimental work. A given cage space occupied by two hostile voles is a much worse environment for both of them than the same amount of space occupied by a large family unit; and the environment of a dominant animal will be quite different from that of the animals who spend their lives being chased or keeping out of harm's way. Repeatable results cannot be expected, however carefully conditions are standardized outside the group, if interactions within it are highly variable. In the field it is even less to be expected that numbers at one time will bear any necessary relation to numbers later on, if only quantity is taken into account and quality is neglected.

Thus the change in the environment which is here postulated as a necessary antecedent to a decline in numbers of the vole is not simply an increase in numbers, but a change in the nature and frequency of the interactions, which at the present time we do not know how to observe, let alone quantify. Furthermore, if there is selection in favor of genotypes that are better able to stand these interactions (7) they will themselves produce a new kind of environment about which population density alone can tell us very little.

## 2. Physiological Changes

Although an unknown blood condition may be associated with them (13), little is known about the supposed physiological changes, and perhaps the most that can be hoped for is to get some measure of their effects. This point can be made more obvious by considering an explanation suggested by Leslie and Ranson (22). These authors showed that a vole population with a fixed age-specific schedule of mortality would tend to decline more rapidly than usual if it entered the non-breeding season with an unusually high proportion of the older animals. If we accept this explanation we also accept the fact of senescence in organisms without trying to explain it, and confine our attention to measuring its demographic effects. The explanation now being offered is the same in principle as that of Leslie and Ranson, the only difference being that the change in the quality of the population is no longer attributed to an increase in the proportion of older animals (4), but to an increase in the proportion of animals that are congenitally less viable. For all that is known at present these changes in constitution may also be too difficult for the ecologist to measure directly, and he may have to study them through their effects on growth rate, survival, reproduction, behavior, and reaction to standard tests of various sorts.

## 3. External Factors

In contrast to hypotheses according to which the animals die a violent death from epidemics, predators, parasites, climatic catastrophes, or shock disease, no specific causes of death are postulated. Nor for the following reasons is it thought to be profitable to try to discover them. At various times in its life an animal has a number of experiences, the last of which, naturally enough, is followed by death. If death comes through a pure accident, such as drowning, most of the animal's previous experiences will be irrelevant to its chances of survival. In other cases, however, many circumstances in its earlier life are likely to affect its probability of dying later on: quality and quantity of food, reproduction, psychological factors, chronic disease, weather, and other hazards. In order to understand a particular death rate it may be more important to examine early events of this sort than those immediately associated with death. Local forces of mortality, whatever they happen to be, will be sufficient to kill off a susceptible population, though the rate at which they do so will presumably vary.

Even when an animal dies under observation in the laboratory it is hard to determine the causes of death. It may be thought that the problem is simpler in the wild, where many deaths occur from accidents of a kind that is easier to understand than the so-called deaths from old age. This impression may be based partly on misapprehension about causes of death (24), partly on non-random sampling. Although some captive animals live long enough to become decrepit, most of them die before reaching old age, and under the harsher conditions in nature relatively more individuals may be expected to die unpredictably early deaths. Secondly the majority of corpses of animals dying in nature are never found at all, and those that are may well result from the simpler forms of accident. At present we do not know; but there is no real justification for assuming that the ecologist can expect to explain the shape of a survival curve in nature until he can do so for one in the laboratory.

This argument should not be pressed to the point where no attempt is made to find out when and how the greatest changes occur in mortality rates, for example during bad weather or at the onset of breeding. Such associations are to be anticipated, but they may contribute only part of the explanation and may not occur universally.

We may now review the course of the argument. We first considered the simplest type of explanation, that a single antecedent condition, such as an outbreak of disease, was both necessary and sufficient to bring about a decline in numbers. No such unique condition was discovered. The next most simple explanation might have been that declines occur for different reasons on different occasions, and if we knew only that animals became scarce now and then there might be some excuse for accepting almost anything as a sufficient explanation, e.g. bad weather one time, predation the next, and so on. No such solution can be regarded as satisfactory when there are enough details to show that the phenomenon is no mere reduction in numbers, but an association of fairly specific effects that are unlikely to follow except from fairly specific antecedents. We therefore had to consider a third type of explanation involving two or more factors in combination, and including at least one necessary and specific condition. This necessary condition is thought to be an interaction capable of increasing the susceptibility of certain generations to a variety of non-specific agents, including chronic disease or parasites, further interactions with other animals, and a range of physical factors that the animals normally tolerate. According to this view both the specific and non-specific conditions must be satisfied, a change in susceptibility being insufficient to bring about a decline in the absence of the normal mortality factors, and the latter alone being insufficient to decimate a normal population, or at least to produce the association of effects that characterize the recurrent type of decline.

It is difficult to refute this interpretation at present, since it states that an unknown kind of interaction produces an unknown change in the average properties of the individuals, whose descendants become more susceptible to unknown and principally local forms of mortality. Part of the difficulty is technical: we seldom see wild voles or find their corpses; they live too long and take up too much space when brought into the laboratory to provide data on longevity and fertility; they have too long a generation time; little is known about their genetics, and so on. Finally, we have not yet learned how to set up experimental populations to give results that are both repeatable and relevant to the problem in nature.

The latter difficulty comes from the fact that wild rodents, even when abundant, live fairly well dispersed. A population of breeding adults must be considered "crowded" at a density of 120 per acre in the best habitats at Lake Vyrnwy, or one vole to 40 sq. yd of ground covered in dense vegetation and interspersed with a network of runways in three dimensions. Elsewhere densities may be still lower (17). Contrary, therefore, to what some authors appear to believe, useful results will not necessarily follow from keeping animals at a density several hundred times that occurring in nature, and at the same time failing to provide a substitute for their runways and cover.

Certain consequences of the hypothesis could be tested by applying experimental methods in the field, and departures from the following predictions would tend to discredit the idea in its present form. (1) If animals are prevented from interacting adversely they should go on increasing until they run out of food. (2) If large enough numbers of animals are continually removed from an expanding population, the survival rate of the remainder should continue to be high; but where an adverse physiological change has occurred no reduction in density should be sufficient to reverse a downward trend. (3) Numbers should continue to increase if animals from an increasing population are successfully transferred to an area from which a declining population has been removed; but numbers should continue to decline if animals from a declining population are transferred to a new area.

Predictions of this kind can so easily go wrong because of unforseen practical difficulties, inadequate knowledge, and faulty logic, that the time and money required to carry them out on voles might not be well spent. Other species, however, might be easier to work with if it is reasonable to believe that the problem in the vole is merely a special case of a far more general phenomenon. We must now examine this possibility.

## Relation to Other Ideas

Andrewartha and Birch (2, p. 656) summarize the principal aspect of their views in the form of three curves for each of two habitats, in one of which (area B) climatic catastrophes happen more frequently than in the other, and reduce the population to lower numbers, from which it recovers more slowly. They say "Taking all three curves into account, one can easily see that the animals would be more numerous, on the average, in area A than in area B." According to this scheme population densities are determined by the severity and frequency of bad weather, and no other factors need be postulated. We may express this point of view as implying that, in instances of this type, variations in weather are both necessary and sufficient to determine population density.

According to Nicholson (26) there is more to it than this, however. He, too, recognizes the importance of the physical factors, but argues that "they act as the tools or *instruments of destruction* used by true reactive factors". (A reactive factor is one that is influenced by changes in population density and influences it in turn.) The really essential point of his argument is that without a dependent variable the proportion of the population destroyed would be unrelated to population density, which therefore would not be "governed". However, since the death rate would be altogether different in the absence of the "instruments of destruction", much semantic difficulty can be avoided by assuming merely that both types of factor are necessary in such cases. Stripped of its surplus terminology, Nicholson's view can, I think, be reduced to the testable proposition that a set of independent variables is a necessary but not a sufficient condition determining a given population density. His other necessary condition, as already stated, is the presence of a reactive factor, and it is here that the trouble arises.

In a definition of considerable importance Nicholson (25) states: "*The action of the controlling factor must be governed by the density of the population controlled*". From this it would seem important to discover factors whose *action* varies with population density; but this is not what Nicholson advises: "Instead we must find which of the factors are influenced, and how readily they are influenced, by changes in the density of the animals". A natural enemy which destroys only 1% of the population would be "wholly responsible for control", whereas climate would not, even if it destroyed 98% of the population, because "its action [is] uninfluenced by the density of the animals". A good many writers have accepted this argument uncritically apparently without recognizing the magnitude of the assumption involved or the almost complete lack of empirical evidence.

The action of a physical factor can be measured only by observing the results of a reaction on the part of the organism, and these results are predictable only if the properties of the organism can be assumed to be constant. In the case of population phenomena we can measure the action of weather only by observing its effects on death rates, birth rates, or other parameters of the population, and it seems unrealistic to assume that the characteristics of the individual animals that make up the population are constant and independent of population density. Similar considerations affect the interpretation of most mortality rates, since even the effects of biotic factors such as parasites can also be explained by changes either in host resistance or in the severity of the factor.

Changes in resistance, systematically related to population density, are entirely consistent with Nicholson's main idea about the regulation of animal numbers; but not with his proposition that the action of the physical factors is independent of population density. This axiom can be abandoned, however, or restated in unambiguous terms, without affecting his main principle; and the main principle of Andrewartha and Birch may also be retained, as their idea that population density is chiefly determined by the action of the physical factors is entirely consistent with this action being governed by some population attribute. Both theories already include enough qualifications to make such a synthesis possible. The vole work suggests that population densities are indeed governed or regulated, but that this is most commonly achieved by the action of the physical factors; and since the action of any factor whatever depends upon the properties of the individuals, it seems a priori improbable that the effects of weather are independent of population density.

It is perhaps worth trying to justify the addition of fresh speculations to a subject already overburdened with them by showing their possible application to one of the many studies in which no evidence was discovered to show that numbers are regulated in the manner predicted a priori (as seems to be the case with all studies that have gone on long enough to rule out mere associations as explanations).

"It is difficult to see what factors may be responsible for regulating populations of *Glossina*. *Unfavourable conditions of climate are presumably independent of density and cannot regulate it* [italics mine]. Competition for blood between individual tsetse flies does not, we believe, take place. We are left to suppose that the "enemies" (using that word broadly) of the fly or the puparium must be responsible for the regulation. But it must be admitted that we have no evidence that any particular enemy becomes more numerous or effective at higher densities of the tsetse population. We have indeed very little knowledge of the causes or mechanisms which prevent an indefinite increase of these insects when external conditions are favourable, but one must certainly suppose that some such factor exists" (3).

This passage shows the remarkable persistence of the fallacy that because climatic factors are themselves unaffected by population density therefore their action is also independent of density (or other parameters). Jackson (19) also failed to realize that the effect of weather on tsetse flies can never be measured in isolation from a system involving individuals whose properties may not be constant. Although he found a long-term statistical relation between saturation deficit and birth and death rates, he could not understand why these parameters often fluctuated in opposite directions in two populations exposed to the same weather. "There is thus little doubt that the short-term fluctuations are governed by something intrinsic in the local populations, which if true is sufficient to put the detailed analysis of the effects of climate forever beyond our grasp." In contrast to this conclusion, the ideas developed in the present paper imply that results such as Jackson's are exactly what one would hope to find in order to understand the effects of climate. His results are consistent with the view that the two populations were significantly different in their properties; and such properties should be easier to investigate when simultaneous samples of animals can be examined from contrasting populations. Indeed the effects of climate are almost certain to be unpredictable until differences in the properties of the animals can be recognized.

At the present time there is an understandable reluctance to believe that the degree of crowding commonly observed in nature could possibly have profound effects on physiological condition. In the case of the tsetse fly, for example, the maximum population density may be only about 1800 ♂ ♂ per sq. mile in some places, with 2–3 times as many ♀ ♀, or about 10 flies per acre (3,19). Nevertheless Buxton (3) was prepared to speculate that tsetse flies might have a form of behavior that regulates their population density through dispersal; and Tinbergen (28) considers that such mechanisms may be fairly universal. As we know so little about behavior it would be wrong to assume that it has no important effects on physiology and genetics, and there is little doubt that individual properties should be taken into account more often than is customary in population studies. Perhaps the most notable exceptions are the work on locust phases (1 and earlier work), and physiological types of tent caterpillar (29).

According to the views given in this final section voles probably exemplify a general law that all species are capable of limiting their own population densities without either destroying the food resources to which they are adapted, or depending upon enemies or climatic accidents to prevent them from doing so. If this is true, self-regulatory mechanisms have presumably been evolved through natural selection, and arguments in support of this view can certainly be advanced. In the present paper, however, the only argument required is the purely methodological one that it is best to start with the fewest and simplest explanations possible, and to add to them only when it is clear that there are fundamental differences between similar phenomena in related species.

To assume that all species are capable of regulating their own numbers is entirely different from believing that all populations are in fact so regulated. In particular the assumption that a self-regulatory mechanism has been evolved by natural selection implies that it has been adapted in relation to a more or less limited range of environmental conditions. In unnatural or atypical situations, therefore, the mechanism will not necessarily prevent abnormal rates of increase or recurrent food crises.

It may be difficult to apply these views to other species until criteria have been established for recognizing instances of self-regulation and distinguishing them from instances of other phenomena. The attempt is nevertheless worth making, for birth rates and death rates are likely to be misinterpreted as long as it is assumed that the properties of the individuals are constant at all population densities.

## Acknowledgments

The substance of this paper was given in some talks at the Department of Zoology, University of British Columbia, in April 1959, and I wish to thank Dr. Ian McTaggart Cowan, Dr. James F. Bendell, and other members of the department for helpful discussions. Dr. W. G. Wellington was also kind enough to read and comment on the manuscript. I am especially grateful to Dr. E. W. Fager for some very useful advice about an earlier draft of this paper, and my colleagues at the Bureau of Animal Population have, as usual, made numerous constructive suggestions that have also been incorporated in the present version.

## References

1. ALBRECHT, F. O., VERDIER, M., and BLACKITH, R. E.   Détermination de la fertilité par l'effet de groupe chez le criquet migrateur (*Locusta migratoria migratorioides* R. et F.). Bull. biol. France, **92**, 349–427 (1958).   *See also* Nature, **184**, 103–104 (1959).
2. ANDREWARTHA, H. G. and BIRCH, L. C.   The distribution and abundance of animals. The University of Chicago Press, Chicago, Ill.   1954.
3. BUXTON, P. A.   The natural history of tsetse flies.   An account of the biology of the genus *Glossina* (Diptera).   Mem. London School Hyg. Trop. Med. No. **10**, 1–816 (1955).
4. CHITTY, D.   Mortality among voles (*Microtus agrestis*) at Lake Vyrnwy, Montgomeryshire in 1936–9.   Phil. Trans. Roy. Soc. London, Ser. B, **236**, 505–552 (1952).
5. CHITTY, D.   Tuberculosis among wild voles: with a discussion of other pathological conditions among certain mammals and birds.   Ecology, **35**, 227–237 (1954).
6. CHITTY, D.   Adverse effects of population density upon the viability of later generations. *In* the numbers of man and animals.   *Edited by* J. B. Cragg and N. W. Pirie.   Oliver and Boyd, Ltd., Edinburgh. 1955. pp. 57–67.
7. CHITTY, D.   Self-regulation of numbers through changes in viability.   Cold Spring Harbour Symposia Quant. Biol. **22**, 277–280 (1958).
8. CHITTY, D.   A note on shock disease.   Ecology.   In press (1959).
9. CHRISTIAN, J. J.   The adreno-pituitary system and population cycles in mammals.   J. Mammalogy, **31**, 247–259 (1950).
10. CHRISTIAN, J. J.   A review of the endocrine responses in rats and mice to increasing population size including delayed effects on offspring.   Naval Med. Research Inst. Lect. Rev. Ser. No. 57–2, 443–462 (1957).
11. CHRISTIAN, J. J. and LEMUNYAN, C. D.   Adverse effects of crowding on reproduction and lactation of mice and two generations of their progeny.   Naval Med. Research Inst. Research Rept. NM 24 01 00.04.01, **15**, 925–936 (1957).
12. CLARKE, J. R.   Influence of numbers on reproduction and survival in two experimental vole populations.   Proc. Roy. Soc. B, **144**, 68–85 (1955).
13. DAWSON, J.   Splenic hypertrophy in voles.   Nature, **178**, 1183–1184 (1956).
14. ELTON, C.   Voles, mice and lemmings: problems in population dynamics.   Oxford University Press, London.   1942.
15. FRANK, F.   Untersuchungen über den Zusammenbruch von Feldmausplagen (*Microtus arvalis* Pallas).   Zool. Jahrb. (Syst.), **82**, 95–136 (1953).
16. FRANK, F.   The causality of microtine cycles in Germany (second preliminary research report).   J. Wildlife Management, **21**, 113–121 (1957).
17. GODFREY, G. K.   Observations on the nature of the decline in numbers of two *Microtus* populations.   J. Mammalogy, **36**, 209–214 (1955).
18. GREEN, R. G. and EVANS, C. A.   Studies on a population cycle of snowshoe hares on the Lake Alexander Area. . . .   J. Wildlife Management, **4**, 220–238, 267–278, 347–358 (1940).
19. JACKSON, C. H. N.   The analysis of a tsetse-fly population. III.   Ann. Eugen., Camb. **14**, 91–108 (1948).
20. LESLIE, P. H.   The properties of a certain lag type of population growth and the influence of an external random factor on a number of such populations.   Physiol. Zoöl. **32**, 151–159 (1959).
21. LESLIE, P. H., CHITTY, D., and CHITTY, H.   The estimation of population parameters from data obtained by means of the capture–recapture method. III.   An example of the practical applications of the method.   Biometrika, **40**, 137–169 (1953).
22. LESLIE, P. H. and RANSON, R. M.   The mortality, fertility and rate of natural increase of the vole (*Microtus agrestis*) as observed in the laboratory.   J. Animal Ecol. **9**, 27–52 (1940).

23. LOCKIE, J. D.   The breeding habits and food of short-eared owls after a vole plague. Bird Study, **2**, 53–69 (1955).
24. MEDAWAR, P. B.   The uniquness of the individual.   Methuen and Co. Ltd., London. 1957.
25. NICHOLSON, A. J.   The balance of animal populations.   J. Animal Ecol. **2**, 132–178 (1933).
26. NICHOLSON, A. J.   An outline of the dynamics of animal populations.   Aust. J. Zool. **2**, 9–65 (1954).
27. SUMMERHAYES, V. S.   The effect of voles (*Microtus agrestis*) on vegetation.   J. Ecology, **29**, 14–48 (1941).
28. TINBERGEN, N.   The functions of territory.   Bird Study, **4**, 14–27 (1957).
29. WELLINGTON, W. G.   Individual differences as a factor in population dynamics: the development of a problem.   Can. J. Zool. **35**, 293–323 (1957).
30. WELLS, A. Q.   The murine type of tubercle bacillus (the vole acid-fast bacillus).   Special Rept. Ser. Med. Research Council, London, **259**, 1–42 (1946).
31. ZIMMERMANN, K.   Körpergrösse und Bestandsdichte bei Feldmaüsen (*Microtus arvalis*). Z. Säug. **20**, 114–118 (1955).

# EVOLUTION IN SEXUAL AND ASEXUAL POPULATIONS*

JAMES F. CROW AND MOTOO KIMURA

University of Wisconsin, Madison, Wisconsin, and National Institute
of Genetics, Mishima-shi, Shizuoka-ken, Japan

It has often been said that sexual reproduction is advantageous because of the enormous number of genotypes that can be produced by a recombination of a relatively small number of genes (for example, *Issues in Evolution*, p. 114–115). The number of potential combinations is indeed great, but the number produced in any single generation is limited by the population size, and gene combinations are broken up by recombination just as effectively as they are produced by it. Furthermore, for a given amount of variability, the efficiency of selection is greater in an asexual population than in one with free recombination since the rate is measured by the total genotypic variance rather than by just the additive component thereof.

On the other hand, unless new mutations occur, an asexual population has a selection limit determined by the best existing genotype, whereas directional selection in a sexual population can progress far beyond the initial extreme, as has been demonstrated by selection experiments. The purpose of this article is to compare sexual and asexual systems as to the rate at which favorable gene combinations can be incorporated into the population, considering the effect of gene interaction, mutation rate, population size, and magnitude of gene effect. Most of the material is not new, but the various ideas have not been brought together in this context and we have introduced some refinements.

## HISTORICAL

The question was first discussed from the viewpoint in which we are here interested by Fisher (1930) and Muller (1932). We shall follow mainly the argument given by Muller.

In an asexual population, two beneficial mutants can be incorporated into the population only if the second occurs in a descendant of the individual in which the first occurred. On the other hand, in a sexual population the various mutants can get into the same individual by recombination. Only if the mutation rate were so low or the population so small that each mutant became established before another favorable mutant occurred would the two systems be equivalent.

The situation is illustrated in figure 1, adapted from Muller's original drawings. The three mutants, A, B, and C are all beneficial. In the asexual

*Paper number 987 from the Division of Genetics, University of Wisconsin; also contribution number 534 from the National Institute of Genetics, Mishima-shi, Japan. This work was aided by grants from the National Institutes of Health (RG-8217 and RG-7666).

Reprinted by permission of The University of Chicago Press and the authors from *The American Naturalist* 99:439–450, 1965.

population when all three arise at approximately the same time only one can persist. In figure 1, A is better adapted than B or C (or perhaps luckier in happening to occur in an individual that for other reasons was more fit than those in which B and C arose) so that A is eventually incorporated. B is incorporated only after it occurs in an individual that already carries A, and C only in an individual that already carries both A and B. In the sexual system, on the other hand, all three mutants are incorporated approximately as fast as any one of them is in the asexual system.

The lower part of the figure shows a small population. Here the favorable mutants are so infrequent that one has time to be incorporated before another occurs. Thus there is no advantage to the sexual system.

In general, several favorable mutants arising at the same time can all be incorporated in a sexual system whereas only one can be without recombination. There is, of course, a high probability of random loss of even a favorable mutation in the first few generations after its occurrence. This problem has been solved by Fisher (1930), but since the result is essentially the same in an asexual and sexual system it is irrelevant to the present discussion.

Muller's verbal argument was made quantitative in later papers (1958, 1964). We have improved Muller's calculations slightly by taking into consideration the decelerating rate of increase in the frequency of a favorable mutant as it becomes common.

## MATHEMATICAL FORMULATION

Consider first a population without recombination. We ignore the large majority of mutants that are unfavorable, for these are eliminated and thus are not incorporated into the population. Our interest is only in mutants that are favorable.

Let $N$ = the population number

$U$ = the total rate of occurrence per individual per generation of favorable mutations at all loci

$g$ = the average number of generations between the occurrence of a favorable mutation and the occurrence of another favorable mutation in a descendant of the first

$x = 1/U$ = the number of individuals such that on the average one favorable mutation will occur

$s$ = the average selective advantage of a favorable mutant

Thus, $g$ is the number of generations required for the cumulative number of descendants of a mutant to equal $x$, this being a number of such size that on the average one mutant will have occurred. Letting $p_i$ be the proportion of individuals carrying the mutant gene in the $i^{th}$ generation, $g$ is given by

$$x = Np_1 + Np_2 + \ldots + Np_g \qquad (1)$$

the summation being continued until there have been enough generations, $g$, to make the total number of mutant individuals equal to $x$. We assume that

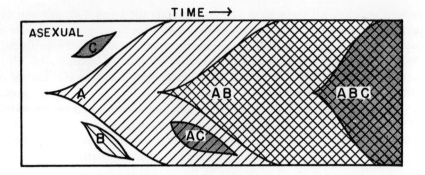

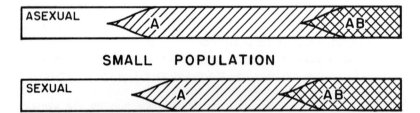

FIGURE 1. Evolution in sexual and asexual populations. The hatched and shaded areas show the increased number of mutant individuals following the occurrence of a favorable mutation. The abscissa is time. Modified from Muller (1932).

$s$ is small, and therefore that $p$ changes very slowly so that it is appropriate to replace addition by integration. This leads to

$$x = \int_0^g Np \, dt \qquad (2)$$

In the absence of recombination, $p$ follows the logistic curve

442                          THE AMERICAN NATURALIST

$$p = \frac{p_0}{p_0 + (1 - p_0)\,e^{-st}} \qquad (3)$$

where $p_0$ is the initial proportion of mutants, as first shown by Haldane (1924). If we start with a single mutant, $p_0 = 1/N$, and (3) becomes

$$p = \frac{1}{1 + (N - 1)\,e^{-st}} \qquad (4)$$

Substituting this for $p$ in (2) and integrating, we obtain

$$x = \frac{N}{s} \ln \frac{N - 1 + e^{sg}}{N}$$

or, rewriting and recalling that $x = 1/U$,

$$g = \frac{1}{s} \ln \left[ N(e^{s/UN} - 1) + 1 \right] \qquad (5)$$

In an asexual population one new mutant that will eventually be incorporated into the population arises every $g$ generations. On the other hand, if reproduction is sexual, all the mutants that occur during this interval can eventually be incorporated. The number of mutants that arise per generation is $NU$, or in $g$ generations, $NUg$. Thus the ratio of incorporated mutations in a sexual population to that in an asexual population is $NUg : 1$, or

$$\frac{NU}{s} \ln \left[ N(e^{s/UN} - 1) + 1 \right] \qquad (6)$$

The favorable genes need not be mutants that are occurring for the first time. They may, for example, be genes brought in by immigrants or previously harmful mutants that have become beneficial because of a changed environment and already exist in the population at low frequencies.

Some numerical results are shown in table 1. For example, if the selective advantage of a favorable mutation is 0.01 and the total rate of occur-

TABLE 1

The relative rate of incorporation of new mutations into the
population with and without recombination

| $\dfrac{U}{s}$ | $N$ | | | | | | |
|---|---|---|---|---|---|---|---|
| | $10^3$ | $10^4$ | $10^5$ | $10^6$ | $10^7$ | $10^8$ | $10^9$ |
| $10^{-7}$ | 1.0007 | 1.01 | 1.12 | 2.38 | 16.7 | 162 | $1.6 \times 10^3$ |
| $10^{-6}$ | 1.007 | 1.09 | 2.15 | 14.4 | 139 | $1.4 \times 10^3$ | $1.4 \times 10^4$ |
| $10^{-5}$ | 1.07 | 1.92 | 12.1 | 116 | $1.2 \times 10^3$ | $1.2 \times 10^4$ | $1.2 \times 10^5$ |
| $10^{-4}$ | 1.69 | 9.75 | 92.6 | 922 | $9.2 \times 10^3$ | $9.2 \times 10^4$ | $9.2 \times 10^5$ |
| $10^{-3}$ | 7.50 | 69.6 | 691 | $6.9 \times 10^3$ | $6.9 \times 10^4$ | $6.9 \times 10^5$ | $6.9 \times 10^6$ |
| $10^{-2}$ | 46.7 | 462 | $4.6 \times 10^3$ | $4.6 \times 10^4$ | $4.6 \times 10^5$ | $4.6 \times 10^6$ | $4.6 \times 10^7$ |
| $10^{-1}$ | 240 | $2.4 \times 10^3$ | $2.4 \times 10^4$ | $2.4 \times 10^5$ | $2.4 \times 10^6$ | $2.4 \times 10^7$ | $2.4 \times 10^8$ |

The ratio of the two rates is given in the body of the table. $N$ is the population number, $U$ is the total rate of occurrence of all favorable mutants, and $s$ is the average selective advantage of such mutants.

rence of such mutations is $10^{-8}$, the ratio $U/s$ is $10^{-6}$. As can be seen from the table, the advantage of recombination is negligible in a population of $10^3$, but the rate ratio is 2.15 in a population of $10^5$ and 1380 in a population of $10^8$. If the selective advantage is smaller, the advantage of a sexual system is greater. Likewise, with a higher mutation rate the advantage is greater.

We have discussed mutants that were beneficial at the time of their first occurrence. Similar considerations are involved when a previously deleterious mutant type is rendered beneficial, such as by a change in the environment.

We do not intend to imply that the very high values in the lower right part of the table are realistic. Doubtless other factors become limiting. But the table does show the general trend and emphasizes the enormous advantage of an evolutionary system with recombination.

It is likely that the probability of a mutant being favorable is greater when the effect of the mutant is small. Thus, with small $s$, $U$ tends to become larger. Since increasing $U$ and decreasing $s$ both have the effect of enhancing the advantage of recombination, the more that evolution proceeds by small micromutational steps, the greater the advantage of sexuality.

It is interesting that $U$ and $s$ enter the formula always in the form $U/s$, and never separately. This exact reciprocal dependence is understandable; for with slow selection the number of generations required for a given gene frequency change is inversely proportional to $s$ (Haldane, 1924). Thus a reduction in $s$ means that proportionately more mutations will occur during the time that one is being incorporated.

Table 1 also shows that the advantage of recombination increases with an increase in the population size. In fact, with large populations the advantage is nearly proportional to the population number.

To summarize: The advantage of a reproductive system that permits free recombination is greatest for the incorporation of mutant genes with individually small effects, occurring at relatively high rates, and in a large population.

## THE EFFECT OF GENE INTERACTION

So far we have been concerned only with mutant genes that are beneficial. We have also assumed that the combination of two mutant genes is more beneficial than either by itself; otherwise there would be no advantage of incorporating the second one.

The situation is quite different with some kinds of gene interaction. Where two or more mutants are individually harmful, but beneficial in combination, sexual reproduction may actually be disadvantageous.

The essential situation is clear with a haploid model, so we shall consider this simpler case. Suppose that the existing wild type in the population is genotype $ab$. The mutant types $Ab$ and $aB$ have fitnesses that, relative to $ab$, are reduced by the proportions $s_1$ and $s_2$. On the other hand, we assume that the double mutant has an enhanced fitness, greater than $ab$ by a proportion $t$. The quantities $s_1$, $s_2$, and $t$ are all taken to be positive.

Both single mutant types, $Ab$ and $aB$, will be found in low frequency in the population, their exact numbers being determined by the ratio of their rate of occurrence by mutation to their rate of elimination by selection. The double mutant, $AB$, will occasionally arise, but infrequently.

However, once such a double mutant does arise, its fate will be quite different in a population with and without recombination. Ignoring the question of chance elimination during the early generations (which, as we said earlier, is not significantly different in the two kinds of populations), an $AB$ double mutant in an asexual population will increase and eventually be incorporated at a rate determined by the value of $t$.

On the other hand, in a sexual population, an $AB$ individual will ordinarily mate with an $ab$ genotype, in which case the progeny will consist of all four genotypes in proportions depending on the amount of recombination. Only if the fitness of the $AB$ type is great enough to compensate for the loss of $AB$ types through recombination will this genotype increase. The relationships can be set forth as follows:

| Genotype | $ab$ | $Ab$ | $aB$ | $AB$ |
|---|---|---|---|---|
| Relative fitness, $w$ | 1 | $1 - s_1$ | $1 - s_2$ | $1 + t$ |
| Frequency | $(1 - x)(1 - y)$ | $x(1 - y)$ | $(1 - x)y$ | $xy$ |

$$\overline{w} = 1 - s_1 x(1 - y) - s_2(1 - x)y + txy$$

$$\frac{\partial w}{\partial x} = y(s_1 + s_2 + t) - s_1$$

$$\frac{\partial w}{\partial y} = x(s_1 + s_2 + t) - s_2$$

These relationships assume that the two loci change independently under the action of natural selection, which is not strictly true unless $(1 + t) = (1 - s_1)(1 - s_2)$; but the formulae are approximately correct for unlinked loci when $s_1$, $s_2$, and $t$ are small.

Gene $A$ will increase when $\partial \overline{w}/\partial x$ is positive and decrease when this is negative. Therefore there is an unstable equilibrium at $y = s_1/(s_1 + s_2 + t)$. Below this value of $y$, $x$ will decrease; above this value, $x$ will increase. The situation is symmetrical for $x$ and $y$ by interchanging $s_1$ and $s_2$. Thus there is no way for the frequency of the $AB$ type to increase unless it somehow gets past the equilibrium point. This problem was discussed extensively by Haldane (1931).

The formulae are identical in a diploid population with complete dominance, on replacement of $x$ by $p^2$ and $y$ by $q^2$, where $p$ and $q$ are the frequencies of the recessive alleles at the two loci (see Wright, 1959, p. 442).

The situation is the familiar bottleneck frequently discussed by Wright (1931 and later). In his metaphor, the population is at one adaptive peak composed mainly of $ab$ genotypes and there is no way for it to go to the higher peak composed mainly of *AB* genotypes without passing through a valley where *Ab* and *aB* types predominate.

There are several ways in which a sexual population might conceivably solve this problem. Some populations have several generations of asexual reproduction intervening between sexual generations. Another possibility would be strong assortative mating among the *AB* types; but the *a priori* probability of the genes that gave the increased fitness also producing the right type of mating behavior seems small indeed. Another possibility is random drift across the adaptive valley because of variable conditions or small effective population number, but this, as Wright (1931 and later) has emphasized, would lead to a considerable lowering of fitness (see also Kimura, Maruyama, and Crow, 1963). Furthermore, Kimura (unpublished) has shown that the probability of joint fixation of two genes such as are being discussed here is very small, even in small populations. For example, in a population of effective size $N = 1000$, the single mutants with 1 per cent selective disadvantage and the double mutant with 5 per cent advantage, the probability of joint fixation is about $2.5 \, p_0 q_0 \times 10^{-6}$, where $p_0$ and $q_0$ are the initial frequencies of the single mutants. The corresponding probability for completely neutral genes is $p_0 q_0$. Note that $p_0 q_0$ is a very small quantity. For individually deleterious but collectively advantageous mutant genes to have a reasonably high probability of joint fixation, the population must be so small that the inbreeding effect causes a serious effect on the viability.

In general, sexual reproduction can be a distinct disadvantage if evolution progresses mainly by putting together groups of individually deleterious, but collectively beneficial mutations. It seems to us that if this type of gene action were the limiting factor in evolution at the time sexual reproduction first evolved, sexual recombination might never have been "invented."

### THE EFFECT OF LINKAGE

Two closely linked genes in a sexual organism can be quite similar to genes in an asexual organism as far as their relations to each other are concerned, for they may stay together for a great length of time. If $r$ is the recombination frequency between two linked genes, they will stay together $1/r$ generations on the average before being separated by crossing over. This can easily be seen by noting that the probability that they will remain together $g$ generations and separate in the next is $(1 - r)^g r$. Then the average number of generations during which they remain together is

$$\bar{g} = r + 2(1 - r)r + 3(1 - r)^2 r + 4(1 - r)^3 r + \ldots$$

$$= r(1 + 2x + 3x^2 + 4x^3 + \ldots)$$

where $x = 1 - r$. But $1 + 2x + 3x^2 + \ldots$ is the derivative of $1 + x + x^2 + x^3 + \ldots = 1/(1 - x)$. Therefore

$$\bar{g} = r \frac{d}{dx} \left( \frac{1}{1 - x} \right) = \frac{1}{r}$$

446                        THE AMERICAN NATURALIST

Thus, two genes linked together with a recombination value of 0.1 per cent would remain linked on the average for 1000 generations before separating.

Consider again the earlier model where the four haploid genotypes, $ab$, $Ab$, $aB$, and $AB$ have fitnesses in the ratio $1 : 1 - s_1 : 1 - s_2 : 1 + t$, and assume that the amount of recombination between the loci is $r$. If the rare $AB$ individual mates with an $ab$ type, which will usually be the case, the proportion of $AB$ progeny will be reduced by a fraction $r$ because of recombination. However, the $AB$ type will increase from these matings if the extra fitness of the $AB$ type is enough to more than compensate for this; that is, if $(1 + t)(1 - r) > 1$, or $t > r/(1 - r)$.

The conditions for increase of $AB$ genotypes in general are a little less stringent because some $AB$ matings are with $AB$, $aB$, or $Ab$ types and in these there is no effect of crossing over. Furthermore, $AB$ types are being added by recombination from $Ab \times aB$ matings. Finally, $\bar{w}$, the average fitness is not 1, but slightly less. However, these do not change the direction of the inequality, so we can still say that a sufficient condition for the double mutant type to increase is $t > r/(1 - r)$. This is also the condition for increase in diploids, where $t$ is now the advantage of the double heterozygote over the prevailing type (Bodmer and Parsons, 1962, p. 73).

In Wright's metaphor, the effect of linkage is to raise the valley between the two adaptive peaks and with extremely close linkage to provide a direct bridge.

For closely linked genes where $r$ is small, the $AB$ type will increase and ultimately become fixed if $t > r$. Thus, the closer the linkage, the greater the tendency to build up coadapted complexes—provided, of course, that such closely linked, mutually beneficial mutants occur. The extreme example is the high degree of functional interdependence within a cistron.

### COADAPTATION

We have seen that asexual organisms are in a better position than sexual species to build up coadapted complexes, except under conditions of close linkage. In an asexual population the mutants accumulate in a certain sequence; first we have mutant $A$, then $AB$, then $ABC$, and so on. In this case the effect of $B$ in the absence of $A$ is irrelevant; it may be beneficial or harmful, or simply be a modifier that is neutral in the absence of $A$. Of all the mutants that arise in the species after $A$ has been incorporated, the one that is most likely to persist is the one that in the presence of $A$ gives the greatest fitness. Therefore, there will be a tendency for combinations to be mutually coadapted, and these genes may be less beneficial or even harmful in other combinations (Cavalli and Maccacaro, 1952). That is to say, they may well be what Mayr has called "narrow specialists."

In a sexual population, on the other hand, genes $A$ and $B$ are likely to be incorporated only if they are beneficial both individually and in combination. The type of gene that is most efficiently selected in a sexual population is one that is beneficial in combination with a large number of genes. We can only guess about the a priori distribution of gene interactions; but it is clear that in a population with free recombination the "good mixers" (that is, those having a large additive component) will be most efficiently selected.

The best opportunity to test these possibilities would be populations exposed to an entirely new environment. Drug resistance in bacteria and insecticide resistance in insects offer such a possibility. Chloramphenicol resistance in *Escherichia coli* is polygenic and has been analyzed by Cavalli and Maccacaro (1952). During the selection for resistance the reproduction was asexual, though recombination was used later for analyzing the genetic basis of the resistance. Recombinants between resistant and susceptible strains were skewed in the direction of greater susceptibility, as were crosses between different resistant strains. The results, therefore, suggest considerable coadaptation with complementary action of the genes accumulated during the selection process.

DDT resistance in Drosophila is also polygenic and has been analyzed genetically (Crow, 1957; King and Somme, 1958). Analysis of variance of the contribution of various chromosomes to the resistance showed an almost complete additivity, as would be expected in a sexual species according to the view we have been discussing. Thus, at least in these two cases, there is good agreement with what our theoretical speculations would predict.

We should emphasize that the genetic variability in sexual populations that have had a long history of selection for the traits under consideration may not have a large additive component. The genes that act additively may already have been incorporated into the population so that those that remain in unfixed condition are the ones that are not responsive to selection; that is, they are genes with complex interactions. Thus it is not surprising if, in a stable natural environment or in an artificial population where selection has been practiced for a long time, the nonadditive components of variance predominate.

### HAPLOIDY VERSUS DIPLOIDY

The evolutionary advantages of recombination can be obtained in haploid as well as diploid species. Yet diploidy is the rule in a great many complex organisms and there must have been a regular trend of evolution from haploidy to diploidy.

At first glance it would appear that there is an obvious advantage of diploidy in that dominant alleles from one haploid set can prevent the deleterious effects of harmful recessive alleles in the other. However, when equilibrium is reached the situation is roughly the same in a diploid as in a haploid. In a haploid species the mutation load will equal the total mutation rate when equilibrium is reached. With diploidy the load will be somewhere between this value and twice this value, depending on the level of dominance. With any substantial heterozygous effect of deleterious recessive genes, the mutation load is nearly twice the mutation rate (Haldane, 1937; Kimura, 1961). So the effect of diploidy is generally to double the mutation load by doubling the number of genes. From this standpoint diploidy certainly offers no advantages, only disadvantages.

However, when the population has reached equilibrium as a haploid, a change to diploidy offers an immediate advantage (Muller, 1932). To be sure, when the population reaches a new diploid equilibrium the advantage is lost; but by then there is no turning back, for a return to haploidy would greatly increase the load by uncovering deleterious recessives. Thus, it is easy to see how diploidy might evolve from haploidy, even if the population did not gain any permanent benefit therefrom.

On the other hand, there are some other possible advantages of diploidy, of which we shall mention two. One that has frequently been suggested is the possibility of overdominance. To the extent that the heterozygote is fitter than either homozygote at some loci there is an advantage of diploidy, provided the average fitness of the diploid population is enough greater than the haploid to compensate for the greater mutation load.

A second possible advantage of diploidy is the protection it affords against the effects of somatic mutation, a possibility that also occurred independently to Muller. The zygote in a diploid species or the post-meiotic cell from which the organism develops in a haploid species might have approximately the same fitness at equilibrium, but the effects of somatic mutation would be quite different. If the soma were large and complicated, as in higher plants and especially animals, a diploid soma might provide a significant protection against the effects of recessive mutations in critical organs.

## THE EVOLUTION OF SEXUALITY

The development of sexual reproduction confers no immediate advantage on the individual in which this occurs. In fact, the result is far more likely to be deleterious. The benefit is only to the descendants, perhaps quite remote, and to the population as a whole. Thus, it seems likely that the selective mechanism by which recombination was established was intergroup selection. Fisher (1930) goes so far as to suggest that sexuality may be the only character that evolved for species rather than for individual advantage.

On the other hand, despite the great evolutionary advantages of sexual reproduction, there are immediate advantages in a return to asexual reproduction. An advantageous type whose recombinant progeny were disadvantageous would have an advantage for its immediate descendants by developing an asexual mode of reproduction, other things being equal. In diploids there is the additional advantage of fixing heterotic combinations.

This all accords with the conventional belief that sexuality developed very early in the evolution of living forms and is therefore found in all major groups; but that numerous independent retrogressions to vegetative reproduction continue to occur, conferring an immediate advantage but a long time evolutionary disadvantage.

144

SUMMARY

In an asexual population two favorable mutants can be incorporated into the population only if one occurs in a descendant of the individual in which the other occurred. In a sexual population both mutants can be incorporated through recombination. A mathematical formulation is given of the relative rates of incorporation of the new mutations with and without recombination. Recombination is of the greatest advantage when the double mutant is more advantageous than either single mutant, when the mutant effects are small, when mutations occur with high frequency, and when the population is large.

On the other hand, for the incorporation of individually deleterious but collectively beneficial mutations, recombination can be disadvantageous. Close linkage has effects similar to those of asexual reproduction. Experimental data on DDT resistance in Drosophila and chloramphenicol resistance in bacteria are cited showing greater development of coadaptation in an asexual system.

The evolution of diploidy from haploidy confers an immediate reduction in the mutation load by concealment of deleterious recessives, but this advantage is lost once a new equilibrium is reached. Thus the development of diploidy may be because of an immediate advantage rather than because of any permanent benefit. On the other hand, there are other possible advantages of diploidy, such as heterosis and protection from somatic mutations.

LITERATURE CITED

Bodmer, W. F., and P. A. Parsons, 1962, Linkage and recombination in evolution. Adv. in Genet. 11: 1–100.

Cavalli, L. L., and G. A. Maccacaro, 1952, Polygenic inheritance of drug-resistance in the Bacterium *Escherichia coli.* Heredity 6: 311–331.

Crow, J. F., 1957, Genetics of insecticide resistance to chemicals. Ann. Rev. Entomol. 2: 227–246.

Fisher, R. A., 1930, The Genetical Theory of Natural Selection. The Clarendon Press, Oxford. 2nd ed., 1958. Dover Pub., New York.

Haldane, J. B. S., 1924, The mathematical theory of natural and artificial selection. Part I. Trans. Cambridge Phil. Soc. 23: 19–41.

1931, A mathematical theory of natural selection. Part VIII. Metastable populations. Proc. Cambridge Phil. Soc. 27: 137–142.

1937, The effect of variation on fitness. Amer. Natur. 71: 337–349.

Kimura, M., 1961, Some calculations on the mutational load. Jap. J. Genet. 36 (Suppl.): 179–190.

Kimura, M., T. Maruyama, and J. F. Crow, 1963, The mutation load in small populations. Genetics 48: 1303–1312.

King, J. C., and L. Somme, 1958, Chromosomal analysis of the genetic factors for resistance to DDT in two resistant lines of *Drosophila melanogaster.* Genetics 43: 577–593.

Muller, H. J., 1932, Some genetic aspects of sex. Amer. Natur. 8: 118–138.

1958, Evolution by mutation. Bull. Amer. Math. Soc. 64: 137–160.

450                    THE AMERICAN NATURALIST

    1964, The relation of recombination to mutational advance.  Mutation
        Res. 1: 2–9.
Tax, Sol, and C. Callender (eds.), 1959, Issues in Evolution.     Vol. 3 of
        Evolution after Darwin.   University of Chicago Press.
Wright, S., 1931, Evolution in mendelian populations.  Genetics 16: 97–159.
    1959, Physiological genetics, ecology of populations, and natural se-
        lection.   Perspect. Biol. Med. 3: 107–151.

# EVOLUTION IN SEXUAL AND ASEXUAL POPULATIONS

## J. MAYNARD SMITH

School of Biological Sciences, University of Sussex, Falmer, Brighton, England

### INTRODUCTION

It was argued by Fisher (1930) that sexual reproduction is the only characteristic of living organisms which owes its presence to the fact that it favors the survival of groups rather than of individuals. It is therefore important to understand precisely what are the advantages conferred on a group by sexual reproduction.

The orthodox answer to this question (e.g., Fisher, 1930; Muller, 1932) is that it accelerates adaptation to a changing environment because it makes it possible to combine in a single descendant mutations originally occurring in distinct individuals. This argument has recently been made quantitative by Crow and Kimura (1965). They conclude that sexual reproduction can accelerate evolution by many orders of magnitude and that its effects are greatest when the evolving population is large, the frequency of beneficial mutations high, and the selective advantages small.

I believe these conclusions to be wrong. My reasons can most easily be illustrated by a counterexample, in which according to the orthodox view sexual reproduction ought to be an advantage, but in which in fact it makes no difference. A comparison of this example with the treatment of Crow and Kimura shows that different assumptions have been made. The validity of the alternative assumptions, and the circumstances in which sexual reproduction is an advantage, are then discussed.

### A COUNTEREXAMPLE

The simplest situation in which sexual reproduction should, according to the orthodox view, acelerate evolution is that in which selection favors two alleles at different loci, both initially rare. Consider therefore the evolution of a haploid population varying at two loci. Initially the population inhabits an environment in which alleles $a$ and $b$ confer the greatest fitness, and are therefore the common alleles at their respective loci. The environment then changes, so that alleles $A$ and $B$ confer the greatest fitness. How far will sexual reproduction accelerate evolution from genotype $ab$ to genotype $AB$?

We need first to find the equilibrium frequencies of the four genotypes before the change of environment. Let these frequencies, and the fitnesses of the four genotypes, be

Reprinted by permission of The University of Chicago Press and the author from *The American Naturalist* 102:469–473, 1968. Copyright 1968 by the University of Chicago.

| Genotype | $ab$ | $Ab$ | $aB$ | $AB$ |
|---|---|---|---|---|
| Fitness | 1 | $1 - H$ | $1 - h$ | $(1 - H)(1 - h)$ |
| Equilibrium frequency | $P_{ab}$ | $P_{Ab}$ | $P_{aB}$ | $P_{AB}$ |

Let the mutation rate from $a$ to $A$ be $\mu_A$, and from $b$ to $B$ be $\mu_B$. Then after selection and mutation have acted, the relative proportions of the four genotypes are:

$$ab : P_{ab}(1 - \mu_A)(1 - \mu_B);$$

$$Ab : [P_{ab}\mu_A(1 - \mu_B) + P_{Ab}(1 - \mu_B)](1 - H);$$

$$aB : [P_{ab}\mu_B(1 - \mu_A) + P_{aB}(1 - \mu_A)](1 - h);$$

$$AB : [P_{ab}\mu_A\mu_B + P_{Ab}\mu_B + P_{aB}\mu_A + P_{AB}](1 - H)(1 - h).$$

Since at equilibrium these proportions do not change, $P_{Ab}/P_{ab}$ is constant from generation to generation, and hence:

$$P_{Ab}(1 - \mu_A)(1 - \mu_B) = [P_{ab}\mu_A(1 - \mu_B) + P_{Ab}(1 - \mu_B)](1 - H).$$

If we assume that $H$ and $h$ are small, but are large compared to the mutation rates, this reduces to

and similarly

and

$$\left. \begin{aligned} P_{Ab} &= P_{ab}\mu_A/H \\ P_{aB} &= P_{ab}\mu_B/h \\ P_{AB} &= P_{ab}\mu_A\mu_B/Hh. \end{aligned} \right\} \tag{1}$$

From (1) it follows that

$$P_{ab} P_{AB} = P_{Ab} P_{aB}. \tag{2}$$

If (2) is to be satisfied, and if the frequencies of genes $A$ and $B$ are $p_A$ and $p_B$, respectively, it can be shown that the frequencies of the genotypes $ab$, $Ab$, $aB$ and $AB$ are $(1 - p_A)(1 - p_B)$; $p_A(1 - p_B)$; $(1 - p_A)p_B$; and $p_A p_B$, respectively. These frequencies arise as a result of recurrent mutation and selection but are the same as would be produced by a single generation of sexual reproduction.

We will now consider the changes in an asexual species after the environment has changed. Let the fitnesses be:

| Genotype | $ab$ | $Ab$ | $aB$ | $AB$ |
|---|---|---|---|---|
| Fitness | 1 | $(1 + K)$ | $(1 + k)$ | $(1 + K)(1 + k)$ |

Let $p_{ab}$, $p'_{ab}$ be the frequencies of $ab$ in two successive generations, and similarily for the other genotypes. If the mutation rates are small compared to $K$ and $k$, then:

$$\left.\begin{aligned}
p'_{ab} &= p_{ab}/T \\
p'_{Ab} &= p_{Ab}(1 + K)/T \\
p'_{aB} &= p_{aB}(1 + k)/T \\
p'_{AB} &= p_{AB}(1 + K)(1 + k)/T.
\end{aligned}\right\} \tag{3}$$

Where $T = 1 + Kp_{Ab} + kp_{aB} + (K + k + Kk)p_{AB}$. From (3), $p'_{Ab}p'_{aB} = p_{Ab}p_{aB}(1 + K)(1 + k)/T$, and $p'_{ab}p'_{AB} = p_{ab}p_{AB}(1 + K)(1 + k)/T$. Hence, if $p_{Ab}p_{aB} = p_{ab}p_{AB}$, then

$$p'_{Ab}p'_{aB} = p'_{ab}p'_{AB}. \tag{4}$$

But it has already been shown (equation (2)) that this independence relationship is satisfied initially, and hence from (4) it will be satisfied throughout the evolution from $ab$ to $AB$.

It is now apparent that sexual reproduction would not alter the rate of evolution, since all that sexual reproduction can do is to restore this independence relationship.

### THE REASON FOR THE DISCREPANCY

Why is it that Crow and Kimura conclude that sexual reproduction can accelerate evolution, whereas in this counterexample discussed it makes no difference? The essential difference between their assumption and mine is that they regard mutation as a unique event, whereas I have treated it as a recurrent event. Before discussing the merits of these alternative assumptions it will be helpful to see how the uniqueness assumption affects their conclusions.

In their notation

$N =$ the population number.

$U =$ the total rate of occurrence per individual per generation of favorable mutations at all loci.

$g =$ the average number of generations between the occurrence of a favorable mutation and the occurrence of another favorable mutation in a descendant of the first.

$x = 1/U =$ the number of individuals such that on the average one favorable mutation will occur.

According to their argument, in an asexual population one new favorable mutation will be incorporated every $g$ generations. In a sexual population, $NUg$ favorable mutations will occur in that time, and all will be incorporated. Hence the relative rates of evolution will be as $NUg:1$.

The statement that $NUg$ favorable mutations will be incorporated in $g$ generations of a sexual species assumes that all these mutations are different. Clearly if particular mutations recur, the conclusion could be wrong by many orders of magnitude. More precisely, it is out by a factor equal to the number of times a particular mutation recurs in $g$ generation in a population of $N$ individuals.

The uniqueness assumption also leads to an underestimate of the rate of evolution of an asexual species. Thus it is assumed that the first individual in a population to undergo a favorable mutation is the *only* individual to leave any descendants many generations later, as is the first of his descendants to undergo a second favorable mutation, and so on. But if, for example, favorable mutations $a \to A$, $b \to B$, and $c \to C$ are all recurrent events, then any $abc$ individual undergoing any of these mutations has a good chance of leaving $ABC$ descendants many generations later.

Notice that the discrepancy introduced by assuming mutations to be unique is greatest when $NUg$ is greatest—that is, when the population is large, the rate of favorable mutations high, and the selective advantages small (and hence $g$ large). These are precisely the conditions listed by Crow and Kimura as those in which sexual reproduction is most advantageous. Thus their conclusions depend critically on their assumption that mutations are unique events.

It is difficult to see what justification there could be for making this assumption. Presumably most favorable mutations are base substitutions. If so, a particular mutation would have a frequency of $10^{-8}$ to $10^{-9}$, in contrast to the frequency of $10^{-5}$ to $10^{-6}$ for the frequency of all harmful mutations in a particular cistron. A frequency of $10^{-8}$ does not make an event unique, particularly when discussing the evolution of sex, which originated among micro-organisms: there can be $10^9$ bacteria in a test tube.

The only mutations which can reasonably be thought of as unique events are those requiring two almost simultaneous events—that is, structural rearrangements. The frequency $U$ of favorable structural rearrangements is likely to be so low as to wipe out the predicted advantage of sexual reproduction.

### THE ADVANTAGES OF SEX

I am satisfied that the treatment of the problem given by Crow and Kimura is misleading. It does not follow that the "counterexample" I have considered is an adequate model either. What is needed is a general treatment similar to that given by Crow and Kimura, but omitting the uniqueness assumption. Pending such a treatment, it is interesting to see what conclusions emerge if we regard the counterexample as essentially correct.

The counterexample considers evolution at two loci, from $ab \to AB$. It is shown that if initially $P_{ab} P_{AB} = P_{Ab} P_{aB}$, then sexual reproduction confers no advantage. It is also shown that if the genetic variance in the initial population was generated by recurrent mutation. then this equation will be satisfied.

Suppose, however, there were initially two environments, in one of which $Ab$ was the fittest (and therefore commonest) genotype, and in the other $aB$ was the fittest genotype. Suppose now that a third environment becomes available for colonization from the two existing ones and that in this new environment $AB$ is the fittest genotype. Then initially $P_{Ab} P_{aB} \gg P_{ab} P_{AB}$, and the increase in frequency of $AB$ will be very much greater if reproduction is sexual.

In this simple case, then, if the genetic variance of a population has been generated by mutation in a uniform environment, sexual reproduction does not accelerate evolution when the environment changes. But if the genetic variance has been generated by selection favoring different genotypes in different environments, then sexual reproduction will accelerate adaptation to a new environment.

In other words, sexual processes are an advantage because they make it possible to bring together in one individual, not merely mutations which have occurred in different ancestors (because the same result can be achieved equally well by recurrent mutation), but different regions of DNA which have been programmed by natural selection in different ancestral populations in different environments.

## SUMMARY

In a simple model case, the rates of evolution in an asexual and a sexual haploid population are compared. It is shown that, if the genetic variance of the population is generated by mutation in a uniform environment, sexual reproduction confers no advantage. But if the genetic variance has arisen because selection has favored different genotypes in different environments, then sexual reproduction will accelerate adaptation to a new environment.

These conclusions differ sharply from those reached by Crow and Kimura (1965). The difference arises because those authors treated mutations as unique events, whereas they are here treated as recurrent events.

LITERATURE CITED

Crow, J. F., and M. Kimura. 1965. Evolution in sexual and asexual populations. Amer. Natur. 99:439–450.
Fisher, R. A. 1930. The genetical theory of natural selection. Clarendon, New York.
Muller, H. J. Some genetic aspects of sex. Amer. Natur. 8:118–138.

# A RÉSUMÉ OF INVESTIGATIONS ON THE EVOLUTION OF MELANISM IN THE LEPIDOPTERA

## By H. B. D. KETTLEWELL

### Genetic Laboratories, Zoology Department, University of Oxford

Apart from flight, the wings in the Lepidoptera are used for developing various pattern and colour devices enabling them to pass the daytime protected from predators.

In the cryptic species, complicated patterns have been built up suitable for concealment on lichened tree trunks, boughs, rocks, reeds or posts, and the phenomenon of 'industrial melanism' is found among this group only. Of the 780 species of Macro-lepidoptera which occur in the British Isles, about seventy are in the process of replacing their populations with dark or black individuals. In the majority of cases the black mutant is inherited as a simple Mendelian dominant. The position of the melanics occurring in other groups, however, is completely different. In those insects which gain protection from mechanisms other than crypsis (warning, threat and flash coloration), or even in those cryptic moths which benefit from resembling dead leaves, the melanics are rare, recessive, sub-lethal and are probably maintained by recurrent mutation. A third group of melanics can be referred to as 'geographic melanics', and they are confined to the Highlands of Scotland, the west coast of Great Britain and Ireland. Their inheritance in the few cases known is dominant (complete or incomplete) or in others multi-factorial; so far never recessive. It will be noted that these areas are comprised of primeval forest, 'unspoilt' countryside, or environments little affected by civilization. In recent years we have been attempting to analyze the relative advantages and disadvantages of the melanics and their light forms and, to date, these studies have been confined to investigations on the so-called industrial melanics. These have, for the most part, been conducted on *Biston betularia* L., the Peppered Moth (Selidosemidae), and one of its melanics *carbonaria* Jordan; its other melanic, *insularia* Th.-Mieg, is complicated and probably determined by a series of alleles and is, except for population frequencies, omitted from this paper.

Reprinted by permission of the Royal Society of London and the author from Proceedings of the Royal Society (London), B. 145:297–303, 1956.

298      H. B. D. Kettlewell (Discussion Meeting)

TABLE 1(*a*). RELEASE EXPERIMENT FIGURES FOR *BISTON BETULARIA*
(MALES ONLY) RUBERY NEAR BIRMINGHAM, 1953

The letters *C*, *T* and *I* stand for *carbonaria*, *typical* and *insularia* respectively throughout
this paper.

| date (1953) | releases | | | | catches | | | | recaptures | | | |
|---|---|---|---|---|---|---|---|---|---|---|---|---|
| | *C* | *T* | *I* | totals | *C* | *T* | *I* | totals | *C* | *T* | *I* | totals |
| 25. vi. | 10 | 12 | 10 | 32 | 8 | 0 | 1 | 9 | — | — | — | — |
| 26. vi. | 0 | 0 | 0 | 0 | 127 | 15 | 7 | 149 | 3 | 1 | 1 | 5 |
| 27. vi. | 33 | 11 | 15 | 59 | 34 | 5 | 1 | 40 | 1 | 0 | 1 | 2 |
| 28. vi. | 37 | 21 | 5 | 63 | 23 | 3 | 3 | 29 | 2 | 0 | 2 | 4 |
| 29. vi. | 0 | 0 | 0 | 0 | 55 | 10 | 1 | 66 | 5 | 4 | 0 | 9 |
| 30. vi. | 68 | 26 | 8 | 102 | 37 | 3 | 2 | 42 | 1 | 0 | 1 | 2 |
| 1. vii. | 90 | 21 | 3 | 114 | 76 | 9 | 2 | 87 | 19 | 2 | 2 | 23 |
| 2. vii. | 74 | 21 | 3 | 98 | 75 | 13 | 4 | 92 | 28 | 6 | 0 | 34 |
| 3. vii. | 68 | 15 | 0 | 83 | 77 | 11 | 10 | 98 | 25 | 3 | 1 | 29 |
| 4. vii | 67 | 10 | 2 | 79 | 66 | 9 | 2 | 77 | 23 | 2 | 0 | 25 |
| 5. vii | 0 | 0 | 0 | 0 | 73 | 3 | 5 | 81 | 16 | 0 | 0 | 16 |
| totals | 447 | 137 | 46 | 630 | 651 | 81 | 38 | 770 | 123 | 18 | 8 | 149 |

TABLE 2(*a*). RELEASE EXPERIMENT FIGURES FOR *BISTON BETULARIA*
(MALES ONLY) DEAN END, DORSET, 1953

| date (1953) | releases | | | | catches | | | | recaptures | | | |
|---|---|---|---|---|---|---|---|---|---|---|---|---|
| | *C* | *T* | *I* | totals | *C* | *T* | *I* | totals | *C* | *T* | *I* | totals |
| 13. vi. | 37 | 38 | 9 | 84 | — | — | — | — | — | — | — | — |
| 14. vi. | 8 | 17 | 2 | 27 | 4 | 17 | 2 | 23 | 4 | 1 | 1 | 6 |
| 15. vi. | 8 | 25 | 1 | 34 | 2 | 27 | 5 | 34 | 2 | 9 | 3 | 14 |
| 16. vi. | 22 | 40 | 0 | 62 | 1 | 34 | 2 | 37 | 0 | 0 | 0 | 0 |
| 17. vi. | 0 | 0 | 0 | 0 | 7 | 58 | 3 | 68 | 7 | 7 | 0 | 14 |
| 18. vi. | 42 | 65 | 3 | 110 | 0 | 30 | 1 | 31 | 0 | 1 | 0 | 1 |
| 19. vi. | 39 | 72 | 0 | 111 | 2 | 26 | 1 | 29 | 2 | 6 | 0 | 8 |
| 20. vi. | 24 | 57 | 0 | 81 | 1 | 44 | 2 | 47 | 1 | 3 | 0 | 4 |
| 21. vi. | 42 | 29 | 0 | 71 | 1 | 13 | 2 | 16 | 1 | 4 | 0 | 5 |
| 22. vi. | 0 | 0 | 0 | 0 | 5 | 13 | 1 | 19 | 5 | 4 | 0 | 9 |
| 23. vi. | 0 | 0 | 0 | 0 | no releases | | | | no captures | | | |
| 24. vi. | 0 | 0 | 0 | 0 | no releases | | | | no captures | | | |
| 25. vi. | 82 | 43 | 0 | 125 | 1 | 11 | 0 | 12 | 0 | 0 | 0 | 0 |
| 26. vi. | 0 | 0 | 0 | 0 | 3 | 8 | 1 | 12 | 2 | 2 | 0 | 4 |
| 27. vi. | 51 | 28 | 0 | 79 | 0 | 8 | 0 | 8 | 0 | 0 | 0 | 0 |
| 28. vi. | 22 | 22 | 0 | 44 | 1 | 20 | 0 | 21 | 1 | 5 | 0 | 6 |
| 29. vi. | 17 | 18 | 0 | 35 | 0 | 14 | 0 | 14 | 0 | 5 | 0 | 5 |
| 30. vi. | 24 | 11 | 0 | 35 | 4 | 11 | 1 | 16 | 3 | 6 | 0 | 9 |
| 1. vii. | 0 | 0 | 0 | 0 | 2 | 9 | 0 | 11 | 2 | 2 | 0 | 4 |
| 2. vii. | 0 | 0 | 0 | 0 | 0 | 7 | 0 | 7 | 0 | 0 | 0 | 0 |
| 3. vii. | 0 | 0 | 0 | 0 | 0 | 0 | 0 | 0 | 0 | 0 | 0 | 0 |
| 4. vii. | 55 | 31 | 0 | 86 | 0 | 0 | 0 | 0 | 0 | 7 | 0 | 7 |
| 5. vii. | 0 | 0 | 0 | 0 | 0 | 9 | 0 | 9 | 0 | 7 | 0 | 7 |
| totals | 473 | 496 | 15 | 984 | 34 | 359 | 21 | 414 | 30 | 62 | 4 | 96 |

The life history of *B. betularia* is as follows: the ova are laid from May to August and the larvae feed from May to October. The species overwinters as a pupa, the imago hatching from May to August. The eggs are laid in masses or 'cakes' in crevices in bark. Dispersal takes place immediately after hatching, the young larvae being airborne on a long thread (Kettlewell 1955 *a*). They feed on most deciduous trees. The female moths rarely come to light, but the males do so freely and they assemble readily to newly hatched females from 9 p.m. (G.M.T.) to dawn. For these reasons the males only are used for mark-release experiments. Investigations have been, and are being, carried out on the following special problems involved:

### RELATIVE CRYPTIC ADVANTAGES OF THE BLACK AND THE LIGHT FORMS

Aviary experiments were carried out using a pair of great tits (*Parus major* L.) at the Madingley Research Station, Cambridge (Kettlewell 1955 *b*). The following points were shown:

(1) The birds ate both forms of the Peppered Moth.

(2) They did this selectively according to the cryptic advantage of the insects and in the order of their conspicuousness as previously scored by us.

(3) The birds rapidly became conditioned to looking for this species and, to overcome this, other species of moths had to be released at the same time.

These aviary experiments were sufficiently encouraging to demand a large-scale mark-release in nature. Accordingly, in the summer of 1953 this was undertaken near the industrial centre of Birmingham where 85 % of the *betularia* population is of the *carbonaria* form. A total of 630 *betularia* were marked and released on to a sample of the only available trunks and boughs. Of these, 447 were *carbonaria*, 137 *typical* and 46 *insularia*. Each was scored for its cryptic efficiency. In this area, it appeared to man that the light form (= the *typical*) was five times more conspicuous than *carbonaria*. Table 1(*a*) shows detailed figures for captures, releases and subsequent recaptures, taken within 24 h of being released. More than twice as many *carbonaria* were recovered as *typicals*. Furthermore, two species of birds (hedge sparrow, *Prunella modularis* L., and robin, *Erithacus rubecula* L.)

| TABLE 1(*b*) | | | | | TABLE 2(*b*) | | | |
|---|---|---|---|---|---|---|---|---|
| | catches | | | | | catches | | |
| | *C* | *T* | *I* | totals | | *C* | *T* | *I* | totals |
| | Birmingham | | | | | Dean End | | | |
| wild population | **528** | **63** | **30** | **621** | (4) | **297** | **17** | **314** |
| percentage phenotype | **85·03** | **10·14** | **4·83** | — | (possible escapes) | **94·6** | **5·4** | — |
| release after 1 day of self-determination | 25 | 2 | 2 | — | 2 | 4 | 1 | — |
| percentage phenotype | 5·72 | 1·48 | 4·34 | — | — | — | — | — |
| percentage return of releases | **27·5** | **13·0** | **17·4** | — | **6·34** | **12·50** | **(26·67)** | — |

## 300     H. B. D. Kettlewell (Discussion Meeting)

were seen to take and eat our releases, and they did this on the majority of occasions in order of conspicuousness as previously scored by me. It was possible to exclude factors other than bird predation as being responsible for the differential figures of the recaptures (Kettlewell 1955 b).

A similar experiment was undertaken in the summer of 1955 in Dean End, a heavily lichened and pollution-free wood in Dorset, where the *carbonaria* form, if it exists, is under 1 % of the population. Of 984 *betularia* released, 496 were *typical* and 473 *carbonaria* (*insularia* 15). Of the *typicals* 12·5 % were retrapped, but only 6·34 % of the *carbonaria*. Fewer individuals were captured here and, assuming equally efficient collecting techniques to those used in the Birmingham experiments, it would appear that table 2 (*a*) indicates that the pitch of predation was higher than in the Birmingham experiments. In table 3 are given the

TABLE 3. BIRMINGHAM RECAPTURES

| date | observed | | | | expected | | |
|---|---|---|---|---|---|---|---|
| | C | T | I | total | C | T | I |
| 25. vi. | 5 | 1 | 2 | 8 | 2·5000 | 3·0000 | 2·5000 |
| 26. vi. | 0 | 0 | 0 | 0 | 0 | 0 | 0 |
| 27. vi. | 0 | 1 | 2 | 3 | 1·6780 | 0·5593 | 0·7627 |
| 28. vi. | 9 | 4 | 2 | 15 | 8·8095 | 5·0000 | 1·1905 |
| 29. vi. | 0 | 0 | 0 | 0 | 0 | 0 | 0 |
| 30. vi. | 17 | 2 | 1 | 20 | 13·888 | 5·0980 | 1·5686 |
| 1. vii. | 41 | 6 | 0 | 47 | 37·1053 | 8·6579 | 1·2368 |
| 2. vii. | 30 | 2 | 1 | 33 | 24·9184 | 7·0714 | 1·0102 |
| 3. vii. | 26 | 2 | 0 | 28 | 22·9398 | 5·0602 | 0 |
| 4. vii | 12 | 0 | 0 | 12 | 10·1772 | 1·5190 | 0·3038 |
| | **140** | **18** | **8** | **166** | **121·4615** | **35·9658** | **8·5726** |

number of recaptures during the whole of both experiments (and not just those released within 24 h), together with their expected values calculated from the frequency of releases of the three phenotypes. It will again be seen that for each day taken separately there is always an excess of *carbonaria* and a deficiency of the light form in the Birmingham experiments (with f. *insularia* lying between both). The reverse is true for the unpolluted wood of Dean End for the majority of releases, and for their sum (table 4). A comparison of the two tables gives valuable information. In the first place, for the Birmingham releases, it will be seen that extending the period over which recaptures were made, the number of *carbonaria* taken is materially increased, whereas this is not so for the other two phenotypes. We have given reasons already for believing that there is no differential migration from an area so that table 3 clearly reflects a difference in the death-rates for the three phenotypes, consequently from this table it can be said that *carbonaria* is at an advantage to *typical* in the Birmingham area. Furthermore, the direct observations of Dr Tinbergen and myself show that the birds ate more *carbonaria* than *typicals* at Dean End and the reverse at Birmingham (Kettlewell, in manuscript). We succeeded in filming seven species of birds doing this.

TABLE 4. DEAN END RECAPTURES

| date | observed | | | | expected | | |
|---|---|---|---|---|---|---|---|
| | C | T | I | total | C | T | I |
| 13. vi. | 6 | 3 | 3 | 12 | 5·2857 | 5·4286 | 1·2857 |
| 14. vi. | 1 | 7 | 2 | 10 | 2·9630 | 6·2963 | 0·7407 |
| 15. vi. | 0 | 1 | 0 | 1 | 0·2353 | 0·7353 | 0·0294 |
| 16. vi. | 8 | 8 | 0 | 16 | 5·6774 | 10·3226 | 0 |
| 17. vi. | 0 | 0 | 0 | 0 | 0 | 0 | 0 |
| 18. vi. | 2 | 8 | 0 | 10 | 3·8182 | 5·9091 | 0·2727 |
| 19. vi. | 1 | 2 | 0 | 3 | 1·0541 | 1·9459 | 0 |
| 20. vi. | 2 | 4 | 0 | 6 | 1·7778 | 4·2222 | 0 |
| 21. vi. | 4 | 4 | 0 | 8 | 4·7324 | 3·2676 | 0 |
| 22. vi. | — | — | — | — | 0 | 0 | 0 |
| 23. vi. | — | — | — | — | 0 | 0 | 0 |
| 24. vi. | — | — | — | — | 0 | 0 | 0 |
| 25. vi. | 2 | 2 | 0 | 4 | 2·6240 | 1·3760 | 0 |
| 26. vi. | — | — | — | — | 0 | 0 | 0 |
| 27. vi. | 1 | 5 | 0 | 6 | 3·8734 | 2·1266 | 0 |
| 28. vi. | 0 | 7 | 0 | 7 | 3·5000 | 3·5000 | 0 |
| 29. vi. | 3 | 8 | 0 | 11 | 5·3429 | 5·6571 | 0 |
| 30. vi. | 2 | 1 | 0 | 3 | 2·0571 | 0·9429 | 0 |
| 4. vii. | 0 | 7 | 0 | 7 | 4·4767 | 2·5233 | 0 |
| | 32 | 67 | 5 | 104 | 47·4180 | 54·2535 | 2·3285 |

TABLE 5. BACKGROUND RECOGNITION IN *BISTON BETULARIA*, $\chi^2_{(1)} = 10·9$

| | black (= *carbonaria*) | white (= *typical*) | total |
|---|---|---|---|
| black background | 38 | 20 | 58 |
| white background | 21 | 39 | 60 |
| total | 59 | 59 | 118 |

It therefore seems almost certain that, not only is selection acting in the two woods, but that it is sufficiently intense for it to have a marked effect on the expectation of life of the three phenotypes.

### OTHER BEHAVIOUR AND CHARACTER DIFFERENCES AT PRESENT BEING INVESTIGATED

*Background recognition*

In order to test whether the dark and the light forms of *betularia* 'chose' to sit on the background on which they were less conspicuous, a simple experiment was devised, details of which have been published (Kettlewell 1955 b). A correct 'choice' of background for both forms was apparent, giving a $\chi^2_{(1)}$ of 10·9 for 118 individuals. It is admitted that this must be repeated using larger numbers. It is suggested that contrast differences arising from stimuli, received from their own colour, and those from the background on which they sit, may be responsible for this (table 5).

302          H. B. D. Kettlewell (Discussion Meeting)

*Viability differences*

A survey of leaf pollution is being undertaken. The method is to wash 6 oz. of leaves taken from the same trees at intervals through the summer. The dried residue is weighed, and there appears to be a correlation between the amount of pollution, the month of the year, aphid density and rainfall. The solid portion is fed back to backcross broods of *betularia*. An increased tolerance has already been shown under adverse conditions in other species (Ford 1937) but not to the effects of air pollution.

*Larval behaviour differences*

Backcross broods from the rare light form occurring in industrial areas, have been separated according to those larvae which were first to reach full growth and those which took longest. The proportion of phenotypes hatching from these time groups has diverged from equality sufficiently to demand further investigation; it is possible that slow feeding is a character of the *carbonaria* form.

*Scent differences*

In Dean End wood, where there are no *carbonaria*, virgin sib females of the black and white forms of *betularia* were placed in separate cages, 3 to 5 ft. apart. We noted behaviour differences of the wild male typical forms which appeared to vary according to the meteorological conditions. There was evidence that in this wood the *typical* males came to *carbonaria* females more freely than the *typical* on warm nights.

SUMMARY

It appears that in the recent past, prior to one hundred years ago, the so-called industrial melanics were absent from collections and records. They are still absent from large areas of western and south-western England, where lichen-covered deciduous trees predominate. Evidence has been provided that, in these areas, melanic mutations would be rapidly eliminated because of their cryptic disadvantages. Nevertheless, in the changed countryside of central and eastern England, the melanic forms are rapidly replacing the light-coloured individuals and even managing to re-establish themselves in their melanic forms in centres from which they have long been absent (*Procus literosa* and *Apamea characterea* in Sheffield). Industrial melanism probably represents an example of transient polymorphism. The majority of these melanic mutants are at the start dominant, and this may well be the result of selection in the past. In the Highlands of Scotland in the old forests containing indigenous pines, the melanics of several species exist in a state of balanced polymorphism. They are, in the few instances known, dominants also. If it can be shown that they are genetically identical mutants to those in the industrial melanics, it may throw light on the origin of the present-day industrial melanics. It is possible that within the past 3000 years, at a time when the British Isles was extensively covered with pine, or at a period when the meteorological conditions were different, that these same cryptic species existed in a state of balanced polymorphism similar to the situation found in Scotland

*Investigations on evolution of melanism in Lepidoptera* 303

today, and that during this period their state of dominance was evolved. If this purely theoretical hypothesis is correct, the Highland melanics (e.g. *Boarmia repandata* ab. *nigricata* and *Lampropteryx suffumata* ab. *piccata*) may well be relict forms.

REFERENCES (Kettlewell)

Ford, E. B. 1937 *Biol. Rev.* **12**, 461.
Kettlewell, H. B. D. 1955*a Entomologist*, **88**, 50.
Kettlewell, H. B. D. 1955*b Nature, Lond.*, **175**, 943.
Kettlewell, H. B. D. 1956 *Heredity* (in the Press).

THE THEORY OF SELECTION FOR MELANISM IN LEPIDOPTERA

BY J. B. S. HALDANE, F.R.S.

*Department of Biometry, University College, London*

Dr Kettlewell's proof that the dark form *carbonaria* of *Biston betularia* has replaced the type, at least in part as the result of selection by bird predators, gives me the right to bring my calculation (Haldane 1924) on this matter up to date.

Assuming random mating, if the relative fitnesses of the genotypes $CC$, $Cc$ and $cc$ are as $1:1-k:1-K$, and the gene frequencies are $pC + qc$, then the annual change in the value of $p$ is

$$\Delta p = \frac{pq(kp - kq + Kq)}{1 - 2kpq - Kq^2}.$$

But $K$ and $k$ are not constants, even in a constant environment. They change with the frequency of other genes (or possibly plasmons). At present in industrial areas, $K$ is positive and $k$ nearly zero, since $C$ is apparently fully dominant. However, on the genetic background of unpolluted areas, $Cc$ is intermediate and $k$ may be about $\frac{1}{2}K$ (Ford 1955).

Before industrial pollution began, $C$ was a rare mutant, rendering the moth conspicuous to birds, and $K$ and $k$ were negative. If $\mu$ was the mutation rate of $c$ to $C$, $p$ was about $\dfrac{2\mu(1-K)}{k-K}$, or perhaps 3 or 4 times the value of $\mu$, say $10^{-5}$. If $k$ is zero the final state in an industrial area would be given by $q^2 = \nu K^{-1}$, where $\nu$ is the rate of mutation of $C$ to $c$. Thus $q$ would be of the order of $10^{-2}$ to $10^{-3}$, with one recessive per 10000 or per million. This, however, would not be achieved until after over $K^{-1}q^{-1}$ years, that is to say, several centuries or millennia, of selection. Dr Kettlewell tells me that at present about 1 % to 10% of recessives are commonly found in industrial areas, so that $q = 0.2$ approximately.

If $1 - K = (1-k)^2$, that is to say, the fitness of the heterozygotes is the geometric mean of that of the homozygotes, the time needed for $p$ to increase from $10^{-5}$ to $0.8$ is $-\dfrac{11.20}{\log_{10}(1-K)}$ years, or 37 years if $K = \frac{1}{2}$, as Kettlewell's Table 3 suggests. If $k = 0$ it is

$$\frac{4 + (1-K)\ln 5}{K} - \frac{\ln(8 \times 10^4)}{\ln(1-K)} \quad \text{(Haldane 1932)},$$

Reprinted by permission of the Royal Society of London from Proceedings of the Royal Society (London), B. 145:303–304, 1956.

J. B. S. Haldane (Discussion Meeting)

or 27 years if $K = \frac{1}{2}$. The effect of dominance is to double the rate of selection at first, but to slow it down greatly when recessives become rare.

I conclude, either that selection is usually much less intense than Kettlewell found, that immigration from unpolluted areas is important (which is unlikely) or that selection has slowed down for a reason which I consider.

It appears that during the last century genes have been selected which have no effect of $CC$, but make $Cc$ nearly as dark as $CC$. Now such genes will only confer an advantage if they are present in $Cc$ animals, and, as shown in the Appendix, the total number of $Cc$ moths, on the hypotheses so far considered, will be of the order of 4 to 6 times the annual population at most, so the frequency of a modifying gene is unlikely to increase even twentyfold. On this hypothesis the selection of modifiers of heterozygotes cannot be explained.

A possible hypothesis is that heterozygotes are or were physiologically fitter than either homozygote. Ford (1940) showed that when partially starved, $Cc$ survived better than $cc$. There is no evidence as to whether $Cc$ is fitter than $CC$. If it is so, or was so for a number of years, then we can suggest that the primary selective process in the more polluted industrial areas was complete by about 1890, leading to a balanced polymorphism with $p = 0.86$ or some neighbouring value, giving about 74 % $CC$, 24 % $Cc$, 2 % $cc$ at hatching. If the fitness of $cc$ was $\frac{1}{2}$ that of $Cc$, as Kettlewell's results suggest, that of $CC$ would have been about 92 % that of $Cc$. In this case selection has had a reasonable opportunity of favouring genes which increase the dominance of $C$. It should be possible to test this hypothesis, at least on genetic backgrounds where $C$ is not fully dominant.

I wish then to emphasize that the problem is not yet fully solved, and that numerical calculations of the type here given are of a certain value if only as suggesting further experiments.

REFERENCES (Haldane)

Ford, E. B. 1940 *Ann. Eugen., Lond.*, **10**, 227–252.
Ford, E. B. 1955 *Moths.* London: Collins.
Haldane, J. B. S. 1924 *Trans. Camb. Phil. Soc.* **23**, 10–41.
Haldane, J. B. S. 1932 *Proc. Camb. Phil. Soc.* **28**, 244–248.

# SELECTION FOR GEOTAXIS IN MONOMORPHIC AND POLYMORPHIC POPULATIONS OF DROSOPHILA PSEUDOOBSCURA

By Theodosius Dobzhansky and Boris Spassky*

THE ROCKEFELLER INSTITUTE

Communicated August 29, 1962

Carson[1, 2] has been successful in obtaining by selection strains of *Drosophila robusta* which differed in their behavior. The behavioral character involved is a complex one, a phototactic response combined with a general vigor and an ability to respond quickly to outside interference. The selection was more effective in populations which were karyotypically monomorphic (i.e., structurally homozygous) than in polymorphic ones in which many individuals were inversion heterozygotes. Carson ascribes this to the blockage of gene recombination in inversion heterozygotes, and to relatively free recombination in the homozygotes. Hirsch and his students[3-5] have devised an apparatus which permits selecting flies which are positively or negatively geotactic, the procedure being easy, accurate, and not time consuming. They have shown that populations of *Drosophila melanogaster* contain enough genetic variance to respond rapidly to the selection. The genetic basis of the geotactic response is complexly polygenic, and Erlenmeyer-Kimling and Hirsch[5] found that at least three of the four pairs of the chromosomes are involved. We have used a similar apparatus, constructed under the supervision of Professor Hirsch, to study the response to selection for positive and for negative

Reprinted by permission of the National Academy of Sciences and the authors from *Proceedings of the National Academy of Sciences* 48:1704–1712, 1962.

geotaxis in chromosomally polymorphic and monomorphic populations of *Drosophila pseudoobscura*.   The apparatus is, very briefly, a classification maze, in which the flies have to make their "choices" of going up or down; a fly which goes 15 times upward ends in the terminal tube No. 1; going always downwards leads to the terminal tube No. 16; going up and down with eqval frequency leads, irrespective of the order, to tubes Nos. 8 or 9, etc.   The selection is made simply by breeding the flies which are found in the uppermost, or in the lowermost tubes.   After some generations of selection the flies become distinctly different in their preferences for upward or downward movements.

*Material and Technique.*—The experimental populations are derived from 12 strains homozygous for the CH gene arrangement, and 12 strains homozygous for the AR gene arrangement, in their third chromosomes.   The wild ancestors of these strains were collected at Piñon Flats, Mount San Jacinto, California, some 15 years ago; the strains were kept in regular mass cultures in a constant temperature room at 16°C.   The three experimental populations were monomorphic for AR, monomorphic for CH, and polymorphic for AR and CH respectively.   The populations were made by intercrossing all the AR strains, or all the CH strains, or all the AR to all the CH strains, and using the hybrids so obtained.   The "monomorphic" populations were, accordingly, structurally homozygous, but were presumably genically heterogeneous.   The polymorphic one was both chromosomally and genically heterogeneous, the initial frequencies of the AR and CH chromosomes being 50 per cent.

In every generation approximately 250 virgin females and 250 males, aged separately 2–10 days on ordinary culture medium, were run through the maze.   The maze stood in a constant temperature room at 20°C, the light being a fluorescent lamp, vertically placed near the terminal tubes of the maze (see Hirsch[3]).   In general, the flies were introduced into the maze in the afternoon, and by next afternoon or morning, almost all of them sorted themselves out in the terminal tubes.   The females and the males were run, of course, separately.   For selection, 25 females and 25 males were taken from the uppermost, or from the lowermost tubes of the maze.   At the beginning of the experiment, the uppermost (No. 1) and the lowermost (No. 16) tubes had too few flies, and then the flies from two, three or more upper or lower tubes were used.   The females and the males of a given selection were placed together in a culture bottle, and transferred to fresh culture bottles daily for about a week, whereupon the parents were discarded.   The oviposition and the development of the progeny took place at 25°C.   When the adults of the next generation hatched, females and males were collected daily, separated, and aged at 16°C until enough flies accumulated to be placed in the maze.

*Experimental Data.*—The results of the experiments are summarized in Tables 1 and 2 in Figures 1 and 2.   It can be seen that the flies in the original populations were either neutral to gravity or only slightly positively geotactic.   The mean values for the females were between 9 and 10, and for the males between 7.8 and 9.4.   The point of neutrality being 8.5, this indicates either a weak positive geotaxis or simply that a fly is more likely to fall down than it is to crawl up in the maze.   The negative selection (moving upward) may have been slightly more rapid in the early generations than the positive selection (moving toward gravity), but by the ninth generation the means of the positive lines were between 10.0 and 11.7, and of the negative lines between 4.7 and 6.4.   Some further progress was accomplished in the next nine generations, and in the 18th generation the means of the positive lines were between 11.4 and 13.0, and of the negative lines between 3.4 and 5.2.   The variation curves of the positive and negative selection lines continued to overlap, but they became, if considered jointly, very distinctly bimodal.

After eight generations of selection, the polymorphic populations were subjected to cytological analysis.   Chromosomes in the salivary gland cell were examined in 150 larvae from the population selected for a positive and 150 from that selected

161

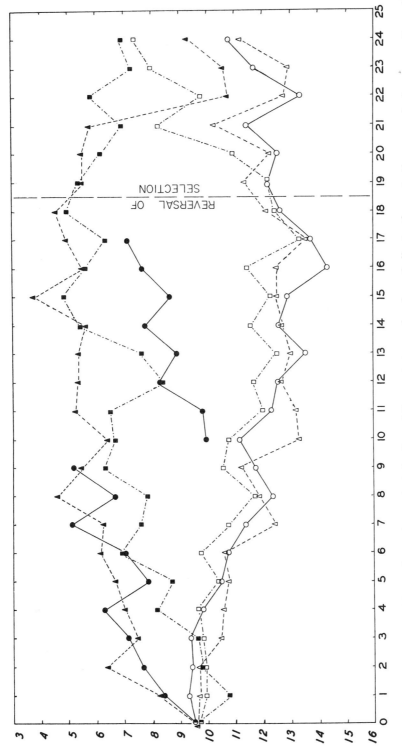

Fig. 1.—Selection for positive and negative geotaxis in *Drosophila pseudoobscura* females. Ordinate, the geotactic score; abscissa, generations of selection. Solid lines and circles, polymorphic populations; dashed lines and triangles, monomorphic AR; dot and dash and squares, monomorphic CH. Black symbols, negative selection; white symbols, positive selection.

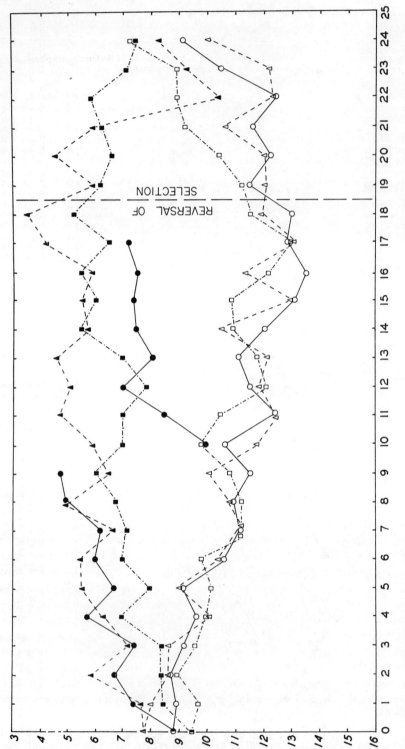

Fig. 2.—Selection for positive and negative geotaxis in *Drosophila pseudoobscura* males.   The meaning of the symbols is given in the caption for Figure 1.

TABLE 1

SELECTION FOR POSITIVE GEOTAXIS IN MONOMORPHIC AND POLYMORPHIC POPULATIONS OF
*Drosophila pseudoobscura*

(The highest possible score is 16, the lowest 1. In Tables 1 and 2, the scores of the females are placed on the left and of the males on the right. Further explanation in text.)

| Generation | Monomorphic AR | | Monomorphic CH | | Polymorphic | |
|---|---|---|---|---|---|---|
| P | $9.67 \pm 0.21$ | $7.77 \pm 0.26$ | $9.72 \pm 0.22$ | $9.45 \pm 0.20$ | $9.51 \pm 0.24$ | $8.80 \pm 0.25$ |
| 1 | $9.63 \pm 0.25$ | $7.97 \pm 0.24$ | $9.89 \pm 0.24$ | $9.62 \pm 0.23$ | $9.25 \pm 0.22$ | $8.92 \pm 0.22$ |
| 2 | $9.63 \pm 0.27$ | $8.54 \pm 0.24$ | $9.85 \pm 0.25$ | $8.90 \pm 0.22$ | $9.41 \pm 0.26$ | $8.67 \pm 0.27$ |
| 3 | $10.35 \pm 0.25$ | $8.57 \pm 0.26$ | $9.72 \pm 0.22$ | $9.45 \pm 0.20$ | $9.29 \pm 0.24$ | $9.10 \pm 0.24$ |
| 4 | $10.43 \pm 0.25$ | $10.03 \pm 0.26$ | $9.66 \pm 0.23$ | $10.00 \pm 0.25$ | $9.85 \pm 0.31$ | $9.26 \pm 0.21$ |
| 5 | $10.69 \pm 0.23$ | $8.99 \pm 0.26$ | $10.24 \pm 0.25$ | $10.16 \pm 0.24$ | $10.46 \pm 0.20$ | $9.11 \pm 0.26$ |
| 6 | $10.65 \pm 0.25$ | $10.38 \pm 0.26$ | $9.62 \pm 0.25$ | $9.76 \pm 0.22$ | $10.70 \pm 0.28$ | $10.53 \pm 0.25$ |
| 7 | $12.23 \pm 0.24$ | $11.18 \pm 0.26$ | $10.68 \pm 0.26$ | $11.11 \pm 0.23$ | $11.29 \pm 0.27$ | $11.59 \pm 0.24$ |
| 8 | $11.85 \pm 0.29$ | $10.81 \pm 0.27$ | $11.67 \pm 0.24$ | $11.14 \pm 0.23$ | $12.23 \pm 0.22$ | $10.91 \pm 0.26$ |
| 9 | $11.16 \pm 0.26$ | $10.00 \pm 0.28$ | $10.44 \pm 0.27$ | $10.74 \pm 0.24$ | $11.68 \pm 0.24$ | $11.43 \pm 0.24$ |
| 10 | $13.22 \pm 0.21$ | $11.73 \pm 0.29$ | $10.66 \pm 0.24$ | $9.76 \pm 0.23$ | $11.09 \pm 0.24$ | $10.55 \pm 0.27$ |
| 11 | $13.15 \pm 0.21$ | $12.39 \pm 0.23$ | $11.98 \pm 0.23$ | $10.42 \pm 0.24$ | $12.23 \pm 0.22$ | $12.36 \pm 0.24$ |
| 12 | $11.67 \pm 0.23$ | $11.79 \pm 0.25$ | $11.62 \pm 0.24$ | $12.05 \pm 0.21$ | $12.52 \pm 0.22$ | $11.41 \pm 0.25$ |
| 13 | $12.90 \pm 0.22$ | $12.08 \pm 0.27$ | $12.42 \pm 0.21$ | $11.72 \pm 0.20$ | $13.45 \pm 0.20$ | $11.06 \pm 0.26$ |
| 14 | $12.57 \pm 0.22$ | $10.41 \pm 0.29$ | $11.52 \pm 0.22$ | $10.84 \pm 0.23$ | $12.51 \pm 0.22$ | $11.98 \pm 0.23$ |
| 15 | $12.42 \pm 0.24$ | $12.96 \pm 0.23$ | $12.18 \pm 0.19$ | $10.87 \pm 0.22$ | $12.90 \pm 0.21$ | $13.07 \pm 0.21$ |
| 16 | $12.44 \pm 0.24$ | $11.26 \pm 0.24$ | $11.39 \pm 0.20$ | $12.12 \pm 0.23$ | $14.21 \pm 0.16$ | $13.50 \pm 0.21$ |
| 17 | $13.55 \pm 0.18$ | $13.08 \pm 0.21$ | $13.27 \pm 0.20$ | $12.85 \pm 0.18$ | $13.78 \pm 0.19$ | $12.73 \pm 0.22$ |
| 18 | $12.02 \pm 0.24$ | $11.79 \pm 0.31$ | $12.37 \pm 0.21$ | $11.45 \pm 0.23$ | $12.52 \pm 0.21$ | $13.00 \pm 0.18$ |

Selection Reversed

| Generation | Monomorphic AR | | Monomorphic CH | | Polymorphic | |
|---|---|---|---|---|---|---|
| 19 | $9.31 \pm 0.19$ | $11.95 \pm 0.24$ | $12.15 \pm 0.22$ | $11.15 \pm 0.22$ | $12.14 \pm 0.23$ | $11.45 \pm 0.21$ |
| 20 | $12.25 \pm 0.23$ | $11.98 \pm 0.23$ | $10.87 \pm 0.24$ | $10.28 \pm 0.24$ | $12.53 \pm 0.21$ | $12.13 \pm 0.24$ |
| 21 | $10.13 \pm 0.17$ | $10.56 \pm 0.17$ | $8.23 \pm 0.27$ | $9.06 \pm 0.28$ | $11.34 \pm 0.29$ | $11.60 \pm 0.27$ |
| 22 | $12.85 \pm 0.19$ | $12.35 \pm 0.22$ | $9.77 \pm 0.23$ | $8.87 \pm 0.23$ | $13.30 \pm 0.19$ | $12.39 \pm 0.28$ |
| 23 | $12.94 \pm 0.20$ | $12.11 \pm 0.24$ | $7.91 \pm 0.24$ | $8.84 \pm 0.25$ | $11.66 \pm 0.24$ | $10.46 \pm 0.26$ |
| 24 | $11.18 \pm 0.25$ | $9.97 \pm 0.29$ | $7.21 \pm 0.20$ | $7.16 \pm 0.20$ | $10.72 \pm 0.23$ | $9.03 \pm 0.24$ |
| 25 | $10.24 \pm 0.26$ | $10.51 \pm 0.26$ | $7.59 \pm 0.21$ | $6.72 \pm 0.21$ | $9.96 \pm 0.21$ | $8.63 \pm 0.23$ |

for a negative geotaxis. The gene arrangements were thus determined in 300 third chromosomes from each population. The negative population proved to have only AR chromosomes, while in the positive one the frequencies were 66.0 per cent AR and 34.0 per cent CH chromosomes. The negative "polymorphic" population has, thus, become a monomorphic AR. It was discarded, and a new population was started, in order to test whether the elimination of CH in the negatively selected polymorphic population might have been accidental.

The initial material for this new polymorphic population was obtained by crossing AR flies from the positively selected monomorphic AR, with CH flies from the negatively selected monomorphic CH population. The $F_1$ flies were run through the maze, and gave a mean score of 9.97 in both sexes. They were, thus, weakly positively geotactic. Since the parents had scores of between 10 and 11 (the AR population), and 6 (the CH population), the performance of the hybrids is intermediate, perhaps with a tendency toward dominance of the positive geotaxis. The new population was subjected to a negative selection, responded quickly (Figures 1 and 2), and after seven generations of selection (corresponding to the 17th generation in the other populations) achieved a record of about 7. A cytological examination showed that it had lost its CH chromosomes, and became monomorphic AR.

At the same time (the 17th generation) the positively selected polymorphic population had 53.0 per cent AR and 47.0 per cent CH. It has increased the fre-

## TABLE 2

SELECTION FOR NEGATIVE GEOTAXIS IN MONOMORPHIC AND POLYMORPHIC POPULATIONS OF
*Drosophila pseudoobscura*

| Generation | Monomorphic AR | | Monomorphic CH | | Polymorphic | |
|---|---|---|---|---|---|---|
| P | 9.67 ± 0.21 | 7.77 ± 0.26 | 9.72 ± 0.22 | 9.45 ± 0.20 | 9.51 ± 0.24 | 8.80 ± 0.25 |
| 1 | 8.18 ± 0.25 | 7.52 ± 0.26 | 10.87 ± 0.26 | 8.34 ± 0.25 | 8.73 ± 0.25 | 7.35 ± 0.23 |
| 2 | 6.24 ± 0.24 | 5.83 ± 0.21 | 9.67 ± 0.27 | 8.38 ± 0.27 | 7.57 ± 0.26 | 6.63 ± 0.23 |
| 3 | 7.37 ± 0.26 | 7.19 ± 0.23 | 9.54 ± 0.24 | 8.39 ± 0.25 | 7.07 ± 0.24 | 7.34 ± 0.25 |
| 4 | 6.98 ± 0.23 | 6.26 ± 0.25 | 8.04 ± 0.25 | 6.97 ± 0.21 | 6.25 ± 0.23 | 5.66 ± 0.21 |
| 5 | 6.64 ± 0.26 | 5.42 ± 0.23 | 8.72 ± 0.27 | 7.92 ± 0.20 | 7.80 ± 0.22 | 6.26 ± 0.26 |
| 6 | 6.06 ± 0.25 | 5.33 ± 0.22 | 6.91 ± 0.25 | 6.94 ± 0.31 | 6.93 ± 0.25 | 5.93 ± 0.26 |
| 7 | 6.11 ± 0.24 | 6.52 ± 0.25 | 7.52 ± 0.25 | 7.12 ± 0.23 | 5.08 ± 0.23 | 6.10 ± 0.22 |
| 8 | 4.60 ± 0.19 | 4.81 ± 0.21 | 7.88 ± 0.26 | 6.64 ± 0.23 | 6.61 ± 0.28 | 4.87 ± 0.26 |
| 9 | 5.45 ± 0.24 | 6.39 ± 0.25 | 6.17 ± 0.22 | 5.96 ± 0.25 | 5.10 ± 0.28 | 4.66 ± 0.25 |
| 10 | 6.35 ± 0.31 | 5.84 ± 0.25 | 6.48 ± 0.23 | 6.59 ± 0.24 | Re-Started | |
| 11 | 5.18 ± 0.24 | 5.70 ± 0.23 | 6.42 ± 0.23 | 6.39 ± 0.22 | 9.97 ± 0.27 | 9.97 ± 0.31 |
| 12 | 5.22 ± 0.27 | 5.08 ± 0.34 | 8.25 ± 0.25 | 7.74 ± 0.30 | 9.89 ± 0.28 | 8.45 ± 0.31 |
| 13 | 5.31 ± 0.22 | 4.57 ± 0.20 | 7.54 ± 0.25 | 6.97 ± 0.27 | 8.15 ± 0.27 | 6.96 ± 0.21 |
| 14 | 5.62 ± 0.21 | 5.65 ± 0.18 | 5.48 ± 0.22 | 5.48 ± 0.23 | 8.91 ± 0.28 | 8.01 ± 0.27 |
| 15 | 3.80 ± 0.19 | 5.42 ± 0.24 | 4.70 ± 0.23 | 5.98 ± 0.25 | 7.76 ± 0.29 | 7.47 ± 0.29 |
| 16 | 5.45 ± 0.24 | 5.83 ± 0.25 | 5.48 ± 0.23 | 5.33 ± 0.23 | 8.61 ± 0.28 | 7.33 ± 0.27 |
| 17 | 4.92 ± 0.25 | 4.13 ± 0.23 | 6.21 ± 0.24 | 6.44 ± 0.25 | 7.61 ± 0.30 | 7.60 ± 0.27 |
| 18 | 4.40 ± 0.18 | 3.41 ± 0.19 | 4.81 ± 0.20 | 5.22 ± 0.21 | 7.06 ± 0.29 | 7.19 ± 0.29 |
| | | | Selection Reversed | | | |
| 19 | 5.43 ± 0.23 | 5.85 ± 0.28 | 5.23 ± 0.24 | 6.17 ± 0.22 | ... | ... |
| 20 | 5.42 ± 0.24 | 4.51 ± 0.23 | 6.14 ± 0.24 | 6.55 ± 0.29 | ... | ... |
| 21 | 5.78 ± 0.23 | 5.88 ± 0.26 | 6.88 ± 0.27 | 6.18 ± 0.22 | ... | ... |
| 22 | 10.83 ± 0.27 | 10.30 ± 0.26 | 5.78 ± 0.25 | 5.72 ± 0.22 | ... | ... |
| 23 | 10.50 ± 0.23 | 9.26 ± 0.21 | 7.12 ± 0.29 | 7.01 ± 0.28 | ... | ... |
| 24 | 9.14 ± 0.25 | 8.28 ± 0.25 | 6.91 ± 0.25 | 7.28 ± 0.22 | ... | ... |
| 25 | 9.00 ± 0.20 | 7.61 ± 0.21 | 6.82 ± 0.22 | 7.25 ± 0.22 | ... | ... |

quency of CH, while the negatively selected population lost its CH chromosomes. Polymorphic AR and CH populations kept in population cages at 25°C, but not selected for geotaxis, reach equilibria at about 70 per cent AR and 30 per cent CH. The conclusion is inescapable that selection for negative geotaxis favors the carriers of AR chromosomes, while that for positive geotaxis gives an advantage to the AR/CH heterokaryotype. The evidence that it is the heterokaryotype, and not simply the carriers of CH chromosomes that is favored, is twofold. In the first place, the AR chromosomes are not lost in the positively selected polymorphic population. Secondly, this population shows a disturbance of the Hardy-Weinberg equilibrium in favor of the heterokaryotype. In the 17th generation of selection, 64 per cent of the larvae examined from this population belonged to the AR/CH heterokaryotype. In this population, the selection has evidently favored a gene pool, which made the AR/CH and CH/CH homokaryotypes semilethal, and thus achieved a population in which almost two thirds of the individuals were the heterokaryotypes AR/CH. Populations of this sort are known in some species of *Drosophila* also in nature.[6, 7]

Since by the 17th generation the selection gains were becoming small, the experiment was redirected as follows. The negatively selected polymorphic population which lost its CH chromosomes was discarded. The remaining five populations were each subdivided in two; in one division the selection was relaxed, the flies being transferred to fresh cultures, generation after generation, without being run through the maze; in the other division the selection was reversed, the old positive populations being now selected for negative geotaxis, and vice versa.

The results of the reversed selection are shown in Tables 1 and 2 and in Figures

TABLE 3

The Geotaxis Scores before and after the Relaxation of Selection

|  | Monomorphic AR ♀ | ♂ | Monomorphic CH ♀ | ♂ | Polymorphic ♀ | ♂ |
|---|---|---|---|---|---|---|
| Positive Selection |  |  |  |  |  |  |
| Before relaxation | 12.07 | 11.79 | 12.37 | 11.44 | 12.52 | 13.00 |
| After relaxation | 10.09 | 9.76 | 12.28 | 10.85 | 11.94 | 11.18 |
| Negative selection |  |  |  |  |  |  |
| Before relaxation | 4.40 | 3.41 | 4.81 | 5.22 | ... | ... |
| After relaxation | 4.71 | 3.59 | 6.19 | 5.68 | ... | ... |
| Difference |  |  |  |  |  |  |
| Before relaxation | 7.67 | 8.38 | 7.56 | 6.22 | ... | ... |
| After relaxation | 5.38 | 6.17 | 6.09 | 5.17 | ... | ... |

1 and 2. The populations responded rapidly; in fact, the back-selection acted even more quickly than the forward selection did in the original populations. After six generations of back-selection (the 24th generation in the Tables and Figures) the differences between the lines which were originally so striking almost disappeared. The relaxation of the selection resulted also in some losses of the differences previously achieved, as can be seen in Table 3. However, the relaxation of the selection gave, unsurprisingly, a smaller degree of convergence than the back-selection.

A cytological examination of the populations in which the selection was relaxed or reversed gave most interesting results. The polymorphic population selected for 18 generations for positive geotaxis, and then having passed 11 generations without selection, contained 50 per cent of AR and of CH chromosomes. Among the 150 larvae examined, 78 were AR/CH heterozygotes, a good fit to the Hardy-Weinberg expectation of 75. The population back-selected for 7 generations in the negative direction after the 18 generations of the positive selection had, in a sample of 200 larvae, 99 AR/CH heterokaryotypes and 101 CH/CH homokaryotypes, and not a single AR/AR. Here the AR chromosomes have evidently become lethal in double dose. This is the more unexpected, since the negative selection in the original polymorphic population resulted in the diminution of CH and in fixation of AR.

The selection has not been equally efficient in the different populations. In Figures 1 and 2 it can be seen at a glance that, while the polymorphic and the monomorphic AR populations were for the most part close at all stages of selection, the monomorphic CH lagged behind. Table 4 makes this fact even more evident.

TABLE 4

Differences between the Geotaxis Scores in Polymorphic and Monomorphic Populations Selected for Positive and Negative Responses

| Generation | Mono AR | Mono CH | Polymorphic | Generation | Mono AR | Mono CH |
|---|---|---|---|---|---|---|
| 1 | 0.95 | 0.15 | 1.22 | 14 | 6.85 | 5.70 |
| 2 | 3.05 | 0.35 | 1.95 | 15 | 8.08 | 6.18 |
| 3 | 2.18 | 0.62 | 1.99 | 16 | 6.21 | 6.35 |
| 4 | 3.60 | 2.32 | 3.60 | 17 | 8.79 | 6.74 |
| 5 | 3.81 | 1.87 | 2.58 | 18 | 8.02 | 6.92 |
| 6 | 4.82 | 2.76 | 4.19 |  | Selection Reversed |  |
| 7 | 5.34 | 3.53 | 5.14 | 19 | 5.00 | 5.95 |
| 8 | 6.62 | 4.15 | 5.83 | 20 | 7.15 | 4.23 |
| 9 | 7.59 | 4.53 | 6.69 | 21 | 4.52 | 2.12 |
| 10 | 6.38 | 3.68 | ... | 22 | 2.04 | 3.57 |
| 11 | 7.83 | 4.78 | ... | 23 | 2.65 | 1.30 |
| 12 | 6.53 | 3.84 | ... | 24 | 1.86 | 0.09 |
| 13 | 7.55 | 4.81 | ... |  |  |  |

This table shows the divergence achieved after various generations of selection between the scores of the populations selected in the opposite directions (females and males combined). The divergence is consistently greater in the monomorphic AR than in the monomorphic CH populations. The selection in the polymorphic population is about as effective as it is in the monomorphic AR, and more so than in the monomorphic CH.

*Discussion.*—The geotactic response of *Drosophila pseudoobscura* is evidently under a genetic control. Although the three initial populations in our experiments were originally approximately neutral to gravity, they responded to both positive and to negative selections, and gave rise to populations the members of which tended to move downward or upward respectively. The nature of the genetic variance which underlies these selection responses constitutes an interesting problem. By the 17th and 18th generations of the selection the increments gained per generation became small, indicating that a plateau was being approached. This did not, however, mean an exhaustion of the genetic variance; on the contrary, the reversal of the selection gave a rapid response, if anything more rapid than that to the original selection, and by the 24th generation the populations were almost back to their preselectional states as far as their geotactic scores were concerned. Some loss of the selectional gains has also occurred in the lines in which the selection was relaxed for 11 generations. This suggests, though does not completely prove, that the genetic variance was in part not simply additive. The modal geotactic reaction of the original populations, which happened to be close to the neutrality point, was a result of a gene pool held in a balanced state. The balance was displaced by the artificial selection, and upon relaxation of this selection, was partly restored by natural selection, perhaps owing to the adaptive advantage of the heterozygous state. This is an example of what Lerner[3] has termed "genetic homeostasis." The remarkably rapid response to the back selection was due to the artificial and the natural selections reinforcing each other.

The selection, both in the plus and in the minus directions, was effective in populations monomorphic as well as polymorphic for the third chromosome gene arrangements, AR and CH. The observed variance was about equally large in all the populations, and it did not undergo any substantial change during the selection. The relatively less rapid selectional gains in the monomorphic CH populations may perhaps be related to the fact that CH chromosomes are not as frequent in nature as AR chromosomes in the geographic region from which the source material was derived.

The behavior of the polymorphic populations under selection is remarkable. The selection for a negative geotactic response favored AR chromosomes, while the heterokaryotype AR/CH induced a positive geotaxis on its carriers. This is the first recorded instance of chromosomal polymorphism derived from natural populations conditioning a behavior difference unconnected with sex; Spiess[9] has, however, discovered differences in mating propensity among karyotypes of *Drosophila persimilis.* It must, however, be made clear that the behavior is not influenced directly by the gene arrangement as such, but rather by the gene contents of the chromosomes having certain gene orders. This is demonstrated by the chromosomal changes observed in the polymorphic populations selected first for a positive geotaxis and then back-selected in the negative direction. The original selection fa-

167

1712          *GENETICS: DOBZHANSKY AND SPASSKY*          Proc. N. A. S.

vored the AR/CH heterokaryotype, and made the homokaryotypes subvital; the back-selection favored an AR chromosome which happened to be lethal in double dose, and resulted in a population which consisted of CH/CH homokaryotypes and AR/CH heterokaryotypes, but lacked AR/AR entirely.

*Summary.*—Using a classification maze constructed by Professor Jerry Hirsch, we have selected populations of *Drosophila pseudoobscura*, for a positive and for a negative geotactic behavior. The three initial populations were respectively monomorphic for AR, monomorphic for CH, and polymorphic for AR and CH gene arrangements in their third chromosomes. All the initial populations were about neutral to gravity, yet all responded both to plus and to minus selection. The plus selection favored AR chromosomes, while the negative selection favored the AR/CH heterokaryotype. Relaxation of the selection resulted in a partial relapse towards the original state. Reversal of the selection gave an almost complete return to the original state. In the polymorphic AR/CH population the back-selection favored an AR chromosome which was lethal in double dose.

* The work reported in this article has been carried out under Contract No. AT-(30-1)-1151 of the U.S. Atomic Energy Commission with the Columbia University, New York.

[1] Carson, H. L., Cold Spring Harbor Symposia on Quantitative Biology, vol. 23 (1958), pp. 291–306.

[2] Carson, H. L., Cold Spring Harbor Symposia on Quantitative Biology, vol. 24 (1959), pp. 87–105.

[3] Hirsch, J., in *Roots of Behavior*, ed. E. L. Bliss (New York: Harper, 1962), pp. 3–23.

[4] Hirsch, J., and L. Erlenmeyer-Kimling, *Science*, **134**, 835–836 (1961).

[5] Erlenmeyer-Kimling, L., and J. Hirsch, *Science*, **134**, 1068–1069 (1961).

[6] Dobzhansky, Th., and O. Pavlovsky, these Proceedings, **41**, 289–295 (1955).

[7] Dobzhansky, Th., and O. Pavlovsky, these Proceedings, **46**, 41–47 (1960).

[8] Lerner, I. M., *Genetic Homeostasis* (New York: John Wiley & Sons, 1954).

[9] Spiess, E. B., and B. Langer, *Evolution*, **15**, 535–544 (1961).

# NATURAL SELECTION IN WATER SNAKES (*NATRIX SIPEDON* L.) ON ISLANDS IN LAKE ERIE

Joseph H. Camin and Paul R. Ehrlich

*Chicago Academy of Sciences, Chicago, Illinois* [1]

Received February 26, 1958

Although in recent years laboratory selection has become a commonplace, natural selection operating in wild populations has been quite difficult to document. Much of the published work has been inconclusive (see summary in Robson and Richards, 1936, for early work) or open to controversy (e.g., Lamotte, Cain and Sheppard, and Sedlmair on *Cepaea*). The present study analyzes all available data on color pattern variation in the water snakes of the Lake Erie islands. These data appear to illustrate a situation in which migration and strong selection pressure combine to give a relatively clear-cut picture of differential elimination of color pattern types from a population.

The uniform medium-gray color of the majority of adult water snakes inhabiting the islands in the western part of Lake Erie (as opposed to the "normal" dark banded type) was first noted by Morse (1904). In 1937 Conant and Clay described the island population as a separate subspecies *Natrix sipedon insularum*, differing from typical *sipedon* primarily in the large percentage of unbanded or weakly banded individuals. In 1954 Camin, Triplehorn and Walter compared the frequencies of various pattern types in wild-caught juveniles with those of the adult population and found a statistically significant decrease in the proportion of banded individuals from the juvenile to the adult population. In the present paper these previous data are reanalyzed and integrated with additional data, principally on frequencies of pattern types in

litters, in order to present a picture of the entire post-natal selection for pattern type.

## MATERIALS AND METHODS

Data from Middle Island are from the collections of Camin, Triplehorn and Walter made in 1949 and Camin and Ehrlich in 1957. Litter data from the Bass Complex islands are from the collections of Camin in 1948 and Camin and Ehrlich in 1957. All other data are from Conant and Clay (1937).

Conant and Clay originally divided the continuous variation in pattern types arbitrarily into four classes A–D (see figure 1), A being unbanded and D being typical banded *N. sipedon sipedon*. For greater precision, Camin *et al.* added the intermediate categories ab, bc and cd. These latter categories are employed here when comparison with Conant and Clay's data is not required. Where necessary for statistical tests, categories were lumped as follows: A = A + ab, B = B, C = bc + C, D = cd + D. A + B and C + D were lumped where the tests required only two classes of individuals. For convenience in the discussion to follow, "banded" and "unbanded" will be used to describe the two halves of the pattern spectrum (e.g., when referring to the effects of migration of "unbanded" individuals, we are including types ab and B snakes, which actually do show some light banding).

"Bass Complex" refers to North Bass, Middle Bass, South Bass, Green and Rattlesnake Islands. Middle-Pelee refers to Middle and Pelee Islands. "Peninsular mainland" refers to collections from Port

[1] Present address of both authors: Department of Entomology, University of Kansas, Lawrence, Kansas.

Evolution 12: 504–511. December, 1958.

Reprinted by permission of The Society for the Study of Evolution and the authors from *Evolution* 12:504–511, 1958.

505          JOSEPH H. CAMIN AND PAUL R. EHRLICH

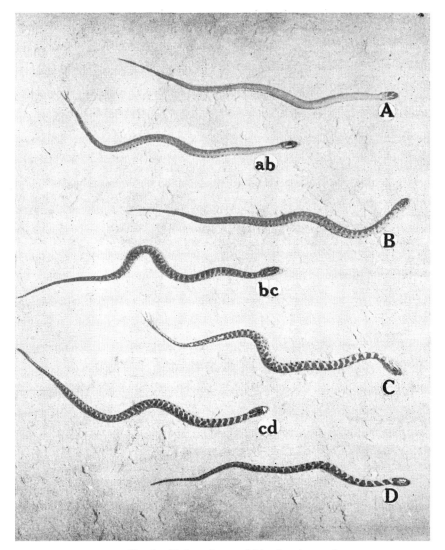

Fig. 1.   Pattern types of island water snakes.

Clinton, Lakeside, Marblehead and Catawba Peninsula (all Ohio).

All pregnant females were isolated and their litters, including those stillborn, were scored as to pattern type. There was no sign of a correlation between pattern type and live birth.

There is no evidence that there is any change in pattern type from birth to maturity. Both Conant and Camin have kept individuals of *N. s insularum* in captivity over periods of several years without noticing any change in pattern.

Individuals of all pattern types have been recorded from the adult population.

## DESCRIPTION OF THE ISLANDS

The Lake Erie islands (fig. 2) vary in area from less than one acre to about fifteen square miles. The islands are wooded, and with a few exceptions (such as a large marsh on Middle Bass) they have little or no inland water. In general the water snakes are confined to the peripheries of the islands where they sub-

NATURAL SELECTION IN SNAKES

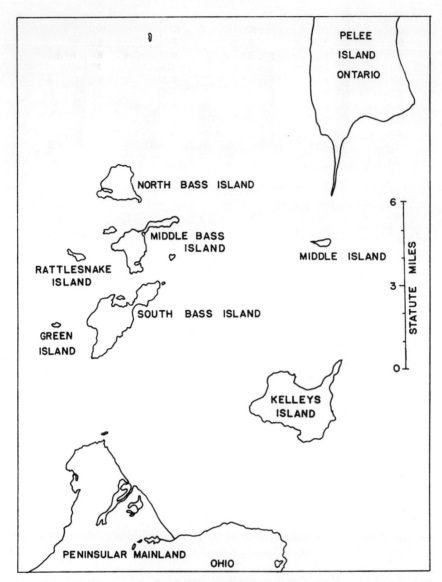

Fig. 2. Map of Lake Erie islands.

sist in large part on *Necturus* and storm-killed fish (Conant, 1951 and unpublished observations). The peripheries of the islands consist of flat limestone rocks (see Conant, 1951, Pl. 26, fig. 1), limestone cliffs or limestone pebble beaches.

The highest point on the islands is on South Bass (about 70 feet above lake level). Middle Island is approximately 15 feet above lake level at its highest.

## GEOGRAPHIC VARIATION

As can be seen from the histograms (fig. 3), there is considerable geographic variation in pattern type. All the Ontario mainland snakes were typically banded *sipedon* and the peninsular mainland samples contained a very few unbanded individuals. The difference between the Ontario and Peninsular

507    JOSEPH H. CAMIN AND PAUL R. EHRLICH

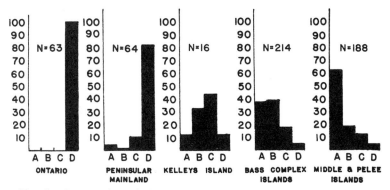

Fig. 3.    Geographic variation (ordinates—per cent of total; abscissas—
pattern types).

samples was not significant by Fisher's exact probability test (P = .123).

The sample from Kelleys I. contains a significantly greater proportion of banded individuals than that from the Bass Complex (chi-square, .01 > P > .001) and the Bass Complex sample has a significantly larger proportion of banded individuals than the one from Middle-Pelee (chi-square, P << .001).

Camin and other biologists in the area have frequently observed snakes swimming several miles from the nearest shore. This would indicate that there is considerable mainland-island and inter-island migration. A major factor in maintaining the geographic variation would appear to be this pattern of migration. Whereas South Bass and Kelleys Islands would probably receive about equal numbers of banded mainland migrants, South Bass doubtless receives additional migrants from the more northerly members of the Bass Complex. Because of their greater distance from shore, these northern islands of the Bass Complex would receive fewer typical *sipedon* migrants from the mainland and thus have populations with a lower proportion of banded individuals. The unbanded southward migrants could account for the fact that South Bass (as well as the Bass Complex as a whole) has a lower proportion of banded individuals than does Kelleys.

Similarly the relative isolation from the mainland of Middle and Pelee Islands could account for the greater proportions of unbanded individuals in their populations.

## EVIDENCE OF SELECTIVE ELIMINATION

Figure 4 shows by histograms the pattern type frequencies of Bass Complex litters and adults and Middle Island litters, juveniles and adults.

The "raw" litter data are presented by histograms in figures 5 and 6. In these figures, the type classification of the female parent is indicated by a vertical line topped by the ♀ symbol. It is interesting to note that in all but one litter the female was of a class closer to the unbanded extreme of the distribution than was the median class of the offspring. A number of genetic explanations could account for this phenomenon, but without further data an hypothesis would have no value.

Because of the restrictions placed on the data by the fact that the litters are samples from the sample of the total gene pool carried by their parents (a type of cluster sampling), it is immediately apparent that simple chi-square analysis would not give a legitimate test of the apparent differences in type frequencies between the litter and adult populations. The young are not mutually independent samplings from the population of young, as the adults are from the adult population; on the contrary, phenotypes of dif-

NATURAL SELECTION IN SNAKES

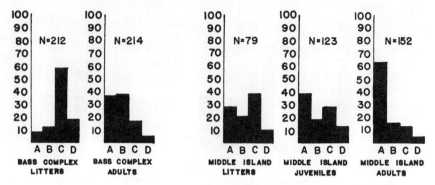

Fig. 4. Comparisons of young and adults (ordinates—per cent of total; abscissas—pattern types).

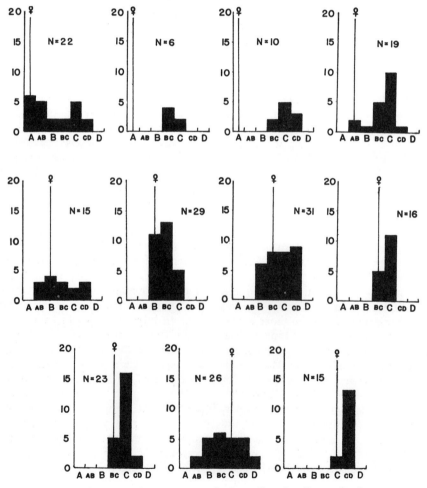

Fig. 5. Distribution of pattern types in Bass Complex litters (ordinates—number of individuals).

509                    JOSEPH H. CAMIN AND PAUL R. EHRLICH

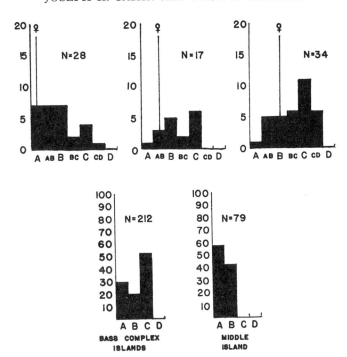

Fig. 6. 1st row: Distribution of pattern types in Middle Island litters (ordinates—number of individuals); 2nd row: Litters classified by female parent type (ordinates—per cent of total).

ferent individuals in the same litter present considerable correlation.

Using a formula[1] for the most conservative estimate of the variance of $\hat{p}$ (an

[1] Mr. David W. Calhoun, biometrician with G. D. Searle and Co., has contributed the following derivation: A simple upper limit for the variance of $\hat{p}$ can be obtained as follows. As a model let us assume each litter is associated with a probability, p, that any individual will be of type "A or B." The individuals making up a single litter form a binomial sample with parameter p. The values of p for different litters may be different, the distribution of these p's for the population of litters being unknown. Assume, finally, that litter size does not depend on p. Then the variance of $\hat{p}$, the proportion of type "A or B" in the pooled sample from all litters, has the form

$$\text{Var } (\hat{p}) = A\Sigma n^2/(\Sigma n)^2 + B/(\Sigma n)$$

where the n's are the individual litter sizes, A is the true variance (unknown) of the distribution of p's among litters and B is the average of the binomial variances pq for individual litters. Neither A nor B can exceed 0.25, and they cannot both assume this value, no matter what the distribution of p. Therefore

$$\text{Var } (\hat{p}) < 0.25[\Sigma n^2/(\Sigma n)^2 + 1/(\Sigma n)].$$

estimate of the parametric proportion of types A + B) in the litter populations, and the binomial variance for the adult populations, the significance of the differences between the litter and adult populations was tested using the Fisher-Behrens test with infinite and 213 degrees of freedom. It was found that the Bass Complex litter population was significantly different (P < .001) from the Bass Complex adult population.

The Middle Island litter population was not found to be significantly different from the Middle Island adult population. This failure to demonstrate a statistically significant difference is doubtless due to the insufficient sampling (3 litters only) of the litter population, since the similarly constituted wild-caught juvenile population is significantly different from the adult population (chi-square; P < .01).

## DISCUSSION

The observed significant differences between the young and adult populations can only be accounted for by differential elimination of the banded pattern types or by pattern changes in the individual snakes. The evidence is overwhelmingly in favor of the former hypothesis.

There are a number of possible explanations for the presence of the unbanded populations on the Lake Erie islands. The environmental conditions of the islands might induce purely phenotypic changes in snakes which matured there. The fact that the unbanded pattern types are found in the litters, and the evidence indicating no change in pattern type of individual snakes throughout life would seem to obviate this possibility.

A high proportion of unbanded pattern types might be maintained by migration from other unbanded populations. However, all known *N. sipedon* populations that could possibly supply migrants are made up of typical banded snakes.

For the frequency of unbanded genotype to be maintained by mutation alone in the observed populations would require directed mutation at a rate far above that known for any locus ever studied in any organism, even if it is assumed that color pattern is a single factor trait.

Genetic drift is not indicated as a factor in maintaining the high frequency of unbanded individuals on the islands for two reasons: First, the snakes are extremely abundant on the islands (seven collectors captured about 400 *N. sipedon* on Middle Island in five hours in 1949; three collectors captured 234 in four hours on South Bass in 1935) so that there is no reason to believe that their effective population size on any of the larger islands would approach the level at which drift would be an important factor. Second, the pattern trend is towards unbanded individuals on all the islands, which indicates a systematic pressure rather than random drift.

Therefore, by a process of elimination, selection alone can reasonably account for the presence of populations with a high proportion of unbanded individuals on the islands.

Although it is not essential to the case in point, the source of the selection pressure is of considerable interest. To the human eye, the unbanded snakes are very effectively cryptically colored when they are on the flat limestone rocks of the island peripheries. In contrast, the banded individuals are highly conspicuous. It seems likely that a visual predator is one of the principal selective influences. Gulls are abundant around the islands and experiments by the authors (carried on with the cooperation of the Lincoln Park Zoo) indicated that gulls would eat young water snakes. Other likely predators are herons (which are abundant in the area), raptors, and (recently) man.

Whatever the selective agents are, it appears that the establishment of a genetic system producing essentially 100% unbanded individuals has been prevented by a continual influx of "banded" genes brought into the island gene pools by a steady flow of mainland immigrants. This balance between strong selection and migration pressures has produced a situation which lends itself extraordinarily well to analysis. Unfortunately the presence of some migrant individuals makes it impossible to determine the exact composition of the non-migrant (selected) adult population.

On examining the works of Conant and Clay (1937) and Conant (1951) it becomes apparent that, in the problem at hand, the subspecies approach has tended to obscure a significant biological problem. Snakes of intermediate pattern types were considered to be intergrades between two distinct biological entities and some of the dynamic aspects of the situation were not considered. This should not be construed as criticism of Conant and Clay, whose careful and de-

511      JOSEPH H. CAMIN AND PAUL R. EHRLICH

tailed analysis has made possible the present study.

It should be noted that as long ago as 1942, Dunn pointed out the value of snakes and other reptiles for studies of selection in operation. It is hoped that this line of investigation will not continue to be neglected.

## SUMMARY

Data are presented indicating post-natal selection for pattern type in water snakes (*Natrix sipedon*) on the islands of Lake Erie. Strong selection, demonstrable without regard to selective agent, has produced a shift towards unbanded pattern types on the islands, while constant migration from the mainland has maintained "banded" genes in the island gene pools. These antagonistic pressures have produced a situation unusually amenable to analysis.

## ACKNOWLEDGMENTS

We wish to thank the following individuals for aid on various aspects of the work: David W. Calhoun, Skokie, Illinois; Roger Conant, Philadelphia Zoological Garden; Henry S. Dybas, Chicago Natural History Museum; Howard K. Gloyd, Chicago Academy of Sciences; Robert W. Hull, Northwestern University; Ernst Mayr, Harvard University; R. Marlin Perkins, Lincoln Park Zoo, Chicago; Loren S. Putnam, Ohio State University; George B. Rabb, Brookfield Zoological Garden, Brookfield, Illinois; and Edward S. Thomas, Ohio State Museum. We would also like to acknowledge the assistance of our wives, Emily F. Camin and Anne H. Ehrlich, in the preparation of the manuscript and figures.

## LITERATURE CITED

CAIN, A. J., AND P. M. SHEPPARD.[2] 1954. Natural selection in *Cepaea*. Genetics, **39**: 89–116.

CAMIN, JOSEPH H., CHARLES A. TRIPLEHORN AND HAROLD J. WALTER. 1954. Some indications of survival value in the type "A" pattern of the island water snakes of Lake Erie. Chicago Acad. Sci. Nat. Hist. Misc., no. 131, 3 pp.

CONANT, ROGER. 1951. Reptiles of Ohio (second edition). University of Notre Dame Press, 284 pp.

——, AND WILLIAM M. CLAY. 1937. A new subspecies of water snake from islands in Lake Erie. Occ. Papers Univ. Michigan Mus. Zool., no. 346, 9 pp.

DUNN, EMMETT REID. 1942. Survival value of varietal characters in snakes. American Naturalist, **76**: 104–109.

LAMOTTE, M.[2] 1951. Recherches sur la structure génétique des populations naturelles de *Cepaea nemoralis* (L.). Bull. Biol. France, Suppl. **35**: 1–239.

MORSE, MAX. 1904. Batrachians and reptiles of Ohio. Proc. Ohio State Acad. Sci., **4**: 95–144.

ROBSON, G. C., AND O. W. RICHARDS. 1936. The Variation of Animals in Nature. Longmans, Green and Co., 425 pp.

SEDLMAIR, H.[2] 1956. Verhaltens-, Resistenz- und Gehäuseunterschiede bei den polymorphen Banderschnecken *Cepaea hortensis* (Müll.) und *Cepaea nemoralis* (L.). Biol. Zentralblatt, **75**: 281–313.

---

[2] These references selected from the extensive literature on the question of selection in *Cepaea*.

# EXPERIMENTAL STUDIES OF THE DISTRIBUTION OF GENE FREQUENCIES IN VERY SMALL POPULATIONS OF *DROSOPHILA MELANOGASTER:* I. FORKED [1]

Warwick E. Kerr and Sewall Wright

*Universidade di São Paulo and The University of Chicago*

Received February 23, 1954 [2]

## Introduction

For quantitative study of the sort of random drift due to inbreeding it is desirable to experiment with segregating genotypes that can be classified without risk of error and with populations that are all of a very small definitely known size.

With respect to the first condition, it is much the most satisfactory if *all* segregating genotypes can be distinguished accurately. This, however, limits severely the number of loci that can be studied. Something can be done where only dominants and recessives can be accurately classified.

Most pairs of alleles with such conspicuous difference in effect as to satisfy the first condition, turn out to be subject to such enormous differences in selection that the accumulation of random deviations, implied by the term random drift, is largely prevented. Selection pressure and the effects of random processes are roughly comparable in magnitude at a given gene frequency if the change in frequency in a generation which the former tends to bring about ($\Delta q$) and the variance increment due in a generation to the latter ($\sigma^2_{\delta q}$) are of the same order (Wright, 1931, 1948). Where the ratio ($\Delta q/\sigma^2_{\delta q}$ is as high as 10 in absolute value, there is not much accumulation of random deviations and hence little random drift. The size of experimental populations in studies of the latter, should be small enough to meet this condition. They should be constant for convenient comparison with theory.

The present experiments (all with *Drosophila melanogaster*) were designed to meet these conditions. Three series were performed. About 120 lines were started in each. In the first series, the sex-linked mutation forked (f) competed with its type allele. Four females (1 f/f, 2 f/+, 1 +/+) and 4 males (2 f/0, 2 +/0) were put in each vial. The second series involved the sex-linked semidominant mutation Bar (B) and its type allele. Each initial vial contained 4 B/+ females and 4 males (2 B/0, 2 +/0). The third series was with the autosomal alleles aristapedia, ss$^a$, and spineless ss; which produce a heterozygote that is close to type. Each initial vial contained 4 ss$^a$/ss females and 4 ss$^a$/ss males. The alleles were thus equally frequent at the beginning of each experiment.

The cultures were allowed to develop until about 2 to 4 days after the offspring began to emerge. The flies hatched up to this time were discarded (in an evening). The flies which appeared next morning (if enough had emerged) were etherized and from among them 4 females and 4 males were taken at random and served as progenitors of the following generation. The etherized flies were put on a porcelain plate and the first 4 males and the first 4 females that happened to be closest to the

[1] Experimental data by W. E. Kerr, under a fellowship of the Rockefeller Foundation, mathematical analysis by S. Wright. Acknowledgment is made to Dr. Th. Dobzhansky for material and for his hospitality during the conduct of these experiments. Acknowledgment is also made to Dr. J. Crow for material and suggestions. Analysis was aided by a grant from the Wallace C. and Clara A. Abbott Memorial Fund of The University of Chicago.

[2] Editor's Note: This paper is the first of a series of three. The others will be published in successive issues of Evolution.

Evolution 8: 172–177. June, 1954.

Reprinted by permission of The Society for the Study of Evolution and the authors from *Evolution* 8:172–177, 1954.

right end of the plate were the flies taken. It was often, however, necessary to wait to the second and sometimes to the third day to obtain 4 of each sex. This procedure was repeated in every following generation in every line. The first series was carried 16 generations, the second 10 and the third 9 generations. In general, all 8 parents in each culture lived until their progeny started to emerge. In some instances one or more died a few days after the culture was started. No new flies were substituted. Lines were discontinued if fixation was attained. A few were discarded on account of mite infection and other accidents. These latter strains have not been included in the statistics presented here. The present paper will be confined to the experiments with the forked.

### FORKED

Table 1 shows the most important results. Among the 96 lines with initial gene frequency (.50 f + .50 f+), 26 were still unfixed at the end of 16 generations. Wild type had become fixed in 41 and forked in 29. There is here only an insignificant suggestion that forked was at a selective disadvantage. There seems, however, to have been a shift toward increasing disadvantage of forked as the experiment proceeded. In the first 8 generations, wild type became fixed in 17 lines, forked in 23, while in the last 8 generations, wild type became fixed in 24 lines, forked in only 6, a difference with a probability from accidents of sampling of less than .01. Nevertheless it is clear that the selection against forked must have been slight to have permitted as much fixation as occurred against its pressure.

This result is in agreement with those of previous experiments. In Ludwin's (1951) experiments, the initial gene frequency of .50 in cultures which contained on the average about 44 males, 51 females

TABLE 1. *The amount of fixation of forked and its type allele in 96 lines, each consisting of 4 ♂'s and 4 ♀'s in each generation and carried 16 generations unless fixed earlier.* The amount of fixation from generation 4 to 16 is compared with the expected amount at a constant rate of 8.9% per generation.

| | Type newly fixed | Not fixed | Forked newly fixed | Total | Observed (fixed) No. (o) | Observed (fixed) % | Calc. No. (c) | (o-c) | $\frac{(o-c)^2}{c}$ |
|---|---|---|---|---|---|---|---|---|---|
| 1 | 1 | 94 | 1 | 96 | 2 | 2.1 | | | |
| 2 | 0 | 92 | 2 | 94 | 2 | 2.1 | | | |
| 3 | 1 | 87 | 4 | 92 | 5 | 5.4 | | | |
| 4 | 5 | 79 | 3 | 87 | 8 | 9.2 | 7.7 | +0.3 | .01 |
| 5 | 3 | 70 | 6 | 79 | 9 | 11.4 | 7.0 | +2.0 | .57 |
| 6 | 1 | 66 | 3 | 70 | 4 | 5.7 | 6.2 | -2.2 | .78 |
| 7 | 5 | 59 | 2 | 66 | 7 | 10.6 | 5.9 | +1.1 | .21 |
| 8 | 1 | 56 | 2 | 59 | 3 | 5.1 | 5.3 | -2.3 | 1.00 |
| 9 | 3 | 52 | 1 | 56 | 4 | 7.1 | 5.0 | -1.0 | .20 |
| 10 | 4 | 47 | 1 | 52 | 5 | 9.6 | 4.6 | +0.4 | .03 |
| 11 | 5 | 39 | 3 | 47 | 8 | 17.0 | 4.2 | +3.8 | 3.44 |
| 12 | 2 | 37 | 0 | 39 | 2 | 5.1 | 3.5 | -1.5 | .64 |
| 13 | 3 | 34 | 0 | 37 | 3 | 8.1 | 3.3 | -0.3 | .03 |
| 14 | 3 | 30 | 1 | 34 | 4 | 11.8 | 3.0 | +1.0 | .33 |
| 15 | 1 | 29 | 0 | 30 | 1 | 3.3 | 2.7 | -1.7 | 1.07 |
| 16 | 3 | 26 | 0 | 29 | 3 | 10.3 | 2.6 | +0.4 | .06 |
| 1–3 | 2 | 273 | 7 | 282 | 9 | 3.2 | | | |
| 4–8 | 15 | 330 | 16 | 361 | 31 | 8.6 | 32.1 | -1.1 | |
| 9–16 | 24 | 294 | 6 | 324 | 30 | 9.3 | 28.9 | +1.1 | |
| 4–16 | 39 | 624 | 22 | 685 | 61 | 8.9 | 61.0 | | 8.37 |

but with enormous variations, fell to .30 in about 2 or 3 months and was still about the same at 6 months. In experiments by Merrill (1953) in populations that rarely exceeded 100 adults and in many cases were down to less than 10 flies, the frequency of forked similarly fell from .50 at the beginning to .30 by 99 days and averaged .33 in counts from 125 days to 270 days. There was no indication of increasing selection against forked in those experiments. Both authors found evidence of important differences in gene frequency among individual cultures which they attributed to random drift.

From inspection of table 1, it appears that the percentage of fixation (including both that of type and forked) rose to generation 4 but did not change consistently thereafter. The average rate for generations 4 to 16 was 8.91% (standard error 1.09%). Assuming theoretical constancy at this figure, the differences between observed and calculated numbers for unfixed and for newly fixed lines yields $\chi^2 = 8.4$, 12 degrees of freedom, probability .70–.80 of being exceeded by accidents of sampling.

The theoretical rate of fixation for a neutral sex-linked gene after a steady rate has been attained has been given as approximately $(2 N_M + N_F)/(9 N_M N_F)$ in which $N_M$ is the effective number of males and $N_F$ that of females. (Wright 1933). This approximation only applies, however, if $N_M$ and $N_F$ are moderately large. The panmictic index $P$ ($= 1-F$ where $F$ is the inbreeding coefficient) measures the amount of heterozygosis relative to that in a random bred stock. The exact recurrence formula derived by the method of path coefficients was given as follows in the paper cited. Primes refer to preceding generations.

$$P = P' - C_1 (2 P' - P'') + C_2 (2 P'' - P''')$$

where

$$C_1 = (N_F + 1)/(8 N_F),$$
$$C_2 = (N_M - 1)(N_F - 1)/(8 N_M N_F)$$

In the present case

$$C_1 = 5/32, \quad C_2 = 9/128.$$

$$P = .6875 P' + .296875 P'' - .0703125 P'''$$

TABLE 2. *The theoretical values of P ($=1-F$), P/P' and the proportional rate of change of P in a population consisting of 4 males and 4 females under sex linked inheritance and no selection*

| Generation | P ($=$1-F) | P/P' | $\Delta$P/P' |
|---|---|---|---|
| 0 | 1 | | |
| 1 | 1 | 1 | 0 |
| 2 | 1 | 1 | 0 |
| 3 | .914062500 | .914062500 | .085937 |
| 4 | .854980469 | .935363248 | .064637 |
| 5 | .788848877 | .922651341 | .077349 |
| 6 | .731885910 | .927789759 | .072210 |
| 7 | .677245259 | .925342665 | .074657 |
| 8 | .627418808 | .925427759 | .073572 |
| 9 | .580946889 | .925931581 | .074068 |
| 10 | .538047138 | .926155468 | .073845 |
| 11 | .498260630 | .926053861 | .073946 |
| 12 | .461439099 | .926099858 | .073900 |
| 13 | .427329066 | .926079014 | .073921 |
| 14 | .395744515 | .926088456 | .073912 |
| 15 | .366492734 | .926084178 | .073916 |
| 16 | .339403833 | .926086117 | .073914 |
| 17 | .314316879 | .926085236 | .073915 |
| 18 | .291084347 | .926085636 | .073914 |
| 19 | .269568980 | .926085455 | .073915 |
| 20 | .249643934 | .926085538 | .0739145 |

The correlation $(1 - P_0)$ between the gametes that united to produce the foundation females was zero and the correlation $(1 - P_1)$ between the gametes that unite to produce their daughters is also zero. If there were no differential fecundity among the foundation flies there would be no correlation between mating males and females and hence $(1 - P_3) = 0$. From this point, however, the inbreeding coefficient rises. For calculation of $P_3$, $P'(= P_2)$, $P''(= P_1)$ and $P'''(= P_0)$ are all assigned the value 1. Table 2 shows the values of $P$, the ratio of successive values $P/P'$ and the percentage change in $P$ per generation $(100 \ (P - P')/(P')$ for 20 generations. It may be seen that $P/P'$ oscillates about the value .9260855. This is approximated to 4 places by the 11th generation and to 7 places by the 19th. Values of $P$ beyond this point can thus be calculated to 6 places by the formula $P = .9260855 \ P'$.

The rate of decrease of heterozygosis after it reaches stability can also be derived at once by equating $P/P'$, $P'/P''$ and $P''/P'''$ and expressing in terms of $x = \Delta P/P'$ (Wright 1933).

$$x^3 + x^2 \ (2 + 2 \ C_1)$$
$$+ \ x \ (1 + 3 \ C_1 - 2 \ C_2)$$
$$+ \ (C_1 - C_2) = 0$$

The solution is .0739145, the limit about which $\Delta P/P'$ oscillates in the successive generations.

The rate of fixation of lines approaches this same value although somewhat more slowly. Actually it has been noted that a practically constant rate 8.91% is attained by $F_4$. As this is 20.5% larger than the theoretical rate, it is implied that the actual variance due to random processes in each generation was 20.5% greater than expected. As the difference is only 1.5 times its standard error, it is not certainly significant. Taking it at face value, the excess might conceivably be due to fluctuating selection but as there is very little average selection it more probably means that the effective size of population

TABLE 3. *The distribution of unfixed classes after stability of form has been reached in a population in which $2N = 12$, no selection; and the distribution in the following generation, including newly fixed classes (each 1/24 of the total unfixed classes of the preceding generation). The frequency in each of the the unfixed classes is 11/12 of its value in the preceding generation, thus maintaining stability of form.*

|  | Unfixed classes | Following generation |
|---|---|---|
| 0 |  | .04167 |
| 1 | .07881 | .07224 |
| 2 | .08985 | .08236 |
| 3 | .09317 | .08541 |
| 4 | .09475 | .08685 |
| 5 | .09554 | .08758 |
| 6 | .09576 | .08778 |
| 7 | .09554 | .08758 |
| 8 | .09475 | .08685 |
| 9 | .09317 | .08541 |
| 10 | .08985 | .08236 |
| 11 | .07881 | .07224 |
| 12 |  | .04167 |
|  | 1.00000 | 1.00000 |

is about 83% of the theoretical value. In an autosomal diploid population the rate of decrease of heterozygosis is $\Delta P/P' = 1/(2N)$ (Wright, 1931). If effective size is defined as $P'/2 \Delta P$, the theoretical effective size with sex linkage and 4 females and 4 males per generation is 6.7646 while the effective size of the experimental population was 5.61. The difference if real can easily be accounted for if 1 or 2 of the 8 flies fail completely to reproduce in each generation.

The distribution of gene frequencies, during the period of constant rate of fixation, must have practically reached equilibrium of form. The actual distribution was not determined because of the lack of visible distinction between $+/+$ and $+/f$. It is of some interest, however, to consider what it must have been. It may suffice to give the distribution for an effective population of 6 and ignore the indicated slight selective differential (Wright, 1931). The standard is considered a population of 6 monoecious diploid individuals with completely random

GENE FREQUENCIES IN SMALL POPULATIONS

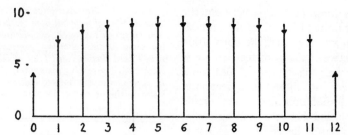

FIGURE 1. The theoretical distribution of gene frequencies (including newly fixed classes) after attainment of stability of form in a population in which $2N = 12$ and selection is absent. Rough estimates for the unfixed classes are given by the ordinates of the curve, $y = 1/12$, unit area (base 12) derived from indefinitely large $2N$. The frequencies $(1/24)$ of the newly fixed classes are given exactly by half the terminal ordinates of this curve.

union of gametes, as it has been shown that the distribution is nearly the same for given $N_e$, irrespective of the system of mating (Wright, 1931).

Let $f(q)$ be the frequency of gene frequency $q$. The class with this gene frequency contributes to the classes of the next generation according to the expansion of $[(1 - q)(f^+) + q(f)]^{12} f(q)$ and thus to the class with gene frequency $q_1$ by

$$\frac{12!}{(2\,Nq)!\,[2\,N(1 - q)]!} q^{2\,Nq_1}(1 - q)^{2\,N(1-q_1)} f(q).$$

The total frequency of $q$ is the sum of all contributions from the 11 values of $q$ from $1/12$ to $11/12$. This must be $11/12$ of its value in the preceding generation if there is equilibrium of the form of the distribution. The equation can be solved algebraically as in a number of simple examples given in the reference cited [3] but it is

[3] We will note that one of these is incorrect as published, viz., that for irreversible mutation in populations of 3 monoecious individuals (p.

probably simplest in this case to start from a rough approximation and iterate, rating up each generation by 12/11, until stability is reached. The resulting distribution is shown in table 3 and figure 1.

While this solution applies to a situation with a slightly lower rate of fixation (1/24 for each allele) than that observed, the form of the distribution apart from the newly fixed classes is substantially correct for 4 ♀'s, 4 ♂'s (12 representative of the locus) for any effective size of parental population not too remote from 6. Indeed with an indefinitely large population in each generation, the form of the distribution is not very different, being approximately uniform for all gene frequencies (Wright, 1931).

118). The correct percentages are 42.40% for $q_a = 1/6$, 21.07% for $q_a = 2/6$, 15.54% for $q_a = 3/6$, 11.99% for $q_a = 4/6$, 9.00% for $q_a = 5/6$, total 100% for unfixed classes. The rate of fixation of A is 17.05% and of a, 4.53% of the unfixed classes.*

TABLE 4. *The history of a line in which an eye color mutation appeared in generation 5 and drifted into fixation in generation 12*

|  |  | $F_4$ |  | $F_5$ |  | $F_6$ |  | $F_7$ |  | $F_8$ |  | $F_9$ |  | $F_{10}$ |  | $F_{11}$ |  | $F_{12}$ |  |
|---|---|---|---|---|---|---|---|---|---|---|---|---|---|---|---|---|---|---|---|
|  |  | f | w$^a$ | f | w$^a$ | f | w$^a$ | f | w$^a$ | f | w$^a$ | f | w$^a$ | f | w$^a$ | f | w$^a$ | f | w$^a$ |
| ♀ | recessive | 2 | — | 1 | 1 | 0 | 0 | 1 | 3 | 0 | 0 | 0 | 2 | 0 | 4 | 0 | 3 | 0 | 4 |
|  | dominant | 2 | — | 3 | 3 | 4 | 4 | 3 | 1 | 4 | 4 | 4 | 2 | 4 | 0 | 4 | 1 | 4 | 0 |
| ♂ | recessive | 1 | — | 1 | 3 | 0 | 4 | 1 | 0 | 0 | 4 | 0 | 2 | 0 | 3 | 0 | 4 | 0 | 4 |
|  | dominant | 3 | — | 3 | 1 | 4 | 0 | 3 | 4 | 4 | 0 | 4 | 2 | 4 | 1 | 4 | 0 | 4 | 0 |

* The last sentence should read: "The rate of fixation of A is 16.31% and of a, 4.34% of the unfixed classes."

A situation that arose in one line (No. 109) in this series is interesting. In the 5th generation the flies taken to be parents of the 6th generation were found to be segregating for an eye color found to behave as an allele of white. This gene drifted in frequency until it became fixed in the 12th generation. The frequencies of f and this gene (apparently $w^a$) were as shown in table 4.

Thus this line had probably become fixed for the type allele of forked by the 9th generation and after the 12 generation for the new eye color mutant.

## DISCUSSION

Populations of 4 males and 4 females per generation are so exceedingly small that experiments such as the present may seem to have no implications for evolution in nature. It must be borne in mind, however, that changes in the underlying multifactorial genetic structure of species probably occur so slowly that an appreciable change in a thousand generations must be considered as an explosively rapid process.

Study in the laboratory of the factors that can contribute to such change is practicable only by stepping up the rates by at least one hundred fold. Thus the interaction between a weak selective advantage of one isoallele over another and a slight random drift, due to inbreeding, can be simulated by using alleles with selective differentials of ten percent or more instead of perhaps only one tenth of a percent or even one hundredth of a percent in populations of only one percent or even one tenth of one percent of the size of a typical natural deme.

In the case of forked, the selective differential is clearly much less than ten percent so that the results of the present paper illustrate random drift from in-

breeding in an almost pure form. More complicated situations will be considered in the later papers of this series.

## SUMMARY

Ninety-six lines of flies (*Drosophila melanogaster*) were started, each from 4 females (1 f/f, 2 f/+, 1 +/+) and 4 males (2 f/0, 2 + /0), and continued to fixation or to the sixteenth generation by random selection of 4 females and 4 males as parents of each new generation. Type ($f^+$) became fixed in 41 lines, forked (f) in 29 lines, and 26 lines were still unfixed at the end. The amount of selection against forked was thus slight, although there was evidence that it was greater in the later generations than at first.

The rate of fixation (of both alleles combined) reached approximate constancy by the fourth generation at 8.9% per generation. This would imply an effective size of population 83 per cent of that expected under sex linkage with 4 females and 4 males per generation but the reduction is of doubtful significance.

In one line, an eye color mutation, probably apricot, appeared in $F_7$ and became fixed in $F_{12}$, three generations after fixation of the type allele of forked.

## LITERATURE CITED

LUDWIN, I. 1951. Natural selection in *Drosophila melanogaster* under laboratory conditions. Evolution, **5**: 231–242.

MERRELL, D. J. 1953. Gene frequency changes in small laboratory populations of *Drosophila melanogaster*. Evolution, **7**: 95–101.

WRIGHT, S. 1931. Evolution in Mendelian populations. Genetics, **16**: 97–159.

——. 1933. Inbreeding and homozygosis. Proc. Nat. Acad. Sci., **19**: 411–420.

——. 1948. On the roles of directed and random changes in gene frequency in the genetics of populations. Evolution, **2**: 279–294.

# AN EXPERIMENTAL STUDY OF INTERACTION BETWEEN GENETIC DRIFT AND NATURAL SELECTION

Theodosius Dobzhansky and Olga Pavlovsky [1]

*Department of Zoology, Columbia University, New York City*

Received January 31, 1957

## Introduction

The role of random genetic drift in the evolutionary process has, for about two decades, been one of the controversial issues in population genetics. Some authors have appealed to "drift" as a convenient explanation of the origin of differences among organisms for which no other explanations seemed to be available. But one's inability to discover the adaptive significance of a trait does not mean that it has none (cf. Dobzhansky, 1956). The hypothesis of random genetic drift should not be used as a loophole; to be accepted it requires a firmer basis than suspicion. Other authors seem to think that drift and natural selection are alternatives. As soon as a gene is shown to have any effect whatever on fitness, the conclusion is drawn that its distribution in populations must be determined solely by selection and cannot be influenced by random drift. But this is a logical non-sequitur. The important work of Aird *et al.* (1954) and of Clarke *et al.* (1956) disclosed that the incidence of certain types of gastro-intestinal ulceration is significantly different in persons with different blood groups. This is, however, far from a convincing demonstration that the observed diversity in the frequencies of the blood group genes in human populations is governed wholly, or even partially, by selection for resistance to ulcers. To make such a conclusion tenable it would have to be demonstrated that the environments in which human racial differences have evolved actually favored greater resistance in certain parts of the

world and lesser resistance in certain other parts. Thus far no evidence has been adduced to substantiate any such claim.

As defined by Wright (1949) random genetic drift includes all variations in gene frequencies which are indeterminate in direction. Such variations are caused by accidents in gene sampling in populations of finite genetically effective size, as well as by fluctuations in the intensity or in the direction of selection, mutation and gene exchange between populations. Wright (1932, 1948, 1948, 1951) as well as the present writer (Dobzhansky, 1937–1941–1951) have stressed that random drift by itself is not likely to bring about important evolutionary progress. Indeed, variations in gene frequencies induced by random drift in small isolated populations are apt to be inadaptive, and hence likely to result in extinction of such populations. However, random drift may be important in conjunction with systematic pressures on the gene frequencies, particularly with natural selection. What is most necessary, then, is the type of experimental evidence that would permit analysis of the interactions between random drift and selection. Such evidence, although difficult to obtain, should be within the range of what is possible. Kerr and Wright (1954) and Wright and Kerr (1954) studied models of Drosophila populations in which the number of the progenitors in every generation was fixed arbitrarily, and in which classical laboratory mutants were used as traits subject to drift and to selection. In the experimental Drosophila populations described in the following pages naturally occurring genetic variants, inversions in the third

[1] The work reported in this article has been carried out under Contract No. AT-(30-1)-1151, U. S. Atomic Energy Commission.

Evolution 11: 311–319.  September, 1957.

Reprinted by permission of The Society for the Study of Evolution and the authors from *Evolution* 11:311–319, 1957.

chromosomes of *Drosophila pseudoobscura* were used. Severe limitation of the population sizes was introduced in some of the populations in only a single generation, at the beginning of the experiments. Experiments so conducted may to some extent reproduce genetic events which occur in natural populations.

## PRELIMINARY EXPERIMENTS

It has been shown (see Dobzhansky, 1949 and 1954, for reviews) that heterozygotes of *Drosophila pseudoobscura* which carry two third chromosomes with different gene arrangements derived from the same locality are, as a rule, superior in Darwinian fitness to the corresponding homozygotes. The situation is more complex when flies of different geographic origins are hybridized. Chromosomal heterozygotes which carry two third chromosomes derived from different geographic regions may or may not exhibit heterosis. Experimental populations, bred in the laboratory in so-called population cages, behave differently depending upon whether the foundation stock of the population consists of flies of geographically uniform or of geographically mixed origin. In the former case, the chromosomes with different gene arrangements usually reach certain equilibrium frequencies. Replicate experiments, conducted with reasonable precautions to make the environments uniform, give results repeatable within the limits of sampling errors. With geographically mixed populations the results do not obey simple rules. The course of natural selection in such populations is often erratic; equilibrium may or may not be reached, or may be reached and then lost; replicate experiments do not give uniform results; heterosis may or may not be present at the start of the experiments, and may or may not develop in the course of selection in the experimental populations.

The indeterminacy observed in the populations of geographically mixed origin is however understandable (Dobzhansky and Pavlovsky, 1953; Dobzhansky, 1954).

Race hybridization releases a flood of genetic variability; the number of potentially possible gene combinations far exceeds the number of the flies in the experimental populations; natural selection perpetuates the genotypes which possess high adaptive values under experimental conditions, but it is a matter of chance which of the possible adaptive genotypes will be formed first in a given population. In some populations these genotypes will happen to be structural heterozygotes, and in others homozygotes.

We have tested about thirty experimental populations of mixed geographic origins, using different combinations of flies from diverse localities (Dobzhansky and Pavlovsky, 1953, and much unpublished data). Among them were two replicate populations, Nos. 119 and 120, which are relevant here. They were started on February 8, 1954, in wood-and-glass population cages used in our laboratory and described previously. The foundation stocks consisted of $F_1$ hybrids between 12 strains derived from flies collected near Austin, Texas in 1953 and 10 strains derived from Mather, California, in 1947. The Texas strains were homozygous for the Pikes Peak (PP) gene arrangement, and the California strains for the Arrowhead (AR) gene arrangement in their third chromosomes. In each of the two cages 2,395 flies of both sexes, taken from the same $F_1$ culture bottles of Texas by California crosses, were introduced. The populations were kept in an incubator at 25° C., samples of eggs deposited in the population cages were taken at desired intervals, larvae hatching from these eggs were grown under optimal conditions in regular culture bottles, and their salivary glands were dissected and stained in acetic orcein.

The course of the events in the populations Nos. 119 and 120 is shown in table 1 and figure 1. The percentage frequencies of PP chromosomes are given in this table, the frequencies of AR chromosomes are the balance to 100 per cent. Each sample is based on determination of the

GENETIC DRIFT AND NATURAL SELECTION

TABLE 1. *Changes in the frequencies (in per cent) of PP chromosomes in two replicate experimental populations of* Drosophila pseudoobscura *of mixed geographic origin (Texas PP by California AR)*

| Days from start | Population No. 119 | Population No. 120 | Chi-Square | P |
|---|---|---|---|---|
| 0 | 50.0 | 50.0 | — | — |
| 35 | 49.3 | 48.7 | 0.02 | 0.90 |
| 70 | 39.0 | 40.7 | 0.08 | 0.75 |
| 105 | 42.3 | 36.7 | 1.01 | 0.35 |
| 250 | 30.0 | 43.7 | 6.01 | 0.01 |
| 300 | 29.0 | 40.7 | 4.50 | 0.03 |
| 365 | 26.3 | 42.0 | 15.60 | 0.001 |
| 425 | 25.0 | 41.7 | 9.37 | 0.002 |

gene arrangement in 300 third chromosomes (150 larvae, taken in 6 subsamples on 6 successive days). The first samples, 35 days from the start, showed little change from the original frequencies, 50 per cent, of the chromosomes. At 70 and 105 days the frequencies of PP diminished, about equally in both populations, as shown by the low chi-square (each chi-

square has one degree of freedom). But at 250 days the frequency of PP diminished in the population No. 119, while it failed to change, or even increased, in No. 120. This situation persisted until April 9, 1955, about 425 days from the start, when the last samples were taken and the populations were discarded. The chi-squares shown in table 1 attest that the outcomes of natural selection in these two experimental populations were clearly unlike. It should be noted that the magnitude of the divergence between the replicate populations Nos. 119 and 120 is not exceptionally great for the type of experiments in which flies from geographically remote localities are involved.

## MAIN EXPERIMENTS

Certain consequences should follow from the above interpretation of the indeterminacy observed in populations of geographically mixed parentage. The indeterminacy should be a function of the genetic variability in the foundation stock

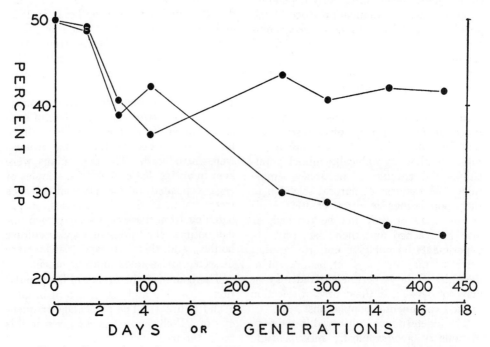

FIG. 1. Changes in the frequencies of PP chromosomes in two replicate experimental populations of mixed geographic origin (Texas by California).

314     THEODOSIUS DOBZHANSKY AND OLGA PAVLOVSKY

of the populations. Chromosomes with PP and AR gene arrangements are recognizable under the microscope; their frequencies are made uniform in the foundation stock of all populations, and we observe changes in their frequencies as the experiment progresses. However, we infer that, apart from this overt variability in the frequency of the gene arrangements, there must exist also a large amount of genic variability released owing to gene recombination in the $F_2$ and later generations of interracial hybrids. Although there is no way of telling by how many genes the races differ, the number of the possible gene combinations must be several to many orders of magnitude greater than the number actually realized. The outcome of selection in the experimental populations should, then, be more variable in small than in large populations.

This working hypothesis is open to experimental test, but the experimental technique must be carefully thought through. One could make some experimental populations smaller than others by keeping them in cages of different sizes and with different amounts of food. The drawback of this would be that the environments of the populations of different sizes would be dissimilar. Therefore, we have chosen to vary the sizes of the foundation stocks of our populations, but to permit them to expand to equal size, which, because of the high fecundity of the flies, they do within a little more than a single generation.

The same 12 Texas PP and 10 California AR strains were used in the main as in the preliminary experiments (see above). $F_1$ hybrids between them, which were necessarily heterozygous PP/AR, were raised in regular culture bottles, and so were the $F_2$ hybrids. In June 1955, 4,000 $F_2$ flies, about equal numbers being females and males and derived equally from the different crosses, were placed in a population cage. Between June 15 and 27, 15 cups with yeasted culture medium were inserted in the cage daily. The flies covered the medium with eggs overnight. The cups with the eggs were then withdrawn and placed in another population cage containing no adult flies. In this manner ten population cages, Nos. 145–154, were obtained on ten successive days. They were descended, then, from the same foundation stock of 4,000 $F_2$ interlocality hybrids. The frequencies of PP and AR chromosomes in the foundation stock are evidently 50–50. These are the "large" populations.

Ten groups of 20 $F_2$ flies each, 10 ♀♀ and 10 ♂♂, were taken from the same $F_2$ cultures which served as the source of the foundation stock for the "large" populations, care being taken to include in each group flies from all the $F_2$ cultures.

TABLE 2.  *Frequencies (in per cent) of PP chromosomes in the experimental populations*

| Large populations | | | Small populations | | |
|---|---|---|---|---|---|
| No. | Oct. '55 | Nov. '56 | No. | Oct. '55 | Nov. '56 |
| 145 | 39.3 | 31.7 | 155 | 37.7 | 18.0 |
| 146 | 42.3 | 29.0 | 156 | 30.7 | 32.0 |
| 147 | 29.3 | 34.7 | 157 | 31.0 | 46.0 |
| 148 | 38.0 | 34.0 | 158 | 32.3 | 46.7 |
| 149 | 33.3 | 22.7 | 159 | 34.3 | 32.7 |
| 150 | 36.0 | 20.3 | 160 | 41.7 | 47.3 |
| 151 | 40.3 | 32.0 | 161 | 37.3 | 16.3 |
| 152 | 41.0 | 22.3 | 162 | 25.3 | 34.3 |
| 153 | 37.0 | 25.7 | 163 | 37.7 | 32.0 |
| 154 | 42.0 | 22.0 | 164 | 25.3 | 22.0 |
| Mean | 37.85 | 27.44 | Mean | 33.33 | 32.73 |
| Variance | 15.30 | 26.96 | Variance | 26.73 | 118.91 |

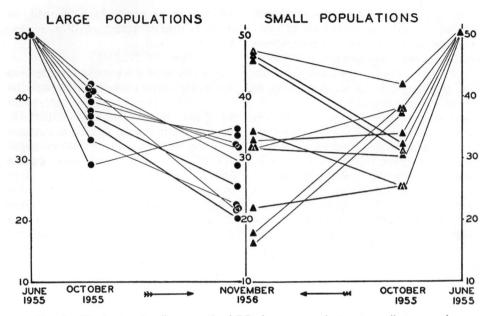

Fig. 2. The frequencies (in percent) of PP chromosomes in twenty replicate experimental populations of mixed geographic origin (Texas by California).

These groups of $F_2$ flies were placed in regular culture bottles and allowed to produce progenies. Each progeny was then transferred to population cages of the same type as those used for the "large" populations. Ten population cages, Nos. 155–164, were thus obtained. They are the "small" populations. It should be reiterated that the "large" and the "small" differed only in the foundation stocks, these being 4,000 and 20 flies respectively. All populations were kept at 25° C. and treated similarly in every way.

In October and November 1955, about 4 generations after the start, the populations were examined; egg samples were taken and the chromosomes in the salivary gland cells of the larvae that hatched from these eggs were studied. The gene arrangements in the chromosomes were determined and scored by Dr. Louis Levine. The results are summarized in table 2 and figure 2. As usual, each sample consisted of 300 chromosomes. The frequencies of PP varied from 29.3% to 42.3% in the "large" populations, and from 25.3% to 41.7% in the "small" ones.

The heterogeneity is significant in both; the chi-square for the "large" is 19.5 and for the "small" ones 35.9, which correspond to probabilities of about 0.02 and of much less than 0.001 respectively. The heterogeneity among the replicate experiments is, of course, not surprising in view of the outcome of the preliminary experiments (table 1), although in these latter a significant heterogeneity first appeared after somewhat more than 4 generations from the start. It may be noted (table 2) that the variance for the "small" populations (26.7) is ostensibly greater than for the "large" ones (15.3), but the F value is not significant. It may also be noted that the frequencies of PP chromosomes have declined from the 50% value in the foundation stock, the decline being somewhat greater in the "small" (33.3%) than in the "large" (37.8%) populations.

The next, and the final, test of the populations was made in November 1956, i.e., more than a year after the first test and about 19 generations after the populations were placed in the population cages. The preliminary experiments

**316** THEODOSIUS DOBZHANSKY AND OLGA PAVLOVSKY

(table 1) show that the populations reach equilibria in the frequencies of PP and AR chromosomes within less than a year from the start. The samples, 300 chromosomes per cage, were taken in the usual manner and scored by one of us (Th. D). The results are reported in table 2 and figure 2.

It may be noted that the mean frequency of PP in the "large" populations is now 27.4% and in the "small" ones 32.7%. These means are not significantly different from each other, but the 1956 mean for the "large" populations is significantly lower than the 1955 mean. The outcomes of natural selection in the "large" and the "small" populations are, then, similar on the average. It is otherwise when the outcomes in the individual populations are considered. As shown in table 2 and figure 2, the frequencies of PP in the "large" populations range from 20.3% to 34.7%, and in the "small" ones from 16.3% to 47.3%. In both instances the heterogeneity is highly significant (the chi-square for the "large" population is 40.4 which, for 9 degrees of freedom, has a negligible probability of being due to chance. Both in the "large" and especially in the "small" populations the variance has increased during the year intervening between the two tests (1955–1956).

Most important of all is, however, that the "small" populations show a heterogeneity significantly greater than the "large" ones. The variances, 118.9 and 27.0, now give an F ratio of 4.4 which is significant at between the 0.025 and 0.010 levels. The greater heterogeneity is evidently due to the different magnitudes of the foundation stocks in these populations. This heterogeneity was indicated already by the tests in October 1955, but it has become significant as the selection continued during the year between the two tests. Finally, it may be pointed out that there appears to be no significant correlation between the status of a given population in 1955 and 1956. For example, No. 160 had the highest frequency of PP in both tests (Table 2), but No. 161 which had the lowest frequency in 1956 had an above average frequency in 1955.

## DISCUSSION

The results of the present investigation can be stated very simply: Although the trait studied (the gene arrangement in the third chromosome) is subject to powerful selection pressure, the outcome of the selection in the experimental populations is conditioned by random genetic drift. The either-selection-or-drift point of view is a fallacy.

In our experiments, the heterozygotes which carry two third chromosomes with different gene arrangements are heterotic; natural selection in the experimental populations establishes equilibrium states at which both gene arrangements occur with certain frequencies; these frequencies are determined by the relative fitness of the homozygotes and heterozygotes. Now, the environments being reasonably uniform in all experimental populations, the outcome of the selection processes in the replicate experiments should also be uniform. And so it is, in experimental populations of geographically uniform origin. But it is not so in geographically mixed populations. In the latter, the selective fates of the chromosomal gene arrangements become dependent upon the polygenic genetic background, which is highly complex and variable because of the gene recombination that is bound to occur in populations descended from race hybrids. Here random drift becomes operative and important. It becomes important despite the populations being small only at the beginning of the experiments, because the foundation stocks in some populations consisted of small numbers of individuals. Thereafter, all the populations expand to equal sizes, fluctuating roughly between 1,000 and 4,000 adult individuals. Such populations can be regarded as small only in relation to the number of gene recombinations which are possible in populations of hybrid origin.

For reasons that are not far to seek, geneticists visualize the evolutionary process usually in terms of the destinies of single genes. With the notable exception of the contributions of Wright (1932 and subsequent work), this is the frame of reference of most of the mathematical theory of population genetics. This makes manageable an otherwise impossibly complex topic, and yet the oversimplified models usually suffice for understanding of microevolutionary processes. But as we move into the realm of mesoevolution (Dobzhansky, 1954), not to speak of macroevolution, it becomes indispensable to consider not only the destinies of single genes but also of integrated genotypes, and finally of the gene pool of Mendelian populations. In our experiments, the foundation stock of the populations consisted of $F_2$ hybrids between rather remote geographic races; a highly variable gene pool arose owing to the hybridization; random drift caused different segments of this gene pool to be included in the foundation stocks of each population, especially in the small ones; natural selection then produced divergent results in different populations, especially again amongst the small ones.

It is now logical to inquire whether the events observed in our experimental populations resemble situations which occur in nature. The excellent work of Dowdeswell and Ford (1952, 1953) and Ford (1954) has disclosed a most suggestive case. Populations of the butterfly *Maniola jurtina* are rather uniform throughout southern England, despite some obvious environmental diversity in different parts of this territory. In contrast to this, the populations of the same species show quite appreciable divergence on the islands of the Scilly archipelago, although these islands are within only a few miles of each other and their environments appear rather uniform. Especially remarkable is the divergence observed between the populations of certain small islands, while larger islands have more nearly similar populations. The small islands happen, however, to be situated between the larger ones. The investigators have estimated

that the populations of the small islands consist of numbers of individuals of the order of 15,000 and that the populations of the large islands must be considerably greater. The authors conclude that the genetic divergence between these populations must be produced entirely by selection, random drift being inconsequential. The evidence is, however, weighed in favor of the view that the genetic divergence was initiated by the island populations being derived from small numbers of immigrants from the mainland or from other islands. These immigrants introduced somewhat different sets of genes on each island, whereupon natural selection built different genetic systems in the different populations.

The divergence between island and mainland populations has been studied also by Kramer and Mertens (1938) and by Eisentraut (1950) in lizards, and by Lowe (1955) in mammals and reptiles. Most data agree in showing that the divergence is greater on smaller than on larger islands, and greater on islands more remote from the mainland than on those which are apt to receive immigrants most frequently. Many authors, including this writer (Dobzhansky, 1937, 1941), interpreted these situations as arising through random drift in populations of continuously small size, or frequently passing through narrow "bottlenecks." This interpretation need no longer be sustained. It is more probable, especially in the light of the experiments described in the present article, that in the island populations we are observing the emergence of novel genetic systems moulded by interaction of random drift with natural selection.

Mayr (1954) has pointed out that conspicuous divergence of peripherally isolated populations of a species is a fairly general phenomenon, well known to systematists. He rightly concludes that this divergence cannot be due entirely to random drift "in the ordinary sense," i.e., to fluctuations of the gene frequencies in populations of persistently small size. Indeed, some of the peripheral populations consist of thousands or even millions of individuals. Mayr's interpretation can be stated best in his own words: "Isolating a few individuals (the 'founders') from a variable population which is situated in the midst of a stream of genes which flows ceaselessly through every widespread species will produce a sudden change of the genetic environment of most loci. This change, in fact, is the most drastic genetic change (except for polyploidy and hybridization) which may occur in a population, since it may effect all loci at once. Indeed, it may have the character of a veritable 'genetic revolution.' Furthermore, this 'genetic revolution,' released by the isolation of the founder population, may well have the character of a chain reaction. Changes in any locus will in turn affect the selective values at many other loci, until finally the system has reached a new state of equilibrium." The outcome of our experiments described above may, in a sense, be regarded as experimental verification of Mayr's hypothesis.

## SUMMARY

Twenty replicate experimental populations of *Drosophila pseudoobscura* were kept in a uniform environment for approximately 18 months. The foundation stocks of all the populations consisted of $F_2$ hybrids between flies of Texas origin which had the PP gene arrangement in their third chromosomes, and flies of California origin with the AR gene arrangement in the same chromosome. In ten of the populations the founders numbered 4,000 individuals; the other ten populations descended from only 20 founders each.

The frequencies of PP and AR chromosomes in all the populations were originally 50 per cent. Eighteen months later, the frequencies of PP varied from about 20 to 35 per cent in the populations descended from the large numbers of founders, and from 16 to 47 per cent in those descended from small numbers of the founders. The heterogeneity of these frequencies of PP chromosomes observed in the replicate populations is statistically highly significant. More important still, the heterogeneity is significantly greater in the populations descended from small numbers of founders than in those descended from large numbers of founders.

Heterozygotes which carry a PP and an AR third chromosome are superior in adaptive value to the PP and AR homozygotes. Therefore, the frequencies of PP and AR chromosomes in the experimental populations are controlled by natural selection. However, the heterogeneity of the results in the replicate populations is conditioned by random genetic drift.

Only some of the possible combinations of the genes of the Texas and California genomes are actually realized in the populations. The segments of the gene pool which arise from race hybridization are smaller, and therefore less uniform, in the populations descended from small than in those descended from large numbers of founders. It may reasonably be inferred that evolutionary changes involving interactions of natural selection and random drift of the kind observed in our experiments are not infrequent in nature.

## ACKNOWLEDGMENTS

We take pleasure in acknowledging our obligations to our colleague Professor Howard Levene, and to Dr. Bruce Wallace of the Long Island Biological Laboratories, for their counsels regarding the statistical and experimental procedures; to Professor Louis Levine for the examination of the chromosomal constitution of the experimental populations in October of 1955; to Mr. and Mrs. B. Spassky for the maintenance of the experimental populations during the two months when both authors were absent from New York; and to many colleagues and friends for many discussions of the problems and issues dwelt upon in the present article.

LITERATURE CITED

AIRD, I., H. H. BENTALL, J. H. MEHIGAN, AND J. A. FRASER ROBERTS. 1954. The blood groups in relation to peptic ulceration and carcinoma of the colon, rectum, breast, and bronchus. Brit. Med. Journ., 2: 315–321.

CLARKE, C. H., J. W. EDWARDS, D. R. W. HADDOCK, A. W. HOWELL EVANS, R. B. McCONNELL, AND P. M. SHEPPARD. 1956. ABO blood groups and secretor character in duodenal ulcer. Brit. Med. Journ., 2: 725–730.

DOBZHANSKY, TH. 1937–1941–1951. Genetics and the Origin of Species. Columbia University Press, New York (1st, 2nd and 3rd editions).

——. 1949. Observations and experiments on natural selection in *Drosophila*. Proc. 8th Internat. Cong. Genetics: 210–224.

——. 1954. Evolution as a creative process. Proc. 9th Internat. Cong. Genetics, 1: 435–449.

——. 1956. What is an adaptive trait? Amer. Naturalist, 20: 337–347.

——. 1957. Genetics of natural populations. XXVI. EVOLUTION (in press).

——, and O. PAVLOVSKY. 1953. Indeterminate outcome of certain experiments on *Drosophila* populations. EVOLUTION, 7: 198–210.

DOWDESWELL, W. H., AND E. B. FORD. 1952. Geographical variation in the butterfly *Maniola jurtina*. Heredity, 6: 99–109.

——, AND E. B. FORD. 1953. The influence of isolation on variability in the butterfly *Maniola jurtina*. Symp. Soc. Exp. Biol., 7: 254–273.

EISENTRAUT, M. 1950. Die Eidechsen der spanischen Mittelmeerinseln und ihre Rassenaufspaltung in Lichte der Evolution. Berlin.

FORD, E. B. 1954. Problems in the evolution of geographical races. In: Evolution as a Process: 99–108.

KERR, W., AND S. WRIGHT, 1954. Experimental studies of the distribution of gene frequencies in very small populations of *Drosophila melanogaster*. EVOLUTION 8: 225–240.

KRAMER, G., AND R. MERTENS. 1938. Rassenbildung bei west-istrianischen Inseleidechsen in Abhangigkeit von Isolierungsalter und Arealgrosse. Arch. Naturgesch., 7: 189–234.

LOWE, CH. H. 1955. An evolutionary study of island faunas in the Gulf of California, Mexico, with a method of comparative analysis. EVOLUTION, 9: 339–344.

MAYR, E. 1954. Change of genetic environment and evolution. In: Evolution as a Process: 157–180.

WRIGHT, S. 1932. The roles of mutation, inbreeding, crossbreeding and selection in evolution. Proc. 6th Internat. Congress Genetics, 1: 356–366.

——. 1948. On the roles of directed and random changes in gene frequency in the genetics of populations. EVOLUTION, 2: 279–294.

——. 1949. Population structure in evolution. Proc. Amer. Philos. Soc., 93: 471–478.

——. 1951. Fisher and Ford on "The Sewall Wright Effect." Amer. Scientist, 39: 452–479.

——, AND W. KERR. 1954. Experimental studies of the distribution of gene frequencies in very small populations of *Drosophila melanogaster*. EVOLUTION, 8: 225–240.

# Evolution of Fitness in Experimental Populations of Drosophila serrata

Abstract. *Changes which enhance adaptedness to the environment occur in experimental populations of* Drosophila serrata *which are acted upon by strong natural selection. The improvement is greater in hybrid than in single-strain populations because genetic variability is greater in the former.*

Evolutionary changes can be observed not only on the geological time scale. Rapid adaptive changes have been found in both natural and experimental populations. Among insects, adaptive changes in the genetic constitution of natural populations, caused by natural selection in changing environments, have been recorded in several species (1); in some cases these genetic changes have also been reproduced experimentally (2). With *Drosophila*, improvements in fitness in carriers of certain chromosomal arrangements have also been observed in the laboratory (2, 3). Experiments devised to observe and measure improvements in the ability of a population to exploit the resources of a particular environment are nevertheless rare (4). The experiments reported here were designed to study changes of this kind.

Two strains of *Drosophila serrata*, derived from impregnated females collected in nature, were used. One was collected near Popondetta, New Guinea, and had been maintained in

the laboratory by mass culture for 1½ years before the beginning of the experiment. The other one was collected in Bulahdelah, about 130 miles north of Sydney, Australia, and had been maintained by mass culture for about 3 years. Six experimental populations were used. Two of the populations were derived from the Popondetta strain and two from the Sydney strain; the other two populations were started with $F_1$ descendents of mass crosses between the Popondetta and the Sydney strains.

One population of each pair was maintained at 25° ± 0.5°C and the other at 19° ± 0.5°C. Each population was started with 150 pairs of flies. The populations were maintained in ½-pint milk bottles, with a ¾-inch layer of medium (cream of wheat and molasses) and with a double piece of toweling, 2 by 7 inches, partially pressed into the medium. The technique has been described in detail elsewhere (5). In short, the adult flies are introduced into a bottle with

fresh medium and transferred to a new bottle at regular intervals. For flies maintained at 25°C, transfer is made on Mondays, Wednesdays, and Fridays; for the others, on Mondays and Fridays. The bottles containing eggs are also kept in the constant-temperature incubators. At 25°C, adult flies start to emerge about the 12th day; at 19°C, about the 16th day. The newly hatched flies are collected and counted on the same days on which the populations are transferred to new bottles and then are added to the bottle with the adult flies. The adult, ovipositing flies are thus always in a single bottle with fresh food, while some 13 other bottles in each series contain eggs, larvae, pupae, and hatching adults. Every second week, on Friday, the adult populations are anesthetized with ether, counted, and weighed; the newborn flies are also weighed on that day before they are added to the adult population.

The adult populations increase in numbers very rapidly because of continuous addition of newly hatched flies. In 5 to 8 weeks they reach a size of about 2000 individuals; then they oscillate around that number during the rest of the experiment. The action of natural selection is very strong, both among the adults and during the immature stages. The number of eggs laid in each bottle is at least 10 times, and perhaps 100 times, larger than the number of flies which can develop on the amount of food available. The adult flies are extremely crowded in the bottle. The surface of the food is covered with several layers of flies attempting to feed and to lay eggs.

The two Sydney populations were discarded after 51 weeks. Their performance is not reported here since it was similar to that of the Popondetta populations and has been reported elsewhere (5). The other four populations were maintained for 70 weeks. The sizes of the adult populations and the numbers of flies hatching per week are shown in Figs. 1 and 2. A trend toward increasing population size is quite apparent. This trend was examined statistically by the regression of population size on time between weeks 17 and 70. During the first 5 to 8 weeks the populations grew in size until they reached the limits imposed by food and space. To dissociate the increase in population size due to the natural growth of the population from

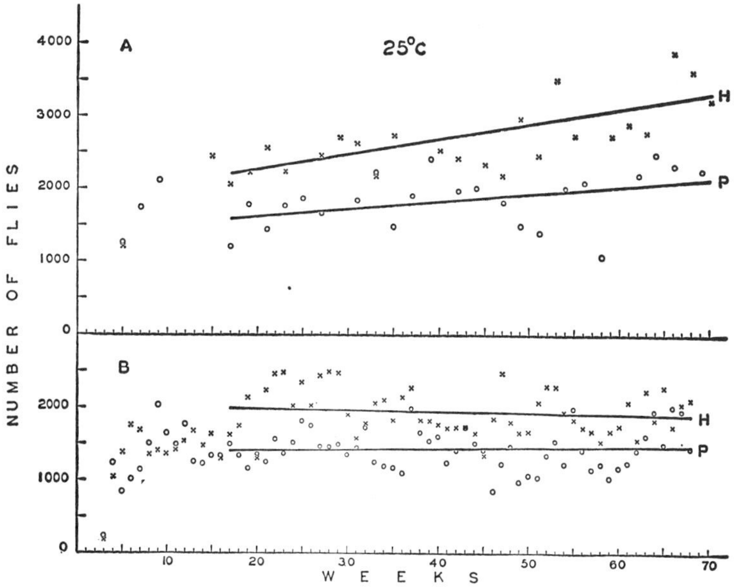

Fig. 1. Population size (*A*) and weekly production (*B*) of two experimental populations of *Drosophila serrata* at 25°C. H, Hybrid population; P, single-strain (Popondetta) population.

Reprinted by permission of the American Association for the Advancement of Science and the author from *Science* 150:903–905, 12 November 1965. Copyright 1965 by the American Association for the Advancement of Science.

the increase caused by the genetic improvement in fitness, the occasional counts made during the first 16 weeks of the experiment were not used in the regression analysis. About five generations must have elapsed during that period at 25°C, and about three generations at 19°C (5). A regression analysis in one time for the number of flies hatched per week was also done for the interval of weeks 16 to 68. The regression lines are drawn in Figs. 1 and 2. Table 1 shows, for the adult flies, the mean population size, $\overline{Y}$, and the regression coefficient of population size on time; time units are weeks. The same parameters for the newborn flies are presented in Table 2. Student's $t$ was used to test the significance of the coefficients of regression. The $t$ values and the probability that such values are due to chance are also included in Tables 1 and 2.

The coefficients of regression of population size on time vary from 8.4 to 20.4, and in all the populations they are significantly different from zero. The populations have evolved toward a superior adaptation to the experimental environment. This evolution occurs gradually during the 54 weeks of the experiment. The improvement during this period seems to be due exclusively to the increased ability of the flies to survive the crowding in the bottles, and their aver-

age longevity is constantly increasing. The coefficients of regression for the number of newborn flies per week are not significantly different from zero, so that no improvement is apparent in the ability of the populations to transform the available food into living flies. Moreover, the differences between the regression coefficients of population size and newborn flies are statistically significant ($P < .05$) for all four populations. Two considerations, not mutually exclusive, may account for this result. During their past history drosophila flies have probably been exposed quite frequently to conditions in which a limited amount of food was available for the number of eggs and larvae present in a particular ecological niche. Under these con-

Table 1. Mean population size, $\overline{Y}$, of four experimental populations of *Drosophila serrata* from weeks 17 to 70, and regression coefficients, $b$, of population size on time (weeks as time units), with $t$ and $P$ values for significance of regression.

| $\overline{Y}$ | $b$ | $t$ | $P$ |
|---|---|---|---|
| | *Single strain at 25°C* | | |
| 1862 | +10.5 | 2.27 | <.05 |
| | *Hybrid at 25°C* | | |
| 2750 | +19.5 | 3.36 | <.01 |
| | *Single strain at 19°C* | | |
| 1724 | + 8.4 | 2.58 | <.02 |
| | *Hybrid at 19°C* | | |
| 2677 | +20.4 | 4.46 | <.001 |

Table 2. Mean number of flies, $Y$, produced per week between weeks 16 to 68 by four experimental populations of *Drosophila serrata*, and regression coefficients, $b$, of the number of flies produced on time (weeks as time units) with $t$ and $P$ values for significance of regression.

| $Y$ | $b$ | $t$ | $P$ |
|---|---|---|---|
| | *Single strain at 25°C* | | |
| 1434 | +1.05 | 0.43 | >.50 |
| | *Hybrid at 25°C* | | |
| 1939 | −2.08 | 0.64 | >.50 |
| | *Single strain at 19°C* | | |
| 795 | +1.87 | 1.20 | >.20 |
| | *Hybrid at 19°C* | | |
| 1244 | +0.69 | 0.30 | >.50 |

ditions, natural selection is expected to produce and to maintain genetic constitutions which allow the populations to exploit maximally the available food sources. Any mutation arising in the experimental populations which would increase their ability to transform food into living matter had probably originated in the past and had been incorporated into the genetic endowment of the population. The second hypothesis is that competition for food during the immature stages was so strong that the maximum genetic improvement had already been achieved during the first three to five generations of the experiment, which are not included in the regression analysis. The higher productivity of the hybrid populations seems to support this hypothesis.

As for the adult flies, competition for space among them may not be so strong as competition for food among the larvae. On the other hand, it is unlikely that during their past history these populations have been living in their natural habitats with available space as limited as it is in the experimental environment. Adult crowding is a new environmental factor for these flies, and evolutionary adaptation is therefore more likely to occur. The genetic variability present in the populations, or arising by mutation and recombination, gives origin, under the action of natural selection, to new genotypes highly fit to survive under crowded conditions. In *The Origin of Species* Darwin wrote that natural selection "tends to the improvement of each creature in relation to its organic, and inorganic conditions of life." When drosophila flies are exposed to a novel condition of life, such as adult crowding, natural selection improves their genetic constitution in relation to that condition.

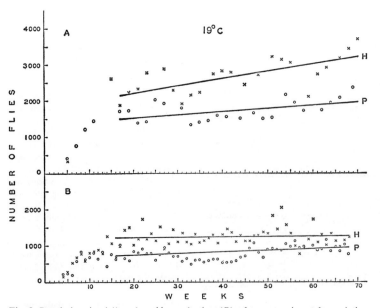

Fig. 2. Population size (*A*) and weekly production (*B*) of two experimental populations of *Drosophila serrata* at 19°C. *H*, Hybrid population; *P*, single-strain (Popondetta) population.

The conflict between adaptive fitness and genetic variability has been pointed out (6). The mutation process furnishes the raw materials from which adaptive changes are constructed, but it produces also a multitude of poorly adapted variants. Under the action of natural selection, those genetic variants in a population which increase the adaptation of the population to the environments in which it lives are preserved. Populations of the same species living in geographically widely separated regions are expected to have different genetic constitutions. Two such populations, one from New South Wales in Australia and the other from New Guinea, were used in these experiments to initiate hybrid populations. The hybrid populations may therefore carry larger amounts of genetic variability. The probability that highly adapted genotypes will be produced during exposure to new environments is greater in the hybrid than in the single-strain populations. Figures 1 and 2 show that the performance of the hybrid populations is superior for both the number of flies produced and the total population size. Similar results have been obtained in other cases (3, 5, 7). Moreover, Table 1 shows that the rate of increase in population size with time is considerably higher in the hybrid populations than in the single-strain populations. In other words, the hybrid populations are evolving faster. The rate of increase in the population size of the hybrid populations is approximately double that of the single-strain populations. The difference between the regression coefficients is statistically significant for flies maintained at 19°C ($t = 2.11$, $P < .05$), but not for flies maintained at 25°C ($t = 1.03$, $P > .20$).

FRANCISCO J. AYALA
*Rockefeller Institute, New York*

**References and Notes**

1. T. Dobzhansky, *Heredity* **1**, 53 (1947); *Evolution* **12**, 385 (1958); E. B. Ford, *Advance Genet.* **5**, 43 (1953); H. B. D. Kettlewell, *Ann. Rev. Entomol.* **6**, 245 (1961).
2. T. Dobzhansky, *Evolution* **1**, 1 (1947).
3. M. W. Strickberger, *Evolution* **17**, 40 (1963); *Genetics* **51**, 795 (1965).
4. See, however, T. Dobzhansky and B. Spassky, *Evolution* **1**, 191 (1947); H. L. Carson, *Proc. Natl. Acad. Sci. U.S.* **44**, 1136 (1958).
5. F. J. Ayala, *Genetics* **51**, 527 (1965).
6. T. Dobzhansky, *Genetics and the Origin of Species* (Columbia Univ. Press, New York, ed. 3, 1951); J. B. S. Haldane, *Amer. Natur.* **71**, 337 (1937); K. Mather, *Biol. Rev. Cambridge Phil. Soc.* **18**, 32 (1943).
7. T. Dobzhansky and O. Pavlovsky, *Heredity* **16**, 169 (1961).
8. Research supported by AEC contract AT-(30-1)-3096-2. T. Dobzhansky provided guidance and criticism and H. Levene statistical advice. The statistical analysis was done by Suzanne Mosby.

16 August 1965

# IV

# Adaptations
# of Populations

In the preceding two sections, we considered the topics of variation in and changes of populations. We now turn to a related topic—the nature of a population's adaptation to its environment. In considering the adaptation of a population, we run the danger of falling into a semantic argument, for it is obviously the individual that is or is not adapted to the environment. However, the death of one or a few maladapted individuals may have little or no effect on the population as a whole and it is the broader unit that is our primary concern. Moreover, if we consider the appearance of a novel adaptation in an individual as an evolutionary experiment, it is clear that the experiment will be judged a success or failure according to its broader implications for the population as a whole.

Adaptations are elicited in response to environmental challenges or opportunities presented at any level from the molecule to the ecosystem. Accordingly, some adaptations may seem rather minor (the ability to metabolize a single molecule) whereas other adaptations may seem to be much broader (the development of flight by formerly wingless insects). However, all adaptations, regardless of their complexity, must meet the same test: to be successful they must increase the ability of the population to survive through time.

The lead paper in this section deals with the evolution of complex life cycles which are divided into two or more ecologically distinct phases, for instance the tadpole and adult stages of frogs. ISTOCK briefly considers the initial constraints on developing a complex life cycle from a simple, one-phased cycle and then formulates a general model for the population dynamics of such a cycle. From this model, he asserts that (1) there is a high degree of independence in the evolution of the different life cycle phases, (2) once achieved, if a complex cycle is to be stable the rates of change of adaptation of both phases must be the same, and (3) over long periods of time the second assertion is unlikely to hold, hence complex life cycles are inherently unstable. Finally, several examples are presented from a variety of phyla which support these assertions. Thus ISTOCK's paper not only elegantly treats a problem of considerable interest; it provides another example of the power and beauty of the model as a tool for the understanding of nature.

The development of a complex life cycle is one mode of niche expansion. Of course, most species with simple life cycles also have adaptations that promote the survival of a population in a diversity of environments. In some cases, as illustrated in the paper by JAIN and MARSHALL, closely related species may have quite different adaptations to ensure survival under a wide range of environmental conditions. The mating system of the two species of wild oats examined in this study is one of predominant self-fertilization accompanied by a small amount of outcrossing. Although both species are adapted to colonizing diverse habitats, the modes of adaptation of the two appear to be quite different, at least in degree. The populations of one species, *Avena fatua*, appear to depend heavily on genetic flexibility in adapting to heterogeneous environments, whereas individuals within populations of *A. barbata* exhibit a greater phenotypic plasticity. Another interesting aspect of this work is the apparent heterozygote advantage at several loci in the first species. Thus overdominance in conjunction with the low frequency of outcrossing, serves to maintain genetic variability in the face of the intense inbreeding resulting from self-fertilization.

Behavioral elements also enter any general consideration of how populations adapt to their environment. One of the most striking modes of adaptation is almost exclusively behavioral in operation—the division of the habitat into defended areas which are termed territories. Usually territories are formed by one or both members of a breeding pair of individuals. Many variations on this theme exist and in the paper by CARRICK one of them—the group territorial system of the Australian magpie—is described and analyzed. Because of geographical variation, not all sites are equally suitable for the establishment of territories. Generally, if the suitability of a habitat varies in a clinal pattern through space, it may be divided into central and marginal areas for purposes of study. When CARRICK did this, he found that breeding success was highest in central areas where permanent groups were formed and much lower in marginal territories that contained an inadequate amount of either cover or feeding area.

It is generally assumed that qualitatively different types of processes occur in the central and marginal portions of a population. For instance, population density tends to be higher in central than in marginal areas whereas the effective rigor of the environment tends to be higher in marginal areas than in the center of a population's distribution. We might therefore hypothesize that the major stresses operating on individuals in the central part of the range relate to intrapopulational factors, whereas in marginal areas the major threats to continued survival have their origins in external factors. If this hypothesis is valid, we would expect to find different patterns of natural selection in the two parts of the population. Further, if there is some isolation of the individuals occupying central and marginal areas, then adaptive differences should evolve which reflect the different selective pressures. These differences do in fact occur as evidenced by CARSON's study of *Drosophila robusta*. This species is characterized by latitudinal clines in both morphology and frequencies of various chromosome inversions, reflecting adaptation to different sets of environmental conditions. Moreover, as one moves toward the marginal areas from the distributional center, the frequency of inversions decreases until at the periphery of the distribution a population is relatively free of chromosomal polymorphism. Since inversions, in heterozygous form, effectively restrict recombination, there is a corresponding increase in the recombination potential at the margins. This provides the population with a greater capacity to adapt rapidly to environmental challenges than would be possible if the extensive inversion system of the central area were present.

Another closely related question is: How does the fitness of a population depend on its adaptive history? Using *Drosophila* populations collected from different geographical regions of Lebanon, Egypt, and Uganda, TANTAWY and MALLAH have measured the response of several quantitative characters to variation in culture temperature. It was found that populations collected in environments that have a large amount of temperature variation respond differently to thermal stress during development than do those populations collected in relatively non-variable environments. Specifically, those populations from variable environments showed less morphological variation and higher viability and therefore greater developmental homeostasis than those populations collected in the stable environments. In the face of environmental change it might be expected that populations from variable environments would be more likely to survive than those populations existing in relatively constant environments. On the other hand, TANTAWY and MALLAH found that the population from the most stable environment was superior to all other populations under the laboratory conditions that most closely approximated its original climate. From this type of evidence it is clear that the gene pool of a population reflects the environmental challenges that meet each new generation.

One means of determining the effective amount of variation in a population at any given time is to measure the phenotypic variability of its component individuals. This is the type of measure employed by LEVINS in the prologue paper and it is used again by CODY in this section to explain clutch size variation in birds. CODY assumes that there is a limited amount of time and energy available to an individual. This time and energy must be allocated among all of the various activities necessary for survival. However, because of environmental and genetic variation, not all individuals follow the same mode of allocation; hence any population contains variation in environmental exploitation patterns. CODY's hypothesis explains how variation in clutch size parallels changes in both the physical and biotic environment.

This conclusion is reinforced by the study of JOHNSON and COOK on variation in the carpel number of buttercups. An analysis of the pattern of geographic variation indicated a high correlation between carpel number and length of the growing season. This correlation is at least partially related to the time required for photosynthesis to produce the materials needed for seed endosperm formation. When plants from different environments are grown under uniform conditions, it is found that there are both genetic and environmental components in the variation of their carpel number, reflecting the adaptation of each population to its original environment. JOHNSON and COOK argue that two factors operate to determine the buttercup's seed production: (1) phenotypic plasticity which maximizes reproductive success of the individual in the presence of environmental variation from year to year, and (2) stabilizing selection for an optimal intermediate carpel number that reflects the average amount of photosynthate that can be produced in the specific environment.

Another aspect of the same general topic is discussed by McLAREN in his study of the relationship between body size and reproduction of arctic chaetognaths (arrow-worms). In some habitats, *Sagitta elegans* matures and reproduces in its first year of life. In other habitats, the same species has a longer prereproductive growth stage and does not become sexually mature until its second year. These divergent patterns of adaptation create a problem since it is easy to demonstrate that if survivorship and total fecundity are fixed, the growth rate of a population can be increased by shortening the period between birth and first reproduction. Assuming that both life histories are optimum for their individual environments, we must ask what factors lead to a two-year maturation period at a large body size in one habitat when the species is physiologically capable of reaching sexual maturity at a smaller size in only one year. McLAREN's approach to this question illustrates the interdigitation of both theory and data that typifies much of population biology.

Evidence for the integration of the gene pool in response to selection for adaptation to the local environment is also available from many different laboratory experiments. One type of experiment, exemplified by the paper of WALLACE and VETUKHIV, involves comparing the fitness of progeny from crosses between geographically distinct populations with that of progeny from intrapopulational matings. Generally it is found that the $F_1$ offspring from interpopulational crosses are superior, but that the $F_2$ progeny have reduced fitness. The superiority of $F_1$ progeny cannot be attributed to an increase in total heterozygosity per se, but rather to heterozygosity for integrated gene complexes. The latter, of course, are broken up by recombination in the $F_1$ individuals, leading to the reduced fitness observed in the $F_2$.

Thus evidence from a variety of sources can be marshalled to demonstrate that through natural selection a population acquires a high degree of adaptation to its environment.

The last topic to be considered in this section is the question of what happens when a deleterious allele enters the population. The usual fate of such genes is elimination by either natural selection or random genetic drift, with the rate of elimination under selection being proportional to the reduction in fitness of genotypes containing the allele. Yet most natural populations of house mice are polymorphic for certain alleles (*t* alleles) which when homozygous are either lethal or cause sterility in males. Studies of this system have shown that between 85 and 99 percent of the functional sperm of heterozygous males contain the *t* allele. Thus selection against the deleterious alleles in the zygotic stage is counterbalanced by selection favoring *t*-bearing gametes.

Deterministic models based on these two opposing selective forces lead to predictions of equilibrium gene frequencies in natural populations that are considerably higher than those actually found. LEWONTIN, in his paper on the male sterile *t* alleles, demonstrates that if the effective size of mouse breeding units is small enough, the combined effects of selection and random genetic drift will produce frequencies closer to those observed in nature. In addition to the attempt to solve this very interesting problem, LEWONTIN's paper also illustrates the use of digital computers to stimulate biological systems.

The male sterile *t* alleles provide an example of the increase in frequency of a deleterious allele which can lead to extinction of the population. LEWONTIN's analysis leads him to the conclusion that interdeme selection is responsible for the continued persistence of these alleles. Although the reality, or unreality, of interdeme or group selection is currently a topic of vigorous debate in some circles of population biology, the *t* allele system does provide one definite example of its operation.

# THE EVOLUTION OF COMPLEX LIFE CYCLE PHENOMENA:
## AN ECOLOGICAL PERSPECTIVE

Conrad A. Istock

*Department of Biology, University of Rochester*

Received June 3, 1966

It seems reasonable to expect ecological theory to supply clear statements about the dominant forces which influence sequences of evolutionary change. This idea proceeds simply from the recognition that natural selection is identical with the interactions between organisms or populations and their secular environments. Such interactions determine probabilities of survival and reproduction as well as population size. This paper contains a theoretical treatment of the ecological and evolutionary exigencies imposed by a complex life cycle.

For the purposes of this paper a complex life cycle is one which involves passage through two or more ecologically distinct phases. This means that there does not exist any overlap among the factors which limit abundance in each phase. Each phase thus has its own set of predator-prey, competitive, physical-environmental, and resource interactions.

The following notation (adapted from Cole, 1954) will be convenient in designating important junctures in the life history of any species which exhibits two ecologically distinct life cycle phases:

0—age 0 or birth,
$\psi$—first age after transfer between "larval" and "adult" environments,
$\alpha$—age of first reproduction,
$\omega$—age of last reproduction,
$\lambda$—age of maximum longevity.

For simplicity, I will take $\psi$ and $\alpha$ to be the same age. While this is certainly not the case in many species it does not alter the sense of any of the following discussions. Thus ages 0 to $(\alpha-1)$ define larval life, ages $\alpha$ to $\omega$ define adult reproductive life, and ages $(\omega + 1)$ to $\lambda$ define postreproductive life.

The initial evolution of a complex life cycle must involve the transfer of one part of the life history of a species from a set of ancestral resources to a new set of supplementary resources (Fig. 1). The transfer would go to completion quickly if the following criteria are met: (1) genetic (potential gene pool) preadaptation for the supplementary environment exists; (2) the set of supplementary resources is sufficient to allow a net energy gain to the species. This implies that adequate demographic balance (*i.e.*, reciprocal numerical repopulation of both environments) is established. This does not necessarily imply resource limitation of the population in either the ancestral or supplementary environments.

Throughout this paper only species with two distinct phases are considered. The expansion of these arguments to cases of more than two phases should not be difficult.

## THEORETICAL ARGUMENT

The life table and table of reproduction serve as a record of the age-specific survival and fertility data for any species population (Deevey, 1947; Birch, 1948; Dublin et al., 1949; Smith, 1954; Fisher, 1958). Such data may describe either the maximum physiological performance of the population under a set of defined physical conditions or its performance under a variety of more natural sets of conditions which involve restrictive biological interactions in addition to the physical factors. The following life table $(l_x)$ and fertility $(m_x)$ definitions will be used:

$l_{x, p}$ = the probability that any given individual will still be alive at age $x$ in a population existing under a

Reprinted by permission of The Society for the Study of Evolution and the author from *Evolution* 21:592–605, 1967.

specified set of physical conditions but free from biological restraints other than innate genetic defects (physiological growth conditions).

$l_{x,e}$ = the probability that any given individual will still be alive at age $x$ in a population existing under the same physical conditions plus an array of externally (interspecific) and internally (intraspecific) imposed biological restraints (equilibrium or natural growth conditions).

$l'_x$ = a new survivorship column which represents a hypothetical combination of larval physiological survivorship and adult equilibrium survivorship. Now, the probability of surviving to age $\psi$ (equal to age $\alpha$ in the fabricated life histories of this paper) is given by the expression $l'_\psi = l_{\psi-1,p} \cdot l_{\psi,e}/l_{\psi-1,e}$, and all succeeding values are given by the expression $l'_x = l'_{x-1} \cdot l_{x,e}/l_{x-1,e}$ (see Table 1 and Fig. 2).

$l''_x$ = a new survivorship column which represents a hypothetical combination of larval equilibrium survivorship and adult physiological survivorship. Now the probability of surviving to age $\psi$ is given by the expression $l''_\psi = l_{\psi-1,e} \cdot l_{\psi,p}/l_{\psi-1,p}$, and all succeeding values by the expression $l''_x = l''_{x-1} \cdot l_{x,p}/l_{x-1,p}$ (see Table 1 and Fig. 2).

$m_{x,p}$ = the mean number of female offspring born to a female during age $x$ in a population existing under physiological conditions.

$m_{x,e}$ = the mean number of female offspring born to a female during age $x$ in a population existing at equilibrium.

It will be seen shortly that these six different columns of data allow the separation of larval and adult life history contributions (see Table 1 for numerical example).

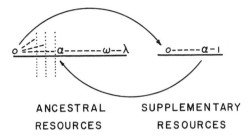

ANCESTRAL       SUPPLEMENTARY
RESOURCES       RESOURCES

FIG. 1. Schematic diagram of initial evolution from a simple to a complex life cycle. The figure depicts the gradual transfer of all immature individuals from the set of ancestral resources to a set of new resources.

Figure 2 shows the distinction between the four types of survivorship using the artificial data in Table 1. It is now possible to use the $l_x$ and $m_x$ definitions to erect the following definitions:

$R_g$ = a gross reproductive rate; it is the sum of some $m_x$ column.

$R_0$ = a net reproductive rate; it is the sum of the cross products of any $l_x$ and $m_x$ columns.

$r$ = an instantaneous rate of increase.

$R_0$ and $r$ are related by the expression $R_0 = e^{r\tau}$, where $\tau$ is the mean duration of one biological generation (Smith, 1954). In this paper $\tau$ is treated as a species characteristic constant. This is certainly not generally true and corrections for density-dependent changes in $\tau$ would have to be included in any practical analyses.

Four different types of net reproductive and instantaneous rates are possible as a result of the foregoing definitions:

$$R_{0,p} = \Sigma\, l_{x,p}\, m_{x,p} = \text{antilog } e^{r_p\tau},$$
$$R_{0,a} = \Sigma\, l'_x\, m_{x,e} = \text{antilog } e^{r_a\tau},$$
$$R_{0,l} = \Sigma\, l''_x\, m_{x,p} = \text{antilog } e^{r_l\tau},$$
$$R_{0,e} = \Sigma\, l_{x,e}\, m_{x,e} = 1;\ r_e = 0.$$

These summations are over the $\alpha$ to $\omega$ age span, the only ages for which $m_x$ values can exist. Using the calculations from Table 1 the relationships of the four net reproductive rates are shown graphically in Figure 3. $R_{0,p}$ is the highest net reproductive rate possible under the defined physical con-

594                                    CONRAD A. ISTOCK

TABLE 1. *Life tables, tables of reproduction, and an estimate of epsilon for a species with a complex life cycle.*

| $x$ | $l_{x,p}$ | $l'_x$ | $l_{x,e}$ | $l''_x$ | $m_{x,p}$ | $m_{x,e}$ | $l_{x,p}m_{x,p}$ | $l'_x m_{x,e}$ | $l''_x m_{x,p}$ | $l_{x,e}m_{x,e}$ |
|---|---|---|---|---|---|---|---|---|---|---|
| 0 | 1.00 | | 1.00 | | | | | | | |
| 1 | .99 | | .70 | | | | | | | |
| 2 | .98 | | .50 | | | | | | | |
| 3 | .97 | | .40 | | | | | | | |
| 4 | .96 | | .30 | | | | | | | |
| 5 | .95 | | .25 | | | | | | | |
| $\alpha$ 6* | .94 | .760 | .20 | .248 | 15.0 | 0.70 | 14.100 | 0.532 | 3.720 | 0.140 |
| 7 | .93 | .646 | .17 | .245 | 40.0 | 1.70 | 37.200 | 1.098 | 9.800 | 0.289 |
| 8 | .92 | .532 | .14 | .242 | 50.0 | 3.00 | 46.000 | 1.596 | 12.100 | 0.420 |
| 9 | .91 | .418 | .11 | .239 | 30.0 | 1.01 | 27.300 | 0.422 | 7.170 | 0.111 |
| $\omega$ 10 | .90 | .304 | .08 | .236 | 10.0 | 0.50 | 9.000 | 0.152 | 2.360 | 0.040 |
| 11 | .85 | | .05 | $R_{g,p} = 145.0$ | | $R_0 = 133.600$ | | 3.800 | 35.150 | 1.000 |
| 12 | .75 | | .03 | | | | | | | |
| 13 | .55 | | .01 | | | | | | | |
| 14 | .15 | | .00 | | | | | | | |
| 15 | .00 | | .00 | | | | | | | |

$$\epsilon = \frac{\ln R_{0,p}/\tau - \ln R_{0,1}/\tau}{\ln R_{0,p}/\tau} = \frac{0.6123 - 0.4450}{0.6123} = 0.273$$

\* $\alpha = \psi$.

ditions. $R_{0,a}$ is the net reproductive rate which results if the larval phase of the life cycle conforms to its physiological survivorship but the adult phase exhibits equilibrium (natural) survivorship and fertility. $R_{0,l}$ is the net reproductive rate when larval survival is of the equilibrium (natural) type but the adult survival and fertility remain physiological. $R_{0,e}$ results when the effects produced by both phases are just sufficient to produce equilibrium for the population as a whole.

It is possible to show that

$$R_{0,p} = R_{0,a} \cdot R_{0,l} \cdot R_{0,e},$$

and thus that

$$r_p = r_a + r_l.$$

The larval effect ($\epsilon$) contributing to decline from $r_p$ to $r_e$ may be defined as

$$\epsilon r_p = r_p - r_l, \tag{1}$$

or

$$\epsilon = (r_p - r_l)/r_p. \tag{2}$$

Similarly the adult effect ($\phi$) may be defined as

$$\phi r_p = r_p - r_a. \tag{3}$$

Adding (1) and (3) and substituting for $r_p$ yields

$$r_p = \epsilon r_p + \phi r_p,$$

or

$$r_p = \epsilon r_p + (1 - \epsilon)r_p. \tag{4}$$

If a population could somehow continuously realize growth at some positive rate $r$ it would grow exponentially according to the expression

$$dN/dt = rN, \tag{5}$$

where $r = r_p$ at maximum growth. Now, if we assume that the addition of each new individual to the population causes some degree of crowding, resulting in a linear suppression of $r_p$ we may write

$$r = r_p - cN_l - gN_a, \tag{6}$$

where $N_l$ is the number of larvae alive, $N_a$ the number of adults alive, and $c$ and $g$ the coefficients of suppression by larvae and adults respectively. Upper limits for $N_i$ and $N_a$ would be $K_l$ and $K_a$; the saturation values or maximum carrying capacities of the larval and adult environments. At equilibrium equation (6) becomes

$$r = r_p - cK_l - gK_a = 0.$$

Substituting for $r_p$ from (4) and rearranging we obtain at equilibrium

$$r = [\epsilon r_p - cK_l]$$
$$+ [(1 - \epsilon)r_p - gK_a] = 0. \tag{7}$$

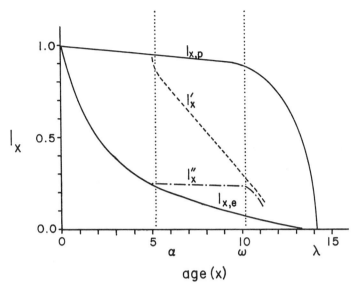

FIG. 2. Graph of physiological, equilibrium (or natural), and two hypothetical composite survivorship curves from the fabricated data in Table 1. All symbols are defined in the text.

For equation (7) to be realized both bracketed expressions must be zero. Biologically this means that both phases of the life cycle are saturating their respective environments indicating that

$$g = (1 - \epsilon) r_p / K_a$$

and

$$c = \epsilon r_p / K_l .$$

Substituting for $c$ and $g$ in (6), substituting for $r_p$ from (4) and simplifying yields

$$r = r_p \left[ \epsilon (1 - N_l / K_l) + (1 - \epsilon)(1 - N_a / K_a) \right],$$

and substituting this into (5) we obtain

$$dN/dt = r_p N \left[ \epsilon (1 - N_l / K_l) + (1 - \epsilon)(1 - N_a / K_a) \right] . \quad (8)$$

Of course $N = N_a + N_l$. Equation (8) contains three unknowns. Therefore a third equation, perhaps either (i) $dN_l/dt = f(N_a, N_l)$ or (ii) $dN_a/dt = f(N_a, N_l)$, is required to describe the rate of population change. These unite the two phases.

Equation (8) is similar in form and derivation to the usual logistic equation

$$dN/dt = r_p N (1 - N/K)$$

for the growth of a population occupying a single environment. There have been many objections to this expression (Smith, 1952; Andrewartha and Birch, 1954; Frank, 1960; Slobodkin, 1961). The same objections apply to equation (8). These expressions can only serve as highly stylized representations.

It is possible to deduce the conditions for the demographic balance which must exist when the population is simultaneously saturating both larval and adult environments. That is, when $\Delta N / \Delta t = 0$: where $\Delta t$ is the average time required for the death of $K_a$ adults. Over this time interval, let $N_m$ be the total number of individuals passing from the larval to the adult portion of the life cycle. By definition $N_m < N_l$. More significantly, $N_m > K_a$ and $N_a R_{g,e} > K_l$ must hold if the population is to maintain the highest possible equilibrium numbers in both environments (Fig. 4). The units in these inequalities must be numbers: mass, volume or energy units are not valid. Alterations of the latter two inequalities make it possible to define the four possible states for a population with a complex life cycle. These are set out in

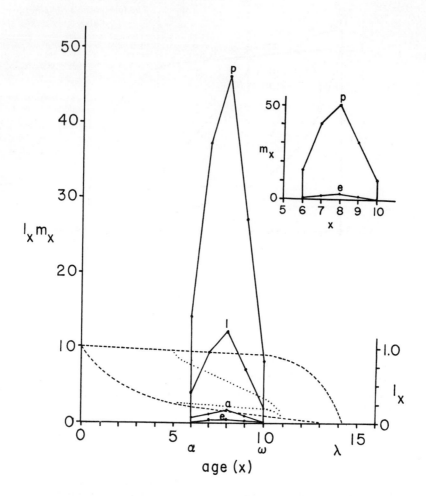

FIG. 3. Graphs of the relationship of the four different $l_x m_x$ curves, and two different $m_x$ curves. The symbols $p$, $l$, $a$, and $e$ identify physiological, larval effect only, adult effect only, and equilibrium respectively. This corresponds to the subscript designations on the four different net reproductive rates (areas under the curves) defined in the text.

Table 2. It is perhaps unlikely that any species continuously realizes Case 1. Case 1 represents the maximum exploitation of the ecological advantages of a complex life cycle and may be called the optimal case.

It should be noted that equations (i) and (ii) cannot be realized in one important way. Under either Case 2 or Case 3 there is no possibility that feedback from the unsaturated phase will elicit greater input from the saturated phase, thus restoring Case 1.

EVOLUTIONARY INDEPENDENCE

In species with complex life cycles the ecologically distinct phases evolve independently of one another to a large degree. This is illustrated by the morphological and physiological adaptations of all species which have such life cycles. Wigglesworth (1954) has amply supported this conclusion with respect to insects. Such independence is incomplete to the degree that some behavioral, developmental, and morphological characteristics necessary for making the

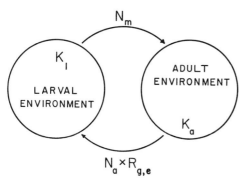

FIG. 4. Schematic representation of the relationship between larval environment, adult environment, and the demographic functions which must unite the two segments of the population in these environments.

TABLE 2. *The four possible complex life cycle states.*

| Case No. | Definition | Ecological interpretation |
|---|---|---|
| 1) | $N_m > K_a$ | Both environments saturated |
|  | $N_a R_{g,e} > K_l$ |  |
| 2) | $N_m > K_a$ | Adult environment saturated |
|  | $N_a R_{g,e} < K_l$ | Larval environment not saturated |
| 3) | $N_m < K_a$ | Adult environment not saturated |
|  | $N_a R_{g,e} > K_l$ | Larval environment saturated |
| 4) | $N_m < K_a$ | Both environments not saturated |
|  | $N_a R_{g,e} < K_l$ |  |

transitions between phases must be maintained. Beyond these restraints each phase will undergo independent adaptation to its respective environment. *If the optimal case is to be maintained indefinitely after it is once achieved it is necessary for the rates of change of adaptation of both phases to be the same.* If these rates are not the same the pattern of Case 1 will be disrupted by reversal of one of the inequalities thus yielding either Case 2 or Case 3. That is, either adult fertility and abundance will become insufficient to saturate the larval environment or, conversely, the rate of metamorphic transition from larvae to adults will become too low to saturate the adult environment. It is important to note that this imbalance would be generated by the evolutionary changes taking place within the species itself and might occur even in a constant environment.

Case 2 or Case 3 may also develop early in the adoption of a complex life cycle if the process of transfer of part of the life history overshoots. This would happen if the supplementary environment is so large that the potential equilibrium is passed and the demand for individuals moving from the ancestral to the supplementary environments comes to exceed the actual supply.

The evolutionary problem posed by a complex life cycle becomes more explicit if some ecologically meaningful way of defining "rate of change of adaptation" can be found. This will be done in terms of the saturation value $K$.

It is probably clear to most ecologists that $K_l$ and $K_a$ are not likely to be simple constants for natural populations. During any single turn through the life cycle $K_l$ and $K_a$ are functions of time and not necessarily monotonic functions (although for some species and habitats such functions might serve as an approximation). Complicated functional relationships arise from the time-related responses of the limiting factors for separate larval and adult populations. It will be necessary to measure these as a sequence of time-specific values throughout the larval and adult seasons respectively. For some field populations it may be possible to relate specific times in the adult reproductive period to specific times in the larval growth period to obtain corresponding values of saturation and corresponding flow rates between phases as illustrated in Figure 5. The arrows which indicate passage between phases are not meant to indicate the mapping of a tight functional relationship. In fact it is unlikely that such a relationship exists for most organisms with complex life cycles. On the other hand, Figure 5 does depict

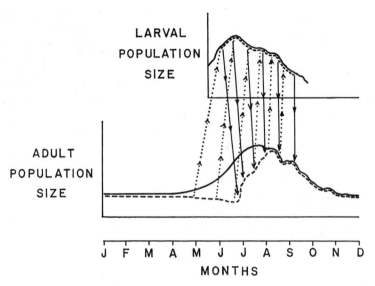

LARVAL
POPULATION
SIZE

ADULT
POPULATION
SIZE

J F M A M J J A S O N D

MONTHS

FIG. 5. Representation of the dynamics of a population with a complex life cycle during one year. The solid lines represent the time-specific larval and adult saturation values and the dashed lines the actual sizes of larval and adult segments of the population. The lines with arrows symbolize transfer between phases. Note that the rate of movement between phases also changes with the season.

a hypothetical example where the inequalities of the optimal case are almost satisfied except for failure to saturate the adult environment in early spring.

Since $K$ will be correlated with the seasons of the year (probably even in the tropics) a new saturation value $K'$ may be defined as

$$K' = \int K_t dt ,$$

where the integration is taken over some seasonal interval suggested by the natural history of the species. This saturation value is of more general applicability to natural populations than is $K$.

A small sequence of estimates of $K'$ might show considerable variation, but this is eliminated if a mean value, $\overline{K}'$, is taken over, say, 100-year blocks of time. Then, $\Delta\overline{K}'/\Delta t$ for time intervals greater than a few hundred years will portray the *rate of change of adaptation*. External changes in the physical and biological environment as well as internal, genetically determined, changes due to natural selection will alter the course of $\overline{K}'$ over evolutionary time.

Thus, the course of larval and adult

adaptation can be represented by $\overline{K}'_l$ and $\overline{K}'_a$ and the Case 1 inequalities become $\overline{N}'_m > \overline{K}'_a$, $(\overline{N_a R_{g,e}})' > \overline{K}'_l$. Once established these must hold over evolutionary time if the complex life cycle is to be maintained. This is shown by the solid lines in Figure 6. The dashed lines in Figure 6 indicate the general dilemma posed by unequal rates of change of adaptation (which in this special case results in neoteny).

Nowhere in the foregoing discussion is it necessary to require that $K_a$ and $K_l$ are set by resource-limitation. This is, however, implicit in a logistic equation, since a linear suppression of growth potential with increasing population size implies intraspecific competition for some finite requisite. However, the use of the saturation level concept in the cases of Table 2 and in all subsequent arguments need not carry this requirement. Any sort of restrictions from enemies, physical-environmental features, resources, or combinations of these are permissable as factors determining the time course of $K$ as used in Figure 5 and associated discussion. The requirement of

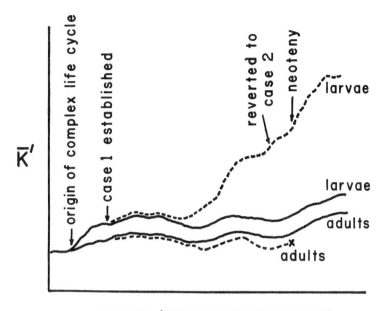

FIG. 6. The solid lines represent an ideal evolutionary history which preserves the complex life cycle once initiated. The dashed lines represent an alternate possibility involving unequal changes in larval and adult adaptation leading to neoteny. The time span is presumed to be in millions or tens of millions of years.

distinct sets of limiting factors for each phase remains.

The foregoing extension of the argument from ecological to evolutionary time spans also invites consideration of the concept of equilibrium population. Over time periods of one to several tens of generations the fluctuations of a natural population could easily make nonsense of the concept of an equilibrium. It has already been argued that over tens of thousands to millions of generations (evolutionary time) the assumption of equilibrium is surely invalid. This made possible the definition of a "rate of change of adaptation." However, over something like 100 generations the utilization of the concept of an equilibrium population is justified. A span of generations which is ecologically long but evolutionarily quite short would accomplish the averaging out of short-term ecological disturbances but not encounter longer gross climatic and biotic changes. It is on this basis that the idea of an equilibrium population is adopted for the evolutionary investigations presented here. Using the mathematics here outlined to analyze the dynamics of a field population with a complex life cycle would perhaps involve a more naive assumption concerning population equilibria. At present it is not certain whether such an assumption would be justified for most species (cf. Hutchinson, 1965).

THE MEANING OF $\epsilon$

Recall that $\epsilon$ expresses the degree to which larval survival in nature is responsible for the suppression of maximum population increase which results in the equilibrium state. The control of the population comes as the result of a certain number of regulatory events. These events are deaths and nonrealized potential births (each event does not, however, contribute the same amount of regulation). These regulatory events are distributed across the

600                                   CONRAD A. ISTOCK

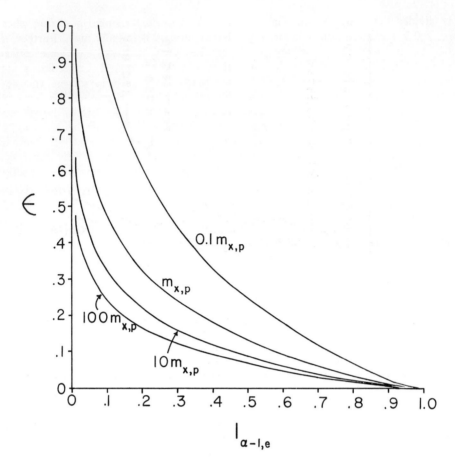

FIG. 7. Relationship between the partitioning of selection upon the complex life cycle character and larval survival in nature. The figure was constructed using a series of tables (like Table 1) with different larval survival patterns. It shows how $\epsilon$ varies with larval survival under four different physiological fertility patterns. For further explanation see text.

two life cycle phases and $\epsilon$ reflects the proportion of total regulation accomplished by larval deaths. Natural selection operates through the same set of deaths and unrealized births. Thus $\epsilon$ is also a reflection of the distribution of these selective events across the two phases. Further, I contend that if we consider the form of the life cycle, including the duration of each phase and the total array of activities in each phase, as a phenotypic trait, $\epsilon$ *becomes a measure of the proportion of total selection upon the life cycle form which occurs during the larval phase.* In other words, the set of regulatory events determining

changes in population size is identical with the set of selective events which influence the changing or unchanging state of the life cycle form. The two sets are identical both because they contain the same array of events and because each specific event (e.g., the first larval death or last nonrealized birth) carries exactly the same proportional effect in each set. Therefore it would follow that selection will be operating to perpetuate any existing form of the life cycle only when $\epsilon = 0.5$. (Note that $\epsilon = 0.5$ means that total selection is equally distributed across the two phases but not that the total number of selective events is equally divided between the two phases.) When $\epsilon > 0.5$ selection would favor any tendency toward reduction or elimination of the larval phase. When $\epsilon < 0.5$ selection would favor reduction or loss of the adult phase. This argument concerning $\epsilon$ as a measure of selection on the life cycle holds for the following reason. Consider a phenotype which substitutes activity in one phase for activity in the other without any net loss in reproductive capacity. If $\epsilon = 0.5$ there is no selective advantage. But if $\epsilon = 0.2$ and the new phenotype prolongs larval life thus entering adult life later than usual and perhaps eliminating some typical adult activities (and exposure to sources of mortality) there is an advantage. Assuming the population as a whole is in equilibrium, giving a net reproductive rate ($R_0$) equal to one, the new phenotype avoids some of the regulatory events concentrated disproportionately during adult life and effectively has a net reproductive rate greater than one. Thus its phenotypic tendencies will increase in relative abundance (provided they are hereditary) and an alteration of the life cycle form will take place. This same argument is also valid if the total population is increasing or decreasing.

Using the $l_{x,p}$ values of Table 1 is possible to numerically evaluate the effect of different values for $l_{\alpha-1,e}$ (the outcome of larval survival in nature) and different sets of values for $m_{x,p}$ on $\epsilon$ as shown in Figure 7. This set of $l_{x,p}$ values should serve as a reasonable representation of any physiological survivorship pattern. The $m_{x,p}$ values represent a rather modest level of reproductive prowess ($R_{g,p} = 145$), while the 0.1 $m_{x,p}$ ($R_{g,p} = 14.5$) and 100 $m_{x,p}$ ($R_{g,p} = 14,500$) represent low and moderately high values. The relationships of Figure 7 indicate the manner in which fertility and larval survival must be balanced in order to bring $\epsilon$ close to 0.5. The curvilinear nature of the relationship is such that any adaptive changes in larval survival which occur when larval survival is initially low have a much greater effect on

$\epsilon$ than equivalent changes occurring when larval survival is initially high. Further, if larval survival increases, a decrease in fertility would be required if selection is not to oppose the persistence of the complex life cycle pattern. Conversely an increase in fertility would be required if larval survival decreases. Four of the salamander species studied by Organ (1961) form a series which at least qualitatively illustrates the expected interaction between fertility and larval survival. Accurate plotting of Organ's data is not possible because the required $m_{x,p}$ data are lacking.

The process by which $\epsilon$ has been calculated involves fabricating an $m_{x,e}$ column such that $R_{0,e} = 1$ (Table 1). It might be argued that it would be ecologically just as meaningful to alter the $l_{x,e}$ pattern between $\alpha$ and $\omega$; that is by varying the adult survival. Actually the adult pattern of natural survivorship does not influence $\epsilon$. Hence, $\epsilon$ is only a function of $l_{\alpha-1,e}$ and physiological gross reproduction. This indicates asymmetry in the way selective forces on the life cycle character emerge from the population dynamics of complex life cycles. Given the innate potential for population increase the survival during the nonreproductive (larval) phase determines the way selection for the life cycle is partitioned among the two phases. The innate potential for increase depends upon physiological survivorship and fertility. Physiological survivorship is a composite of larval and adult genetic properties; physiological fertility is an adult genetic characteristic; while $l_{\alpha-1,e}$, the third factor determining $\epsilon$, is due to the adaptive complex of the larvae for dealing with the realities of larval life in nature. Physiological survivorship is perhaps nearly constant, while physiological fertility and larval survival in nature are subject to largely independent evolutionary tendencies.

Independent evolutionary changes in one phase of a complex life cycle will always change $\epsilon$. This is so because these adaptive changes (whether increasing or decreasing adaptation) alter survival and reproductive probabilities and thus the distribution of regulation and selection. Since adaptation affects the allowable population size one might expect a relationship to exist between $\epsilon$ and the four complex life cycle states given in Table 2. A population persisting long under Case 1 should manifest $\epsilon$ values which fluctuate around 0.5. Case 2 corresponds to $\epsilon < 0.5$ and Case 3 to $\epsilon > 0.5$. These conjectures concerning Cases 2 and 3 assume that in the unsaturated phase individuals have all resources in abundance and are scarce enough to make deleterious relationships with enemies less operable. Epsilon cannot be specified for Case 4, though this case will probably be ephemeral. Nevertheless, $\epsilon$ is a far more sensitive indicator of the evolutionary dynamics of a complex life cycle than the inequalities in Table 2. This is true because a unidirectional change in the distribution of selection on the two phases would be recorded by measurements of $\epsilon$ before any actual reversals among the inequalities became detectable.

Over evolutionary time a complex life cycle must be maintained by balancing the flow rates between phases despite the independent adaptation of each phase. Ideally these rates are sufficient to maximize the exploitation of both environments. However, there is no obvious reason why an increase in the adaptation of one phase will promote a corresponding change in the adaptation of the other phase. Hence it appears that *complex life cycles are inherently unstable over evolutionary time* whether in a changing or unchanging environment.

## The Alteration of Complex Life Cycles

It is possible to think of populations of species with a two-phase life cycle as if they contained three different classes of genotypic tendencies. (1) Some genotypes tend toward a repeated completion of the life cycle and approach maximization of energy extraction in each phase. (2) Other genotypes tend toward a reduction or loss

of the adult phase. These would be genotypes which spend less time, less of their development, or less activity in this phase and thereby accomplish an increase in survival by less expression of all or some adult traits. (3) Still other genotypes might tend toward the reduction or loss of the larval phase.

As long as Case 1 (Table 2) is energetically advantageous and can be realized demographically, Class 1 genotypes will predominate or exist exclusively. Whenever Case 1 is not fulfilled the species population as a whole will be less abundant than if Case 1 were realized. Under such circumstances genotypes of one of the other two classes, if available, would possess a greater relative fitness than the Class 1 genotypes and a reduction in one phase would occur. In effect nature may play a trick on many species. First a pathway to resource expansion is offered through fission of the life cycle. This produces ecological and evolutionary independence which in turn generates a situation favoring partial or complete dissertion of one part of the life cycle. In laboratory experiments with blowflies, Nicholson (1960) has, to a very limited extent, produced such effects by continuous maintenance of Case 2.

Where the rate of change of adult adaptation exceeds that of the larvae the interjection of a stage of asexual reproduction near the end of the larval phase could at least temporarily counter selection favoring elimination of the larval stage. Asexuality is energetically the most efficient sort of reproduction. Larval asexual reproduction would be a property of a Class 1 genotype.

## Complex Life Cycle Phenomena

There are numerous examples which suggest that the foregoing argument is relevant. Partial or total reduction of one life cycle phase is common among animals which have or have had complex life cycles. The Cnidaria primitively possessed the polypoid-medusoid life cycle yet throughout the Class Hydrozoa there is a remarkable tendency toward reduction or loss of one phase (Hyman, 1940). The Class Anthozoa illustrates complete loss of the medusoid and the Class Scyphozoa the reduction of the polypoid while forms such as *Aurelia* illustrate the interjection of asexual reproduction between larval (polypoid) and adult (medusoid) phases. In the Crustacea there is a clear tendency toward reduction or loss of free-swimming larvae (Snodgrass, 1956). Among Echinoderms the primitive condition is not clear but in many cases the larval stages do not feed (Hyman, 1955). The Insects are replete with examples: Ephemeroptera, many Plecoptera, Trichoptera, many Lepidoptera, Diptera, and others (Comstock, 1920).

The mayflies (Ephemeroptera) offer an almost perfect example. Adults of modern mayflies serve for dispersal and other mechanics of reproduction, but in terms of energy capture the adults are quite extinct. It is not difficult to imagine how selection leading to the reduction of the terrestrial adult arose from the increasing adaptation of the nymph to virtually unexploited aquatic environments of the Carboniferous. The intensity of past selection against the adult in mayflies may be indicated by the fact that some of the most abundant species are either parthenogenic or ovoviviparous (Needham et al., 1935); characteristics which represent rather extreme ways of amplifying and guarding the adult reproductive potential.

The mode of growth in insects would seem to obviate against the loss of the larval stage. However, such loss has occurred in several dipteran families; Muscidae (Tsetse fly), Hippoboscidae, and Nycteribiidae (Comstock, 1920). In the evolution of insect life cycles the need for demographic balancing of two phases might be met temporarily by adjustment of the number and duration of the immature instars, or conversely by alteration of adult longevity and fertility. The former appears among the Odonata (Corbet, 1963). The dragonflies are, however, quite contrary to theoretical expectation because there are no examples where one phase has been very seriously reduced. This leads to the suspicion that there may exist the possibility of coordinated evolution among the phases of a complex life cycle. This implies that the rates of change of adaptation in the two phases are tightly interlocked, perhaps through feedback mechanisms which involve the partitioning and overlapping utilization of a finite number of genetic sites. While possibily avoiding the dilemma of evolutionary independence, such a mechanism would retard evolutionary change in general. It may be less occult to argue that the Odonata early became well adapted in both phases, before any drastic stresses due to evolutionary independence developed and that since the late Paleozoic there has been no opportunity for either phase to undergo sufficient evolutionary change to cause disruption of the life cycle.

Many superb illustrations of life cycle evolution are provided by the Amphibia. Here there exists an entire continuum, ranging from the complete loss of the adult phase (neoteny) in some salamanders to the complete loss of free-living larvae in other salamanders and some frogs.

Many other groups possess complex life cycles or derived patterns but a complete review will not be attempted. Hardy (1954) has reviewed the great variety of instances in which neoteny may have been a dramatic evolutionary innovation. The large number of examples given by Hardy might make one suspicious that a convenient mask for ignorance has been widely employed. However, so many of Hardy's examples do involve complex life cycles that it may well be that the wealth of examples is in fact instructive.

The entire argument of the present paper leads to the contention that complex life cycles are inherently unstable over evolutionary time and that such life cycles lead to extreme shifts in evolutionary trend, such as neoteny, in those few cases

604                                    CONRAD A. ISTOCK

where extinction does not occur first. Hardy refers to this as "escape from specialization" and so it may have been in many instances. But we have as yet no means for measuring specialization, and this is required to justify Hardy's phrase. "Change of adaptation" would be a less dramatic but more appropriate phrase.

During the evolution of life there may have been intervals when the adoption of complex life cycles by free living organisms was particularly frequent. The colonization of Precambrian and early Paleozoic seas, the evolution to freshwater later in the Paleozoic, and the progressive association of insects and flowers in the early Cenozoic may be examples of such times. The continual adaptive radiation of life may have progressively reduced the frequency with which opportunities for the adoption of a complex life cycle occurred. Opportunity for the adoption of complex parasitic life cycles may, however, have increased over geological time. It is curious that few if any complex life cycles with marine and terrestrial phases exist.

SUMMARY

A complex life cycle exists when the individuals of a species consistently pass through two or more ecologically distinct phases. Only the case with two phases (e.g., larval and adult) is considered in this paper. Manipulation of various life table and fertility measures make it possible to: (1) separate the larval and adult effects on the decline from maximum population growth to equilibrium; (2) derive a logistic equation for the growth of a population with a complex life cycle; and (3) define four possible states in which such a population might exist, one of which allows maximum realization of the ecological advantages of such a life cycle.

To a great extent the evolutionary adaptations of the different phases of a complex life cycle are independent. Such independence is likely to make complex life cycles generally unstable over evolutionary time by moving the population away from maximum realization of the ecological advantages of such a life cycle. This will generate selective forces favoring a reduction or loss of one phase or the other. It is possible to interpret the degree to which the larval and adult phases are not equally responsible for population regulation as a measure of the degree to which selection is operating to maintain the complex life cycle character. There are characteristics of many present day species which seem to be the result of reduction or loss of one part of a complex life cycle.

LITERATURE CITED

ANDREWARTHA, H. G., AND L. C. BIRCH. 1954. The distribution and abundance of animals. Univ. Chicago Press, Chicago.

BIRCH, L. C. 1948. The intrinsic rate of natural increase of an insect population. J. Anim. Ecol. 17: 15–26.

COLE, L. C. 1954. The population consequences of life history phenomena. Quart. Rev. Biol. 29: 103–137.

COMSTOCK, J. H. 1920. An introduction to entomology. Comstock Publ. Assoc., Ithaca.

CORBET, P. S. 1963. A biology of dragonflies. Quadrangle Books, Chicago.

DEEVEY, E. S. 1947. Life tables for natural populations of animals. Quart. Rev. Biol. 22: 283–314.

DUBLIN, L. I., A. J. LOTKA, AND M. SPIEGELMAN. 1949. Length of life: A study of the life table. Ronald Press, New York.

FISHER, R. A. 1958. The genetical theory of natural selection. Dover Publ., New York.

FRANK, P. W. 1960. Prediction of population growth form in Daphnia pulex cultures. Amer. Natur. 94: 357–372.

HARDY, A. C. 1954. Escape from specialization. In J. Huxley, A. C. Hardy, and E. B. Ford [eds.] Evolution as a process. George Allen and Unwin, London.

HUTCHINSON, G. E. 1965. The ecological theater and the evolutionary play. Yale Univ. Press, New Haven.

HYMAN, L. H. 1940. The invertebrates: protozoa through ctenophora. Vol. I. McGraw-Hill, New York.

——. 1955. The invertebrata: Echinodermata, the coelomate Bilateria. Vol. IV. McGraw-Hill, New York.

NEEDHAM, J. G., J. R. TRAVER, AND G. HSU. 1935. The biology of mayflies. Comstock Publ. Assoc., Ithaca.

NICHOLSON, A. J. 1960. The role of population dynamics in natural selection. In S. Tax [ed.] Evolution after Darwin. Univ. Chicago Press, Chicago I: 477–521.

ORGAN, J. A. 1961. Studies of the population dynamics of the salamander genus *Desmognathus* in Virginia. Ecol. Monogr. **31**: 189–220.

SLOBODKIN, L. B. 1961. Growth and regulation of animal populations. Holt, Rinehart, and Winston, New York.

SMITH, F. E. 1952. Experimental methods in population dynamics: a critique. Ecology **33**: 441–450.

——. 1954. Quantitative aspects of population growth. *In* E. Boel [ed.] Dynamics of growth processes. Princeton Univ. Press, Princeton.

——. 1963. Population dynamics in *Daphnia magna* and a new model for population growth. Ecology **44**: 651–653.

SNODGRASS, R. E. 1956. Crustacean metamorphosis. Smithsonian Misc. Collections, 4260.

WIGGLESWORTH, V. B. 1954. The physiology of insect metamorphosis. Cambridge Univ. Press, Cambridge.

# POPULATION STUDIES IN PREDOMINANTLY SELF-POLLINATING SPECIES. X. VARIATION IN NATURAL POPULATIONS OF *AVENA FATUA* AND *A. BARBATA*\*

## S. K. JAIN AND D. R. MARSHALL

Department of Agronomy, University of California, Davis, California

The maintenance and utilization of genetic variation in predominantly self-pollinating species has recently been examined in detail both theoretically and experimentally. An increasing body of evidence indicates that populations of inbreeders contain substantial stores of genetic variability and possess a well-integrated population structure (Allard, Jain, and Workman, 1966). Further, the patterns of population differentiation and variability found in nature indicate that the observed polymorphism is often adaptive and fits these species for both the opportunistic settlement and enduring occupation of temporally and spatially diverse habitats (Allard, 1965; Kannenberg and Allard, in press). However, further quantitative studies are necessary to confirm these observations and, more particularly, to elucidate the relationships between the population ecology and genetics of predominantly inbreeding species.

The present study is concerned with the comparative ecogenetics of two species of wild oats, *Avena fatua* L. (common wild oat; $2n = 42$) and *A. barbata* Brot. (slender wild oat; $2n = 28$). These species have a number of features in common. Both are predominantly autogamous, annual adventive grasses capable of occupying a diversity of habitats. Both were introduced into California less than 200 years ago during the mission period (1769–1823) and now form an important component of the California annual type vegetation complex (Talbot, Biswell, and Hormay, 1939; Robbins, 1940). Further, they have widely overlapping ranges of distribution. There are, however, some differences in this regard. *A. fatua* occurs more commonly in lower regions with deep, more fertile, and heavier alluvial soils as a weed in agricultural fields, along the roadsides, fence lines, etc., while *A. barbata* tends to dominate in the more elevated, grazed rangelands with poorer and lighter soils. Where the distribution ranges overlap, the two species often occur in pure stands in adjacent, yet sharply delimited areas, and in a few other regions they occur in mixed stands with a rather complex mosaic pattern (hereafter referred to as pure and mixed sites, respectively).

Despite the basic similarities between *A. fatua* and *A. barbata*, particularly in their ability to colonize and occupy diverse habitats, preliminary observations on variation at several marker loci and the breeding system in the two species indicated that they differ markedly with respect to poly-

\*This work was supported by a grant (GM 10476) from the National Institutes of Health (USPHS).

Reprinted by permission of The University of Chicago Press and the authors from *The American Naturalist* 101:19–33, 1967.

20                                THE AMERICAN NATURALIST

morphism and the level of natural outcrossing. *A. barbata* appears to be monomorphic and to have a lower rate of natural outcrossing than *A. fatua* which has previously been shown to maintain polymorphism and heterozygosis despite as low as 3 to 5 % outcrossing (Imam and Allard, 1965). The systematic study of such a pair of coexisting species provides an excellent opportunity to analyze the effect of differences in polymorphism, quantitative variability, and mating system on the adaptive strategies encountered in predominantly self-pollinated species.

This paper reports for both species quantitative estimates of (1) the degree of polymorphism at three marker loci, and (2) phenotypic variation for two quantitative characters in a large number of natural populations, and (3) the within population genetic variability in the pure vs. mixed sites.

### MATERIALS AND METHODS

#### Polymorphism and phenotypic variation

The survey of polymorphism and phenotypic variation in natural populations was carried out during the early summer of 1965. Samples were collected in the foothills of the Vaca Mountain Range of the Central Valley at 17 different locations (region I, designated A to Q) along Highway 128 (Fig. 1) and at five locations (region II, designated 1 to 5) along Highway 101 in the coastal region. Wild oats are distributed in this area more or less in continuous stands, along with other annual herbaceous species belonging to the genera *Festuca*, *Bromus*, *Hordeum*, *Erodium*, and *Medicago*, in varying proportions among different sites. The sites were chosen for reasonable accessibility and adequate range in the density and relative proportions of *A. fatua* and *A. barbata* arising from the variation in soil type, slope, grazing intensity, etc. At locations D, E, F, and G, two or more sites (denoted by a numeral subscript) were sampled using a linear transect along the slope in order to study the microgeographic variation for both qualitative and quantitative characters.

Samples were drawn by taking all plants within a central area at each site. The sampling area was varied from site to site depending on plant density to provide samples of 100 to 200 individuals. All samples were scored for the relative proportions of *A. fatua* and *A. barbata* and for several qualitative characters—lemma color (black vs. grey or white); pubescence of lemma, rachilla and node (presence vs. absence); and the presence vs. absence of purple spot on outer glume. Loci $B/b$ (black vs. grey or white lemma) and $H_1/h_1$ (pubescent vs. nonpubescent lemma) have been studied by several workers (see Coffman, 1961); the mode of inheritance of node hairiness and the glume spot character is now being investigated. A few samples were also scored for awn form and texture, panicle shape and other floral characters for which the results indicated no variation in this region within both species. Genetic variation for most of these simply inherited characters has been noted in various *Avena* species by Coffman (1961), Suneson (personal communication) and others. For quantitative variation,

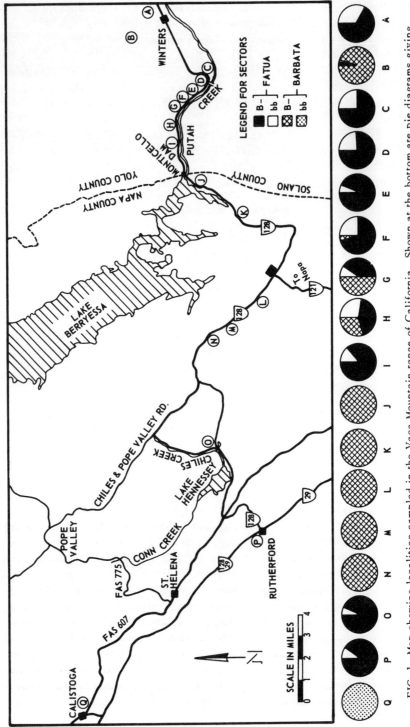

FIG. 1. Map showing localities sampled in the Vaca Mountain range of California. Shown at the bottom are pie diagrams giving the proportions of black and gray lemma colors in A. *fatua* and A. *barbata*.

22                                THE AMERICAN NATURALIST

length of primary panicle and spikelet number on the primary panicle were recorded for a random subsample of 50 to 100 individuals at each site.

It is important to note that the characters (marker loci) were not chosen because they were known to show variation in *Avena fatua* but rather for convenience in scoring and simple inheritance. We did not find one of the marker loci reported by Imam and Allard (1965) polymorphic since all individuals observed had pubescent rachilla. Moreover, we made a search for polymorphic loci in *Avena barbata* in order to estimate outcrossing rates in nature, but failed to find one. Thus, if there is any bias in the sample of our characters, it would have been in favor of polymorphic loci in *barbata*.

In another set of samples, collected later in the seedling stage from several sites, seedlings of both species were scored for the pubescent vs. nonpubescent leaf sheath character. Inheritance studies in *A. fatua* involving 35 segregating families showed this character to be under monogenic control $(\chi_{[1]}^2 = 0.027)$ with pubescent $(Ls_1)$ dominant over nonpubescent $(ls_1)$.


### Genetic Variability

This portion of the study was based on progenies derived from the plants collected at sites $D_2$, H, and A (Fig. 1) during the summer of 1964. A brief description of these sites, chosen because they are predominantly *fatua*, mixed, and predominantly *barbata*, respectively, is given below.

| Site | Description |
|------|-------------|
| $D_2$ | Virtually no *barbata*; moderately dense stand; approximately one acre plot on roadside; gentle east facing slope |
| H | *A. fatua* and *A. barbata* in nearly 7 : 3 ratio; dense stand; steep south facing slope |
| A | *A. barbata* and *A. fatua* in nearly 9 : 1 ratio; sparse stand; lightly wooded, grazed ranch area; steep west facing slope |

The sampling procedure was similar to that described above. In this case, however, the sampling area was varied to provide a minimum sample of 200 plants.

In the winter of 1964-65, a total of 600 families (a family deriving from 10-12 seeds of the same panicle) were grown in a field nursery at Davis with a completely randomized design. Replication was not possible due to the small numbers of seed set per plant in nature at these sites. Spacing was one foot between and within rows. Families with seven or more mature plants were scored for lemma color, lemma pubescence, and leaf sheath pubescence. Measurements were made on a single plant basis in the same families for panicle length, spikelet number/panicle, and mean seed size (determined by the mean length of five seeds per individual). These single plant data were used to estimate the within- $(\sigma_w^2)$ and between- $(\sigma_b^2)$ family components of variance for each species and site.

VARIATION IN SELF-POLLINATING SPECIES 23

## RESULTS

### Polymorphism

The data on the relative proportions of *A. fatua* and *A. barbata* and the degree of polymorphism recorded in each species are summarized in Table 1 and shown in part in the sectorial diagrams (Fig. 1). The samples studied included a range of pure *A. barbata* and *A. fatua* sites and several mixed sites in which the relative frequency of *A. barbata* was extremely variable both among sites and along the linear transects at locations F and G. Over the wide range of sites studied in region I, all *A. barbata* samples observed so far showed monomorphism. Alleles *B*, *H*, and *ls$_1$* were fixed at all sites except Q where the entire sample had grey lemma and pubescent leaf sheath (i.e., genotypically *bbLs$_1$-*). This is in sharp contrast to *A. fatua* samples which were clearly highly polymorphic at all three loci scored. Similarly, observations on the presence or absence of node hairiness and a purple spot on the outer glume showed *A. barbata* to be monomorphic and *A. fatua* highly polymorphic for these characters at almost all sites. The frequency of bb individuals within *A. fatua* varied without a regular clinal pattern over larger regions, but locally showed a high degree of correlation with varying soil types (G. L. Stebbins, unpublished data) which suggests that the differences in the degree of polymorphism observed in *A. fatua* populations have developed in response to and are maintained by natural selection. This point will be considered further below.

### Genotypic frequencies

The observed genotypic frequencies and estimates of the recessive allelic frequencies in *A. fatua*, based on progeny test data, for sites D$_2$, H, and A are shown in Table 2 together with the estimated values of the fixation index, $\hat{F}$ (where $\hat{F} = 1 - \{\hat{R}/2\hat{q}(1 - \hat{q})\}$; $\hat{R}$ = the observed level of heterozygosity; $\hat{q}$ = frequency of recessive allele). The estimates of $\hat{F}$, which provide a meaningful measure of departure from Hardy-Weinberg proportions (Wright, 1965; Workman and Jain, 1966) were compared with the expected equilibrium value of $F$ (assuming no selection, $F_e = [(1 - t)/(1 + t)]$ for two different levels of outcrossing ($t = 0.05$, $0.02$). These values represent the range of outcrossing most commonly observed at the lemma color locus (Imam and Allard, 1965) and also at the loci governing the lemma pubescence and leaf sheath pubescence (Jain and Marshall, unpublished) in natural populations. The $\chi^2_{(3)}$ values for comparing the $\hat{F}$ and $F_e$ values combined over loci are 21.37 (D$_2$), 0.285 (H), and 0.148 (A) with $t = 0.05$, and for $t = .02$ these are 27.20 (D$_2$), 1.196 (H), and 0.690 (A). Thus, there is a significant excess of heterozygotes at site D$_2$ (pure *A. fatua*) over the levels expected with no selection. Similar results were obtained for several pure *A. fatua* populations by Imam and Allard (1965). Hence, natural selection involving heterozygote advantage appears to be a major factor in the maintenance of polymorphism in *A. fatua*, particularly within the pure

TABLE 1

Relative proportion of *barbata* and estimates of phenotypic frequencies* showing morphism in *fatua vs barbata*

| | Site | A | B | C | D1 | D2 | D3 | D4 | E1 | E2 | F1 | F2 |
|---|---|---|---|---|---|---|---|---|---|---|---|---|
| Fatua | $bb$ | .273 | .332 | .231 | .169 | .099 | .455 | .309 | .084 | .078 | .082 | .174 |
| | $b_1b_1$ | .556 | .229 | .091 | .028 | .036 | .090 | 0 | .057 | .078 | .019 | .023 |
| | $ls_1ls_1$ | .645 | ... | ... | .245 | .270 | .298 | .383 | ... | ... | ... | ... |
| Barbata (% of total and phenotype) | | .890 ($BH_1$) | 0 | 0 | 0 | 0 | 0 | 0 | 0 | 0 | 0 | .246 ($BH_1$) |
| Sample size | | 340 | 310 | 121 | 106 | 111 | 100 | 123 | 106 | 116 | 157 | 114 |

| | Site | F3 | F4 | F5 | F6 | F7 | G1 | G2 | G3 | H | I | J |
|---|---|---|---|---|---|---|---|---|---|---|---|---|
| Fatua | $bb$ | .215 | .292 | .024 | .506 | .364 | .297 | .143 | .061 | .381 | .141 | 0 |
| | $b_1b_1$ | 0 | .028 | 0 | .405 | .280 | .297 | .143 | .080 | .626 | .050 | 0 |
| | $ls_1ls_1$ | ... | ... | ... | .238 | .318 | .158 | ... | 0 | .358 | .137 | 0 |
| Barbata (% of total and phenotype) | | .046 ($BH_1$) | 0 | 0 | .048 ($BH_1$) | .010 ($BH_1$) | .145 ($BH_1$) | .933 ($BH_1$) | .516 ($BH_1$) | .300 ($BH_1$) | 0 | 1.00 ($BH_1$) |
| Sample size | | 130 | 140 | 124 | 83 | 129 | 110 | 104 | 155 | 137 | 120 | 100 |

| | Site | K | L | M | N | O | Q | Region II 1 | 2 | 3 | 4 | 5 |
|---|---|---|---|---|---|---|---|---|---|---|---|---|
| Fatua | $bb$ | 0 | 0 | 0 | 0 | .067 | 0 | .490 | .245 | .248 | .164 | .407 |
| | $b_1b_1$ | 0 | 0 | 0 | 0 | 0 | 0 | .130 | .078 | .129 | .019 | .180 |
| | $ls_1ls_1$ | 0 | 1.00 | 0 | 1.00 | .295 | 1.00 | .523 | .576 | .583 | .438 | .470 |
| Barbata (% of total and phenotype) | | 1.00 ($BH_1ls_1$) | 1.00 ($BH_1ls_1$) | 1.00 ($BH_1ls_1$) | 1.00 ($BH_1ls_1$) | ... | 1.00 ($bH_1Ls_1$) | ←—— not scored ——→ | | | | 0 |
| Sample size | | 113 | 112 | 30 | 30 | 120 | 121 | 100 | 129 | 101 | 103 | 128 |

*These are relative proportions of recessives ($bb$, $b_1b_1$, $ls_1ls_1$) among *fatua* individuals.
Number of adult plants scored for species, lemma color, and lemma pubescence. Leaf sheath hairiness was scored on larger samples during the seedling stage.

TABLE 2

Observed genotypic frequencies in *A. fatua*

| Genotype | Site | | | | | |
|---|---|---|---|---|---|---|
| | D2 | | H | | A | |
| | Frequencies | Statistic* | Frequencies | Statistic* | Frequencies | Statistic* |
| BB | 0.712 | $\hat{q} = 0.219$ | 0.548 | $\hat{q} = 0.417$ | 0.667 | $\hat{q} = 0.303$ |
| Bb | 0.138 | $\hat{F} = 0.597$ | 0.071 | $\hat{F} = 0.854$ | 0.060 | $\hat{F} = 0.858$ |
| bb | 0.150 | | 0.381 | | 0.273 | |
| No. of Progenies | 80 | | 42 | | 33 | |
| $H_1 H_1$ | 0.583 | $\hat{q} = 0.334$ | 0.312 | $\hat{q} = 0.657$ | 0.444 | $\hat{q} = 0.278$ |
| $H_1 h_1$ | 0.167 | $\hat{F} = 0.625$ | 0.062 | $\hat{F} = 0.862$ | 0 | $\hat{F} = 1$ |
| $h_1 h_1$ | 0.250 | | 0.626 | | 0.556 | |
| No. of Progenies | 12 | | 16 | | 9 | |
| $Ls_1 Ls_1$ | 0.775 | $\hat{q} = 0.162$ | 0.571 | $\hat{q} = 0.395$ | 0.291 | $\hat{q} = 0.355$ |
| $Ls_1 ls_1$ | 0.125 | $\hat{F} = 0.539$ | 0.071 | $\hat{F} = 0.851$ | 0.064 | $\hat{F} = 0.860$ |
| $ls_1 ls_1$ | 0.100 | | 0.358 | | 0.645 | |
| No. of Progenies | 80 | | 42 | | 31 | |

*$F$ is estimated as $1 - \hat{R}/2\hat{q}(1 - \hat{q})$ where $\hat{R}$ = observed level of heterozygosity, $\hat{q}$ = frequency of recessive allele.

sites in region I. However, the situation appears to be somewhat different in the mixed stands (A and H). Although the data showed an excess of heterozygotes at both sites, the difference between the observed and expected levels at equilibria in the absence of selection was not statistically significant. Yet, estimates of phenotypic frequencies (Table 1) and recessive allelic frequencies (Table 2) indicate that there is a consistently higher degree of polymorphism in the mixed stands of both species. Hence, other factors such as disruptive selection in time, frequency-dependency or viability interactions among individuals (e.g., see Dempster, 1955) may be important in maintaining polymorphism in certain mixed sites.

A similar analysis of outcrossing rates and genotypes frequencies has not yet been possible in *A. barbata* due to monomorphism for all marker characters scored; samples from both H and A had all *A. barbata* individuals with $BB \ H_1 H_1 \ ls_1 ls_1$ genotype. However, the lack of visible polymorphism does not necessarily indicate lack of genetic variability as shown by the quantitative analysis of variability in natural populations presented next.

### Phenotypic Variation

The phenotypic variability in *A. fatua* and *A. barbata* populations at pure vs. mixed sites is compared in Table 3. Both the mean and coefficient of variation (C.V.) of panicle length and spikelet number show variation among different sites within and between locations and between the two species. The mode of distribution is also different in the two species as shown for panicle length in Fig. 2. *A. fatua* has a unimodal distribution approaching

26                          THE AMERICAN NATURALIST

## TABLE 3

Phenotypic variation in pure and mixed natural populations of *fatua* and *barbata*

| Stand | Site | fatua | | | | Site | barbata | | | |
|-------|------|-------|---|-------|---|------|---------|---|-------|---|
| | | Spikelet no. | | Panicle length | | | Spikelet no. | | Panicle length | |
| | | Mean | C.V. | Mean | C.V. | | Mean | C.V. | Mean | C.V. |
| Pure | E1 | 7.69 | 0.51 | 9.91 | 0.40 | K | 11.36 | 0.55 | 15.08 | 0.40 |
| | E2 | 6.26 | 0.40 | 8.17 | 0.33 | L | 7.95 | 0.68 | 10.79 | 0.48 |
| | F1 | 13.98 | 0.44 | 15.22 | 0.25 | Q | 6.50 | 0.43 | 8.93 | 0.44 |
| | F4 | 9.26 | 0.38 | 10.10 | 0.28 | *R2 | 5.96 | 0.43 | 9.26 | 0.36 |
| | F5 | 7.06 | 0.34 | 8.13 | 0.33 | *R4 | 3.47 | 0.89 | 4.77 | 0.42 |
| | F6 | 10.34 | 0.46 | 11.18 | 0.29 | *R5 | 6.24 | 0.46 | 8.39 | 0.39 |
| | *1 (region II) | 2.48 | 0.35 | 4.45 | 0.40 | *S4 | 12.14 | 0.44 | 17.21 | 0.29 |
| | *5 (region II) | 8.18 | 0.43 | 9.78 | 0.38 | *T | 10.72 | 0.51 | 13.26 | 0.32 |
| | *KK1 | 14.68 | 0.18 | 13.47 | 0.30 | *U | 2.82 | 0.43 | 5.21 | 0.50 |
| | *0 | 7.58 | 0.48 | 10.42 | 0.45 | *Z | 28.02 | 0.47 | 25.13 | 0.46 |
| | | fatua | | | | | barbata | | | |
| Mixed | F2 | 9.23 | 0.34 | 10.73 | 0.24 | | 13.75 | 0.43 | 16.86 | 0.30 |
| | F3 | 9.36 | 0.42 | 11.12 | 0.26 | | 17.83 | 0.19 | 18.59 | 0.25 |
| | G1 | 7.42 | 0.35 | 8.41 | 0.31 | | 11.06 | 0.47 | 14.34 | 0.31 |
| | G2 | 4.86 | 0.32 | 7.07 | 0.38 | | 10.64 | 0.52 | 13.69 | 0.40 |
| | G3 | 4.62 | 0.43 | 5.84 | 0.40 | | 10.32 | 0.76 | 12.21 | 0.51 |
| | *R1 | 4.23 | 0.45 | 7.56 | 0.32 | | 5.54 | 0.44 | 11.19 | 0.34 |
| | *R3 | 11.70 | 0.29 | 17.30 | 0.45 | | 13.60 | 0.49 | 14.12 | 0.61 |
| | *S1 | 14.60 | 0.38 | 15.20 | 0.21 | | 9.58 | 0.55 | 16.81 | 0.34 |
| | *S2 | 9.21 | 0.41 | 9.76 | 0.27 | | 6.56 | 0.54 | 10.55 | 0.32 |
| | *KK2 | 6.52 | 0.32 | 8.39 | 0.32 | | 9.02 | 0.38 | 14.30 | 0.40 |

*These sites were studied in spring 1966 for quantitative variation in order to include several different locations in the rank tests. Wilcoxon's T test for signed ranks of paired values in mixed sites showed C.V. for *barbata* to be significantly higher (one tailed test; spikelet no., P < .05; panicle length, P < .005) than C.V. for *fatua*.

normality in most cases whereas *A. barbata* seems to have platykurtic and often multimodal distribution. The same difference was observed for seed size and spikelet number and the degree of kurtosis and skewness tended to vary among pure and mixed sites depending on their respective means.

The estimates of coefficient of variation given in Table 3 are in most cases larger for *A. barbata* than *A. fatua*. In particular, note in the case of mixed sites that the estimates of C.V. from matched samples are larger for *A. barbata* in 16 out of a total of 20 comparisons. Although the sampling distribution of coefficient of variation was derived by McKay (1932), the appropriate tests of significance do not seem to be available for such comparisons. Van Valen (1965) used the ratio of squared C.V.'s for F-test and discussed briefly the various other tests for inequality of variances. For the present set of estimates from pure sites (unmatched samples) and mixed sites (matched samples), the distribution-free rank tests (Mann-Whitney's U and Wilcoxon's T) were used, respectively, to test whether in these regions *A. barbata* is phenotypically more variable than *A. fatua*. For both panicle length and spikelet number and comparing within the pure and mixed

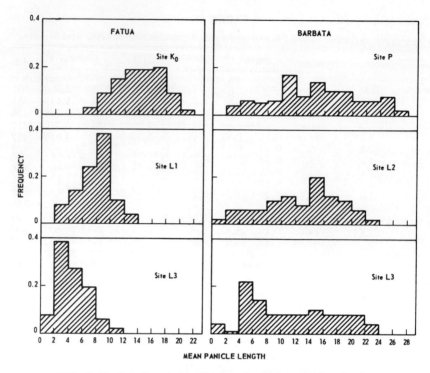

FIG. 2. Panicle length distributions in *A. fatua* and *A. barbata* from three localities each. Localities are shown in Fig. 1.

sites, the ranks showed the C.V.'s for *A. barbata* to be significantly larger (P < .05, in each of four tests) than *A. fatua*. Assuming independence of these two characters (the estimates of phenotypic correlation coefficient being nearly zero in most samples), these probabilities could be combined using Pearson's $P_\lambda$ test (see Rao, 1952, p. 44) to give a $\chi^2$-test (P < .001) which effectively measures the consistency of results from several such independent tests of the same hypothesis.

### Genetic Variability

Data on *A. fatua* and *A. barbata* families grown under a common nursery environment are given in Table 4 for three quantitative characters. It can be seen that the overall means are different for the two species; *A. barbata* has a smaller mean seed size, larger panicle, and greater spikelet number. Further, both species show a significantly wide range in family means for each character at all three sites indicating that there is a great deal of genetic variability among families in *A. fatua* as well as *A. barbata*. However, there are also some notable differences between species in this regard as exemplified by the distributions of family means shown in Fig. 3. *A. fatua* generally shows a wider range in family means, and, similar to the pattern observed in Fig. 1, has a more symmetrical and normal distribution

28                          THE AMERICAN NATURALIST

## TABLE 4
### Estimates of between- and within-family variability

| Site | Character | Species | Range of family means | Grand mean | $S_b{}^2$ | d.f. | $S_w{}^2$ | d.f. |
|------|-----------|---------|----------------------|-----------|-----------|------|-----------|------|
| D2 | Seed size | A. fatua | 1.14–1.75 | 1.47 | 0.0322 | 120 | 0.0160 | 991 |
| H | | A. fatua | 1.16–1.65 | 1.38 | 0.0168 | 56 | 0.0126 | 401 |
| | | A. barbata | 1.13–1.62 | 1.27 | 0.0096 | 18 | 0.0091 | 124 |
| A | | A. fatua | 1.18–1.49 | 1.31 | 0.0061 | 28 | 0.0103 | 212 |
| | | A. barbata | 1.09–1.50 | 1.22 | 0.0090 | 62 | 0.0105 | 417 |
| D2 | No. of | A. fatua | 24.8–94.6 | 50.9 | 182.62 | 72 | 222.18 | 768 |
| H | spikelets | A. fatua | 32.3–80.4 | 55.1 | 163.81 | 38 | 237.66 | 335 |
| | | A. barbata | 53.1–77.3 | 64.1 | 54.67 | 11 | 186.80 | 97 |
| A | | A. fatua | 39.1–73.0 | 56.3 | 96.29 | 17 | 259.75 | 164 |
| | | A. barbata | 33.0–81.1 | 60.5 | 62.29 | 41 | 209.01 | 341 |
| D2 | Panicle | A. fatua | 20.4–30.6 | 25.3 | 9.69 | 72 | 17.30 | 768 |
| H | length | A. fatua | 18.6–32.4 | 24.2 | 8.51 | 38 | 15.46 | 335 |
| | | A. barbata | 27.1–32.8 | 30.3 | 3.24 | 11 | 13.72 | 97 |
| A | | A. fatua | 21.9–29.0 | 26.9 | 4.57 | 17 | 16.46 | 164 |
| | | A. barbata | 22.3–33.4 | 29.8 | 4.22 | 41 | 16.86 | 341 |

than A. barbata. Also, it should be noted that the range of family means is larger in pure than mixed sites in both species.

Assuming that the underlying distributions are similar in the two species, the estimates of between- and within-family components of variance could be compared for A. fatua vs. A. barbata using Van Valen's corrected F-test based on the ratio of the C.V.$^2$ (Van Valen, 1965) and the probabilities combined by $P_\lambda$ test over sites. The values of $\chi^2$ for the $P_\lambda$ tests of significance are given in Table 5. The results generally parallel those for the comparisons among family means above. With respect to both $s_b{}^2$ and $s_w{}^2$, A. fatua is clearly more variable than A. barbata. This point is well illustrated for the within-family component of variance by the distributions shown in Fig. 3. There are two possible explanations for the observed difference in $s_w{}^2$ between species. First, if the within family variation is largely genetic, A. fatua families may be more heterozygous and hence show greater variation through segregation than A. barbata families. On the other hand, if $s_w{}^2$ arises from mainly nongenetic sources, the smaller values of $s_w{}^2$ for A. barbata suggests that barbata is phenotypically more stable than fatua. However, it will be seen that the latter explanation is not in agreement with the results presented earlier (Table 3) which showed that A. barbata was significantly more variable phenotypically than A. fatua. Hence, these results lead to the conclusion that natural populations of A. fatua contain significantly greater amounts of within-family genetic variability than populations of A. barbata. This conclusion is supported by the evidence from within family selection in A. fatua presented by Imam and Allard (1965), which indicated that much of the within family variance in this species was heritable. Moreover, since A. barbata is phenotypically more variable than A. fatua, one would expect that the estimates of $s_w{}^2$ shown in Table 4 represent an underestimate of the relative difference in

224

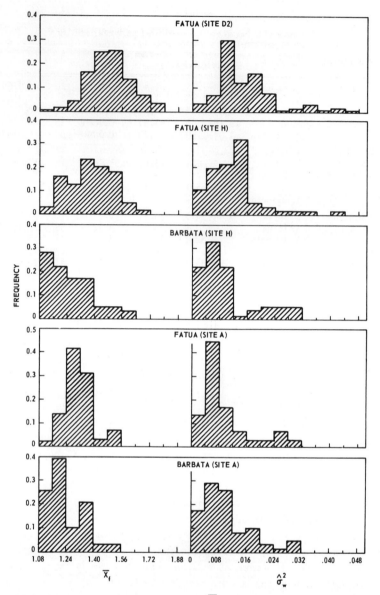

FIG. 3. Distributions of family means ($\overline{X}_f$) and within-family variances ($\hat{\sigma}_w^2$) of seed size at several localities in A. *barbara* and A. *fatua.*

within family genetic variability between the two species. Selection experiments within families such as the one reported by Imam and Allard (1965) have been undertaken to obtain more critical evidence on this point.

Table 5 also gives the chi-square values (combined over sites) for the comparisons of variability in pure vs. mixed sites. Both the between and within family components of variance are generally significantly higher in

30                    THE AMERICAN NATURALIST

TABLE 5

Chi-squares* for $P_\lambda$ test of significance on between- and
within-family variances ($S_b^2$, $S_w^2$)

| Statistic | Seed size | Panicle length | Spikelet no. | |
|---|---|---|---|---|
| | *barbata* vs *fatua* (based on mixed sites H and A; d.f. = 4) | | | Total $\chi^2$ ——————— (d.f. = 12) |
| $S_b^2$ | 3.27 | 11.62‡ | 15.34‡ | 30.23‡ |
| $S_w^2$ | 4.71 | 13.82‡ | 18.42‡ | 36.95§ |
| | Pure vs. mixed, within *fatua* (d.f. = 4) | | | Total $\chi^2$ ——————— (d.f. = 12) |
| $S_b^2$ | 16.59‡ | 9.79† | 9.21 | 35.59§ |
| $S_w^2$ | 10.60† | 7.01 | 5.63 | 23.24† |
| | Pure vs. mixed, within *barbata* (d.f. = 2) | | | Total $\chi^2$ ——————— (d.f. = 6) |
| $S_b^2$ | 1.39 | 3.21 | 2.41 | 7.01 |
| $S_w^2$ | 4.61 | 4.61 | 4.61 | 13.83† |

*The $\chi^2$-values computed from combining probabilities derived from Van Valen's corrected F-tests are greater than or equal to those given in this table. Significance levels .001, .01 and .05 are shown by †, ‡, § respectively.

pure than mixed sites in both species. However, consideration of the data in Tables 4 and 5 indicate that there is a difference between the two components of variation in this regard. The within-family component is reduced to a lesser extent in moving from pure to mixed sites than the between-family component, particularly in *A. barbata*. Such a result would be expected if the genetic component of variation within individual species is lowered in mixed sites whereas the nongenetic component is not reduced to the same extent.

DISCUSSION

The quantitative study of natural variation in *A. fatua* and *A. barbata* confirmed our previous subjective observations and suggests that the two species differ markedly in population structure. Populations of *A. fatua* are highly polymorphic for several marker loci investigated and contain substantial stores of genetic variability. The populations of *A. barbata*, on the other hand, were found to be predominantly monomorphic for all these loci. The evidence presented from quantitative data appears to be consistent with the findings on marker loci which showed that *A. barbata* has relatively a smaller genetic component of total phenotypic variability than *A. fatua* in these regions. The differences in the observed pattern of natural variation between the two species raise two important questions. First, what is the nature of the intrapopulational selective forces which lead to monomorphism and greater genetic homogeneity in *A. barbata*? In view of the large size and almost continuous distribution of the populations studied, drift appears to be an unlikely factor in allelic fixation. Further, the observed monomorphism cannot be attributed to the absence of alternative alleles in nature since both B and b were found at different sites, and seed samples collected from the soil surface at sites J and L contained a few ($< 0.10\%$) bb seeds among the B− samples. Also, a few *barbata* specimens collected from Sonoma County and held in the Agronomy herbarium at the University of California, Davis, were all found to differ from our own collections in being phenotypically $Ls_1$− B− (hairy leaf sheath and black lemma).

Whether the alternative alleles fail to establish themselves due to a selective disadvantage or chance elimination is now being tested by transplant experiments. Seeds carrying the reciprocal alleles have been sown at sites J, K, L, and Q. Such a test is suggested by the thesis that the widespread polymorphism in *A. fatua* may be due, in part, to frequent introgression of different alleles from cultivated oats, *A. sativa* L. (hexaploid, $2n = 42$), a factor allowing widespread multiple introductions of new alleles into *A. fatua* which is ineffective in the case of tetraploid *A. barbata*. Alternatively, the selective values of the reciprocal alleles might be such as to result in greater viability differences between the homozygotes in *A. barbata* than *A. fatua* which, in the absence of very strong heterozygote advantage, is particularly unfavorable for the maintenance of polymorphism under heavy inbreeding (Hayman, 1953; Jain and Allard, 1966).

Second, what differences, if any, in the adaptive strategies undertaken by the two species might be associated with the observed differences in population structure? Thoday (1953), Lewontin (1957), Levins (1965), and many others, have pointed out that populations can adapt to the multiplicity of environments encountered in nature either by individual buffering, whereby each organism in the population is capable of adapting to a variety of environments, or by populational buffering, where the population is genetically variable and each genotype is adapted to a specific environment. That *A. barbata* is genetically less variable but phenotypically more variable than *A. fatua* in nature suggests that relative importance of these mechanisms might differ in the two species. *A. barbata* appears to rely less on populational buffering and more on individual buffering, particularly phenotypic flexibility or phenomorphism, than *A. fatua*. However, it is likely that both mechanisms play a significant role in both species, the difference being one of degree rather than kind.

The above hypothesis is supported by results obtained from the comparisons of variability in pure and mixed sites. Since the two species have more or less similar requirements, the niche occupied by each species would be narrower in mixed than pure stands due to the stabilizing selection imposed by species competition. The "niche width" is defined after Van Valen (1965) as the "total multidimensional space used by a species or segment of a community." Thus, since both species appear to adapt to heterogeneous environments, at least in part, through genetic diversity, it could be expected that the genetic, and therefore phenotypic, variation would be lower in mixed stands (narrower niche). Further, as *A. barbata* appears to rely less on genetic diversity and more on phenotypic plasticity, it could be expected that the decrease in genetic variation would be proportionately less in this species. As noted previously, consideration of the data in Tables 3, 4, and 5 confirms these expectations. The developmental flexibility of *A. fatua* and *A. barbata* is now being evaluated in a series of controlled environments. Preliminary analysis of variation for some vegetative characters showed that *A. barbata* has greater plasticity than *A. fatua*.

However, it should be emphasized here that ecological factors, such as differential germination, etc., (see Harper, 1965) may be as important, if not more important, than the mating system and population structure in determining the modes of adaptation of these species. For example, Morley (1959), in discussing the concepts of fitness and long-term flexibility as a function of variation in relation to the distribution of *Trifolium subterranean* (a highly self-fertilized legume) vs. *Phalaris tuberosa* (a cross-fertilizing grass) in Australia, pointed out "the difference is not one of uniformity or variability, plasticity or homeostasis." It is largely that subterranean clover has a prodigious potential for seed production and efficient mechanisms for seed and seedling survival. Thus, the effects of many climatic, biotic, and genetic factors on both inter- and intrapopulational selective values must be taken into account in order to evaluate the mode of variability in a species and its optimal strategy for survival and successful colonization.

## SUMMARY

Quantitative estimates were made of the degree of polymorphism at three marker loci and the amount of phenotypic and genetic variability for three quantitative characters in several natural populations of two wild oat species, *Avena fatua* and *A. barbata*. The results showed that, for all the simply inherited characters studied, *A. barbata* was largely monomorphic whereas *A. fatua* was highly polymorphic for at least five different marker loci. Evidence was presented for heterozygote advantage as a factor maintaining polymorphism in certain populations of *A. fatua*. Estimates of between and within-family variability suggested that while both species have a substantial genetic component of total variability, there is a relatively larger nongenetic component in *A. barbata* accounting for its greater overall phenotypic variation in nature. The differences in the modes of variation and population structure between the two species are briefly discussed in relation to their adaptive strategies. It was postulated that *A. barbata* relies less on genetic diversity and more on phenotypic plasticity than *A. fatua* in adapting to heterogeneous environments.

## ACKNOWLEDGMENTS

The authors wish to express sincere thanks to Drs. R. W. Allard, R. M. Love, and G. L. Stebbins for their helpful criticisms of the manuscript. One of us (D. R. Marshall) is indebted to the University of Sydney for financial support in the form of the Thomas Lawrence Pawlett Travelling Scholarship.

LITERATURE CITED

Allard, R. W. 1965. Genetic systems associated with colonizing ability in predominantly self-pollinated species, p. 49–75. *In* H. G. Baker and G. L. Stebbins [eds.], The genetics of colonizing species. Academic Press, New York.

Allard, R. W., S. K. Jain, and P. L. Workman. 1966. The population genetics of inbreeding species. Advances in Genetics, vol. 14 (in press).

Coffman, F. A. 1961. Oat and oat improvement. Monograph Series, American Society of Agronomy, Madison.

Dempster, E. R. 1955. Maintenance of genetic heterogeneity. Cold Spring Harbor Symp. Quant. Biol. 20:25–32.

Harper, J. L. 1965. Establishment, aggression, and cohabitation in weedy species, p. 243–268. *In* H. G. Baker and G. L. Stebbins [eds.], The genetics of colonizing species. Academic Press, New York.

Hayman, B. I. 1953. Mixed selfing and random mating when homozygotes are at a disadvantage. Heredity 7:165–183.

Imam, A. G., and R. W. Allard. 1965. Population studies in predominantly self-pollinated species. VI. Genetic variability between and within natural populations of wild oats from differing habitats in California. Genetics 51:49–62.

Jain, S. K., and R. W. Allard. 1966. The effects of linkage, epistasis, and inbreeding on population changes under selection. Genetics 53: 633–659.

Kannenberg, L. W., and R. W. Allard. 1967. Population studies in predominantly self-pollinated species. VIII. Genetic variability in the *Festuca microstachys* complex. Evolution (in press).

Levins, R. 1965. Theory of fitness in a heterogeneous environment. V. Optimal genetic systems. Genetics 52:891–904.

Lewontin, R. C. 1957. The adaptations of populations to varying environments. Cold Spring Harbor Symp. Quant. Biol. 22:395–408.

McKay, A. T. 1932. Distribution of the coefficient of variation and the extended t-distribution. Proc. Roy. Statist. Soc., Sec. A, 95:695–699.

Morley, F. H. W. 1959. Natural selection and variation in plants. Cold Spring Harbor Symp. Quant. Biol. 24:47–56.

Rao, C. R. 1952. Advanced methods in biometric research. John Wiley & Sons, New York.

Robbins, W. W. 1940. Alien plants growing without cultivation in California. Calif. Agr. Exp. Sta. Bull. No. 637.

Talbot, M. W., H. H. Biswell, and A. L. Hormay. 1939. Fluctuations in the the annual vegetation of California. Ecology 20:394–402.

Thoday, J. M. 1953. Components of fitness. Symp. Soc. Exp. Biol. 7:96–113.

Van Valen, L. 1965. Morphological variation and width of ecological niche. Amer. Natur. 99:377–390.

Workman, P. L., and S. K. Jain. 1966. Zygotic selection under mixed random mating and self-fertilization: Theory and problems of estimation. Genetics 54:159–171.

Wright, S. 1965. The interpretation of population structure by F-statistics with special regard to systems of mating. Evolution 19:395–420.

# Ecological Significance of Territory in the Australian Magpie,

## *Gymnorhina tibicen*

### Robert Carrick

*Division of Wildlife Research, C.S.I.R.O., Canberra, Australia*

Much has been written on the possible significance of territorialism in birds and other animals; but, while some of the functions of territory appear self-evident enough, actual proof of their operation in nature has been difficult to obtain. In a comprehensive review of this subject, which cites the relevant literature to that time, Hinde (1956) was still able to write: "There is no direct evidence that territory limits the total breeding population in all habitats. . . . Territorial behaviour may reduce disease, but this is unlikely to be a significant consequence except in some colonial species. . . . The functions of territorial behaviour are extremely diverse, and the quality of the evidence available for assessing them is little different from that available to Howard." This last point is still substantially true, half a century after Howard. Wynne-Edwards (1962) has given a fully documented account of the territory habit, which he rightly interprets as no different in purpose from the other forms of social behavior that constitute the homeostatic machinery whereby populations of animals are widely dispersed and excessive increase of numbers, with consequent depletion of food and other resources, is prevented.

The two main questions arise from each side of the population equation, and each contains several others. *Firstly*, does territorialism reduce productivity (fecundity) significantly below the biotic potential of the species? To what extent does it do so, and how is the reduction achieved? Are adult females unable to breed through denial of suitable nest sites, mates, or food supply? Or is maturity prevented by lack of the necessary proximate stimuli, or even by inhibitory factors? *Secondly*, does territorialism buffer its adherents from important causes of mortality? Does it prevent or reduce the risk of starvation, i.e. what is the relation between territory and food supply? Does it confer safety from predators or protection from disease?

A main difficulty of research on this problem is that the effects of territorialism usually have to be inferred from the study of the territorial individuals alone; there is no nonterritorial element in the same species, or at least it is barely visible, to serve as a control and provide comparative data on natality and mortality under the two systems. This stems from the fact that those individuals that fail to attain territorial status are either excluded from the habitat that the species requires for food, shelter, and reproduction, and so they succumb, or else they live cryptically in and around the margins of the preferred habitat. In the case of the strongly territorial Australian Magpie (*Gymnorhina tibicen*), however, there is a large and obvious overflow

Proc. XIII Intern. Ornithol. Congr.: 740–753. 1963

Reprinted by permission of The American Ornithologists' Union and the author from *Proceedings XIII International Ornithological Congress* 2:740–753, 1963.

population outside the wooded breeding territories that is not territorial, at least in the same sense as the breeding birds, and that can maintain its numbers without recourse to migration. This stems mainly from the fact that this species is primarily an insectivorous ground-surface feeder, but is versatile enough to explore other food sources and even resorts to carrion and pasture foliage when necessary. The controlled experiment that we would like to set up in so many other species exists naturally.

Fig. 1. Adult cock Australian Magpie (*Gymnorhina tibicen*) giving the aggressive carol at the boundary of its territory. Photo by E. Slater.

*G. tibicen* (Fig. 1) is a member of the Australo-Papuan family Cracticidae, allied to the Corvidae. It stands about 9 inches high; and its adult plumage pattern, with jet black underparts and white nape, rump, and wing-flash, advertises the fact that predation on it is unlikely to be important; so exposed habitats can be used. A reasonable solution to the problem of diurnal shelter from the elements, especially heat and wind, can usually be found even in open country, and these individuals resort to communal night roosts some distance from their feeding grounds. This magpie is a sedentary species, with conspicuous behavior; it is not shy and it is readily trapped. Its aggressive carol, energetic defense of the territorial boundary, and readiness to attack intruders, including ornithologists, further assist field study (Fig. 1). The immature first-year birds are distinguished by their grayish, not black, plumage, and the sexes by the grayish lower nape and rump and the shorter bill of the female. It nests typically in trees, but shows considerable adaptability.

Fig. 2. The central part of the study area at Gungahlin, Canberra. Open savannah woodland (*Eucalyptus* spp., exotic conifers, and deciduous trees) and adjacent pasture are the habitat for permanent breeding territories. Photo by C. Totterdell.

The scene of the present study is 5 sq miles of open savannah, woodland, and pasture (Fig. 2 and 3) around Gungahlin, the headquarters of the Division of Wildlife Research, C.S.I.R.O., outside Canberra, Australia. The native gums, among which *Eucalyptus blakeleyi* predominates, form sparse cover with ground feeding places throughout and around them; exotic trees, including conifers and elms, are planted more compactly, and offer equally acceptable nest sites to the magpie. The study area was chosen to include samples of breeding habitat with intervening open ground. The basis of this study is individual color banding of territorial birds and group banding of others; over 650 of the former, and 2,500 of the latter, have been banded during 1955–62. Adults and young in territories on the study area have been banded annually, and in the four winters 1957, 1958, 1960, and 1961, about

80 percent of the nonterritorial birds living in the treeless pasture habitat have been banded. Since 1955, some 220 territorial groups have been studied. The area of woodland cover around Gungahlin (Fig. 2), which contains two-thirds of the territorial breeding groups in the study area, has been most intensively studied; every magpie there is color banded, i.e. about 150 birds in 40–45 territories. Over 1,000 specimens for dissection have been taken from comparable open and wooded terrain several miles from the study area, and experiments involving manipulation of internal or external environment

Fig. 3. A marginal part of the study area at Gungahlin, Canberra. The open pasture is populated by nonbreeding flock birds and groups in open territories; marginal territories form around isolated trees or bushes. Photo by C. Totterdell.

have been made mainly outside the study area. Counts of the territorial birds in the area, with identification of color-banded individuals, are made every 3 months, and the free-flying juveniles still present in February receive their color combination then.

This is a preliminary account of the main findings that relate to the ecological significance of territorialism. These results are based on extensive data from birds of known identity and history, and a full account of this study will be published in a future issue of *C.S.I.R.O. Wildlife Research.*

### SOCIAL ORGANIZATION AND USE OF HABITAT

The Australian Magpie forms social territorial groups of 2–10 birds. Most territories fall within the 5- to 20-acre range, with an average of about 10

744                    ECOLOGY: POPULATION STUDIES

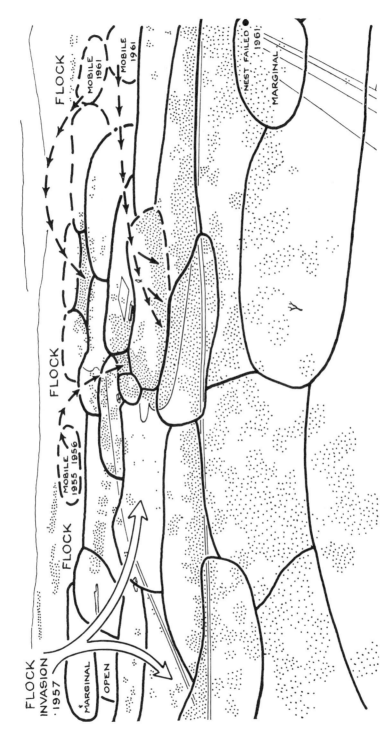

Fig. 4. The territories in the central part of the study area (Fig. 2). Most are occupied by permanent groups; the two types of marginal territory are shown at top left (inadequate cover) and bottom right (inadequate pasture); small arrows show where mobile groups attempted to nest, and the large arrow shows where flock birds invaded breeding territories in the hard winter and spring of 1957.

acres, but smaller areas are held where surrounding pressure is strong, and larger ones at the margins of the territorial area where there is no neighboring group. A group of two birds is always adult cock and hen; there may be six adults in a group, with any combination of sexes but a maximum of three breeding individuals of either sex in one group. The average number of adults per group is three, and males seldom outnumber females. Bigamy is common, and trigamy occurs. There is no relation between the size and quality of the territory and the number of birds that occupy it. At any time a large territory may have a small group, and vice versa; groups can fluctuate in time within the range of 2–10 birds without change of boundary.

The upper limit of territory size is, by observation, the largest area that the group can obtain and hold effectively; the better territories contain far more nest habitat and shelter than the group can use, and may well contain a food surplus also, although this requires to be tested by experimental alteration of food level. In a few instances the constant lateral pressure at territory boundaries enabled a group to increase its area when a neighboring group departed, but this gain was later surrendered, presumably through inability to defend the larger area. The lower limit of territory size is set by the amount of feeding pasture required to sustain the group, for a much smaller area than this can contain superabundant cover. Thus, territory size is largely determined by group size, although it is difficult to see what determines the level of the latter, which is similar throughout the range of the black-backed and white-backed forms of *G. tibicen* in eastern Australia. It is tempting to suggest that the group is limited by the number of birds that the dominant member can control, but the Western Australian Magpie (*G. dorsalis*) differs in having groups of up to 26 birds, with as many as six adult males in some groups, that occupy territories of 30–150 acres, and there are apparently no flocks (Robinson, 1956).

In many changes of territory ownership, no healthy reigning group has been dispossessed, regardless of the size of its territory or the relative strength of opponent groups. The members of defending and attacking groups fight as a team, with the advantage strongly in favor of the former.

It is convenient to recognize five social categories based on the quality of habitat occupied by each (Fig. 4 and 5), but these form a graded series and the system is anything but static, for birds and groups in the poorer environments are continually striving to improve their position in the habitat scale. Groups compete for tree cover with adjoining pasture feeding areas, which results in the open and marginal woodland, and also some open pasture, becoming subdivided into territories that are held for periods and defended with a tenacity proportionate to their quality as places to breed and feed.

1) *Permanent* groups hold territories that provide an adequate or surplus amount of all requirements all the year round. There are many more trees than the small number of birds requires for shelter, roosting, or nesting, and seasonal weights give no indication of food shortage at any time. Birds

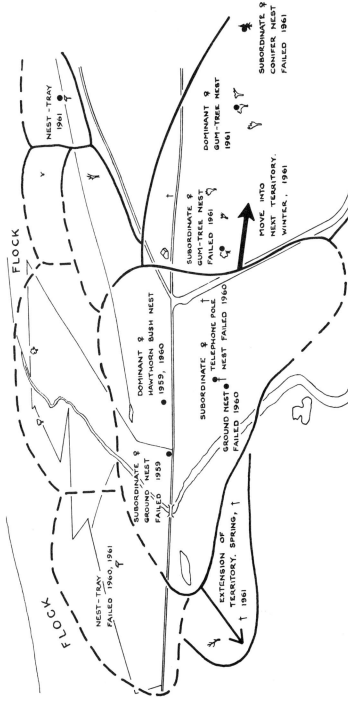

Fig. 5. The territories in a marginal part of the study area (Fig. 3). The marginal territory in the center was occupied in 1959 and 1960 by a cock with two hens; the dominant hen nested in the single hawthorn bush and the subordinate one made abortive attempts elsewhere; in 1961, this group succeeded to the permanent territory on the right, but interference by the dominant hen still prevented the subordinate one from breeding successfully. A group of two cocks and three hens found the center territory inadequate for breeding in 1961, despite an extension to include a dead tree. A similar variability of response was shown by the open groups at top left and top right, and only the latter nested on the artificial tray provided.

remain in these optimal territories all day and all year, and make no attempt to move. Virtually all successful breeding is done by these birds. A permanent group may contain birds of all ages.

2) *Marginal* groups occupy territories with an inadequate amount of either cover or feeding area. They form around one or two small trees or bushes (or even artificial nest sites such as telegraph poles or tall wireless masts) on the outskirts of better cover; also in open woodland poorly defended by the surrounding groups but with inadequate pasture for feeding at all seasons. Attempts to breed rarely succeed to the point of fledging. Marginal groups usually consist of adult birds only.

3) *Mobile* groups commute between a separate feeding area in the open and a nesting–roosting area among trees. The latter is held against the strong opposition of neighboring groups, and mobile groups exist mainly during the breeding season. Breeding always fails, usually at an early stage, and mobile groups do not contain first-year birds.

4) *Open* groups form in areas of treeless pasture that provide adequate feeding all year, except possibly during severe drought or hard frost. They roost in the denser woodland that is not otherwise used by this species; the daily flight is usually within a mile, and members of the same open group may go to different roosts. An open group can last several years, and some become mobile groups in spring. Open groups contain only adult birds, but they make no attempt to nest.

5) *Flock* birds are nonterritorial. They are birds of all ages and both sexes, and some may have bred as members of territorial groups now disbanded. They form loose flocks of a few up to several hundred individuals that feed in open pasture and roost in woods. More intensive study might well reveal that most flock adults are in fact in open groups with varying degrees of attachment to feeding area or constancy of membership, but more stable during the breeding season. The flocks show slight mobility throughout the year, and about half of the open terrain in the study area is occupied and the other half left untenanted by them at any one time. They do not attempt to nest.

### CHANGES OF STATUS

In this territorial system, there is considerable temporal and spatial stability of groups and individuals; in May 1962, 16 of the original 38 permanent groups present in 1955 still occupied the same territory, and 20 percent of males and 18 percent of females were in the territories where they were first banded as adults in 1955 or early 1956. These figures are rather low because they include losses from human activities that would not occur over most of the magpie's range. This stability is maintained by constant vigilance in a dynamic situation in which there is continual daily effort all the year round, with an upsurge of activity in July to October, i.e. before and during breeding, on the part of both groups and individuals to improve their social status.

Individual changes may result in increase, replacement, or decrease in the members of a group. Most birds leave their natal territory during their first year, some in the second, and a few in the third, but a small proportion continues to live and breed there. More females than males do this, and the oldest hen that has remained in the parental territory is now almost 7 years old, while the oldest cock is 3½ years old. It is exceptional for an adult to be added to an existing group, but this has occurred when a sick hen was unable to repel a flock hen that became established in the group before the resident hen recovered. Members of a group repel their own sex, but each sex supports the other once a contest is under way. When a vacancy is created, as by mortality, for either sex, a replacement by one or more birds of the same sex may occur; this is more usual in the case of females than males, presumably because of the greater ability of the latter to hold on to their territory. Mortality causes decrease in a group, and either sex may emigrate from a group in an inadequate territory to one in a better territory where there is a sex vacancy for it.

A group preformed in the flock, or one in occupation of a poor habitat, may succeed in forcing its way into a better habitat, thus creating a new territory. Loss of the dominant adult, usually the male, often leads to break-up and displacement of a group by a new one. A group seldom becomes too large, but in one case a group of 3 males, 4 females, and 3 immatures became subdivided and the adult male and female, which separated from the others, continued to occupy part of the original territory. Expansion of territory with change in the composition of the group can occur when a neighboring group goes out and the territory is not immediately claimed by an incoming group; unless the first territory is small, the group is not usually able to defend the expanded area effectively and has to surrender all or part of it eventually.

### THE GONAD CYCLE AND BREEDING

In the Canberra region, egg laying extends from August through October, and some seasons start earlier than others. This is preceded by increased epigamic activity of adult males from July onward, when many immatures are evicted from territorial groups and many open and marginal groups make determined attempts to secure adequate tree cover for nesting. The female alone selects the nest site and builds the nest; copulation occurs only at her invitation. The clutch contains 1–6, average 3, eggs, and some re-laying after failure occurs in earlier seasons, but little in a normal one. The cock does not brood, but may feed the hen on the nest and may play a variable part in feeding the young.

Males of all ages and all environments and social positions have motile sperm in the breeding season. Testes are largest in adult males in permanent territories, and much smaller in territory or flock 1-year-olds. Where nutrition is adequate, as it always seems to be, physical environmental stimuli alone appear capable of bringing the testis to maturity, after which age and social status in that order determine how far development will proceed. Testis size and sperm production do not appear to be affected by antagonistic relations between groups, or between a group and trespassing individuals, or within the group.

No 1-year-old female has been known to ovulate. Some 2-year-old hens breed, but even in permanent groups some females of this age or even older may not breed. In spring the ovary undergoes partial development in every case, and the final rapid increase in size of oocytes, with associated nest-building behavior, depends on the presence of certain critical stimuli as well as the absence of inhibiting factors. To attain ovulation, the hen must be a member of a social group in a territory that offers an acceptable nest site, but the threshold value of the latter in different individuals varies from a high tree to a low bush or post, and in one exceptional case the ground. Tradition is probably important, and preliminary experiments in open territories with artificial sites in the form of wooden trays on poles, bare or decorated with foliage, and with small trees, suggest that foliage as such sometimes has valency. Male stimulation of the female does not occur, for hens whose adult cocks were caponized with oestrogen implants and made effeminate to the point of building nests and soliciting, continued to build and lay (infertile eggs) normally on the same dates as control groups.

Even in the presence of adequate proximate stimuli, oocyte development and nest building can be inhibited by emotional factors, such as intrusion of a strange magpie of either sex into the territory, an undue amount of boundary fighting, or domination by another female of the same group. The psychosomatic effect of alien individuals, even on hens in first-grade permanent territories, has been observed as it occurred naturally in several situations, notably in 1957 when flock birds, which overran some territories (Fig. 4) during the frosty winter and were not evicted by spring, caused inhibition of nesting among the resident hens; this effect has been confirmed experimentally. The response of individual hens to similar stimulatory and inhibitory factors in the environment varies widely.

No open group has reached the stage of nest building. The breeding performance of mobile groups varies from failure to commence building to an occasional successful hatching, but, because of predation while the adult is absent at the feeding ground, no hen in a mobile group has been able to fledge its young. Those mobile hens that become sufficiently established to build and lay often lose their eggs from the direct attack of neighboring magpies; or else the eggs become addled, or eggs or nestlings fall to predators when the hens are engaged in boundary fights or are absent in the feeding area. The most common predator of eggs and nestlings is the Australian Raven (*Corvus coronoides*). Marginal groups often fail to nest, but a small percentage rear young to the free-living stage. It is the permanent groups that produce the annual increment to the population, but even their breeding

750          ECOLOGY: POPULATION STUDIES

TABLE 1.—NUMBERS OF *Gymnorhina tibicen* IN THE GUNGAHLIN STUDY AREA

| Status<br>When Censused | TERRITORY[a]<br>AUG.–SEPT. | | FLOCK[b]<br>MAY–JULY | | TOTAL IN<br>POPULATION | |
|---|---|---|---|---|---|---|
| | No. | Percent | No. | Percent | No. | Percent |
| **ADULT FEMALES** | | | | | | |
| 1957[c] | 92 | 36 | 161 | 64 | 253 | 100 |
| 1958 | 103 | 35 | 189 | 65 | 292 | 100 |
| 1960 | 112 | 39 | 178 | 61 | 290 | 100 |
| 1961 | 111 | 40 | 168 | 60 | 279 | 100 |
| **AVERAGE DURING 1957–61** | | | | | | |
| Males | 79 | 21 | 296 | 79 | 375 | 100 |
| Females | 107 | 38 | 174 | 62 | 281 | 100 |
| Total adults | 186 | 28 | 470 | 72 | 656 | 100 |
| (Sex ratio ♂ : ♀) | (43 : 57) | | (63 : 37) | | (57 : 43) | |
| 1st-year birds[d] | ca. 15 | | ca. 70 | | ca. 85 | |
| Total population | ca. 200 | | ca. 540 | | ca. 740 | |

[a] Territory birds include all hens that have an opportunity to breed, i.e. permanent, marginal, and mobile groups.

[b] Flock birds are nonterritorial individuals plus open groups.

[c] Owing to improved methods of observation and trapping in subsequent years, the numbers for 1957 may be rather low.

[d] Counts taken in midwinter.

rate is reduced by aggression between groups and by sex dominance within groups, as well as by the usual factors not directly associated with social territorialism. The extent to which this system reduces breeding to one-quarter of the potential it would have in the absence of territorial capitalism of breeding sites and sociosexual aggression and dominance is shown in Tables 1 and 2.

## ANNUAL PRODUCTIVITY AND MORTALITY

In a good breeding season about one juvenile magpie per adult territorial female reaches the free-flying stage in January, and the number is much

TABLE 2.—DEGREE OF BREEDING FAILURE CAUSED BY TERRITORIALISM

| Year | 1958 | | 1960 | |
|---|---|---|---|---|
| | No. | Percent | No. | Percent |
| Total number adult females in study area | 292 | 100 | 290 | 100 |
| Nonbreeding females in flocks | 189 | 65 | 178 | 61 |
| Failing females in territories, due to intergroup aggression | 16 | 6 | 21 | 7 |
| and intragroup dominance | 13 | 5 | 14 | 5 |
| Total reduction of nests | 218 | 76 | 213 | 73 |

lower in poor seasons. The high survival of adult birds during the course of this study indicates that a low annual death rate, especially in the permanent territorial groups, is adequate to cancel the normal increase from natality.

Starvation has not been evident in this study, although birds of all ages in the wide range of habitats, but each with good feeding pasture, have shown significant differences of body weight throughout the year. The same is true of stomach contents and fat reserves.

Predation by crows and hawks occurs up to the free-flying stage, and is more severe in poorer cover, but natural losses among older birds, even including those due to feral cats, are not considered serious. The Peregrine Falcon (*Falco peregrinus*) has occasionally hunted the area and taken adult flock birds in the open. Immature *Homo sapiens* of all ages take a steady but small toll of nestlings, which are popular if illegal pets, and of adults, which afford target practice in the absence of other game and, in the case of the cock during the breeding season, engender retaliation for their unprovoked attacks on people. Territories on main roads consistently lose their juveniles, and an occasional adult, in traffic accidents, and rabbit traps and other human agencies also account for a small number of birds, mainly in territories.

Diseases of many kinds have been identified during this study, some of them lethal, and at least one is considered to be an important primary cause of death. This is *Pasteurella pseudotuberculosis*, which killed large numbers of flock birds during the cold wet winter of 1956, but, being contact-spread, did not cause a single death among the territory individuals, all of which were banded, in woodland closely adjacent to open pasture where dead and dying birds could be picked up daily at the height of the epidemic. The flock birds exposed to this infection showed no sign of debility, as compared with territory birds, that might have predisposed them to mortality, and the conditions that favor the disease appear to occur too infrequently for development of resistance to it. During the harder winter of 1957, the food on the more exposed pastures became unavailable, and many flock birds concentrated on softer ground and haystacks, where they picked up the spores of the fungus *Aspergillus*, which became a secondary cause of death of some importance that year. Both of these diseases and several others take a constant low-level toll of magpies.

## CONCLUSIONS

Territorialism and associated sociosexual interactions limit breeding to about one-quarter of the adult population of *G. tibicen*.

Territorialism buffers that element of the population against important mortality from disease, and probably also protects it from predation.

The completeness of the territorial habit in *G. tibicen*, in which the social group lives permanently within its territory, indicates that the food supply of this area is always adequate; nor is there evidence that flock birds come up against the food limit.

ACKNOWLEDGMENTS

I am much indebted to F. N. Ratcliffe and the Executive of the Commonwealth Scientific and Industrial Research Organisation, Australia, for enabling this study to be done. I am also grateful, among many others, to my wife, who has been mainly responsible for identifications of banded birds, to W. J. M. Vestjens, who has borne the brunt of the trapping and collection of specimens and breeding data, to Mrs. Amy Bernie for maintenance of records and analysis of data, to R. Mykytowycz for pathological examinations, and to I. C. Rowley and K. Keith for assistance during the earlier years.

During the discussion after this paper was read at the Congress, significant questions and comments were made by David Lack of Oxford and Richard F. Johnston of Kansas.

SUMMARY

A study of population ecology in the Australian Magpie (*Gymnorhina tibicen*) during 1955–62 at Gungahlin, Canberra, is based on 650 birds individually color-banded and 2,500 others banded; 220 territorial groups have been studied, and three field experiments done on proximate factors in the stimulation and inhibition of breeding. A preliminary account of the evidence on the ecological significance of territorialism is given in this paper.

Open savannah woodland and adjacent pasture are permanently occupied by breeding groups of 2–10 birds, with a maximum of 3 adults of each sex; an average territory is 10 acres. Similar social groups also hold marginal territories that are deficient in feeding pasture or tree cover for shelter and nesting. Open treeless pasture supports a large nonbreeding element, including former breeders, in the form of slightly nomadic flocks and some territorial groups that may become mobile in spring between separate feeding and breeding areas. Successful breeding is virtually confined to the permanent groups, and productivity is low; territorialism reduces breeding to one-quarter of its potential. Groups and individuals in the poorer habitats make constant efforts to improve their status; the causes of changes in the composition or status of groups are described.

Testes mature in all situations, but the response of individual females to the environmental situation is more variable. The adult ovary requires adequate stimuli from group status and suitable nest site. It can be inhibited by sociosexual factors, such as conflict with neighboring groups or intruders in the territory, or by dominance within the group, which cause a psychosomatic reaction involving ovarian repression.

In this species, territorialism has led to a high degree of numerical and spatial stability. It buffers the permanent occupants of the preferred habitat from important disease mortality, and probably also from predation.

LITERATURE CITED

HINDE, R. A. 1956. The biological significance of the territories of birds. Ibis 98: 340–369.

ROBINSON, A. 1956. The annual reproductory cycle of the magpie, *Gymnorhina dorsalis* Campbell, in south-western Australia. Emu 56:233–336.

WYNNE-EDWARDS, V. C. 1962. Animal dispersion in relation to social behaviour. Oliver and Boyd, Edinburgh. 653 p.

# THE GENETIC CHARACTERISTICS OF MARGINAL POPULATIONS OF DROSOPHILA

## HAMPTON L. CARSON

Department of Zoology, Washington University, St. Louis, Missouri

## INTRODUCTION

The natural population of any particular species, at a given time, is an assemblage of organisms distributed in space and, as such, has an areal structure, or geometry. Perhaps the oldest of the sciences which deal with the description and interpretation of natural populations is that of plant and animal geography. This science treats primarily the distribution of organisms in space and ordinarily the basic data are derived from "present-day" distributions, based on records documented by preserved specimens in museums and herbaria. Although some aspects of this science, and some workers, concern themselves with the annual or perennial ebb and flow of populations, the principal ramifications of the science are into the field of interpretative historical geography, based on inferences from the peculiarities of present-day distributions. The historical aspects of this approach have in recent years been given a special stimulus through the introduction of the technique of analyzing pollen horizons (see review in Cain, 1944).

Paleontology has also traditionally dealt with populations in space and time, although the time involved and the taxonomic level dealt with are such that these data are in most cases of little help in understanding the structure of existing natural populations. Species populations in space and time are also legitimate study material for the ecologist; both micro- and macro-ecological factors are powerful determinants of the past and present distribution pattern of a given species.

Species populations, and especially those sub-populations which exist within the species, have become the realm of the new science of population genetics. As a science dealing with the experimental study of evolution, population genetics has scarcely left the laboratory and theoretical stages of its development, yet it is the dynamics of populations in a state of nature that one wishes ultimately to interpret and predict. Certain key data are required by the population geneticist and it is of course his hope, as a newcomer to the study of species populations, that these data may already have been gathered.

Unfortunately, this in general does not appear to be the case. For example, the time parameter of most interest to the geneticist is the time from one generation to the next. Obviously a plant with the annual habit will have a geographical distribution which could, under certain conditions, change rapidly in only a few years, whereas a plant which replaces itself on the average of once every 40

years can be represented much more accurately on a distribution map. In the latter case, a detailed map of distribution, prepared for the current year will in all probability still be valid a decade later.

Persons who prepare distribution maps, furthermore, appear to be extraordinarily preoccupied with the "original" range of the organism before the advent of modern civilization. Such treatment certainly serves well the ends of the student of phylogeny and history of the group but the practice tends to submerge some of the most significant problems that may be open to attack by the population geneticist. There are few organisms indeed which have not been faced by the many-faceted, severe and unprecedented environmental challenges posed by modern human civilization. The few thousand years since the spread of human populations have witnessed the emergence of innumerable evolutionary novelties, ranging all the way from the specific products of conscious human selection to the weeds, both plant and animal, which have attached themselves to man. Except in key cases, like that of industrial melanism (see Ford, 1953), there has been little or no interpretation from the point of view of population genetics, of these striking evolutionary events.

Studies of distribution are perhaps inclined more toward documenting ecological effects on populations rather than recording fluctuations of populations with time. This is probably because techniques which enable us to measure the effects of various ecological factors are better developed than those dealing with population sizes. Data on actual effective population sizes are of course exceedingly rare and are at best first approximations. It is more surprising, however, that data on relative population sizes in different parts of a species range, population densities, are likewise scarce. Species populations are often treated as if the density of the individuals which comprise them was the same throughout the range. Such is apparently not the case and these varying densities quite obviously affect prominently the genetic characteristics of the natural populations.

Examples of the inadequacy of existing data on natural populations for the genetically trained observer could be multiplied. Such an accounting, however, is not necessary to emphasize the importance of the gathering of certain kinds of data. Suffice it to say that the population geneticist who wishes to investigate directly the genetic material of natural populations must be prepared to obtain

Reprinted by permission of the Long Island Biological Association and the author from *Cold Spring Harbor Symposium on Quantitative Biology* 20:276–286, 1955.

not only genetic but ecological and distributional data as well.

The purpose of the present discussion is to direct the thoughts of the population geneticist to populations at the edge or margin of the range of the species. A working concept of a marginal population will be developed following which certain facts relative to the genetic structure of marginal versus central populations will be presented. Special attention will be paid to certain data derived from studies of *Drosophila* populations which indicate that the genetic characteristics of marginal populations differ, in some cases, from that portion of the species population which occupies a more central position. The proposition will be offered that the marginal populations of certain species of *Drosophila* appear to possess a genetic system which is considerably more open for gene recombination than the populations found in the center of the species range. This appears to be a by-product of adaptive evolution in central populations through chromosomal polymorphism. The net result is nonetheless to confer on marginal populations a relatively high evolutionary potential.

## THE CONCEPT OF THE MARGINAL POPULATION

What is meant in this paper by a marginal population may best be made clear by recourse to a specific example. For this purpose it is convenient to consider a well-known, characteristic, and extensively mapped species of tree from eastern North America, the American Elm (*Ulmus americana* L.). Plants are generally so much better known than animals from a geographical point of view that one may best use an example of plant distribution as a point of departure. This case is, furthermore, of special interest in that this tree forms sap exudations, or slime fluxes, which apparently form the principal breeding sites of *Drosophila robusta*. This species of fly has received a relatively large amount of attention from the point of view of the genetics of natural populations. This work will be referred to later in the present paper. Referring to the distribution of *Ulmus americana* in an exemplary way (Fig. 1) it may be seen that it is a fairly simple matter to circumscribe the periphery of the distribution of this tree. The map, more than the usual one of this sort, shows the topographical (in the sense of Cain, 1944) distribution. Thus it is absent from the marine margin of some of the area of the eastern and southern coastal plain as well as from sections of the Appalachian and Ozark plateaus. In the upper middle west, the range is much less continuous, being dissected at the margin as the tree pushes westward onto the great plains, following the river valleys. Disjunct, or "island" patterns are formed because the tree is absent from certain areas in Minnesota, Iowa, Missouri and Kansas. The east and south margins have a similar character in that the border of the species is essentially a marine one. The coastal strip forms an abrupt barrier for the species; no conceivable colonization, other than that of small offshore islands, mostly in the coastal plain, could occur in this direction. The result is that the tree grows in complex, stable ecological associations right up to the primary barrier, the sea. Such a margin is geographically and ecologically highly stabilized. For the most part it is as rigid and fixed as a natural boundary can be. The genetic material of the species is being faced here with an insuperable barrier. Such a margin is static both in space and time; it resembles the kind of margin which exists in familiar laboratory populations such as cultures of *Paramecium* or population cages of insects. This particular margin, at least, is a closed system.

The margin existing along the western edge of the species forms a strong contrast to the above. Here, like other elements and communities associated with the eastern deciduous forest, the American Elm is limited by the great plains. This margin, however, differs from the eastern one in that at all points the boundary of the species is highly dissected. Precise data are lacking but it is apparent to even the casual observer that as one proceeds westward the tree becomes more and more characteristic of the river bottoms and is increasingly absent from the higher river-bluff ravines which are its characteristic habitat further east. A diffuse distribution has been converted into one which is essentially linear or dendritic (cf. Blair, 1953).

At such a margin, perennial fluctuations in the extent of the range may also be expected. A series of dry years may roll the species back but such an event may well be followed by expansion and even range extension when conditions are reversed. Such fluidity at the margin is conducive to the formation of "island" marginal populations. Such populations are perhaps best designated as "peripheral isolates" (Mayr, 1954). No term, however, appears to exist which will distinguish between ancient and recent isolates, although the population geneticist finds himself more concerned with the latter.

The static and dynamic margins described above may be likened to abrupt sea cliffs and a low tidal flat, respectively. The organismal tide, rising against cliffs, is turned back abruptly; no pockets of moisture remain after its advance and the margin between sea and cliffs is always sharp. A flat, on the other hand, allows the tide to sweep over it for considerable distances; these tides then periodically recede over a similar or even greater distance, leaving many channels which communicate with the main body of water. Isolated pools are formed which may persist for a time but are periodically swamped by a new succession of high tides or remain permanently isolated until they become extinct through dessication.

Although it is thus possible to draw strong contrasts between such dynamic margins and static

FIGURE 1. Distribution of the American Elm, *Ulmus americana*. (This map is reproduced by courtesy of the United States Forest Service.)

ones, there are certain margins which appear to be intermediate between these types. In fact, no sort of typological thinking is intended in the formation of the above rough classifications. In the case of *Ulmus americana*, another margin is obvious; this is an internal margin, the line where the species stops at the base of the Appalachian uplift. Thus, the tree is absent at higher elevations in the Great Smoky Mountains, although it is an abundant element of the flora in the geographically nearby lowlands.

It has been the contention of many students of geographical distribution that marginal phenomena are recapitulated on a mountainside and this appears to be essentially true. There is, nonetheless, an important difference. The type of fluctuations which occur over large areas, as in the west, are here telescoped into a small space. Actual physical distance between isolate and main population may play an important role in the effectiveness of the

isolation, especially in highly motile organisms. Thus altitudinal marginal phenomena may indeed lack one of the most important features of a truly dynamic one, the strong potentiality for marginal isolation.

Such local ecological or altitudinal margins as those mentioned above, as well as the internal margins between subspecies will not be considered in the present discussion. In the latter situations, the true genetic nature of the initial isolates in divergent speciation may be obscured. The interbreeding of formerly isolated entities is a powerful source of genetic recombination and, as such, has received detailed attention (*e.g.*, Anderson, 1949). It is the purpose of this paper to consider the genetic nature of such isolates during and just after their formation, not the phenomena which surround their reunion.

The peripheral ecotone margin is of the greatest significance for the population geneticist as he contemplates present-day distribution of organisms in space and time because it is in just such populations that isolation may occur most readily. Such cessation of gene flow is a necessary prerequisite for speciation and the formation of peripheral isolates appears to be one of the most prominent ways that this flow can be interrupted. In this manner, pioneers from the body of the species make their advances. Instances of such ebb and flow may be observed in the patterns of distribution of present-day organisms, but probably few such isolates have any future other than extinction (*e.g.*, Lewis, 1953) or re-swamping. The situation nonetheless contains the crucial ingredients which could lead to the formation of evolutionary novelties and it is of particular importance that marginal populations, as the direct progenitors of such isolates, be better known genetically.

## GENETIC CHARACTERISTICS OF MARGINAL POPULATIONS OF DROSOPHILA

Studies of the geographical distribution of natural populations of *Drosophila* species, like those of many other insects, are beset with many difficulties. Animals in general, being capable of movement, present very different technical problems from plants. In the case of *Drosophila*, which continues to be exceptionally valuable material for the study of genetic characteristics, not only has knowledge of the ecology of the organisms been proceeding slowly but only the bare essentials of geographical distribution are available. For certain of the well-studied species, those of which quantitative samples have been studied, we are now in possession of enough facts to enable us to prepare approximate geographical ranges. Thus for *Drosophila robusta*, *D. pseudoobscura*, *D. persimilis* and *D. willistoni* we are now able to designate certain populations as marginal and certain others as central. The discussion which follows will of necessity be confined to such species.

*Drosophila robusta*. This species is one of the most characteristic members of the family Drosophilidae found in the deciduous forest of the eastern United States. Its populations have been the object of considerable study from the genetic (gene arrangements and morphology), ecological and distributional point of view (see review of Carson, 1952; see also Levitan, 1955). This species breeds extensively on the sap exudations of various trees of the deciduous forest, especially *Ulmus americana*. Very much less is of course known about the distribution of the fly than about the distribution of its principal host species. Nevertheless, *D. robusta* appears to be coextensive with *Ulmus americana* over most of the range of the latter. The boundary populations of the fly are less well known but it does not appear to occur north of the United States except in southern Ontario.

As mentioned earlier, it is probable that population densities decrease as the margin of a species is approached. The question arises whether data exist on *Drosophila* populations which might permit estimation of varying relative population densities of any species. A rather large number of collections of *Drosophila* have been made in eastern North America using fermenting bananas as an attrahent and data on the number of flies caught by this method are available in the literature and in unpublished files of various collectors.

There are many drawbacks to using these data as an indication of densities. Not only is there variation in the conditions under which the collections were made (*e.g.*, microhabitats, season, time of day, calendar year, zeal of collecting and so forth) but other intangible factors enter in. Thus the condition of the bait, varying bait preferences on the part of the flies, and the presence or absence of fortuitous local "hatches" of flies all may seriously affect the number of specimens of any given species which are caught. It is apparent that only large collections of flies, preferably made at all seasons could be admissable as data on which a calculation of relative population density of any species in an area could be based.

Even under the above circumstances, the per cent of any species in the total flies caught is misleading because certain species, especially those associated with man, show opportunistic breeding and can build up locally or seasonally to enormous numbers which swamp the ecologically more balanced population sizes of the native species. Thus at certain times and places, a collection of *Drosophila* may consist largely of the cosmopolitan species *D. melanogaster* or *D. hydei*. Of the truly native species, those which breed on fungus likewise tend to show enormous periodic fluctuations in numbers, depending on the availability of the substrates on which they breed (*e.g.*, *D. occidentalis* at Aspen Valley, Yosemite National Park, California, in July 1954, Cooper and Dobzhansky, 1955).

In general contrast to the gross instability from season to season and place to place of the above cases, are the population characteristics of those flies which belong to the affinis group of the genus (*sensu lato*: including the affinis and obscura subgroups). In the eastern United States there are four well-known members of the affinis subgroup (*D. affinis*, *D. algonquin*, *D. athabasca* and *D. narragansett*). In the western part of their ranges, these species are replaced principally by *D. pseudoobscura* but also by *D. persimilis*, *D. miranda* and *D. azteca*. *D. athabasca* tends to have a somewhat boreal distribution so that its range extends rather far westward in the north (see Patterson and Wagner, 1943). The affinis group thus forms the most stable and abundant element in *Drosophila* populations in most of the continental United States. In almost every area in which extensive collections have been made, some member of this group is the ascendent species of the genus.[1] Members of this group, furthermore, overlap one another and thus extend across the biome margin between the eastern deciduous forest and western grassland.

The affinis group is found abundantly with *Drosophila robusta* in all parts of the range of the latter species. In fact, the affinis group extends well beyond it both to the north (into Canada) and south (into central Florida) and to the west (to the west coast). In the east, the time of greatest seasonal abundance of this group approximately corresponds with the greatest seasonal abundance of *Drosophila robusta*. All of these above characteristics make the numbers of affinis group flies caught a relatively good measure of the success of sampling of native species of *Drosophila* in general and provides as stable a yardstick as could be hoped for in estimating the relative abundance of *D. robusta*, especially if all-season records are available. It is not claimed that the affinis group itself does not vary in density in various parts of the range; there are certainly enormous variations in this regard. It is nevertheless true that the affinis group is generally most abundant in those parts of its range where *D. robusta* is most abundant. This indicates that the major ecological requirements of the two groups are somewhat similar and the known facts about their breeding habits appear to bear out this contention (Carson and Stalker, 1951).

It therefore appears to be reasonable that a rough estimate of the relative density of *Drosophila robusta* in different geographical areas will be given by the proportion of *D. robusta* captured relative to the affinis group. The domestic species, fungus breeders, infrequent species or species with restricted distributions have been excluded in the calculation of relative density, thus reducing the number of variables. Table 1 gives the percentage of *Drosophila robusta* out of the total of the robusta and affinis group caught in a series of large collections. In every case, an attempt has been made to utilize either summer-season or year-round samples and to include data based on the collection of at least 1000 members of the two groups. If *D. colorata*, the only other member of the robusta group in North America, was recognized by the worker identifying the flies, the number of these was added to the total as it is probable that *D. colorata* replaces *D. robusta* ecologically in certain areas, especially the north-central middle west.

Reference to Table I will show that the lowest densities of *D. robusta* are found in Oklahoma and Texas whereas the highest are found in eastern Tennessee and Missouri. The former localities are generally near the margin of the species range whereas the latter are more central geographically. The

figure for eastern Nebraska is unexpectedly high and is taken to indicate that the center of abundance of the species extends from the southern Appalachians through the middle west in a northwesterly direction. Williams and Miller (1952) have reported a number of eastern species of *Drosophila*, including *D. robusta*, from the extreme northwestern corner of the state.

Data are also presented in Table 1 which show the results of collections made in the Great Smoky Mountains National Park and vicinity in July of 1947 (Stalker and Carson, 1948). Collections were made at six different altitudes from 1000 to 6000 feet and were made daily over a period of a week. These data are included here because the manner in which the collections were taken make them reasonably comparable. They show strikingly the precipitous decline (45.4% to zero) of *D. robusta* at the telescoped altitudinal margin of the species in this area.

Genetic variation of two sorts has been studied quantitatively in *Drosophila robusta*: morphological variation and variation in gene arrangement frequencies (see review of Carson, 1952). Initial data on both types of variation indicated the existence of clines within the species. These have been viewed mostly as north-south clines; indeed the evidence indicates that there is a northern and southern phenotype and a gradual intergradation in between.

Chromosomal variation is due to inversions and there are some 14 different gene arrangements distributed in various parts of the range of the species. When considered in the form of gene frequencies, these arrangements fall into clinal patterns, suggesting that they are closely associated with the adaptive capacities of the species. More recently, however, the writer (1955) has re-examined much of the older data and some new data from a different point of view. Inversions are viewed as sections of the chromosome in which recombination in heterozygous individuals is to a large measure inhibited. A study of the effects of various inversion combinations on crossing over (Carson, 1953) has made it possible to estimate the effects on a female fly of a given chromosomal constitution, or karyotype.

As in each case the chromosomal constitution of all of the chromosomes of the set were observed, it has been possible, through measurements, to determine the amount of euchromatin in each female which has free crossing over, that is, unencumbered by the existence of a heterozygous inversion having a suppressive effect. As these calculations are made on the basis of actual measurements in the salivary gland chromosomes, the amount of chromatin which is blocked by inversions of different size is directly measured. For any given female, it has been possible to give a figure, the index of free

---

[1] A prominent exception to this statement is the ascendency of *D. mulleri* and *D. aldrichi* in Texas. These, however, are cactus-breeding forms and occupy a niche which is not widespread in North America.

TABLE 1. DENSITY OF *Drosophila robusta* RELATIVE TO THE AFFINIS AND ROBUSTA GROUPS IN VARIOUS PARTS OF EASTERN NORTH AMERICA

| Geographical location and date of collection | Source of data | Total number of affinis group* and robusta† group captured | Per cent robusta |
|---|---|---|---|
| Eastern Oklahoma (total of all collections) | Patterson, 1943 | 1,075 | 2.2 |
| Aldrich Farm, Austin, Texas, 1938-1941 | Patterson and Wagner, 1943 | 5,669 | 3.3 |
| Texas (total of all collections) | Patterson, 1943 | 12,046 | 3.7 |
| Itasca State Park, northern Minnesota, Summer, 1950-1952 | Spieth (unpub.) | 3,898 | 5.5 |
| Mississippi-Louisiana, June, 1950 | Stalker (unpub.) | 3,545 | 6.0 |
| Ohio, various locations, July, 1939 | Stalker and Spencer (unpub.) | 12,688 | 6.3 |
| Englewood Cliffs, New Jersey, 1948-1949 | Levitan, 1954 | 5,745 | 6.4 |
| Rochester, New York, July, 1940 | Stalker (unpub.) | 1,755 | 6.6 |
| Georgia-Alabama, various locations, April, 1946 | Stalker (unpub.) | 1,531 | 7.1 |
| Coopers Rock State Forest, W. Virginia, 1952-1954, all seasons | Dorsey and Carson, 1955 | 10,482 | 9.0 |
| Cheboygan, Michigan, July, 1954 | Miller (unpub.) | 1,479 | 9.8 |
| Eastern Nebraska, various locations | Williams and Miller, 1952 and Miller (unpub.) | 8,322 | 16.0 |
| Unaka Mountain, Tennessee-N. Carolina, 2200-4800 ft., 1950-52, 1954 | Stevenson, 1952 and unpub. | 19,618 | 18.7 |
| St. Louis, Missouri, Olivette Woods, 1946-49 | Stalker and Carson (unpub.) | 26,099 | 20.2 |
| Eastern Tennessee, various locations, summer | Patterson, 1943 | 2,418 | 48.5 |
| Great Smoky Mountain National Park and vicinity, July 8-15, 1947 (daily collections at all stations) | Stalker and Carson, 1948 and unpub. | | |
| 6000 ft. | | 201 | 0.0 |
| 5000 ft. | | 276 | 0.0 |
| 4000 ft. | | 1,366 | 2.6 |
| 3000 ft. | | 1,138 | 4.3 |
| 2000 ft. | | 1,360 | 16.4 |
| 1400-1000 ft. | | 1,550 | 45.4 |
| Grand totals | | 122,261 | 13.1 |

\* *D. affinis*; *D. athabasca*; *D. algonquin*; *D. narragansett*
† *D. robusta*; *D. colorata*

crossing over, which indicates the amount of euchromatin available to the process of crossing over. Thus, in a structural homozygote, the index is 100 per cent, and in a fly heterozygous for a short inversion covering, for example, 10 per cent of the total euchromatic genome length, the index would be 90 per cent.

A total of 614 egg samples of female flies of *Drosophila robusta* from wild populations have been assigned an index of free crossing over. The wild parents of these flies came from nine geographical areas within the range of the species. Frequency distribution histograms of these indices were prepared for each of these nine populations. Analysis of the data reveals that populations which are centrally-located with respect to the range of the species have relatively very low indices of free crossing over. This reflects the fact that the frequency of individuals which are heterozygous for a number of relatively long inversions is very great in such populations. As one approaches the margins of the species distribution this situation changes. Populations from the margin of the species range tend to be much more homozygous for gene arrangement

and consequently have much higher indices of free crossing over. The data fall into a continuous series but may be grouped into three statistically significant groups from central, intermediate and marginal areas.

Recently a large sample of *D. robusta* from the extreme northwest corner of the range (Dawes County, Nebraska) has been obtained (Carson, 1956). This highly marginal population proved to be essentially homozygous for gene arrangement. The two largest submarginal populations previously studied (Carson, 1955) were only relatively homozygous (85% free crossing over), whereas in the Nebraska case homozygosity is almost complete (of 1868 chromosome arms tested, only two individual instances of an inverted arrangement were found). Marginal homozygosity for gene arrangement in this species, therefore, appears to be a more complete and striking phenomenon than had previously been suspected.

MARGINAL POPULATIONS IN OTHER DROSOPHILA SPECIES

The situation which has been described in *Drosophila robusta* seems to be paralleled by data on the marginal populations of the tropical South American species *Drosophila willistoni* (da Cunha *et al.*, 1950; Townsend, 1952; da Cunha and Dobzhansky, 1954). The latter authors have discussed the proposition that the degree of chromosomal polymorphism in a population is a function of the number of ecological niches occupied and exploited by a species. These authors point out that although the facts of inversion distribution in *D. willistoni* support the concept in the main, there is at least one notable exception. This is the so-called "Bahia race" of *D. willistoni* which has a uniformly low frequency of inversions although on the basis of the hypothesis, considerable variation would be expected. Another exception to the general application of this hypothesis is the situation which exists in various parts of the range of *Drosophila pseudoobscura* in the western United States (Dobzhansky, 1944). In the Colorado Plateau region, for example, there exists a tendency for the populations to be strongly homozygous for gene arrangement (see map in Dobzhansky, 1951), whereas populations on all sides of this one have a greater diversity of gene arrangements. Such a population appears to be ecologically marginal in much the same sense as desert populations of *Drosophila willistoni*. In general, however, the distribution of the polymorphism within *D. pseudoobscura* does not show a direct correlation between the amount of polymorphism and the variety of niches apparently occupied by the species. Although the chromosomal polymorphism is high in the Sierra Nevada mountains it is also high near the southeastern border of the species in Texas.

*D. persimilis* (Dobzhansky, 1948; Spiess, 1950) is much more regular in its behavior. There are north-south clines and clines of frequencies with altitude which resemble *Drosophila robusta* in that there is a strong tendency towards structural homozygosity both as one goes northward and as altitude is attained. Data on *Drosophila subobscura* from western Europe (Stumm-Zollinger, 1953) are generally less extensive and make no attempt specifically to sample marginal populations. It is nevertheless noteworthy that the degree of chromosomal polymorphism is less in populations from Switzerland than it is in collections from lower altitudes in France.

## CONCLUSIONS

The hypothesis of da Cunha and Dobzhansky (1954) that the amount of chromosomal polymorphism in a species of *Drosophila* is a function of the number of ecological niches occupied or exploited by that species appears in general to be supported by the facts. Thus, where a species is apparently the most successful and where it has relatively the highest population densities, its environmental mastery appears to be reflected in a high degree of chromosomal polymorphism.

Adoption of the above as a working hypothesis implies the corollary expectation that in areas where the species is less ascendent and less well adapted to its environment there will be a correspondingly lower degree of chromosomal polymorphism. Evidence has been adduced which indicates that marginal populations, or populations in areas where there are relatively fewer ecological niches available for a small yeast-feeding fly, do in fact have less chromosomal polymorphism.

The contention may be entertained that the homozygosity for gene arrangement which is observed at the periphery is due to genetic drift operating in small populations, thus fixing certain arrangements in the homozygous condition. This is considered to be an unlikely explanation. In *D. robusta*, at least, clines of inversion frequencies are very regular and gradual and, as one approaches the margin, homozygosity appears to be acquired in a consistent and orderly fashion. This suggests that the margins are, in large measure, in contact genetically with the main body of the species and suggests that drift plays a minor role, if any, in the establishment of homozygosity at the margin.

There are, nevertheless, a number of exceptions to the ecological niche hypothesis of da Cunha and Dobzhansky; several have already been mentioned. An additional prominent exception is the presence of a very low degree of polymorphism in most of the cosmopolitan species of the genus *Drosophila*. So far as is known, such world-wide forms as *D. melanogaster*, *D. immigrans*, *D. hydei*, *D. virilis*, *D. busckii* and others have generally much less chromosomal polymorphism than in the native species which have been discussed. These species come from three different subgenera so that their particular chromosomal mechanism does not seem to bear any relation to their taxonomic position. Certain of them, furthermore, as for example, *D. virilis*, have certain very close relatives (*e.g.*, *D. montana*, Moorhead, 1954) which display a very high degree of chromosomal polymorphism. A similar case involving *D. polymorpha* and *D. cardinoides* has been described by da Cunha, Brncic and Salzano (1953). The latter species, which shows some tendency to be associated with man-made habitats, has considerably less chromosomal polymorphism than the very closely related *D. polymorpha* which tends to be a forest species. Clearly, the manner in which the genetic system of the cosmopolitan or domestic species is adjusted to the environment is different from that of many of the "native" species. These exceptions require an explanation.

The assumption is often made, although sometimes merely implied, that chromosome inversions and other chromosome aberrations found in natural populations are basically equivalent, in their evolutionary importance, to gene mutations. The adoption of such a view is made easy by the fact that the experimental methods used for producing one kind of hereditary change may also be used to produce the other. In fact, one often hears the statement that there is no difference in kind between "structural" chromosome changes and gene mutations. Both types of change are commonly used in the manipulations of the geneticist who is primarily concerned with more classical problems of chromosome mechanics and genetic function. From the viewpoint of population genetics, this view has certain misleading consequences.

Almost thirty years of study of chromosome inversions has brought forth overwhelming evidence that naturally-occurring inversions resemble gene mutations in only one important way from the point of view of population genetics; this is that they behave as single units in inheritance. The principal cytogenetic effect of an inversion is its effect on recombination by crossing over rather than through direct point effects on the phenotype. Inversions thus represent in large measure frozen combinations of genes which are suddenly packaged or crystallized by virtue of the occurrence of the inversion. These combinations, which one is tempted to look upon as associations of genes of small individual effect, or polygenes, are maintained in natural populations by a superior fitness of the structurally heterozygous condition.

Inversions, therefore, appear to function primarily as restrictors of recombination through their effects on crossing over. A new rigid group of linked genes is produced which is effectively isolated from recombination. When a high degree of inversion heterozygosity is reached in a population, as in certain central populations of *Drosophila robusta*, the majority of the chromatin is effectively prevented from intrachromosomal recombination. Restriction of this sort results in genetic specialization; the number of recombining units in the genotype is often drastically reduced. A new mutation occurring in such a milieu finds itself restricted to a relatively small number of genotypic combinations.

The concentration of inversions within a species or a population has often been taken as a measure of the genetic diversity present. According to the view being developed here, chromosomal polymorphism should rather be emphasized as an adaptive mechanism which restricts the release and expression of genetic variability. The variability which may exist is locked by the inversions in specialized combinations. It is conceivable, for example, that two populations might be identical in the amount of gene variability which they possess, yet if one of these is relatively more heterozygous for inversions, the variability in this population is not so available for welding into new genotypes by recombination. This may be viewed as an automatic by-product of the inversion type of genetic specialization.

How much effective crossing over occurs in individuals from populations where chromosomal polymorphism is very extensive? Such crossing over must, in very large measure, be confined to structurally homozygous chromosome sections. Two sorts of homozygous sections are found in an individual from a central population where chromosomal polymorphism is high. First, there are those sections which are entirely free of inversions and are homozygous in all individuals. Unfortunately, few precise data are available on the amount of crossing over which occurs in such sections. In *D. robusta*, however, where inversions are found in all chromosomes, these sections are in many cases short distal segments; others occur between independent inversions. Study of the latter type of region (Carson, 1953) has shown that crossovers are in some cases not obtained at all or, if exchanges do occur, the products do not appear to be fully viable, at least under natural conditions.

Similar chromosome sections in which crossing over is effectively absent between adjacent independent inversions have been identified in *D. polymorpha* (da Cunha, private communication), *D. americana* (Carson and Blight, 1952; Blight, 1955) and in *D. guaramunu* (Brncic, 1953). In view of the above cases, and in the absence of systematic data on this point, caution must be exercised in assuming completely free recombination in homozygous sections in chromosomes which differ by one or more inversions. Chromosomes completely or essentially free of inversions, however, would be expected to display normal, if not increased recombination (see Levine and Levine, 1954). Thus *D. pseudoobscura, D. persimilis* (Dobzhansky, 1944), *D. nebulosa* (Pavan, 1946; da Cunha, Brncic and Salzano, 1953) and other species which have inversions concentrated primarily in one chromosome of the set appear, even in central populations, to keep open an extensive avenue of recombination in the other chromosomes. This appears to be less true of highly polymorphic populations of *D. willistoni* and *D. robusta*. These species tend to have crossing over blocked throughout all of the chromosomes.

A second major source of recombined genotypes in central populations is in paired chromosome sections homozygous for the various gene arrangements. Such homozygotes are viable and are continually produced. It seems likely, however, that recombination between such chromosome sections would not be a rich source of variability for adjustment through recombination of polygenes. These sections exist in the population because of the superior fitness of the sectional heterozygotes. Selection would thus be expected to operate continually to perfect the heterotic qualities of these sections when in heterozygous combination with alternative gene arrangements. This would be especially true when the frequency of heterozygotes in natural populations is high. As the frequency of inversion heterozygotes decreases and the frequency of structurally homozygous chromosomes becomes higher as the margin is approached, one would expect a

284                      *HAMPTON L. CARSON*

system of adjustment based on free recombination of polygenes to replace the system based on sectional heterosis.

The inversion systems of species with extensive central polymorphism, like *D. robusta* and *D. willistoni*, have a means of escape from the specializing tendency which a high amount of chromosomal polymorphism confers on a population. This escape mechanism consists of relatively homozygous marginal populations where recombinations of polygenes throughout the genome is permitted on a large scale. Thus, should the adaptive response based on superior fitness of heterozygotes be reversed, a particular chromosome or chromosome set could, through selection for sectional homozygosity, rapidly regain a more open system of recombination. Regional differentiation of chromosomal characteristics, with relative structural homozygosity at the margin thus provides a solution to the ancient evolutionary dilemma with which the organism is continually faced. This is the maintenance of a high adaptive level and at the same time the preservation of a balance between too much recombination, which may destroy adaptive gene complexes, and too little, which restricts the ability of the organism to change genetically in response to drastically changed conditions.

If the view that chromosomal polymorphism essentially represents specialization is valid, one might logically expect that sectional heterozygosity would in some instances become permanently fixed at some high level of developmental homeostasis, and be incapable of being reversed. Such a condition could result from a balanced condition in which sectional homozygotes are lethal or have greatly reduced viability. Dobzhansky and Pavlovsky (1955) have described a case in a Honduran population of *D. tropicalis* which approximates this situation. Homozygotes are apparently formed in every generation but die off before the adult stage is reached. This case is particularly interesting in that this condition has not been found in other populations of the species.

The above case appears to be about as far as this type of fixation of the karyotype has gone in *Drosophila*, but it is of interest to mention in this connection the situation which exists in the purely thelytokus parthenogenetic fly, *Lonchoptera dubia* (Stalker, 1954, 1956). The substantial amount of sectional rearrangement found between the homologues of this fly may well have originated as a heterotic system before the loss of syngamy, in much the same manner in which it has originated in natural populations of *Drosophila*. In this case, however, the avenues of escape have been shut; the process of genetic specialization has proceeded to its logical conclusion and the entire genome of the species has become fixed, with a large part of it as a series of permanent complex sectional heterozygotes, each of which is essentially a clone.

The fixed or nearly fixed heterotic systems found in *Lonchoptera* and *D. tropicalis* are not very far removed from the conditions found in central populations of *D. willistoni* and *D. robusta*. In these latter populations there is apparently already little opportunity for new syntheses by recombination of polygenes, whereas in the marginal populations of these same species, recombination may proceed in a much more effective manner, for the reasons detailed above.

Cosmopolitan species, such as *D. melanogaster*, have only a low degree of natural chromosomal polymorphism and thus in this sense their genetic system resembles that of marginal populations of the native species discussed above. Abundant evidence is available on the capacity of *D. melanogaster* to respond to selection for quantitative characters. Responses are often rapid and sustained over many generations (Mather, 1943; Robertson and Reeve, 1952; Scossiroli, 1954; Rasmuson, 1955 and others). These responses have been widely ascribed to the action of selection on an intensively recombining system of polygenes.

A recombining system similar to that found in *D. melanogaster* is thus visualized as existing in marginal populations as opposed to central ones. Adaptive novelties are considered most likely to be synthesized by recombination under conditions observed in marginal populations. Such novelties, once synthesized, might spread back into the body of a species, where a replacement, at least in part, of older endemic types might occur. This explanation has, in fact, been evoked by Dobzhansky and da Cunha (1954) to explain the origin of the structurally uniform Bahian race of *D. willistoni*.

Cosmopolitan species may have originated as such novelties. They may represent adaptive types which were originally synthesized in the marginal populations of their endemic ancestors. By virtue of their novel characteristics and the ubiquity of their niche, they have become world-wide and the relative lack of chromosomal polymorphism may reflect the nature of the populations from which they originated. *D. pseudoobscura*, *D. nebulosa* and other forms in which heterosis is essentially confined to one chromosome retain a rather open recombination system even in their relatively polymorphic populations. They thus appear to occupy a position intermediate between the highly endemic species on the one hand and the cosmopolitan species on the other.

## Summary

1. Only slight attention has been given to specific studies of the genetic characteristics of populations at the margin of distribution of a species relative to more centrally located populations. The concept of a dynamic as opposed to a static marginal population is discussed and the key position of the former in evolutionary problems emphasized.

2. Studies of the geographical distribution and

genetic characteristics of various species of *Drosophila* are reviewed. Particular attention is given to the consideration of data on *D. robusta* which show that marginal populations of this species are relatively homozygous for gene arrangement, whereas central populations show extensive polymorphism due to inversions.

3. The view is presented that central populations with a high degree of chromosomal polymorphism suffer drastic reduction in ability to undergo recombination by crossing over, whereas marginal populations have relatively free crossing over.

4. Reduction in recombination potential is viewed as a form of genetic specialization. Central populations of endemic species like *D. robusta* or *D. willistoni*, which show chromosomal polymorphism through the genome, are less likely to foster the formation of major adaptive novelties than are marginal populations of the same species.

5. Cosmopolitan species of *Drosophila*, like *D. melanogaster*, are relatively free of chromosomal polymorphism; their genetic system thus resembles an endemic marginal population in that there is a free system of crossing over.

6. The suggestion is made that cosmopolitan species may have originally evolved from endemic ancestors in marginal situations, and have retained the open system of recombination characteristic of their progenitors.

ACKNOWLEDGMENTS

The writer wishes particularly to thank Drs. D. D. Miller, R. Stevenson, W. P. Spencer, H. T. Spieth and H. D. Stalker for generously making available unpublished records of some of their collections of *Drosophila*. The work of the author is supported by grants from the National Science Foundation (NSF-0421) and the Office of Naval Research, Department of the Navy (NR-164-220).

REFERENCES

ANDERSON, E., 1949, Introgressive Hybridization. New York, John Wiley and Sons, Inc.

BLAIR, W. F., 1953, Population dynamics of rodents and other small mammals. Adv. Genet. *5:* 2-41.

BLIGHT, W. C., 1955, A cytological study of linear populations of *Drosophila americana* near St. Louis, Mo. Washington University, St. Louis; thesis.

BRNCIC, D., 1953, Chromosomal variation in natural populations of *Drosophila guaramunu*. Z. indukt. Abstamm.-u. Vererb-lehre *85:* 1-11.

CAIN, S., 1944, Foundations of Plant Geography. New York, Harper and Brothers.

CARSON, H. L., 1952, Contrasting types of population structure in *Drosophila*. Amer. Nat. *86:* 239-248.

1953, The effects of inversions on crossing over in *Drosophila robusta*. Genetics *38:* 168-186.

1955, Variation in genetic recombination in natural populations. J. Comp. Cell. Physiol. *45:* suppl. 2, 221-236.

1956, Marginal homozygosity for gene arrangement in *Drosophila robusta*. Science *123:* 630-631.

CARSON, H. L., and BLIGHT, W. C., 1952, Sex chromosome polymorphism in a population of *Drosophila americana*. Genetics *37:* 572.

CARSON, H. L., and STALKER, H. D., 1951, Natural breeding sites for some wild species of *Drosophila* in the eastern United States. Ecology *32:* 317-330.

COOPER, D. M., *and* DOBZHANSKY, TH., 1956, Studies on the ecology of *Drosophila* in the Yosemite Region of California. I. The occurrence of species of *Drosophila* in different life zones and at different stations. Ecology *37:* (in press).

DA CUNHA, A. B., BRNCIC, D., and SALZANO, F. M., 1953, A comparative study of chromosomal polymorphism in certain South American species of *Drosophila*. Heredity *7:* 193-202.

DA CUNHA, A. B., BURLA, H., and DOBZHANSKY, TH., 1950, Adaptive chromosomal polymorphism in *Drosophila willistoni*. Evolution *4:* 212-235.

DA CUNHA, A. B., and DOBZHANSKY, TH., 1954, A further study of chromosomal polymorphism in *Drosophila willistoni* in its relation to environment. Evolution *8:* 119-134.

DOBZHANSKY, TH., 1944, Chromosomal races in *Drosophila pseudoobscura* and *Drosophila persimilis*. Carnegie Inst. Wash. Publ. *554:* 47-144.

1948, Genetics of natural populations. XVI. Altitudinal and seasonal changes produced by natural selection in certain populations of *Drosophila pseudoobscura* and *Drosophila persimilis*. Genetics *33:* 158-176.

1951, Genetics and the Origin of Species. 2nd ed. New York, Columbia University Press.

DOBZHANSKY, TH., and PAVLOVSKY, O., 1955, An extreme case of heterosis in a Central American population of *Drosophila tropicalis*. Proc. Nat. Acad. Sci. Wash. *41:* 289-295.

DORSEY, C. K., and CARSON, H. L., 1956, Selective response of wild Drosophilidae to natural and artificial attrahents. Ann. Ent. Soc. Amer. *48: 49:* 177-181.

FORD, E. B., 1953, The genetics of polymorphism in the Lepidoptera. Advanc. Genet. *5:* 43-87.

LEVINE, R. P., and LEVINE, E. E., 1954, The genotypic control of crossing over in *Drosophila pseudoobscura*. Genetics *39:* 677-691.

LEVITAN, M., 1954, Drosophilidae in New York and New Jersey. Amer. Midl. Nat. *52:* 453-457.

1955, Studies in linkage in populations. I. Associations of second chromosome linkages in *Drosophila robusta*. Evolution *9:* 62-74.

LEWIS, H., 1953, The mechanism of evolution in the genus *Clarkia*. Evolution *7:* 1-20.

MATHER, K., 1943, Polygenic inheritance and natural selection. Biol. Rev. *18:* 32-64.

MAYR, E., 1954, Change of genetic environment and evolution. In: Evolution as a Process, London, George Allen and Unwin, Ltd.

MOORHEAD, P. S., 1954, Chromosome variation in giant forms of *Drosophila montana*. Univ. Tex. Publ. *5422:* 106-129.

PATTERSON, J. T., 1943, The Drosophilidae of the Southwest. Univ. Tex. Publ. *4313:* 7-216.

PATTERSON, J. T., and WAGNER, R. P., 1943, Geographical distribution of species of the genus *Drosophila* in the United States and Mexico. Univ. Tex. Publ. *4313:* 217-281.

PAVAN, C., 1946, Chromosomal variation in *Drosophila nebulosa*. Genetics *31:* 546-557.

RASMUSON, M., 1955, Selection for bristle numbers in some unrelated strains of *Drosophila melanogaster*. Acta Zool. Stockh. *36:* 1-49.

ROBERTSON, F. W., and REEVE, E. C. R., 1952, Studies on quantitative inheritance. I. The effects of selection of wing and thorax length in *Drosophila melanogaster*. J. Genet. *50:* 414-447.

SCOSSIROLI, R. E., 1954, Effectiveness of artificial selection under irradiation of plateaued populations of *Drosophila melanogaster*. Union Intern. Sci. Biol. ser. B, No. *15:* 42-66.

STALKER, H. D., 1954, Banded polytene chromosomes in the ovarian nurse cells of adult Diptera. J. Hered. 45: 259-264.
    1956, On the evolution of parthenogenesis in *Lonchoptera* (Diptera). Evolution 10: (in press).
STALKER, H. D., and CARSON, H. L., 1948, An altitudinal transect of *Drosophila robusta* Sturtevant. Evolution 2: 295-305.
STEVENSON, R., 1952, Altitudinal distribution of species of the genus *Drosophila* (Diptera) on Unaka Mountain, Tennessee-North Carolina. J. Tenn. Acad. Sci. 27: 97-103.
STUMM-ZOLLINGER, E., 1953, Vergleichende Untersuchung uber die Inversionshaufigkeit bei *Drosophila subobscura* in Populationen der Schweiz und Sudwesteuropas. Z. Indukt. Abstamm.-u. Vererb. Lehre 85: 382-407.
SPIESS, E. B., 1950, Experimental populations of *Drosophila persimilis* from an altitudinal transect of the Sierra Nevada. Evolution 4: 14-33.
TOWNSEND, J. I., JR., 1952, Genetics of marginal populations of *Drosophila willistoni*. Evolution 6: 428-442.
WILLIAMS, D. D., and MILLER, D. D., 1952, A report on *Drosophila* collections in Nebraska. Bull. Univ. Nebr. State Mus 3: 1-19.

## DISCUSSION

LEVITAN: Without meaning to detract from Dr. Carson's excellent description of greater homozygosity for arrangement in the marginal populations discussed, I would like to raise the following question: Would it not be a better test of the hypothesis suggested if it were based on comparisons of populations with the same degree of chromosomal polymorphism (or if the degree of such heterogeneity were taken into account in the calculations)? This question arises because the homozygosity is traceable to two factors: 1) High frequencies of certain arrangements, and 2) a smaller amount of polymorphism (fewer inversions). For possible cause and effect implications, it should be realized that the latter factor may be the result of an entirely different aspect of evolution from the former. To illustrate: In *D. robusta* the absence of 2L-3 from Florida-Georgia populations considerably increases the homozygosity merely because three kinds of heterozygotes (2L/2L-3, 2L-1/2L-3 and 2L-2/2L-3) cannot occur. Even small amounts of 2L-3 would undoubtedly raise the index of homozygosity for this marginal population to those in places much closer to the center of distribution. The absence of this arrangement ( and others, as described in Carson and Stalker, 1947) may be the result of its inability to penetrate an ecological barrier quite some distance removed from the marginal area and for reasons quite different from those which determine which populations shall be marginal and which central. This point also applies to the *D. pseudoobscura* data, where the degree of heterozygosity is generally even more dependent on the degree of heterogeneity for arrangements.

CARSON: Your basic point is certainly valid. The index, however, was devised as a means of expressing the total effect of inversions on recombination as actually observed in the populations studied. It was not designed to test specifically any

hypothesis of the cause of the inversion distributions. It may well be that calculations corrected as Dr. Levitan suggests might provide a somewhat better basis for examining the hypothesis referred to.

DOBZHANSKY: Dr. Carson has stated that his method of evaluation of the polymorphism due to inversions in *Drosophila* populations is related to that used by da Cunha and myself. Dr. Carson's method is much superior to ours. We simply count the mean number of heterozygous inversions which an individual carries: Dr. Carson estimates the proportion of the chromosome length in which the recombination is suppressed and in which it is free. One should note that this is not merely a technical refinement but a novel point of view. For inversions in *Drosophila* populations mean gene complexes which are inherited as supragenic units of adaptive polymorphism; the absence of inversions indicates a freedom of formation of novel gene combinations. Thus, a species may contain races or Mendelian populations which have evolved the genetic equipment necessary to master all the accessible ecological niches in the territory in which they live; and also marginal races and populations which act as scouts out to explore new possibilities of adaptive conquests of new environments. The analysis of the relations between the chromosomal polymorphism and the environment in Brazilian populations of *Drosophila willistoni*, made by da Cunha and myself, has on the whole confirmed our hypothesis according to which such correlations are expected to exist. Some exceptions have, however, been found in which the polymorphism proved to be not as extensive as expected. The existence of such exceptions was, in a sense, encouraging, since it showed that the hypothesis used did not belong to the class of hypothesis which cannot be contradicted by observations. Dr. Carson's work offers, however, an opportunity to do further tests of the hypothesis, and perhaps to discover the phenomena which are responsible for the apparent exceptions.

WALLACE: If a population fails to establish or to maintain a balanced polymorphic system utilizing chromosomes of different gene arrangements, its individual members will be structural homozygotes. Gene recombinations will be enhanced by this homozygosity. One does not yet know, however, what is cause and what is effect in the general absence of polymorphism within marginal populations.

CORDEIRO: In connection with Dr. Carson's important contribution to the knowledge of the genetic structure of marginal populations of *Drosophila*, I wish to call your attention to some results of the work done by Dr. Townsend and myself, and my colleagues, C. P. Jaeger, E. C. Jaeger and J. Peterson in Porto Alegre, Brazil. My data in the work with Jaeger and Jaeger showed that Rio Grande de Sul populations of *Drosophila willistoni* conceal significantly lower percentages of lethal and semilethal genes in comparison with those of central populations of the same species analyzed by Pavan and colleagues (in 794 homozygous strains for the second chromosome in Rio Grande de Sul, 32.24 ± 1.6 are lethals and semilethals, for tropical Brazil, 41.2 ± 1.1 in 2004 strains).

The work done by Townsend and myself in 1954, not yet analyzed statistically, apparently confirms these findings both for lethals and for heterogeneity of chromosome arrangements.

These results clearly agree with the lower chromosome heterogeneity for inversions in the edges of a species distribution such as that presented by Dr. Carson.

Considering the deleterious average effect of lethals in heterozygous condition, as I showed for

this species in 1952, and the recently finished work of C. P. Jaeger and myself showing that lethal bearing heterozygotes have a lower homeostatic response to cold temperature effects (+4°C for 12 hours) ($\chi^2$ of dif. = 72.015 in 21 different combinations) it appears that our data parallel and confirm the hypothesis of da Cunha and Dobzhansky, and Carson's interpretations presented today.

The edges of distribution of *D. willistoni* are both climatically rigorous in winter and have a homogeneous flora. This pushes the species toward uniformity of chromosomal arrangements and discards a great part of the semidominant lethals that seem to contribute to genetic variability.

# STUDIES ON NATURAL POPULATIONS OF *DROSOPHILA*.

## I. HEAT RESISTANCE AND GEOGRAPHICAL VARIATION IN *DROSOPHILA MELANOGASTER* AND *D. SIMULANS*

A. O. Tantawy and G. S. Mallah

*Faculty of Agriculture, University of Alexandria, Alexandria, Egypt, U.A.R.*

Received January 8, 1960

Under laboratory conditions quantitative characters in *Drosophila*, such as body size or fecundity, are very sensitive to environmental changes, e.g., temperature fluctuations or changes in quality or quantity of food. In nature, the same situation is found where changes in annual temperature or humidity affect the type of flora as well as the size of *Drosophila* fauna.

It is well known that there is a correlation between some quantitative characters and the geographical distribution of animals. Thus, the pioneer work of Timofeeff-Ressovsky (1933) showed that strains of *Drosophila funebris* and *Drosophila melanogaster* derived from different geographical regions react differently to temperature. Studies on the morphology of wild populations as those reported by Dobzhansky (1937), Reed and Reed (1947) on *Drosophila pseudoobscura* and *Drosophila persimilis*, Stalker and Carson (1947, 1948 and 1949) on *Drosophila robusta*, Prevosti (1955) on *Drosophila subobscura*, demonstrated that wing length and other traits decrease in size with geographical distribution from north to south.

The early work of Dobzhansky and his collaborators showed that natural populations of *Drosophila pseudoobscura* in different geographical localities differed in the frequency of various inversions in the third chromosome. Further work by Dobzhansky revealed that within one locality, populations of *Drosophila pseudoobscura* exhibited seasonal variations in respect to the frequency of different inversions.

Laboratory investigations designed to test the reaction of various gene arrangements to different temperature conditions have been carried out by Dobzhansky in a series of papers on *Drosophila pseudoobscura*, Kalmus (1945) on *Drosophila melanogaster*, Dubinin and Tiniakov (1945) on *Drosophila funebris*, Moos (1955) and others on *Drosophila pseudoobscura*, and Spiess (1958) on *Drosophila persimilis*. They all found that various genotypes react differently to various temperatures.

The present study, the first of a projected series dealing with natural populations of *Drosophila* in the Middle East and surrounding areas, was designed to test an hypothesis concerning the nature of developmental homeostasis. The hypothesis to be tested can be expressed as follows: progeny

Evolution **15**: 1–14.  March, 1961

Reprinted by permission of The Society for the Study of Evolution and the authors from *Evolution* 15:1–14, 1961.

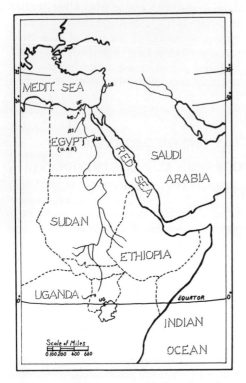

FIG. 1. Different geographical regions from which populations of *Drosophila melanogaster* and *Drosophila simulans* were captured.

of euryokous populations (i.e., populations that have a wide tolerance for various environmental factors) are better able to withstand the upper and lower limits of experimental laboratory conditions than progeny of stenokous populations.

## TECHNICAL PROCEDURE

*Collecting technique.* All collections of *Drosophila* in the present investigation and in the future, have been and will be carried out by exposing cans measuring 6×8 in., each containing one pound of ripe bananas which was mashed, autoclaved, and then inoculated with a suspension of baker's yeast. At the time of collection, i.e., in the early morning and late afternoon, Dobzhansky and Epling (1944), about a dozen of these cans were placed on the ground in the shade of trees to attract the flies. The *Drosophila* were collected with the aid of collect-

ing nets and were then transferred into vials containing cornmeal-molasses-agar medium.

In the laboratory the flies were etherized. Males of *Drosophila melanogaster* and *Drosophila simulans* were classified as to species by examining the genitalia. Females were placed in individual culture bottles and classified by examination of their male progeny.

*Localities.* Natural populations of *Drosophila melanogaster* and *Drosophila simulans* were sampled from several localities, as shown in figure 1, one each from Lebanon (Safa Valley, 3,500 ft altitude) Uganda (Namulonge, 3,775 ft altitude) and three populations from Egypt (approximately at sea level). The Egyptian populations were captured from: the University of Alexandria Farm, Alexandria; Wadi-El-Natroon, an isolated desert area halfway between Alexandria and Cairo (92 km southwest of Cairo); Luxor, about 550 km south of Cairo. *Drosophila melanogaster* as well as *Drosophila simulans* were found in all these localities except Luxor, where only *Drosophila melanogaster* was found. However a *simulans* population from Beni-Swef, about 112 km south of Cairo, was substituted for this one. These localities are designated as: LB, UG, UF, WD, LX, and BS, respectively.

Most of the collecting was done during July and August in 1956, by placing the cans under grape vines, fig, or palm trees. Dobzhansky et al. (1957) did a preliminary survey collection of the *Drosophila* fauna in

TABLE 1. *Monthly averages of percentages of humidity and temperature in different geographical regions in 1956*

| Locality | Humidity % | Temperature ° C |
|----------|------------|-----------------|
| LB | 60.21 ± 8.91 | 16.15 ± 7.38 |
| UF | 69.17 ± 7.02 | 20.04 ± 6.35 |
| WD | 63.66 ± 12.52 | 21.55 ± 6.95 |
| BS | 54.83 ± 15.24 | 21.90 ± 7.30 |
| LX* | 29.12 ± 14.05 | 25.49 ± 9.52 |
| UG | 72.94 ± 2.95 | 27.34 ± 1.34 |

* % humidity and temperature were not recorded from September to December.

Egypt and obtained the frequency distribution of adults of *Drosophila melanogaster* and *Drosophila simulans* captured from the above mentioned regions as well as other localities in Egypt. Average percentages of humidity and temperatures recorded in 1956 for all localities are presented in table 1, indicating that the Uganda locality shows the highest percentage of humidity and temperature which are constant through the year, and that the Lebanon locality is the coldest, with wider fluctuations.

*Experimental.* Ten captured fertilized females each of *Drosophila melanogaster* and of *Drosophila simulans* were chosen at random from each locality and placed in separate culture bottles for two days, and then transferred into fresh bottles every other day for a week in order to establish the original foundation populations. At every generation, the offspring of the ten females from each locality were intercrossed to obtain ten new bottles. In other words, males from the first bottle were intercrossed with virgin females of the second bottle, males from the second bottle with females of the third bottle, and so on to produce the first and second new bottles, respectively. Such a procedure was made to obtain the first nine bottles. The tenth new bottle was obtained by intercrossing males of the first bottle with virgin females of the tenth bottle. Progeny of the first generations of these females were not used in order to avoid any possible influence of the original environmental conditions in which females had survived.

The five different populations of *Drosophila melanogaster* and of *Drosophila simulans* were exposed to the following temperatures: 10°, 15°, 18°, 22°, 25°, 28°, 30°, and 31° C. Populations of *Drosophila melanogaster* were examined also at 31.5° C and those of *Drosophila simulans* at 30.5° C (the upper limits of temperature at which progeny can be obtained in these species). These temperatures were held constant to within 0.1° C.

Within a given temperature and locality virgin females from each of the bottles were

intercrossed with males from other bottles to maintain the foundation stock as heterozygous as possible. Samples of flies were taken at random from each bottle (20 pairs) and were placed in oviposition bottles; thus one hundred oviposition bottles were used for all the populations at a given temperature. Eggs were collected from these bottles at a known temperature and cultured at the same temperature.

From each of the oviposition bottles samples of eggs were obtained and cultured in five food vials. To prevent competition in the larval stage not more than seventy eggs were introduced into each vial which contained the normal food culture. Collection and culturing of eggs were carried out on four successive days and after emergence adults were counted and classified as to sex.

From the populations emerging from each of the two vials during the first two days, ten males and ten females were obtained at random on each day, in order to measure wing and thorax length. Thus a total of 400 males and females from each locality in each temperature were examined. The total number of flies emerging from all vials on the four days was used to get an estimate of the percentage of emergence and sex-ratio in the progeny.

Measurements of wing and thorax length were obtained by the method described by Robertson and Reeve (1952) and used by the senior author as described in previous publications, Tantawy (1959). At a given temperature, all populations were treated at the same time in the same manner and to minimize environmental fluctuations the methods recommended by Robertson and Reeve were used.

## RESULTS AND DISCUSSION

*Wing and thorax length.* It was known from the work of Mellanby (1954) that some insects can become acclimatized to changes in temperature. Smith (1957) found that in individuals of *Drosophila subobscura* acclimatization takes place and depends on whether animals are homozygous or heterozygous, the latter showing more acclimatization.

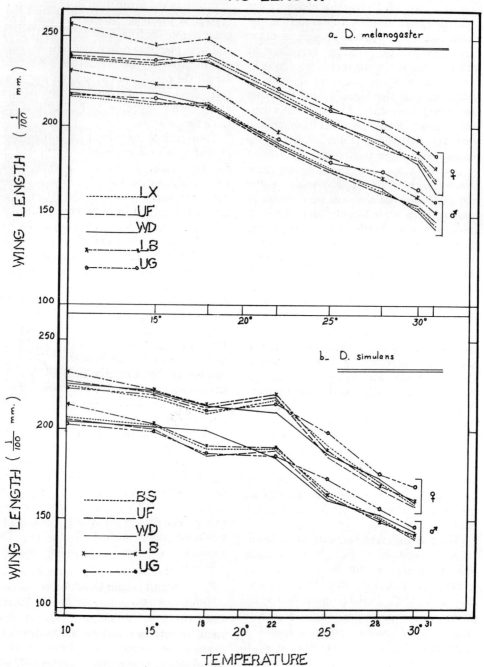

FIG. 2. Wing length in *Drosophila melanogaster* and *Drosophila simulans* at various temperatures. Units of measurement are 1/100 mm.

Our results secured from the present experiment on the effects of various degrees of temperature on body size, i.e., wing and thorax length, in *Drosophila melanogaster* and *Drosophila simulans* are presented in figure 2 a and b for both species, respectively. Results obtained for thorax length are not given since they show a similar pattern of behavior as that obtained in the wing length.

The results as presented in figure 2 a and b indicate clearly that *Drosophila melanogaster* is significantly larger in wing length at any given temperature than is *Drosophila simulans*, and in both species the females are larger than the males. Various degrees of temperature show highly significant effects on body size; wing length is longer at the lower temperatures and decreases gradually with the increase of temperature. The average percentage of decrease, for both sexes in all populations of *Drosophila melanogaster*, from the lowest to the highest degrees, is 31.03 per cent and 18.66 per cent for wing and thorax length, respectively, and 31.79 per cent and 22.89 per cent in *Drosophila simulans* for both dimensions, respectively. Such results indicate that although *Drosophila melanogaster* is bigger in size than *Drosophila simulans*, both species were affected similarly by temperature changes, especially in regard to wing length. Such a phenomenon of changing wing length with various degrees of temperature are in agreement with the results of Stalker and Carson (1947) working on *Drosophila robusta* and Pantellouris (1957) on *Drosophila melanogaster*.

Considering the different populations from the various geographical regions, the results indicate that in both species populations from Lebanon are larger in wing length than other populations, at almost every temperature. Such a population is morphologically larger than that from Uganda where the lower temperature prevails, but the situation is reversed at the higher temperatures, where UG populations show superiority in size to all other populations. Other populations captured from Egypt do not show any significant differences between them and showed almost the same size as UG populations, except at the higher temperatures where the latter ones show longer wing length. These results will be discussed later.

Thorax length of all populations behaved almost in the same manner as wing length and figure 3 a and b for *Drosophila melanogaster* and *Drosophila simulans* shows a highly positive correlation between the two measurements. The results are presented as log of wing plotted against log of thorax which indicate also that wing length is affected more than thorax length, particularly at the extreme temperatures. Such a point can be illustrated more clearly when measurements for both dimensions are expressed as a ratio of wing/thorax length. The results for wing/thorax ratio in *Drosophila melanogaster* and *D. simulans* indicate that with an increasingly cold climate, wing length is longer relative to thorax length than it is at higher temperatures, a fact which agrees fairly well with the findings of Stalker and Carson (1947) and Pantellouris (1957). It has also been shown by Reeve and Robertson (1953) that changes of temperature during the pupal stage may have profound effects on wing length but not on thorax length.

*Phenotypic variance.* Phenotypic variance of wing length is expressed as the coefficient of variation and the results are presented in figure 4 a and b for *Drosophila melanogaster* and *D. simulans*.

The results as presented in figure 4 indicate that temperature has a highly significant effect on variability of wing length in all populations studied. Such variation is high at the two extremes of the temperature; higher temperatures show more effects on phenotypic variation than lower or intermediate ones. The smallest coefficients of variation appear when flies were exposed to intermediate temperatures. The results also indicate that UG populations are the highest in phenotypic variance at almost every temperature, but are the lowest at the highest temperatures. LB populations show more

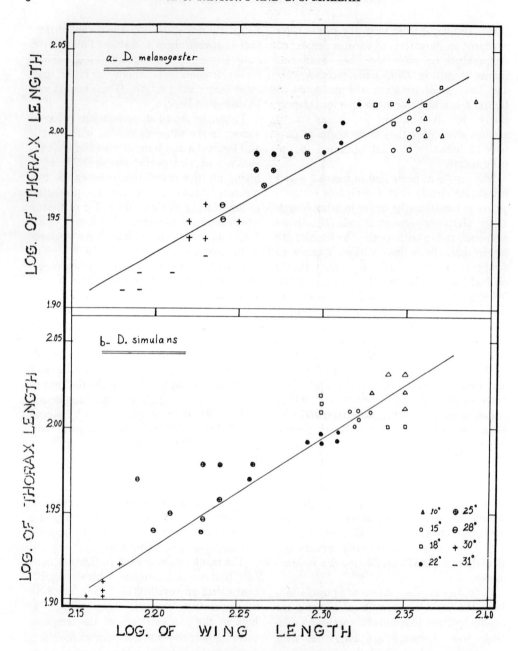

Fig. 3. Log of wing length plotted against log of thorax length in all populations of *Drosophila melanogaster* and *Drosophila simulans*.

uniformity in wing length than other populations but become the most variable at the highest temperature.

Such differences in phenotypic variance will be discussed later, but it would be of great interest to know whether the variance is a reflection of different responses of similar genotypes, or whether it is a reflection of

# COEFFICIENTS OF VARIATION FOR WING LENGTH

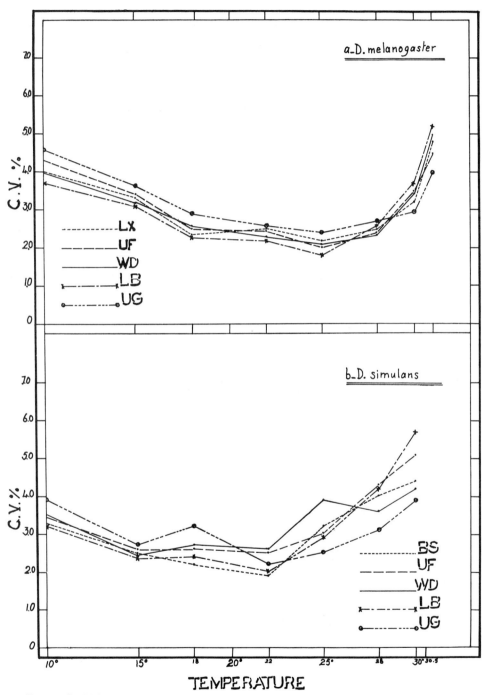

FIG. 4. Coefficients of variation for wing length of all populations of *Drosophila* in respect to different degrees of temperature.

8              A. O. TANTAWY AND G. S. MALLAH

# PERCENTAGE OF EMERGENCE

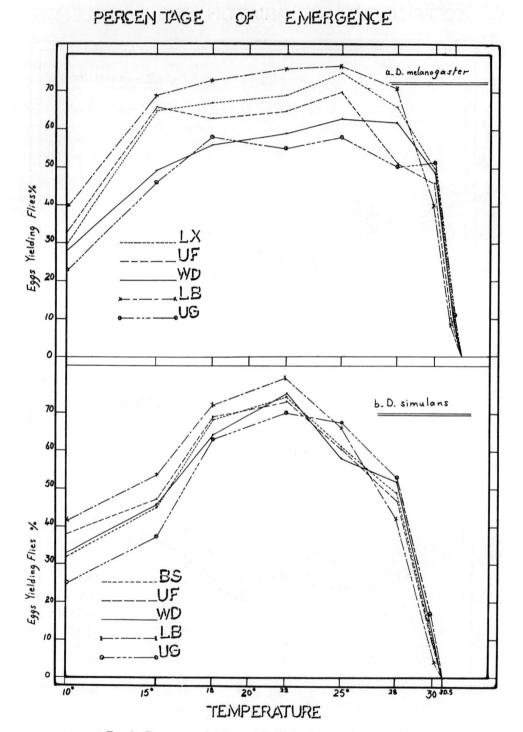

FIG. 5. Percentage of emergence in all populations of *Drosophila*.

a wider range of genotype within a given population. This point we hope to investigate in the near future.

*Percentage of emergence.* Percentage of emergence is measured by the number of adult flies that hatched from a certain number of eggs cultured in food vials. The results obtained are presented in figure 5 a and b for *Drosophila melanogaster* and *D. simulans.*

The results as shown in figure 5 demonstrate that different temperatures have various effects on the percentage of emergence. In all the populations studied the percentage of emergence is about 25–40 per cent at the lowest temperature, increasing gradually with the increase of temperature. The maximum percentage of emergence can be seen at 25° C, i.e., 58–76 per cent in *Drosophila melanogaster* and at 22° C, i.e., 69–79 per cent in *D. simulans*, which shows that optimal conditions for both species may be different. At higher temperatures, the percentage of emergence decreases gradually to 8 per cent and 5 per cent in both species. Complete lethality of pupae occurs at 31.5° C in *Drosophila melanogaster* and 30.5° C in *D. simulans*, thus showing a temperature difference between these sibling species.

Populations from the extreme north and extreme south end of the range differ in their per cent emergence in the same way as they differ in wing length. Populations from LB show higher percentage of emergence at almost every temperature, except that at highest temperatures where UG populations show the best viability.

If we plot percentage of emergence against the coefficients of variation for wing length the results demonstrate a highly significant negative correlation between such characters in both species. It is of interest to note that, at lower temperatures, LB populations are superior to UG populations where the former show a higher percentage of emergence and lower variation for wing length, but at the higher temperature the situation is reversed.

*Optimal conditions and geographical distribution.* There is extensive evidence on

*Drosophila* species other than *Drosophila melanogaster* and *Drosophila simulans* which indicates that wing length shows an increase in northern geographical regions, e.g., Stalker and Carsons (1947, 1948 and 1949) on *Drosophila robusta*, Dobzhansky (1948) on *Drosophila pseudoobscura* and Prevosti (1955) on *Drosophila subobscura.*

Our results, summarized in figures 2, 4, and 5, suggest that the optimal temperatures for *D. melanogaster* and *D. simulans* are 25° C and 22° C, respectively. The values of the various characters studied at these optimal temperatures are shown in table 2, the localities being arranged in north to south order.

The results thus presented in table 2 indicate that northern populations, i.e., LB, are significantly larger in size, less variable and more viable than those from the extreme south, i.e., UG populations. In *D. simulans* there is a gradient of size from north to south, while in *D. melanogaster* flies from central Egypt are the smallest. Such differences in behavior and the insignificant differences between some of the Egyptian populations and that from Uganda could be explained on the basis of possible immigration throughout the Nile Valley. LB populations are isolated from the Egyptian ones by the Sinai Desert. If we consider LB populations as northern populations and all other populations, i.e., from Egypt and Uganda, as southern ones, we find significant differences between them in every respect; the former populations are larger, less variable and more viable than the latter ones, which agrees well with the findings of other investigators.

It seems probable, therefore, from such results, that the geographical differences in morphology are the results of an adaptation to climate and such adaptation may be of indirect effect. Dobzhansky (1937) stated that the morphological phenotype may be the by-product of some more fundamental physiological adaptation. Annual mean temperature as well as percentage humidity are the more obvious environmental conditions, which show correlations with the

TABLE 2.  *Morphological differences between males and females of* Drosophila melanogaster
*and* Drosophila simulans *in mean wing and thorax length, at their optimal temperatures,
with their respective coefficients of variation (C.V.%).   Units of measurement are
1/100 mm.   Percentages of emergence are also presented.*

| Popula-tion | Wing Length* | | | | Thorax Length* | | | | Percentage of emergence |
| | Males | | Females | | Males | | Females | | |
| | Size | C.V. | Size | C.V. | Size | C.V. | Size | C.V. | |
| --- | --- | --- | --- | --- | --- | --- | --- | --- | --- |
| *Drosophila melanogaster* | | | | | | | | | |
| LB | 183.41 | 1.86 | 211.09 | 1.70 | 93.69 | 2.40 | 106.11 | 2.19 | 76.18 |
| UF | 175.59 | 1.97 | 203.19 | 2.11 | 89.48 | 2.59 | 102.39 | 2.19 | 68.70 |
| WD | 176.10 | 2.29 | 202.60 | 1.97 | 91.40 | 3.37 | 104.74 | 2.45 | 63.13 |
| LX | 176.16 | 2.36 | 203.78 | 1.99 | 90.81 | 2.64 | 103.87 | 2.22 | 73.89 |
| UG | 180.03 | 2.50 | 210.27 | 2.36 | 91.54 | 3.41 | 105.03 | 2.57 | 58.11 |
| *Drosophila simulans* | | | | | | | | | |
| LB | 190.91 | 2.17 | 220.16 | 1.87 | 95.63 | 2.96 | 109.95 | 2.36 | 79.91 |
| UF | 189.36 | 2.77 | 218.66 | 2.19 | 94.75 | 2.84 | 108.39 | 2.27 | 72.59 |
| WD | 184.97 | 2.73 | 209.63 | 2.49 | 91.20 | 3.52 | 104.54 | 3.03 | 74.84 |
| BS | 189.44 | 2.25 | 217.98 | 1.79 | 94.81 | 2.86 | 108.86 | 2.66 | 74.83 |
| UG | 185.96 | 2.58 | 215.52 | 1.99 | 92.41 | 3.21 | 107.31 | 2.47 | 69.49 |

* Each mean is taken from 200 pairs of adult flies.

phenotypic appearance of the animal. Other environmental conditions such as type of flora may have some effects on such adaptation. In sum, we find that animals which are adapted to a given temperature are less phenotypically variable than those not adapted.

*Sex-ratio.* It is a known fact that wild populations of *Drosophila* give a sex-ratio almost of 1:1 under optimal conditions. When environmental conditions are changed the ratio is also changed.

There are some exceptional situations reported in which some wild-type females captured from nature give rise to a highly abnormal sex-ratio. Thus, Magni (1954), Moriwaki et al. (1957) working on *Drosophila bifasciata*, Cavalcanti and Falcau (1954) on *D. prosultans*, Stalker (1957) on *D. paramelanica* and Malogolowkin et al. (1959) on *D. willistoni*, all reported abnormal sex-ratio arising from some wild females. Malogolowkin et al. (1959) attributed such an abnormal situation to the action of an agent which is transmitted by

the female to all her eggs and is lethal in XY zygote.

In the present investigation, all hatched flies were classified to sex and the results for the various sex-ratios at the different temperatures are presented in figure 6 a and b for *Drosophila melanogaster* and *D. simulans*, where locality and total number of adults counted are also shown.

The results as shown in figure 6 indicate an influence of temperature on sex-ratio. At lower and higher temperatures in both species there are significant differences between sexes; females predominate, while at milder temperatures the ratio is almost one to one. During the experiment it was noticed that at the two extremes of temperature, particularly at the higher one, pupae fail to develop into adults. It was observed that adults attempted to emerge from the pupae, but only succeeded in dragging their heads and thorax out of the pupal case.

One may conclude from these results, that females are the stronger sex in resisting

FIG. 6.   Sex-ratio for all populations of *Drosophila* under various degrees of temperature; populations and number of adults counted in each locality are also illustrated.

# SEX RATIO

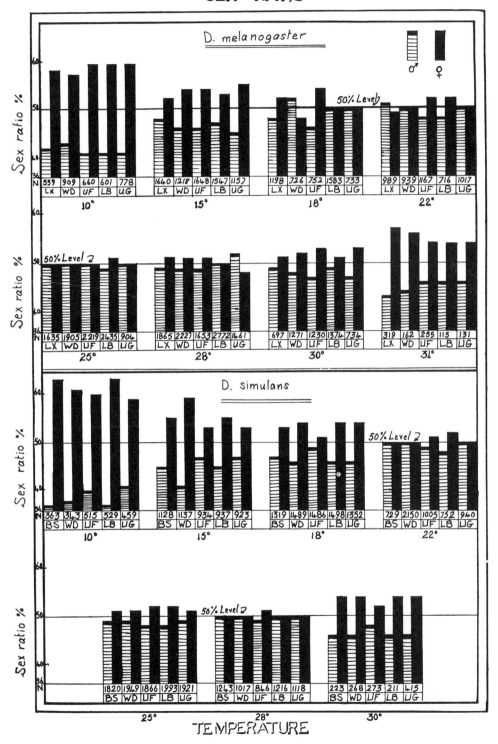

TEMPERATURE

changes in temperatures and are also better buffered than males. Such resistance became apparent in the immature stages of adults, particularly in the pupal stage.

## Conclusions

The earliest studies of geographical variation in different species of *Drosophila* have been reviewed by Stalker and Carson (1947). It has been found that size of an animal differs according to altitude and northern animals are larger in size than southern ones

Our results as reported, show clearly that body size and percentage of emergence as well as sex-ratio can be altered by changing temperature conditions; the latter two characters are the more sensitive ones. Such alteration in the new laboratory conditions depends to a great extent on the original climatic conditions in which flies had survived. Thus, LB populations of *Drosophila melanogaster* and *Drosophila simulans* are well adapted to the colder and milder degrees of temperature and UG populations to the warmer ones. Such populations are larger in wing length and thorax length with low phenotypic variances and higher viability under their adapted conditions. These findings are in general agreement with those of Lerner (1954) who stated that the poorest adapted individuals have higher variability. Since variability is usually regarded as a measure of homeostasis, on the assumption that a less variable phenotype indicates superior homeostatic buffering properties which result in a high general adaptedness in a range of environments, one may conclude that LB populations which are euryokous populations are more adapted to wider changes in environmental conditions than that of UG populations which are stenokous populations. An analysis of the geographical distribution of the two populations, shows that LB populations inhabit regions characterized by medium summer temperature and colder winter with a lower percentage of humidity, while UG populations were captured from a region where the temperature is 27° C almost constant

throughout the year with a higher degree of humidity. Thus indicating that stenokous populations are better adapted only to a temperature similar to that of their native conditions. This is expected since natural selection acts more strongly on the euryokous populations than on the stenokous ones, therefore the former populations are able to adapt themselves to wider alterations of climatic conditions, i.e., they are more homeostatic. Results obtained in the present investigation are in agreement with those reported by Lewontin (1956 and 1957) who has equated homeostasis with fitness, which indicate that the physiological and morphological responses of a homeostatic individual are adaptive so as to favor survival.

The reaction of LB and UG populations to the temperatures, showing different adaptation to the extremes, gives rise to the following questions:

1. What would be the response to selection in populations of both localities under optimal conditions as well as colder and warmer temperatures?

2. Do crosses between and within different populations, under the previously mentioned conditions, yield the same degree of heterosis?

Such points will be investigated in future experiments.

## Summary

1. Natural populations of *Drosophila melanogaster* and *Drosophila simulans* were captured from different geographical regions in Lebanon, Egypt, and Uganda.

2. Offspring of such populations were reared under different temperatures ranging from 10° to 31.5° C in *Drosophila melanogaster* and to 30.5° C in *Drosophila simulans*.

3. Wing and thorax length are greater at lower temperatures, decreasing gradually with increasing temperature, while the percentage of emergence is lower at the two extremes of temperature and significantly higher at optimal conditions.

4. Wing/thorax ratio is about 2 under

optimal conditions, increasing at lower temperatures and decreasing at higher ones.

5. Phenotypic variance of wing length is higher at both extremes, and much higher at warmer temperatures.

6. Complete sterility, i.e., eggs failing to produce adults, occurs at 31.5° C in all populations of *Drosophila melanogaster* and at 30.5° C in *Drosophila simulans*.

7. Lebanon populations, i.e., northern populations, are more vigorous, less variable and more viable than all other populations studied at almost every temperature, while populations from Uganda show superiority to all other populations only at the higher temperatures, i.e., their original climatic conditions.

8. Extremes of temperature adversely affect sex-ratio. At the two extremes of temperature females appear to be the stronger sex and are significantly more numerous than males. At milder temperature the sexes occur in equal numbers.

### Acknowledgments

The authors wish to express their gratitude to Professor Th. Dobzhansky of Columbia University, New York, U.S.A., with whom all the collection of flies were made during his invited visit to Alexandria University in 1956; to the American University in Beirut for providing facilities for capturing flies in Lebanon; and to Dr. T. H. Coaker of the Cotton Research Station, Namulonge, Uganda, for sending samples of flies.

We wish to thank Dr. M. Demerec, Director of the Biological Laboratory, Cold Spring Harbor, New York, who gave the senior author a Summer Fellowship in 1959 which enabled him to use the laboratory and library facilities.

Finally, we are very indebted to Professors Th. Dobzhansky and R. C. Lewontin for their valuable suggestions during the preparation of the manuscript.

### Literature Cited

Cavalcanti, L. A. G., and P. M. Falcau. 1954. A new type of sex-ratio in *Drosophila prosaltans*. Duda Proc. IXth. Inter. Congr. Genet., Part II: 1233–1235.

Dobzhansky, Th. 1937. Genetic nature of species differences. Amer. Nat., **71**: 404–420.

——. 1948. Genetics of natural population. XVI. Altitudinal and seasonal changes produced by natural selection in certain populations of *Drosophila pseudoobscura* and *Drosophila persimilis*. Genetics, **33**: 158–176.

——, and C. Epling. 1944. Taxonomy, geographical distribution and ecology of *Drosophila pseudoobscura* and its relative. Carnegie Inst. Wash. Publ. No. 544: 1–46.

——, G. S. Mallah, A. O. Tantawy, and A. M. Mourad. 1957. Collection of *Drosophila* species in Egypt. Drosophila Inform. Serv., **31**: 116–117.

Dubinin, N. P., and G. G. Tiniakov. 1945. Seasonal cycles and the concentrations of inversions in populations of *Drosophila funebris*. Amer. Nat., **79**: 570–572.

Kalmus, H. 1945. Adaptive and selective responses of a population of *Drosophila melanogaster* containing e and e+ to differences in temperature, humidity and selection for developmental speed. J. Genet., **47**: 58–63.

Lerner, I. M. 1954. Genetic Homeostasis. Oliver and Boyd, Edinburgh.

Lewontin, R. C. 1956. Studies on homeostasis and heterozygosity. 1. Of *Drosophila melanogaster*. Amer. Nat., **90**: 237–256.

——. 1957. The adaptations of populations to varying environments. Cold Spr. Harbor Symp. Quant. Biol., **22**: 395–408.

Magni, G. E. 1954. Thermic cure of cytoplasmic sex-ratio in *Drosophila bifasciata*. Caryologia (Suppl.), **6**: 1213–1216.

Malogolowkin, C., D. F. Poulson, and E. Y. Wright. 1959. Experimental transfer of maternally inherited abnormal sex-ratio in *Drosophila willistoni*. Genetics, **44**: 57–74.

Mellanby, K. 1954. Acclimatization and thermal death point in insects. Nature, **173**: 582.

Moos, J. R. 1955. Comparative physiology on some chromosomal type in *Drosophila pseudoobscura*. Evolution, **9**: 141–151.

Moriwaki, D., and O. Kitagawa. 1957. "Sexratio" in *Drosophila bifasciata*. Jap. Jour. Genet., **32**: 208–210.

Pantellouris, E. M. 1957. Size response of developing *Drosophila* to temperature changes. J. Genet., **55**: 507–510.

Prevosti, A. 1955. Geographical variability in quantitative traits in populations of *Drosophila subobscura*. Cold Spr. Harbor Symp. Quant. Biol., **20**: 294–299.

Reed, S. C., and E. W. Reed. 1947. Morphological differences and problems of speciation in *Drosophila*. Evolution, **2**: 113–133.

Reeve, E. C. R., and F. W. Robertson. 1953. Studies in quantitative inheritance. II. Analysis of a strain of *Drosophila melanogaster* selected for long wing. J. Genet., **51**: 276–316.

ROBERTSON, F. W., AND E. C. R. REEVE. 1952. Studies in quantitative inheritance. I. The effects of selection of wing length and thorax length in *Drosophila melanogaster*. J. Genet., **50**: 414–448.

SMITH, J. MAYNARD. 1957. Temperature tolerance and acclimatization in *Drosophila subobscura*. J. Exp. Biol., **34**: 85–96.

SPIESS, E. B. 1958. Chromosomal adaptive polymorphism in *Drosophila persimilis*. II. Effects of population cage conditions on life cycle components. EVOLUTION, **12**: 234–245.

STALKER, H. D. 1957. Sex-ratio in *Drosophila paramelanica*. Genetics, **42**: 399.

—— AND H. L. CARSON. 1947. Morphological variation in natural populations of *Drosophila robusta* Sturtevant. EVOLUTION, **1**: 237–248.

—— AND ——. 1948. An altitudinal transect of *Drosophila robusta* Sturtevant. EVOLUTION, **2**: 295–305.

—— AND ——. 1949. Seasonal variation in the morphology of *Drosophila robusta* Sturtevant. EVOLUTION, **3**: 330–343.

TANTAWY, A. O. 1959. Selection limits with sibmating in *Drosophila melanogaster*. Genetics, **44**: 287–296.

TIMOFEEFF-RESSOVSKY, N. Y. 1933. Uber die relative vitalitat von *Drosophila melanogaster* Meigen und *Drosophila funebris* Fubricuis unter verschiedenen Zuchtbedingungen, in Zusammenhang mit den Verbreitaagsarealen diesser Arten. Arch. Naturgesch. N.F., **2**: 285–290.

# A GENERAL THEORY OF CLUTCH SIZE

MARTIN L. CODY

*Leidy Laboratory of Biology, University of Pennsylvania, Philadelphia*

Accepted June 11, 1965

It is possible to think of organisms as having a certain limited amount of time or energy available for expenditure, and of natural selection as that force which operates in the allocation of this time or energy in a way which maximizes the contribution of a genotype to following generations. This manner of treatment of problems concerning the adaptation of phenotypes is called the "Principle of Allocation" (Levins and MacArthur, unpublished), and one of its applications might be the formulation of a general theory to account for clutch size in birds. At this stage we will assume that clutch size is a hereditary phenotypic characteristic which can be affected to a greater or lesser extent by the prevailing environmental conditions and which exhibits the normal variability of such characteristics. Lack (1954) discusses the validity of several hypotheses which attempt to account for clutch size and its variation under different circumstances and conditions, all of which were rejected in favor of his now widely accepted theory that clutch size is adapted to a limited food supply. This paper is an attempt to show that this and other existing hypotheses when taken singly are inadequate in some respect to account for all the data, that each holds for some particular set of conditions, and that each is but a part of the complete explanation. The theories will be dealt with individually and it will be shown that as environment varies so will the factors which determine clutch size.

## PRESENTATION OF THE THEORY

It is known that in temperate regions, because periodic local catastrophes reduce and maintain populations below the carrying capacity, $\bar{K}$, of the habitat, natural selection is proceeding to maximize $r$, the reproductive rate (Fisher, 1929, whose fundamental theorem is density independent). In these regions any phenotypic variation which enables parents to leave more offspring will be selected for. Any increase in clutch size, up to a limit determined by natural resources, would suffice to increase the reproductive rate. In the tropics, however, with a more climatically stable environment where the advent of such catastrophes is rare, populations will be at saturation densities, and any adaptive variations which will increase the carrying capacity $\bar{K}$ will usually be favored by natural selection (MacArthur, 1962). Increasing $\bar{K}$ is equivalent to increasing the population density with the same resources, or maintaining the population density with decreased resources. Whereas in unstable regions all energy was perforce utilized to increase $r$, an individual living in a stable environment well suited to the needs of the species would need to spend much less energy on maximizing $r$ than individuals living elsewhere. By the "Principle of Allocation," maximum contribution to future generations will be achieved by those individuals which utilize, to increase $\bar{K}$, some of the energy conserved by reducing $r$. Such individuals will be favored by natural selection over others which do not allocate surplus energy to this end. We can guess suitable recipients for the conserved energy, possible candidates for its use being predator avoidance, more successful intraspecific competition (i.e., reduction in resource density necessary for maintained existence), or perhaps devoting more energy per individual to the raising of the young. All these considerations could serve to increase the contribution to future generations. Such energy requirements or drains, together with the number of eggs laid, may

EVOLUTION **20**: 174–184. June, 1966

Reprinted by permission of The Society for the Study of Evolution and the author from *Evolution* 20:174–184, 1966.

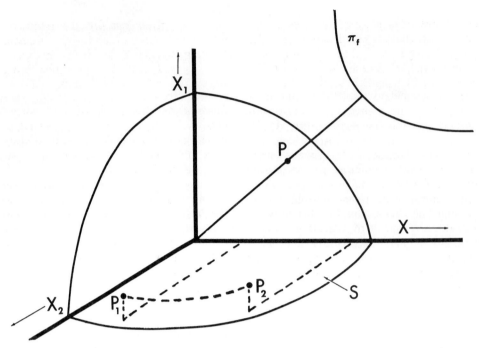

Fig. 1. Three-dimensional graph showing the point of intersection $P$ of the surface of phenotypes $S$ with the "adaptive function" $\pi_f$. The phenotype $P$ receives benefits proportional to its intercepts on the axes $X$, $X_1$, and $X_2$, resulting from dividing its energy between clutch size, avoiding predators and competitive ability respectively.

all be operating simultaneously and can be considered as acting along the axes of a multidimensional graph. Distance along the axes represents not the actual amount of energy spent, but the advantage gained by the individual who spends that amount of energy on that particular requirement. Measurable quantities such as clutch size can be substituted as units for the purpose of this argument. Representing increasing clutch size along the $X$-axis, two other energy drains can be represented along $X_1$ and $X_2$ in a three-dimensional figure (Fig. 1). All possible allocations of energy to these three requirements—clutch size, predator avoidance, and competition—can be represented as points comprising a surface $S$ and the volume under it in the figure. Every point of the surface $S$ can be considered as a phenotype having the strategy indicated by the proportions of the available energy to be spent on the factors represented by the three axes. Using the

coordinates shown in the figure, phenotypes at the vertices of the solid farthest out along the axes, will be concentrating their energy on either laying many eggs, avoiding enemies, or competing more efficiently for resources. Since a jack-of-all-trades policy often brings greater returns than a specialist policy, the ability to avoid predators will rise appreciably when a large clutch is sacrificed for a slightly smaller one. Reasoning likewise with the other two combinations of axes, we deduce the convex nature of the surface $S$ which, together with the enclosed space, represents all possible phenotypes. We can now consider the strategy which maximizes the number of descendants for a particular species and environment and is favored by natural selection over the many alternatives as that point where a surface $\pi$ touches $S$ tangentially. $\pi$ is an "adaptive function" for the environmental conditions, the position of which varies in relation to the surface as

176                                    MARTIN L. CODY

the relative importance of the coordinates changes. $\pi_f$ consists of all points of equal fitness, $f$ (see Levins, 1962), and the most fit phenotype, or most apt strategy, is that represented by a point $P$ which lies both on $S$ and the $\pi_f$ with largest $f$. The fitness or suitability, $f$, of a phenotype for certain conditions increases with the perpendicular distance of $\pi_f$ from the origin, because the farther out a point is on lines radiating from the origin, the greater are the advantages obtained along the axes (bigger intercepts) and the more fit becomes the phenotype. So the one point which lies farthest from the origin on $S$ and on the farthest $\pi$ indicates the best strategy. Different environments will select different optimum phenotypes. As the relative importance of one coordinate, say competitive ability, increases, the adaptive surface $\pi$ will rotate toward that coordinate, resulting in an optimal phenotype which has sacrificed some egg-laying ability for increased competitive ability. So the position of $P$ and hence clutch size, the intercept of $P$ on the $X$-axis, will vary with the environmental conditions.

EXISTING THEORIES OF CLUTCH SIZE

That a bird is limited physiologically from laying more eggs is a view which finds little acceptance today. There are numerous instances of birds laying more eggs than their normal clutch when eggs are removed at laying. And yet there are groups, e.g., Procellariiformes, which lay one egg and usually do not replace it if lost. This seems a great waste of reproductive potential, and this theory might be the correct answer to account for the low $r$, especially as petrels lay eggs notably large for the size of the bird. But then, if natural selection has brought the ruddy duck (*Oxyura jamaicensis*) to lay a clutch three times its own weight (Kortright, 1943), surely the same could apply to a petrel given the same environmental conditions if it were advantageous to the species. It is apparent that this group of birds, living in the most stable coastal environment, are at a fairly constant maximum density as determined by the resources, and the importance of increasing $r$ is small. Denoting $X_1$ and $X_2$ as shown in Fig. 1, large $X_2$ and small $X_1$ (predation being low) intercepts indicate strategy $P_1$ as shown, having a very small $X$ intercept (clutch size).

The second hypothesis, again not a popular one, states that clutch size is limited by the number of eggs a parent can cover. This seems plausible when we consider that many ground-nesting birds have large clutches, this being a nest-site obviously conducive to holding many eggs. However, most of the large clutches of ground-nesters belong to gallinaceous birds, in which the young are not heavily dependent on the parents for food. Therefore, the largest number of eggs which can be covered, or young which can be brooded (shelter probably being very important), whichever is the lower, will determine clutch size. This being a limitation which does not vary with environment, we expect clutch size to be invariably high (large $X$ intercept). Ground-nesters which do feed young have much smaller clutches (*Caprimulgus, Sterna, Alauda*).

A third theory is that clutch size is adjusted "to balance mortality," but it has been pointed out by Lack (1947, 1949, 1954) that there is no proven mechanism to carry out this adjustment, convenient though such a system would be. The "balancing mortality" theory implies altruism, that birds possess a self-regulatory mechanism whereby recruits just compensate for losses. We cannot see how natural selection could operate in successive years to favor that clutch which would bring the population back to its optimum. Birds which laid larger clutches would naturally come to predominate, if conditions allowed the survival of these clutches, to the detriment of any or all altruistic members of the population which lay the supposedly optimal clutch for that season. There is perhaps one conceivable way in which a population could balance its mortality, and that is a behavioral one. There have been certain cases documented in which popula-

CLUTCH SIZE IN BIRDS                                    177

TABLE 1. *Effect of variations in food supply on clutch size.*

| Species | Conditions average or below | Conditions above average | Reference |
|---|---|---|---|
| Nutcracker, *Nucifraga caryocatactes* | poor nutcrop previous year, av. clutch = c/3 | good nutcrop av. clutch = c/4 | Swanberg, *in* Lack, 1954 |
| Barn owl, *Tyto alba* | normal clutch = c/3 in this part of Africa | clutch size during mouse plague = c/7 | Fuggles-Couchman, *in* Moreau, 1944 |
| *Ploceus velatus* | dry season, 10% c/4, 90% c/3 | good rainfall, 90% c/4, 10% c/3 | Hoesch, *in* Moreau, 1944 |
| Bay-breasted warbler, *Dendroica castanea* | non-budworm years 4 c/4, 8 c/5, 5 c/6 av. = c/5.1 | budworm years 1 c/4, 5 c/5, 15 c/6, 3 c/7, av. = c/5.8 (significantly higher) | MacArthur, 1958 |

tion density has been shown to be inversely proportional to clutch size, but it is just as difficult to see how natural selection could accomplish this. Kluijver (1951) showed this relation for *Parus major*, and also that the same inverse relation holds for numbers of broods and density. Given that this relationship obtains, and is adhered to by all members of the population, here is a possible and sufficient mechanism to ensure a constant optimum density, on the average. Thus a greatly depleted population will have a correspondingly high clutch size, and as density increases under the influence of this high clutch, the latter will decrease accordingly. Large or small overwinter losses can be accommodated in this way. Many examples of density-fecundity relationships are given by Wynne-Edwards (1962), observed both in laboratory and field populations. We would now interpret this as follows, that as population density increases, numbers approach $\overline{K}$, and advantage is removed from high $r$ with a corresponding reduction in clutch size. The greatest difficulty in assessing the value of such relationships is that of divorcing density and food supply, and it is undoubtedly the latter which is the more appropriate factor in many cases; the inversely proportional density and clutch size may be an incidental result of the directly proportional food supply and clutch size.

Lack's (1954) views that parents rear the average maximum number of young possible, given the prevailing conditions and food supply, that one clutch size is optimal for a species in a locality in any particular year, and that this is the clutch size that will be favored by natural selection in that year is supported by much data for temperate passerines and near-passerines. It is also supported indirectly by observed variances in clutch size with food supply (Table 1). Evidence does show one optimum clutch size per season, as revealed either by the greatest number of fledglings reared from intermediate clutch size (as in *Apus apus*, Lack and Lack, 1951) or by the greatest post-fledging survival from an intermediate clutch size in those species which show approximately the same fledging success for several clutch sizes (*Sturnus vulgaris* and *Parus major*, Lack, 1954). Examples of variation in clutch size with food supply are assembled in Table 1, which illustrates how independent of rigid genetic control clutch size may become. Influence of food-gathering conditions, not on clutch size but on differential survival, is seen in swifts (Lack and Lack, 1951) in which c/3 and c/2 yield 0.9 and 1.0 fledglings, respectively, in a bad year (below average sunshine) and 2.3 and 1.9 fledglings, respectively, in a good year. Non-passerines are also subject to a food limitation, as is seen in the case of the short-eared owls (*Asio flammeus*), snowy owls (*Nyctea nyctea*) and pomatorhine skuas (*Stercorarius pomarinus*), all of which prey on lemmings (*Dicrostonyx*) in northern Alaska. Population density is one per three to four square miles, one per two to four square miles, and 18 per square mile, respectively, in peak lemming years, zero, one per two to four square miles, and four per square mile in intermediate years, and no breeding takes place in years of low density (Pitelka *et al.*, 1955). It is agreed here that because of the adaptive nature of clutch size, parents are rearing as many young as will maximize their contribution to the next generation and that in the above cases the limiting factor is food.

## Clutch Size and Latitude

The increase of clutch size with latitude is a phenomenon which has been recognized by ornithologists for many years (Moreau, 1944, pp. 286–287). The only reasonable attempt to account for this trend is that of Lack (1947) who maintained that food supply is limiting in the tropics as in the temperate zones. He accounted for the increase in clutch size by considering that increasing day length from the equator gave parents a longer time per day to find food, and consequently larger broods could be reared. Support for this was forthcoming from data on the raven (*Corvus corax*) and the crossbill (*Loxia curvirostra*), both of which nest before the March equinox in northern Europe and show an increase in clutch size toward the equator. The theory does not easily account for species which feed young and do not increase clutch size with latitude (many Corvidae, Sulidae, Falconiformes, Charadriiformes), or species which do not feed young and do increase clutch size with latitude (Anatidae —see Fig. 2.4, Rallidae). Even more interesting are the tropical species which nest before the equinox (many tropical Passerines nest in the dry season, January to March). These show a large increase in clutch size from the equator northward, although day length decreases with north latitude (Skutch, 1954, 1960). It is also interesting that nocturnal mammals show increased litter size with latitude (Lord, 1960).

The more stable an environment is for a species, the greater the incidence of selec-

tion for $\overline{K}$ in populations of that species, and the more inter- and intraspecific competition will occupy the time and energy of the species, with a consequent reduction in clutch size. We therefore expect that clutch size will be inversely proportional to the climatic stability of the habitat, and as this stability decreases on moving north or south from the equator, clutch size will increase correspondingly. The latitude/ clutch size graphs in Fig. 2 illustrating this relationship have been compiled from sources listed in the bibliography. A discussion of the individual examples mentioned in the figure footnote will be found below, as well as discussion of differences in the distribution of points and steepness of slopes. We may now relate these graphs to the theoretical model presented earlier. Degree of environmental stability, as we infer this to be directly proportional to energy spent on competition, may be represented along the $X_2$ axis in Fig. 3, and all points of equal stability on $S$ are given by the intersection of $S$ and a plane perpendicular to $X_2$ and parallel to $X$ and $X_1$.

Before we can denote the path described on $S$ by the optimal phenotype as the adaptive function changes from one suitable at high latitudes to one suitable at low latitudes, we need to know the relationship between $X_2$ and $X_1$, the axis along which energy spent avoiding predation is represented. Students of tropical birds have often remarked on the heavy predation losses sustained by their subjects at breeding. Skutch (1949, 1954, 1960), perhaps the most experienced observer in this field, emphasized that nest predation in the tropics is far greater than in temperate counterparts, to the extent that he has postulated the necessity for a reduced number of trips to the nest with food for the young, and hence a better chance of escaping the detection of a watching predator, as a possible reason for low clutch size in the tropics. He further observed that the habit, apparently widely developed among forest birds, of bringing to the nest large morsels seldom and thereby cutting visits to a minimum, might be an adaptation

CLUTCH SIZE IN BIRDS

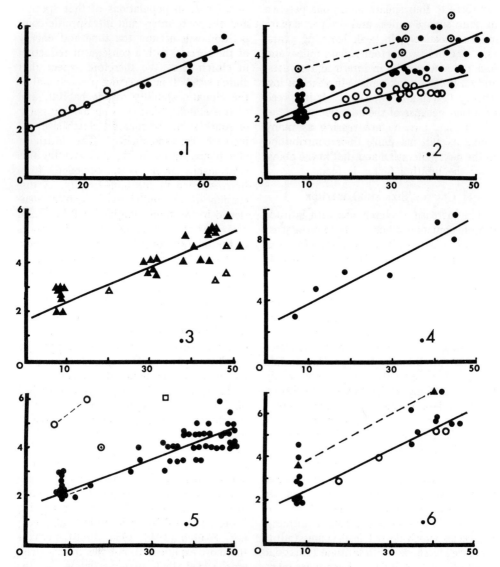

Fig. 2. Graphs of clutch size (ordinate) against latitude (abscissa).

2.1—the genus *Emberiza*. ◯ = species nesting in Africa south of the equator; ● = species nesting in Europe and Asia. The two sets of points fit the same line.

2.2—the family Tyrannidae. ◯ = South American species; ● = North American species ($p \ll$ 0.001 that the lines fitting these two sets of points have the same slope); ⊙ = the genus *Myiarchus* (hole nesters); ⊙---⊙ = *Myiarchus tuberculifer*.

2.3—the family Icteridae. ▲ = North American species; △ = South American species.

2.4—the genus *Oxyura* (family Anatidae), worldwide distribution.

2.5—the "superfamily" Thraupidae plus Parulidae, in Central and North America. ●---● = *Myioborus miniatus*; ◯---◯ = *Tanagra lauta* (hole nester); ⊙ = *Tanagra luteicapilla* (niche nester); ▢ = *Prothonotaria citrea* (hole nester).

2.6—the family Trogloditidae. ◯ = South American species; ● = North American species; ▲---▲ = *Troglodytes aedon*.

180                                    MARTIN L. CODY

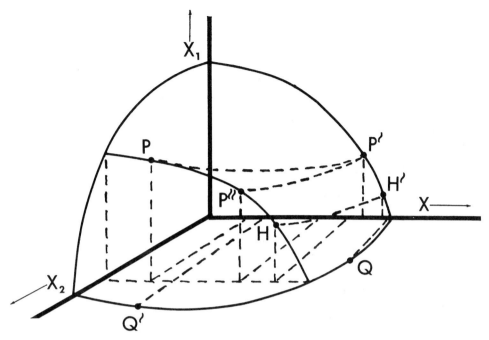

Fig. 3. Paths traced by the adaptive function from temperate to tropical latitudes for mainland open-nesting passerines ($P'$----$P$), predation-free species ($P'$----$P''$), hole-nesters ($H'$----$H$) and island-nesting species ($Q$----$Q'$).

to reduce nest predation. The work of Snow (1962) on *M. manacus*, in which the young of only 19 per cent of 227 nests reached fledgling over five years of observation confirms this high rate of loss to nest enemies, as at least 158 of these failures could be attributed to predation. Such losses from this cause are not nearly so great in temperate regions (Lack, 1954). If we now let $P'$ be the strategy of a species nesting in the temperate, with low predation, low stability, and therefore a high clutch, the optimal phenotype will describe a curve $PP'$, where $P$ represents the strategy in the tropics, a region of high predation and high stability, resulting in a small intercept on $X$ and a low clutch size.

## PREDICTIONS FROM THE THEORY

Let us first consider stable environments. We have asserted above that reduced clutches in the tropics are the indirect result of climatic stability. If this is indeed so, and we have correctly deduced the most pertinent factors involved, then we should be able to predict that reduced clutch sizes will be found in any environment characterized by its stable conditions. Moreau (1944), when comparing species inhabiting evergreen forests in equatorial Africa with close relatives occupying more seasonal habitats at the same latitude (and therefore receiving the same amount of light per day), found that in eight cases the forest birds had lower clutches, in two cases the opposite, and in 12 instances no change in clutch size could be detected (by *t*-test, these data have a 75 per cent probability of significance). Specifically, a caprimulgid which nests in the forest lays one egg, while all other members of its family in the Old World and in North America lay two eggs.

Oceanic islands, well known for the great climatic stability they enjoy, ought to show decreased clutches from the mainland at the same latitude, and indeed this is the case (Table 2). See also Lack (1947, pp.

CLUTCH SIZE IN BIRDS                    181

TABLE 2. *Differences between island and mainland clutch sizes at the same latitude.*

| Species or genus | For temperate islands off the coast of New Zealand[1] | | Species or genus | For tropical islands in the Caribbean[2] | |
|---|---|---|---|---|---|
| | Average mainland clutch | Average island clutch | | Average mainland clutch | Average island clutch |
| *Anas* | 8 (3 sp.) | 3.5(1 sp.) | *Saltator albicollis* | 2.0 | 2.5 |
| *Bowdleria punctata* | 3.1 | 2.5 | *Tangara gyrola* | 2.0 | 2.0 |
| *Gerygone* | 4.5(1 sp.) | 4.0(1 sp.) | *Habia rubica* | 2.3 | 2.0 |
| *Petroica macrocephala* | 3.5 | 3.0 | *Cacicus cela* | 2.0 | 2.0 |
| *Miro australis* | 2.6 | 2.5 | *Coereba flaveola* | 2.5 | 2.5 |
| *Anthornis melanura* | 3.5 | 3.0 | *Empidonax euleri* | 2.0 | 3.0 |
| *Cyanoramphus novaezelandeae* | 6.5 | 4.0 | *Elaenia flavogaster* | 2.3 | 2.5 |

[1] Species considered were either indigenous to the offshore islands and had a mainland relative in the same genus, or were subspecifically distinct on the island. The difference between the mainland and island means is 90 per cent significant, by *t*-test.

[2] Species on isolated West Indian islands are compared to the mainland, and also the extreme southerly Lesser Antillean islands (isolated) are compared to Trinidad, which is very close to the mainland. The means are not significantly different.

308–309). To exhibit an "island effect" (i.e., reduced clutch size), the island must be sufficiently isolated that mainland immigrants, which lay a larger clutch, do not swamp the island population, and the typical island clutch size is kept at the lower level. I have taken the subspeciation of island forms as an indication of sufficient isolation to fulfill this requirement. As well as possessing an impoverished fauna in general, most islands have no predators whatsoever, either on adult birds (most island bird lists are without accipiters or falcons) or on nests (snakes and mammals, among the chief nest predators at lower latitudes, are poor colonizers and are absent from most islands), a fact which probably accounts for the evolution of many flightless species (rails and ducks) on islands. Lack of predation puts island strategies in the $XX_2$ plane in the figure, and if $Q$ represents the strategy on an island at the same latitude as the temperate mainland but having a much milder, fairly stable climate, and $Q'$ the strategy on a tropical island, perhaps even more stable than the opposite mainland, $Q'Q$ is the path of optimum strategies of island birds from high latitudes to the equator. Consequently, although temperate islands should have reduced clutch sizes, tropical island clutch sizes, if different at all, will be only slightly

higher or slightly lower than those on the mainland, depending on the relative increase of predation on the mainland which determines the $X$-intercept of $P$, or the relative increase of stability on the island which will alter the $X$-intercept of $Q$. This prediction is also verified in Table 2 which shows that in some cases lack of predation permits a larger clutch size on tropical islands not compensated for by increased stability on the island. In many others the difference in clutch size will be perhaps only fractional (of an egg), requiring a detailed study of many nests to reveal it.

Coastal areas of continents are more stable climatically than central regions, and as we would expect if the theory is correct, clutch size increases from the coast inland (Lack, 1947, for Europe). This phenomenon is well observed in the United States, which has an extremely mild west coast, in contrast to the center of the continent where violent storms are of common occurrence. Thus, many birds (see, for example, Bent, 1938, p. 302, for the great horned owl, *Bubo virginianus*) lay their largest clutches in the midwest (between about 86° and 96° east longitude), an area which includes those states most familiar with severe winters and storms. A study by Johnston (1960) of clutch size in song sparrows, *Melospiza melodia*, revealed not only a gradual latitudinal increase from Baja California (3.05 eggs) to Alaska (4.17), but an increase from the Pacific coast east to Ohio (4.15) at which latitude the coastal sparrows lay 3.65 eggs. Presumably by taking advantage of the coastal climate, a few hummingbirds (Trochilidae) reach British Columbia, while one species, *Selasphorus rufus*, reaches Alaska (61° N). Mountainous areas are more unstable and unpredictable in their climate than adjacent lowlands, which accounts for the general trend for species nesting at high altitudes to lay larger clutches. In the Sierra Nevada, song sparrows (Johnston, 1960) at a median latitude of 38° N lay an average clutch of 3.99 eggs, which would not be found on the coast south of about 58° N.

A further instance of climatic stability affecting clutch size is found in South America, whose narrow and tapered configuration, especially below the tropics, where the influence will be most important, allows the closer proximity of inland areas to the surrounding oceans and results in a considerably milder more stable climate in this country compared to similar latitudes in North America. The Humboldt current up the west coast will have an additional ameliorating influence. We expect that the slope of the latitude clutch size graph will be steeper in North America than in the southern half of the continent, and this is exactly the situation which exists (Fig. 2). Africa, on the other hand, has a much larger and wider land mass, and Fig. 2 shows an equal slope for both north and south of the equator there. Large sea-birds live in coastal and hence quite stable environments, and have few predators, and so in tropical and temperate waters alike there will be a tendency to increase $\overline{K}$ not $r$, because of the stable conditions in which these birds live. Implications that this might be the case come from the work of Nelson (1964) on *Sula bassana*, which suggests (but does not prove as yet) that food is not the limiting factor of clutch size. It is possible that the $X_2$ axis in Fig. 1 might more appropriately denote effort

spent on an individual chick, measurable as weight at fledging, as even slightly smaller chicks at fledging would perhaps be at a disadvantage in its competitive ability during the next few years.

The Peruvian booby, *Sula variegata*, is a guanay-producing species which feeds in the waters of the Humboldt current off western South America. Every seven years or so the cold waters of this current are met by warm waters ("El Niño") from the northeast at a time when these birds are feeding young, and a food shortage results during which colonies are abandoned and the young boobies starve (Murphy, 1936). So far as this species is concerned conditions are unstable, and selection will be proceeding for $r$. In fact this species lays one to four eggs, and six out of seven years rears three young as often as two (other species of *Sula* which lay two eggs seldom rear both young). This is no doubt made possible by the rich food supply of the Humboldt current, and is seen graphically as equivalent to moving from $P_1$ to $P_2$ in Fig. 1.

The bay-breasted warbler, *Dendroica castanea*, Cape May warbler, *D. tigrina*, and the Tennessee warbler, *Vermivora peregrina*, are the North American warblers which depend on an unstable food supply. These species are largely dependent on irregular spruce-budworm outbreaks (MacArthur, 1962) for food during their breeding season, and as we would expect lay larger clutches (of five to six, five to seven, and five to six eggs, respectively) than other member of the Parulidae (normal clutch size four, rarely five, eggs). Another exception to the usual four eggs is the prothonotary warbler, *Prothonotaria citrea*, which is a hole-nester and lays a six-egg clutch.

A second prediction concerns predation-free species. It can be seen from Fig. 3 that if a species does not experience the increased predation in the tropics that most passerines do, the line $P'P$ would be altered to $P'P''$, $P''$ having the same $X_2$-intercept as $P$, but an intercept on $X_1$ equal or nearly equal to that of $P'$ and an $X$-intercept closer to that of $P'$. Thus we can predict that species which are relatively free from predators will have a smaller temperate-tropical increase in clutch size. This is exactly the situation observed by Lord (1960) in North American mammals, in which no statistically significant increase in litter size with latitude could be found in predatory species (*Vulpes, Felis, Mustela*).

Hibernating animals would manage to avoid predation during winter and showed a less steep slope than did non-hibernating prey species, all these being statistically significant.

A third and final prediction may be made for hole nesters. Hole-nesting birds would escape much of the predation suffered by species nesting in open or exposed situations. For instance in the red-breasted merganser (*Mergus serrator*), which in Europe commonly nests in holes in banks, rocks, and tree roots, 91 per cent of hatched young survived, whereas for six species of open-nesting ducks this figure averages 58 per cent (from data in Lack, 1954). We can predict not only that clutch size will be higher in the tropic and temperate zones alike, but also that, as nest predation is higher in the tropics and the relative advantage of hole-nesting over open nests is greater there, the latitude/clutch size slope will be less steep for these hole nesters than for the open nesters. As this has been represented in Fig. 3, $P$ and $P'$ move down curves of points of equal stability to strategies $H$ and $H'$, but $PH$ will be greater than $P'H'$ due to the greater relative advantage gained in the more stable-greater predation region. Lack (1948) showed not only that hole nesters lay a larger clutch by nearly two eggs on the average, for mid-European passerines, but that strategies between $P'$ and $H'$ exist, as intermediate stages of nest exposure, i.e., roofed and niche sites, between hole and open sites, which expose the nest to more predation and a higher chance of failure, result in intermediate clutch sizes. Tropical hole nesters also have higher clutches. The genus *Myiarchus* comprises the only tyrannid flycatchers to nest in holes in decayed stumps (Skutch, 1960, p.

398), and these species are responsible for the higher clutches of the family (Fig. 2.2). Similarly, of the Central American Thraupidae the only member for which clutch data exist and which nests in a hole is the Bonaparte euphonia, *Tanagra lauta*. While the other members of its genus, and indeed its family, lay two to three and rarely more eggs in this region (Skutch, 1954, p. 249), this species lays five to six eggs. The hole-nesting Ramphastidae (toucans) lay three to four eggs, compared to the two eggs which comprise a full clutch for the vast majority of tropical birds and likewise with the jacamars Galbulidae laying an average of 2.6 eggs (Skutch *et al., in litt.*). Indications that the slope of the graphs for hole-nesters is more gradual are obtained from limited data, but hole-nesting Alcenidae increase their clutch size from four to five or six (ratio 1 : 1.4) from Central America to the United States, while most of the graphs given show a ratio of 1 : 2.5 for that range of latitude.

## SUMMARY

The principle of allocation of time and energy is used to formulate a general theory to account for clutch size in birds. "Advantages" are figured as the axes of a three-dimensional graph, and phenotypes allocating their energy in particular ways as points in space forming a surface and enclosed solid.

In the temperate zones most energy is used to increase the reproductive rate $r$. In the tropics the carrying capacity of the habitat is more important, resulting in a smaller clutch size. Different phenotypes will be more fit in different environments, as optimum allocation of energy differs.

Previous theories of clutch size are discussed, and incorporated into this general theory. Increase of clutch size with latitude is analyzed, and accounted for by the theory.

Predictions are made that all stable environments, the tropics, islands, coasts, will favor reduced clutches. Examples are quoted in which instability of conditions results in increased clutch size. The situa-

184                                    MARTIN L. CODY

tion of predation-free species is examined, and it is predicted that the clutch size of such species will remain relatively unchanged with latitude changes. These predictions seem to be verified in all cases where data are available to test them.

### ACKNOWLEDGMENTS

I am deeply indebted to Dr. Robert MacArthur for his assistance throughout the preparation of this paper. I am also grateful to Dr. Mike Rosensweig and Dr. Harry Recher for reading the manuscript and offering many useful suggestions.

### LITERATURE CITED

BENT, A. C. 1938. Life histories of North American birds of prey (Part 2). Bull. U. S. Nat. Mus., **170**: 1–482.

BOND, J. 1947. A field guide of birds of the West Indies. Macmillan, New York.

CAYLEY, N. W. 1956. What bird is that? Angus and Robertson, Sydney.

DELACOUR, J. 1959. The waterfowl of the world. Country Life, London.

FISHER, R. A. 1929. Genetical theory of natural selection. Oxford Press.

GOODALL, J. D., A. W. JOHNSON, AND R. A. PHILIPPI. 1946. Las aves de Chile. Buenos Aires.

HERKLOTS, G. A. C. 1961. The birds of Trinidad and Tobago. Collins, London.

JOHNSTON, R. F. 1960. Variation in breeding season and clutch size in song sparrows of the Pacific coast. Condor, **56**: 268–273.

KORTRIGHT, F. H. 1943. The ducks, geese and swans of North America. Amer. Wildlife Inst., Washington.

KLUIJVER, H. N. 1951. The population ecology of the Great Tit *Parus m. major* L. Ardea, **39**: 1–135.

LACK, D. 1947. The significance of clutch size. Parts I and II. Ibis, **87**: 302–352.

——. 1948. The significance of clutch size. Part III. Ibis, **90**: 25–45.

——. 1949. Comments on Mr. Skutch's paper on clutch size. Ibis, **91**: 455–458.

——. 1954. The natural regulation of animal numbers. Clarendon Press, Oxford.

LACK, D., AND E. LACK. 1951. The breeding biology of the swift *Apus apus*. Ibis, **93**: 501–546.

LEVINS, R. 1962. Theory of fitness in a heterogeneous environment. 1. The fitness set and adaptive function. Amer. Nat., **96**: 361–373.

LORD, R. D. JR. 1960. Litter size and latitude in North American mammals. Amer. Midl. Nat., **64**: 488–499.

MACARTHUR, R. H. 1958. Population ecology of some warblers of Northeastern coniferous forests. Ecology, **39**: 599–619.

——. 1962. Some generalized theorems of natural selection. Proc. Nat. Acad. Sci., **48**: 1893–1897.

MOREAU, R. 1944. Clutch size: A comparative study, with special reference to African birds. Ibis, **86**: 286–347.

MURPHY, R. C. 1936. Oceanic birds of South America. Macmillan, New York.

NELSON, B. 1964. Factors influencing clutch size and chick growth in the North Atlantic gannet *Sula bassana*. Ibis, **106**: 63–77.

OLIVER, W. R. B. 1955. New Zealand birds. Reed, Wellington.

PITELKA, F. A., P. Q. TOMICH, AND G. W. TREICHEL. 1955. Ecological relations of jaegers and owls as lemming predators near Barrow, Alaska. Ecol. Monogr., **25**: 85–117.

POUGH, R. H. 1949. Audubon land bird guide. Doubleday, New York.

——. 1957. Audubon water bird guide. Doubleday, New York.

SKUTCH, A. F. 1949. Do tropical birds rear as many young as they can nourish? Ibis, **91**: 430–455.

——. 1954. Life histories of Central American birds. Pacific Coast Avifauna, **31**: 1–448.

——. 1960. Life histories of Central American birds. II. Pacific Coast Avifauna, **34**: 1–593.

SNOW, D. 1962. Field study of the black and white manakin *Manacus manacus*. Zoologica, **47**: 65–104.

WYNNE-EDWARDS, V. C. 1962. Animal dispersion in relation to social behaviour. Oliver and Boyd, Edinburgh.

# "CLUTCH SIZE" IN BUTTERCUPS

Michael P. Johnson[1] and Stanton A. Cook

Department of Biology, University of Oregon, Eugene, Oregon 97403

## INTRODUCTION

The question of natural regulation of clutch size in birds has been dealt with in some detail. The various hypotheses are discussed by Lack (1954), whose conclusions represent the now generally accepted theory that clutch size is related to a limited food supply. More specifically, there will be selection toward some "optimum" clutch size, which represents the maximum number of nestlings that can be furnished the necessary quantity of food from the prevailing environment. Clutch sizes less than the optimum value will have their genetic material represented in lesser frequency than those with the optimum number. On the other hand, the probability of success of the individual nestlings is reduced as clutch size exceeds the optimum value. Reproductive success is not enhanced by increasing clutch size if it leads to reduced fitness of the nestlings. While selection for an optimum clutch size may be strong, clutch size is not usually constant throughout a population at any given point in time. Moreover, the mean clutch size may vary from season to season within the same population. This variation reflects genetic differences in the first case, and environmental differences in the second. These environmental and genetic differences may be extended to account for interspecific and geographic variation. Examples of these types of variation are given in Lack (1954) and Cody (1966).

Certain data suggest an analogous regulation in angiosperms. Harper (1964) has pointed out that seed size is one of the least plastic of plant characters. Many examples of constancy in seed size (usually measured as weight) are given in Harper (1961, 1964) and Bradshaw (1965). These observations have in general been made when the effects of changes in density are studied. Other related plant characters (such as seeds/capsule, seeds/plant, flowers/plant, and capsules/plant) are greatly reduced in number with increasing density and the associated decrease in resources available to each individual. Since the major portion of the weight of a seed is food-storage tissue, one may conclude that there is some optimum amount of food reserve which will normally insure the necessary seedling vigor. An effective strategy for plants would then be similar to that of

[1] Present Address: Department of Biological Science, Florida State University, Tallahassee, Florida 32306.

Reprinted by permission of The University of Chicago Press and the authors from *The American Naturalist* 102:405–411. 1968. Copyright 1968 by the University of Chicago.

birds: maximize "clutch size" without exceeding the number that can be provided the necessary amount of energy. A strong case for this type of regulation of reproduction in plants has not previously been made.

Benson (1948) indirectly pointed out a pattern of geographical variation in *Ranunculus flammula* L. that is suggestive of the type of regulation proposed by Lack. He observed that carpel number (and hence seed number, since only one seed is produced per carpel) decreases with an increase in latitude. This observation was based largely on the examination of herbarium material, where the nature of the variation (environmental or genetic) could not be determined. Following the Lack theory, one can hypothesize that this variation is the result of selection for an "optimum" carpel number in response to the variation in the length of the growing season associated with latitudinal changes. The length of the growing season would affect the total amount of photosynthate available for food-storage tissue in the seeds. If this is true, then a similar pattern of variation would be expected with changes in elevation.

## METHODS AND MATERIALS

*Ranunculus flammula* L. has wide geographical and altitudinal ranges and, associated with these, a wide range of morphological forms. In western North America the species ranges from about lat 30° to 70°N and from sea level to 10,000 feet in elevation. In the populations sampled, usually only one flower is produced by each ramet, which is the functional individual. In addition, only one seed per carpel is produced. A measure of carpel number is therefore a good indicator of the maximum possible seed set (clutch size) for the individual being measured. The variation in carpel number was measured and analyzed in the following manner.

Seven populations were sampled along a transect from the Oregon coast to an elevation of 5,616 feet in the Cascade Mountains (Table 1). These populations occur in a narrow latitudinal band. Flowers in fruit were dissected and the carpel number was determined. In addition, plants were transplanted from five of the populations to the greenhouses at the University of Oregon. Carpel numbers were measured for three seasons, twice in one season, and at two subhabitats representing the two moisture extremes at the Florence population. All other field measurements were made during the 1965 flowering season at what was estimated to be peak flowering for the given population. For all field samples the mean number of carpels, mean number of fertile carpels, and fertility percentage are given in Table 1. The transplanted material was maintained at Eugene for a minimum of 2 years before measurement, to reduce residual field environmental effects.

Two environmental variables were used as indicators of the length of the growing season: (1) elevation, as determined from topographic maps; and (2) length of the frost-free period in days, as determined from Department of Commerce data for the station nearest the population sampled. While neither of these variables should by any means be considered

## TABLE 1

### LIST OF POPULATIONS STUDIED AND VARIABLES MEASURED

| POPULATION | $E'$ | $\bar{X}_1$ | $\bar{X}_2$ | $P$ | $N$ | $\bar{X}_3$ | $N$ | \multicolumn{7}{c}{PAIRWISE ANALYSES OF VARIANCE BETWEEN MEAN FIELD CARPEL NUMBER} |
|---|---|---|---|---|---|---|---|---|---|---|---|---|---|---|
| | | | | | | | | 1 | 2 | 3 | 4 | 5 | 6 | 7 |
| 1. Miller Lake | 5,616 | 13.9 | 5.3 | 38.6 | 47 | ... | ... | ... | ... | ... | ... | ... | ... | ... |
| 2. Horse Lake | 5,200 | 11.2 | 7.9 | 70.5 | 30 | 16.0 | 10 | 3 | ... | ... | ... | ... | ... | ... |
| 3. Malone Spring | 4,150 | 16.9 | 16.1 | 95.0 | 20 | 18.3 | 10 | 3 | 3 | ... | ... | ... | ... | ... |
| 4. Mohawk Valley | 468 | 17.7 | 14.0 | 78.9 | 19 | .. | .. | 3 | 3 | 0 | ... | ... | ... | ... |
| 5. Cleawox Lake | 80 | 27.6 | 20.0 | 72.4 | 46 | 33.7 | 67 | 3 | 3 | 3 | 3 | ... | ... | ... |
| 6. Coos Bay | 50 | 23.9 | 22.2 | 92.9 | 62 | 36.7 | 3 | 3 | 3 | 3 | 3 | 2 | ... | ... |
| 7. Florence (a) | 20 | 26.7 | 23.5 | 88.3 | 30 | 40.0 | 42 | 3 | 3 | 3 | 3 | 0 | 1 | ... |

FLORENCE SAMPLES

| POPULATION | $\bar{X}_1$ | $\bar{X}_2$ | $P$ | $N$ | a | b | c | d | e |
|---|---|---|---|---|---|---|---|---|---|
| b) 1962 | 27.8 | 24.9 | 89.8 | 29 | 0 | ... | ... | ... | ... |
| c) 1964 | 28.1 | 24.4 | 86.6 | 30 | 0 | 0 | ... | ... | ... |
| d) 1965a | 23.8 | 19.9 | 83.9 | 57 | 3 | 3 | 1 | ... | ... |
| e) 1965b | 22.8 | 17.0 | 74.7 | 39 | 3 | 3 | 3 | 3 | ... |

NOTE.—Samples 1–7a taken at peak flowering in 1965. $E'$ = elevation (feet); $\bar{X}_1$ = mean field carpel number; $\bar{X}_2$ = mean cultivated carpel number; $\bar{X}_3$ = mean seed set; $N$ = sample size; $P$ = percentage of seed set; 0 = not significant; 1 = $p < .05$; 2 = $p < .01$; 3 = $p < .001$.

408                     THE AMERICAN NATURALIST

a precise measure of the length of the growing season, each would be expected to represent a reasonable indicator.

### RESULTS AND DISCUSSION

It is apparent from Table 1 that there is a reduction in carpel number with an increase in elevation. From the analyses of variance it is seen that, with the exception of two cases, the differences between mean field carpel numbers are significant. The mean cultivated carpel numbers parallel the values of the field measurements, but they are consistently higher. A genetic component of variation is demonstrated by the observation that population samples vary in carpel number when grown in a uniform environment. The marked increase in carpel number under cultivation demonstrates that carpel number may be modified by environmental conditions. Further observations may be made of the environmental effects by examining the multiple samples taken at Florence. The samples of 1962, 1964, and 1965 (Table 1) were all taken at peak flowering and do not differ significantly in mean carpel number. The samples 1965a and 1965b were taken late in the season from the wet and dry subhabitats, respectively. These two samples are not significantly different in carpel number from each other, but both are significantly different from the three peak flowering samples (1962, 1964, and 1965). At this locality there is no observed significant difference in carpel number between seasons or between subhabitats sampled at the same time during a single season, but a significant difference is observed between samples from different times during the season.

An alternative hypothesis for the regulation of carpel number is selection in response to variables (pollinators, genetic factors) which affect fertility. From the same material used to determine carpel number, seed set was also determined. The percentage of seed set was transformed, using the arc-sine transformation (Snedecor, 1956). Regression analyses of mean carpel number on transformed fertility were computed and the regressions found not significant. The correlation coefficients between fertility and carpel number are given in Table 2. When mean carpel number (as measured in the field or in a uniform environment) is regressed on either of the indicators of length of growing season (elevation or number of days

TABLE 2

CORRELATION COEFFICIENTS BETWEEN CARPEL NUMBER AND ELEVATION IN
FEET (I), NATURAL LOG OF ELEVATION (II), MAXIMUM NUMBER OF DAYS
BETWEEN FROSTS (III), AND FERTILITY PERCENTAGE USING THE
ARC-SINE TRANSFORMATION (IV)

|  | Mean Field Carpel Number | Mean Cultivated Carpel Number |
|---|---|---|
| I............ | −.8747 | −.9786 |
| II........... | −.9324 | −.9985 |
| III.......... | .8649 | .9662 |
| IV........... | .3267* | .0437* |

* Not significant at the .05 level.

between frosts), the regression is significant. There is a better fit with elevation when elevation is transformed to logarithms. The correlation coefficients between carpel number and the environmental variables are given in Table 2. The results of the regression analyses are given in Table 3, and the regression curves are given in Figures 1 and 2.

These data, in demonstrating a decrease in carpel number with an increase in elevation, are consistent with the previously cited observation of Benson. With the correlations between elevation, latitude, and the number of days between frosts, it appears reasonable to suggest that carpel number is regulated in part by the length of the growing season. The length of the growing season would be expected to affect the total amount of energy available to the plants for the production of food reserves necessary for seed germination and seedling establishment. It is to be expected that other environmental factors (for example, available soil nutrients) which limit accumulation of suitable food reserve will also affect carpel number. While each plant has genetic limitations to prevent the production of seeds in greater number than can be supplied adequate food reserve, there also exists a flexibility for the production of greater numbers of seeds under more favorable availability of requisite resources. This provides the plants with the opportunity to take maximum advantage of the available resources. The analogy of this to the Lack theory should be obvious.

In addition to carpel number, the percentage of seed set is also of importance in determining clutch size. There were no observations of plants under cultivation having markedly reduced fertility. Genetic factors affecting fertility are therefore considered to be of little importance in this instance. *R. flammula* is self-incompatible, and marked differences in numbers and kinds of pollinators were observed between the populations (Johnson, 1966). The results of the Florence subsampling show that the percentage of seed set differs within a single season and between subhabitats during a single season in such a way as to suggest seasonal and spatial paucity of insects. The lower mean carpel number at the end of the season (note in Table 1 the 1965 *a* and *b* Florence populations) may be attributed to two classes which increase in frequency toward the end of the season:

TABLE 3

VALUES OF $F$ AND $p$ OF THE REGRESSIONS OF MEAN CARPEL NUMBER ON ELEVATION IN FEET (I), NATURAL LOG OF ELEVATION (II), AND MAXIMUM OF DAYS BETWEEN FROSTS (III)*

|  | I | II | III |
|---|---|---|---|
| Mean field carpel number: |  |  |  |
| $F$ | 16.29 | 33.30 | 14.85 |
| $p$ | $<.01$ | $<.01$ | $<.05$ |
| $r^2$ | .7651 | .8694 | .7481 |
| Mean cultivated carpel number: |  |  |  |
| $F$ | 67.80 | 1008 | 42.17 |
| $p$ | $<.01$ | $<.01$ | $<.01$ |
| $r^2$ | .9576 | 1.9970** | .9336 |

* Also given is coefficient of determination ($r^2$) for each.

** 0.9970

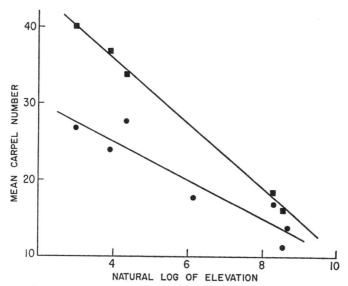

FIG. 1.—Mean carpel number plotted against the natural log of the elevation. Upper regression curve for means of cultivated plants (*squares*). Lower
regression curve for means of field measurements (*circles*).

(1) plants flowering in their first year (*R. flammula* being a perennial), and
(2) plants which are flowering a second time during the same season. In
both cases, only part of the season has been available for the accumulating
of food reserve for endosperm tissue.

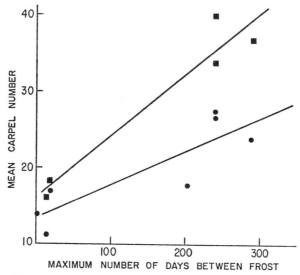

FIG. 2.—Mean carpel number plotted against maximum number of days
between frosts. Upper regression curve for means of cultivated plants (*squares*).
Lower regression curve for means of field measurements (*circles*).

## SUMMARY

The variation in carpel number in *Ranunculus flammula* was analyzed. Both genetic and environmental components of variance were observed and discussed. Significant correlations between length of growing season and carpel number were observed. It was concluded that the genetic component of the variation results from selection toward some "optimum" carpel number consistent with the amount of food reserve that can be accumulated by the plant for endosperm tissue in the environment in which this selection occurs. The plasticity of individuals for carpel number allows for annual fluctuations in environment. An analogy is made with clutch size regulation in birds.

## ACKNOWLEDGMENTS

This work was supported by the National Science Foundation (grant GB-399) and was completed during the tenure of the senior author as a postdoctoral trainee at Stanford University (NIH grant 2G-365-R1). The authors thank Dr. Peter H. Raven, Stanford University, for his valuable suggestions during the preparation of the manuscript.

### LITERATURE CITED

Benson, L. 1948. A treatise on the North American Ranunculi. Amer. Midland Natur. 40:1–261.

Bradshaw, A. D. 1965. Evolutionary significance of phenotypic plasticity in plants. Advances Genet. 13:115–155.

Cody, M. L. 1966. A general theory of clutch size. Evolution 20:174–184.

Harper, J. L. 1961. Approaches to the study of plant competition. Soc. Exp. Biol. Symp. 15:1–39.

———. 1964. The nature and consequence of interference amongst plants. XI Int. Congr. Genet., Proc., p. 465–482.

Johnson, M. P. 1966. Developmental flexibility and ecological amplitude in *Ranunculus flammula* L. Unpublished Ph.D. thesis. Univ. Oregon.

Lack, D. 1954. Natural regulation of animal numbers. Clarendon Press, Oxford.

Snedecor, G. W. 1956. Statistical methods. Iowa State Coll. Press, Ames.

# ADAPTIVE SIGNIFICANCE OF LARGE SIZE AND LONG LIFE OF THE CHAETOGNATH *SAGITTA ELEGANS* IN THE ARCTIC

IAN A. McLAREN[1]

*Marine Sciences Centre, McGill University, Montreal, Quebec*

*Abstract.* Zooplankton of high latitudes generally develop more slowly, reach a larger size, and live longer than related forms in warmer seas. Existing explanations are reviewed and a new one offered. Where generation length is set by marked seasonality of food supply, as in the arctic, high fecundity and associated large size and slow development may be selected for. It is shown from analysis of generation length, fecundity, and natural mortality of the chaetognath *Sagitta elegans* that its biennial life cycle in the eastern Canadian Arctic is of optimal length.

## INTRODUCTION

It is generally true that marine zooplankters of high latitudes develop more slowly, reach a larger size, and live longer than related forms in warmer seas. Since development rate may be slower even in the presence of abundant food, some authors (e.g. Digby 1954) have simply concluded that high-latitude forms are not particularly well adapted to living at low temperatures. However, Dunbar (1957), in his review of the subject, feels that "differences in the type of life cycle are probably at the root of the ultimate (as opposed to the proximate) causes for the differences between groups in this respect."

Several authors have pointed out the obvious relationship between life cycles and environmental periodicity. Since food in arctic seas may be abundant only during a very restricted season (Bogorov 1958), especially for phytophagous zooplankton (Grainger 1959), it is not surprising that many forms have annual life cycles in the arctic, as compared with several generations per year elsewhere. However, biennial life cycles (examples in Dunbar 1957) do not seem explicable in the same way. More generally, other authors (e.g. Connell and Orias 1964; Paloheimo and Dickie 1965) have deduced in a variety of arguments that large size and associated slow growth and low metabolism may confer advantages on animals faced with periodic food shortages.

Dunbar (1960) went further and suggested that development of large, slow-growing, slow-respiring individuals in the arctic might reflect "natural selection at the level of the ecosystem," whereby lower rates of increase are selected to prevent overutilization of resources and "lethal oscillations" of the system. However, he offered no quantitative arguments to explain how ordinary selection pressures could be overcome by this group-selection process.

This paper describes a quite different way in which large size and slow growth may be adaptive in highly seasonal northern waters. Although referring only to a single species of marine plankter, I believe the arguments are very general, and may apply to other poikilotherms in the arctic and perhaps in seasonal environments elsewhere.

[1] Present address: Biology Department, Dalhousie University, Halifax, Nova Scotia.

A series of published and unpublished collections are analyzed here by a variety of means. Fieldwork has been supported by the Fisheries Research Board of Canada and the National Research Council of Canada. The paper has been written under a Canada Council Fellowship. I am grateful to J. C. Carter, J. H. Fraser, and A. J. Southward for supplying specimens and data.

## SEASONAL AND GEOGRAPHIC VARIATIONS IN SIZE AND LIFE CYCLE OF *S. elegans*

Among zooplankters that have several generations per year size varies seasonally as a function of temperature during development (McLaren 1963). The size-temperature response may vary geographically within species (McLaren 1965) and this is clearly true of populations of the chaetognath *Sagitta elegans* from the Canadian Arctic and the western North Atlantic (Fig. 1).

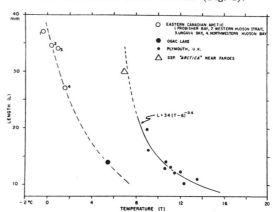

FIG. 1. The relationship between mean of samples of mature *Sagitta elegans* and estimated mean temperature during their development.

The points and curve relating mature body size to temperature for animals off Plymouth are from McLaren (1963, fig. 7). The point for the Faroes population is based on animals collected in March 1937, and described by Fraser (1939) as "commonly reaching up to 30 mm

Reprinted by permission of Duke University Press and the author from *Ecology* 47:852–855, 1966.

288

and over." Dr. Fraser kindly examined a dozen specimens and writes (personal communication) that the two
largest (29 and 32 mm) were mature. Fraser (1939)
also gives a table of temperatures at 0 and 100 m depth
for stations at which the large animals were collected,
all of which may be averaged to suggest a temperature
of 7.4 ± 1.0°C (mean and 95% fiducial limit) at the time
of sampling. Perhaps a better estimate of temperature
*during* development is given by averaging all available
records of temperature during January, February, and
March 1937, from the area bounding Fraser's collection
sites (61° to 63°N by 03° to 08°W) as listed in the
Bulletin Hygrographique (Intern. Council Explor. Sea
1939). This estimate (6.9 ± 0.5°C) does not differ from
the above. It is thus reasonable to suggest as on Fig. 1
that adult size around the Faroe Islands reaches about
30 mm at a temperature during development of 7°C.
Although the Faroe animals were believed by Fraser
(1939) to be "subspecies *arctica*," they seem to belong to
the same size-temperature category as those from Plymouth.

Size data from the eastern Canadian Arctic are from
Dunbar (1962). Mean lengths of mature (stage III)
animals are determined from his figures as follows:
Frobisher Bay (his Fig. 6); west end Hudson Strait
(his Fig. 2b, c, d, and e combined); Ungava Bay (Fig.
5); northwestern Hudson Bay (Fig. 2a). Growth appears to be all but suspended in the arctic winter (see
his Fig. 3), and I therefore assume that the growth season extends from mid-June to mid-September. For all
these regions, mean temperature during this season was
estimated for the upper 50 m (from which almost all of
Dunbar's samples were taken) by graphing all available
data (Dunbar 1958; Barber and Glennie 1964). Temperatures were taken as isothermal at −1.7°C in mid-
June, before records were available.

The point for Ogac Lake, the warm, landlocked head
of a fiord on Baffin Island (see Dunbar 1958), is accurately fixed for animals born in spring and maturing in
summer from size and temperature data in McLaren
(1961).

Although the accuracy of individual points might be
questionable, Figure 1 shows clearly that the response of
size to temperature is shifted in the expected direction in
the colder environment. However, the shift is only
"partial," since the animals of normal arctic waters (Ogac
Lake is abnormally warm) still average much larger than
those from southern waters. Further, Dunbar (1962)
showed that the large arctic form is biennial, whereas the
smaller form off Plymouth has five or six generations
per year (Russell 1932). Elsewhere (McLaren 1963)
it has been shown that size, generation length, and
fecundity are negative functions of temperature, and that
it is advantageous for *S. elegans* to be small and fast-
developing when food is more-or-less continuously adequate. In the arctic, abundant food (e.g., nauplii of
small copepods) for newborn *S. elegans* (which are only
about 2 mm long) occurs only during the seasonal phytoplankton maximum. The life cycle must be annual or
some multiple thereof. The legitimate question is why
*S. elegans* matures in 2 yr at a larger size rather than in
1 yr at a smaller size, as it is "forced" to do in the
abnormally warm environment of Ogac Lake (McLaren
1961, Dunbar 1962). This could be effected by a further
shift in the temperature response (see Fig. 1) so that
maturity would occur at a smaller size. To answer this
question, data are required on fecundity and natural mortality rates.

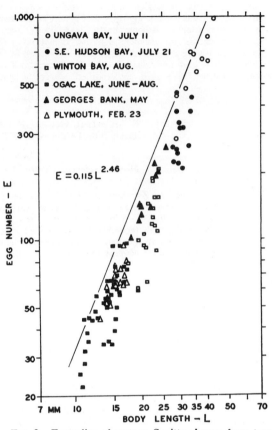

Fig. 2. Fecundity of mature *Sagitta elegans* from two
semilandlocked fiords (Ogac Lake, Winton Bay) and two
offshore areas in the eastern Canadian Arctic, and from
Georges Bank, off Massachusetts, and from off Plymouth,
England.

## FEDUNDITY OF *S. elegans*

Figure 2 shows counts of eggs in mature *S. elegans*
from four localities in the eastern Canadian Arctic and
from two temperate regions. In a previous paper (Mc-
Laren 1963) fecundity was calculated by plotting ovary
length against body length (because of available published measurements) and in turn relating egg number
to ovary length. Since eggs may have been shed by some
ovaries, this indirect means of determining fecundity
could have resulted in errors. To obtain the data on
Figure 2, ovaries were stripped from the formalin-
preserved animals and all eggs counted under magnification. To ensure maximal counts ovaries were included
from the earliest available sampling dates in the arctic
season, and some ovaries from all localities were included
that had large eggs, but did not otherwise appear to be
fully expanded. As well as release of eggs, there is
another source of reduced counts. Even the most expanded ovaries contained very small eggs or oocytes
clustered along the oviduct. In some ovaries these appeared distinct in outline and "healthy"; in others, some
appeared to be undergoing resorption. For these reasons
the line in Figure 2 is drawn by eye through near-
maximal points as a measure of potential fecundity. The
logarithmic slope of this line (2.46) is steeper than previously estimated (1.8, in McLaren 1963). The propor-

tion of potential fecundity that is actually achieved is unknown, but there is a suggestion that it may be the same in all populations. Among arctic populations, where spawning occurs in summer, negative deviations from the line in Figure 2 are smallest in the early sample from Ungava Bay, and individuals in the later samples from other localities have shed, or resorbed, about the same maximal proportion of their eggs.

It thus appears that egg production by *S. elegans* is the same function of adult size wherever the animal is found, and regardless of the generation length. It may not seem intuitively reasonable that the relationship of egg number and body size is thus independent of the local adaptive circumstances. The relationship may be imposed by shape restrictions in the animal; presumably these could be modified, but then we would no longer be dealing with the "same" animal morphologically, ecologically, and presumably taxonomically.

### Natural Mortality Rate in the Arctic

From extensive collections taken in a number of seasons and localities and graphed by Dunbar (1962, his Fig. 2, 5) it is possible to determine numbers and sizes of 1-yr-old (his group "B") and 2-yr-old (his group "A" age classes. The combined data are given in Figure 3,

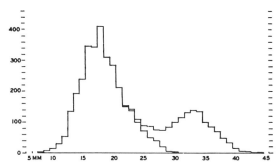

Fig. 3. Size-frequency distribution of combined samples of arctic *Sagitta elegans* graphed by Dunbar (1962). The members of the two groups were separated on the original graphs by dividing intermediate (minimal frequency) size classes equally between the two groups.

and the total counts are 3,170 and 1,216 respectively. For two reasons this may be taken as a maximal measure of mortality in the second year of life. First, data from Frobisher Bay (Dunbar's Fig. 6) are excluded, because 1-yr-olds seem badly underrepresented there—perhaps, according to Dunbar, for hydrographic reasons. Second, excessive post-spawning mortality may have reduced the numbers of 2-yr-olds in samples taken later in the summer.

### Rate of Increase in the Arctic

By integration of potential fecundity as a function of size (Fig. 2) and size-frequency distributions (Fig. 3) it can be estimated that the average 2-yr-old could produce about 543 eggs, whereas the average 1-yr-old, if it matured at this age, could only produce 138 eggs. Again, the latter estimate must be taken as maximal, since 1-yr-olds grow demonstrably during summer when the mature 2-yr-olds have ceased to grow (see Dunbar 1962, his Fig. 2, 5).

The instantaneous coefficient of increase ($r$) of a hermaphroditic species (Cole 1964) may be given as: $r = \ln$ (egg no. $\times$ proportion eggs surviving to maturity)/generation length. Since it must be assumed that

*S. elegans* in the arctic are neither increasing nor decreasing over any meaningful time span, and since samples are available from several years and localities, their coefficient of realized rate of increase on an annual basis may be written:

$$r = \frac{\ln\left[(543)\left(\frac{1}{543}\right)\right]}{2} = 0.$$

For animals maturing in their first year, this expression becomes:

$$r = \frac{\ln\left[(138)\left(\frac{1}{543}\times\frac{3,170}{1,216}\right)\right]}{1} = -0.43$$

This would result in an annual decrease of the population of about 35%. Note that the same conclusion may be reached as long as the same proportion of eggs is shed by large and small animals, which seems to be the case (see above).

If maturation is adaptively delayed until the animals are 2 yr old, it might be wondered if a further delay would be advantageous. There is no way to determine this directly, but an approach may be made by assuming that mortality rate (1,216/3,170) and mean length increase (14 mm) are the same in the third year as in the second. A shift of each 2-yr-old size-class in Figure 3 by 14 mm, and integration of the resulting size-frequency distribution with Figure 2 (and its extrapolation) leads to a mean fecundity of 1,318 eggs. Then,

$$r = \frac{\ln\left[(1,318)\left(\frac{1}{543}\times\frac{1,216}{3,170}\right)\right]}{3} = -0.02$$

There would thus still be a small population decrease, but by the same reasoning further delays would be increasingly successful. At this point the naïveté of the analysis must be stressed. Very large specimens, assuming growth rate is in fact undiminished with length increase, might be structurally or ecologically disharmonious. For example, it can be shown that the ovaries would exceed the length of the body cavity in most of the imaginary 4-yr-olds.

*S. elegans* thrives with a 1-yr cycle in Ogac Lake, which is highly atypical both hydrographically and biologically (McLaren 1961). For the arctic seas in general, although the above argument may be quantitatively imprecise in detail, it may be concluded that large size and the 2-yr cycle are not signs of poor adaptation, but are optimal solutions to living in highly seasonal conditions.

### Literature Cited

Barber, F. J., and C. J. Glennie. 1964. On the oceanography of Hudson Bay, an atlas presentation of data obtained in 1961. Can. Dept. Mines Tech. Surv., Mar. Sci. Br., MS Rep. Ser. No. 1.

Bogorov, B. G. 1958. Perspectives in the study of seasonal changes of plankton and the number of generations at different latitudes, p. 145-158. *In* A. A. Buzzati-Traverso (ed.). Perspectives in marine biology. Univ. California Press.

Cole, L. C. 1954. The population consequences of life history phenomena. Quart. Rev. Biol. 29: 103-137.

Connell, J. H., and E. Orias. 1964. The ecological regulation of species diversity. Amer. Naturalist 98: 399-414.

Digby, P. S. B. 1954. The biology of the marine planktonic copepods of Scoresby Sound, East Greenland. J. Animal Ecol. 23: 298-338.

Dunbar, M. J. 1957. The determinants of production in

northern seas: a study of the biology of *Themisto libellula* Mandt. Can. J. Zool. **35**: 797-819.

———. 1958. Physical oceanographic results of the "Calanus" expeditions in Ungava Bay, Frobisher Bay. Cumberland Sound, Hudson Strait, and northern Hudson Bay, 1949-1955. J. Fish. Res. Bd. Can. **15**: 155-201.

———. 1960. The evolution of stability in marine environments. Natural selection at the level of the ecosystem. Amer. Naturalist **94**: 129-136.

———. 1962. The life cycle of *Sagitta elegans* in arctic and subarctic seas, and the modifying effects of hydrographic differences in the environment. J. Mar. Res. **20**: 76-91.

Fraser, J. H. 1939. The distribution of Chaetognatha in Scottish waters in 1937. J. Cons. Intern. Explor. Mer **14**: 24-34.

Grainger, E. H. 1959. The annual oceanographic cycle at Igloolik in the Canadian Arctic. I. The zooplankton and physical and chemical observations. J. Fish. Res. Bd. Can. **16**: 453-501.

International Council for the Exploration of the Sea. 1939. Bull. Hydrogr. for 1937.

McLaren, I. A. 1961. The hydrography and zooplankton of Ogac Lake, a landlocked fiord on Baffin Island. Ph.D. thesis, Yale Unversity, New Haven.

———. 1963. Effects of temperature on growth of zooplankton, and the adaptive value of vertical migration. J. Fish. Res. Bd. Can. **20**: 685-727.

———. 1965. Some relationships between temperature and egg size, body size, development rate, and fecundity, of the copepod *Pseudocalanus*. Limnol. Oceanogr. **10**: 528-538.

Paloheimo, J. E., and L. M. Dickie. 1965. Food and growth of fishes. I. A growth curve derived from experimental data. J. Fish. Res. Bd. Can. **22**: 521-542.

Russell, F. S. 1932. On the biology of Sagitta. The breeding and growth of *Sagitta elegans* Verrill in the Plymouth area, 1930-31. J. Mar. Biol. Ass. U. K. **18**: 131-145.

# ADAPTIVE ORGANIZATION OF THE GENE POOLS OF DROSOPHILA POPULATIONS

## BRUCE WALLACE AND M. VETUKHIV

The Biological Laboratory, Cold Spring Harbor, New York; Columbia University, New York

## INTRODUCTION

That genes interact during the development of an individual is an elementary fact of genetics. This interaction makes it impossible, at least in theory, for selection within Mendelian populations to modify the frequency of one gene independently of all others. Any alteration in the frequencies of alleles at one locus should lead to the modification of frequencies of alleles at numerous other loci. Superimposed upon the developmental interactions are the uncertainties of the interacting combinations themselves resulting from gene recombination and cross-fertilization. Selection cannot favor for long a given allele in a given genetic background; rather, it must act upon a different array of gene combinations in each generation. The interdependence of genes during development and the kaleidoscopic alteration of gene combinations between successive generations result in an internal coherence of gene interactions representative of local gene pools. These pools are integrated through the generation-by-generation coadaptation of segregating, interacting elements.

## LEVELS OF INTEGRATION

As a result of the nature of experimental techniques applied, three levels of integration have been demonstrated for gene pools. The simplest example is that based upon epistatic interactions between homozygous loci. This situation is exemplified by two populations essentially homozygous for the gene combinations $AABB$ and $A'A'B'B'$, respectively, whereas the gene combinations $A-B'-$ and $A'-B-$ are demonstrably inferior in some way. This is roughly the model proposed by Dobzhansky (1941) in which different species represent the populations with different integrated systems (see, too, Sturtevant, 1948). As an example one might refer to the platyfish-swordtail crosses of Gordon (1950) in which a gene causing a dark spot in one species was found to produce melanotic tumors in the interspecific hybrids. Perhaps an even more striking case involving two strains of one species has been reported by Reeve and Robertson (1953). In this instance many individuals of one strain of D. melanogaster were found to be homozygous for a gene (gene combination?) that behaved as a lethal when made homozygous by standard genetic techniques using a second, genetically-marked strain. Obviously this gene was not behaving as a lethal in the background of the original strain.

A second level of integration was described by Dobzhansky (1950) in his analysis of natural populations of D. pseudoobscura. At this level, integration involves heterozygosis for chromosomal inversions. When chromosomes with two different gene arrangements derived from the same geographical locality are used as components of artificial populations, virtually the same equilibrium frequencies are established in all instances regardless of the initial frequencies. When chromosomes of the same two arrangements are collected from two different geographical localities, one may replace the other in an artificial population or, in different populations, a variety of equilibria may be established (Dobzhansky and Pavlovsky, 1953).

The equilibria established in artificial populations result from the selective superiority of heterozygotes carrying chromosomes with different gene arrangements. This superior adaptive value of heterozygotes in certain artificial environments seems to be present from the outset when all chromosomes are derived from the same population; it is not initially present but may arise in populations containing chromosomes from different geographical localities. The integration in this instance is more complex than the simple epistatic interactions between homozygous loci described in the first example. Here, the experimental techniques emphasize the local coadaptation of specific combinations of genes characterizing the different chromosomal rearrangements; this coadaptation is revealed through the adaptive superiority of individuals heterozygous for these gene combinations. Presumably this coadaptation also involves epistatic interactions since the superiority of inversion heterozygotes can be modified by the alteration of genetic material beyond the confines of the inversion (Levine, 1955).

A third level of coadaptation has been suggested by a number of lines of evidence. This is the integration of entire gene pools through selection based on the action of genes in the heterozygous condition. In our own work this model was suggested by an analysis of irradiated, experimental populations of D. melanogaster. A large number of tests were made on a number of these populations to determine the effect of various second chromosomes on the viability of individuals carrying them (1) in the homozygous condition and (2) in random heterozygous combinations. Thirty generations after a single large X-ray exposure, one irradiated population was found to differ from its control in having a higher frequency of chromosomes with various deleterious effects (lethals, semilethals, and subvitals). These same chromosomes

Reprinted by permission of the Long Island Biological Association and the senior author from
*Cold Spring Harbor Symposium on Quantitative Biology* 20:303–309, 1955.

when carried by individuals in random heterozygous combinations resulted in higher viabilities than did those of the control population. Similarly, within two continuously irradiated populations there was a steady accumulation of chromosomes with deleterious effects on viability when homozygous; there was not, however, a corresponding, continual decline in the viability of individuals carrying random combinations of these chromosomes (Wallace and King, 1951, 1952). These results suggested that genes are found within populations because they have been retained as a result of selective properties they exhibit in heterozygous individuals. Any particular allele at any locus will be retained or eliminated by virtue of its average adaptive value when in combination with various other alleles at that or other loci present in the gene pool of the population as suggested by Wright long ago (1931).

The model of a gene pool containing numerous series of "isoalleles" as a result of selection favoring heterozygous individuals is more complex than that based on selection for homozygosis. The model promises to be a useful one, nevertheless: Selection for heterozygosity at a number of loci would automatically result in an integrated pool of co-adapted alleles (coadapted, that is, between as well as within loci), as Lerner (1954) has pointed out; indeed, Lerner has suggested that selection may demand an obligate level of heterozygosity. The variability that is revealed through gene recombination as specific interactions supports the model (Wallace et al., 1953). The plateaus frequently encountered in artificial selection programs despite the existence of genetic variability within the experimental lines is most easily explained by this model (Lerner, 1954). The contrast in magnitude of the environmental component of phenotypic variance of homozygous and heterozygous individuals offers a basis upon which selection may operate in retaining heterozygous individuals; these individuals are much less affected by environmental variations (Robertson and Reeve, 1952; Dobzhansky and Wallace, 1953; and Moos, 1955). Furthermore, the extent of genetic variability carried in a gene pool of this sort and its availability for immediate selection offer an opportunity for the rapid evolutionary changes of the type described by Mayr (1953).

Obviously, an adequate experimental verification of the integration of gene pools as outlined above will entail tests of many sorts. The experiments reported below were designed to test whether genes present in the gene pool of one local population interact in novel ways with those from other pools. Further, if these novel interactions were detected, the experiments were to indicate the roles of heterozygosity and recombination in determining these interactions. These experiments were done independently by the two authors; the similarity of purpose, technique, and results has led us to this joint presentation.

## MATERIALS AND METHODS

The basic experimental approach of the studies described below is best described by the question: What is the frequency with which larvae of different genotypes survive to adulthood in crowded cultures under conditions of rigorous competition for food? Experimental procedures differed from experiment to experiment; complete technical details are to be found elsewhere (Vetukhiv, 1953, 1954; Wallace, 1955). In brief, a given number of freshly hatched larvae were transferred to each of a number of vials containing a measured amount of culture medium; the final data consist of the number of adults hatched in these vials (with the exception of the first experiment with *D. melanogaster* in which the number of adults hatched by the eleventh day is given). For different species different numbers of larvae were placed in each vial. In the experiments performed by Vetukhiv, half of the larvae in each vial were of the genotype to be tested; the other half were control larvae homozygous for a recessive mutation. Kalmus' medium and measured quantities of fresh yeast were used in these analyses. In the studies on *D. melanogaster* measured quantities of regular *Drosophila* medium or of blackstrap molasses-agar-propionic acid medium were used. In these latter experiments mutant larvae were not used as competitors.

The genotypes of the tested flies consisted solely of combinations of genes obtained from natural populations. For each species a number of geographical strains were used (Table 1); each strain was represented by a number of lines derived originally from different fertilized females captured in the field.

Tests of three species, *D. pseudoobscura*, *D. willistoni*, and *D. paulistorum*, involved individuals obtained by crossing different lines from the same locality, hybrid individuals obtained by crossing lines from different populations, and the $F_2$ individuals obtained from each of these two crosses.

The experiments with *D. melanogaster* included many more different sorts of crosses; in some instances four different populations were involved in the same hybrid ("double-cross" hybrids). These crosses were used specifically to test the relative roles of heterozygosity and recombination in deter-

TABLE 1. THE GEOGRAPHICAL ORIGINS OF THE FLIES OF THE DIFFERENT SPECIES USED IN THESE EXPERIMENTS

| *D. melanogaster* | *D. pseudoobscura* |
|---|---|
| Experimental 1* | Mather, California |
| Experimental 3* | Piñon Flats, California |
| Massachusetts | Bryce Cañon, Utah |
| New York | Ferron Cañon, Utah |
| Virginia | Gunnison, Colorado |
| California | *D. paulistorum and D. willistoni* |
| Chile | Belem, Para, Brazil |
| Israel | Icana, Amazonas |
| | Cantareira, Sao Paulo |

*See Wallace and King (1951).

TABLE 2. SCHEMATIC LIST OF THE 61 COMBINATIONS OF
GENES FROM FOUR POPULATIONS STUDIED IN THE FIRST
EXPERIMENT

The flies used came from the experimental populations 1
and 3, Massachusetts, and New York. The number of
combinations studied and the amount of heterozygosity and
recombination for each of the generalized crosses are also
listed. Matings with $F_1$ hybrid males are indicated (*).

| Crosses | Number | Heterozygous loci | Derived chromosomes |
|---|---|---|---|
| aa × aa | 4 | 0% | 0% |
| aa × bb | 6 | 100% | 0% |
| aa × bc | 12 | 100% | 50% |
| ab × cd | 3 | 100% | 100% |
| ab × ac | 12 | 75% | 100% |
| ab × ab | 6 | 50% | 100% |
| aa × ab | 12 | 50% | 50% |
| ab* × ab | 6 | 50% | 50% |

FIGURE 1. Schematic representation of two pairs of chromosomes carried by individuals differing in proportions of "heterozygous" loci and in the degree of genetic recombination. The terms "heterozygous loci," "derived chromosomes," and "derived haploid sets" (D) are defined in the text.

mining larval survival. The absence of crossing-over in male Drosophila permitted an analysis of gene recombination in the absence of intra-chromosomal recombination. To obtain crossover chromosomes from both parents in certain crosses, it was necessary to use special "$F_3$" males obtained by two consecutive backcrosses to hybrid females; these males transmitted many crossover chromosomes identical to those transmitted by hybrid females. A schematic list of the crosses made for these studies is given in Tables 2 and 3. Figure 1 shows diagrammatically the genotypes for two chromosomes of the flies produced by the various types of crosses.

Certain terms are convenient in the discussion of the experiments with D. melanogaster. 'Heterozygous" loci are defined as those at which the two alleles have been derived from different populations; for each of the crosses listed in Tables 2 and 3 it is possible to calculate the proportion of heterozygous loci. (In every instance, however, where homologous loci are occupied by alleles from the same population these have come from two different lines of that population.) A "derived" (as opposed to a "natural") chromosome is one that carries, as a result of crossing-over in an inter-popu-

TABLE 3. SCHEMATIC LIST OF THE 150 COMBINATIONS OF
GENES FROM FIVE POPULATIONS STUDIED IN THE SECOND
EXPERIMENT

The flies used came from Chile, Israel, Virginia, California, and New York. The number of combinations studied and the amount of heterozygosity and recombination for each of the generalized crosses are also listed. Matings with $F_1$ hybrid males are indicated (*).

| Crosses | Number | Heterozygous loci | Derived chromosomes |
|---|---|---|---|
| aa × aa | 5 | 0% | 0% |
| aa × bb | 10 | 100% | 0% |
| aa × bc | 30 | 100% | 50% |
| ab × cd | 15 | 100% | 100% |
| aa × ab | 20 | 50% | 50% |
| ab* × xcc | 30 | 100% | 0% |
| ab* × xcd | 30 | 100% | 50% |
| ab* × xab | 10 | 50% | 50% |

lation $F_1$ hybrid female, segments derived from two different populations. A "derived" haploid set is one transmitted in the gamete of an inter-population $F_1$ hybrid male and, consequently, consists of chromosomes from different populations. Since crossing-over does not occur in these males, each chromosome of a "derived" haploid set is a "natural" chromosome.

The studies on larval survival showed that the different genotypes tested do indeed behave differently. To lessen the likelihood that the viability studies gave a biased and untrue picture of overall adaptive values, Vetukhiv has continued his studies by an analysis of the fecundity of females of different genotypes. Flies to be tested were allowed to develop under nearly optimal conditions. Several females of each genotype together with a number of males were kept in vials with cardboard spoons of Drosophila medium. By exchanging spoons daily and counting the eggs deposited, daily and lifetime production of ovipositing females were determined. The results of these studies are summarized in the present paper; a detailed account of these experiments will be published elsewhere.

## RESULTS

### Species other than D. melanogaster

The studies of Vetukhiv deal with four classes of genotypes for each of the three species of Drosophila. The four genotypes are (1) those characteristic of local populations (intra-$F_1$), (2) $F_1$ hybrids obtained by crossing flies of different populations (inter-$F_1$), (3) $F_2$ individuals obtained by mating intra-$F_1$'s, and (4) $F_2$ individuals obtained from inter-$F_1$'s. The three species were D. pseudoobscura, D. willistoni, and D. paulistorum. The results of these studies are given in Table 4.

TABLE 4. PER CENT SURVIVAL OF DROSOPHILA LARVAE UNDER SEVERE CONDITIONS

Genotypes tested: Intra-population $F_1$ and $F_2$ obtained by crossing between strains of the same population; inter-population $F_1$ and $F_2$ obtained by crossing between strains of different populations.

| | $F_1$ | $F_2$ |
|---|---|---|
| D. pseudoobscura | | |
| Intra | 59.6 | 59.6 |
| Inter | 70.4 | 49.2 |
| D. willistoni | | |
| Intra | 59.9 | 57.2 |
| Inter | 68.3 | 51.5 |
| D. paulistorum | | |
| Intra | 54.7 | 53.1 |
| Inter | 58.0 | 51.3 |

Although some crosses between strains appear not to follow the general pattern, it is apparent from the data in Table 4 that larvae of different genotypes differ in their ability to survive under the conditions of the experiment. On the average, inter-population $F_1$ hybrid larvae survived better than did larvae obtained by crossing different lines from the same geographical locality. This higher viability of $F_1$ hybrid larvae was not retained by their offspring; on the contrary, the average survival of these inter-$F_2$ individuals was consistently lower than that of larvae formed by crossing lines derived from within the same locality. The breakdown of viability in the $F_2$ generation of inter-population hybrids indicates that genes found within local populations are retained by virtue of their mutual, selectively favorable interactions. This agrees with the results expected on the coadaptation hypothesis. Similarly, the lack of any comparable breakdown in the $F_2$ generation of the intra-population line-hybrids supports the hypothesis. On the other hand, the higher viability of $F_1$ inter-population hybrid larvae relative to that observed for larvae obtained by crossing between lines of the same population is difficult to explain. By definition, coadaptation can hardly be the explanation for this higher viability since there can be no coadaptation between genes of isolated populations.

There remains the possibility that the observed increase in survival of inter-population hybrid larvae is an example of Dobzhansky's "luxuriance" (1950), a spurious heterosis. Heterosis that is adaptively meaningful must affect many factors of reproductive importance or, at the very least, increase the combined effect of these factors. A test was made, therefore, of the fecundity of D. pseudoobscura females with genotypes comparable to those of the larvae discussed above; the results of this study are given in Table 5.

The data in Table 5 parallel precisely those of Table 4. Females obtained by crossing different lines from the same locality lay fewer eggs per day and fewer eggs per lifetime than do hybrid females obtained by crossing between lines of different

TABLE 5. EFFECT OF GENOTYPE ON EGG PRODUCTION IN D. pseudoobscura

Intra- and inter-population $F_1$ and $F_2$ obtained as in Table 4.

| | Eggs/day/female | Eggs/life/female |
|---|---|---|
| Intra $F_1$ | 15.2 | 642.1 |
| Inter $F_1$ | 19.0 | 810.5 |
| Intra $F_2$ | 16.5 | 679.2 |
| Inter $F_2$ | 15.6 | 553.3 |

populations. On the other hand, the fecundity of intra-$F_2$ females exceeds that of the inter-$F_2$ females. As in the case of larval viability, there is no apparent change from intra-$F_1$ to intra-$F_2$. The agreement between the results of these two types of analyses re-inforces the conclusion that genes within local gene pools are coadapted. At the same time, it indicates that the heterosis of inter-population $F_1$ hybrids is not spurious.

### Studies with D. melanogaster

The results of the experiments with D. melanogaster permit some further insight into the phenomenon of heterosis. In the experiments with D. pseudoobscura and other species Vetukhiv found that the inter-population $F_1$ hybrid larvae possessed the highest survival rate. Was this simply an indication that these larvae had the highest proportion of heterozygous loci and, hence, the least expression of deleterious mutations? By using a number of different populations in one experiment, it was

TABLE 6. MEAN NUMBER OF FLIES PRESENT AT 11TH DAY IN VIALS OF EXPERIMENT I GROUPED ON THE BASIS OF THE PROPORTION OF "HETEROZYGOUS" LOCI AND DERIVED CHROMOSOMES

These figures indicate the number of adults hatching from 200 larvae when 40 larvae were placed in each of 5 vials. For comparative purposes the material is presented in the same form as Figures 1 and 2.

| derived chromosomes | | "Heterozygous" loci | | | |
|---|---|---|---|---|---|
| | | 100% | 75% | 50% | 0% |
| 0% | N | 154.38 ±2.34 | | | 148.13 ±2.91 |
| | D | not tested | | | |
| 50% | N | 140.06 ±2.20 | | 142.36 ±2.17 | |
| | D | not tested | | 142.25 ±3.10 | |
| 100% | N | 140.58 ±3.96 | 135.77 ±2.00 | 133.42 ±3.53 | |
| | D | | | | |

possible to obtain larvae of a number of genotypes in which the proportions of heterozygous loci equalled that of the inter-population $F_1$ hybrids. These additional genotypes supply the answer to our question.

The results of two experiments with *D. melanogaster* are summarized in Tables 6 and 7. In these tables the tested larvae have been grouped according to proportions of heterozygous loci and of recombinant chromosomes or derived haploid sets. The significance of these data is shown diagrammatically in Figures 2 and 3 where arrows have been drawn between classes of larvae whose differences in survival exceed those expected by chance (5% level); the arrows point to the classes with the fewer survivors.

These data bring out two important facts. First, inter-population $F_1$ hybrids have higher average viabilities than do flies obtained by crossing different lines of the same population. This is certainly true in the second experiment (Table 7, Fig. 3) and is most likely true in the first as well (Table 6) although the observed difference in numbers of survivors was not significant ($p = .07$). Second, this is the only type of larvae whose average viability is consistently higher than that of individuals from local populations. Among the various classes of larvae which are 100 per cent heterozygous are found the highest and the lowest viabilities of the experiments. Heterozygosity alone does not result in an increase in viability.

TABLE 7. MEAN NUMBER OF FLIES HATCHING IN VIALS OF EXPERIMENT II GROUPED ON THE BASIS OF THE PROPORTION OF 'HETEROZYGOUS" LOCI AND DERIVED CHROMOSOMES

These numbers indicate the number of adults surviving from 300 larvae when 25 larvae were placed in each of 12 vials. For comparative purposes the material is presented in the same form as Figures 1 and 3.

"Heterozygous" loci

| derived chromosomes | | | 100% | 75% | 50% | 0% |
|---|---|---|---|---|---|---|
| 0% | N | | 171.80 ±1.94 | | | 156.00 2.95 |
| | D | | 159.13 ±1.13 | | | |
| 50% | N | | 165.30 ±1.17 | | 161.00 1.52 | |
| | D | | 148.43 ±1.05 | | 159.00 1.90 | |
| 100% | N | | 146.73 ±1.61 | not tested | not tested | |
| | D | | | | | |

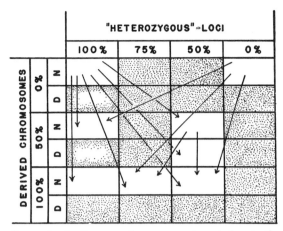

FIGURE 2. A diagrammatic representation of the significance of the data given in Table 6. Arrows connect classes of larvae which produced significantly different average numbers of adults by the 11th day ($p < .05$); each arrow points toward the class with the lower number.

The results of these experiments indicate that local populations of *D. melanogaster*, despite the continual, world-wide transport of individuals of this species by man, undergo genetic differentiation. This differentiation consists of building up coadapted and integrated gene combinations that can be disrupted by inter-population gene recombination and chromosomal segregation. In spite of this local coadaptation, inter-population $F_1$ hybrids in our studies possessed the highest average viabilities. This heterosis cannot be ascribed to coadaptation nor can it result from heterozygosity alone. This heterosis must be ascribed to heterozygosity for different but integrated gene systems.

To describe the relationship between two inte-

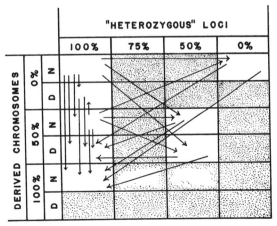

FIGURE 3. A diagrammatic representation of the significance of the data in Table 7. Arrows connect classes of larvae producing significantly different average numbers of surviving adults ($p < .05$); each arrow points toward the class with the lower number.

grated systems in an inter-population $F_1$ hybrid, it is probably best to use Mather's term (1943) "relational balance." These systems are not coadapted for two reasons: (1) Coadaptation is a phenomenon unique to local populations; (2) coadaptation results from "natural" selection acting in a succession of generations and the consistent production of individuals with well-adapted phenotypes must be one of its attributes. By definition, inter-population hybrids are not of local populations. Furthermore, the $F_2$ and later (Brncic, 1954) generations arising from inter-population hybrids exhibit a striking loss of viability.

The successful utilization of relational balance within a coadapted or integrated system requires that it be restricted to manageable proportions; this is probably the role of inversions in *Drosophila* populations. (This does not imply that inversions are the only method by which this utilization might be achieved.) Simply by limiting the amount of chromosomal material involved and by preventing recombination within certain segments of the chromosomes, these inversions enable the integrated combinations to persist from generation to generation within a cross-fertilizing species. For the chromosomal segments included within an inversion—without neglecting the fact that these must act in harmony with the rest of the genotype—a population with two different gene arrangements actually represents the intimate co-existence of two isolated populations and their $F_1$ hybrids. This is the picture suggested, too, by speculations on the role of inversions based on their geographical distributions (Wallace, 1953, 1954; see, however, Levitan, Carson, and Stalker, 1954).

### DISCUSSION

These experiments and the related ones by Brncic (1954) make the concept of a single wild-type or "normal" genotype of a species untenable. The establishment of harmoniously integrated genetic systems is not characteristic of species but of local populations. These systems come about through the selective advantage possessed by certain gene combinations, through the disruption of these favored combinations each generation by recombination, and through re-selection of new combinations in the succeeding generation. This is a never-ending process. Important in the determination of combinations to be favored are the interactions occurring between genes at the same or different loci; these interactions are important, however, only where they occur—within local populations. Within these populations (recalling the spatial ramifications of these populations as a result of the migration of individuals from one to the other) the gene pool established by selection is one that maximizes the frequency with which these interactions are utilized by the individuals of each generation.

That coadaptation can be a rapid process has

been indicated in a number of studies. For example, heterozygotes carrying "deleterious" chromosomes from an irradiated population possessed higher average viabilities than did heterozygous individuals carrying "better" chromosomes from a non-irradiated population (Wallace and King, 1951); this situation existed by the thirtieth generation after irradiation, the time of the earliest tests. Dobzhansky and his co-workers (Dobzhansky and Pavlovsky, 1953; Levene, Pavlovsky and Dobzhansky, 1954) have reported sharp changes in selective forces observed in experimental populations containing chromosomes from different geographical localities. King (this volume) has found a situation in studies of DDT resistance that parallels the viability effects reported above; coadaptation in this case must have arisen within a dozen or so generations. Wallace *et al.* (1953) showed that recombination between chromosomes derived from two populations isolated from one another for 60 generations gave results distinguishable from those obtained by recombination between chromosomes derived from the same population.

The model of an integrated gene pool presented in the second section of this paper was based not only upon specific, intra-population gene interactions but also upon selection of heterozygotes. The experiments described above are sufficient to establish the existence of special interactions; they do not, however, deal with intra-population heterozygosis. Selection for heterozygotes is indicated by the rapidity with which coadaptation arises within isolated populations. The concluding paragraphs will consider briefly this aspect of the model.

Earlier in this Symposium, Dobzhansky described what he called the "Classical" and "Balance" Hypotheses of population structure. These two models are identical to those which Wallace and his co-workers (Wallace *et al.*, 1953) tried to distinguish between experimentally by means of an analysis of the variation which arose as a result of gene recombination. Since these two models are not mutually exclusive, the results were not unambiguous. They do indicate, however, that if the Balance Hypothesis is not correct, there are specific and unexpected gene interactions that make it seem as if it were. Mather (1954) has stressed, too, the impossibility of distinguishing the two models in the presence of these interactions.

Finally, then, we might mention a further study on these interactions. Dobzhansky (this volume), in discussing the homeostatic properties of heterozygous individuals, assured us that the virtual absence of the environmental component of variance in no way implied that all heterozygous individuals are identical (see Wallace and Madden, 1953; Dobzhansky and Spassky, 1953; and Dobzhansky, Spassky and Pavlovsky, 1955). Real differences do exist between the viabilities of individuals heterozygous for different chromosomal combinations. Wallace and King (1952) compared the differences in viability of individuals heterozygous for combinations of second chromosomes when one chromosome was common to both pairs with the differences between individuals heterozygous for independent pairs of second chromosomes. (These comparisons consist of the mean successive differences of |a/b— b/c| and of |a/b—c/d|.) No significant difference was found between the two mean successive differences in a test of about 300 observations in each series. These studies have been extended considerably and the m. s. d. has been converted into variance (Wallace, unpub.). It now appears that the variance observed between combinations possessing a common chromosome is 80 per cent (one experimental population) to 90 per cent (four populations) as large as the variance between independent combinations. Not only are there real differences between different heterozygous individuals but the vast majority of these differences are to be ascribed to the individual combinations rather than to either of two chromosomes of the combinations. The magnitude of this type of interaction, the rapidity with which gene pools become integrated, the unexpected variations revealed by gene recombination, and the superior homeostatic properties of heterozygous individuals lead us to believe that not only are the gene pools of local populations genetically integrated but also that the selective advantage of heterozygous individuals is an essential part of this adaptive organization.

## SUMMARY

Various experimental techniques have revealed three levels of integration within the gene pools of local populations: (1) integration based upon epistatic interactions between homozygous loci, (2) coadaptation of different gene arrangements within local populations involving both heterosis and epistasis, and (3) the integration of entire gene pools through selection for heterozygosity.

Experiments with four species of *Drosophila* in which the viability or fecundity of various types of inter-population hybrids was studied indicates that the local gene pools are indeed integrated. These studies have no direct bearing on the problem of intra-population heterozygosity but further evidence is listed which indicates that selection of heterozygous individuals forms an integral part of this adaptive organization.

## REFERENCES

BRNCIC, D., 1954, Heterosis and the integration of the genotype in geographical populations of *Drosophila pseudoobscura*. Genetics 39: 77-88.
DOBZHANSKY, TH., 1941, Genetics and the Origin of Species. 1st Edition. Columbia Univ. Press, New York.
1950, Genetics of Natural Populations. XIX. Origin of heterosis through natural selection in populations of *Drosophila pseudoobscura*. Genetics 35: 288-302.
DOBZHANSKY, TH., and PAVLOVSKY, O., 1953, Indeterminate outcome of certain experiments on *Drosophila* populations. Evolution 7: 198-210.

DOBZHANSKY, TH., and SPASSKY, B., 1953, Genetics of natural populations. XXI. Concealed variability in two sympatric species of *Drosophila*. Genetics 38: 471-484.
DOBZHANSKY, TH., PAVLOVSKY, O., SPASSKY, B., and SPASSKY, N., 1955, Genetics of natural populations. XXIII. Biological role of deleterious recessives in populations of *Drosophila pseudoobscura*. Genetics (in press).
DOBZHANSKY, TH., and WALLACE, B., 1953, The genetics of homeostasis in *Drosophila*. Proc. Nat. Acad. Sci. Wash. 39: 162-171.
GORDON, MYRON, 1950, Heredity of pigmented tumours in fish. Endeavour 9: 26-34.
LERNER, I. MICHAEL, 1954, Genetic Homeostasis. Oliver and Boyd, Edinburgh. 134 pp.
LEVENE, H., PAVLOVSKY, O., and DOBZHANSKY, TH., 1954, Interaction of adaptive values in polymorphic experimental populations of *Drosophila pseudoobscura*. Evolution 8: 335-349.
LEVINE, LOUIS, 1955, Genotypic background and heterosis in *Drosophila pseudoobscura*. (in ms.)
LEVITAN, M., CARSON, H. L., and STALKER, H. D., 1954, Triads of overlapping inversions in *Drosophila robusta*. Amer. Nat. 88: 113-114.
MATHER, K., 1943, Polygenic inheritance and natural selection. Biol. Rev. 18: 32-64.
1954, The genetical units of continuous variation. Proc. 9th Intern. Cong. Genetics. Part I. Caryologia 6 (suppl.).
MAYR, E., 1953, Change of genetic environment and evolution. In: Evolution as a Process, ed. by J. Huxley. Allen and Unwin, London.
MOOS, J., 1955, Comparative physiology of some chromosomal types in *Drosophila pseudoobscura* (in ms.).
REEVE, E. C. R., and ROBERTSON, F. W., 1953, Studies in quantitative inheritance. 11. Analysis of a strain of *Drosophila melanogaster* selected for long wings. J. Genet. 51: 276-316.
ROBERTSON, F. W., and REEVE, E. C. R., 1952, Heterozygosity, environmental variation, and heterosis. Nature, Lond. 170: 286.
STURTEVANT, A. H., 1948, Evolution and function of genes. Amer. Sci. 36: 225-236.
VETUKHIV, M., 1953, Viability of hybrids between local populations of *Drosophila pseudoobscura*. Proc. Nat. Acad. Sci. Wash. 39: 30-34.
1954, Integration of the genotype in local populations of three species of *Drosophila*. Evolution 8: 241-251.
WALLACE, B., 1953, On coadaptation in *Drosophila*. Amer. Nat. 87: 343-358.
1954, Coadaptation and the gene arrangements of *Drosophila pseudoobscura*. IUBS Symp. on Gen. of Pop. Struct. IUBS Series B. Vol. 15: 67-94.
1955, Inter-population hybrids in *Drosophila melanogaster*. Evolution (in press).
WALLACE, B., and KING, J. C., 1951, Genetic changes in populations under irradiation. Amer. Nat. 85: 209-222.
1952, A genetic analysis of the adaptive values of populations. Proc. Nat. Acad. Sci. Wash. 38: 706-715.
WALLACE, B., KING, J. C., MADDEN, C. V., KAUFMANN, B. T., and McGUNNIGLE, E. C., 1953, An analysis of variability arising through recombination. Genetics 38: 272-307.
WALLACE, B., and MADDEN, C. V., 1953, The frequencies of sub- and supervitals in experimental populations of *Drosophila melanogaster*. Genetics 38: 456-470.
WRIGHT, S., 1931, Evolution in Mendelian populations. Genetics 16: 97-159.

## DISCUSSION

DEMPSTER: This comment refers to a comparison of flies having second chromosomal combinations indicated diagrammatically as a/b, b/c, c/d, etc. Let us assume that other chromosomes were equally similar or different in the various kinds of comparisons and that variance due to non-genetic sources has been removed in the analysis. In this case, individuals having one chromosome in common can be thought of as half-sibs whose common parent is completely homozygous. It should be clearly understood that this refers only to two-fifths of the genome so that epistatic variance may be decreased relative to additive variance, although there might also be a slight compensatory effect due to epistatic interactions between the tested second chromosomes and the constant marked ones which could appear as additive variance.

According to Dr. Clark Cockerham's model, and with the reservations noted above, the correlation between genotypic values of individuals having one chromosome in common would be one-half if all variance were of the simple additive type, one-quarter if it were all of the two locus additive by additive type, one-eighth if it were all of the three locus additive by additive by additive type, and so on for higher order interactions. However, the correlation would be zero if all the variance were of the dominance type or if it were all of any epistatic type in which dominance is involved. Since the standard deviation of those differences due to second chromosomes only between individuals having one second chromosome in common is estimated by Dr. Wallace as about 95 per cent of that of individuals without any second chromosome in common, the ratio of the corresponding variances would be about 90 per cent. Therefore, the genetic correlation between individuals with one second chromosome in common is about .10. It seems clearly impossible to explain the smallness of this value on any reasonable additive hypothesis and it therefore appears that dominance variance or epistatic effects involving dominance variance at one or more of the interacting loci on the second chromosome must be responsible. At the dominant loci, dominance might be either complete, or nearly complete, or over-dominance could be responsible.

It is exceedingly difficult to eliminate sources of bias in an experiment of this kind where the interpretation depends on relatively small differences between two variances. The measurements of chromosomal combinations were made by comparing them with heterozygotes appearing in the same cultures. Thus the measured differences between genotypes a/b and c/d might be represented very approximately by the following expression where the genotypic symbols are replaced by the relative proportions of survivors of individuals of the corresponding constitutions:

$$\left\{ a/b - \tfrac{1}{2} \left[ CyL/a + CyL/b \right] \right\} -$$
$$\left\{ c/d - \tfrac{1}{2} \left[ CyL/c + CyL/d \right] \right\}$$

The expected value of this difference is indicated symbolically as follows where letters refer to the average contributions of chromosomes to the measurements and $i$ refers to the interaction contributions involving chromosomes designated by subscripts:

$$\left\{ \tfrac{1}{2} (a + b - c - d) + i_{ab} - i_{cd} \right\} -$$
$$\tfrac{1}{2} \left\{ i_{Cya} + i_{Cyb} - i_{Cyc} - i_{Cyd} \right\}$$

By comparison the expected value where one chromosome is in common would be of the following form:

$$\left\{ \tfrac{1}{2} (a - c) + i_{ab} - i_{cd} \right\} - \tfrac{1}{2} \left\{ \quad \right\} i_{Cya} - i_{Cyc}$$

The model of Cockerham refers to the quantities in the first brackets in each expression, whereas the quantities in the second bracket of each is extraneous. These second bracket terms would be expected to make independent contributions to the variance of the difference. This contribution is twice as great where no chromosome is common as in the case where one chromosome is common. It would seem, therefore, that this might account in part for the observed correlation. The new experiments proposed by Dr. Wallace in which comparisons of various chromosomal combinations will be made with individuals of the genotype CyL/Pm should provide some very welcome information on this point. There might be some bias in the opposite direction were insufficient allowance made for all sources of variation, genetic as well as non-genetic, not due to second chromosomes.

I think a more direct test of the dominance explanation might be made were two pairs of chromosomes controlled so that differences of the following types, among others, might be compared, where the first pairs of letters in brackets refer to second chromosomes and the second pairs to third chromosomes.

[a/b;c/d] — [a/e;c/f]
with
[a/b;c/d] — [a/b;g/b]
and
[a/b;c/d] — [i/j;c/d]

# INTERDEME SELECTION CONTROLLING A POLYMORPHISM IN THE HOUSE MOUSE*†

R. C. LEWONTIN

Department of Biology, University of Rochester, Rochester, New York

One of the most interesting natural polymorphisms, both from the genetic and evolutionary standpoint, is that found at the T (Brachy, short tail) locus in mice. Mutations at this locus are nearly ubiquitous in natural populations and the frequencies of these mutant alleles are so high as to constitute a real polymorphism.

The main features of this polymorphism have been reviewed by Lewontin and Dunn (1960). Briefly, of the sixteen alleles so far studied, thirteen ($t^{w1, 3, 4, 5, 6, 10, 11, 12, 13, 14, 15, 16, 17}$) are unconditional prenatal lethals. It is these lethal alleles whose population dynamics are investigated in the paper of Lewontin and Dunn. The three remaining alleles ($t^{w2, 7, 8}$) have no apparent viability effect, are completely male sterile and it is these three which will be investigated in the present paper.

Despite the strong selection against these alleles as homozygotes because of their lethality or sterility, they are maintained in populations by an aberrant ratio of + and $t$ gametes in the effective sperm pool of heterozygous males. Between 85 and 99 per cent of the functional sperm of $+/t^w$ males carry the $t^w$ allele, the exact degree of transmission distortion depending upon the $t^w$ allele involved. Ratios of $t$ and + in ova are, on the other hand, normal. A complete table of transmission ratios for the alleles so far studied is contained in Lewontin and Dunn.

There is, finally, a suggestion of heterosis in males (Dunn, Beasley and Tinker, 1958) but this is only a suggestion, based as it is on a small sample and involving only one allele, $t^{w11}$.

Leaving aside the moot point of heterosis, the polymorphism for $t^w$ alleles is maintained by the balance between loss of alleles in homozygotes and replacement of these alleles by the aberrant segregation ratio in heterozygous males. As Lewontin and Dunn have shown, the observed frequencies of $t^w$ lethal alleles in natural populations do not correspond closely to those predicted by the simple algebra of this balance. The observed frequencies of these lethal alleles are uniformly lower than the predicted equilibrium

*This paper is dedicated to Professor L. C. Dunn in recognition of his long and distinguished contribution to the science of genetics.
†This investigation was performed under Atomic Energy Commission Contract AT(30-)2620.

Reprinted by permission of The University of Chicago Press and the author from *The American Naturalist* 96:65–78, 1962.

values and we proposed in our 1960 paper that this discrepancy is due to the effect of genetic drift operating in small family groups.

Recently, interest has turned from the lethal $t^w$ alleles to those causing male sterility. Despite a superficial resemblance, the population dynamics of these sterile alleles has certain interesting differences from the case of the lethal alleles, and it is these differences that I wish to explore in this paper. In particular, the sterile $t^w$ alleles provide an example of the importance of interdeme selection in controlling the genetic structure of a species.

## THE PROBLEM

In a recent paper Dunn and Levene (1961) discuss what is known about one particular sterile allele, $t^{w2}$. This allele is present in an enclosed population of mice maintained by Dr. Howard Schneider at the Rockefeller Institute for Medical Research. The population originated from a sample of wild mice captured in New York and Philadelphia in 1944. It was maintained at a size of 75-125 individuals during 1944-50, and about 50-60 from 1951 to 1959, but was reduced in size during each summer, once possibly to an effective size of only four. Thus, there is a considerable genetic bottle-neck every year, and moreover, it is not at all certain that the large winter breeding population is indeed one panmictic unit. There may be some family structure even though the physical conditions are not conducive to the formation of isolates.

Small samples from this population taken in January and June, 1952, showed the presence of a lethal $t$ allele, $t^{w1}$ and a sterile allele $t^{w2}$. Larger samples taken in June, 1955, and June, 1959, failed to reveal the lethal allele and it is assumed that this has been lost. The frequency of the allele $t^{w2}$ in the population, as estimated from the two large samples of 1955 and 1959, is .37 and is based on over 200 mice tested. There is no significant heterogeneity between the two samples, so it is probable that this is an accurate estimate of equilibrium frequency.

Finally, the transmission ratio of $t^{w8}$ : + from $t^{w2}/+$ males has been estimated from all four samples. In the 1952 samples this ratio was 95 per cent $t^{w2}$ to 5 per cent +, but the subsequent large samples gave a ratio of 85 per cent $t^{w2}$ to 15 per cent +. The difference between these is highly significant and no obvious reason for the difference can be given. It is the lower figure of .85 for the transmission advantage of $t^{w2}$ that is assumed for calculation in this paper.

Dunn and Levene show that the gene frequency of a sterile $t$ allele at equilibrium should be simply $\hat{q} = 2m - 1$ where $m$ is the transmission ratio of the $t^w$ allele in heterozygous males. Applying this formula to $t^{w2}$, the prediction is that $\hat{q} = .70$ while in fact the observed $\hat{q}$ is .37, and has been for some time. What is the source of this discrepancy? It may be that selection against homozygotes in the form of prenatal death would help to account for the difference. No such lethality has been observed, but it has not been carefully looked for. Another possibility is that the transmission ratio is lower under population conditions than under test mating conditions, and again it must be said that no check can be easily made of this hypothesis.

Lewontin and Dunn, in their investigation of the effect of small population size on the frequency of lethal $t^w$ alleles, found that inbreeding resulted in a lowering of the frequency of these alleles over the whole population from what was predicted by the deterministic equation (Bruck, 1957). Whether or not such inbreeding would account for the situation in the $t^{w2}$ population, as opposed to the other alternatives suggested above, it seemed interesting to investigate the effects of such small population size on sterile $t$ alleles.

### THE MONTE CARLO METHOD

The method employed here, as for the earlier investigation of the lethal $t$ alleles, is that of Monte Carlo simulation of populations. The method is discussed in some detail by Lewontin and Dunn. In brief a digital computer (IBM 650) was programed to simulate the processes of meiosis, random union of sperm and egg, and selection in a finite population. At the beginning of a run the following information is supplied to the computer:

$N\male$ : number of adult males maintained.
$N\female$ : number of adult females maintained.
m    : proportion of $t$ gametes from a heterozygous male.

In addition, the fact that $t^w/t^w$ males transmit no gametes is also supplied to the computer. No other selective forces were assumed to be operating. The program is set in operation and generation after generation computed until one of four conditions occurs:

(1) The population is all homozygous +/+.
(2) The population is all homozygous $t/t$.
(3) All *males* are homozygous $t/t$, if this occurs before condition 2.
(4) Some preset number of generations has elapsed (usually 100).

Each generation the program prints out the generation number, the number of adult male and female parents of each genotype, the gene frequencies among adults and the gene frequencies in ova and sperm.

Because ova and sperm are chosen each generation by a random process, no two runs of the machine give an identical result even if all the initial parameters are identical. Thus, making 200 runs is equivalent to setting up 200 independent populations all with the same values of population size and segregation ratio. These replicated populations then produce an empirical distribution of gene frequencies analogous to the results of replicated experiments.

Two sets of runs were made in the present study. The first, designated as small populations, maintained two males and six females with an initial

68                    THE AMERICAN NATURALIST

composition of one +/$t$ male, one +/+ male, four +/+ females and two +/+
females. This family structure of two males and six females was chosen
to be comparable with the studies of Lewontin and Dunn on lethal alleles.
In all, 221 replicated runs of small populations were made.

The *large populations* maintained 12 males and 12 females started
initially with six +/+ males, six +/$t$ males, six +/+ females and six +/$t$
females. This population structure was chosen as a possible one for a
bottleneck population. Only 59 replicated runs were made of these populations.

The previous studies with lethal alleles showed that the results are
insensitive to the initial composition of the population over a wide range
so that no runs were made varying the initial composition.

Throughout, the value of m = .85 was preset and no other selective
forces were imposed.

### RESULTS OF THE MONTE CARLO TRIALS

#### 1. *Small population*

*The Stable Distribution of Gene Frequencies.* Even though all runs are
started with the same population composition in the first generation, no two
runs will be identical in subsequent generations because of the random
processes involved. This is illustrated in figure 1. The abscissa in each
histogram is the frequency, $q$, of the $t$ allele in the population. These
frequencies are multiples of 1/16 since with two males and eight females
there are only 16 genes at this locus in the population. On the ordinate
of each histogram is the proportion of populations (runs) showing a particular gene frequency. *Only unfixed populations are shown*, that is, populations in which the $t$ and + alleles are still segregating. The fixed population will be dealt with below.

In the first generation, of course, all the runs have the same gene frequency since the initial composition of the population was the same for all.
Immediately in the second generation, however, a frequency distribution is
formed and this continues to flatten out resulting in a more or less stable
form by the fifth generation. There are rather wild fluctuations in the histograms as generations go on, because the total number of unfixed populations
gets smaller and smaller. By the ninth generation, the last shown in the
figure, there are only 59 out of the original 221 populations still segregating
(see below). The appearance of such a *stable distribution* of unfixed
classes is in accord with the prediction of Wright (1937).

To get a clearer idea of this stable distribution, the distributions of individual generations after the fifth have been lumped to give an average
stable distribution of unfixed classes shown in figure 2(a). The total
histogram in figure 2(a) is the average stable distribution when all unfixed
classes are considered. The shaded portion of the histogram results from
removing from the distribution those populations in which all males are
homozygous $t/t$. Such populations disappear from the species in the next
generation since all males are sterile. Obviously this correction affects

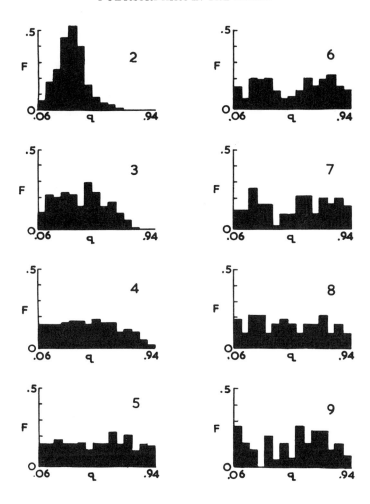

FIGURE 1. Frequency distributions of gene frequencies in successive generations. The ordinate shows the proportion of all populations (runs) having a given
gene frequency. The abscissa shows the values of q, the frequency of the $t$ allele.
Only unfixed classes are shown. Data from 221 "small populations."

only those classes in which the frequency of the $t$ allele is high. The
appropriate statistics for the corrected and uncorrected distributions are:

$$uncorrected: \quad \bar{q} = .523 \qquad s_{q_2}^2 = .0730$$
$$corrected: \quad \bar{q} = .461 \qquad s_q = .0630$$

There is a distinct suggestion of bimodality in figure 2(a). This is
brought out more clearly in figure 2(b) in which adjacent gene frequency
classes have been grouped. Because of the odd number of classes, the
frequency 15/16 is not grouped and the height of this class in the histogram has been doubled to make it comparable with other classes. Again
the appearance of bimodality is confirmed in both the corrected and un-

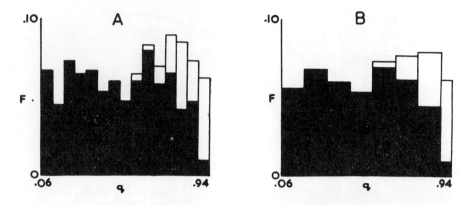

FIGURE 2. Stable distribution of gene frequency for unfixed classes in "small populations." Ordinate is relative frequency of a given class, abscissa is in gene frequency, q, of *t* allele. Shaded portion is distribution corrected for populations in which males are all homozygous *t* but females are not. 2A is raw frequency distribution; 2B is grouped by averaging pairs of adjacent classes except the last.

corrected distributions. One mode appears at q = .1875 − .2500 and one at q = .6875 − .7500. This bimodality is probably real, based as it is on 550 observations.

*Rates of Fixation.* As was pointed out earlier, runs are terminated when one of three genetic conditions occurs: complete homozygosity for + alleles, complete homozygosity for *t* alleles or complete *male* homozygosity for *t* alleles with females still segregating. For the small populations one of these three conditions had occurred for every population by the end of generation 24. Figure 3 is a plot of the cumulative fixation rates for these runs. On the abscissa are the generation numbers and on the ordinate, the proportion of the original 221 populations which has been fixed by a given generation. The solid (uppermost) curve is the fixation rate from all causes combined. As the curve shows, no population segregating for *t* was left by the end of the 24th generation. By generation six, half of all the populations had become fixed from one cause or another.

The three lower curves are a breakdown of the sources of fixation making up the total. The broken line (second highest curve) is the cumulative fixation due to male homozygosity for *t* alleles. Irrespective of whether females are still segregating for + and *t*, if males are all homozygous the population has reached fixation by *extinction*, since all males are sterile. As the curve shows, slightly in excess of 70 per cent of the original populations become extinct from this cause. This population extinction also obviously results in extinction of the *t* alleles carried by them. Although it makes no difference to the outcome of the process, there are usually two sorts of populations represented by this broken line. In some, males have become homozygous but females are still segregating, while in others, males and females have become simultaneously homozygous. In fact this latter case is rare compared with the former, and this is shown in the lowest

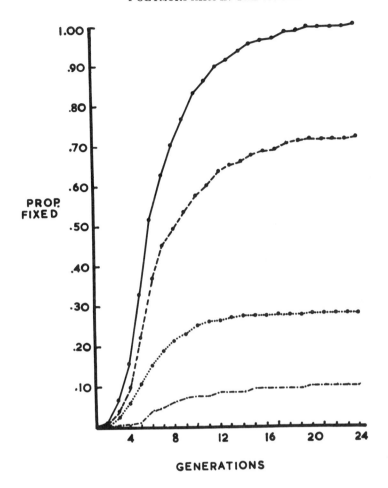

FIGURE 3. Proportions of "small populations" fixed in successive generations. Solid line: total of all types of fixation; broken line: all males *t/t, including* cases of females all *t/t*; dotted line: all individuals +/+; mixed line: all males *and* females *t/t*.

curve of figure 3 (mixed dots and dashes). Only ten per cent of all populations become simultaneously fixed for *t* in males and females, and this is to be expected since there are three times as many females as males in the population. It should be noted that the reverse case, in which females are all homozygous but males still segregate, does not result in extinction since *t/t* females are fully fertile, as far as is known.

Finally fixation at the other end of the scale may occur. The dotted line of figure 3 shows that eventually about 30 per cent of the populations become fixed at +/+.

In summary, for small populations, all *t* alleles are lost by generation 24. About 30 per cent of this loss is due to random fixation of + alleles, the remaining 70 per cent being due to random fixation of *t* alleles in males with the resultant extinction of the population.

## 2. *Large populations*

"Large populations" of 12 males and 12 females were replicated only 59 times, but these populations persisted for many more generations so that the total information on the stable distribution of gene frequencies is in fact greater than for small populations. Figures 4(a) and 4(b) are ungrouped and grouped stable frequency distributions of unfixed populations. These are based upon the distribution after generation ten, in order to avoid the effect of the initially imposed gene frequency.

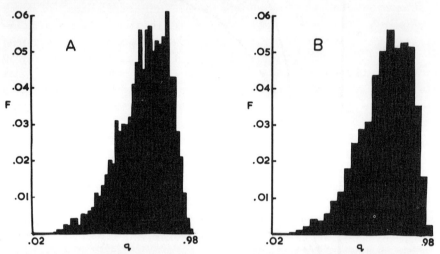

FIGURE 4. Stable gene frequency distribution of unfixed classes for "large populations." 4A: raw frequency distribution; 4B: grouped by averaging pairs of adjacent classes except the first.

Because of the relatively slow rate of fixation in these populations (see below) and the large number of observations (3871) represented in the stable frequency distribution, only a trivial difference in the distribution results from correcting it for populations in which males but not females, are fixed at $t/t$. Thus, only the uncorrected distribution is shown. The appropriate statistics for this distribution are:

$$\bar{q} = .6895$$
$$s_q^2 = .0231$$

The comparisons with the "small populations" are clear. The mean for the "large populations" is quite close to the deterministic prediction of $q = .70$ while the small population mean of .523 (uncorrected) is far too small. The large population distribution is much more peaked around its mean as evidenced by its lower variance (.0231 as compared to .0730) and this effect is also apparent from a simple comparison of the shapes of the distributions. A population size of 12 males and 12 females is, as expected, rather more like the deterministic model than smaller populations. Nevertheless, even with 12 males and 12 females there is an obvious

effect of genetic drift.   The probability is approximately .13 that such a
population will have a gene frequency of .50 or less.

The other interesting feature of the "large population" distribution is
the absence of any frequency less than $7/48 = .1458$.   In theory, of course,
a population will occasionally have such a low frequency and even become
fixed for the + allele, but in our sample of 3871 population generations this
has never occurred.

FIXATION RATES

The cumulative total fixation rate for the "large populations" is shown
in figure 5.   The curve is rather irregular and shows a curious plateau between generation 30 and 60.   There is no reason in theory for such a plateau
and this may be discounted as an effect of sampling error since only 59
populations have been run for the large size.   It is curious, however, that
in the study of lethal alleles made by Lewontin and Dunn, sample sizes
were usually this small or smaller, but no such erratic fixation curves
were observed.

As is to be expected, the rate of fixation is lower for these "large populations" than for the small ones, so that after 100 generations 48 per cent
of the populations are still segregating for + and $t$ alleles.   The most
striking difference lies in the fact that *all fixation in "large populations"
is of the male $t/t$ type.*   As intimated in the previous section, drift toward
fixation of + alleles is so small that it has not been observed.   The obvious
conclusion from this observation is that extinction is the inevitable result
of the presence of a $t$ allele in a population of our "large" size.

COMPARISON OF LETHAL AND STERILE $t$ ALLELES

There are striking differences between the population dynamics of lethal
and sterile $t$ alleles, both in the stable gene frequency distributions and in
the types and rates of random fixation in small populations.

The most obvious difference in stable frequency distribution is that
lethal $t$ alleles never reach a frequency greater than .50, while sterile
allele gene frequencies cover the ranges 0 to 1.   This results simply from
the fact that no gene can ever reach a gene frequency greater than .50
unless there are some homozygotes in the population.   A concomitant of
this fact is the greater variance of gene frequencies for sterile alleles.   In
a population with two males and six females, the variance of the stable
frequency distribution of sterile alleles was .0630 after correction for
homozygous $t/t$ males.

No runs for lethal alleles with m = .85 were made by Lewontin and Dunn,
but an examination of table 7 of that paper shows that the standard deviation of gene frequency falls off linearly with increasing m for a given
population size.   Extrapolation from the table then provides the approximate
figure of .030 for the variance of lethal gene frequency in populations of
two males and sex females with m = .85.

Just as in the case of lethal alleles, the effect of random drift falls off
markedly as the size of family increases from two males and six females

74                              THE AMERICAN NATURALIST

to twelve males and twelve females. For sterile alleles the variance
drops from .063 to .023 and the slightly bimodal distribution of figure 2
changes to the sharply peaked distribution of figure 4. For lethal alleles,
a roughly comparable change occurs when population size increases from
two males and two females to ten males and ten females, the variance
falling from .010 to .006 (m = .95).

A second aspect of the stable distribution of gene frequencies, is the
change that occurs in the mean as population size decreases. The deterministic prediction for the sterile allele frequency is .70. The "large populations" were close to this ($\bar{q}$ = .6895), but the "small populations" had a
mean gene frequency of .523 including populations with all males sterile
and .461 excluding such populations. This radical fall in gene frequency
of unfixed populations is also observed in the case of lethal $t$ alleles. In
broad outline, then, the effect of various population sizes on the stable
distribution of gene frequencies is the same for sterile and lethal $t$ alleles.

The striking difference between the two kinds of alleles is manifest in
the pattern of fixation of genes due to genetic drift. The situation for
lethal alleles can be easily summarized. Fixation is always of wild-type
alleles so that small family size results in a loss of lethal $t$ alleles, and
thus a reduction of genetic load on the population. We are led to expect,
then, that lethal $t$ alleles will finally disappear from mouse populations
although the rate of loss is slowed considerably by reinfection of wild
type populations from the immigration of heterozygous males.

Moreover, since the rate of loss is greater for all alleles with a lower
segregation distortion, we expect only those $t$ alleles with a very high
value of m to remain in the species for any considerable period.

The situation for male sterile $t$ alleles is much more complicated. This
complication arises from the existence of two sorts of fixation. One of
these, fixation at all wild type alleles, results in loss of $t$ genes but the
other, fixation of $t$ genes in males, results in the *elimination of mouse
populations* as well as $t$ alleles. The relative frequency of these two
types of fixation will depend on both the family structure of the mouse
population and the intensity of the segregation distortion.

Figure 3 shows that with a very small family size, two males and six
females, all families reach fixation in 24 generations. About 30 per cent
of the families become pure wild type, while the other 70 per cent become
*extinct*. If the assumption of Lewontin and Dunn is correct, that a geographical population of the house mouse is made up of a large number of
small family units, then such a population will lose its $t$ alleles at the expense of a tremendous mortality of breeding units. As population size
rises the extinction of breeding units becomes less rapid. Figure 5 shows
that after 25 generations only about 17 per cent of the family units have
become extinct when breeding size is 12 males and 12 females. However,
the rate of extinction *relative to* the rate of *fixation of wild type genes*
goes up dramatically. In fact, as the figure shows, not a single population
was fixed for the wild type gene. Thus, although extinction is less rapid

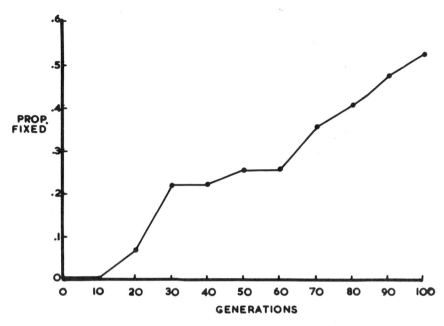

FIGURE 5. Proportion of "large populations" fixed at all males $t/t$ at successive ten generation intervals.

in larger family units, it has no effect on the frequency of the $t$ allele over the whole population. Added to this is the fact that the mean frequency of $t$ among unfixed populations is higher in large family groups than in small ones. The net result is that populations made up of these larger family groups will have a constant low rate of family extinction coupled with a frequency of sterile males in unfixed families of close to 50 per cent. One effect of such a high proportion of non-reproducing males is to make the population less effective in colonizing new areas. The other would be to make it more susceptible to crashes in population size when unfavourable conditions for breeding arose.

Because the rate of family extinction is fairly low, there will be replacement of extinguished families by immigrants from the rest of the population, and the entire process will be cyclic. The polymorphism for the population as a whole will be a relatively stable one.

In contrast to this is a population made up of very small family groups of the order of two males and six females. Here the rate of family extinction is quite high, but pure wild type families are being formed at the same time. These wild type families can be reinfected with $t$ allels by immigration of heterozygous males, so that the rate of loss of $t$ alleles will be slowed down. Nevertheless, in the long run, the polymorphism is unstable.

The population size as a whole will be much smaller than for the case of large families because of the wholesale extinction of family groups, but this effect will lessen as the proportion of unfixed families in the population decreases. Eventually, when the $t$ allele is lost from the entire population, population reproductive potential will rise well above that of segregating populations. During the process of $t$ allele loss, however, the population runs a great risk of becoming completely extinguished.

Sterile $t$ alleles may be regarded as analogous to parasites which infect the host at a high rate and which, if they become too frequent, may cause extinction of the host. Looked at in this way, the host (mouse) populations can cope with the parasitic gene in one of two ways. The first incorporates the parasitic gene as a permanent component of the population but renders it relatively avirulent, since the rate of extinction of large families is quite low. The second, through very small family size, cures the population of the parasitic infection, but the cure is a drastic one with the attendant risk that the virulent parastic gene will extinguish the host.

The success of the $t$ allele as a parasitic gene also depends upon its transmission ratio. Lewontin and Dunn have shown that, for lethal $t$ alleles, selection among populations will lead to a higher and higher value of m. This is because $t$ alleles with low transmission values of segregation distortion are lost from the population more rapidly due to the fixation of wild type alleles. The same is not true for sterile alleles. As the value of m increases, the distribution of unfixed classes is skewed more and more toward higher frequencies of $t$ alleles. This does have the effect of decreasing the loss of $t$ alleles by fixation of wild type genes, but at the same time it increases the extinction rate of mouse populations from fixation of $t$ alleles in males. A successful parasite is one which does not kill its host and thus extinguish itself. The net results is that those $t$ alleles will last longest in mouse populations which minimize fixation at all wild type and which simultaneously keep the extinction rate of mouse populations to a reasonable level. We should expect to find, then, that the distribution of transmission ratios among sterile $t$ alleles in populations is displaced toward lower values of m from the distribution of lethal $t$ alleles.

The lethal alleles reported by Lewontin and Dunn have a mean transmission ratio of .959 and range from .895 to .998 (table 1 of their paper). The three sterile alleles, $t^{w2}$, $t^{w7}$ and $t^{w8}$ have ratios respectively of .850, .938 and .876 (table 1 of Lewontin and Dunn reports the earlier figure of .950 for $t^{w2}$). The sample is small but suggestive. All three sterile alleles are below the mean for lethal alleles and two, $t^{w2}$ and $t^{w8}$ have the lowest value of m ever found in a population. The mean value of m for sterile alleles, .885, is significantly different from that for lethal alleles ($t = 3.74$, 14 d.f., $P < .01$), but too much weight should not be attached to such a meager sample.

## INTERDEME SELECTION

There have been many suggestions, notably by Wright (1959) that some genes may increase in frequency in a population even though they make the probability of survival of the population less. That is, the effect of intra-population selection is not always beneficial to the population. It is not easy to define the fitness of a population as a whole, but one reasonable definition would be the average time to extinction (Thoday, 1953; Lewontin, 1961). On such a criterion the lethal $t$ alleles may or may not reduce the fitness of mouse populations, although they certainly place a very large lethal load on the population.

Sterile $t$ alleles, however, are clearly an example of genes deleterious to the population, since they are the direct cause of population extinction. Although lowering the fitness of homozygous males, these genes have a net genic selective advantage due to their segregation distortion. *Intra-populations* selection favors such genes yet they will be lost from the species eventually by *interdeme* selection. In small family units the interdeme selection operates at the level of the family, causing extinction of $t$ bearing families. In large family-unit populations the process is slower and operates at the level of the entire population. Genetic drift is not effective in producing wild type families, but the segregation of $t$ alleles in the population can maintain itself under adverse conditions, and reduces the returning power of such populations if they have been reduced to low numbers by some catastrophe. That is, the rate of increase, $r$, will be low because of the high frequency of sterile males.

## SUMMARY

Certain populations of house mice carry a gene, $t$, which makes homozygous males sterile. These are maintained in the population because heterozygous males produce sperm, a large preponderance of which carry the mutant allele. An investigation has been made of the fate of such genes in natural populations. The results are:

(1) In small families the mutant allele may be lost by random fixation of wild type alleles.

(2) More often it is the $t$ allele which becomes fixed in males. This results in extinction of the family.

(3) The rate of extinction compared with the rate of fixation of wild type genes *increases* as family size *increases*.

(4) The polymorphism will be stable in large families and unstable in small ones but such small families run a great risk of extinction.

(5) The most favorable condition for maintenance of sterile $t$ alleles in small populations is that of an *intermediate* transmission ratio as compared with the high ratios expected in lethal alleles. This comparison agrees with the observed segregation ratios in lethal and sterile alleles from wild populations.

The sterile $t$ alleles are an example of the control of the genetic composition of a species by interdeme selection operating through the frequent extinction of demes carrying such alleles.

## LITERATURE CITED

Bruck, D., 1957, Male segregation ratio advantage as a factor in maintaining lethal alleles in wild populations of house mice. Proc. Natl. Acad. Sci. U. S. 43: 152-158.

Dunn, L. C., A. B. Beasley and H. Tinker, 1958, Relative fitness of wild
    house mice heteroxygous for a lethal allele.    Am. Naturalist
    92: 215-220.
Dunn, L. C., and H. Levene, 1961, Population dynamics of a variant *t*
    allele in a confined population of wild house mice.    Evolution
    15: 385-393.
Lewontin, R. C., 1961, Evolution and the theory of games.    J. Theoret.
    Biol.  1: 382-403.
Lewontin, R. C., and L. C. Dunn, 1960, The evolutionary dynamics of a
    polymorphism in the house mouse.  Genetics 45: 705-722.
Thoday, J. M., 1953, Components of fitness.    Symp. Soc. Exptl. Biol.
    7: 96-113.
Wright, S., 1937, The distribution of gene frequencies in populations. Proc.
    Natl. Acad. Sci. U. S., 23: 307-320.
    1959, Physiological genetics, ecology of populations and natural
    selection.  Perspect. Biol. Med. 3: 107-151.

# V

# Interactions
# Between
# Populations

It could be said that interactions between populations are of interest to population biologists; but that would be a little like saying that *Drosophila* is of interest to entomologists. Until relatively recently this area of research has been in the exclusive domain of the ecologist, and the genetic consequences of encounters between two or more distinct populations have usually either been ignored or discounted. Thus even though it is apparent that interactions such as predation and competition are potent agents of natural selection, there are relatively few measures of their effects on the gene pools of either natural or laboratory populations and still fewer measures of subsequent changes in the mode of environmental exploitation of the interacting populations. Recently, however, some inferential approaches to questions of this type have been made and the first paper in this section deals with one such treatment.

It is argued by MacARTHUR and LEVINS that specific community structures have arisen through two major factors: (1) the extent and distribution of environmental patchiness (heterogeneity) and (2) the degrees of resource specialization of the interacting populations. Their analysis provides one mechanism to explain the fact that as an environment gradually changes from one geographical or temporal point to another, the structure of a community also changes.

Two types of predictions are possible from the model erected by MacARTHUR and LEVINS. First, populations whose individuals specialize on different types of resources can coexist in both time and space if the diversity of the resource supply matches that of the resource demand. Second, populations whose individuals are generalists and therefore require variety within a given resource category will engage in competition. The end result of this competition is expected to be habitat displacement with each of the generalist populations exploiting habitats that have different mixes of the required resources.

Although neither of these predictions is either novel or surprising, the theoretical basis from which they emerge is new. A large part of the inherent beauty and satisfaction of this model is derived from the manner in which old observations and intuitive explanations are recast in a new and more objective framework that causally relates the properties of a population to its spatial distribution in a varying environment.

Other predictions that may be derived from the model are more unexpected than those just discussed. For instance, it can be predicted that resource specialists will be relatively less affected by an environmental change than the resource generalists. Further, given information on the nature of the environment and the pool of species upon which natural selection may act, it is in theory possible to identify optimal species combinations for maximum utilization of the environment.

The theory of competition has been of such commanding importance to research in this area of biology for so long that the paucity of hard evidence for the existence and quantitative significance of competition between natural populations is often overlooked. Competitive exclusion is often invoked to explain a set of observations in nature. However, in many instances it may be argued that such an explanation is based on tenuous and untestable assumptions about either the history of the populations or the factors which regulate population size. Moreover, in some cases alternate mechanisms serve equally as well to explain the same observations. Why then is competition theory so frequently invoked?

Part of the appeal of this theory is that it is broad enough to explain a wide variety of interactions between populations on the same trophic level. This feature is particularly attractive in enabling an investigator to generalize his results to other populations of the same type or even to very different kinds of populations. Moreover the lack of much concrete evidence for the reality of competition can be explained by the notion that the process is so subtle that its effects require very sensitive and long-term measurements against a background of fluctuating selection intensities and intrapopulational stochastic variations. This explanation not only permits the use of competition theory in cases where competition has not been demonstrated, but also, if true, it precludes direct falsification of hypotheses based on an assumption of competition. Because of the theoretical importance of competitive interactions between populations, several papers have been selected to illustrate some of the approaches used in studies of competition.

The paper by CONNELL presents one of the few unequivocable demonstrations of competitive exclusion ever made under natural conditions. With a series of very elegant field experiments, it is clearly shown that the horizontal zonation of two species of intertidal barnacles is established by interspecific competition. In this investigation individuals of the species in the upper zone were overgrown and dislodged from the rock surface when they encroached on the space being occupied by individuals of the species in the lower zone. Thus the distribution of the two populations is determined by interference competition in which the access of individuals of one population to a jointly required environmental resource is prevented by activities of the members of a second population. Usually, interference competition progresses through a direct action by the members of one population on those of the second.

The other type of competitive interaction is exploitation competition. Exploitation differs from interference competition in that the interaction between the two populations is mediated through the quantity of environmental resources and therefore is usually not the result of a direct action of one population on a second. Although several lines of evidence can be marshalled to argue for the reality and significance of interference competition in nature, the only solid evidence for exploitation competition between two animal populations has been acquired in laboratory experiments utilizing highly simplified and therefore artificial environments. This fact cannot be taken as either a criticism of the use of laboratory experiments in ecological studies or as an argument against the significance of exploitation competition. It does, however, indicate that generalization of experimental laboratory results to field situations must be done wih great care.

The most extensive investigation of competition between any two populations has been carried out with the flour beetles *Tribolium confusum* and *T. castaneum*, chiefly in the laboratory of Thomas Park at the University of Chicago. Park found that under conditions of high temperature and high humidity, *T. castaneum* was able to exclude *T. confusum*, whereas with a regimen of low temperature and humidity the opposite result was obtained. Under intermediate conditions of temperature and humidity, in some cultures *T. castaneum* would win and in other cultures *T. confusum* would be the sole survivor. This observation led to the development of a mathematical model describing the outcome of competition as a stochastic or random process. At this point genetic investigations of *Tribolium* competition were initiated; the results of one of the first of these is presented in the paper by LERNER and DEMPSTER. It was found that if the competition cultures were started with a large enough number of beetles to ensure that the replicate cultures had the same genetic composition (i.e., a representative sample of the gene pool of the foundation population), the results of competition could be completely specified. Moreover, different inbred lines differed in their competitive ability. These investigations underline perhaps more clearly than any others the necessity of fusing the fields of population genetics and ecology.

Recent studies have extended the investigation of competition between species of *Tribolium* to a variety of different environments. Moreover it has become clear that the primary mechanism of the competition is cannibalism on the eggs and pupae of both species by the larvae and adults of both species. Thus the pattern is one of interference rather than exploitation and some investigators prefer to view the interaction between the two flour beetles as a mutual prey-predator system rather than as competition per se.

In the last few years, a great deal of important research on plant competition has been performed by HARPER and his colleagues and students. One of the general approaches taken by this group is illustrated in the paper by HARPER and McNAUGHTON which describes an experimental investigation of the population dynamics of 5 species of poppies. Density-dependent mortalities were determined for each species, both in isolation and in combination with each of the four potential competitors. This design made it possible to evaluate the outcome of competition as a function of interactions both within and between populations. Therefore the results of the experiments may be used to assess the self-regulation of population size in a number of different environments and also to directly study the process of competition between pairs of populations with similar environmental exploitation patterns.

Among the more important findings of HARPER and McNAUGHTON was that in mixed stands there is much less self-regulation of population size when the density of a given population is low. In other words, an increase in density results in a reduced chance of establishment and therefore in a decreased competitive ability. These results constitute an example of the frequency dependent effectiveness of competition as an agent of natural selection. They also indicate that coexistence may occur under continued competition as proposed in the next paper.

PIMENTEL, FEINBERG, WOOD, and HAYES, in the last paper of the series on competition, argue that coexistence and not exclusion may result from competition occurring in a complex environment that allows time for genetic adaptation. Although unable to achieve coexistence between competing blowfly and housefly populations, they did succeed in demonstrating genetic changes that supported parts of their initial hypothesis.

Thus the investigation of competition constitutes one of the most active areas of population biology today. Not only do many significant questions remain unanswered, but many more questions need to be posed.

The presence of an ecologically similar species poses potential challenges to a population through competition. However, if in addition to being ecologically similar the challenger is closely related, a nexus of other problems may arise, chiefly the maintenance of reproductive isolation. The paper by LEVIN and KERSTER documents one of these problems and its solution, in an area where two members of the flowering plant genus *Phlox* are sympatric. Even though the two populations were separated by strong gametic incompatibility barriers, pollen flow from one population to the other could occur because both flowered at the same time and both were visited by the same insect pollinators. The analysis of a flower color polymorphism in one of the populations not only provides a good example of contrasting modes of adaptation with and without the presence of a closely related species, but in addition illustrates the highly complex nature of some adaptive systems.

While the potency of competition as a major determinant of community structure is still a subject of discussion and disagreement, the corresponding effects of predation have long been recognized. Recently, however, several studies have been published that show effects of surprising magnitude. In one of these, BROOKS relates the presence or absence of introduced plankton-feeding fish to radically different structures of the zooplankton in different lakes. The predation by these fish is both size specific (small individuals not being eaten) and habitat specific (the shallow, littoral areas of the lakes being avoided) and as a result there is selection against large open-water plankters. Large zooplankton tend to feed on the same foods that small zooplankton eat as well as on larger food items. BROOKS hypothesizes that competition for food among the small zooplankton exerts a selective pressure for increased body size, thereby enlarging the total supply of food. According to this hypothesis, the size structure of the zooplankton reflects stabilizing selection (Section III) for decreased size to escape fish predation and increased size to escape exploitation competition. As discussed earlier, it is difficult either to prove or disprove such competition, yet the limited amount of data that are available appear to be consistent with this interpretation. Especially notable is the relationship which is drawn between predation and the presence or absence of polymorphism in certain species of zooplankton.

The paper by BREEDLOVE and EHRLICH exemplifies another effect of predation, in this case between a butterfly and a small perennial plant. Eggs laid by the butterfly on the immature inflorescences hatch to produce larvae that feed on the flower parts. The result of this interaction on the plant population is a reduced seed production and therefore a lowered reproductive rate. Obviously, a prey population that lacks the ability to reproduce in the presence of continued predation is doomed to extinction. But just as obviously, a predator (or parasite) population that eliminates its food supply is equally doomed to local extinction. The analysis of this type of system has led to the development of the theory of coevolution. In the face of strong predation, there is intense selection on the prey population to reduce its availability to the predator or to protect its reproductive process by some other method. On the other hand the predator must be able to respond to a reduced availability of its prey by feeding on alternate food sources or by adapting to the change in the original prey population.

The population is the basic biological unit of communities and ecosystems. In the earlier sections of these readings, we concentrated on developing an understanding of the structural properties of this unit. In the present section, our emphasis has been different. By combining pairs of populations, we have seen structural properties emerge that are not found in the component populations themselves. This means, of course, that we cannot develop a knowledge of communities and ecosystems by studying only populations, just as a poem by T. S. Eliot is not necessarily suggested by a dictionary of the English language. But on the other hand, without an understanding of words and their meaning, there could be no poetry.

## COMPETITION, HABITAT SELECTION, AND CHARACTER DISPLACEMENT IN A PATCHY ENVIRONMENT

By Robert MacArthur and Richard Levins

DEPARTMENTS OF BIOLOGY, UNIVERSITY OF PENNSYLVANIA AND UNIVERSITY OF PUERTO RICO

*Communicated by G. E. Hutchinson, April 27, 1964*

It is well known that related species often differ in either habitat[1] or size, and thereby avoid competitive elimination. The way in which they differ is related to the specialized ways they have of using resources, which ways in turn control numbers of coexisting species and other aspects of the evolution of the community. The detailed reasons for these assertions are given in the following paragraphs.[2] Briefly, the argument is as follows. Among species which specialize on a single uniform resource, only the most effective one will survive and that species will be found wherever the resource occurs, in abundance determined by the density of the resource. Other such pure specialist species will be found, one to a uniform resource; these will normally differ in morphology, but will not in general be affected by one another's distributions. On the other hand, species which specialize on a particular *proportion* of mixture of two or more particular resources will be found only where their favored proportion is found, and will be replaced by other species in other habitats where the proportion of the mixture changes to one on which the new species are more effective. Of this mixed-resource type of species there can be as many[3] as there are proportions of the resources which can be counted on from season to season—i.e., very many in stable climates and fewer in unpredictable climates.

To make these ideas more precise, we first consider an imaginary habitat in which there is a scattering of uniform units or grains of resource 1 and another

Reprinted by permission of the National Academy of Sciences and the authors from *Proceedings of the National Academy of Sciences* 51:1207–1210, 1964.

scattering of uniform grains of resource 2.   In such an environment we can distinguish as "fine-grained" an individual or a species which utilizes both resources in
the proportion in which they occur.   (If the actual grain size of the resources were
so fine that the species could not discriminate and select, then the species would
have to be "fine-grained," hence the terminology.)   An individual or a species will
be called "coarse-grained" if it discriminates and selects only grains of one of the
resources.   These are the pure specialists of the first paragraph.   Notice that if
individuals are sedentary, as trees are, it is possible for individuals to be coarse-
grained, spending their lives on soil of a single type, while the species is fine-grained,
with individuals not selecting soil types.   Normally, coarse-grained utilization will
be expected only where the time and energy lost due to neglecting the other possible
resource is slight compared with the benefits of specialization.[4]   Pursuing species
with relatively large foods are usually of this sort.

   If now we plot the quantity of resource 1 along the abscissa of a graph and the
quantity of resource 2 along the ordinate, then each habitat, with a certain quantity
of each resource, determines a point in the graph.   We assume here that the resources are consumable and renewing, like prey species.   (Other kinds of resources,
like nest sites, can be analyzed similarly.[5])   Then the process of competitive elimination consists in one species reducing the resources to such a low level that the
other cannot harvest sufficiently to maintain its population.   As a first approximation, each species will increase when and only when its joint resource supply is
sufficiently dense.   Thus, for fine-grained species $x$ and $y$, and resource populations
$R_1$ and $R_2$, we might have

$$\frac{dx}{dt} = [i_1(R_1 - c_1) + i_2(R_2 - c_2)]x \qquad \frac{dR_1}{dt} = f(x,y,R_1,R_2)$$

$$\frac{dy}{dt} = [j_1(R_1 - d_1) + j_2(R_2 - d_2)]y \qquad \frac{dR_2}{dt} = g(x,y,R_1,R_2).^{*}$$

(We have included the equations for $dR_1/dt$ and $dR_2/dt$ for completeness; actually,
they are not needed in the following analysis.)   Here the $c$'s and $d$'s are the threshold
densities of resources below which the species have a net loss of energy and the $i$'s
and $j$'s measure the effectiveness with which the species utilize their resources to
reproduce.   For coarse-grained species $V$ (specializing on $R_1$) and $W$ (specializing
on $R_2$), these equations would be of the form

$$\frac{dV}{dt} = [a(R_1 - m)]V \qquad \frac{dW}{dt} = [b(R_2 - n)]W.$$

In either case we can plot the lines $dx/dt = 0$ and $dy/dt = 0$ or $dV/dt = 0$ and
$dW/dt = 0$ on the graph, and they might[6] look as in Figure 1 or Figure 2.   Notice
$x$ and $y$ can increase in environments lying *beyond* these lines, not within them as in
the familiar[7] competition graphs.   Thus, if there were a species $z$ with isocline
$dz/dt = 0$ as in Figure 1, it could come to equilibrium with species $x$ at resource
level $P$, but such an equilibrium would be subject to invasion by species $y$ which
can still increase with resources at this level.   Then a new equilibrium, $Q$, will be
reached in which $y$ has replaced $z$.   Notice that since two lines determine a point,
two species at most[8] will normally be able to coexist; similarly, with three resources

---

* The biological meaning of these equations would be clearer if they were written in the form

$$\frac{dx}{dt} = [i_1R_1 + i_2R_2 - c]x \; ; \frac{dy}{dt} = [j_1R_1 + j_2R_2 - d]y$$

The intercepts written on Fig. 1 would then be modified to

$$R_1 = \frac{c}{i_1} \text{ and } R_2 = \frac{c}{i_2}$$

320

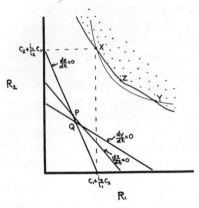

FIG. 1.—The lines, $dx/dt = 0$, $dy/dt = 0$, and $dz/dt = 0$ marking the inner boundaries of the areas in which species $x$, $y$, and $z$ can increase. $R_1$ and $R_2$ are the quantities of resource 1 and resource 2, respectively. Point $x$, with coordinates ($c_1 + i_2c_2/i_1$, $c_2 + i_1c_1/i_2$), and points $y$ and $z$, with coordinates similarly defined by the intercepts of the respective lines, then determine the isoclines $dx/dt = 0$, $dy/dt = 0$, and $dz/dt = 0$, completely. Other possible species might lie at other points in the stippled region. The light curve intersecting the stippled area at $x$ and $y$ is an equilateral hyperbola for reference purposes. See text for further explanation.

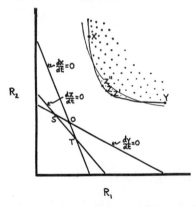

FIG. 2.—The meaning of the lines and stippled area is as in Fig. 1. In Fig. 2 the stippled area is more convex than an equilateral hyperbola, and species $z$ can effectively invade the community consisting of $x$ and $y$ which comes to equilibrium at point O.

and three dimensions it will take three planes to determine a point, so that at most three species can coexist, and so on.[9] Finally, notice that if, as in Figure 2, species $z$ has isocline $dz/dt = 0$ crossing the $x$ and $y$ isoclines inside O, then there will be two alternative equilibria $S$ and $T$, each resistant to colonization by any of the other spccvis whose isoclines are drawn. Such alternatiee communities, each resistant to invasion, may be found among islands, but where a large species pool exists, normally one combination is optimal. Thus, when $z'$ and $z''$ are available, they will replace $y$ and $x$, respectively, and so on.

To find optimal species combinations and to see how natural selection operates, we construct a set rather like the fitness set described by Levins.[10] We plot on the graphs points whose coordinates are the isocline intercepts (e.g., $c_1 + (i_2/i_1)c_2$, $c_2 + (i_1/i_2)c_1$). Each species then determines a point, and the set of available species—the species pool—determines a cloud of points which, for simplicity, we assume to be fairly solid and continuous in outline (see Fig. 2).

The isocline analysis shows that the equilibrium species are those whose isoclines have small intercepts. Hence, the optimal combinations consist of some species on the inner boundary of the sets in Figures 1 and 2. To see which these will be, we find that shape of boundary which would have all its species isoclines passing through the same point. All of the species on such a boundary would be equally good competitors. This shape of boundary is an equilateral hyperbola. In fact, an isocline passing through $(a,b)$ with slope $m$ has the intercepts $x = a - b/m$, $y = b - ma$. As $m$ varies, these values of $x$ and $y$ are the coordinates of points in the figures describing species whose isoclines all intersect at $(a,b)$. But for these points $(x-a)/b = -l/m* = a/(y-b)$ so that $(x-a)(y-b) = ab$ is the equation of a boundary consisting of equally good competitors. Thus, if the boundary of the set stippled in the figures bulges uniformly more than an equilateral hyperbola, a single, jack-of-all-

$$* \frac{1}{m}$$

321

1210          *ZOÖLOGY: MACARTHUR AND LEVINS*          Proc. N. A. S.

trades will be favored (Fig. 2). If the set is flatter—less convex—than the hyperbola, as in Figure 1, then the specialists at either end of the boundary will be favored. In the latter case the species will be coarse-grained; in the former the optimal species is relatively fine-grained. As we change from one habitat to another of slightly differing relative suitability for the two resources, the values of $i_1$, $c_1$, $i_2$, $c_2$, etc., change, and so the fitness set in Figure 2 becomes transformed into a new one. The same species will still be the best specialists, but in general the optimal jack-of-all-trades will change. Hence this type of species will show habitat selection.

In most real habitats, grains of resource are not uniform. For these, it is still useful to talk about fine- and coarse-grained species, but to be precise we must refer to fine- and coarse-grained *differences* between species. Thus among birds, warblers eat smaller food than temperate zone tanagers, and hence the two groups have coarse-grained differences and suitable habitats will contain representatives of each. However, different warblers eat the same food species, only in slightly different proportions; hence among warblers there are fine-grained differences and habitat selection resulting in each species consuming insects in a slightly different location within a forest or in a slightly different forest type. With these distinctions in mind, all the preceding analysis still holds true.

Since pursuing species with large items of food can efficiently specialize, these tend to be separated by coarse-grained differences. Thus, weasels tend to be found in sympatric forms of many sizes, as do accipiters among the hawks and other pursuing predators. But species which spend most of their time searching, especially for small items, cannot afford to overlook many. For these the fitness set, stippled in the figures, will tend to be very convex, and fine-grained differences with marked habitat selection will predominate. Most small birds, grazing mammals, and, among the hawks, perhaps the buteos fall into this category.

Both authors were supported by grants from the National Science Foundation. Drs. Joseph Connell, G. E. Hutchinson, and W. John Smith made valuable suggestions.

[1] Habitat here includes microhabitat (e.g., layer in a forest), and both small- and large-scale geographic separations.

[2] A fuller account will appear as part of a larger publication by Levins and MacArthur on the evolution of the niche.

[3] The number of such species will be proportional to a spatial diversity divided by a temporal diversity at any point. The amount of overlap has been discussed by G. E. Hutchinson, *Am. Naturalist*, **93**, 145 (1959).

[4] The concept of grain is treated in more detail by R. Levins and R. MacArthur, *op. cit.*

[5] Levins, R., and R. MacArthur, *op. cit.* For such species will be governed by equations of the form $dx/dt = i_1 x[K_1 - P_1(x,y, \ldots)] + i_2 x[K_2 - P_2(x,y, \ldots)]$; $dy/dt = j_1 y[K_1 - P_1(x,y, \ldots)] + j_2 y[K_2 - P_2(x,y, \ldots)]$. $K_1$ and $K_2$ are the quantities of two kinds of nest sites, and $P_1$ and $P_2$ are the number in use. We then plot $dx/dt = 0$ and $dy/dt = 0$, etc. in a graph whose coordinates are $P_1$, $P_2$.

[6] If the resources are not alternatives but are both required, or if they alternate in time, then the lines will bow in; see Levins, R., and R. MacArthur, *op. cit.*

[7] Slobodkin, L. B., *The Growth and Regulation of Animal Populations* (New York: Holt, Rinehart and Winston, 1961).

[8] At most two because it is infinitely improbable that three or more independent lines will pass through the same point. Even if three did pass through the point, the two most closely parallel to the coordinate axes will alone persist.

[9] This theorem does not depend upon the specific form of the equations.

[10] Levins, R., *Am. Naturalist*, **96**, 361 (1962).

# THE INFLUENCE OF INTERSPECIFIC COMPETITION AND OTHER FACTORS ON THE DISTRIBUTION OF THE BARNACLE *CHTHAMALUS STELLATUS*

Joseph H. Connell

*Department of Biology, University of California, Santa Barbara, Goleta, California*

## Introduction

Most of the evidence for the occurrence of interspecific competition in animals has been gained from laboratory populations. Because of the small amount of direct evidence for its occurrence in nature, competition has sometimes been assigned a minor role in determining the composition of animal communities.

Indirect evidence exists, however, which suggests that competition may sometimes be responsible for the distribution of animals in nature. The range of distribution of a species may be decreased in the presence of another species with similar requirements (Beauchamp and Ullyott 1932, Endean, Kenny and Stephenson 1956). Uniform distribution is space is usually attributed to intraspecies competition (Holme 1950, Clark and Evans 1954). When animals with similar requirements, such as 2 or more closely related species, are found coexisting in the same area, careful analysis usually indicates that they are not actually competing with each other (Lack 1954, MacArthur 1958).

In the course of an investigation of the animals of an intertidal rocky shore I noticed that the adults of 2 species of barnacles occupied 2 separate horizontal zones with a small area of overlap, whereas the young of the species from the upper zone were found in much of the lower zone. The upper species, *Chthamalus stellatus* (Poli) thus settled but did not survive in the lower zone. It seemed probable that this species was eliminated by the lower one, *Balanus balanoides* (L), in a struggle for a common requisite which was in short supply. In the rocky intertidal region, space for attachment and growth is often extremely limited. This paper is an account of some observations and experiments designed to test the hypothesis that the absence in the lower zone of adults of *Chthamalus* was due to interspecific competition with *Balanus* for space. Other factors which may have influenced the distribution were also studied. The study was made at Millport, Isle of Cumbrae, Scotland.

I would like to thank Prof. C. M. Yonge and the staff of the Marine Station, Millport, for their help, discussions and encouragement during the course of this work. Thanks are due to the following for their critical reading of the manuscript: C. S. Elton, P. W. Frank, G. Hardin, N. G. Hairston, E. Orias, T. Park and his students, and my wife.

### Distribution of the species of barnacles

The upper species, *Chthamalus stellatus,* has its center of distribution in the Mediterranean; it reaches its northern limit in the Shetland Islands, north of Scotland. At Millport, adults of this species occur between the levels of mean high water of neap and spring tides (M.H.W.N. and M.H.W.S.: see Figure 5 and Table I). In southwest England and Ireland, adult *Chtham-*

Reprinted by permission of Duke University Press and the author from *Ecology* 42:710–723, 1961.

*alus* occur at moderate population densities throughout the intertidal zone, more abundantly when *Balanus balanoides* is sparse or absent (Southward and Crisp 1954, 1956). At Millport the larvae settle from the plankton onto the shore mainly in September and October; some additional settlement may occur until December. The settlement is most abundant between M.H.W.S. and mean tide level (M.T.L.), in patches of rock surface left bare as a result of the mortality of *Balanus,* limpets, and other sedentary organisms. Few of the *Chthamalus* that settle below M.H.W.N. survive, so that adults are found only occasionally at these levels.

*Balanus balanoides* is a boreal-arctic species, reaching its southern limit in northern Spain. At Millport it occupies almost the entire intertidal region, from mean low water of spring tides (M.L.W.S.) up to the region between M.H.W.N. and M.H.W.S. Above M.H.W.N. it occurs intermingled with *Chthamalus* for a short distance. *Balanus* settles on the shore in April and May, often in very dense concentrations (see Table IV).

The main purpose of this study was to determine the cause of death of those *Chthamalus* that settled below M.H.W.N. A study which was being carried on at this time had revealed that physical conditions, competition for space, and predation by the snail *Thais lapillus* L. were among the most important causes of mortality of *Balanus balanoides.* Therefore, the observations and experiments in the present study were designed to detect the effects of these factors on the survival of *Chthamalus.*

## METHODS

Intertidal barnacles are very nearly ideal for the study of survival under natural conditions. Their sessile habit allows direct observation of the survival of individuals in a group whose positions have been mapped. Their small size and dense concentrations on rocks exposed at intervals make experimentation feasible. In addition, they may be handled and transplanted without injury on pieces of rock, since their opercular plates remain closed when exposed to air.

The experimental area was located on the Isle of Cumbrae in the Firth of Clyde, Scotland. Farland Point, where the study was made, comprises the southeast tip of the island; it is exposed to moderate wave action. The shore rock consists mainly of old red sandstone, arranged in a series of ridges, from 2 to 6 ft high, oriented at right angles to the shoreline. A more detailed description is given by Connell (1961). The

other barnacle species present were *Balanus crenatus* Brug and *Verruca stroemia* (O. F. Muller), both found in small numbers only at and below M.L.W.S.

To measure the survival of *Chthamalus,* the positions of all individuals in a patch were mapped. Any barnacles which were empty or missing at the next examination of this patch must have died in the interval, since emigration is impossible. The mapping was done by placing thin glass plates (lantern slide cover glasses, $10.7 \times 8.2$ cm, area 87.7 cm$^2$) over a patch of barnacles and marking the position of each *Chthamalus* on it with glass-marking ink. The positions of the corners of the plate were marked by drilling small holes in the rock. Observations made in subsequent censuses were noted on a paper copy of the glass map.

The study areas were chosen by searching for patches of *Chthamalus* below M.H.W.N. in a stretch of shore about 50 ft long. When 8 patches had been found, no more were looked for. The only basis for rejection of an area in this search was that it contained fewer than 50 *Chthamalus* in an area of about 1/10 m$^2$. Each numbered area consisted of one or more glass maps located in the 1/10 m$^2$. They were mapped in March and April, 1954, before the main settlement of *Balanus* began in late April.

Very few *Chthamalus* were found to have settled below mid-tide level. Therefore pieces of rock bearing *Chthamalus* were removed from levels above M.H.W.N. and transplanted to and below M.T.L. A hole was drilled through each piece; it was then fastened to the rock by a stainless steel screw driven into a plastic screw anchor fitted into a hole drilled into the rock. A hole 1/4" in diameter and 1" deep was found to be satisfactory. The screw could be removed and replaced repeatedly and only one stone was lost in the entire period.

For censusing, the stones were removed during a low tide period, brought to the laboratory for examination, and returned before the tide rose again. The locations and arrangements of each area are given in Table I; the transplanted stones are represented by areas 11 to 15.

The effect of competition for space on the survival of *Chthamalus* was studied in the following manner: After the settlement of *Balanus* had stopped in early June, having reached densities of 49/cm$^2$ on the experimental areas (Table I) a census of the surviving *Chthamalus* was made on each area (see Figure 1). Each map was then divided so that about half of the number of

TABLE I. Description of experimental areas*

| Area no. | Height in ft from M.T.L. | % of time sub-merged | POPULATION DENSITY: NO./CM² IN JUNE, 1954 | | | Remarks |
|---|---|---|---|---|---|---|
| | | | Chthamalus, autumn 1953 settlement | | All barnacles, undisturbed portion | |
| | | | Undisturbed portion | Portion without Balanus | | |
| MHWS............... | +4.9 | 4 | — | — | — | — |
| 1.................... | +4.2 | 9 | 2.2 | — | 19.2 | Vertical, partly protected |
| 2.................... | +3.5 | 16 | 5.2 | 4.2 | — | Vertical, wave beaten |
| MHWN............... | +3.1 | 21 | — | — | -- | — |
| 3a................... | +2.2 | 30 | 0.6 | 0.6 | 30.9 | Horizontal, wave beaten |
| 3b................... | " | " | 0.5 | 0.7 | 29.2 | "      "      " |
| 4.................... | +1.4 | 38 | 1.9 | 0.6 | — | 30° to vertical, partly protected |
| 5.................... | +1.4 | " | 2.4 | 1.2 | — | "   "   "   "   " |
| 6.................... | +1.0 | 42 | 1.1 | 1.9 | 38.2 | Horizontal, top of a boulder, partly protected |
| 7a................... | +0.7 | 44 | 1.3 | 2.0 | 49.3 | Vertical, protected |
| 7b................... | " | " | 2.3 | 2.0 | 51.7 | "      " |
| 11a.................. | 0.0 | 50 | 1.0 | 0.6 | 32.0 | Vertical, protected |
| 11b.................. | " | " | 0.2 | 0.3 | — | "      " |
| 12a.................. | 0.0 | 100 | 1.2 | 1.2 | 18.8 | Horizontal, immersed in tide pool |
| 12b.................. | " | 100 | 0.8 | 0.9 | — | "      "      "      "      " |
| 13a.................. | -1.0 | 58 | 4.9 | 4.1 | 29.5 | Vertical, wave beaten |
| 13b.................. | " | " | 3.1 | 2.4 | — | "      "      " |
| 14a.................. | -2.5 | 71 | 0.7 | 1.1 | — | 45° angle, wave beaten |
| 14b.................. | " | " | 1.0 | 1.0 | — | "      "      "      " |
| MLWN............... | -3.0 | 77 | — | — | -- | — |
| MLWS............... | -5.1 | 96 | — | — | - . | — |
| 15.................... | +1.0 | 42 | 32.0 | — | -- | ⎰Chthamalus of autumn, 1954 set- |
| 7b................... | +0.7 | 44 | 5.5 | 3.7 | -. | ⎱tlement; densities of Oct., 1954. |

* The letter "a" following an area number indicates that this area was enclosed by a cage; "b" refers to a closely adjacent area which was not enclosed. All areas faced either east or south except 7a and 7b, which faced north.

Chthamalus were in each portion. One portion was chosen (by flipping a coin), and those Balanus which were touching or immediately surrounding each Chthamalus were carefully removed with a needle; the other portion was left untouched. In this way it was possible to measure the effect on the survival of Chthamalus both of intraspecific competition alone and of competition with Balanus. It was not possible to have the numbers or population densities of Chthamalus exactly equal on the 2 portions of each area. This was due to the fact that, since Chthamalus often occurred in groups, the Balanus had to be removed from around all the members of a group to ensure that no crowding by Balanus occurred. The densities of Chthamalus were very low, however, so that the slight differences in density

between the 2 portions of each area can probably be disregarded; intraspecific crowding was very seldom observed. Censuses of the Chthamalus were made at intervals of 4-6 weeks during the next year; notes were made at each census of factors such as crowding, undercutting or smothering which had taken place since the last examination. When necessary, Balanus which had grown until they threatened to touch the Chthamalus were removed in later examinations.

To study the effects of different degrees of immersion, the areas were located throughout the tidal range, either in situ or on transplanted stones, as shown in Table I. Area 1 had been under observation for 1½ years previously. The effects of different degrees of wave shock could not be studied adequately in such a small area

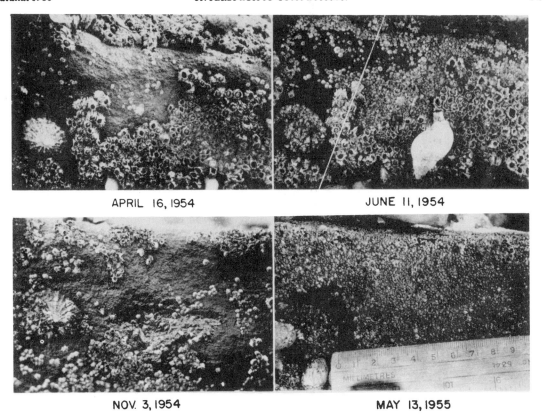

APRIL 16, 1954                                JUNE 11, 1954

NOV. 3, 1954                                  MAY 13, 1955

Fig. 1. Area 7b. In the first photograph the large barnacles are *Balanus,* the small ones scattered in the bare patch, *Chthamalus.* The white line on the second photograph divides the undisturbed portion (right) from the portion from which *Balanus* were removed (left). A limpet, *Patella vulgata,* occurs on the left, and predatory snails, *Thais lapillus,* are visible.

of shore but such differences as existed are listed in Table I.

The effects of the predatory snail, *Thais lapillus,* (synonymous with *Nucella* or *Purpura,* Clench 1947), were studied as follows: Cages of stainless steel wire netting, 8 meshes per inch, were attached over some of the areas. This mesh has an open area of 60% and previous work (Connell 1961) had shown that it did not inhibit growth or survival of the barnacles. The cages were about 4 × 6 inches, the roof was about an inch above the barnacles and the sides were fitted to the irregularities of the rock. They were held in place in the same manner as the transplanted stones. The transplanted stones were attached in pairs, one of each pair being enclosed in a cage (Table I).

These cages were effective in excluding all but the smallest *Thais.* Occasionally small *Thais,* ½ to 1 cm in length, entered the cages through gaps at the line of juncture of netting and rock surface. In the concurrent study of *Balanus* (Con-

nell 1961), small *Thais* were estimated to have occurred inside the cages about 3% of the time.

All the areas and stones were established before the settlement of *Balanus* began in late April, 1954. Thus the *Chthamalus* which had settled naturally on the shore were then of the 1953 year class and all about 7 months old. Some *Chthamalus* which settled in the autumn of 1954 were followed until the study was ended in June, 1955. In addition some adults which, judging from their large size and the great erosion of their shells, must have settled in 1952 or earlier, were present on the transplanted stones. Thus records were made of at least 3 year-classes of *Chthamalus.*

## Results

### The effects of physical factors

In Figures 2 and 3, the dashed line indicates the survival of *Chthamalus* growing without contact with *Balanus.* The suffix "a" indicates that the area was protected from *Thais* by a cage.

714                      JOSEPH H. CONNELL                Ecology, Vol. 42, No. 4

In the absence of *Balanus* and *Thais,* and protected by the cages from damage by water-borne objects, the survival of *Chthamalus* was good at all levels. For those which had settled normally on the shore (Fig. 2), the poorest survival was on the lowest area, 7a. On the transplanted stones (Fig. 3, area 12), constant immersion in a tide pool resulted in the poorest survival. The reasons for the trend toward slightly greater mortality as the degree of immersion increased are unknown. The amount of attached algae on the stones in the tide pool was much greater than on the other areas. This may have reduced the flow of water and food or have interfered directly with feeding movements. Another possible indirect effect of increased immersion is the increase in predation by the snail, *Thais lapillus,* at lower levels.

*Chthamalus* is tolerant of a much greater degree of immersion than it normally encounters. This is shown by the survival for a year on area 12 in a tide pool, together with the findings of Fischer (1928) and Barnes (1956a), who found that *Chthamalus* withstood submersion for 12 and 22 months, respectively. Its absence below M.T.L. can probably be ascribed either to a lack of initial settlement or to poor survival of newly settled larvae. Lewis and Powell (1960) have suggested that the survival of *Chthamalus* may be

favored by increased light or warmth during emersion in its early life on the shore. These conditions would tend to occur higher on the shore in Scotland than in southern England.

The effects of wave action on the survival of *Chthamalus* are difficult to assess. Like the degree of immersion, the effects of wave action may act indirectly. The areas 7 and 12, where relatively poor survival was found, were also the areas of least wave action. Although *Chthamalus* is usually abundant on wave beaten areas and absent from sheltered bays in Scotland, Lewis and Powell (1960) have shown that in certain sheltered bays it may be very abundant. Hatton (1938) found that in northern France, settlement and growth rates were greater in wave-beaten areas at M.T.L., but, at M.H.W.N., greater in sheltered areas.

At the upper shore margins of distribution *Chthamalus* evidently can exist higher than *Balanus* mainly as a result of its greater tolerance to heat and/or desiccation. The evidence for this was gained during the spring of 1955. Records from a tide and wave guage operating at this time about one-half mile north of the study area showed that a period of neap tides had coincided with an unusual period of warm calm weather in April so that for several days no water, not even waves, reached the level of Area 1. In the period

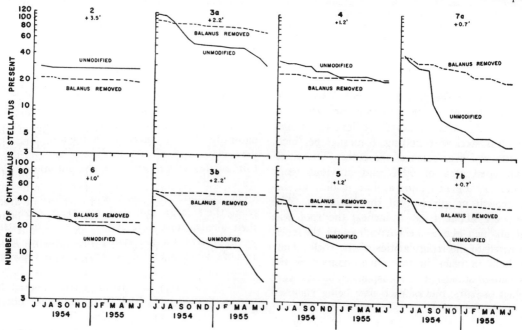

FIG. 2. Survivorship curves of *Chthamalus stellatus* which had settled naturally on the shore in the autumn of 1953. Areas designated "a" were protected from predation by cages. In each area the survival of *Chthamalus* growing without contact with *Balanus* is compared to that in the undisturbed area. For each area the vertical distance in feet from M.T.L. is shown.

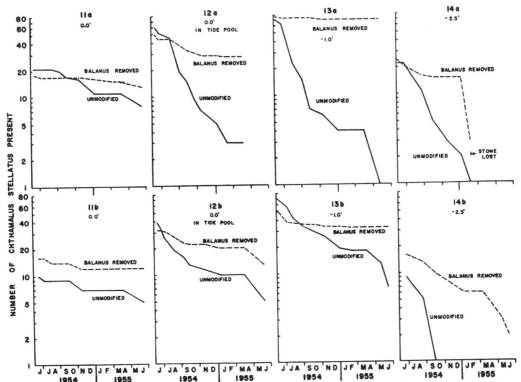

Fig. 3. Survivorship curves of *Chthamalus stellatus* on stones transplanted from high levels. These had settled in the autumn of 1953; the arrangement is the same as that of Figure 2.

between the censuses of February and May, *Balanus* aged one year suffered a mortality of 92%, those 2 years and older, 51%. Over the same period the mortality of *Chthamalus* aged 7 months was 62%, those 1½ years and older, 2%. Records of the survival of *Balanus* at several levels below this showed that only those *Balanus* in the top quarter of the intertidal region suffered high mortality during this time (Connell 1961).

### Competition for space

At each census notes were made for individual barnacles of any crowding which had occurred since the last census. Thus when one barnacle started to grow up over another this fact was noted and at the next census 4-6 weeks later the progress of this process was noted. In this way a detailed description was built up of these gradually occurring events.

Intraspecific competition leading to mortality in *Chthamalus* was a rare event. For areas 2 to 7, on the portions from which *Balanus* had been removed, 167 deaths were recorded in a year. Of these, only 6 could be ascribed to crowding between individuals of *Chthamalus*. On the undisturbed portions no such crowding was

observed. This accords with Hatton's (1938) observation that he never saw crowding between individuals of *Chthamalus* as contrasted to its frequent occurrence between individuals of *Balanus*.

Interspecific competition between *Balanus* and *Chthamalus* was, on the other hand, a most important cause of death of *Chthamalus*. This is shown both by the direct observations of the process of crowding at each census and by the differences between the survival curves of *Chthamalus* with and without *Balanus*. From the periodic observations it was noted that after the first month on the undisturbed portions of areas 3 to 7 about 10% of the *Chthamalus* were being covered as *Balanus* grew over them; about 3% were being undercut and lifted by growing *Balanus;* a few had died without crowding. By the end of the 2nd month about 20% of the *Chthamalus* were either wholly or partly covered by *Balanus;* about 4% had been undercut; others were surrounded by tall *Balanus*. These processes continued at a lower rate in the autumn and almost ceased during the later winter. In the spring *Balanus* resumed growth and more crowding was observed.

716              JOSEPH H. CONNELL            Ecology, Vol. 42, No. 4

In Table II, these observations are summarized for the undistributed portions of all the areas. Above M.T.L., the *Balanus* tended to overgrow the *Chthamalus,* whereas at the lower levels, undercutting was more common. This same trend was evident within each group of areas, undercutting being more prevalent on area 7 than on area 3, for example. The faster growth of *Balanus* at lower levels (Hatton 1938, Barnes and Powell 1953) may have resulted in more undercutting. When *Chthamalus* was completely covered by *Balanus* it was recorded as dead; even though death may not have occurred immediately, the buried barnacle was obviously not a functioning member of the population.

TABLE II. The causes of mortality of *Chthamalus stellatus* of the 1953 year group on the undisturbed portions of each area

| Area no. | Height in ft from M.T.L. | No. at start | No. of deaths in the next year | PERCENTAGE OF DEATHS RESULTING FROM: | | | |
|---|---|---|---|---|---|---|---|
| | | | | Smothering by *Balanus* | Undercutting by *Balanus* | Other crowding by *Balanus* | Unknown causes |
| 2......... | +3.5 | 28 | 1 | 0 | 0 | 0 | 100 |
| 3a........ | +2.2 | 111 | 81 | 61 | 6 | 10 | 23 |
| 3b........ | " | 47 | 42 | 57 | 5 | 2 | 36 |
| 4......... | +1.4 | 34 | 14 | 21 | 14 | 0 | 65 |
| 5......... | +1.4 | 43 | 35 | 11 | 11 | 3 | 75 |
| 6......... | +1.0 | 27 | 11 | 9 | 0 | 0 | 91 |
| 7a........ | +0.7 | 42 | 38 | 21 | 16 | 53 | 10 |
| 7b........ | " | 51 | 42 | 24 | 10 | 10 | 56 |
| 11a....... | 0.0 | 21 | 13 | 54 | 8 | 0 | 38 |
| 11b....... | " | 10 | 5 | 40 | 0 | 0 | 60 |
| 12a....... | 0.0 | 60 | 57 | 19 | 33 | 7 | 41 |
| 12b....... | " | 39 | 34 | 9 | 18 | 3 | 70 |
| 13a....... | -1.0 | 71 | 70 | 19 | 24 | 3 | 54 |
| 13b....... | " | 69 | 62 | 18 | 8 | 3 | 71 |
| 14a....... | -2.5 | 22 | 21 | 24 | 42 | 10 | 24 |
| 14b....... | " | 9 | 9 | 0 | 0 | 0 | 100 |
| Total, 2-7.. | — | 383 | 264 | 37 | 9 | 16 | 38 |
| Total, 11-14.. | — | 301 | 271 | 19 | 21 | 4 | 56 |

In Table II under the term "other crowding" have been placed all instances where *Chthamalus* were crushed laterally between 2 or more *Balanus,* or where *Chthamalus* disappeared in an interval during which a dense population of *Balanus* grew rapidly. For example, in area 7a the *Balanus,* which were at the high population density of 48 per cm², had no room to expand except upward and the barnacles very quickly grew into the form of tall cylinders or cones with the diameter of the opercular opening greater than

that of the base. It was obvious that extreme crowding occurred under these circumstances, but the exact cause of the mortality of the *Chthamalus* caught in this crush was difficult to ascertain.

In comparing the survival curves of Figs. 2 and 3 within each area it is evident that *Chthamalus* kept free of *Balanus* survived better than those in the adjacent undisturbed areas on all but areas 2 and 14a. Area 2 was in the zone where adults of *Balanus* and *Chthamalus* were normally mixed; at this high level *Balanus* evidently has no influence on the survival of *Chthamalus.* On Stone 14a, the survival of *Chthamalus* without *Balanus* was much better until January when a starfish, *Asterias rubens* L., entered the cage and ate the barnacles.

Much variation occurred on the other 14 areas. When the *Chthamalus* growing without contact with *Balanus* are compared with those on the adjacent undisturbed portion of the area, the survival was very much better on 10 areas and moderately better on 4. In all areas, some *Chthamalus* in the undisturbed portions escaped severe crowding. Sometimes no *Balanus* happened to settle close to a *Chthamalus,* or sometimes those which did died soon after settlement. In some instances, *Chthamalus* which were being undercut by *Balanus* attached themselves to the *Balanus* and so survived. Some *Chthamalus* were partly covered by *Balanus* but still survived. It seems probable that in the 4 areas, nos. 4, 6, 11a, and 11b, where *Chthamalus* survived well in the presence of *Balanus,* a higher proportion of the *Chthamalus* escaped death in one of these ways.

The fate of very young *Chthamalus* which settled in the autumn of 1954 was followed in detail in 2 instances, on stone 15 and area 7b. The *Chthamalus* on stone 15 had settled in an irregular space surrounded by large *Balanus.* Most of the mortality occurred around the edges of the space as the *Balanus* undercut and lifted the small *Chthamalus* nearby. The following is a tabulation of all the deaths of young *Chthamalus* between Sept. 30, 1954 and Feb. 14, 1955, on Stone 15, with the associated situations:

| | |
|---|---|
| Lifted by *Balanus* | : 29 |
| Crushed by *Balanus* | : 4 |
| Smothered by *Balanus* and *Chthamalus* | : 2 |
| Crushed between *Balanus* and *Chthamalus* | : 1 |
| Lifted by *Chthamalus* | : 1 |
| Crushed between two other *Chthamalus* | : 1 |
| Unknown | : 3 |

This list shows that crowding of newly settled *Chthamalus* by older *Balanus* in the autumn mainly takes the form of undercutting, rather than of smothering as was the case in the spring. The reason for this difference is probably that the *Chthamalus* are more firmly attached in the spring so that the fast growing young *Balanus* grow up over them when they make contact. In the autumn the reverse is the case, the *Balanus* being firmly attached, the *Chthamalus* weakly so.

Although the settlement of *Chthamalus* on Stone 15 in the autumn of 1954 was very dense, 32/cm², so that most of them were touching another, only 2 of the 41 deaths were caused by intraspecific crowding among the *Chthamalus*. This is in accord with the findings from the 1953 settlement of *Chthamalus*.

The mortality rates for the young *Chthamalus* on area 7b showed seasonal variations. Between October 10, 1954 and May 15, 1955 the relative mortality rate per day $\times$ 100 was 0.14 on the undisturbed area and 0.13 where *Balanus* had been removed. Over the next month, the rate increased to 1.49 on the undisturbed area and 0.22 where *Balanus* was absent. Thus the increase in mortality of young *Chthamalus* in late spring was also associated with the presence of *Balanus*.

Some of the stones transplanted from high to low levels in the spring of 1954 bore adult *Chthamalus*. On 3 stones, records were kept of the survival of these adults, which had settled in the autumn of 1952 or in previous years and were at least 20 months old at the start of the experiment. Their mortality is shown in Table III; it was always much greater when *Balanus* was not removed. On 2 of the 3 stones this mortality rate was almost as high as that of the younger group. These results suggest that any *Chthamalus* that managed to survive the competition for space with *Balanus* during the first year would probably be eliminated in the 2nd year.

Censuses of *Balanus* were not made on the experimental areas. However, on many other areas in the same stretch of shore the survival of *Balanus* was being studied during the same period (Connell 1961). In Table IV some mortality rates measured in that study are listed; the *Balanus* were members of the 1954 settlement at population densities and shore levels similar to those of the present study. The mortality rates of *Balanus* were about the same as those of *Chthamalus* in similar situations except at the highest level, area 1, where *Balanus* suffered much greater mortality than *Chthamalus*. Much of this mortality was caused by intraspecific crowding at all levels below area 1.

TABLE III. Comparison of the mortality rates of young and older *Chthamalus stellatus* on transplanted stones

| Stone No. | Shore level | Treatment | Number of *Chthamalus* present in June, 1954 | | % mortality over one year (or for 6 months for 14a) of *Chthamalus* | |
|---|---|---|---|---|---|---|
| | | | 1953 year group | 1952 or older year groups | 1953 year group | 1952 or older year groups |
| 13b | 1.0 ft below MTL | *Balanus* removed | 51 | 3 | 35 | 0 |
| | | Undisturbed | 69 | 16 | 90 | 31 |
| 12a | MTL, in a tide pool, caged | *Balanus* removed | 50 | 41 | 44 | 37 |
| | | Undisturbed | 60 | 31 | 95 | 71 |
| 14a | 2.5 ft below MTL, caged | *Balanus* removed | 25 | 45 | 40 | 36 |
| | | Undisturbed | 22 | 8 | 86 | 75 |

TABLE IV. Comparison of annual mortality rates of *Chthamalus stellatus* and *Balanus balanoides**

| Area no. | *Chthamalus stellatus*, autumn 1953 settlement | | |
|---|---|---|---|
| | Height in ft from M.T.L. | Population density: no./cm² June, 1954 | % mortality in the next year |
| 1................ | +4.2 | 21 | 17 |
| 3a............. | +2.2 | 31 | 72 |
| 3b............ | " | 29 | 89 |
| 6............... | +1.0 | 38 | 41 |
| 7a............. | +0.7 | 49 | 90 |
| 7b............. | " | 52 | 82 |
| 11a............. | 0.0 | 32 | 62 |
| 13a............. | −1.0 | 29 | 99 |
| 12a............. | (tide pool) | 19 | 95 |
| | *Balanus balanoides*, spring 1954 settlement | | |
| 1 (top)......... | +4.2 | 21 | 99 |
| 1:Middle Cage 1.. | +2.1 | 85 | 92 |
| 1:Middle Cage 2.. | " | 25 | 77 |
| 1:Low Cage 1.... | +1.5 | 26 | 88 |
| Stone 1......... | −0.9 | 26 | 86 |
| Stone 2......... | " | 68 | 94 |

* Population density includes both species. The mortality rates of *Chthamalus* refer to those on the undisturbed portions of each area. The data and area designations for *Balanus* were taken from Connell (1961); the present area 1 is the same as that designated 1 (top) in that paper.

In the observations made at each census it appeared that *Balanus* was growing faster than *Chthamalus*. Measurements of growth rates of the 2 species were made from photographs of

718               JOSEPH H. CONNELL          Ecology, Vol. 42, No. 4

the areas taken in June and November, 1954. Barnacles growing free of contact with each other were measured; the results are given in Table V. The growth rate of *Balanus* was greater than that of *Chthamalus* in the experimental areas; this agrees with the findings of Hatton (1938) on the shore in France and of Barnes (1956a) for continual submergence on a raft at Millport.

TABLE V. Growth rates of *Chthamalus stellatus* and *Balanus balanoides*. Measurements were made of uncrowded individuals on photographs of areas 3a, 3b and 7b. Those of *Chthamalus* were made on the same individuals on both dates; of *Balanus*, representative samples were chosen

|  | CHTHAMALUS | | BALANUS | |
|---|---|---|---|---|
|  | No. measured | Average size, mm. | No. measured | Average size, mm. |
| June 11, 1954................. | 25 | 2.49 | 39 | 1.87 |
| November 3, 1954.............. | 25 | 4.24 | 27 | 4.83 |
| Average size in the interval....... | | 3.36 | | 3.35 |
| Absolute growth rate per day x 100 | | 1.21 | | 2.04 |

After a year of crowding the average population densities of *Balanus* and *Chthamalus* remained in the same relative proportion as they had been at the start, since the mortality rates were about the same. However, because of its faster growth, *Balanus* occupied a relatively greater area and, presumably, possessed a greater biomass relative to that of *Chthamalus* after a year.

The faster growth of *Balanus* probably accounts for the manner in which *Chthamalus* were crowded by *Balanus*. It also accounts for the sinuosity of the survival curves of *Chthamalus* growing in contact with *Balanus*. The mortality rate of these *Chthamalus*, as indicated by the slope of the curves in Figs. 2 and 3, was greatest in summer, decreased in winter and increased again in spring. The survival curves of *Chthamalus* growing without contact with *Balanus* do not show these seasonal variations which, therefore, cannot be the result of the direct action of physical factors such as temperature, wave action or rain.

Seasonal variations in growth rate of *Balanus* correspond to these changes in mortality rate of *Chthamalus*. In Figure 4 the growth of *Balanus* throughout the year as studied on an intertidal panel at Millport by Barnes and Powell (1953), is compared to the survival of *Chthamalus* at about the same intertidal level in the present study. The increased mortality of *Chthamalus* was found to occur in the same seasons as the in-

creases in the growth rate of *Balanus*. The correlation was tested using the Spearman rank correlation coefficient. The absolute increase in diameter of *Balanus* in each month, read from the curve of growth, was compared to the percentage mortality of *Chthamalus* in the same month. For the 13 months in which data for *Chthamalus* was available, the correlation was highly significant, P = .01.

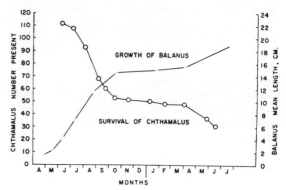

FIG. 4. A comparison of the seasonal changes in the growth of *Balanus balanoides* and in the survival of *Chthamalus stellatus* being crowded by *Balanus*. The growth of *Balanus* was that of panel 3, Barnes and Powell (1953), just above M.T.L. on Keppel Pier, Millport, during 1951-52. The *Chthamalus* were on area 3a of the present study, one-half mile south of Keppell Pier, during 1954-55.

From all these observations it appears that the poor survival of *Chthamalus* below M.H.W.N. is a result mainly of crowding by dense populations of faster growing *Balanus*.

At the end of the experiment in June, 1955, the surviving *Chthamalus* were collected from 5 of the areas. As shown in Table VI, the average size was greater in the *Chthamalus* which had grown free of contact with *Balanus*; in every case the difference was significant (P < .01, Mann-Whitney U. test, Siegel 1956). The survivors on the undisturbed areas were often misshapen, in some cases as a result of being lifted on to the side of an undercutting *Balanus*. Thus the smaller size of these barnacles may have been due to disturbances in the normal pattern of growth while they were being crowded.

These *Chthamalus* were examined for the presence of developing larvae in their mantle cavities. As shown in Table VI, in every area the proportion of the uncrowded *Chthamalus* with larvae was equal to or more often slightly greater than on the crowded areas. The reason for this may be related to the smaller size of the crowded *Chthamalus*. It is not due to separation, since *Chthamalus* can self-fertilize (Barnes and Crisp

TABLE VI. The effect of crowding on the size and presence of larvae in *Chthamalus stellatus*, collected in June, 1955

| Area | Treatment | Level, feet above MTL | Number of Chthamalus | DIAMETER IN MM | | % of individuals which had larvae in mantle cavity |
|------|-----------|------|------|------|------|------|
| | | | | Average | Range | |
| 3a...... | Undisturbed | 2.2 | 18 | 3.5 | 2.7-4.6 | 61 |
| " ...... | *Balanus* removed | " | 50 | 4.1 | 3.0-5.5 | 65 |
| 4....... | Undisturbed | 1.4 | 16 | 2.3 | 1.8 3.2 | 81 |
| "....... | *Balanus* removed | " | 37 | 3.7 | 2.5-5 1 | 100 |
| 5....... | Undisturbed | 1.4 | 7 | 3.3 | 2.8-3.7 | 70 |
| "....... | *Balanus* removed | " | 13 | 4.0 | 3.5-4.5 | 100 |
| 6....... | Undisturbed | 1.0 | 13 | 2.8 | 2.1-3.9 | 100 |
| "....... | *Balanus* removed | " | 14 | 4.1 | 3.0-5.2 | 100 |
| 7a & b.. | Undisturbed | 0.7 | 10 | 3.5 | 2.7-4.5 | 70 |
| "    .. | *Balanus* removed | " | 23 | 4.3 | 3.0-6.3 | 81 |

TABLE VII. The effect of predation by *Thais lapillus* on the annual mortality rate of *Chthamalus stellatus* in the experimental areas*

| Area | Height in ft from M.T.L. | % mortality of Chthamalus over a year (The initial numbers are given in parentheses) | | | | | |
|------|------|------|------|------|------|------|------|
| | | a: Protected from predation by a cage | | | b: Unprotected, open to predation | | |
| | | With Balanus | Without Balanus | Difference | With Balanus | Without Balanus | Difference |
| Area 3.. | +2.2 | 73 (112) | 25 (96) | 48 | 89 (47) | 6 (50) | 83 |
| Area 7.. | +0.7 | 90 ( 42) | 47 (40) | 43 | 82 (51) | 23 (47) | 59 |
| Area 11.. | 0 | 62 ( 21) | 28 (18) | 34 | 50 (10) | 25 (16) | 25 |
| Area 12 . | 0† | 100 ( 60) | 53 (50) | 47 | 87 (39) | 59 (32) | 28 |
| Area 13.. | −1.0 | 98 ( 72) | 9 (77) | 89 | 90 (69) | 35 (51) | 55 |

*The records for 12a extend over only 10 months; for purposes of comparison the mortality rate for 12a has been multiplied by 1.2.
†Tide pool.

1956). Moore (1935) and Barnes (1953) have shown that the number of larvae in an individual of *Balanus balanoides* increases with increase in volume of the parent. Comparison of the cube of the diameter, which is proportional to the volume, of *Chthamalus* with and without *Balanus* shows that the volume may be decreased to ¼ normal size when crowding occurs. Assuming that the relation between larval numbers and volume in *Chthamalus* is similar to that of *Balanus*, a decrease in both frequency of occurrence and abundance of larvae in *Chthamalus* results from competition with *Balanus*. Thus the process described in this paper satisfies both aspects of interspecific competition as defined by Elton and Miller (1954): "in which one species affects the population of another by a process of interference, i.e., by reducing the reproductive efficiency or increasing the mortality of its competitor."

### The effect of predation by Thais

Cages which excluded *Thais* had been attached on 6 areas (indicated by the letter "a" following the number of the area). Area 14 was not included in the following analysis since many starfish were observed feeding on the barnacles at this level; one entered the cage in January, 1955, and ate most of the barnacles.

*Thais* were common in this locality, feeding on barnacles and mussels, and reaching average population densities of 200/m² below M.T.L. (Connell 1961). The mortality rates for *Chthamalus* in cages and on adjacent areas outside cages (indicated by the letter "b" after the number) are shown on Table VII.

If the mortality rates of *Chthamalus* growing without contact with *Balanus* are compared in and out of the cages, it can be seen that at the upper levels mortality is greater inside the cages,

at lower levels greater outside Densities of *Thais* tend to be greater at and below M.T.L. so that this trend in the mortality rates of *Chthamalus* may be ascribed to an increase in predation by *Thais* at lower levels.

Mortality of *Chthamalus* in the absence of *Balanus* was appreciably greater outside than inside the cage only on area 13. In the other 4 areas it seems evident that few *Chthamalus* were being eaten by *Thais*. In a concurrent study of the behavior of *Thais* in feeding on *Balanus balanoides*, it was found that *Thais* selected the larger individuals as prey (Connell 1961). Since *Balanus* after a few month's growth was usually larger than *Chthamalus*, it might be expected that *Thais* would feed on *Balanus* in preference to *Chthamalus*. In a later study (unpublished) made at Santa Barbara, California, *Thais emarginata* Deshayes were enclosed in cages on the shore with mixed populations of *Balanus glandula* Darwin and *Chthamalus fissus* Darwin. These species were each of the same size range as the corresponding species at Millport. It was found that *Thais emarginata* fed on *Balanus glandula* in preference to *Chthamalus fissus*.

As has been indicated, much of the mortality of *Chthamalus* growing naturally intermingled with *Balanus* was a result of direct crowding by *Balanus*. It therefore seemed reasonable to take the difference between the mortality rates of *Chthamalus* with and without *Balanus* as an index of the degree of competition between the species. This difference was calculated for each area and is included in Table VII. If these differences are compared between each pair of adjacent areas in and out of a cage, it appears that the difference, and therefore the degree of competition, was greater outside the cages at the upper shore levels and less outside the cages at the lower levels.

720           JOSEPH H. CONNELL          Ecology, Vol. 42, No. 4

Thus as predation increased at lower levels, the degree of competition decreased. This result would have been expected if *Thais* had fed upon *Balanus* in preference to *Chthamalus*. The general effect of predation by *Thais* seems to have been to lessen the interspecific competition below M.T.L.

## DISCUSSION

"Although animal communities appear qualitatively to be constructed as if competition were regulating their structure, even in the best studied cases there are nearly always difficulties and unexplored possibilities" (Hutchinson 1957).

In the present study direct observations at intervals showed that competition was occurring under natural conditions. In addition, the evidence is strong that the observed competition with *Balanus* was the principal factor determining the local distribution of *Chthamalus*. *Chthamalus* thrived at lower levels when it was not growing in contact with *Balanus*.

However, there remain unexplored possibilities. The elimination of *Chthamalus* requires a dense population of *Balanus,* yet the settlement of *Balanus* varied from year to year. At Millport, the settlement density of *Balanus balanoides* was measured for 9 years between 1944 and 1958 (Barnes 1956b, Connell 1961). Settlement was light in 2 years, 1946 and 1958. In the 3 seasons of *Balanus* settlement studied in detail, 1953-55, there was a vast oversupply of larvae ready for settlement. It thus seems probable that most of the *Chthamalus* which survived in a year of poor settlement of *Balanus* would be killed in competition with a normal settlement the following year. A succession of years with poor settlements of *Balanus* is a possible, but improbable occurrence at Millport, judging from the past record. A very light settlement is probably the result of a chance combination of unfavorable weather circumstances during the planktonic period (Barnes 1956b). Also, after a light settlement, survival on the shore is improved, owing principally to the reduction in intraspecific crowding (Connell 1961); this would tend to favor a normal settlement the following year, since barnacles are stimulated to settle by the presence of members of their own species already attached on the surface (Knight-Jones 1953).

The fate of those *Chthamalus* which had survived a year on the undisturbed areas is not known since the experiment ended at that time. It is probable, however, that most of them would have been eliminated within 6 months; the mortality rate had increased in the spring (Figs. 2

and 3), and these survivors were often misshapen and smaller than those which had not been crowded (Table VI). Adults on the transplanted stones had suffered high mortality in the previous year (Table III).

Another difficulty was that *Chthamalus* was rarely found to have settled below mid tide level at Millport. The reasons for this are unknown; it survived well if transplanted below this level, in the absence of *Balanus*. In other areas of the British Isles (in southwest England and Ireland, for example) it occurs below mid tide level.

The possibility that *Chthamalus* might affect *Balanus* deleteriously remains to be considered. It is unlikely that *Chthamalus* could cause much mortality of *Balanus* by direct crowding; its growth is much slower, and crowding between individuals of *Chthamalus* seldom resulted in death. A dense population of *Chthamalus* might deprive larvae of *Balanus* of space for settlement. Also, *Chthamalus* might feed on the planktonic larvae of *Balanus;* however, this would occur in March and April when both the sea water temperature and rate of cirral activity (presumably correlated with feeding activity), would be near their minima (Southward 1955).

The indication from the caging experiments that predation decreased interspecific competition suggests that the action of such additional factors tends to reduce the intensity of such interactions in natural conditions. An additional suggestion in this regard may be made concerning parasitism. Crisp (1960) found that the growth rate of *Balanus balanoides* was decreased if individuals were infected with the isopod parasite *Hemioniscus balani* (Spence Bate). In Britain this parasite has not been reported from *Chthamalus stellatus*. Thus if this parasite were present, both the growth rate of *Balanus,* and its ability to eliminate *Chthamalus* would be decreased, with a corresponding lessening of the degree of competition between the species.

### The causes of zonation

The evidence presented in this paper indicates that the lower limit of the intertidal zone of *Chthamalus stellatus* at Millport was determined by interspecific competition for space with *Balanus balanoides*. *Balanus*, by virtue of its greater population density and faster growth, eliminated most of the *Chthamalus* by directing crowding.

At the upper limits of the zones of these species no interaction was observed. *Chthamalus* evidently can exist higher on the shore than *Balanus* mainly as a result of its greater tolerance to heat and/or desiccation.

The upper limits of most intertidal animals are probably determined by physical factors such as these. Since growth rates usually decrease with increasing height on the shore, it would be less likely that a sessile species occupying a higher zone could, by competition for space, prevent a lower one from extending upwards. Likewise, there has been, as far as the author is aware, no study made which shows that predation by land species determines the upper limit of an intertidal animal. In one of the most thorough of such studies, Drinnan (1957) indicated that intense predation by birds accounted for an annual mortality of 22% of cockles (*Cardium edule* L.) in sand flats where their total mortality was 74% per year.

In regard to the lower limits of an animal's zone, it is evident that physical factors may act directly to determine this boundary. For example, some active amphipods from the upper levels of sandy beaches die if kept submerged. However evidence is accumulating that the lower limits of distribution of intertidal animals are determined mainly by biotic factors.

Connell (1961) found that the shorter length of life of *Balanus balanoides* at low shore levels could be accounted for by selective predation by *Thais lapillus* and increased intraspecific competition for space. The results of the experiments in the present study confirm the suggestions of other authors that lower limits may be due to interspecific competition for space. Knox (1954) suggested that competition determined the distribution of 2 species of barnacles in New Zealand. Endean, Kenny and Stephenson (1956) gave indirect evidence that competition with a colonial polychaete worm, (*Galeolaria*) may have determined the lower limit of a barnacle (*Tetraclita*) in Queensland, Australia. In turn the lower limit of *Galeolaria* appeared to be determined by competition with a tunicate, *Pyura*, or with dense algal mats.

With regard to the 2 species of barnacles in the present paper, some interesting observations have been made concerning changes in their abundance in Britain. Moore (1936) found that in southwest England in 1934, *Chthamalus stellatus* was most dense at M.H.W.N., decreasing in numbers toward M.T.L. while *Balanus balanoides* increased in numbers below M.H.W.N. At the same localities in 1951, Southward and Crisp (1954) found that *Balanus* had almost disappeared and that *Chthamalus* had increased both above and below M.H.W.N. *Chthamalus* had not reached the former densities of *Balanus* except at one locality, Brixham. After 1951, *Balanus* began to return in numbers, although by 1954 it had not reached the densities of 1934; *Chthamalus* had declined, but again not to its former densities (Southward and Crisp 1956).

Since *Chthamalus* increased in abundance at the lower levels vacated by *Balanus*, it may previously have been excluded by competition with *Balanus*. The growth rate of *Balanus* is greater than *Chthamalus* both north and south (Hatton 1938) of this location, so that *Balanus* would be likely to win in competition with *Chthamalus*. However, changes in other environmental factors such as temperature may have influenced the abundance of these species in a reciprocal manner. In its return to southwest England after 1951, the maximum density of settlement of *Balanus* was 12 per cm$^2$; competition of the degree observed at Millport would not be expected to occur at this density. At a higher population density, *Balanus* in southern England would probably eliminate *Chthamalus* at low shore levels in the same manner as it did at Millport.

In Loch Sween, on the Argyll Peninsula, Scotland, Lewis and Powell (1960) have described an unusual pattern of zonation of *Chthamalus stellatus*. On the outer coast of the Argyll Peninsula *Chthamalus* has a distribution similar to that at Millport. In the more sheltered waters of Loch Sween, however, *Chthamalus* occurs from above M.H.W.S. to about M.T.L., judging the distribution by its relationship to other organisms. *Balanus balanoides* is scarce above M.T.L. in Loch Sween, so that there appears to be no possibility of competition with *Chthamalus*, such as that occurring at Millport, between the levels of M.T.L. and M.H.W.N.

In Figure 5 an attempt has been made to summarize the distribution of adults and newly settled larvae in relation to the main factors which appear to determine this distribution. For *Balanus* the estimates were based on the findings of a previous study (Connell 1961); intraspecific competition was severe at the lower levels during the first year, after which predation increased in importance. With *Chthamalus*, it appears that avoidance of settlement or early mortality of those larvae which settled at levels below M.T.L., and elimination by competition with *Balanus* of those which settled between M.T.L. and M.H.W.N., were the principal causes for the absence of adults below M.H.W.N. at Millport. This distribution appears to be typical for much of western Scotland.

722                                      JOSEPH H. CONNELL                                  Ecology, Vol. 42, No. 4

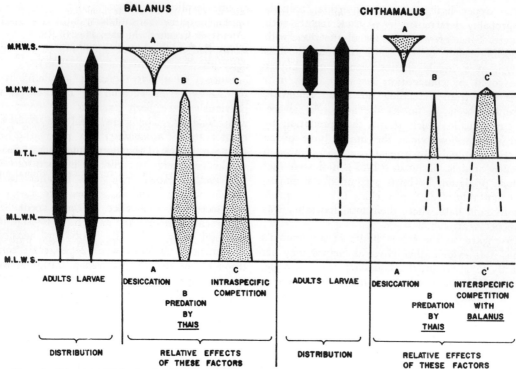

Fig. 5. The intertidal distribution of adults and newly settled larvae of *Balanus balanoides* and *Chthamalus stellatus* at Millport, with a diagrammatic representation of the relative effects of the principal limiting factors.

## Summary

Adults of *Chthamalus stellatus* occur in the marine intertidal in a zone above that of another barnacle, *Balanus balanoides*. Young *Chthamalus* settle in the *Balanus* zone but evidently seldom survive, since few adults are found there.

The survival of *Chthamalus* which had settled at various levels in the *Balanus* zone was followed for a year by successive censuses of mapped individuals. Some *Chthamalus* were kept free of contact with *Balanus*. These survived very well at all intertidal levels, indicating that increased time of submergence was not the factor responsible for elimination of *Chthamalus* at low shore levels. Comparison of the survival of unprotected populations with others, protected by enclosure in cages from predation by the snail, *Thais lapillus,* showed that *Thais* was not greatly affecting the survival of *Chthamalus*.

Comparison of the survival of undisturbed populations of *Chthamalus* with those kept free of contact with *Balanus* indicated that *Balanus* could cause great mortality of *Chthamalus*. *Balanus* settled in greater population densities and grew faster than *Chthamalus*. Direct observations at each census showed that *Balanus* smothered,

undercut, or crushed the *Chthamalus;* the greatest mortality of *Chthamalus* occurred during the seasons of most rapid growth of *Balanus*. Even older *Chthamalus* transplanted to low levels were killed by *Balanus* in this way. Predation by *Thais* tended to decrease the severity of this interspecific competition.

Survivors of *Chthamalus* after a year of crowding by *Balanus* were smaller than uncrowded ones. Since smaller barnacles produce fewer offspring, competition tended to reduce reproductive efficiency in addition to increasing mortality.

Mortality as a result of intraspecies competition for space between individuals of *Chthamalus* was only rarely observed.

The evidence of this and other studies indicates that the lower limit of distribution of intertidal organisms is mainly determined by the action of biotic factors such as competition for space or predation. The upper limit is probably more often set by physical factors.

### References

Barnes, H. 1953. Size variations in the cyprids of some common barnacles. J. Mar. Biol. Ass. U. K. **32:** 297-304.

————. 1956a. The growth rate of *Chthamalus stellatus* (Poli). J. Mar. Biol. Ass. U. K. **35**: 355-361.

————. 1956b. *Balanus balanoides* (L.) in the Firth of Clyde: The development and annual variation of the larval population, and the causative factors. J. Anim. Ecol. **25**: 72-84.

———— and H. T. Powell. 1953. The growth of *Balanus balanoides* (L.) and *B. crenatus* Brug. under varying conditions of submersion. J. Mar. Biol. Ass. U. K. **32**: 107-128.

———— and D. J. Crisp. 1956. Evidence of self-fertilization in certain species of barnacles. J. Mar. Biol. Ass. U. K. **35**: 631-639.

Beauchamp, R. S. A. and P. Ullyott. 1932. Competitive relationships between certain species of freshwater Triclads. J. Ecol. **20**: 200-208.

Clark, P. J. and F. C. Evans. 1954. Distance to nearest neighbor as a measure of spatial relationships in populations. Ecology **35**: 445-453.

Clench, W. J. 1947. The genera *Purpura* and *Thais* in the western Atlantic. Johnsonia **2**, No. 23: 61-92.

Connell, J. H. 1961. The effects of competition, predation by *Thais lapillus,* and other factors on natural populations of the barnacle, *Balanus balanoides.* Ecol. Mon. **31**: 61-104.

Crisp, D. J. 1960. Factors influencing growth-rate in *Balanus balanoides.* J. Anim. Ecol. **29**: 95-116.

Drinnan, R. E. 1957. The winter feeding of the oystercatcher (*Haematopus ostralegus*) on the edible cockle (*Cardium edule*). J. Anim. Ecol. **26**: 441-469.

Elton, Charles and R. S. Miller. 1954. The ecological survey of animal communities: with a practical scheme of classifying habitats by structural characters. J. Ecol. **42**: 460-496.

Endean, R., R. Kenny and W. Stephenson. 1956. The ecology and distribution of intertidal organisms on the rocky shores of the Queensland mainland. Aust. J. mar. freshw. Res. **7**: 88-146.

Fischer, E. 1928. Sur la distribution geographique de quelques organismes de rocher, le long des cotes de la Manche. Trav. Lab. Mus. Hist. Nat. St.-Servan **2**: 1-16.

Hatton, H. 1938. Essais de bionomie explicative sur quelques especes intercotidales d'algues et d'animaux. Ann. Inst. Oceanogr. Monaco **17**: 241-348.

Holme, N. A. 1950. Population-dispersion in *Tellina tenuis* Da Costa. J. Mar. Biol. Ass. U. K. **29**: 267-280.

Hutchinson, G. E. 1957. Concluding remarks. Cold Spring Harbor Symposium on Quant. Biol. **22**: 415-427.

Knight-Jones, E. W. 1953. Laboratory experiments on gregariousness during setting in *Balanus balanoides* and other barnacles. J. Exp. Biol. **30**: 584-598.

Knox, G. A. 1954. The intertidal flora and fauna of the Chatham Islands. Nature Lond. **174**: 871-873.

Lack, D. 1954. The natural regulation of animal numbers. Oxford, Clarendon Press.

Lewis, J. R. and H. T. Powell. 1960. Aspects of the intertidal ecology of rocky shores in Argyll, Scotland. I. General description of the area. II. The distribution of *Chthamalus stellatus* and *Balanus balanoides* in Kintyre. Trans. Roy. Soc. Edin. **64**: 45-100.

MacArthur, R. H. 1958. Population ecology of some warblers of northeastern coniferous forests. Ecology **39**: 599-619.

Moore, H. B. 1935. The biology of *Balnus balanoides.* III. The soft parts. J. Mar. Biol. Ass. U. K. **20**: 263-277.

————. 1936. The biology of *Balanus balanoides.* V. Distribution in the Plymouth area. J. Mar. Biol. Ass. U. K. **20**: 701-716.

Siegel, S. 1956. Nonparametric statistics. New York, McGraw Hill.

Southward, A. J. 1955. On the behavior of barnacles. I. The relation of cirral and other activities to temperature. J. Mar. Biol. Ass. U. K. **34**: 403-422.

———— and D. J. Crisp. 1954. Recent changes in the distribution of the intertidal barnacles *Chthamalus stellatus* Poli and *Balanus balanoides* L. in the British Isles. J. Anim. Ecol. **23**: 163-177.

————. 1956. Fluctuations in the distribution and abundance of intertidal barnacles. J. Mar. Biol. Ass. U. K. **35**: 211-229.

# INDETERMINISM IN INTERSPECIFIC COMPETITION

By I. Michael Lerner and Everett R. Dempster

Department of Genetics, University of California, Berkeley

*Communicated March 26, 1962*

The extensive experiments of Park and his associates[1-4] on competition between two species of flour beetles, *Tribolium castaneum* and *T. confusum*, have become one of the most-quoted examples of indeterminism in biology. When populations of the two species are kept together in cultures containing whole-wheat flour and yeast, one species invariably displaces the other. Under high temperature and high relative humidity, *T. castaneum* (hereafter designated *CS*) is the winner; when both temperature and humidity are low, *T. confusum* (designated *CF*) wins. At intermediate regimens, such as represented by 29°C and 70 per cent humidity, in

Reprinted by permission of the National Academy of Sciences and the authors from *Proceedings of the National Academy of Sciences* 48:821–826, 1962.

the various experiments reported by Park's group (the first four in Table 1), *CS* emerged as the successful competitor in some 84 per cent of the cultures while *CF* won in 16 per cent of them. The indeterminacy is provided by the apparent unpredictability as to which species will win in any given culture. This situation has been analyzed on the basis of a stochastic model,[6] presumably on the assumption that, as stated by Cole,[7] Park "has discovered environmental conditions under which the two species are so nearly evenly matched that stochastic elements take over and mediate the outcome." The term *stochastic* here, to refer to a statistical authority in this field,[8] is synonymous with "probabilistic" and "was intended to draw attention explicitly to the random . . . aspect of population changes, due partly to the intrinsically discrete structure of populations, and in contrast with some older so-called 'deterministic' formulations." In Park's[9] own words: "The outcome of the struggle appears to be determined by something comparable to a toss of a coin." Recently Mayr,[10] in his provocative essay on cause and effect in biology, referred specifically to the Tribolium experiments as an example of unpredictability of the results of complex ecological interactions.

We wish to submit here the view that in competition experiments of the type

TABLE 1

Outcome of Competition Experiments between *T. castaneum* (CS) and *T. confusum*
(CF) Maintained at 29°C and 70% Relative Humidity
(All life stages transferred monthly)

| Reference | Initial population | Number of winning cultures | |
|---|---|---|---|
| | | CS | CF |
| Park[1] | 2 pairs of each species | 12 | 6 |
| Kennington[2] | " | 19 | 1 |
| Park[3] | " | 24 | 4 |
| Park and Lloyd[4] | " | 9 | 1 |
| Lerner and Ho[5] | 10 pairs of each species | 20 | 0 |

described, the apparent indeterminacy is largely the result of genetic heterogeneity among the founders of the populations in the different cultures, and that proper specification of the genotypes makes the results of replicate competing cultures predictable with near certainty in each individual case. This view, foreshadowed by the previous demonstration[5] of intraspecific genetic variation in competitive ability of Tribolium, is supported by the deterministic outcome of competition trials in which the genetic variability from culture to culture has been greatly reduced. This reduction has been accomplished in two types of experiments. In the first of these, a larger number of parental animals was introduced into each culture, and in the second, additionally, highly inbred lines were utilized. It should be noted in this connection that normally outbreeding organisms maintained in the laboratory as very large populations, in sharp contrast to those propagated, as in our inbred lines, by brother-sister matings, are likely to become only slightly or moderately inbred, even over periods of tens or perhaps hundreds of generations.

The first type of evidence is only mildly suggestive. As previously reported,[5] in repeating Park's experiments under the same conditions, except for initiating the competition cultures with ten pairs of beetles of each species instead of two,

*CS* emerged the winner in all 20 replicates (see Table 1). The obvious interpretation, should this difference be considered significant (the P value is 0.04 using Fisher's[11] exact method for one-tailed contingency tests), is that the small sample of four beetles from a genetically heterogeneous population of *CS* used in establishing cultures has a lower probability of including representatives with superior genotypes for competitive ability than the larger samples of 20. More generally stated, the aggregate genetic effects in competition of sets of 20 genotypes taken at random are much more uniform from culture to culture than are the aggregate effects of sets of four genotypes, so that in the former case the average superiority of *CS* would almost invariably (and in our 20 tests always) prevail. Similarly,

TABLE 2

Outcome of Competition Experiments between *T. castaneum* (CS) and *T. confusum* (CF) Maintained at 29°C and 70% Relative Humidity.

(All cultures initiated with 10 pairs of each species. Adults discarded at monthly transfer. Some of the results shown have already been reported by Lerner and Ho.[5])

| Generations inbred at outset of experiments | Competitors | Won by CS | Won by CF | Outcome uncertain |
|---|---|---|---|---|
| 0 | CS synth-CF synth | 89 | 1* | 0 |
| 13 | CS 2-CF 9 | 10 | 0 | 0 |
| | CS 2-CF 11 | 10 | 0 | 0 |
| | CS 12-CF 9 | 10 | 0 | 0 |
| | CS 12-CF 11 | 9 | 1 | 0 |
| | CS (2 × 12)-CF 9 | 10 | 0 | 0 |
| | CS (2 × 12)-CF 11 | 10 | 0 | 0 |
| | CS 2-CF (9 × 11) | 7 | 1 | 2† |
| | CS 12-CF (9 × 11) | 0 | 10 | 0 |
| | CS (2 × 12)-CF (9 × 11) | 10 | 0 | 0 |
| 16–18 | CS 3-CF 1 | 0 | 10 | 0 |
| | CS 3-CF 11 | 0 | 10 | 0 |
| | CS 5-CF 1 | 10 | 0 | 0 |
| | CS 5-CF 11 | 8 | 0 | 2‡ |
| | CS (3 × 5)-CF 1 | 10 | 0 | 0 |
| | CS (3 × 5)-CF 11 | 10 | 0 | 0 |
| | CS 3-CF (1 × 11) | 0 | 10 | 0 |
| | CS 5-CF (1 × 11) | 0 | 10 | 0 |
| | CS (3 × 5)-CF (1 × 11) | 10 | 0 | 0 |
| | CS synth-CF (1 × 11) | 20 | 0 | 0 |
| 18 | CS synth-CF (9 × 11) | 10 | 0 | 0 |
| | CS 12-CF synth | 0 | 10 | 0 |
| | CS 12-CF (9 × 11) | 0 | 10 | 0 |

* The CF winning culture was infected with *Nosema*, see Lerner and Ho.[5]
† Percentages CS at termination were 54 and 79, respectively.
‡ Percentages CS at termination were 61 and 67, respectively.

under environments in which *CF* has more than a trivial advantage, larger foundation populations should lead to invariable victories for *CF*.

Evidence from the second type of experiment, based in part on published results and in part on new data, is presented in Table 2. Procedures followed in the 320 competition cultures reported require some amplification. As has been noted in our previous publication,[5] Park's standard technique of transferring all life stages of the competing beetles to fresh medium monthly has been modified, the adults being discarded at each transfer. The outcome of competition was found to be identical with that using Park's original method (in both instances, however, starting with ten pairs of beetles of each of the species) but in general arrived at much more rapidly. This modification has been adopted as a timesaving device.

We have found, however, that even under these conditions the period of complete elimination of one of the species is very much prolonged in the few situations to be seen in Table 2 when the outcome is not completely determinate for the whole set of replicates.

The synthetic populations of the two species in which the unsuccessful attempt to select directly for competitive ability has been previously described are represented in the table as *CS synth* and *CF synth*, respectively. The other designations refer to various inbred lines (e.g., *CS 2, CF 1*, etc.) propagated by brother-sister matings for the number of generations specified *prior* to the initiation of the experiment. When the initial competitors were $F_1$ crosses between these inbred lines, the appropriate designation (e.g., *CS (2 × 12)*) is shown.

Examination of the data in the table (populations in a few of the cultures have not yet reached 100 per cent of the winning species, but all of these have approached this state within a few per cent) clearly shows that when genetic heterogeneity of the founding population is largely eliminated, so is most of the "indeterminacy." The further the inbreeding progresses, the more true this is. Had, for instance, the experiments initiated after 16 or more generations of inbreeding been treated as a single set of replicates, the outcome of the cultures carried to the terminal point would be given as 78 wins for *CS* and 60 wins for *CF*. Considering subsets only, within each group of replicates the winning species is invariably the same. Identification of the genotype apparently removes the random effect regarding the outcome, though it should be, of course, noted that the details of the eliminatory process of one of the species, such as duration and pattern, may still be mediated by stochastic events within the populations.

The kinds of factors responsible for lack of uniformity of outcome in replicated competition experiments may be briefly considered. Indeterminacy may result from interculture differences existing at the initiation of populations in such factors as phenotypic differences in fitness traits, ages, genotypes for reproductive or competitive ability, possible infections of parental individuals, and variation in quantity and quality of food provided. Other influences, similar in affecting cultures as units but different in that they are still unresolved in newly established populations, include, for example, temperature and humidity to the extent that their variations from culture to culture are inadequately controlled.

Contrasting with these factors are influences dependent on accidents, coincidences, and, in general, chance phenomena within the individual populations themselves. Certainly belonging to this class are such events as may be traceable to the indeterminacy of behavior of small particles postulated in the theory of quantum mechanics. As has been often noted, variations of individual atoms or small groups of atoms may in some instances create ultimate effects of great magnitude, notably but by no means exclusively exemplified by gene mutation. A molecular accident could, conceivably, affect slightly the stimulus threshold of a neuron, in consequence of which the path taken by a beetle in its wanderings through the medium may be modified, and perhaps deflected from an egg that otherwise would be eaten. In addition there may be innumerable events which, while in an ultimate sense determinate, are uncorrelated in any direct or systematic manner with conditions existing at the initiation of a culture, and are generally so complex as to defy predictability or detailed analysis. Such minor factors as the positions of the beetles at the initiation of a culture, or their tendency, perhaps because of a minor injury, to turn to the right or left on meeting an obstacle, would probably have no effect on the average on the outcome of competition, but in a particular culture might to a degree determine patterns of mating and predation. Events of this general kind, even though conceivably already predetermined at the initiation of individual cultures, could affect the numbers of individuals within each population in a manner susceptible to characterization and interpretation by stochastic models.

In actual experiments there must be indeterminacy with respect to influences of both kinds, those acting within populations and those affecting populations as units, although one may outweigh the other. Neyman, Park, and Scott,[6] in discussing stochastic models applicable to the competition experiments of Park and associates, considered the possibility that indeterminacy of outcome of a culture may exist so long as the ratio of the numbers of individuals of the two species remains within certain definite limits. Such a formulation implies indeterminacy due predominantly to internal factors of the type described in the preceding paragraph, that is, of individual populations themselves. In such case, the drift of the numerical ratio of individuals of the two species to one limit or the other is in any culture due to chance occurrences within it. But, on the other hand, should the genotypes of the founders of the population in actual fact constitute the major influence determining the outcome, such a shift in numerical ratio would be only the result of the competitive values already possessed by the initial genotypes.

In our experiments, within-species genetic variation was demonstrably of overriding importance, inasmuch as the ability of the species to win depended on the particular inbred lines used in a given trial, and the outcome was completely deterministic where genotypic variation was adequately restricted. As a corollary it can be concluded that chance phenomena within our individual populations were so feeble in their ultimate effects as to alter the outcome in few, if any, instances. Therefore it seems reasonable to suggest that in the experiments, differing from ours in some respects, of Park and his associates genotypic variability, which was not closely controlled, may also have been of major importance and responsible at least in part for the observed indeterminacy. Hardin[12] in discussing Park's results wrote: "With certain fixed values for the environmental parameters the experimenters have been unable to control conditions carefully enough to obtain an invariable result." He evidently presumed the influences affecting populations as a unit to be chiefly responsible for the indeterminism. Had Hardin not restricted himself to "conditions," but considered also the possibility of variation among individual genotypes, his conclusion would have been anticipatory of our experiments. It should be stated, however, that the existence of minor residual sources of uncontrolled variation within populations, no doubt, could, even where genotype and other influences affecting populations were very closely controlled, lead to indeterminacy in exceedingly closely matched competitions.

The view elaborated here lends great emphasis to the importance of the genotypes of founders of initially small isolates or Mendelian populations, as has been previously advocated by Mayr,[13] or, more generally, ascribes a significant role to genetic drift. Other indeterminate situations, directly related to genotype, also

341

826 *ZOÖLOGY: LERNER AND DEMPSTER* Proc. N. A. S.

occur, as was clearly brought out in the *Drosophila pseudoobscura* experiments of Dobzhansky and associates[14-16] where drift, occasioned by the fact that only a small proportion of possible recombinants is represented in finite populations, was demonstrated. Our results also suggest that an assumption of indeterminism within experimental populations should not be taken lightly where genotypic variability has not been carefully controlled or not investigated to determine its adequacy to explain the observed results.

*Summary.*—Data are presented to indicate that indeterminacy of outcome of interspecific competition experiments may be largely a reflection of random selection of the genotypes of founder populations.

[1] Park, T., *Ecol. Monographs*, **18**, 265 (1948).

[2] Kennington, G. S., *Physiol. Zoöl.*, **26**, 179 (1953).

[3] Park, T., *Physiol. Zoöl.*, **27**, 177 (1954).

[4] Park, T., and M. Lloyd, *Am. Naturalist*, **89**, 235 (1955).

[5] Lerner, I. M., and F. K. Ho, *Am. Naturalist*, **95**, 329 (1961).

[6] Neyman, J., T. Park, and E. L. Scott, *Proc. 3rd Berkeley Symp. Math. Stat. Prob.*, **4**, 41 (1956).

[7] Cole, L. C., *Science*, **132**, 348 (1960).

[8] Bartlett, M. S., *Stochastic Population Models in Ecology and Epidemiology* (New York: John Wiley & Sons, Inc., 1960), p. 3.

[9] Park, T., in *The Numbers of Man and Animals* (Edinburgh: Oliver & Boyd, Ltd., 1955).

[10] Mayr, E., *Science*, **134**, 1501 (1961).

[11] Fisher, R. A., *Statistical Methods for Research Workers* (6th ed.; Edinburgh: Oliver & Boyd, Ltd., 1936).

[12] Hardin, G., *Science*, **131**, 1292 (1960).

[13] Mayr, E., in *Evolution as a Process*, ed. J. S. Huxley *et al.* (London: George Allen & Unwin, Ltd., 1954).

[14] Dobzhansky, Th., and O. Pavlovsky, *Evolution*, **7**, 198 (1953).

[15] *Ibid.*, **11**, 311 (1957).

[16] Dobzhansky, Th., and N. P. Spassky, these Proceedings, **48**, 148 (1962).

# THE COMPARATIVE BIOLOGY OF CLOSELY RELATED SPECIES LIVING IN THE SAME AREA

## VII. INTERFERENCE BETWEEN INDIVIDUALS IN PURE AND MIXED POPULATIONS OF *PAPAVER* SPECIES

### By JOHN L. HARPER* and I. H. McNAUGHTON†

*Department of Agriculture, University of Oxford*

(*Received 3 January* 1962)

(With 6 figures in the text)

### SUMMARY

Seeds of *Papaver rhoeas, P. dubium, P. lecoqii, P. argemone* and *P. apulum* were sown in garden plots at a range of densities in pure stands and mixtures of two species. The plants reacted to density by a reduced chance of establishment and a plastic reduction of plant weight and capsule numbers — the species did not differ in their reactions to density in pure stands.

In mixed populations the chance of establishment of a species was reduced when its own density in the mixture was increased — the density of the associated species exerted a less significant influence.

The species in lower proportion in a mixture gave the more successful establishment from seed — and it is argued that the persistence of mixed populations is therefore favoured in comparison with pure stands.

### INTRODUCTION

The presence of two or more closely related species living together in the same area poses two types of problem. The continued co-existence‡ of the species as distinct entities presupposes that some form of barrier to inter-breeding occurs between them; the continued cohabitation§ of two species without one succeeding at the expense of another implies some type of biological difference between the species which permits them to evade a decisive struggle for existence. In the first paper of this series the occurrence of mixed populations of species of *Papaver* was described (McNaughton and Harper, 1960*a*). In the distribution of the five British species *P. rhoeas, P. dubium, P. lecoqii, P. argemone* and *P. hybridum*, the presence of two or more species in the same habitat is the rule, only *P. rhoeas* being at all commonly found alone. The other species are almost always found associated with *P. rhoeas*, often with other species of the genus present as well, and on occasion all five species may be present in the same habitat. The first three papers of this series have described the isolating mechanisms which permit these species to remain as distinct specific entities when co-existing.

* Present address: Dept. of Agricultural Botany, University College of N. Wales, Bangor.
† Present address: Scottish Plant Breeding Station, Pentlandfield, Midlothian.
‡ Species are said to *co-exist* if individuals (or their products) ever come into such proximity during their breeding season that all the processes normally leading to fertilization could reasonably be considered possible (Cain, 1953).
§ Species are said to *cohabit* if individuals (or their products) ever come into such proximity that a struggle for existence could reasonably be considered possible (Harper *et al.*, 1961).

E NP    Reprinted by permission of the Trustees of the New Phytologist and the authors from New Phytologist 61:175–188, 1962.

The aim of the experiments described in this paper was to determine what differences in the behaviour of poppies permit them to persist together in mixtures in which one species does not succeed at the expense of the others. The poppies were chosen because their annual habit and relative ease of culture make them convenient material for experimental investigation, particularly in field plots.

Because all plant species have the power of exponential increase, and yet over a period of time their density varies only within relatively narrow limits, it has been argued that the growth of populations must be limited by their size (Harper *et al.*, 1961; Harper, 1960). As the density of a population increases so the rate of increase is slowed down by some controlling or stabilizing consequence of the increasing density of the population. Two species may cohabit in stable mixture only if the population of each reacts specifically to the controlling influences of its own density (Harper *et al.*, 1961). To understand the cohabitation of species it becomes necessary, therefore, to study the reaction of each species to its own density and to compare this with its reaction to the density of associated species.

### Experimental methods

Early experimental studies of the behaviour of poppy populations in field plots were frustrated because of the large numbers of poppy seedlings emerging from buried seed in the arable land sites which we had chosen. Eventually a walled garden long laid down to grass was chosen for this experiment. Its soil proved to have no effective buried seed of poppies present in it. The area chosen was dug, the turf buried one spit deep and the larger stones and debris removed. A heavy fertilizer application was made to the area to mask, as far as possible, any heterogeneities in nutrient status of the proposed experimental plots. The garden was long and narrow with a tall building at one end which shaded the southern half of the area. It was divided transversely into three blocks and the whole experiment was replicated in each block. Each block was divided into eighty plots, each 35 cm square. The plots were sown with various densities and combinations of four of the British species of *Papaver*: *P. rhoeas*, *P. dubium*, *P. lecoqii*, *P. argemone* and a fifth species, *P. apulum* which was obtained from Botanic Gardens and is native in the Mediterranean regions. Three of the species, *P. rhoeas*, *P dubium* and *P. lecoqii* are assigned by Fedde (1909) to the section Orthorhoeades and *P. argemone*, and *P. apulum* to the Argemonorhoeades.

Two sowing rates were employed, 25 seeds per plot and 200 seeds per plot. Each plot receiving 25 seeds of species A also received either 25 or 200 seeds of species A, B, C, D or E. Each plot receiving 200 seeds of species A also received either 25 or 200 seeds of A, B, C, D or E. Thus each species was sown in pure stand at densities of $25^A+25^A$, $200^A+25^A$ and $200^A+200^A$ seeds and each mixture of two species was sown at densities of $25^A+25^B$, $25^A+200^B$, $200^A+25^B$ and $200^A+200^B$. This design permits:

(i) comparison between pure stands of different species over comparable ranges of density,
(ii) comparison between mixtures and pure stands at constant total density, and
(iii) comparison between mixtures of different proportions of the same two species.

The seed used in this experiment was all collected from natural populations in the Oxford area during the previous season except for seed of *P. apulum*. A complication was introduced into the experimental procedure because of the high proportion of dormant seed in samples from wild poppy populations (Harper and McNaughton, 1960). This dormancy has the consequence that the number of seeds germinating immediately after sowing is smaller than the number of seeds sown. In order to obtain comparable densities of seedlings it was necessary to sow seeds in excess of the density of seedlings required. An estimate of the proportion of non-dormant seed in each seed sample obtained from germination tests made in the laboratory, was used to calculate the number of seeds of each species which required to be sown in order to obtain comparable populations. A detailed statistical examination of the counts of plants on the plots (see Table 1 and p. 178) confirmed that this weighting procedure had been successful. In the garden plots more seeds germinated than in the laboratory tests, but the weighting procedure assured comparable establishment of the different species. In subsequent discussion of these experiments density of sowing is described in terms of the number of 'effective' seeds sown and this accounts for the peculiar feature that more than 100% 'establishment' was sometimes obtained.

The seed samples were mixed thoroughly with fine sand and the mixture dispersed over each plot. Seeds were sown on 19 April 1957, and the first seedlings emerged about 3 weeks later.

No detailed counts could be made of the number of seedlings emerged from mixed sowings because of the extreme difficulty of distinguishing some of the species at the seedling stage; *P. dubium* and *P. lecoqii* and *P. argemone* and *P. apulum* are particularly confusing pairs. The plots were weeded throughout the growing season but weeds were not a serious problem. In the first 3 weeks of August there were frequent heavy rainstorms which resulted in lodging of the plants. The experiment was harvested on 22 August 1957. Because the growth periods of the species are not completely synchronous it is clearly impossible to choose a harvest date at an absolutely comparable stage of growth for each species. At harvest, *P. rhoeas* was still flowering whereas others (notably *P. argemone*), had ceased flowering and their capsules had dehisced.

At harvest the plants were cut at ground level and the following values determined for each species separately:

(*a*) number of plants per plot,
(*b*) total dry weight per plot,
(*c*) total number of capsules per plot.

It proved impracticable to determine seed output per plant because the capsules ripen in succession over 4 or 5 weeks and each dehisces when mature so that most of the seeds are lost. There was some evidence that first formed capsules ripened more seeds than those formed later in the season on the same plant.

## EXPERIMENTAL RESULTS

1. *The response of pure stands of* Papaver *species to density*

The poppies reacted to density by increased mortality and also by a reduction in individual plant size. These effects are considered separately.

*The influence of the density of sowing on the mortality of* Papaver *species.* The relationship between the number of seeds sown and the number of plants present at maturity was strikingly non-linear — see Fig. 1. The chance that a seed would produce a plant was diminished as the density of sowing was increased. A regression equation $Y = bx + cx^2$ was fitted to the relationship between the number of seeds sown and the number of

178        J. L. Harper and I. H. McNaughton

plants present at harvest. In this equation *b* may be taken as a measure of the chance that a seed will produce a plant irrespective of the influence of density and *c* represents a measure of the role of density in affecting establishment. The regression was fitted separately to each block for each species except *P. argemone* for which there were a large number of missing values. The results were consistent with the assumption that the regression adequately approximated to the data (see Table 1).

Table 1. *Regression equations relating number of plants per plot* (Y) *to the number of 'effective' seeds sown* (x = *number of 'effective' seeds*)

|  | b | c |
|---|---|---|
| Block A (southernmost, sheltered) | $Y = 25.484x - 1.247x^2$ | |
| Block B (intermediate) | $Y = 19.653x - 0.986x^2$ | |
| Block C (northernmost, exposed) | $Y = 10.336x - 0.372x^2$ | |

The values for *b* and *c* did not differ significantly between species, indicating (i) that the species did not differ significantly in the number of plants produced per 'effective' seed sown, and (ii) the influence of density on establishment was the same for all species in pure stands.

However, *b* differed significantly between blocks ($P<0.05$) and there was some suggestion that this was also true for *c* ($P<0.1$). Thus position in the garden did affect the chance that a seed would give rise to a plant — the southern sheltered block offering the

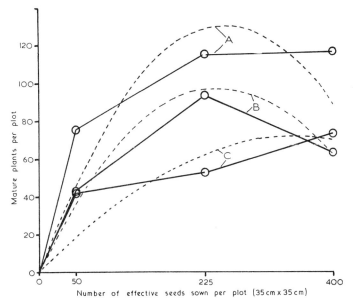

Fig. 1. The relationship between the density of seeds sown and the density of mature plants at harvest based on mean values from five species of *Papaver*. The three dotted curves are calculated regressions (see Table 1) for three blocks A, B and C of the experiment in different parts of the experimental garden.

most favourable and the northern block the least favourable conditions for establishment. These block effects are illustrated in Fig. 1.

*The influence of sowing density on dry weight per plant.* The relationship between the number of seeds sown and the dry weight of plants at harvest involved a decline in individual plant weight as density was increased. Regression equations $Y = a+bx+cx^2$ were fitted separately to each block for each variety. In the equations the term $a$ describes the dry weight per plant irrespective of the action of density and $b$ and $c$ describe the linear and quadratic components of the reaction to density.

There was strong evidence ( $P = <0.01$) of real differences between the values of $a$ for the four species examined (see Table 2). The extent of decline in dry weight per plant was adequately described without the quadratic term which was not significant at $P = <0.1$ and the value of $b$ did not differ significantly between species.

Table 2. *Regression equations relating dry weight per plant* (Y) *to the number of effective seeds sown per plot*

(*a*) Means of three blocks

| | |
|---|---|
| P. rhoeas | $Y = 6.11 - 0.0058x$ g |
| P. dubium | $Y = 4.28 - 0.0058x$ g |
| P. lecoqii | $Y = 4.09 - 0.0058x$ g |
| P. apulum | $Y = 1.91 - 0.0058x$ g |

(*b*) Means of four species

| | |
|---|---|
| Block A (southernmost, sheltered) | $Y = 2.953 + 0.007x$ g |
| Block B (intermediate) | $Y = 4.812 - 0.020x$ g |
| Block C (northernmost, exposed) | $Y = 2.523 - 0.018x$ g |

Individual plant weight was significantly influenced by the position of blocks ($P = <0.05$) the smallest plants being found in the southernmost shaded block where the plant establishment had been most successful.

*The influence of plant density on capsule number per plant.* The regression equation $Y = a+bx+cx^2$ was fitted to each block for each species. The number of capsules per plant decreased as density was increased and the rate of decline did not differ significantly between species. However, there were marked differences in the values of $a$ for the different species — indicating significant differences in the number of capsules borne by plants of the different species irrespective of the influences of density (Table 3).

Table 3. *Regression equations relating capsule number per plant* (Y) *to the density of plants per plot* (x)

| | |
|---|---|
| P. rhoeas | $Y = 10.700 - 0.0044x$ |
| P. apulum | $Y = 9.669 - 0.0044x$ |
| P. lecoqii | $Y = 4.568 - 0.0044x$ |
| P. dubium | $Y = 2.772 - 0.0044x$ |

Pure stands of the poppy species react to increasing density by an increasing risk of mortality and reduced vegetative growth. Increasing density caused a comparable reduction in establishment of all species. The species differed in the growth made before maturity. Increasing density reduced this growth to the same extent in all species. The species did not differ either in success of establishment or plastic response to density. In contrast, different environments, represented by the three blocks in different positions in the garden produced differences both in establishment and subsequent growth and significantly influenced the density response curves for both these parameters.

2. *The response of mixed populations of poppies to density*

The experimental design permitted a comparison of the chance of survival of poppy species in all possible combinations of two species over a range of densities. Each pair of species was present in each block of the experiment sown:

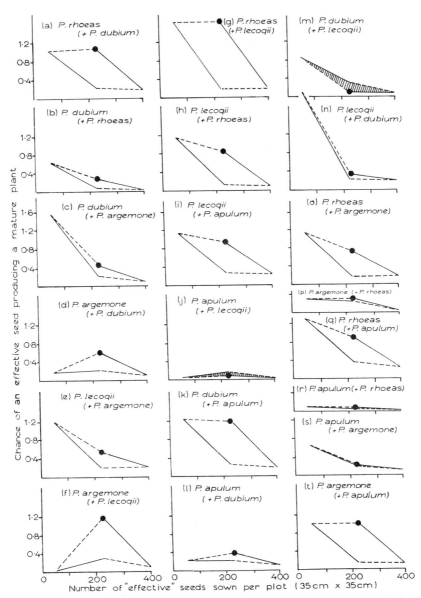

Fig. 2. The influence of density on 'self-' and 'alien-thinning' in two species populations of *Papaver*. The extreme densities, 50 and 400 'effective' seeds per plot were composed of equal numbers of 'effective' seeds of each species. The intermediate density of 225 'effective' seeds per plot was obtained either with a preponderance (8 : 1) of one species or the other. The difference between the chance of a seed producing a mature plant at the two differently constituted intermediate densities reflects the different degrees of thinning produced in predominantly 'self' and predominantly 'alien' populations. In each figure the broken line indicates 'alien-thinning' and the continuous line 'self-thinning'. Cases in which 'alien-thinning' was more intense than 'self-thinning' are shown cross-hatched.

(i) in equal proportions at low density ($25^A + 25^B$ seeds per square foot),

(ii) in equal proportions at high density ($200^A + 200^B$ seeds per square foot), and

(iii) in two different proportions at an intermediate density ($25^A + 200^B$ or $200^A + 25^B$).

The chance that a seed would produce a plant in each of these combinations is plotted against the *combined* sowing density of the two species in Figs. 2a-t. The term 'self-thinning' is used to describe the reduction in the chance that a seed of a given species will form a mature plant which is brought about by an increase in the density of that species. Thus a measure of 'self-thinning' of A is obtained by comparing the performance of A in $(A_{25} + B_{25})$ with that in $(A_{200} + B_{25})$. The term 'alien-thinning' describes the reduction in the chance of a seed forming a mature plant caused by an increase in the density of the associated species. Correspondingly, the measure of 'alien-thinning' is given by comparison of A in $(A_{25} + B_{25})$ with A in $(A_{25} + B_{200})$.

A further measure of 'self-thinning' of A is given by comparing $(A_{25} + B_{200})$ with $(A_{200} + B_{200})$ and of 'alien-thinning' by comparing $(A_{200} + B_{25})$ with $(A_{200} + B_{200})$. In almost all cases shown in Fig. 2 it can be seen that 'self-thinning' is a more drastic process than 'alien-thinning'; *the density-induced establishment risk for each species in a mixture is largely controlled by its own density*. The only marked exception to this rule is the case of *P. dubium* in mixture with *P. lecoqii*, in which case 'alien-thinning' is slightly stronger than 'self-thinning' (see discussion).

### 3. *The relative aggressiveness of the species of* Papaver

In the foregoing analysis each species was considered separately for its reaction in various mixtures. It is also possible to compare the relative performance of two species in mixtures. This may be done visually by making a point to point comparison of the paired diagrams in Fig. 2 (Figs. 2 a and b, c and d, e and f, etc.) or by a statistical test. Since within each block regressions of plant number on density in pure stands are not significantly different for the four species (*vide supra*), direct comparisons between plant numbers for two species in any mixture are valid. Thus where $A_{25}$ denotes the number of plants of species A established at maturity from low density of sowing (25 seeds per square foot) and $A_{200}$ denotes the number of plants of A established at maturity from the high density of sowing (200 seeds per square foot) we may make four comparisons between any two species in mixture:

(*a*) $A_{25}$-$B_{25}$, in which the two species were sown in mixture both at low densities;

(*b*) $A_{200}$-$B_{200}$ in which the species were sown at high densities;

(*c*) $A_{200}$-$8B_{25}$ in which A was sown at eight times the density of B; and

(*d*) $8A_{25}$-$B_{200}$ in which A was sown at one-eighth the density of B.

The comparisons involved three blocks and except in cases where plots were lost, 2 degrees of freedom were available for Student's *t* test. The *t* values for the tests of all species combinations are shown in Table 4.

These results and the visual comparison in Fig. 2 show that *P. apulum* suffered the heavier proportion of total mortality in any mixture of which it was a component; there was only one exception to this rule in the twelve situations studied. The order of aggressiveness of the four species when sown in equal proportions appears to be: *P. rhoeas* > *P. lecoqii* > *P. dubium* > *P. apulum*, irrespective of the density of sowing. In most cases an increase in density from $A_{25} + B_{25}$ to $A_{200} + B_{200}$ exaggerated the differential between the species. A change in proportions of A and B, however, sometimes reversed the differences

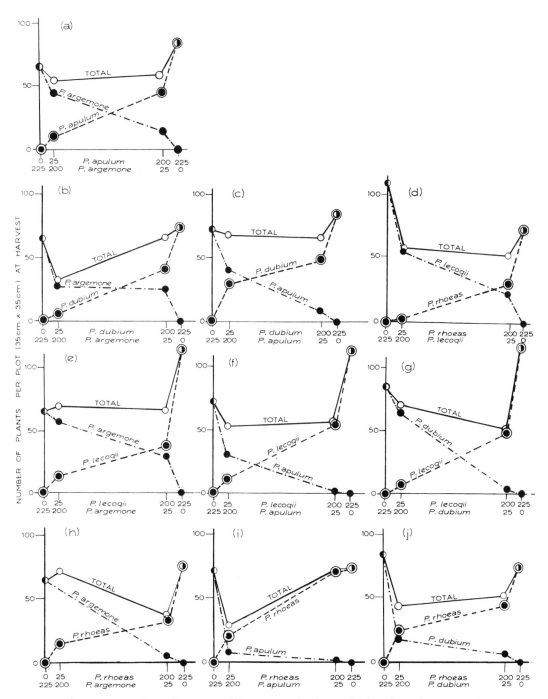

Fig. 3. The numbers of plants surviving to maturity from mixed sowings of poppy species at constant density and varied proportions. The figures on the horizontal scales indicate the number of seeds of each species sown on the plot.

between the species. The order of aggressiveness of the species broadly resembled the order of dry weights of the species in pure stand — the heavier species being the more lethal in mixtures (cf. Table 2).

Table 4. *A comparison by Student's* t *test of the relative success of establishment from seed of species of* Papaver *in various two species mixtures sown at different densities and proportions (see text)*

| | Species in mixture | | | | |
|---|---|---|---|---|---|
| Comparison | A | B | d.f. | t | P |
| | P. apulum | P. dubium | 2 | −4.12 | <0.1 |
| | P. apulum | P. lecoqii | 2 | −3.91 | <0.1 |
| | P. apulum | P. rhoeas | 2 | −2.96 | <0.1 |
| A₂₅-B₂₅ | P. dubium | P. lecoqii | 2 | −2.21 | |
| | P. dubium | P. rhoeas | 2 | −0.50 | |
| | P. lecoqii | P. rhoeas | 1 | −0.63 | |
| | P. apulum | P. dubium | 2 | −1.91 | |
| | P. apulum | P. lecoqii | 2 | −4.86 | <0.05 |
| | P. apulum | P. rhoeas | 2 | −6.72 | <0.05 |
| A₂₀₀-B₂₀₀ | P. dubium | P. lecoqii | 2 | −91.00 | <0.01 |
| | P. dubium | P. rhoeas | 2 | −2.64 | |
| | P. lecoqii | P. rhoeas | 1 | −19.00 | <0.05 |
| | P. apulum | P. dubium | 2 | −11.32 | <0.01 |
| | P. apulum | P. lecoqii | 2 | −1.76 | |
| | P. apulum | P. rhoeas | 2 | −2.31 | |
| A₂₀₀-8B₂₅ | P. dubium | P. lecoqii | 1 | −0.31 | |
| | P. dubium | P. rhoeas | 2 | −1.48 | |
| | P. lecoqii | P. rhoeas | 2 | −2.58 | |
| | P. apulum | P. dubium | 2 | +1.57 | |
| | P. apulum | P. lecoqii | 2 | −4.17 | <0.1 |
| 8A₂₅-B₂₀₀ | P. apulum | P. rhoeas | 2 | −11.30 | <0.01 |
| | P. dubium | P. lecoqii | 1 | −9.33 | <0.1 |
| | P. dubium | P. rhoeas | 2 | +0.47 | |

*4. The response of mixed populations of poppies to changes in proportion at constant density*

The design of this experiment permits a comparison of two species in mixture at constant combined density but varied proportions $A_0 + B_{225} : A_{25} + B_{200} : A_{200} + B_{25} : A_{225} + B_0$. Fig. 3 shows the influences of changes in proportion of two species on the total number of plants present at harvest and the composition of this population. In no case did a mixed sowing produce as great a number of mature plants as one of the components in pure stands. Moreover, mixed stands contained less plants than either corresponding pure stand with two exceptions which involved the poorly replicated *P. argemone*.

Fig. 4 illustrates the changes in total weight per plot at harvest associated with changed proportions of the species sown. The influence of numbers of plants has now been partially masked by large differences in their weight — *P. argemone* and *P. apulum* being small plants and *P. rhoeas*, *P. dubium* and *P. lecoqii* forming heavier plants (Table 2) in their longer growing season. The total dry weight of mixtures was usually intermediate between the weights of the two pure stands.

From observations (i) that mixed stands produced fewer plants than pure stands and (ii) that mixed stands produced a dry weight per plot close to that predicted from the weight produced in pure stands, it follows that plants in mixed stands achieved greater individual dry weights.

The dry weight yield per plot from various combinations of species is illustrated in Fig. 5. The highest yields were obtained from mixtures of smooth capsuled species, and the lowest yields from mixtures of spiny capsuled species.

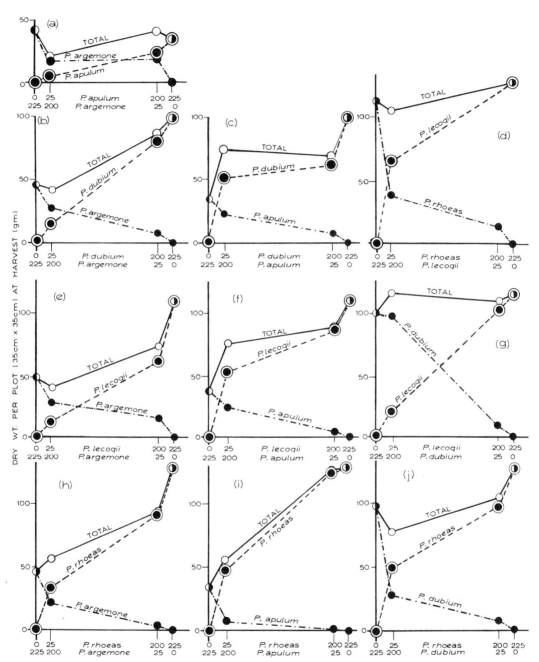

Fig. 4. The weight of plants per plot at harvest derived from mixed sowings of poppy species at constant density and varied proportions (cf. Fig. 3). The figures on the horizontal scales indicate the number of seeds of each species sown on the plot.

## *Interference between individuals*

### DISCUSSION

#### *Establishment of poppy populations*

It is convenient to regard the abundance of a species in an area as determined by (i) the availability of 'seed', (ii) the ability of the species to tolerate the physical and biotic features of the environment such as frost, drought, soil type, predators, grazing animals and (iii) the ability of the species to withstand 'interference' from other plants. There are of course interactions between these factors — but they provide a convenient framework for discussion.

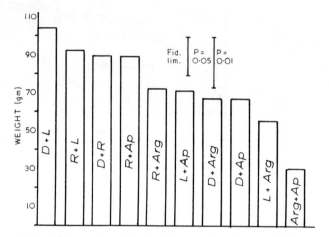

Fig. 5. Dry weight yields per plot of various two species mixtures of *Papaver*. The values shown represent the yield averaged over blocks and densities. R = P. rhoeas, D = P. dubium, L = P. lecoqii, Ap = P. apulum, Arg = P. argemone.

The experiments which have been concerned with the reaction of poppy populations to the density of sowing permit the analysis of the three classes of causal factors which contribute to the abundance of poppies. Sowing a range of seed densities permits the study of the reaction of a species to availability of seed. The size of populations which develop may be analysed in their relation to numbers of seed by a regression which separates those causes of mortality which are independent of the interference from neighbours (ii above) from those causes of mortality which are 'determined' by density (iii above).

The results of the experiments with pure stands show:

(i) That the presence of poppies in the experimental garden was dependent on an external supply of seed — no poppies developed on control plots to which no seed had been added.

(ii) Apart from influences of density, the environmental conditions of the experimental garden offered different chances of establishment to the poppies sown in different places. A seed was more than twice as likely to produce a mature plant when sown in the southernmost sheltered part of the garden as in the northernmost exposed part.

(iii) The more seeds sown, the greater was the chance that a seed failed to produce a mature plant. Such density-regulated establishment clearly conferred self-regulating properties on the pure populations. Moreover the regulatory mechanism seemed to act with approximately equal force on the four species *P. apulum, P. rhoeas,*

*P. dubium* and *P. lecoqii* (probably also *P. argemone*), placing an upper limit on population size of seventy to ninety plants per 35 cm square. This is of the same order of density as many naturally occurring 'dense' stands.

It is interesting that, *after allowance had been made for different amounts of dormant seeds*, no differences in establishment could be detected between species — either with or without the influences of density. Measured in terms of population parameters the species were indistinguishable in these experiments.

### Mixed populations

An examination was made of the establishment of the poppies in mixed populations to separate the effects of density from the effects of proportion.

Increasing density brought with it reduced chance of establishment in the majority of mixtures as in pure stands. However, the population did not react as a uniform whole to density, but each component species suffered mainly according to its own abundance in the mixture. The experimental design made it possible to compare the density-induced failure to establish which was caused by 'self-thinning' with that due to 'alien-thinning' (see Fig. 2). In almost every case the species in greater abundance in a mixture suffered the greater thinning. In two species mixtures of *P. rhoeas*, *P. dubium* and *P. lecoqii*, 'self-thinning' was more pronounced than 'alien-thinning' — the only exception was *P. dubium* in the presence of *P. lecoqii*. In two species mixtures of *P. rhoeas*, *P. dubium* or *P. lecoqii* with *P. apulum* or *P. argemone* 'self-thinning' was again more intense than 'alien-thinning'; and this also occurred in mixtures of *P. apulum* with *P. argemone*. The two spiny-capsuled species *P. apulum* and *P. argemone* showed decreased mortality in the presence of smooth-capsuled species so that here again the species sown in greatest abundance suffered the greatest mortality risk.

The order of the species in agressiveness towards the establishment of each other was essentially the same as that of their vegetative vigour. It was, in decreasing order of aggressiveness and dry weight:

$$P.\ rhoeas > P.\ lecoqii \lesseqgtr P.\ dubium > P.\ apulum$$

The pattern of establishment in mixed populations is not wholly revealed by the analysis of Fig. 2. A consideration of Fig. 3 illustrates a greater complexity. When populations were maintained at constant density, but the proportions of two species sown were varied it was found that the greatest density of plants was regularly obtained from pure stands. In the absence of interference between individuals, either due to 'self-' or 'alien-thinning' the theoretical expectation of population size obtained from mixed sowings is shown in Fig. 6a.

In fact, this situation was only approximately realized in one case — that of mixtures of *P. lecoqii* with *P. dubium*. In most of the remaining fifteen mixtures the situation was closer to that shown in Fig. 6b.

The replacement of 25 seeds in a pure sowing of 225 seeds by 25 seeds of an alien species resulted in a disproportionately reduced establishment of the majority species. This may be interpreted *either* as excessive 'self-thinning' on the part of the part of the majority species *or* as excessive 'alien-thinning' by the minority species. The consequence, also predictable from Fig. 2, is that the species in minority in a mixture was always at an advantage over the majority species, by virtue of its lower mortality risk. This further implies that pure stands were unstable with respect to mixtures and that

## Interference between individuals

*mixtures possessed self-stabilizing properties.* Only the mixtures of *P. dubium* and *P. lecoqii* were clear exceptions to this rule and it is remarkable that these two are rarely found wild in mixed stands (McNaughton and Harper, 1960*a*). It is especially interesting that throughout the analysis of the results of this experiment, *P. dubium* and *P. lecoqii* behaved in a remarkably similar manner. In particular they behaved in mixed stands as if they formed a pure stand — their reactions to 'self-' and 'alien-thinning' did not differ significantly, i.e. they reacted to each other's presence much as they reacted to their own. These two species are very similar in other respects, hybridize readily and are often confused (McNaughton and Harper, 1960*b*).

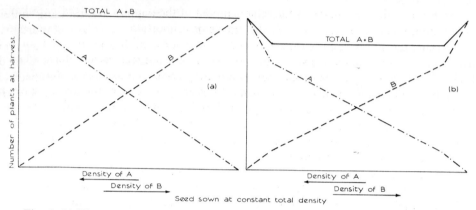

Fig. 6. (a) The theoretical relationship between sowing density and plant numbers in a mixed population of two species A and B at constant combined density and changing proportions with no inter- or intra-specific interference influencing establishment. (b) Typical actual relationship corresponding to (a), with inter- and intra-specific interference influencing establishment (cf. Fig. 3).

### The plasticity of individuals in poppy populations

As the density of populations was increased, the size of individuals, measured as dry weight or as the number of capsules produced per plant, declined. In pure stands the influence of density on plasticity was the same irrespective of the species of poppy sown. In mixed stands the analysis of the plastic response to density was made extremely complex because of the processes of 'self-' and 'alien-thinning' which distorted the relationship between sowing density and ultimate density.

It is unfortunate that it was not found feasible to measure seed output per plant in these experiments so that the relationship between the ratio of seed sown into a plot and that obtained from the plot could be compared (*vide* De Wit, 1960, 1961). However, it may be argued that this information is largely irrelevant to understanding the continued cohabitation of a pair of *Papaver* species for, so long as 'self-thinning' is more vigorous than 'alien-thinning' and the minority species has the lower mortality risk, then the proportions of seeds produced by a mixture at the end of a growing season will be within wide limits irrelevant to the proportions of plants present in the subsequent year.

De Wit (1961) has shown that two species with non-synchronous growth cycles may form stable mixtures — the physiologic analysis of such a situation has been made for the two species *Trifolium repens* and *T. fragiferum* by Harper and Clatworthy (in press). Among the species of *Papaver* considered in this paper the major obvious difference in growth cycles is between the members of the Argemonorhoeades (*P. argemone* and *P. apulum*) and the members of the Orthorhoeades (*P. rhoeas*, *P. dubium* and *P. lecoqii*).

188   J. L. HARPER AND I. H. McNAUGHTON

Flowering is earlier in *P. argemone* and *P. apulum* than in the three smooth-capsuled species and the spiny-capsuled species lose their leaf earlier in the season. The different growth rhythms of the Orthorhoeades and Argemonorhoeades might be sufficient to permit the cohabitation of pairs of species composed of one species from each section of the genus. However, differences in growth period are not apparent between members of the same section of the genus, yet associations of pairs of species from the same sections are very common in the field. It is suggested that the observed differences in 'alien-' and 'self-thinning' of such mixtures are sufficient to permit indefinite cohabitation of these species pairs in more or less stable mixture.

No evidence is offered of the mechanism by which 'alien-' and 'self-thinning' differ. If, as already noted by McNaughton (1959) 'damping-off' is the main cause of mortality, then one might look for species specificity among pathogens to account for the observed patterns of thinning in mixed populations. This interpretation of the mechanism of excess 'self-thinning' compared with 'alien-thinning' is then paralleled by the observed high incidence of *Puccinia graminis* in pure stands of wheat varieties, and low incidence in mixed stands (Hanna, 1956, discussed by Harper *et al.*, 1961). Investigations of this aspect of the problems are continuing.

The experiments described in this paper have relevance both to the manner of regulation of natural populations and to the linked problems associated with 'Gause's Law'. These two general problems have been considered in relation to higher plants in a previous essay (Harper *et al.*, 1961). The main significance of the experimental results described in the present paper lies in the demonstrations (i) that poppy populations have self-regulatory properties operating primarily through mortality (though also through plasticity). (ii) that there is a general tendency for the species composing mixed populations to regulate their numbers independently, and (iii) that pure stands suffer excessive mortality from the substitution of a small number of a related species.

### ACKNOWLEDGMENTS

We are greatly indebted to Mr. J. F. Scott and Dr. J. M. Walker of the Unit of Biometry, University of Oxford, for valued help with the analysis of experimental results. We also wish to thank Mr. R. Bowerman and Miss D. McKellar for technical assistance.

### REFERENCES

CAIN, A. J. (1953). Geography and co-existence in relation to the biological definition of species. *Evolution*, **7**, 76.

FEDDE, F. (1909) Papaveraceae, in *Das Pflanzenreich*, **4**, 366.

HARPER, JOHN L.. (1960). Factors controlling plant numbers, in *The Biology of Weeds*, ed. John L. Harper. Blackwell Scientific Publications, Oxford.

HARPER, JOHN L. (1961). Approaches to the study of plant competition in *Mechanisms in Biological Competition*, ed. F. L. Milthorpe. *Symp. Soc. Exp. Biol.*, **15**, 1.

HARPER, JOHN L., CLATWORTHY, J. N., McNAUGHTON, I. H. & SAGAR, G. R. (1961). The evolution and ecology of closely related species living in the same area. *Evolution*, **15**, 209.

HARPER, JOHN L. & McNAUGHTON, I. H. (1960). The inheritance of dormancy in inter- and intra-specific hybrids of *Papaver*. *Heredity*, **15**, 315.

McNAUGHTON, I. H. (1959). The comparative biology of closely related species living in the same area with special reference to the genus *Papaver*. D.Phil Thesis, Oxford University.

McNAUGHTON, I. H. & HARPER, JOHN L. (1960a). The comparative biology of closely related species living in the same area. I. External breeding barriers in *Papaver* species. *New Phytol.*, **59**, 15.

McNAUGHTON, I. H. & HARPER, JOHN L. (1960b). The comparative biology of closely related species living in the same area. III. The nature of barriers isolating sympatric populations of *Papaver dubium* and *P. lecoqii*. *New Phytol.*, **59**, 129.

DE WIT, C. T. (1960). On competition. *Versl. Landbouwk, Onderz*, **66**, 1.

DE WIT, C. T. (1961). Space relationships within populations of one or more species, in *Mechanisms in Biological Competition*, ed. F. L. Milthorpe. *Symp. Soc. Exp. Biol.*, **15**, 314.

# SELECTION, SPATIAL DISTRIBUTION, AND THE COEXISTENCE OF COMPETING FLY SPECIES*

DAVID PIMENTEL, EDWIN H. FEINBERG†, PETER W. WOOD, AND JOHN T. HAYES

Department of Entomology and Limnology, Cornell University, Ithaca, N.Y.

The competitive exclusion principle states that two species requiring the same resources cannot coexist. This principle is based on the assumption that the competing species themselves and their biotic environment remain genetically constant. From what is known about natural selection and evolution this is a broad assumption. We propose that situations exist in which two species might compete yet still coexist (Pimentel, 1965).

For example, interspecific competitors may change genetically so that both species coexist and utilize the same particular thing in the ecosystem—be it food, space, or other necessary resources. Let us assume that both species are fairly evenly balanced but that species A is slightly superior to species B.

As the numbers of the stronger species are increasing, the numbers of the weaker species are declining and becoming sparse. The abundant individuals of species A at this stage must contend principally with intraspecific competitive selection because there is a greater chance for individuals of this species to interact with their own kind than individuals of the sparse species. Concurrently, species B which is contending primarily with interspecific competitive selective pressure would evolve and improve its ability to compete with its more abundant cohort species A. As species B improves as a competitor its numbers increase and finally B becomes the more abundant species. Thus, the original trend is reversed. After many such oscillations, each change decreasing in intensity, a state of relative stability should result.

Time is essential for such evolution of coexistence to take place between competitors. As mentioned, if two species are fairly similar then fewer changes are necessary to make species B an equal or better competitor than species A. When species A is much stronger than species B, then species B declines rapidly and often does not have sufficient time to evolve.

Although Haldane (1932) did not specifically consider the coexistence of competing species, he pointed out that individuals of a rare species are engaged in competing with other species and struggling against the abiotic

*This study was supported in part by research grants of the National Science Foundation (Environmental Biology G-8903 and GB-549) and the National Institutes of Health (Allergy and Infectious Diseases AI-02914-04).

†Present address: Division of Systematic Biology, Stanford University, Stanford, California.

Reprinted by permission of The University of Chicago Press and the authors from The American Naturalist 99:97–109, 1965.

environment. Then natural selection is operating effectively, the rare species evolves and becomes better able to contend with its competitors and
other environmental factors. This is not usually so with a dominant species, reported Haldane, because these individuals are found in dense associations in which intraspecific selection may be biologically advantageous
for the individual but ultimately disastrous for the species (see also Huxley, 1948). Certainly such intraspecific competition would seldom be
favorable for a species especially relative to its ability to compete against
the sparse species.

The chances of the sparse species persisting and not dwindling to extinction because of competitive pressure depends upon the variability in
the sparse species population, and how much time is available for evolution
and subsequent improvement. With suitable variability and sufficient time
the sparse species under interspecific selective pressure should be able to
make the necessary changes so that it can meet the pressures of its competitor.

The evolutionary adjustment between the competing species would function in either a non-random or random distribution. The sparse species, non-
randomly distributed in scattered small colonies, would have an advantage
because this distribution provides the most favorable opportunity for evolutionary advance (Wright, 1937).

Further evidence in support of this idea comes from the existence of
genotypic strains of *Tribolium confusum* and *Tribolium castaneum*, which
have different competitive abilities. Lerner and Ho (1961) report that either
*T. confusum* or *T. castaneum* will win in competition depending on which
genotypic strains are competed against one another. To keep these two
competing species co-existing in a laboratory situation would require only
the manipulation of a proportion of the genotypes making up each species
population; competitive ability can be selected for (Moore, 1952).

Our aim in this study was to experimentally investigate the idea that the
dominant species in competition remains relatively static in its interspecific competitive ability and that the sparse species evolves to become
the better competitor and eventually the dominant species.

## METHODS

The selection of the housefly (*Musca domestica* L.) and the blowfly
(*Phaenicia sericata* [Meig.]), as experimental animals for use as biological
models, was based on many factors. Both species occupy similar niches in
nature. Their larvae have been observed competing in carnivore, human
(Kilpatric and Schoof, 1956), and chicken dung (R. Axtell, personal communication) and in garbage sludge (Quarterman et al, 1949) and we have observed them in carrion. Neither fly is cannibalistic nor predaceous in any
stage. The adults of both species feed on sugars and require protein for
egg production. Their life cycles are similar; at 80 F the life cycle of both
the housefly and blowfly is about 14 days.

The housefly and blowfly used were collected in the Ithaca area. At intervals, new wild flies were added to the wild and experimental population

TABLE 1

The addition of wild flies of the housefly and blowfly adults to
the multicell population system.

| Week added | Blowfly | | Housefly | |
|---|---|---|---|---|
| | Number added | Cell added to | Number added | Cell added to |
| (The following additions were both males and females.) | | | | |
| 15 | 14 | 15 | 14 | 15 |
| 22 | 19 | 13 | 19 | 13 |
| 22 | 19 | 14 | 19 | 14 |
| 23 | 40 | 8 | 40 | 14 |
| 25 | 32 | 8 | 32 | 13 |
| (The following additions were males.) | | | | |
| 39 | 7 | 14 | 20 | 15 |
| 46 | 25 | 2 | 10 | 16 |
| 46 | 25 | 2 | 10 | 16 |
| 46 | 25 | 2 | 10 | 16 |
| 48 | 25 | 13 | 48 | 10 |
| 49 | 25 | 8 | 10 | 11 |

in the multi-cell cage (table 1) to prevent any possible significant loss of
genes due to inbreeding. The wild flies were maintained under conditions
of husbandry similar to that of the experimental populations.

Populations of both the housefly and blowfly were maintained in population cages which forced both species to occupy the same niche—serving
the same role as herbivore and saprophyte and utilizing the same food and
space. The single-cell population cages consisted of Tri-State plastic
boxes (3.75 × 5.25 × 7.5 inches). To ventilate the cages 100 mesh bronze-
screening covered two openings (1.12 inches diameter) on each side and
one opening (1.5 × 2.5 inches) on the lid. In the cages, the larval and adult
stages of both species of flies depended upon the same food source; adult
flies oviposited directly onto the food which was held in glass shell vials
(1 by 2.4 inches high). The vials were filled 3/4 full with the gel (440 g
dried non-fat-milk, 365 g brewer's yeast, 12 g agar, and 4000 ml water).
About one gram of liver was placed on the surface of the cooled gel. Although the larvae of both species survived on either gel or liver alone, the
liver-gel combination was used because growth was better. One vial per
day was added to a cage until a total of seven vials was present; thereafter, the oldest vial was removed as a fresh one was introduced. The vials
were held off the bottom of the cage by a screen rack. Since the larval
stage of the housefly and blowfly is between four and five days, the larvae
had left the vials and pupated on the bottom of the cage by the time the oldest vial was removed seven days later. Larvae, which for any reason remained in the oldest vial, were discarded with the medium. Larvae which
were forced out of the vial prematurely either crawled into an adjoining vial
or fell to the bottom of the cage and died. Unless otherwise noted all populations were fed a lump of sugar as additional food for the adult flies.

100 THE AMERICAN NATURALIST

The multi-cell population cage, designed to provide an adequate space-time environment, consisted of 16 plastic boxes (3.75 × 5.25 × 7.5 inches) joined to make one large cage (Pimentel et al, 1963). The boxes in 4 by 4 arrangement were connected by 1.5 inch lengths of plastic tubing (0.25 inch inside diameter). This design permitted the flies to disperse slowly throughout the cage. Events taking place in one cell had limited influence upon populations in adjoining cells; we estimate that it would take at least four weeks for overcrowding in one side of the multi-cell cage to be passed on through the intervening cells and influence populations on the opposite side of the cage.

The adult fly populations were censused weekly. For censusing, the flies were lightly anesthetized with carbon dioxide bubbled through water. The increased moisture level reduced the drying effect and a normal exposure time of five minutes caused no mortality. The use of carbon dioxide as an anesthetic was compared with nitrogen to determine if either might have an effect upon the outcome of interspecific competition between the housefly and blowfly; no significant (Chi square test) influence was recorded.

All populations were maintained under controlled temperature conditions (83 ± 3 F). The cages were evenly and continuously lighted from above.

To determine the genetic status of the population while eliminating the chances of continued genetic change, a test should measure competitive ability instantaneously. Unfortunately we did not have such a test, so we had to establish a series of populations for this test. To measure any genetic change in the fly species housed in the multi-cell population cage, samples of each fly species were withdrawn after 38 weeks of interaction. Stocks of these two experimental fly strains were then cultured. The test used to detect possible genetic evolution in the experimental strains, involved competing the various combinations of fly strains in single-cell population cages similar to those previously described. Five replicates for each of the following combinations were started with 25 pairs of day-old adults of each species; wild housefly against wild blowfly, experimental housefly against wild blowfly, wild housefly against experimental blowfly, and experimental housefly against experimental blowfly. These cages were started with seven food vials. The vials were left in until the first census seven days later, when the routine of replacing a vial each day was started. Adult flies were censused weekly. We hoped that by reducing the available space and resulting size of the populations the outcome of competition would be determined before additional genetic changes occurred.

RESULTS

Data obtained from the housefly population maintained for 40 weeks in a single-cell cage provided a standard of the housefly density without interspecific competitive interference. This population was started with 50 pairs of adult flies. After nine weeks, a lump of sugar was added to the cage weekly. This raised the average adult numbers from 121 to 267, and pupal density from 267 to 327 per week. The sugar increased the standing crop of adult flies by increasing their longevity, rather than significantly increasing the number of pupae produced.

The density changes of the blowfly populations were studied in three single-cell cages for an average period of 32 weeks to provide a single-species standard. Each blowfly population was started with 50 pairs of adult flies. The average density of the three blowfly populations was 113, significantly lower than the 267 average recorded for the housefly populations. The average number of blowfly pupae produced per week in the three populations was 328, agreeing favorably with the 327 recorded for the housefly. These data and other unpublished results, indicate that the blowfly is less tolerant of high adult densities than the housefly and the more active blowfly larvae often trap adult flies which attempt to feed in the food vials.

To study competition in single-cell cages four housefly-blowfly populations were established using 50 wild housefly and 50 wild blowfly adults in each cage. Each cage was started with seven food vials. In the two competitions won by the housefly, its density averaged 192 and the blowfly's, 22. In the two competitions won by the blowfly, its density averaged 97 and the housefly's 22. The average survival period of the populations which went to extinction was 86 days for the housefly and 92 days for the blowfly. The two to two win record, the average densities, and the time required for extinction indicate how evenly matched the housefly and the blowfly were under these experimental conditions (table 2).

TABLE 2

Interspecific competition between strains of housefly and blowfly populations in single-cell cages.

| Populations | Total number | Competitions won by the housefly | | | | Competitions won by the blowfly | | | |
|---|---|---|---|---|---|---|---|---|---|
| | | Number | Mean density | | Mean extinction time (days) | Number | Mean density | | Mean extinction time (days) |
| | | | House-fly | Blow-fly | | | Blow-fly | House-fly | |
| WHF[1]/WBF[2]* | 4 | 2 | 192 | 22 | 92 | 2 | 97 | 22 | 86 |
| WHF/WBF | 5 | 4 | 363 | 30 | 103 | 1 | 147 | 104 | 141 |
| EHF[3]/WBF | 5 | 3 | 319 | 26 | 132 | 2 | 135 | 151 | 354 |
| WHF/EBF[4] | 5 | 0 | ... | ... | ... | 5 | 164 | 143 | 99 |
| EHF/EBF | 5 | 0 | ... | ... | ... | 5 | 110 | 128 | 193 |

*The first four competitive populations set up.
[1]Wild housefly.
[2]Wild blowfly.
[3]Experimental housefly.
[4]Experimental blowfly.

In the multi-cell cage 100 houseflies of both sexes were released in one corner cell and in the diagonally opposite corner 100 blowflies of both sexes were released. The housefly population spread quickly and was in all 16 cells by the sixth week. The housefly population increased rapidly, reached a density of 413 per cell at the fourteenth week and averaged 277 houseflies per cell for the first 50 weeks (figure 1). The blowfly population averaged 25 per cell for the first 50 weeks and never reached a density greater than 78. As it struggled for survival at this relatively low density, the blowfly population was concentrated in a few cells along one side of the cage. Starting at week 55 the blowfly population began an explosive increase. During the next ten weeks the blowfly population averaged 240 compared with 13 for the declining housefly population. The housefly population went to extinction during the sixty-fifth week and the system was discontinued at the sixty-ninth week.

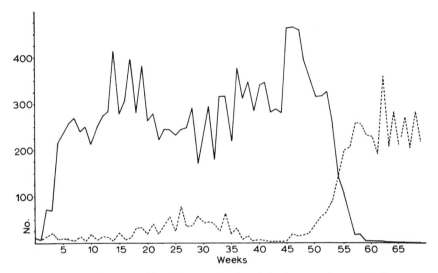

FIGURE 1. Competition between the housefly (———) and blowfly (— — — —) in the 16-cell cage.

A genetic test for the competitive ability of the populations in this multi-cell cage was made at the thirty-eighth week or about 19 generations after the system was started. A sample of 15 adult blowflies from three cells and 25 adult houseflies from 16 cells was withdrawn from different locations in the population cage. Most of the flies removed were females and since they had mated, this increased the proportion of the variability sampled.

In competing the *wild housefly* and the *wild blowfly* populations, the housefly won four and lost one. The average density of the winning housefly populations was 363, the average density of the losing blowfly population was 30 and it went to extinction in a period of 103 days. The average density of the winning blowfly population was 147, the average density of the losing housefly population was 104 and it went to extinction in a period of 141 days (table 2). Although more housefly populations won in this test than won in the initial competition carried out in the single-cell cages when the housefly and the blowfly split winning two to two, the difference be-

SELECTION IN COMPETING SPECIES        103

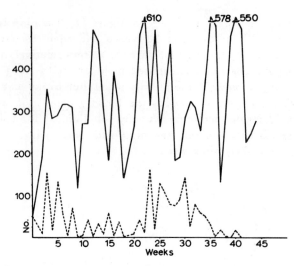

FIGURE 2. Population trends of competition between the housefly (————) and
blowfly (— — — —) won by the housefly in a single-cell cage.

tween the two sets of experiments is not significant (Chi square). This is
due to normal variations within the small number of replicates. Population
trends of competitions won by the housefly in this test and competitions
won by the housefly in the other test combinations are graphed in figure 2;
normally blowfly numbers never exceeded those of the housefly. In the only
contest won by the blowfly in this series, the blowfly gradually overtook
the more dense housefly population and finally caused its extinction (figure
3). This was typical of other competitions won by the blowfly.

Competition between the *experimental housefly* and *wild blowfly* resulted
in the housefly winning three and the blowfly winning two; however, one
contest (figure 4) might be considered a draw because the two species co-

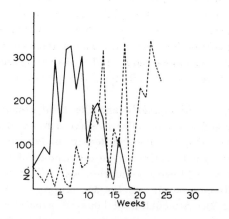

FIGURE 3. Population trends of competition between the housefly (————) and
blowfly (— — — —) won by the blowfly in a single-cell cage.

104           THE AMERICAN NATURALIST

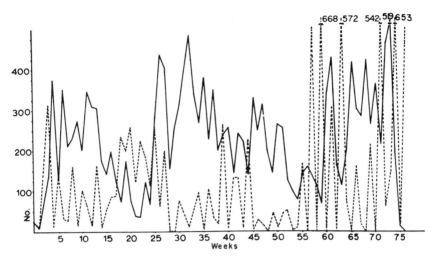

FIGURE 4. Alternation in dominance by the experimental housefly (————) and wild blowfly (— — — —) in competition with one another in a single-cell cage.

existed for 536 days. The average density of the three winning experimental housefly populations was 319; the losing wild blowfly populations averaged 26 and went to extinction in an average period of 132 days. The average density of the two winning wild blowfly populations was 135; the losing experimental housefly populations averaged 151 and went to extinction in an average period of 354 days. The density of the blowfly population which won in 171 days averaged 146 compared with a housefly density of 77. The difference in the outcome of the tests using this combination of experimental housefly versus wild blowfly was not significantly (Chi square) different from the outcome of competition between wild housefly versus wild blowfly.

In the genetic test competing the *wild housefly* and the *experimental blowfly*, the blowfly won all five contests. The competitive ability of the experimental blowfly when matched against the wild housefly was significantly better (0.01 per cent level) than that exhibited by the wild blowfly when it was competed against the wild housefly. The average density of the winning blowfly populations was 164; the losing housefly populations averaged 143 and went to extinction in an average period of 99 days (table 2).

Competition between the *experimental housefly* and the *experimental blowfly* resulted in the blowfly winning all five, however, one contest (figure 5) might be considered a draw because the two species coexisted for 519 days. The competitive ability of the experimental blowfly when matched against the experimental housefly was significantly greater (0.01 per cent level) than that exhibited by the wild blowfly when it was competed against the experimental housefly. These results further demonstrate the improved competitive ability of the experimental blowfly. The average density of the winning experimental blowfly populations was 110; the losing experimental housefly populations averaged 128 and went to extinction in an average

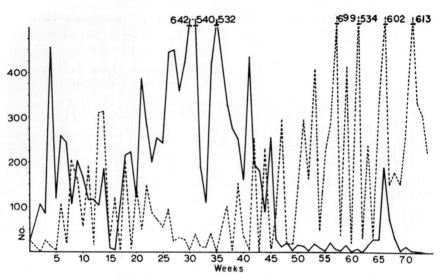

FIGURE 5. Alternation in dominance by the experimental housefly (————) and experimental blowfly (— — — —) in competition with one another in a single-cell cage.

period of 193 days. Excluding the results of the one population graphed in
figure 5, the housefly populations went to extinction in an average period of
112 days. Note that the losing housefly populations had greater average
densities than the winning blowfly populations, but still the housefly lost.
This was due in part to the initial lower density of the blowfly and its relatively slow rate of increase which was typical of most competing blowfly
populations (figure 3).

These results substantiate the evidence that in the multi-cell cage the
initially sparse experimental blowfly population evolved to become an improved competitor. This improvement eventually made it possible for the
blowfly to dominate the housefly in the multi-cell cage. Such a trend in the
multi-cell cage also could have resulted if the experimental housefly population had simply deteriorated. We know this did not occur because the
competitive ability of the experimental housefly was equal to that of the
wild housefly as measured in the competitive genetic tests.

Further evidence concerning the improvement of the experimental blowfly
population can be demonstrated by comparing the density data of the five
wild housefly versus wild blowfly populations plus the five experimental
housefly versus wild blowfly populations with the density data of the five
wild housefly versus experimental blowfly populations plus the five experimental housefly versus experimental blowfly populations. The density of
all the housefly populations against all the wild blowfly populations averaged 282, whereas the density of all the housefly populations against all
the experimental blowfly populations averaged only 136.

The competing housefly and blowfly populations which survived for about
a year and one half in the single-cell population cages are graphed individually (figures 4 and 5), because of the patterns of continued alternate

106                    THE AMERICAN NATURALIST

dominance exhibited by each species. For example, in figure 4 which reflects the contest between an experimental housefly strain and wild blowfly
strain, first the blowfly dominated, then the housefly and vice versa 10
times until the housefly went to extinction. If minor changes are ignored,
there seem to be three periods of clear dominance by the housefly. The
average density of the populations during the 536 day period was 225 for
the housefly and 124 for the blowfly. Note that these densities are intermediate when compared with densities of populations in the contests won
by either the housefly or blowfly. The average density of the winning
housefly population was about 340 and the density of the losing housefly
populations was about 130. The average density of the winning blowfly
population was about 140 and the density of the losing blowfly populations
was about 30.

The other single-cell system, which persisted for about a year and a half,
competed experimental houseflies against experimental blowflies (figure 5).
Initially the housefly dominated, then the blowfly and vice versa six times
until the housefly went to extinction. If minor changes are ignored, two
periods of clear dominance by the housefly are evident. The average density of the winning blowfly population was 147; the losing housefly population averaged 155. These densities are quite close.

The pattern of change in dominance exhibited by each fly species in the
two population systems graphed in figures 4 and 5 is interesting. The
periods of housefly dominance lasted between 15 and 25 weeks, whereas
the blowfly was dominant for somewhat shorter periods. Since both species
have a two week life cycle, from five to 12 generations passed during each
period of dominance. This number of generations provided ample time for
evolution in the sparse species. This picture of alternate dominance of
first one species and then another as noted in these two populations (figures 4 and 5) was what we expected in the 16-cell population system. The
reason for this occurring in the two single-cell systems was probably the
almost equal competitive ability between the fly stocks. Only a small
amount of genetic change was needed before these two species would reverse their dominance in density.

Because we suspected that the changes in dominance from the housefly
to the blowfly and vice versa were due to genetic change, an attempt was
made to measure this change. At week 52, populations in both single-cell
cages were at an appropriate stage for a test. At this time the housefly was
dominant in one and the blowfly was dominant in the other. Twenty-five females, which had an opportunity to mate, were removed from each population. These were cultured for two generations and a sufficient number of
flies was available to set up half or five of the replicate populations.
About two weeks later the remaining five replicate test populations were
set up. The populations were started and maintained by the same procedures used to test competitive ability in the stocks removed from the multi-
cell system. The population trends in this test were analyzed after the

populations had persisted for ten weeks, since a longer period might have led to further evolutionary changes.

If the mechanism proposed in this paper were operating, then in the population system (figure 4) in which the housefly dominated at the fifty-second week, the blowfly should have emerged the winner in these tests. At the tenth week the blowfly had caused the extinction of three of the 10 housefly populations whereas no housefly population caused the extinction of any blowfly population. The average density per system of the blowfly population in all 10 populations for the experimental period was 130, whereas the housefly populations averaged only 65. The trends apparent in the parent population (figure 4) substantiated the trend in the genetic test, that is, the blowfly population increased and became the dominant species at about this same time.

Samples of the housefly and blowfly were removed from the population system graphed in figure 5. The blowfly was the dominant species at this time. As expected, the housefly became dominant. After ten weeks the housefly caused the extinction of three of the 10 blowfly populations and the blowfly caused the extinction of one housefly population. The housefly in all ten populations for the ten-week experimental period had an average density of 86 adults per cage, whereas the blowfly averaged 83. The difference in this series was not as striking as in the previous test, and the parent population also did not show any dramatic change in dominance. The housefly population in the parent cage (figure 5) made one unsuccessful attempt to recover dominance.

Following the withdrawal of stocks from both parent populations, the amplitude of the fluctuations exhibited by the populations increased (figures 4 and 5). We suspect that the parent populations were adversely affected by the procedure of removing stocks from them.

### DISCUSSION

The coexistence of the housefly and blowfly populations in the 16-cell system did not occur. A 30-cell system is now under study. More space and larger populations should provide the necessary time for evolution and coexistence of these species in the same ecological niche. The preliminary trends in the 16-cell system, however, were most encouraging. We had predicted that the sparse species would evolve and become a better competitor and that the dominant species would remain relatively the same in its interspecific competitive ability. This happened. The sparse blowfly population evolved and became a significantly better competitor; the dominant housefly population remained static in its competitive ability.

Although the results were most encouraging we regret that more than one 16-cell population system was not used. Our procedure was dictated by the time required for maintenance and study of such systems.

A question which we raised was that of adding wild genes to the population to prevent inbreeding and deterioration. This procedure may have added a favorable set of genes. To avoid this possibility in the two single-

108 THE AMERICAN NATURALIST

cell population systems which persisted for more than 70 weeks, no outside genes were added. Both still evolved in a manner similar to the multi-cell system. For this reason, we feel confident that selection and evolution were responsible for the change in dominance in the multi-cell system and not the introduced genes.

The persistent alternation of dominance in the two single-cell population systems which existed for more than 70 weeks or more than 35 fly generations suggested that the feed-back mechanism was operating here. The experimental populations set up from stocks removed from these two parent populations also substantiated this. The results from all the tests reported here tend to support the idea proposed that two competing species can occupy the same niche, but more research is needed to understand the mechanism.

## SUMMARY

Interspecific competitors may change genetically with the result that competing species can coexist in the same ecosystem. As a competing species becomes the dominant species, it is at an evolutionary disadvantage because intraspecific competition is the main selective force acting on it. The sparse species, however, because it is under selective pressure from interspecific competition has an evolutionary advantage. Given sufficient time a genetic adjustment between the competing species should result.

To test this theory two competitors, the housefly and blowfly, were released in opposite corners of a multi-celled cage. At first the housefly population suppressed the blowfly population, but in time the blowfly increased, became the dominant species and eventually caused the extinction of the housefly. A genetic check on the blowfly population when it started its comeback showed that it had evolved into a more effective competitor than the housefly. To see if these two species can evolve, coexist and occupy the same niche, a multi-cell cage with increased space-time structure is now under investigation.

## LITERATURE CITED

Haldane, J. B. S., 1932, The causes of evolution. Longmans, Green and Co., New York, London, and Toronto. 235 p.
Huxley, J., 1943, Evolution and modern synthesis. Harper & Bros., New York and London. 645 p.
Kilpatrick, J. W., and H. F. Schoof, 1956, Fly production in treated and untreated privies. Publ. Health Rep. (U. S.) 71: 787-796.
Lerner, J. M., and F. K. Ho, 1961, Genotype and competitive ability of *Tribolium* species. Am. Naturalist 45: 329-343.
Moore, J. A., 1952, Competition between *Drosophila melanogaster* and *Drosophila simulans*. II. The improvement of competitive ability through selection. Proc. Natl. Acad. Sci. U. S. 38: 813-817.
Pimentel, D., 1965, Population ecology and the genetic feed-back mechanism. Proc. Intern. Congr. Genet., 11th. (in press).

Pimentel, D., W. P. Nagel and J. L. Madden, 1963, Space-time structure of
    the environment and the survival of parasite-host systems. Am.
    Naturalist 97: 141–167.
Quarterman, K. D., W. C. Baker and J. A. Jensen, 1949, The importance of
    sanitation in municipal fly control. Am. J. Trop. Med. 29: 973–982.
Wright, S., 1937, The distribution of gene frequencies in populations. Proc.
    Natl. Acad. Sci. U. S. 23: 307–320.

# NATURAL SELECTION FOR REPRODUCTIVE ISOLATION IN *PHLOX*

Donald A. Levin and Harold W. Kerster

*Department of Biological Sciences, University of Illinois at Chicago Circle, Chicago, Illinois*

Received October 24, 1966

Divergence in the genic and chromosomal architecture of local populations from the population system norm has been documented in numerous plant and animal species (cf. Grant, 1963, 1964; Mayr, 1963; Ford, 1965). The stimulus for such divergence may be provided by one of an array of environmental challenges. The immediate presence of a potentially interbreeding congener, or one which competes for biotic or physical resources of the environment may constitute such a challenge. A shift in the adaptive mode of one of the congeners could intensify existing external and internal barriers to gene exchange, or could permit the two species more efficiently to exploit their habitats. Population divergence in areas of congener sympatry, which may involve morphological, physiological, ecological, or ethological traits, has been termed "character divergence" (Darwin, 1859) and "character displacement" (Brown and Wilson, 1956; Wilson, 1965). The term "Wallace effect" has been applied to shifts in population structure whose primary adaptations are to strengthen reproductive isolating barriers (Grant, 1966).

## Description of the Study

The eastern alliance of the plant genus *Phlox* (Polemoneaceae) is a favorable object for investigating character displacement in perennial or long-lived organisms. The alliance displays extensive inter- and intrapopulation heterogeneity, broad zones of polyspecies sympatry, weak to moderate ecological differentiation, overlapping flowering periods, and various degrees of reproductive isolation. Populations may exhibit polymorphisms in vegetative and reproductive characteristics, as well as in crossing behavior and karyology.

Inter- and intrapopulation variation in corolla pigmentation is particularly striking. This variation is expressed in a multitude of color phases ranging from deep lavender or red-pink to white. Most populations are comprised almost exclusively of pigmented forms in which the color is manifested in an array of nuances and intensities. The frequency of dimorphic populations, i.e., those containing pigmented and non-pigmented color phases, ranges from less than 1% to 10%, depending on the taxon. White-flowered plants maintain their notable character through successive seasons in the experimental garden and greenhouse; the hues displayed by pigmented corollas are subject to environmental modification. An analysis of pigment inheritance in a series of annual *Phlox* cultivars suggests that pigment synthesis is under complex polygenic control (Kelly, 1920).

Exceptions to typical color structure may be found in populations of several species, especially *P. pilosa* L. This *Phlox* inhabits much of the eastern United States and is composed almost entirely of populations in which the white corolla phase is rare or absent. There are, however, discrete populations or populations systems in which the white phase prevails. These populations, which contain tens to hundreds of plants, are comparable to the norm in all respects except corolla pigmentation. Although very sporadic in occurrence, such colonies often occur in habitats supporting congeners with similar ecological requirements, typical corolla form and pigmentation, and overlapping flowering periods. We do not mean to imply, however, that all biotically sympatric *P. pilosa* populations deviate from their biotically allopatric allies.

EVOLUTION **21**: 679–687. December, 1967

Reprinted by permission of The Society for the Study of Evolution and the authors from *Evolution* 21:679–687, 1967.

680                    DONALD A. LEVIN AND HAROLD W. KERSTER

The congener of particular interest in this discussion is *P. glaberrima* subsp. *interior* Wherry. *Phlox glaberrima* L. and *P. pilosa* are conspicuous elements of the late spring and early summer prairie floras of Illinois, Indiana, and adjacent states. The species have similar ecological tolerances as evidenced by the frequent formation of contiguous or confluent populations. In spite of these spatial associations, opportunities for interspecific gene exchange are precluded by seasonal isolation, *P. pilosa* being in fruit before *P. glaberrima* commences flowering. If some unusual climatic event afforded an opportunity for interbreeding, hybridization could occur as the species are obligate outbreeders and interfertile (Levin, 1963, 1966; Levin and Kerster, 1967). The incompatibility barriers, however, are formidable.

*Phlox pilosa* is composed of several morphologically, ecologically, and chromosomally distinct phylads (Wherry, 1955; Levin, 1966; Smith and Levin, 1967). A late-flowering race of *P. pilosa* subsp. *pilosa* [= *P. argillacea* Clute and Ferris] is of special significance with respect to hybridization with *P. glaberrima*. This race, indigenous to the sand prairies of northeastern Illinois and northwestern Indiana, consistently flowers 3 weeks later than the norm. Thus the flowering period of this *Phlox* overlaps that of *P. glaberrima* for as long at 2 weeks. The opportunities for hybridization are multiple as populations of these phloxes are often juxtaposed or intermixed, and are pollinated by the same pollinators (Grant and Grant, 1965; Levin and Kerster, 1967). The general floral mechanisms of *P. pilosa* and *P. glaberrima* render them especially suited for Lepidoptera pollination, butterflies being the most important group (op. cit.).

The corolla color structure of populations of the late-flowering *P. pilosa* typically is similar to that of standard populations, red-pink being the predominant or sole phase. The color structure is often reversed, however, in populations where this *Phlox* is in contact with *P. glaberrima*.

The frequency of the white phase appears to be related to the proximity of the congener. As populations of the two taxa become more distant, the frequency of the white phase decreases abruptly. These observations suggest that there is a compelling relationship between white phase predominance and the presence of *P. glaberrima*.

The investigations reported here were undertaken to determine whether *P. glaberrima* was the stimulus for the local displacement of the pigmented phase of *P. pilosa* by the white phase, and to ascertain the adaptive significance of the white phase.

EXPERIMENTAL PROCEDURES

Lepidoptera pollinators are capable of differentiating between species pairs on the basis of flower color and form, and scent (cf. Grant, 1949, 1963; Dronamraju, 1960; Faegri and van der Pilj, 1966). Of particular interest is their ability to distinguish between a number of colors including red-pink and white. The similarity of corolla pigmentation of *P. glaberrima* and typical *P. pilosa*, and the pollinator-discernible difference between *P. glaberrima* and the white phase of *P. pilosa* suggested that flower color displacement in *P. pilosa* might be an adaptation to aid pollinator discrimination and flower-constancy.

The merits of this hypothesis were tested using a pollen "tracer" technique which permits an objective and quantitative appraisal of interspecific pollen flow. The pollen grains of *P. glaberrima* and *P. pilosa* are well-marked by virtue of large, discontinuous, differences in pollen diameter, the average of the former being 55 microns as compared to 30 microns in the latter (Levin and Kerster, 1967). By examining pollen on the stigma of the species in populations comprised of the two phases of *P. pilosa*, and *P. glaberrima*, the flow of pollen between the species and the role of flower color differences in regulating that flow can be ascertained with facility.

The population chosen for pollen flow investigations, located in a sand prairie in southern Cook County, Illinois, contained

371

NATURAL SELECTION FOR REPRODUCTIVE ISOLATION 681

over 150 plants of each species. The population was 70 meters long and 20 meters wide. The species were biotically sympatric in approximately 50% of the area under investigation, *P. pilosa* inhabiting the more xeric sites in the area of allopatry. *Phlox pilosa* was represented almost exclusively by the white phase so that it was necessary to introduce a series of red-pink transplants in order to achieve some measure of color balance. The transplants were introduced in a random fashion in the microhabitats supporting the white phase. The red-pink phase comprised 25% of the modified *P. pilosa* population.

Collections for pollen analysis were performed on June 21, 1966, a time of maximum overlap in species flowering periods. In all, 238 flowers of the white phase and 238 flowers of the red-pink phase of *P. pilosa* were collected from 50 plants of each phase, the plants being located in various sectors of the study area. The stigma of each flower was removed and stained in a solution of aniline-blue in lactophenol for 24 hours. Each stigmata containing over 25 pollen grains was examined for foreign grains. Over 300 stigma of *P. glaberrima* were treated in a similar fashion.

Consideration was given to the problem of whether pollinator discrimination also might occur in dimorphic populations of *P. pilosa*. The pollen of the red-pink and white phases is comparable in size, color and sculpture. Pollinator favor or disfavor, however, might be detected by differential seed production of the two phases. Reproductively mature inflorescences were collected from red-pink and white-flowered plants in 13 populations with typical color structure, and in 3 populations in which white-flowered plants were the predominant form. Nearly 3500 flowers were collected for capsule and seed analyses.

## RESULTS

An examination of stigma of red-pink and white-flowered *P. pilosa* revealed a striking pollinator preference for the red-

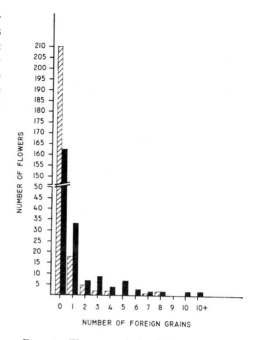

FIG. 1. The numerical distribution of *P. glaberrima* pollen grains on stigma of the red-pink phase (solid bars) and white phase (cross-hatched bars) of *P. pilosa*.

pink form when making an interspecific move from *P. glaberrima*. This preference was manifested in the percentage of stigma with *P. glaberrima* grains and by the total alien pollen load. Thirty per cent of the stigma of the red-pink form carried contraspecific pollen in contrast to 12% of the white form. The distribution of alien pollen loads on the stigma of the two phases is depicted in Figure 1. It is significant to note that 4.8 times as many grains were transported from *P. glaberrima* to the red-pink phase as to equal numbers of the white phase. Foreign pollen loads on *P. pilosa* were distributed in a manner which suggests that the usual number of *P. glaberrima* grains deposited by a single pollination is one (Fig. 1; Levin and Kerster, 1967). Accordingly, we may infer that pollinator moves from *P. glaberrima* to the red-pink phase of *P. pilosa* were nearly five times as frequent as moves to the white phase.

DONALD A. LEVIN AND HAROLD W. KERSTER

Pollen flow to *P. glaberrima* greatly exceeded that to *P. pilosa*, color notwithstanding. Thirty-seven per cent of the stigma examined bore contraspecific pollen with an average of 14.7 grains per "contaminated" stigma. The number of contraspecific grains on *P. glaberrima* stigma varied from 1 to 38. These data, as well as those presented above, indicate that interspecific pollen flow in the study area was more extensive in 1966 than in 1965 (Levin and Kerster, 1967). The overall balance with respect to direction of alien pollen transport, however, did not change significantly.

Seed-set data suggest that pollinators strongly favor the red-pink phase of *P. pilosa* over the white phase in populations where the typical color structure prevailed. The average seed-set per capsule in the red-pink phase was 2.0 as compared to 1.4 in the white phase. Even in colonies where white predominated, its seed production per capsule lagged behind that of red-pink. The average seed-set for the white phase, as compiled from a series of populations containing from 85% to 97% "white" plants, was 1.8 per capsule. The red-pink phase continued to average 2.0 seeds per capsule in spite of its low frequency. The difference in seed-set between the two forms may not entirely be attributable to pollinator color preferences, although such preferences ostensibly are very important. Butterflies have well-developed visual sense, and favor vividly colored blossoms to those which are white or faintly colored (Faegri and van der Pilj, 1966).

## DISCUSSION AND CONCLUSIONS

The eastern *Phlox* alliance is composed of 18 species whose ranges generally are extensive, thereby creating broad zones of polyspecies sympatry. Although the potential for hybridization between many species combinations is rather great, a series of ecological, seasonal, ethological, incompatibility and sterility barriers severely limits this event (Erbe and Turner,

1962; Levin, 1963, 1966, 1967a, b, unpubl.; Levin and Smith, 1965, 1966; Levin and Kerster, 1967). Ecological and seasonal barriers normally preclude pollen flow between sympatric species. In localized areas where edaphic or climatic conditions afford opportunities for such flow, one may find a correspondingly local divergence in the floral pigmentation of one of the species pair. The divergence is particularly conspicuous in the case of interfertile species pairs, but also occurs among intersterile species.

The often compelling relationship between congener proximity and species divergence suggests that certain patterns of variation in flower pigmentation are a consequence of character displacement. In view of the trait involved, one might surmise that local divergence in corolla pigmentation strengthens ethological barriers and thus conserves the reproductive potential of the species. The merits of this hypothesis were validated by data which disclosed that interspecific pollen flow between congeners with comparable corolla pigmentation far exceeded flow between the same congeners with contrasting pigmentation. The reader will recall that nearly five times as much alien pollen was carried to the red-pink phase of *P. pilosa* as to the white phase. In view of the magnitude of the pollen load differential and pollinator preference, we may infer that pollen flow to *P. glaberrima* also is related to corolla pigmentation, and that the bulk of alien pollen which it receives comes from the red-pink phase of *P. pilosa*.

We may now ask whether character displacement was stimulated by a need to impede introgression, or was stimulated by a need to reduce pollen wastage. Stringent incompatibility barriers all but eliminate the potential for hybridization. Interspecific crosses rarely are effectual, and seeds are produced only when *P. pilosa* serves as the maternal parent (Levin, 1966). Since the bulk of the pollen in the population in question is towards *P. glaberrima*, relatively few alien grains will be deposited on stigma of *P. pilosa*, and only a small percentage of these grains will be able to surmount the incompatibility barriers. Nevertheless, there is evidence that genes have trickled from *P. glaberrima* to *P. pilosa* (Levin, 1964, unpubl.). Characteristics of *P. glaberrima* such as glabrous corolla tube and imbricate corolla lobes were found in populations of *P. pilosa*, although examination of bispecific populations from 1962 through 1966 failed to reveal the existence of $F_1$ hybrids or recent backcross derivatives. Not all mixed populations, however, showed evidence of past hybridization. It seems unlikely that divergence in flower color arose solely in response to a need for stronger reproductive barriers. However, we cannot discount the possibility that displacement is related to gene exchange and low hybrid fitness (Wilson, 1965). Wilson (op. cit.) contends that species with imperfect internal isolating barriers will either fuse or displace reproductively in areas of species contact depending on the level of gene flow and fitness of hybrids.

Interspecific pollen flow data suggest that the pollinating mechanism of *Phlox* is somewhat inefficient (Levin and Kerster, 1967). The foreign pollen load on stigma of *P. glaberrima* indicates that typically one or two *P. pilosa* grains are transferred per pollinator move. We may assume that the pollen load carried on intraspecific moves is comparable to that carried on interspecific moves. The relatively large size of *Phlox* pollen and the organ of dispersal, i.e., a smooth butterfly proboscis (Grant and Grant, 1965), contribute to the diminutive pollen load. The butterfly inserts its proboscis into several flowers on a single plant, but most or all of the pollen carried from the previously visited plant is deposited on the first flower (Levin and Kerster, 1967). The species is self-incompatible, so that most pollinations are ineffectual as they are self-pollinations.

The paucity of intraspecific pollen flow is portrayed in the percentage of flowers which form capsules. Collections made dur-

ing 1965 and 1966 revealed that only 60% of the flowers formed capsules and that seed-set per capsule averaged 2.0, three being the maximum. If seed-set per flower is considered, it becomes apparent that seed production is only 40% of the maximum. Can *P. pilosa* afford to lose potentially effectual grains to another species?

The variability in flower-color genes necessary for a character displacement response is usually available. Maintenance of the white phase of *P. pilosa* at low levels is quite common; one or a few of such plants usually can be found in any colony composed of a few hundred plants. Seed-set data indicate that "white" plants, however, are at a distinct selective disadvantage in typical populations. The average seed-set per capsule for the red-pink phase was 2.0 as compared to 1.4 in the white phase. Accordingly, the relative fitness value of the white phase is .70 for this stage of the life cycle; for every 100 seeds produced by the red-pink flowers, the same number of white flowers produce 70 seeds. The retention of the white phase in *P. pilosa* populations might be attributed to the recessive nature of white corolla color, relatively high mutation rates in the polygenes controlling pigment synthesis, or to a selective advantage accorded during the vegetative stage of the life cycle.

The white phase of *P. pilosa* is more highly adapted to co-exist with *P. glaberrima* than is its red-pink ally. We may assume that pollen wastage by the red-pink phase is nearly five times as great as that by the white phase. This supposition is based on the inference that pollinator movements between *P. glaberrima* and red-pink phase are nearly five times greater than between the former and the white phase. Presumably at the time of initial postglacial contact between the species, populations of *P. pilosa* "carried" the white phase in very low frequency. As a consequence of this contact, local colonies of *P. pilosa* experienced differential pollen wastage which resulted in a gradual displacement of the red-pink phase by the white.

Interesting color-sympatry correlations exist between other species of eastern *Phlox*. *Phlox pilosa* and *P. amoena* Sims, a close ally, are sympatric throughout much of the southeastern United States, but generally remain spatially isolated because of different ecological requirements. Close spatial associations and hybridization are observed in southern Tennessee and northern Alabama, where diverse habitats often are in juxtaposition (Levin and Smith, 1966). Many populations of *P. pilosa* in this region contain a high proportion of the white phase, in contrast to the typical red-pink phase.

The color-sympatry correlation may involve entire population systems rather than single populations as illustrated by *P. bifida* Beck and *P. pilosa*. These species typically are seasonally isolated and differ markedly in ecological tolerances, *P. bifida* inhabiting rocky woodland slopes and ledges in dry soils and *P. pilosa* inhabiting more mesic sites in prairies and woodland borders. Deeply pigmented forms typically comprise approximately 99% of the population of both species. There is, however, a late-flowering race of *P. bifida* whose populations are often near or in contact with those of *P. pilosa* in the sand prairies of Illinois and western Indiana. Populations of this race of *P. bifida* are composed almost exclusively of a white-flowered phase. Pollen "tracer" studies show that when contiguous or confluent, pollen is transferred from one species to another (Levin, unpubl.).

An examination of corolla pigmentation in regions of sympatry and allopatry of *P. cuspidata* Scheele and *P. drummondii* Hook. reveals that a color-sympatry association may occur at the subspecies level of divergence. *Phlox drummondii* is composed of six subspecies, five of which are completely or largely allopatric with respect to *P. cuspidata*. The sixth, subspecies *drummondii*, is almost completely sympatric. It is particularly interesting to note that subsp. *drummondii* displays a red corolla while its allies all have pink corollas as does *P. cuspidata*. Natural hybridization between *P. cuspidata* and *P. drummondii* subsp. *drummondii* occurs infrequently. Hybrids are relatively few in number and are sterile (Levin, 1967).

Ethological barriers are the most efficient pre-mating barriers as related to the conservation of reproductive potential (Grant, 1966). The strengthening of ethological barriers would be particularly advantageous to species whose hybrids are adaptively inferior, or to species which can ill afford the loss of gametes involved in actual or potential hybridization (Grant, 1963). Perhaps the latter is the case in *Phlox*.

As we have seen, corolla color displacement may be a highly localized phenomenon or may involve population systems of various magnitudes. Displacement may involve single populations, races or subspecies. Displacement may occur between species which hybridize and exchange genes readily (*P. pilosa* and *P. amoena*), which interbreed but form sterile hybrids (*P. cuspidata* and *P. drummondii*), which rarely hybridize but exchange some genes (*P. pilosa* and *P. glaberrima*), and between species which never hybridize (*P. pilosa* and *P. bifida*). It is significant to note that flower color displacement has occurred irrespective of species' abilities to exchange genes. We must recognize that whether or not hybridization ensues, pollen will flow between intermixed species pairs and the flow may be substantial. We therefore maintain that *Phlox* can ill afford the loss of pollen typically incurred in confluent or adjacent colonies, and that color displacement is the product of selection for ethological isolation, the latter enhancing pollinator discrimination and thereby reducing pollen wastage. The presence of a congener which competes with a species for domestic pollen ostensibly has served as the stimulus for color divergence.

The reinforcement of ethological barriers in areas of sympatry has been described in *Microhyla* (Blair, 1955), *Pseudacris*

(Mecham, 1961), *Hyla* (Littlejohn, 1965), and *Drosophila* (Dobzhansky and Koller, 1938; Dobzhansky, 1951; Dobzhansky et al., 1957; Dobzhansky et al., 1964; Ehrman, 1965), *Erebia* (Lorković, 1958), and *Peromyscus* (McCarley, 1964). Artificial selection for reproductive isolation leading to a strengthening of interstrain or inter-specific ethological barriers also has been demonstrated in *Drosophila* (Koopman, 1950; Wallace, 1954; Knight et al., 1956).

Grant (1966) has designated the secondary and supplementary process of selection for reinforcement of existing reproductive isolating mechanisms as the "Wallace effect." The term refers only to those mechanisms which are operative in the parental generation. The "Wallace effect" may manifest itself in the form of enhanced ethological or incompatibility barriers. Selection for reproductive isolation is most effective in short-lived organisms such as annual plants or ephemeral animals where a loss of reproductive potential could have grave consequences (Dobzhansky, 1958; Stebbins, 1958). Evidence suggesting the occurrence of the "Wallace effect" has been obtained exclusively from short-lived organisms (see Grant, 1966, for a discussion and critique of the evidence for the "Wallace effect").

The role of corolla color displacement is reducing pollen wastage, and the selective advantage of this reduction have been clearly demonstrated in *Phlox*. The evidence presented above indicates that the "Wallace effect" indeed occurs in perennial plants. Therefore, the suggestion that selection for reproductive isolation would be relatively ineffective in perennial plants (Dobzhansky, 1958; Stebbins, 1958) is open to conjecture. If effectual pollen was at a premium in a perennial, a shift in the adaptive mode of that plant which would conserve its reproductive potential indeed would be at a selective advantage. Color displacement in *Phlox* must be interpreted as selection for reproductive isolation.

## Summary

Populations of the eastern species of *Phlox* typically are composed of organisms with pigmented corollas. A small percentage of these populations show color dimorphism, i.e., they contain pigmented and non-pigmented or white forms. The white phase often comprises less than 1% of such populations. Exceptions to the normal color structure occur in a number of species, especially *P. pilosa*. Discrete populations or population systems are known to occur in which the white phase is the predominate or sole form. Although such populations are infrequent, they often grow in habitats supporting a congener with similar ecological requirements and flowering period. This congener often is *P. glaberrima*.

The relationship of color displacement and congener presence was studied in an assemblage comprised of *P. glaberrima* and the two phases of *P. pilosa*. The pollen of both species is well-marked so that an objective, quantitative appraisal of interspecific pollen flow can be made with facility. An examination of the stigma *P. glaberrima* and *P. pilosa* disclosed that there was considerable interspecific pollen flow. It was most enlightening to find that while 30% of the pigmented phase of *P. pilosa* bore alien pollen, only 12% of the white phase bore such pollen. Moreover, 4.8 times as many grains were transported from *P. glaberrima* to flowers of the pigmented phase as to equal numbers of flowers of the white phase. Thus it appears that color divergence aids pollinator discrimination and conserves reproductive potential.

Character displacement in the eastern *Phlox* alliance occurs irrespective of the species' abilities to exchange genes. Displacement occurs between species which are incapable of hybridization, but are capable of exchanging pollen.

We conclude that *Phlox* can ill afford the loss of pollen typically incurred in bispecific populations, and that color displacement is the product of selection for

DONALD A. LEVIN AND HAROLD W. KERSTER

enhanced ethological isolation. The presence of a congener which competes for domestic pollen ostensibly has served as the stimulus for color divergence.

## ACKNOWLEDGMENTS

The work reported here was aided by National Science Foundation grant GB-4326 to the first author.

## LITERATURE CITED

BLAIR, W. F. 1955. Mating call and stage of speciation in the *Microhyla olivacea-M. carolinensis* complex. Evolution **9**: 469–480.

BROWN, W. L., JR., AND E. O. WILSON. 1956. Character displacement. Systematic Zool. **5**: 49–64.

DARWIN, C. 1859. On the origin of species by means of natural selection. First ed. John Murray, London.

DOBZHANSKY, TH. 1951. Genetics and origin of species. Third ed. Columbia Univ. Press, New York.

——. 1958. Species after Darwin. *In* S. A. Barnett [ed.], A century of Darwin. Heinemann, London.

DOBZHANSKY, TH., L. EHRMAN, O. PAVLOVSKY, AND B. SPASSKY. 1964. The superspecies *Drosophila paulistorum*. Proc. Nat. Acad. Sci. **51**: 3–9.

DOBZHANSKY, TH., AND P. C. KOLLER. 1938. An experimental study of sexual isolation in *Drosophila*. Biol. Zentralbl. **58**: 589–607.

DOBZHANSKY, TH., L. EHRMAN, AND O. PAVLOVSKY. 1957. *Drosophila insularis*, a new sibling species of the wilistoni group. Univ. Texas Publ. **9**: 39–47.

DRONAMRAJU, K. R. 1960. Selective visits of butterflies to flowers: a possible factor in sympatric speciation. Nature **186**: 178.

EHRMAN, L. 1965. Direct observation of sexual isolation between allopatric and between sympatric strains of the different *Drosophila paulistorum* races. Evolution **19**: 459–464.

ERBE, L., AND B. L. TURNER. 1962. A biosystematic study of the *Phlox cuspidata-P. drummondii* complex. Amer. Midl. Natur. **67**: 257–281.

FAEGRI, K., AND L. VAN DER PILJ. 1966. The principles of pollination ecology. Pergamon Press. New York.

FORD, E. B. 1965. Ecological genetics. Second ed. John Wiley and Sons, New York.

GRANT, V. 1949. Pollination systems as isolating mechanisms in flowering plants. Evolution **3**: 82–97.

——. 1963. The origin of adaptations. Columbia Univ. Press, New York.

——. 1964. The architecture of the germplasm. John Wiley and Sons, New York.

——. 1966. The selective origin of incompatibility barriers in the plant genus *Gilia*. Amer. Natur. **100**: 99–118.

GRANT, V., AND K. GRANT. 1965. Flower pollination in the *Phlox* family. Columbia Univ. Press, New York.

KELLY, J. P. 1920. A genetical study of flower form and color in *Phlox drummondii*. Genetics **5**: 189–248.

KNIGHT, G. R., A. ROBERTSON, AND C. H. WADDINGTON. 1956. Selection for sexual isolation within a species. Evolution **14**: 14–22.

KOOPMAN, K. F. 1950. Natural selection for reproductive isolation between *Drosophila pseudoobscura* and *Drosophila persimilis*. Evolution **4**: 135–148.

LEVIN, D. A. 1963. Natural hybridization between *Phlox maculata* and *P. glaberrima* and its evolutionary significance. Amer. J. Botany **50**: 714–720.

——. 1966. The *Phlox pilosa* complex: crossing and chromosome relationships. Brittonia **18**: 142–162.

——. 1967a. Variation in *Phlox divaricata*. Evolution **21**: 92–108.

——. 1967b. Hybridization between annual species of *Phlox*: population structure. Amer. J. Botany **54**: 1122–1130.

LEVIN, D. A., AND H. W. KERSTER. 1967. Interspecific pollen exchange in *Phlox*. Amer. Natur. **101**: in press.

LEVIN, D. A., AND D. M. SMITH. 1965. An enigmatic *Phlox* from Illinois. Brittonia **17**: 254–266.

—— AND ——. 1966. Hybridization and evolution in the *Phlox pilosa* complex. Amer. Natur. **100**: 289–302.

LITTLEJOHN, M. J. 1965. Premating isolation in the *Hyla ewingi* complex (Anura: Hylidae). Evolution **19**: 234–243.

LORKOVIĆ, Z. 1958. Some peculiarities of spatially and sexually restricted gene exchange in the *Erebia tyndarus* group. Cold Spr. Harb. Symp. Quant. Biol. **23**: 319–325.

MAYR, E. 1963. Animal species and evolution. Harvard Univ. Press, Cambridge, Massachusetts.

MCCARLEY, H. 1964. Ethological isolation in the coenospecies *Peromyscus leucopus*. Evolution **18**: 331–332.

MECHAM, J. S. 1961. Isolating mechanisms in anuran amphibians. *In* W. F. Blair [ed.], Vertebrate speciation. Univ. Texas Press, Austin, Texas.

SMITH, D. M., AND D. A. LEVIN. 1967. Karyotypes of eastern North American *Phlox*. Amer. J. Botany **54**: 324–334.

STEBBINS, G. L. 1958. The inviability, weakness

and sterility of interspecific hybrids. Advances in Genet. **9:** 147–215.

WALLACE, B. 1954. Genetic divergence of isolated populations of *Drosophila melanogaster*. Proc. Ninth Internat. Congr. Genet., Caryologia, suppl. vol., p. 761–764.

WHERRY, E. T. 1931. The eastern short-styled phloxes. Bartonia **12:** 24–53.

——. 1955. The genus Phlox. Morris Arbor. Mono., III, Philadelphia.

WILSON, E. O. 1965. The challenge from related species. *In* H. G. Baker and G. C. Stebbins [eds.], The genetics of colonizing species. Academic Press, New York.

# THE EFFECTS OF PREY SIZE SELECTION
# BY LAKE PLANKTIVORES

## John Langdon Brooks

### Abstract

Although the biomass of the planktivorous fish in any lake is but a few per cent of that of the plant and animal plankton, these fish exert a potent influence upon the composition of these lower trophic levels. The vulnerability of the zooplankton to predation, together with the high degree of selectivity exercised by the planktivores in their choice of prey items are responsible for this pervasive effect. Freshwater planktivores appear to prefer large Cladocera, especially *Daphnia*. Trout and yellow perch, facultative planktivores, switch to non-planktonic food when large *Daphnia* are not available. Freshwater populations of the primarily marine genus *Alosa* are obligate planktivores, shifting to progressively smaller zooplankters as the larger, preferred items become scarce. Within each prey category there is strong preference for the largest items. In an experimental observation of *Alosa* sp. feeding on a small calanoid copepod, the survival time of each instar was inversely proportional to its mean body length.

The strong preferences evinced by lacustrine planktivores can shift the competitive balance between the zooplanktonic herbivores, all of which exploit the same supply of particulate food. Whenever or wherever planktivores are absent, large zooplankters like *Daphnia pulex* are numerically dominant. When planktivory is more intense the large zooplankters are cropped sufficiently to allow smaller, hitherto suppressed, species to become numerous. The interest displayed by facultative planktivores toward decreasing sizes of prey is considered in relation to the shape-size polymorphism characteristic of most limnetic *Daphnia*.

The effect alluded to in the title relates to determination of the qualitative as well as quantitative composition of the animal plankton of open-water communities of lakes by selective predation of planktivorous fish. The biomass of piscine planktivores may on the average be only a few per cent of that of the combined phytoplankton and zooplankton. Yet, the active selection of prey by these vertebrate carnivores does exert a decisive influence directly upon the composition of the animal plankton, and thus indirectly on the quantity and, perhaps to some extent, quality of the phytoplankton. This effect upon phytoplankton will not, however, be discussed here (see Brooks, in press).

It seems advisable to preface this consideration of the significance of selection, especially size-selection, with a brief notice of some of the characteristics peculiar to open-water communities, as opposed to those of terrestrial ones. The most striking difference is in the size of green plants relative to the animals that feed upon them. The algae, either individual or colonial, are small relative to the animals that feed by one or another semi-automatic means of collecting and concentrating these algae. Terrestrial green plants on the other hand are large, often enormous relative to the invertebrate herbivores, and in forests at least are large relative to the vertebrate herbivores as well. These large plants provide terrestrial ecosystems with complex three-dimensional systems of substrata. These substrate systems are of sufficient temporal stability to have permitted the structure and behavior of associated animals to evolve in relation to the characteristics of the substrata. This has resulted in the use of special parts of this three-dimensional nexus for feeding, for reproductive behavior, and for seeking protection from beasts on the next higher level of the food web. The tiny algae, while concentrated in the upper, illuminated water layers, determine no temporally stable "fine-grained" spatial pattern within the ecosystem, in relation to which the planktonic herbivores could have evolved behavior patterns. While the phytoplankton may be patterned in space by their various orientations in wind-driven currents, these patterns have a short temporal stability. The wind-generated spiral vortices may

Reprinted by permission of the Society of Systematic Zoology and the author from *Systematic Zoology* 17:273–291, 1968.

serve to some degree to concentrate the algae, making feeding easier for any zooplankter that can locate itself in these temporary concentrations. But an ability to concentrate in these temporary concentrations of food would entail the serious disadvantage of making the concentrated zooplankton more easily preyed upon by fish.

It may seem laboring the obvious to insist that these algae provide no place for the herbivores to hide, but it is a peculiar and decisive aspect of open-water systems that planktonic herbivores of all sizes and kinds are naked to the predations of the planktivores. A planktivorous fish, therefore, can in a matter of minutes see the entire array of prey available on any particular day. While the array in lakes is nothing like as diverse as that in most parts of the ocean, the two dominant groups of crustaceans, cladocerans and copepods, do present a series of alternative food items at most seasons. Rotifers are numerous in the plankton, but so small as to be of interest to fish only in their few days after hatching.

### SELECTIVE FEEDING BY LAKE PLANKTIVORES

There are innumerable studies of feeding habits of both marine and freshwater planktivores. In those studies in which analyses of stomach contents have been compared with analyses of the zooplankton available to be eaten, a strong bias in the selection of prey has always been apparent. Most of these studies have not been primarily concerned with the role of prey size in this selection by planktivores (but see Lindström, 1955), the main subject of this paper, although some insight into the role of size can be gained from a knowledge of the size of the prey species. To illustrate the general nature of the selectivity that characterizes feeding by lake planktivores, I shall briefly summarize the results of the excellent studies in Lago Maggiore of northern Italy. Before doing so, however, some further comments must be made on the manner in which planktivores feed.

All planktivorous fish have closely spaced gillrakers, as can be seen in Figure 1, the lower left panel of which depicts the first branchial arch of the planktivorous *Alosa pseudoharengus,* while the right panel depicts the comparable arch of the closely related *Alosa mediocris* that feeds principally on small fish. Obviously, it would avail a fish constructed like *A. mediocris* naught to catch zooplankters, because they would escape from the pharynx with the respiratory current. However, most zooplankters that could be caught by *Alosa pseudoharengus* would probably be retained in its pharynx until swallowed. Observations on the feeding behavior of this species of *Alosa* will be reported below. Galbraith (1967) has carefully examined the width of the space between the gillrakers of rainbow trout (*Salmo gairdneri*) in relation to the size of zooplankters in their stomachs. While he gave about 1.3 mm as the lower size limit of the zooplankters (*Daphnia*) generally eaten, about half of the gillrakers-spaces were less than 1.1mm. He concluded that the trout could not have been indiscriminately gulping water and then straining out the zooplankton with this pharyngeal seive, because zooplankters as small as 1.1mm being common in the lake, would have been retained by the gillrakers and been common in the stomach as well. He backed this conclusion with observations that only large adults were taken from swarms of *Daphnia* in which the small immature instars were common. Although some people not too familiar with the subject have expressed the belief that most planktivorous fish depend solely upon pharyngeal straining to remove the plankton from the surrounding medium, all studies of freshwater planktivores have shown this not to be so. Although a few marine fish, such as the Atlantic menhaden (*Brevoortia tyrannus*), do have a feeding behavior that involves pharyngeal straining to remove particulate matter (in large part phytoplankton) from the water, this is not a common method. In most marine planktivores (*Clupea harengus,* for example) and all lacustrine ones which

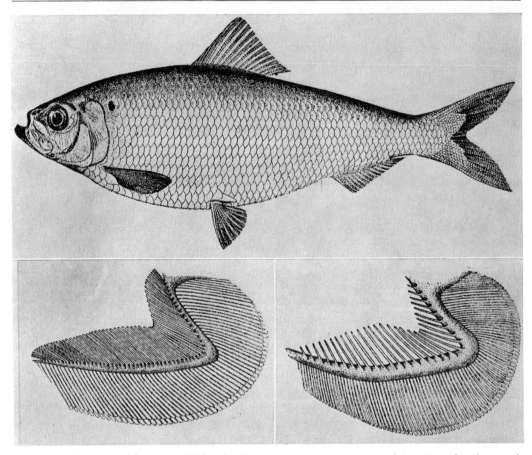

FIG. 1.—*Alosa pseudoharengus* (Wilson). Top, mature specimen, 300mm long. Note that the mouth opens obliquely. Bottom left, first branchial arch, with closely spaced gill rakers that act as a plankton sieve. Compare with (bottom right) the widely spaced gill rakers of *A. mediocris,* a species that feeds primarily upon small fish. From Brooks and Dodson, 1965.

have been observed, the fish actively selects each plankter that it ingests. As all fish must take in mouthsful of water for respiration, it requires little modification of behavior to suck in a mouthful of water that also has a large zooplankter in it (see Hardy, 1956; Hildebrand, 1963).

The open-water community of Lago Maggiore is well suited to provide an illustration of the selective feeding behavior of planktivores, because the zooplankton of this large (212km²), deep (mean depth = 177m), oligotrophic lake has been carefully studied over a period of years by my late friend, Vittorio Tonnolli, whose recent untimely death is mourned by all who were privileged to know him. Against this background of knowledge of the zooplankton, the food habits of the lakes' planktivores, being studied by Berg and Grimaldi, are especially meaningful. An initial estimate of dominance among species of zooplankters can be gained from the mean annual percentage composition. If one considers all life stages of the calanoid copepod *Eudiaptomus vulgaris* (nauplii, all copepodite stages, and adults), this species dominates the plankton at all seasons. Adults alone of *Eudiaptomus vulgaris* constituted about 40% of the zooplankton (excluding immature stages of this species), while adults of the cyclopoid, *Cyclops strenuus,* comprised about 8%. Among the Cladocera, *Daphnia hyalina* (counting all instars) was nearly as abundant as the *Eudiaptomus* adults, amounting to 36%, while another cladoceran, *Diaphanosoma brachyurum,* comprised some 14%. Two species of large predaceous Cladocera, *Bythrotrephes longimanus* and *Leptodora kindtii,* together made up only 1% of the annual value (Tonnolli, 1962; 1957–58 values). There are marked seasonal differences in the abundance of these species not indicated by the above mean values. The populations of the copepods persist throughout the year with some seasonal fluctuations. *Eudiaptomus* adults and copepodites occur at all times in the thousands or ten-thousands per mean cubic meter of the upper 50m of the water column (adults between 500 and 5000/cubic meter). *Daphnia hyalina* (all instars), on the other hand, is present in the same volume of water in somewhat greater numbers than *Eudiaptomus* adults from May through July and again from September to November, but is rarer during late summer when individuals are counted in hundreds, and still rarer during the winter period—January through April. At this time the lake temperature is minimal, about 6° C, as this lake just south of the Alps never freezes. There are fewer than about 100 *Daphnia* per cubic meter. The other herbivorous cladoceran, *Diaphanosoma brachyurum,* was taken only as scattered individuals during this winter period, while the two predaceous cladocerans were absent from December to June. At the height of the abundance of the latter in late summer these were seldom more than about 30 per cubic meter each of *Bythrotrepes* and *Leptodora.*

There are now four species of fish in Lago Maggiore that are primarily planktivorous throughout their lives, two *Coregonus,* an *Alosa,* and a species of the cyprinid genus *Alburnus.* Although two stocks of coregonids have been introduced into Lago Maggiore, we will consider only one, "bondella," deriving from the Lake Neuchâtel population of *Coregonus mac-*

*rophthalmus* Nusslin. This has rapidly become the more numerous of these two very similar species, even though it is the more recent introduction (1950). The other important planktivore that has been studied is a freshwater population of the normally anadromous Mediterranean shad *Alosa ficta* Duhamel (Berg and Grimaldi, 1966a, b).

Cladocerans are the principal food of the coregonids. As soon as *Daphnia hyalina* begins to increase in the spring (end of April), it becomes their principal food. From this time until November, Cladocera comprise 90% or more of the organisms in the stomachs, *Daphnia hyalina* being essentially the sole food of the *Coregonus* during their growth season. In late summer when the density of the *Daphnia* population declines (largely due to predation), *Coregonus* supplements its *Daphnia* ration with either or both of two other large cladocerans, *Sida crystallina* and *Bythrotrephes longimanus.* To exploit these ancillary food sources requires changes in feeding behavior. *Sida crystallina,* an herbivore, is rare in the open waters of lakes, its populations being largely restricted to a peripheral zone, the outer fringes of the littoral vegetation. The coregonids must move inshore to feed upon *Sida. Bythrotrephes,* on the other hand, is a large (ca. 5mm), predatory species, restricted to the open waters, but at its most abundant is rare, as noted above. Much water must be searched by a *Coregonus* in order to half fill its stomach with this prey. It is only in the winter months when the cladoceran populations fail, that *Coregonus* eats *Cyclops strenuus,* the adults of which are available year around at about half the density as those of *Eudiaptomus vulgaris.* But even in winter *Coregonus* does not feed on this latter copepod, which with all its immature stages is much the commonest crustacean in Lago Maggiore.

The *Alosa,* however, does eat some *Eudiaptomus* during the winter months, but even then the less abundant and smaller *Cyclops strenuus* is eaten about five times as frequently. Possibly as a result of its evolution in the sea where copepods are an important element in the diet of most herring-like fish, this lacustrine *Alosa* is relatively more dependent on copepods than are the coregonids, which like most freshwater planktivores eat cladocerans more than copepods. (In Lake Baikal, the venerable ocean among freshwaters, the large calanoid *Epischura baikalensis* is the principal zooplanktonic herbivore of the lake proper, there being no Cladocera. The two planktivores that have evolved in the lake feed largely upon these copepods. See Kozhov, 1963.) In the springtime in Lago Maggiore, *Alosa* unlike *Coregonus* does not switch to *Daphnia* immediately, but continues to feed primarily upon *Cyclops* until the *Daphnia* population has become very dense. In June and July it feeds primarily upon *Daphnia*, but when the density of the *Daphnia* population falls in late summer, *Alosa* at first supplements its diet with *Bythotrephes* (in years when it is available), then shifts back to *Cyclops*, much sooner than *Coregonus* does. It never has more than a scattering of *Sida* in its stomach, which is consistent with the knowledge that *Alosa* (as we will also see in a North American species) tend to avoid the littoral, remaining in the offshore waters.

It is apparent from this account that these two kinds of planktivores are highly selective in their choice of prey. Berg and Grimaldi were not concerned with the attributes of the zooplankton that cause their selection, but both size and method of locomotion appear relevant attributes. The selection by both fish of the large, but rare, *Bythotrephes* exemplifies the significance of prey size, of which more is said below. With regard to locomotion it is worth passing comment that the abundant *Eudiaptomus*, with its large-sized adults, is not eaten by the coregonids, and although eaten by *Alosa* is never taken in proportion to its abundance. The small cyprinid planktivore *Alburnus alburnus* ("bleak") when offered *Daphnia, Bosmina*, and *Diaptomus* by Ivlev (1961) always selected its prey in that order, even though the second cladoceran, *Bosmina*, was much smaller than the

*Diaptomus* (but neither species nor sizes were definitely stated). Furthermore, the cladoceran *Diaphanosoma brachyurum* is fairly common in Lago Maggiore except in the early months of the year, but is not eaten by either planktivore. It may be permissible to speculate that these two zooplankters (calanoid copepods and *Diaphanosoma*) escape the attention of potential predators because both tend to hang relatively immobile from their large antennae and both can make sudden jumps. While it is true that calanoid copepods may glide through the water while hanging suspended, this slow and even glide contrasts with the frequent, jerky movements that characterize the locomotion of both *Daphnia* and *Cyclops*—frequent movements that may register in the optic field of a searching fish (see Lindström, 1955).

## SIZE SELECTION BY LAKE PLANKTIVORES

The role of prey size in the selection of zooplankters by lake planktivores was given special attention in two recent studies that have at the same time considered the consequences that such size-biased selection has upon the composition of the zooplankton. Galbraith and the author, using different approaches, have reached similar conclusions. Galbraith (1967) measured the length of plankters found in the stomachs of rainbow trout (*Salmo gairdneri*) and yellow perch (*Perca flavescens*) and compared their sizes with the size range of the zooplankters living in the two Michigan lakes where the fish were taken. His investigation continued over several years so that the effects of predation could be evaluated. The author has approached the problem of size-dependent selection by freshwater populations of *Alosa pseudoharengus* in a different way (Brooks and Dodson, 1965; Brooks, in preparation). An experimental study of the feeding of a small population of *Alosa* on mixed lake plankton was made in the summer of 1966 to aid in the assessment of the results of *Alosa* predation in several Connecticut

278                                                                                              SYSTEMATIC ZOOLOGY

lakes. These investigations of feeding by *Alosa* will be reported first.

The hope of making such an experimental study seemed dim, due to the difficulty of capturing any of the pelagic *Alosa* in lakes. However, the anadromous stocks of various *Alosa* (*A. sapidessima, A. pseudoharengus,* and *A. aestivalis*) entering the Connecticut River are large, and young-of-the-year can be captured unharmed by seining. During mid-August 1966 a school of about 70 young *Alosa pseudoharengus,* was maintained in a large tank in the riverside Essex Marine Laboratory.[1] This tank, 242cm (8′) long, 35cm wide, and filled to a depth of about 30cm, contained approximately 250 liters. During the first week the only food available to the *Alosa* was the sparse plankton in the river water circulated through their tank. On the eighth and tenth days zooplankton netted in nearby Bashan Lake (see Brooks and Dodson, 1965) was added to the tank. The following brief account of the differential survival of the various kinds and sizes of zooplankters from Bashan Lake in the presence of a small population of alewives is based upon the second addition of lake plankton. Sampling on the previous day had indicated that no zooplankters had survived into the ninth day from the first addition of plankton.

The 65 alewives (5 had been killed at the end of the first experiment for stomach analyses) used in this experiment were from 3.3 to 5.1cm in standard length. All but five were between 3.5 and 4.5cm, and the mean length was about 4cm. They were probably 2 to 3 months old. When undisturbed they swam slowly in a compact school. Examination of Figure 1 will reveal that the mouth of the alewife opens obliquely upward and the eyes are placed

above the middle of the head. Observations of the fish indicated that they usually moved slightly upward to feed, occasionally moving to the side. For the first few minutes after the plankton was introduced into the tank the school broke up, each fish making small darting movements after its prey ("frenzied feeding"). But after about 10 minutes the school had completely reformed and persisted then to the end of the one-hour long period of observation. The fish continued to feed actively while schooling, and their feeding movements were readily observed. Each fish was seen frequently to alter its course slightly from the horizontal swimming path by heading upward briefly and then dropping back into the horizontal course it had been pursuing. Close observation at the moment when the head tipped upward always revealed a planker at an angle of 45° above and 1cm ahead of the tip of the snout at that moment. The mouth then opened and the zooplankter was sucked in. These movements appeared relatively effortless.

The zooplankton of Bashan Lake, collected in several vertical tows from slightly above the bottom to the surface, was dominated by some of the species common in Connecticut lakes. *Daphnia catawba* and *Epischura nordenskiöldi* were present but not abundant. The most numerous copepod was *Diaptomus minutus*. These three species are depicted in the upper panel of Figure 4. Several other relatively rare crustaceans were present but will not be considered here. The two cyclopoids *Mesocyclops edax* and *Cyclops bicuspidatus thomasi,* depicted for Crystal Lake, Figure 4, are not usually found in Bashan. After collection the sample was brought immediately to the laboratory. The *Daphnia* caught in the surface film were skimmed off and the dead ones siphoned from the bottom. A control indicated that there was no non-predatory mortality during the time course of the experiment. Immediately after the water with the concentrated plankton was carefully mixed with the water in the tank, the plankton density in

[1] It is a pleasure to acknowledge my indebtedness to Mr. William Boyd, Director of the Essex Marine Laboratory, for permission to use its facilities; to my former colleague Dr. Sanford Moss, for the use of the specially equipped tank; to my assistants, Mr. Leonard Milstone and Mr. Christopher Smick, for their help with the experimental procedures.

the experimental tank was sampled and sampling was repeated at 15-minute intervals thereafter, until one hour had elapsed. In an attempt to prevent localized concentrations of plankton a glass plate 20cm in diameter was slowly passed from one end of the tank to the other just before the samples were taken. At each sampling four one-liter samples were collected in random sequence at each of four equidistant positions along the length of the tank at randomly chosen depths, but avoiding the bottom and the surface.

The aim of the experiment was to determine the relationship between visible body length and survival in the presence of the *Alosa* school. The *Daphnia* disappeared first, possibly have been consumed during the initial period of frenzied feeding. There was a mean of four *Daphnia catawba* (all sizes) initially, and none remained by the time of the 15-minute sampling.[2] *Epischura*, the calanoid copepod adults of which are even larger than *Daphnia*, survived slightly longer. (The smallest size of *Epischura* that could be distinguished from *Diaptomus* is 700$\mu$ long.) These large copepods were initially present at a mean density of 4/liter, a density maintained through the first 15 minutes, but none were found at the 30-minute sampling, nor thereafter. The numbers of these species were too low to do anything but confirm the common observation that large *Daphnia* are taken by fish more readily than are large calanoid copepods of roughly the same size. This was noted above, for example, in Lago Maggiore where neither *Coregonus* nor *Alosa* fed upon the relatively large *Eudiaptomus vulgaris* to an extent proportional to its abundance, if at all.

It was the *Diaptomus* population that furnished favorable material for a quantita-

[2] It should be noted, however, that at the completion of the hour-long experiment, 100 of the 250 liters in the tank were strained through fine plankton netting in order that the density of the rarer zooplankters might be evaluated. Among the nauplii, one adult and five immature *Daphnia* occurred —an average of about one for each twenty liters of water.

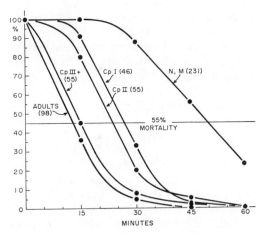

FIG. 2.—The time course of predatory mortality in size-(=life-stage-)-categories of *Diaptomus minutus* when fed upon by *Alosa pseudoharengus* in an experimental tank. N, M, nauplii and metanauplii; Cp I, Cp II, etc.; first copepodite instar, second copepodite instar, etc. The numbers in parentheses indicate the mean number per liter in the initial sampling; subsequent values are percentages of these initial values. The point at which each curve intercepts the 55% mortality line indicates the time required before each size category sustains a 55% decline below the initial value. The gentle slope of the curve for the smallest size category indicates that such individuals are preyed upon at a lower rate than are individuals in the four larger size-categories, the curves for all of which have similar, steep slopes.

tive study. Initially there was an average of over 400/liter, and their life stages (nauplius to adult) ranged in sizes from ca. 0.2 to 0.8mm. Although the shape does change somewhat as a *Diaptomus* grows from nauplius to adult—from the shape of a small ovoid to that of a large ovoid with a small extension on one end—we will consider that these differences in shape are negligible, and that as far as the fish is concerned, size is the only significant variable.

After counting and measuring the zooplankters remaining at each sampling, it was found that there were five age-size categories, the survivorship of which could be followed: (1) nauplii and metanauplii, (2) copepodite I, (3) copepodite II, (4) copepodite III and over, (5) adults. In Figure 2 the mean number surviving in

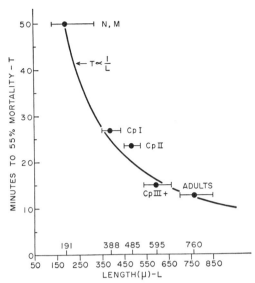

FIG. 3.—Relationship between body size in life stages of *Diaptomus minutus* and susceptibility to predation by *Alosa pseudoharengus*. Susceptibility to predation is measured as time required to reduce initial population of each category by 55% (as measured in Fig. 2). Points indicate the mean length of individuals in each category, the range of value being indicated by the horizontal bars. The line is part of the hyperbola through the N, M value. T, time to 55% mortality, L, length of organisms. Other symbols as in Figure 2.

each category at each sampling time is expressed as a percentage of the initial values (given in parentheses) for each. The difference between the survival of the adults and larvae is striking. At the end of 15 minutes 65 per cent of the adults had been consumed, whereas, the decrease in number of nauplii and metanauplii was undetectable. It was only after 30 minutes of predation that the numbers of the larvae had begun to decrease, and by that time the population of adults had decreased to less than 10 per cent of its original density. The values for the intermediate size-categories fell between these two curves in such a way as to justify drawing the set of smooth curves as given in the graph. The picture that emerges is one of predation concentrated first on the larger prey and then, as the large forms become scarcer, on progressively smaller ones.

In order to examine more precisely the relationship between size of prey and intensity of predation upon items of that size when a choice of sizes is offered, the time required for the consumption of some fraction of the initial population should be plotted against size. The level of predatory loss (or survival, however one wishes to view the matter) chosen should fall within the range covered by the straight-line portions of all curves. The level of 55 per cent mortality (45 per cent survival) was, therefore, selected and the time at which each size-category had decreased to this level was noted. This time to 55 per cent mortality was plotted against the mean size for each category (Fig. 3) with the complete size range for each category indicated. If size (L, for length) were the principal determinant of predation among these life stages of *Diaptomus*, it might be expected that the time (T) to reach any given level of predatory loss would be inversely proportional to the length, i.e.,

$$T \, \alpha \, \frac{1}{L}.$$

As the population of the larval forms with a mean body length of $191\mu$ was reduced to the 55 per cent level in 50 minutes, the population of a form twice as long ($382\mu$) should suffer a similar percentage loss in one-half the time, i.e., 25 minutes. The time to 55 per cent mortality for the first stage copepodites, the mean length of which is $388\mu$, is 26.5 minutes. Populations of zooplankters four times as long as the mean larval length ($764\mu$) should survive only one quarter as long, i.e., 12.5 minutes. The adults (mean length, $760\mu$) do, indeed, survive only 12.5 minutes. The hyperbole* drawn in the graph expressed this theoretical relationship. The closeness of the observed points to this theoretical expectation encourages the interpretation that size (as visible body length) is indeed the major determinant of predatory mortality in this system where strong shape differences are not a factor. Previous observa-

* hyperbola

tions in natural ecosystems had led us to expect some such relationship (although one would hardly have dared hope to discern such a simple one) between prey size and susceptibility to predation by *Alosa pseudoharengus*. The validity of this relationship for other planktivores that select their prey visually should be tested.

The interest displayed by rainbow trout (*Salmo gairdneri*) and yellow perch (*Perca flavescens*) in an array of zooplankters is of quite a different nature from that characteristic of the alewife. Although calanoid and cyclopoid copepods and other cladocerans are indicated as being present in the plankton of the two Michigan lakes Galbraith (1967) investigated, both trout and perch selected only large *Daphnia*. When *Daphnia* at least 1.3mm long were not available, these "planktivores" lost their interest in plankton, and sought other food. The *Daphnia*, assignable to several species, in each lake ranged from 0.4 to 2.9mm in length. Yet, of more than 11,000 *Daphnia* measured from the fish stomachs, few were under 1.3mm in length. During the summer when approximately half of the *Daphnia* in the lakes were less than 1.3mm long, 96 per cent of those eaten by trout and 82 per cent of those eaten by yellow perch were larger than 1.3mm. One can conclude that the prey selection by these planktivores has a strong size bias that can only be explained by the individual selection of each food item. Galbraith made a pertinent observation when he caught some trout that he had observed feeding in a concentrated swarm of *Daphnia*. Although all sizes of *Daphnia* occurred in the swarm, the stomachs contained only large ones above 1.3 mm. This natural experiment demonstrates beyond question that the trout were making individual selections of the large *Daphnia* and ignoring the smaller ones. Results virtually identical with those of Galbraith were found by Brynildson (1958) in his more general investigation of the stomach contents and feeding habits of brook, brown, and rainbow trout (*Salvelinus fontinalis, Salmo trutta,* and *Salmo gairdneri,*

resp.) in some Wisconsin lakes; namely that *Daphnia* was the preferred food and that specimens less than 1mm in length were rarely eaten.

Observations of postjuvenile feeding behavior in freshwater populations of the primarily marine genus *Alosa* thus reveal a sustained interest in planktonic food. These fish can accordingly be designated *obligate* planktivores. On the other hand, observations of yellow perch and of several freshwater species of *Salmo* reveal a much more restricted interest in the array of zooplankters. Both *Salmo* and *Perca* show interest in large *Daphnia* only. If these food items are not available, these fish quickly switch from plankton to some other food source within the lake. Most freshwater species of planktivores would fall into this class of *facultative* planktivores. All evidence suggests that for both obligate and facultative planktivores selection is strongly biased toward the largest items available within any acceptable category of food items.

### EFFECTS UPON SPECIES COMPOSITION OF THE ZOOPLANKTON

These strong preferences evinced by the planktivores will quite obviously affect the species composition of the zooplankton. Whenever there is heavy predation upon only one of a series of competitors, the populations of the others will in general increase. The decided preference shown by most planktivores for *Daphnia* relative to *Diaptomus*, for example, certainly helps account for the relative numerical dominance of these copepods. One is led to suspect that in the virtual absence of predation upon the *Daphnia*, they would in many circumstances be more numerous than the calanoids. However, while one can speculate upon the effect that selective predation must have in maintaining the observed specific composition of a particular ecosystem, it has been possible to be certain of the effects of selective predation only in those ecosystems where there is known to have been a marked increase or decrease in the intensity of planktivory.

Several examples of the consequences for the plankton of the introduction of stocks of planktivores, i.e., of an increase in planktivory, will now be considered.

*Alosa aestivalis*, ecologically equivalent in its feeding behavior to its close relative *Alosa pseudoharengus*, was inadvertently introduced into a small Connecticut lake (area, 80 hectares; maximum depth, 14m) and had become abundant by 1955. A quantitative sampling of the plankton in 1964 was compared with a similar sampling that had been made in 1942 when there were no demonstrable *Alosa* in the lake (Brooks and Dodson, 1965). The 1942 sampling revealed a zooplankton assemblage characteristic of lakes of the region—the large calanoid copepod, *Epischura nordenskiöldi*, the smaller and more numerous *Diaptomus minutus*, the large cyclopoid *Mesocyclops edax*, and the smaller, ubiquitous species *Cyclops bicuspidatus thomasi*. *Daphnia catawba* was the sole dominant cladoceran. In the upper panel of Figure 4 the characteristic appearance of these dominants can be seen. Their place on the scale, as indicated by each arrow, shows the mean length of the smallest egg-bearing instar. In the lower panel is seen the composition of the zooplankton after the *Alosa* population had been established for ten years (1964). The tiny cladoceran *Bosmina longirostris* now shares dominance with two cyclopoid copepods, the tiny *Tropocyclops prasinus* and *Cyclops bicuspidatus thomasi*, the latter being the only one of the three dominant at the present time that was even detected in the open-water plankton sampling of 1942. Numerical dominance within the zooplankton assemblage has shifted conspicuously to species of small body size; the modal length having decreased from 0.8 to 0.3mm. This shift is entirely to be expected as a result of feeding behavior of *Alosa pseudoharengus*. In the experiment *Daphnia catawba* was not detectable after the first 15 minutes of feeding, and all *Epischura* as well as the larger instars of *Diaptomus minutus* had virtually disappeared after 30 minutes

of feeding. After 60 minutes zooplankters of the size of the smallest *Bosmina* were being eaten.

It might be wondered why there are any crustaceans at all in an "alewife" lake. To answer this question it must be remembered that the total biomass of the planktivores is but a small fraction of that of their herbivorous prey and that the number of planktivorous fish is minute in comparison with the numbers of their prey. Furthermore, the *Alosa* swim in large schools, removing the largest zooplankters from the water through which they are passing. This concentration of feeding in a comparatively small volume of the lake at any one time allows the rapidly growing zooplankters, especially the Cladocera, time to mature and reproduce successfully in those portions of the water mass that have not been recently visited by the *Alosa*. For example, in a cubic meter of water not searched by planktivores for a week in midsummer a hundred first instar *Daphnia catawba*—should they have been present—could have matured and possibly released their first broods of young. The population of these parthenogenetic *Daphnia* would still be so sparse as to be undetectable by usual sampling methods and too sparse to be completely eliminated by the fish. It is thus possible, even probable, that in alewife lakes even populations of *Daphnia* do persist.

All three dominants in alewive lakes, unlike the limnetic plankton (i.e., *Daphnia*, *Epischura*, *Diaptomus*) that was so quickly replaced, thrived in the littoral zone and near the bottom, regions avoided by the pelagic *Alosa*. This littoral region provides a refugium for *Bosmina* and *Tropocyclops*, and especially for *Cyclops bicuspidatus thomasi*, the adults of which are even larger than those of *Diaptomus minutus* which were so readily eaten. The persistence of this medium-sized cyclopoid seems attributable to the fact that the adults live (or can live) close to the shore and bottom of the lake and, thus, are likely to escape being eaten. Only the small, immature instars can be found in the open waters of Crystal Lake.

Thus, the introduction of an obligate planktivore into a small lake eliminated from numerical dominance in the open waters all but the very smallest crustaceans, those maturing there at lengths of 0.3 and 0.45mm respectively. The New England lakes in which *Alosa* populations have become established naturally are all similarly dominated by *Bosmina longirostris* and one or two of several small cyclopoids. It is noteworthy that *Bosmina longirostris* appears as a dominant in any pond or lake in North America or Eurasia where predation is intense.

We now have to consider the effect of the establishment of a facultative planktivore in a small lake. As we have noted above in the section on food habits, these facultative planktivores concentrate their planktivory upon *Daphnia*, most especially upon individuals over about 1.3mm in body length (head and carapace). The effects of the predation of such fish should find clearest reflection in the *Daphnia* populations. It was apparent in the case of *Alosa* introductions that elimination of the *Daphnia* permitted the small, and previously suppressed competitor, *Bosmina longirostris*, to achieve dominance. As the facultative planktivores tend to lose interest in zooplankters of a size much larger than the critical size of *Bosmina longirostris* (0.3 mm), one would anticipate that the introduction of facultative planktivores would lead to the elimination of large *Daphnia* and their replacement by medium-sized or small species of *Daphnia*, the smallest of which is much larger than *B. longirostris*. Lacustrine members of another daphniid genus, *Ceriodaphnia*, fall between the smallest *Daphnia* spp. and *Bosmina longirostris* (see Fig. 4). There are eight species of *Daphnia* in the lakes of eastern North American (Brooks, 1957), the largest of which, *D. pulex*, has a body length often just somewhat short of 2mm at the onset of maturity, while the smallest, *D. ambigua*, is clearly less than 1mm at this critical in-

star. Reif and Tappa (1966) reported that five years after the introduction of smelt into a Pennsylvania lake (263 hectares) *D. pulex* had been eliminated and replaced by the somewhat smaller *D. dubia* that lives largely in the surface water where smelt do not feed.

The introduction of facultative planktivores into Sporley Lake, Michigan, as reported by Galbraith, provides as excellent illustration of the shifts in dominance among competing species of zooplanktonic herbivores resulting from an increase in size-dependent predation pressure. Sporley Lake is small, having an area of only 30 hectares and a maximum depth of 12 meters. The circumstance that the littoral vegetation is poorly developed and the shallow bottom is sand is significant, because it means that the facultative planktivores are more dependent upon the zooplankton than might be the case if the biota of the littoral zone were richer. In summer there is little oxygen in the bottom two meters. The previous fish fauna and the zooplankton had been eliminated by poisoning with toxaphene in the fall of 1955, and the lake remained toxic to fish until 1959. However, a population of *Daphnia pulex* established itself the season following the poisoning (1956) and during the next summer about half the population was larger than 2mm in length, some individuals reaching 2.9mm. The same size range was obtained in 1958 and 1959, and although there was not such a large proportion bigger than 2mm, the mean size was at least 1.5mm. In the fall of 1959 rainbow trout were stocked (40 fingerlings and 13 trout of 7 to 9 inches per acre), and in addition a population of fatheaded minnows (*Pimephales promelas*) was detected the next year. In 1962 illegally introduced smelt (*Osmerus mordax*) were detected. In the summer of 1960, following the introduction of the trout, there were very few *Daphnia pulex* larger than 2mm, and, for the first time a few specimens of another species of *Daphnia*, the smaller *D. retrocurva*, were found. The bulk of the *Daphnia* during

SYSTEMATIC ZOOLOGY

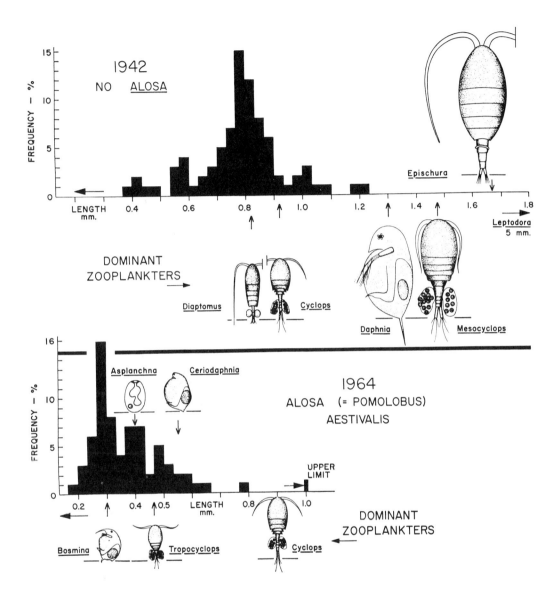

F<small>IG</small>. 4.—The composition of the crustacean zooplankton of Crystal Lake (Stafford Springs, Connecticut) before (1942) and after (1964) a population of *Alosa aestivalis* had become well established. Each square of the histogram indicates that 1 per cent of the total sample counted was within that size range. The larger zooplankters are not represented in the histograms because of the relative scarcity of mature specimens. The specimens depicted represent the mean size (length from posterior base lines to the anterior end) of the smallest mature instar. The arrows indicate the position of the smallest mature instar of each dominant species in relation to the histograms. The predaceous rotifer, *Asplanchna priodonta*, is the only non-crustacean species included; other rotifers were present but not included in this study. Copepod nauplii and metanauplii are not represented in the histograms. From Brooks and Dodson, 1965.

that summer was between 1.0 and 1.7mm. By 1964 and 1965, when the populations of all three facultative planktivores were established, the plankton was again sampled. The size distribution of the *Daphnia* was even more affected, the mean size having dropped to 0.8mm, and there were only a few individuals larger than 1.3mm (4.7%) (this being, it will be remembered, the lower limit to the size of the *Daphnia* generally found in the stomachs of the rainbow trout). Furthermore, the species composition had completely altered. *D. pulex* no longer was found in the samples, its place being taken by the somewhat smaller *Daphnia galeata* and the even smaller *D. retrocurva*. Both of the latter are strongly cyclomorphic species (see next section).

The average size of *D. pulex* at the onset of maturity in Sporley Lake was reported by Galbraith to be 1.8mm before 1960. The summer after the trout were introduced a few reproduced at 1.2mm, but the predation on *Daphnia* of this size was so intense that the population of *D. pulex* could not reproduce itself. In 1964 *D. galeata* and *D. retrocurva* began to reproduce at 0.8mm.

Galbraith further noted that in the presence of the planktivores (i.e., in 1964, 1965) the volume of the standing crop of *Daphnia* (*D. galeata* and *D. retrocurva*) was lower than it had been during the earlier, fish-free years. And he added, "Concurrently there was an increase in the numbers and volume of *Bosmina, Chydorus*, and (to a lesser extent) copepods" (1967:9). The results of this elimination of *Daphnia pulex*, the large-sized dominant during the fish-free years, has been its replacement by a variety of slightly smaller competitors, as the size-efficiency hypothesis predicts will occur whenever predation is less intense than that exerted by *Alosa* in a small lake (Brooks and Dodson, 1965).

It might be of interest to note that a somewhat similar shift in the species of *Daphnia* in a Connecticut Lake (Wononskopomuc, 143 hectares) was noted a year after it had become apparent that a population of *Alosa* was established and several

years after the planktivorous sockeye salmon (*Onchorhynchus nerka*) had been introduced. Whereas *D. pulex*, previously the sole species of *Daphnia*, had occupied all depths of the lake, the year following the known establishment of the populations of alewives (summer of 1966), *D. pulex* was restricted during summer stratification to water just above the bottom in this 31m-deep lake. In the warm upper layers, the cyclomorphic species, *D. dubia* and *D. galeata*, were common (see Brooks, 1964). In the cool water just below the thermocline there is now a sizeable population of that small, cold stenotherm, *Daphnia longiremis*. Whether or not this is a stable association can be determined only by sampling over the next several years.

EFFECTS ON INTRASPECIFIC POLYMORPHISM

A noteworthy aspect of the planktonic Cladocera is their remarkable intraspecific morphological variation, or polymorphism. In temperate lakes the morphs of these short-lived crustaceans replace each other seasonally, with the most exuberant shapes being characteristic of midsummer. In *Daphnia* these forms usually bear a thin, transparent, midsagittal extension on their head called a helmet. In certain species of Eurasian *Bosmina* the antennules are elongated in midsummer, or there is a large, remarkably transparent hump on the dorsum of the carapace. The author has recently suggested (Brooks, 1965) that the significance of this seasonal cycle of body shape (cyclomorphosis) lies in its relation to the closely correlated changes in body size at the onset of maturity. The midsummer individuals of *Daphnia*, bearing the tallest helmets, begin to produce eggs when the size of the visible part of the body (including eye, legs, and brood pouch) is at its annual minimum. In view of what has been said above about size-dependent predation, which is often most intense under midsummer conditions, the adaptive significance of small size at the onset of maturity will be apparent. Because of the oft-noted fact that many planktivores rapidly lose interest in plankton as its size decreases toward 1mm, any mechanism that would depress the size at maturity to about 1mm or slightly below would be of considerable adaptive value. The various transparent peripheral structures evolved by species of several genera of Cladocera all are alike in growing, at midsummer, relatively more rapidly than the visible central body. Their rapid growth is considered by this hypothesis to be a mechanism whereby a high metabolic rate (of positive value in adults for rapidly converting food into eggs) is prevented from increasing the size of the visible body, during the period of immature growth, by means of the drain which the rapid growth of the transparent structures makes upon assimilation. On the other hand, during the cooler seasons when predation is less intense the helmet grows at the same relative rate as, or even more slowly than, the central body, allowing this visible part to attain its maximum size at the onset of maturity. The advantage of a planktonic herbivore's being large at times other than midsummer is the greater feeding effectiveness that goes with large size (see Brooks and Dodson, 1965; Burns, in press; Burns and Rigler, 1967).

This postulated relationship between helmet size, visible body size at the onset of maturity, and the intensity of predation upon morphs of a variable *Daphnia* has been recently tested by Green (1967) in equatorial Lake Albert, the northernmost lake in Africa's western Rift Valley. As would be expected from its geographical position, there is essentially no seasonal change in the physical and chemical parameters of the lake water. The polymorphism of its *Daphnia lumholzi* is not seasonal; rather, the smaller helmeted morphs, and the larger, non-helmeted morphs can be found in the lake at all times of the year—but always in different parts of the lake. The larger, non-helmeted, morph, called "*monacha*" by Green, is the sole and abundant form in the open waters of the middle of the lake, while the

smaller, helmeted morph, "*lumholzi*," is abundant near the shore where the lake is less than 20 meters deep, and in the shallow lagoons along the shore. In the stretches of water between these two sorts of ecological situations the two morphs can be found in varying ratios, *monacha* decreasing toward shore, *lumholzi* decreasing away from the shore.

The chief planktivore in Lake Albert is the characin *Alestes baremose* (Joannis) which is restricted in its distribution to the shallower waters of the lake, to that marginal zone of the lake where the water is less than 20 meters deep. Green made stomach analyses of *Alestes* taken from a lagoon where helmeted *lumholzi* were four times as abundant as *monacha*. Of the zooplankters in the stomach, 89 per cent were *monacha*, while there were no helmeted *lumholzi*—a strong bias toward *monacha*! The mean carapace length of the specimens of *monacha* from the plankton of this lagoon was 1.06mm, and of helmeted *lumholzi*, 0.91. The mean carapace length of the *monacha* from the *Alestes* stomach, however, was 1.28mm, indicating a strong tendency to select the largest individuals of *monacha* from the entire array of zooplankters, especially since the *Daphnia* constituted less than 1 per cent of a plankton assemblage dominated by cyclopoid copepodites and nauplii. Green has made some further relevant observations on egg number and volume of the morphs, for the details of which his fascinating paper should be consulted.

This stable, ecogeographical polymorphism within Lake Albert, therefore, is maintained by the intralacustrine pattern of predation. The intense inshore predation on the larger *monacha* favors the persistence of the smaller, helmeted *lumholzi* there, while in the middle of the lake, where the intensity of predation is much lower, the large non-helmeted *monacha* form thrives to the exclusion of the smaller helmeted *lumholzi*, presumably because of the greater feeding effectiveness of the larger morph.

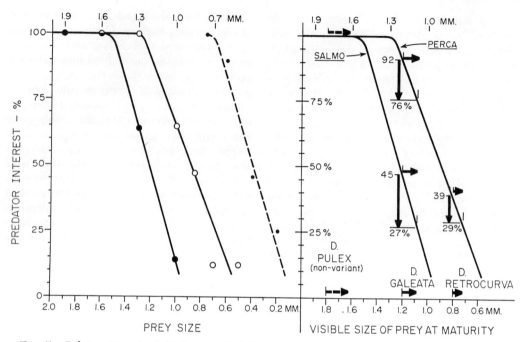

Fig. 5.—Relative interest of freshwater planktivores in prey of various sizes and its relation to size polymorphism in species of limnetic *Daphnia. Left-hand panel:* the solid lines denote the relative interest in *Daphnia* of *Salmo gairdneri* (solid circles) and *Perca flavescens*, calculated from the data of Gallbraith (1967). The dashed line indicates the interest of *Alosa pseudoharengus* in various sizes of *Diaptomus minutus. Right-hand panel:* horizontal arrows representing a ten per cent reduction in body size at the onset of maturity in the cyclomorphic species, *D. galeata* and *D. retrocurva*, are placed in relation to the interest curves for *Salmo* and *Perca*. Vertical arrows represent the relative loss of predator interest in the smaller as compared with the large morph. The arrow for the non-cyclomorphic *D. pulex* indicates the result of a hypothetic reduction of ten per cent in the size at the onset of maturity.

These observations on the feeding behavior of quite unrelated freshwater planktivores (the tropical characin *Alestes baremose*; species of *Salmo* and *Perca* of temperate waters) on *Daphnia* reveal a markedly lower interest in items, the length of which is less than 1mm as compared with that evinced in items only 0.5mm longer. This relationship of predator interest to absolute size of prey is of relevance here because the large morph in all of the variable limnetic *Daphnia* is at the threshold of sustained predator interest. The relatively small decrease in visible body size at the onset of maturity (ca. 10%) that can be achieved by the rapid relative growth of transparent body projections will place the small adults below this threshold

of sustained predator interest. Such a decrease in predation might be decisive for the survival of the prey population.

This relationship of relative predator interest in *Daphnia* of different body sizes can be represented diagrammatically using the scant body of relevant data. The solid lines in the lefthand panel of Figure 5 indicate the relative interest of *Salmo gairdneri* (solid circles) and *Perca flavescens* (open circles) in *Daphnia* of various sizes as estimated from the measurements that Galbraith (1967) presents in his Figure 3 (relating prey size to predator size). His graph gives the total length (head and carapace) of *Daphnia* in the stomachs of more than twenty specimens of each species of planktivore. Both planktivores commonly took *Daphnia* over 2mm in length, but examination of his other data on size distribution of *Daphnia* in the lakes indicates that prey items of this size were often rare and likely absent from the waters searched in the filling of these stomachs. Therefore, the absence of *Daphnia* over 2mm could indicate merely that these sizes were not available to the fish. *Daphnia* up to 1.9mm were present in fair numbers in the lakes during the years represented, and all of the *Salmo* and all but one of the yellow perch contained *Daphnia* 1.9mm long. The number of stomachs containing *Daphnia* of smaller sizes was compared to this standard number of stomachs with *Daphnia* of 1.9mm to give an index of relative predator interest. These ratios, expressed as percentages, are plotted in Figure 5. *Perca flavescens* retains full interest in *Daphnia* down to 1.3mm, while *Salmo* loses interest at about 1.5mm. The steepness of the slope indicates the rapid decrease in interest over this relatively small range of prey sizes from 1.5 to 0.6mm. This lack of interest in the smaller *Daphnia*, of course, has been manifested in the face of an abundance of these smaller sizes in the lake. As a control on the rate of loss of predator interest, the comparable values from the experimental observation of the obligate planktivore, *Alosa pseudoharengus*, feeding upon the small calanoid copepod *Diaptomus minutus* are included in the lefthand panel of Figure 5. The data are derived from those presented in Figure 3. Prey size is as given in that graph and the reciprocal of the number of minutes to 55 per cent mortality is used as an index of predator interest. The value for the adults was taken to indicate "complete" interest (only, of course, relative to the smaller instars). The index of predator interest in the smaller sizes is plotted as a percentage of interest in the adults. The slope of the dashed line drawn through these points for *Diaptomus* indicates that the interest which the various sizes of this smaller copepod hold for an obligate planktivore decreases with decreasing prey size at a rate very similar to the rate at which the facultative

planktivores *Salmo* and *Perca* lose interest in the smaller sizes of *Daphnia*. (It must be remembered that *Salmo* and *Perca*, to all intents, would never feed upon *Diaptomus*.)

The relationship between the loss of planktivore interest in *Daphnia*, as the size of this prey decreases and the visible body size at maturity of the largest and smallest morphs of two species of cyclomorphic *Daphnia*, is represented in the righthand panel of Figure 5. The predator interest curves of *Salmo* and *Perca* are repeated in this panel and the dimensions of *Daphnia galeata* and *Daphnia retrocurva* are indicated in relation to them. *D. galeata* is one of the most successful limnetic species of the genus, occurring as a numerically dominant component of the zooplankton of a large proportion of the temperate lakes of Eurasia and North America (Brooks, 1957). Its success may be due to the fact that the individuals of every population of this species can develop into either large or (visibly) small morphs, depending upon the seasonally varying environmental conditions. In midsummer, individuals of *D. galeata* have rapidly growing transparent helmets and mature at a size sufficiently small visually for the population to reproduce itself in the face of moderate predation. At other seasons slower growth produces large, non-helmeted morphs which enjoy the competitive particle-gathering advantages of large size (Brooks, 1965; Brooks and Dodson, 1965; Burns, in press). Populations of large *Daphnia* can persist at these seasons because predation pressure is low.

The base of the horizontal arrow labelled "*D. galeata*" is at 1.2mm while the tip reaches to 1.08mm. The first value, 1.2mm, is a reasonable estimate of visible body length (carapace and base of head including eye) at the onset of maturity for the large, non-helmeted morph characteristic of spring and fall populations. The older mature instars grow larger, of course, to sizes well above the threshold of full interest for *Perca*, even for *Salmo*. The length of the arrow represents a ten per cent reduction in visible body size at the onset of maturity. This assignment of ten per cent for *D. galeata* is an estimate based upon the value obtained in the sole cyclomorphic population analysed, *D. retrocurva* in Brooks, 1965. This value is conservative, as the comparable value for the *D. lumholzi* of Lake Albert would appear to be twice as large, from the measurements given by Green (1967). Such a reduction as this latter—one-fifth of the visible body length at the onset of maturity—may be near the upper limit that can be achieved through the rapid relative growth of transparent protuberances during the immature instars.

This horizontal arrow is also drawn in relation to the curves for *Salmo* and *Perca*. The base of each arrow indicates the relative predator interest in the large morph, while the tick dropped from the tip of each arrow indicates the relative interest in the visually smaller helmeted morph. The vertical arrows indicate the decrease in the interest of each planktivore occasioned by this ten percent decrease in visible size of the prey. These decreases, of the order of 15 to 20 per cent, indicate that the decrease in visible body size achieved by growth reapportionment without a diminution of the metabolic rate (especially, rates of feeding and egg production) could be of significant advantage to a population of zooplankters striving to maintain itself in the face of moderately heavy midsummer predation by facultative piscine planktivores of the types characteristic of freshwater lakes.

Within the area of northern North America, to which it is confined, the smaller *D. retrocurva* is rather less common than the larger *D. galeata* with which it often coexists. There is some evidence to suggest that *D. retrocurva* is more frequently a dominant at times and in lakes where predation is relatively heavy (Hall, 1964; Galbraith, 1967). The arrow labelled "*D. retrocurva*" represents a ten per cent reduction in the visible size of the helmeted morph from the value of 0.8mm which is

taken as a reasonable estimate of the visible size at the onset of maturity of the large, non-helmeted morph characteristic of spring and fall (Brooks, 1965). The individuals of the first mature instar of *D. retrocurva* are too small to engage the interest of *Perca* or *Salmo*, but in the spring and fall populations numerous individuals grow to a size sufficient to attract the full attention of *Perca*. In the population from Bantam Lake, Connecticut, one of the few in which the size distribution has been carefully analysed, individuals of the abundant April and May populations can attain a visible body size of nearly $1,500\mu$. Twenty-five per cent of the specimens taken during April were visually larger than about $1,300\mu$. In July and August individuals with a visible body size of about $725\mu$ are seen to bear eggs, and nearly 75 per cent of the mature individuals are visually smaller than the mean size at the onset of maturity in April (Brooks, 1968). None were larger than about $1,200\mu$, an upper limit almost certainly set by the predatory removal of larger individuals. The planktivores in large, but shallow, Bantam Lake are of the "yellow perch" type and the midsummer destruction of *Daphnia* larger than about $1,200\mu$ is predictable from the curve of predator interest. Returning to the righthand panel of Figure 5, we find that the *D. retrocurva* arrow intercepts only the *Perca* curve. The ten per cent reduction in the visual size of the smallest mature instar secures a ten per cent loss of predator interest. The elimination of the large mature females in midsummer, shifts the burden of maintaining the population onto the smaller egg bearers. Therefore, the initiation of egg production by individuals less likely to be devoured might be of decisive significance for the survival of the population.

The predator interest curves suggest an explanation for the fact that the size at the onset of maturity in the strongly polymorphic limnetic Cladocera are all within a limited size range. If the extreme modification of the patterns of relative growth can produce a reduction of about ten per cent in the visible body size at the onset of maturity, then the larger morph cannot be much larger than the threshold size of full predator interest. Otherwise, the smaller morph will not have an enhanced survival value. For example, a species maturing at the size of *D. pulex* would not profit by possessing the ability to reduce its size at the onset of maturity by ten per cent during the time of maximum predation pressure because the smaller morph—slightly over 1.6mm—would still be of maximum interest to both types of planktivores. Such a hypothetic reduction is indicated in Figure 5 by the interrupted arrow labelled "*D. pulex.*" One can see, therefore, that *D. pulex* can enjoy the competitive advantages of very large size (for a limnetic *Daphnia*) but it can do so only in lakes where planktivores are sparse. It is quickly eliminated when planktivory increases. Therefore, if a species is to profit from the evolution of this mechanism for visible-size polymorphism, the larger morph for a limnetic species must be no more than about 1.3 to 1.5mm. The smallest polymorphic *Daphnia* belong to the Eurasian species *D. cucullata*, and the smallest midsummer morphs have a visible length of about $700\mu$, just below the smallest *D. retrocurva*. This is the lower limit; further decreases would bring little increase in survival but mean a great loss in food gathering ability. The smallest known *Daphnia* are non-variant dwarfs of *D. cucullata* that live only in European fish ponds where the level of planktivory is very high. They are so poor at food gathering, however, that they do not exist except where intense predation eliminates all larger competitors.

The survival advantage of being below the threshold size of full predator interest can be even more dramatically expressed if it is stated in terms of the relative numbers of *Daphnia* above and below the threshold that are eaten, rather than in terms of the numbers of fish interested in eating the various sizes of prey items. Galbraith (1967) expressed his observations of the size relations of the over 5,000 *Daphnia* eaten by rainbow trout and yellow perch (which we have considered above in a different way) thus: "In spite of the fact that 46 per cent of the *Daphnia* population in Sporley Lake and 58 per cent in Stager Lake consisted of these small individuals [less than 1.3mm], 96 per cent of those eaten by trout and 82 per cent by perch were larger than 1.3mm." The advantages to a *Daphnia* of appearing less than 1.3mm are obvious.

This paper is an outgrowth of research supported by grants GB 1207 and GB 6004 from the National Science Foundation.

REFERENCES

BERG, A., AND E. GRIMALDI. 1965. Biologia della due forme di coregone (*Coregonus* sp.) del Lago Maggiore. Mem. Ist. Ital. Idrobiol., 18:25–196.

BERG, A., AND E. GRIMALDI. 1966a. Biologia dell'agone (*Alosa fictus lacustris*) del Lago Maggiore. Mem. Ist. Ital. Idrobiol., 20:41–83.

BERG, A., AND E. GRIMALDI. 1966b. Ecological relationships between planktophagic fish species in the Lago Maggiore. Verh. Internat. Verein. Limnol., 16:1065–1073.

BROOKS, J. L. 1957. The systematics of North American *Daphnia*. Mem. Conn. Acad. Arts Sci., 13:1–180.

BROOKS, J. L. 1964. The relationship between the vertical distribution and seasonal variation of limnetic species of *Daphnia*. Verh. Internat. Verein. Limnol., 15:684–690.

BROOKS, J. L. 1965. Predation and relative helmet size in cyclomorphic *Daphnia*. Proc. Nat. Acad. Sci., 53:119–126.

BROOKS, J. L. 1967. Cyclomorphosis, turbulence and overwintering in *Daphnia*. Verh. Internat. Verein Limnol., 16:1653–1659.

BROOKS, J. L. In press. Eutrophication and changes in the composition of the zooplankton. Proc. International Symposium on Eutrophication.

BROOKS, J. L., AND S. I. DODSON. 1965. Predation, body size, and composition of plankton. Science, 150:28–35.

BRYNILDSON, O. M. 1958. Lime-treatment of brown-stained lakes and their adaptability for trout and largemouth bass. Ph.D. dissertation, University of Wisconsin.

BURNS, CAROLYN W. In press. The relationship between body size of filter-feeding Cladocera and the maximum size of particle ingested. Limnol. Oceanogr.

BURNS, CAROLYN W., AND F. H. RIGLER. 1967. Comparison of filtering rates of *Daphnia* in lakewater in suspensions of yeast. Limnol. Oceanogr., 12:492–502.

GALBRAITH, M. G., JR. 1967. Size-selective predation on *Daphnia* by rainbow trout and yellow
perch. Trans. Amer. Fish. Soc., 96:1–10.

GREEN, J. 1967. The distribution and variation
of *Daphnia lumholzi* (Crustacea: Cladocera) in
relation to fish predation in Lake Albert, East
Africa. J. Zool., 151:181–197.

HALL, D. J. 1964. An experimental approach to
the dynamics of a natural population of *Daphnia
galeata mendotae*. Ecology, 45:94–111.

HARDY, SIR ALISTER. 1956. The open sea. Its
natural history: Part I, The world of plankton.
The new naturalist series. Collins, London.
335 pp. + xv.

HILDEBRAND, S. F. 1963. Family Clupeidae
(pp. 257–381), in "Fishes of the western North
Atlantic." Memoir 1, Part 3. Sears Foundation
for Marine Research, New Haven.

IVLEV, V. S. 1961. Experimental ecology of the
feeding of fishes. (Trans. from Russian by D.
Scott). Yale Univ. Press, New Haven. 302 pp.
+ viii.

KOZHOV, M. 1963. Lake Baikal and its life.
Junk, The Hague. 344 pp.

LINDSTRÖM, T. 1955. On the relation fish size–
food size. Report, Institute of Freshwater Research, Drottningholm, No. 36:133–147.

REIF, C., AND D. W. TAPPA. 1966. Selective
predation: smelt and cladocerans in Harveys
Lake. Limnol. Oceanogr., 11:437–438.

TONOLLI, V. 1962. L'attuale situazione del po-
polamento planctonico del Lago Maggiore. Mem.
Ist. Ital. Idrobiol., 15:81–134.

*Department of Biology, Osborn Memorial
Laboratories, Yale University, New Haven,
Connecticut 06520.*

# Plant-Herbivore Coevolution: Lupines and Lycaenids

**Abstract.** *Predation on lupine flowers by larvae of a lycaenid butterfly was studied by comparison of inflorescences exposed to and protected from infestation, and by comparison of lupine populations exposed to different degrees of attack. The lycaenids caused striking reduction in seed set, indicating that this small herbivore could act as a potent selective agent in lupine populations.*

Coevolutionary interactions between plants and herbivores have been studied (*1*) and may be a major source of organic diversity (*2*). The selective effect of herbivore attack on plants, except the most extreme attacks which lead to extensive defoliation, are usually discounted as having little influence on plant populations. Also discounted is the primary role of plant biochemicals as herbivore poisons (*3*). Kemp (*4*) described an example of extreme selection for procumbency in pasture plants under heavy grazing. A seemingly insignificant herbivore, the small (wing length ± 14 mm) lycaenid butterfly *Glaucopsyche lygdamus* Doubleday, may have a profound effect on the reproductive capacity of the herbaceous perennial lupine *Lupinus amplus* Greene. This supports the contention that plants are under powerful evolutionary attack by herbivores, an attack not apparent to the casual observer.

Lupine populations in the vicinity of Gothic and Crested Butte, Gunnison County, Colorado, were investigated in June and July of 1968. Female butterflies oviposited only on pubescent portions of immature inflorescences of *L. amplus*. No oviposition was observed on an inflorescence in which some flowers were opened. A comparison of two inflorescence types, both of which occur on the same plants, was made on 7 July. Eggs and egg shells were counted on 125 inflorescences without open flowers (Fig. 1) and 130 inflorescences which had open flowers at the base only (Fig. 1). The unopened portion of the inflorescence presented an oviposition environment to a female butterfly which we are unable to distinguish from an immature inflorescence, except for the presence of opened flowers below, and increased distance from, the crown of the lupine plant. Table 1 shows the very significant difference (*P* ≪ .01) in egg distribution on the two types of inflorescences. Note that since the eggs and egg shells remain attached after the flowers open, all of the eggs found at this time on open flowers may have been laid on the inflorescence when it was immature.

Larvae feed primarily on the wing and keel of the corolla and the stamens which are contained within the keel (54 of 78 larvae observed were feeding in these areas). Other parts of the flower, including the ovary, are less frequently attacked. Flowers attacked by lycaenids often do not reach anthesis and subsequently absciss.

One hundred immature inflorescences (of the type shown in Fig. 1) on 36 plants of the Gothic population were tagged on 5 July. Egg counts were made on all inflorescences and roughly half were designated controls. Controls either had no eggs on them, or had unhatched eggs removed. The tagged inflorescences were censused subsequently on 6, 9, 11, 14, and 17 July. Great care was taken not to damage the flowers. Periods between censuses were not long enough to permit egg hatch, so that we could, by removing all new eggs at each census, keep the controls free of attack by *G. lygdamus* larvae. On 17 July all inflorescences were collected and examined microscopically for damage. Floral scars were counted to give the total number of flowers which could have been produced on the inflorescence (potential production). At this date all inflorescences were fully mature and each flower had ovarian development. The lycaenid larvae found ranged in size from small (newly hatched) to large

Fig. 1. (Left) Inflorescence of *Lupinus amplus* without open flowers; (right) inflorescence with open flowers at base and unopened flowers at apex.

Reprinted by permission of tne American Association for the Advancement of Science and the authors from *Science* 162:671–672, 8 November 1968. Copyright 1968 by the American Association for the Advancement of Science.

Table 1. Distribution of *Glaucopsyche* eggs on the two types of inflorescences shown in Fig. 1.

| Number of eggs | Number of inflorescences | |
|---|---|---|
| | No open flowers | Open flowers |
| 0 | 43 | 120 |
| 1 | 53 | 8 |
| 2 | 14 | 2 |
| 3 | 9 | 0 |
| 4 | 3 | 0 |
| 5 | 1 | 0 |
| 6 | 1 | 0 |
| 7 | 0 | 0 |
| 8 | 1 | 0 |

(presumably last instar). Most larvae, however, were intermediate in size. Clearly, further damage would have been done if the inflorescences had been permitted to progress to seed set. We feel, however, that such damage would have been relatively minor since the ovaries were all well developed and were subject to little attack.

Eight inflorescences were destroyed in the course of the study, leaving 41 controls and 51 exposed to attack. A total of 111 eggs were laid on the exposed inflorescences, 2.18 per inflorescence. The 41 control inflorescences had a potential production of 967 mature flowers. This group actually produced 693, or 71.66 percent of potential. The experimental group had a potential production of 1433 mature flowers and actually produced 533, or 37.19 percent of potential. Of these mature flowers 138 were so badly damaged that they would have abscissed without setting seed, so that a more realistic estimate of realized potential in the experimental group is 395/1433,

or 27.56 percent. Both experimental groups (with and without damage) are, of course, highly significantly different from the controls ($P \ll .01$).

A sample of 100 large inflorescences was taken on 15 July from the Crested Butte population of *L. amplus* on which *G. lygdamus* is rarely seen. This population of lupines is essentially continuous with that at Gothic, some 5 miles (8 km) away. Of a potential of 4169 flowers, 3149 (75.53 percent) were realized, and 3091 (74.14 percent) were judged sufficiently undamaged to set seed. Only 11 egg shells or larvae were found on these plants. In contrast, an additional sample of 100 large inflorescences from the Gothic population, where *G. lygdamus* was abundant, was censused on 16 July. Of a potential of 4277 flowers, 2434 (57.31 percent) matured. Of these 2152 (50.67 percent) matured and were judged sufficiently undamaged to set seed. On these inflorescences 126 *G. lygdamus* egg shells or larvae were found. The differences between the two areas are highly significant ($P \ll .01$).

The damage done to the Gothic population of *L. amplus* by this small butterfly is stunning. In 1968 nearly 50 percent of the potential seed production was destroyed by *G. lygdamus*, which has been abundant at Gothic in every season since 1960 except 1964–65 (when no observations were made). There is no reason to believe that the 1968 density was unusual. Presumably the lupines have been subject to a long-term attrition of their seed production. This has a drastic selective effect on the plant population. Lupines are dependent on having an abundance of seeds widely distributed in the soil

since they germinate only upon disturbance and scarification.

We can guess at one selective response of the plant to *Glaucopsyche* attack—advancement of flowering time. The Gothic population of *L. amplus* seems to have been pushed to its earliest limit, as many examples of frost-killed and damaged inflorescences were observed this year. The butterflies oviposit strictly on the immature inflorescences (Table 1), indicating that plants on which flowers mature before the adult butterflies emerge, or early in the flight season, would be least subject to damage. There is no other obvious reason for the early flowering, as seed production is completed with more than a month of growing season remaining. At this time, other explanations cannot be excluded.

DENNIS E. BREEDLOVE
*Department of Botany, Botanical Gardens, University of California, Berkeley 94720*

PAUL R. EHRLICH
*Department of Biological Sciences, Stanford University, Stanford, California 94305*

**References and Notes**

1. For example D. Janzen, *Evolution* **20**, 249 (1966).
2. P. R. Ehrlich and P. H. Raven, *ibid.* **18**, 586 (1965); P. R. Ehrlich, *Oreg. State Univ. Biol. Colloq.*, in press.
3. For example, C. H. Muller, *Bull. Torrey Bot. Club* **93**, 332, 351 (1966); Z. *Pflanzenkr. Pflanzenpathol.*, *Pflanzenschutz* **74**, 333 (1967); and personal communication: Professor Muller considers the toxic compounds of plants to be "primarily metabolic wastes."
4. W B. Kemp, *J. Heredity* **28**, 328 (1937).
5. We thank J. A. Hendrickson, R. W. Holm, and P. H. Raven, for criticizing our manuscript. Supported by NSF grant GB-5645 and by a Ford Foundation grant.

5 August 1968

# VI

# Epilogue

Any research, no matter how important, is history by the time it is published. Thus, although the valid findings presented in the papers discussed earlier will continue to be valid, and may even have a great influence on the future direction of population biology, they constitute a description of the state of the science in times past. We cannot predict the future of population biology with any degree of confidence. But, we can turn the question around and ask instead: What is the challenge of the future? What are the major areas of our ignorance? What are the important areas that remain to be explored? These questions are, or at least should be, asked every time an investigator designs a piece of research.

A more general answer to these questions is also possible. Our collection of readings closes with a paper that provides one such answer. In the final paper, HUTCHINSON considers some of the basic constraints on life imposed by the biogeochemical structure of our planet, sketches the environmental relations of current topics in population biology, and finally outlines a major direction that research in population biology must take if it is to respond to the void of our present ignorance. In one sense then, HUTCHINSONS's paper is a statement of the challenge of the future for population biology.

# THE INFLUENCE OF THE ENVIRONMENT

## By G. Evelyn Hutchinson

DEPARTMENT OF BIOLOGY, YALE UNIVERSITY

The biosphere, or part of the earth within which organisms live, is a region in which temperatures range not far from those at which water is liquid. It receives a radiation flux of wavelength >3200 Å from the sun or has the products of photosynthesis made available by gravity as in the dark depths of the ocean. Numerous interfaces are present in most parts of the biosphere. It is geochemically characterized by atmophil elements in relative quantities such that both oxidized (Eh $\simeq$ 0.5 volt) and quite reduced (Eh $\simeq$ 0.0 volt) regions are both easily possible often within a few millimeters of each other as in lake sediments. Conditions for such a region on a planet are fairly critical, and would probably always involve loss of the initial gaseous phase with reformation of the atmosphere from frozen or chemically combined material.

Chemically, living organisms are mainly made of cosmically common, light, easily soluble atmophil and lithophil elements. The special properties of the several important elements, such as hydrogen bridge formation, the formation of long carbon chains, the possible existence of —COOH and of —NH$_2$ in the same molecule, the easily oxidized and reduced system —SH HS— $\rightleftharpoons$ —S—S—, the high energy phosphate bond and various other less striking properties exhibited by common biophil elements (of which phosphorus, with an odd atomic number between Si and S, is the rarest) are obviously fundamental. Without these properties life as we know it would be impossible.

The reduction of magnesium concentration in the earth's crust, as compared with the mantle, and the consequent approximate equalization of the amounts of Na, K, Mg, and Ca provide a geochemical rather than a purely chemical example of the "fitness of the environment" to use Henderson's phrase. However, it is difficult to be sure we know we are talking sense in this field without comparative instances, or whether we are involved in problems like the insoluble metaphysical question of childhood, Why am I not someone else? The exploration of the surface of Mars may give, long before the National Academy is celebrating another centenary, some welcome contrasting information. Meanwhile it is reasonable to suppose that extreme rarity and extreme insolubility, leading to a very low concentration of some elements within living tissues, do limit their functional importance.

If we consider an average mammalian liver cell of diameter about 23.4 $\mu$, of volume, assuming a spherical form, of about 6700 $\mu^3$, and of mass, if a density rather more than unity be assumed, of about $7 \times 10^{-9}$ gm, we can obtain from published analyses[1] a rough idea of the mean number of atoms per cell as follows.

| | |
|---|---|
| >$10^{14}$ | **H, O** |
| $10^{12}$–$10^{14}$ | **C, N** |
| $10^{10}$–$10^{12}$ | **S, P, Na, K, Mg, Cl, Ca, Fe,** Si |
| $10^8$–$10^{10}$ | **Zn,** Li, Rb, **Cu, Mn,** Al, Fe, Br |
| $10^6$–$10^8$ | Sn, Ti, Mo, **Co, I,** Pb, Ag, B, Sr, Ni, V, Sc, Cd, ?**Cr, Se** |
| $10^4$–$10^6$ | U, Hg, Be ... } |
| $10^2$–$10^4$ | ............ } 40 additional reactive natural elements probably in these rows. |
| $10^0$–$10^2$ | Ra |

Reprinted by permission of the National Academy of Sciences and the author from *Proceedings of the National Academy of Sciences* 51:930–934, 1964 and by permission of The Rockefeller University Press from *The Scientific Endeavor.*

The elements known to have a function in mammals, other than in maintaining the integrity of skeletal structures (as do F, and possibly[2] Sr and Ba), are given in boldface type. It is evident that the probability of an element having a function decreases with decreasing concentration. When such a table was published twenty years ago, there were 9 elements in the $10^6$–$10^8$ atoms per cell category with only cobalt functional; now there are analytic data for 14 and a presumption that chromium and selenium, which with iodine are now known to be functional, fall here. Evidently about a quarter of the elements with $10^6$–$10^8$ atoms per cell may have a function. In the next two rows we might guess probabilities of 0.1– 0.01 of function. This may imply one or two surprises. What is interesting is that although cobalt is enriched relative to nickel in liver, as in nearly all tissues of higher animals, over its concentration in the lithosphere, or for that matter in plants, it is still little more abundant than lead and less so than molybdenum. To use an element such as cobalt, the biochemistry of utilization must be reasonably specific. There are plenty of atoms of various kinds around in such concentrations that they could play a part as antimetabolites as well as significant functional roles in enzyme systems. It is possible that this sets the lower limits of concentration at which biochemically significant substances occur. There might be too many commoner accidental and potentially interfering materials around for any very important substance to work practically at $10^4$ atoms or molecules per cell. The variety of elementary composition may thus set the standard of purity within which biochemical evolution has occurred.

We may roughly divide most of the biosphere into a purely liquid part, and solid-liquid and solid-gaseous parts, corresponding to (1) the open ocean, (2) the sea bottom, margin, and inland waters, and (3) the colonized land surfaces. In the first, it is possible that iron, which is almost insoluble under oxidizing conditions in inorganic aqueous systems, usually limits the amount of living matter, while in the last, water supply is the most important determinant. In the water-solid systems, including lakes and neritic marine environments, phosphorus, nitrogen, and other elements may be limiting.

The whole plant community can, since it is interconnected through the $CO_2$ and $O_2$ of the atmosphere, be regarded as an extremely inefficient (efficiency not much more than 0.1% in most cases in nature) photosynthetic machine. The details of the biochemistry of photosynthesis have been elucidated in recent years in most impressive studies by various investigators. We are, however, still rather ignorant of the quantitative details of the over-all biogeochemical process. It is evident that both the ocean[3] and the plant cover[4] of the continents play a major part in regulating the $CO_2$ content of the atmosphere, but this regulation is not sufficient to prevent a slow rise[5] due partly, but perhaps not entirely, to the production of the gas by combustion of fossil fuels.

The use of plant material by animals as food is ordinarily a much more efficient process than the photosynthetic capture of the radiation flux from the sun, and allows the existence of a considerable mass of and extraordinary diversity of animals. This diversity is however clearly in part due to the diversity and structural complexity of higher plants. A large part of contemporary ecological research is devoted to elucidation of the general principles that permit the coexistence of very large numbers of species together in a single locality.

The complexity of communities has fascinated naturalists from before Darwin, who described it classically. Only recently has it become apparent what a wealth of quantitative relationships can be seen in the complex structure. Remarkable and quite diverse types of theory, some of which have proved of considerable value in empirical studies, have been developed to deal with this sort of problem, though we still have an enormous amount to learn. While ordinarily the principle of competitive exclusion,[6] which can be phrased in abstract geometrical terms as the statement that two coexisting species do not occupy the same niche, is a good point of departure so long as it is not applied in too naive a manner. The claim may be made that the principle is inapplicable in practice because there would never be a possibility of demonstrating that the niche requirements of two species were, or were not, exactly the same. Actually what is involved is the question as to whether in competition two species could be so nearly equivalent that one would not replace the other in any reasonable time, such as the lifetime of an observer, the period of existence of relevant scientific records, or the period during which the average state of the habitat remained unchanged. The possibility that two competing species might be exactly matched contradicts what has been called the axiom of inequality,[6] that two natural bodies are never exactly the same. The possibility that in very large populations where the dynamics are essentially deterministic, they might be so nearly evenly matched that competition would proceed too slowly to detect, has been seriously suggested for phytoplankton associations, the multispecific nature of which seems otherwise paradoxical.[7] In this, as in other aspects of ecology, the role of time, or of the rates at which things can happen, has been inadequately studied.

In general the speed at which things happen in a very small organism will depend on physical processes of which ordinary diffusion is likely to be the most critical. In larger organisms the celestial mechanics of the solar system, giving days, tidal periods, lunar months, and years, can introduce apparently arbitrary rates into the life of an organism which will interact with rates set by small-scale physical processes. The extent of various kinds of biological clocks is one of the most important phenomena recently discovered in biology. The evidence from odd cases in which periodic processes occur pathologically[8] suggests that the full significance of the gearing of organisms, including ourselves, to the cycle of day and night is not even yet apparent. Moreover a case perhaps could be made for supposing that sometimes clocks can exist which, having evolved in relation to the environment, are no longer set to be synchronous with external periodicities. The human female reproductive cycle, shared by a number of primates, has long suggested a lunar month in spite of the lack of synchrony. Possibly it represents a lunar clock no longer set by the moon; an effect of moonlight on the reproductive cycle of some tropical mammals, including prosimians, has been noted.[9]

Even more extraordinary are the clocks regulating the three species of seventeen-year and the three of thirteen-year cicadas.[10] Here apparently synchrony is adaptive, so that three species bear the brunt of predation, with the different broods emerging so irregularly that there is little chance of a permanent increase in predator population.

Individual cases of a striking kind can, as these, be given at least hypothetical, though very plausible, explanations. We still lack, however, a really clear understanding of the relationship of rates of living and of evolution to the rates of physical change in the universe.

There are two extreme possible ways of evolution in relation to time. Since natural selection will go faster when generations succeed each other faster, one way is the evolution of progressively smaller and more rapidly reproducing organisms. However, the smaller an organism the less it can do. An alternative path gives large, slower reproducing organisms in which, when a nervous system capable of learning is developed, a premium is put on experience. Even in organisms such as plants, which do not learn in the ordinary sense of the word, a perennial can wait about at least metaphorically for a favorable season for reproduction. In the first case the time scale is set by the physical processes of diffusion; in the other extreme case, presumably by some function of the rate at which various things, such as learning, can occur.

In a varying environment, the time taken to learn about a seasonal or otherwise infrequent event will partly depend on the incidence of that event. Some sea birds seem to need several years' experience to learn how to get food for their chick or chicks.[11] The advantage of this learning must be great enough to offset the extra prereproductive mortality, which inevitably accompanies a delay in breeding.

It has recently been suggested that the great intraspecific competition on the limited feeding grounds near nesting sites puts a premium on expertness during the reproductive season and, until this has been acquired, attempts at breeding are wasteful and, to some extent, dangerous. Where mortality is lowest, possibly of the order of 3 per cent per annum in the albatrosses, the period prior to reproduction may be nine years, even though these immense birds have reached maximum size in their first year. In a case like this, learning can obviously only take place during the special period of reproduction, and expertness takes several years to acquire. But it is not clear why human learning of perennial activities should take so long when most of the individual events in our sensory and nervous systems take times measured in milliseconds, rather than months, while on the motor side, a good pianist can play ten notes a second if he has real cause to do so.

In the present and most legitimate excitement over the reading of genetic codes, it is important to remember that lexicography and grammar are not literature, even though the fixing of meaning to symbols and the rules of their ordering make literature possible. The literature of living organisms is very varied, and is perhaps most exciting in the epic or evolutionary forms in which organisms are continually changing in response to selection by a changing environment. Deduction from the possible molecular states of organisms is hardly likely to be an efficient way of exploration; an empirical approach to events is equally needed. A real ecology of time, relating the rates at which things happen in organisms, whether rapid physiological changes or the very slow changes of phylogenesis to the rates of the outside world, is so far only approached at the short-time physiological end. In the immediate future, as argon-potassium dating develops, it will be possible to study evolutionary rates of certain well-known phyletic lines, notably in the Tertiary mammals, with greatly increased precision. Details of variation in evolutionary rates will become accessible and should add enormously to our knowledge of organic change under long time spans. This aspect of biology is likely to be one of immense importance as the Academy moves into its second century of high scientific endeavor.

[1] Hutchinson, G. E., *Quart. Rev. Biol.*, **18**, 331 (1943); with additional data for Sc: Beck, G., *Mikrochemie ver. Mikrochim. Acta*, **34**, 62 (1948); for Be, B, Co, Hg: Forbes, R. M., A. R. Cooper, and H. H. Mitchell, *J. Biol. Chem.*, **209**, 857 (1954); for Si: Gettler, A. O., and C. J. Umberger, *Amer. J. Clin. Pathol.*, Tech. Sect., **9**, 1 (1945); for F: Gushchin, S. K., *Vopr. Pitaniya*, **19**, 71 (1960); for I: Gustun, M. J., *Vopr. Pitaniya*, **18**, 80 (1959); for As: Herman, M. A., T. J. Wiktor, and A. A. van Hee, *Bull. Agr. Congo Belge*, **51**, 403 (1960); for Br: Moruzzi, Giovanni, *Boll. Soc. Ital. Biol. Sper.*, **11**, 725 (1936); and for Cd: Voĭnar, A. O., *Akad. Nauk SSSR, Tr. Konf. Mikroelement*, **1950**, 580 (1952).

[2] Rygh, O., *Bull. Soc. Chim. Biol.* (Paris), **31**, 1052 (1949).

[3] Revelle, R., and H. E. Suess, *Tellus*, **9**, 18 (1957); Bolin, B., and E. Eriksson, in *The Atmosphere and the Sea in Motion* (Rockefeller Institute Press, 1959), p. 130; Eriksson, E., and P. Welander, *Tellus*, **8**, 155 (1956).

[4] Lieth, H., *J. Geophys. Res.*, **68**, 3887 (1963); Bolin, B., and C. D. Keeling, *J. Geophys. Res.*, **68**, 3899 (1963).

[5] Callendar, G. S., *Tellus*, **10**, 243 (1958); Bolin, B., and C. D. Keeling, *loc. cit.*

[6] Hardin, G., *Science*, **131**, 1292 (1960).

[7] Riley, G. A., in *Marine Biology 1*, Am. Inst. Biol. Sci. (1963), p. 70; Hutchinson, G. E., *Am. Naturalist*, **95**, 137 (1961).

[8] Richter, Curt P., these Proceedings, **46**, 1506 (1960).

[9] Cowgill, U. M., A. Bishop, R. J. Andrew, and G. E. Hutchinson, these Proceedings, **48**, 238 (1962); Harrison, J. L., *Bull. Raffles Mus.*, **24**, 109 (1952).

[10] Alexander, R. D., and T. E. Moore, *Misc. Publ. Mus. Zool., Univ. Mich.*,1 21, 1 (1962); Dybas, H. S., and M. Lloyd, *Ecology*, **43**, 444 (1962).

[11] Ashmole, N. P., *Ibis*, **103b**, 458 (1963).